Introduction to Computers and Information Processing

3rd Edition

Introduction to Computers and Information Processing

Larry Long

Prentice-Hall International, Inc.

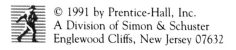 © 1991 by Prentice-Hall, Inc.
A Division of Simon & Schuster
Englewood Cliffs, New Jersey 07632

Printed in the United States of America
10 9 8 7 6 5 4

ISBN 0-13-485947-2

Prentice-Hall International (UK) Limited, *London*
Prentice-Hall of Australia Pty. Limited, *Sydney*
Prentice-Hall Canada Inc., *Toronto*
Prentice-Hall Hispanoamericana, S.A., *Mexico*
Prentice-Hall of India Private Limited, *New Delhi*
Prentice-Hall of Japan, Inc., *Tokyo*
Simon & Schuster Asia Pte. Ltd., *Singapore*
Editora Prentice-Hall do Brasil, Ltda., *Rio de Janeiro*
Prentice-Hall, Inc., *Englewood Cliffs, New Jersey*

To the *instructors* whose dedication to the principles
of education have enabled thousands to enter the age
of information with confidence

To the *students* with the will to accept challenge
and the foresight to seize opportunity

Overview

Contents

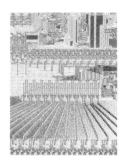

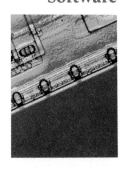

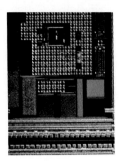

We are in transition from an industrial society to an information society. The forces driving this transition are the computer and the people who strive to exploit its seemingly endless capabilities in their work and in their leisure.

The chapters, fourteen in all, offer an overview of information technology and applications. Two of the seven appendices provide conceptual coverage of computer history and numbering systems. The remaining appendices will help you learn to operate microcomputers and use a variety of popular software packages, including MS-DOS (operating system), WordPerfect (word processing), Lotus 1-2-3 (electronic spreadsheet), and dBASE III Plus (database).

Once you have read and understood the material in this text and have had hands-on experience with computers, you will be poised to play an active role in the "computer revolution."

Getting the Most from This Text

The layout and organization of the text and its content are designed to present concepts in an interesting, logical, and informative manner, and to be used as a reference for the reinforcement of classroom lectures.

A good way to approach each chapter is to

1. Look over the Student Learning Objectives on the chapter opener.
2. Turn to the end of the chapter and read the Summary Outline and Important Terms.
3. Read over the major headings and subheadings and think of how they are related.
4. Read the chapter and note the important terms in **boldface** type and in *italic* type.
5. Relate photos and photo captions to the text. (One picture is worth a thousand words.)
6. Go over the Summary Outline and Important Terms again, paying particular attention to the boldface terms.
7. Take the Self-Test. Reread those sections you do not fully understand.
8. Answer the questions in the Review Exercises.

Color is used throughout the book to add another dimension to the learning process. There are many instances where concepts are reinforced and made easier to understand with the judicious use of color. We call this the *functional use of color.*

The Learning Assistance Package

Introduction to Computers and Information Processing is supported by a comprehensive learning assistance package. The package is detailed in the "Preface to the Instructor." Ask your instructor about the availability of these supplements.

You, Computers, and the Future

Whether you are pursuing a career as an economist, a social worker, an attorney, a dancer, an accountant, a computer specialist, a sales manager, or virtually any other career from shop supervisor to politician, the knowledge you gain from this course ultimately will prove beneficial. Keep your course notes and this book; they will prove to be valuable references in other courses and in your career. The chapter material addresses a broad range of computer concepts that you will encounter frequently in other classes, at work, and even at home.

The use of computers for information processing is in its infancy. You are "getting in on the ground floor" by taking this course. Each class you attend and each page you turn will be a learning experience to help you advance one step closer to an understanding of how computers are making the world a better place in which to live and work. You also will be gaining the knowledge necessary to become an active participant in what is the most exciting decade of technological innovation and change in recorded history.

Preface to the Instructor

The introductory computer course traditionally has posed one of the greatest teaching challenges. To be effective, we must continually change our lecture style. Sometimes we are historians. Much of the time we are scientists presenting technical material. On occasion we are sociologists commenting on social issues. In the same course we toggle between lecture and lab. Moreover, we are teaching an ever-increasing amount of material to students with a wide range of career objectives, many of whom are computerphobics.

Introduction to Computers and Information Processing and its comprehensive teaching/learning system are designed to help you meet this challenge. In the book I have attempted to motivate students by projecting the message that computers are more than just productivity tools; they also can be a continuing source of enjoyment and personal gratification. The teaching/learning system, which is the most comprehensive of its kind, is described briefly in this preface and in detail in the Instructor's Resource Manual portion of the Annotated Instructor's Edition (AIE) of the text. The AIE consists of the student text with lecture-oriented material in the margins.

Target Course

The target course for this text and its teaching/learning system

1. Provides overview coverage of introductory computer and information processing concepts (as opposed to comprehensive coverage).
2. Accommodates students from a broad spectrum of disciplines and interests.
3. Introduces students to microcomputers and one or more of the following: MS-DOS, WordPerfect, Lotus 1-2-3, dBASE III Plus, BASIC programming. (BASIC is covered in a separate booklet.)

Features

- *Step-by-step software tutorials.* Students can progress to an intermediate level of competency in MS-DOS, WordPerfect, Lotus 1-2-3, and dBASE III Plus by working through the keystroke tutorials, one step at a time. Numerous hands-on exercises provide students with an opportunity to build their skills. Once completed, the tutorials are designed to serve as a reference for common software functions.
- *Readability.* All elements (feature boxes, profiles, photos, figures, memory bits, and so on) are integrated with the text to create a reading and study rhythm that complements and reinforces learning.
- *Teachability.* Teachability of a text is that quality that permits instructors to present lectures in a logical and coherent manner.
- *Applications-oriented.* Throughout the book, concepts are presented in the context of computer applications.

- *Presentation style.* The text and all supplements are written in a style that remains pedagogically sound while communicating the energy and excitement of computers to the student.
- *Functional use of color.* Color is used functionally to relate ideas to one another and to illustrate the text.
- *Currency-plus.* The material is more than current, it's "current-plus"—anticipating the emergence and implementation of computer technology.
- *Flexibility.* The text and its teaching/learning system are organized to permit maximum flexibility in course design and in the selection, assignment, and presentation of material.
- *Chapter pedagogy.* Chapter organization and pedagogy are consistent throughout the text. The chapter is prefaced by Student Learning Objectives. In the body of the chapter, all major headings are numbered (1–1, 1–2, and so on) to facilitate selective assignment and to provide an easy cross-reference to all related material in the supplements. Important terms and phrases are highlighted in boldface type. Words and phrases to be emphasized appear in italics. Informative boxed features, "Profiles," photos, and "Memory Bits" (outlines of key points) are positioned strategically to complement the running text. Each chapter concludes with a Summary Outline and Important Terms, Review Exercises (concepts and discussion), and a Self-Test.

The Third Edition

The revisions embodied in *Introduction to Computers and Information Processing* reflect advancing technology and the evolution of college curriculums. The major changes are summarized below.

- *Introduction to Computers and Information Processing* is published in two versions: the student text and the Annotated Instructor's Edition.
- Four completely new appendices demonstrate, via interactive tutorials, the features and functions of MS-DOS, WordPerfect 5.X, Lotus 1-2-3 2.2, and dBASE III Plus. Another new appendix covers using a microcomputer.
- The coverage of I/O and data storage is now split into two separate chapters.
- The history chapter has been replaced with a pictorial overview in Appendix A.
- Two chapters on personal computing and micro software (generic coverage of word processing, desktop publishing, spreadsheet, graphics, and database) have been added.
- A chapter on computers in society has been added.
- BASIC has been removed from the main text and offered as a supplement at a nominal cost.
- Profiles of people who have had a major influence on computers and the computer industries now appear in each chapter.

Organization

Introduction to Computers and Information Processing consists of 14 chapters and seven appendices. The chapters, which are divided into five parts, address concepts relating to information technology and present many examples of the application of this technology. The first two appendices cover those major topics most often omitted from computer survey courses—computer history and numbering systems. Appendix C provides a overview of using microcomputers. The remaining appendices present explanations and keystroke tutorials for MS-DOS, WordPerfect, Lotus 1-2-3, and dBASE III Plus. BASIC programming is covered in *BASIC for Introductory Computing*, a supplemental booklet by Larry and Nancy Long.

The glossary is comprehensive. That is, terms that are not in the text but which may be encountered by the student in future courses or at work are included.

The *Introduction to Computers and Information Processing* Teaching/Learning System

The Annotated Instructor's Edition (AIE).   The AIE is a four-color instructor's version of *Introduction to Computers and Information Processing* that includes lecture points, teaching tips, supplemental material, in-class discussion questions, supplemental examples, warnings, quotes, cross-references to other components of the teaching/learning system, and much more—all in the margin of the text! The AIE also contains an Instructors Resource Manual (IRM) section. The IRM tells you how to acquire and use all the teaching and learning materials; provides tips on preparation, teaching, and delivery; and presents a pedagogical summary of the text. (Lecture notes and solutions are in the *Instructor's Manual and Test Item File*.)

Computer-Assisted Presentation System (CAPS).   CAPS is an integrated set of animated graphics, sometimes called "electronic transparencies," that are used with a PC and a screen-image projector to enhance and facilitate classroom lectures. The "transparencies" contain key lecture points and appropriate graphics, and can be recalled and displayed as needed.

Instructor's Manual and Test Item File (IM&TIF).   The *IM&TIF* contains lecture outlines for each chapter and appendix in the text and each learning module in *BASIC for Introductory Computing*, solutions to exercises (main text, *Study Guide*, and the BASIC supplement), and the test item file (main text and BASIC supplement).

Test Item File Diskettes.   The Test Item File Diskettes are used in conjunction with Prentice Hall DataManager software and the hard copy in the *IM&TIF*.

Instructor's Manual on a Disk.   The chapter and appendix lecture outlines of the *IM&TIF* are included on a disk in generic ASCII format.

Study Guide.   The *Study Guide* is a supplementary book designed to support the student learning objectives in the text. It contains self-tests and hand-in exercises for material in the text and in the BASIC supplement. It also contains a "Guide to *The New Literacy* Videotape Series."

Microcomputer Software: Step by Step. This hands-on lab book by Ted Kalmon, Larry Long, and Nancy Long (Englewood Cliffs, N.J.: Prentice Hall, 1990) provides step-by-step instructions, tutorials, and exercises for MS-DOS, WordPerfect, Lotus 1-2-3, and dBASE III Plus. This book is made available for those students who wish to learn about these software packages in greater depth than they are presented in the main text. It takes beginners to an advanced level of competency.

BASIC for Introductory Computing. This booklet (90 pages) by Larry and Nancy Long (Englewood Cliffs, N.J.: Prentice Hall, 1990) can be purchased with the main text at a nominal extra cost.

Prentice Hall DataManager. PH DataManager is an integrated IBM-PC–compatible test-generation and classroom-management software package. The package permits instructors to design and create tests, to maintain student records, and to provide practice testing for students.

Computerized Testing Service. This call-in service provides customized exams by return mail.

Color Transparency Acetates. One hundred and twenty color transparency acetates, which support material in the text and the Annotated Instructor's Edition, are offered to facilitate in-class explanation. (Over 50% supplement the figures in the text.)

Prentice Hall/New York Times Contemporary View Program. This annual compilation of approximately 20 pertinent and timely articles on computers and automation is available to students. Instructors get a free subscription to *The New York Times* for classroom use.

Full-Function Word Processing Software. Webster's New World Writer and its 100,000-word-plus Spelling Checker are available at a nominal cost.

Videotape Series—*The New Literacy: An Introduction to Computers*. *The New Literacy* is a 13-tape, 26-segment video series on the use and application of computer and information technology.

Video Software Tutorials—*The Video Professor*. This series includes video tutorials for MS-DOS, WordPerfect, Lotus 1-2-3, dBASE III Plus, Microsoft Word, and others.

ABC News/Prentice Hall Video Library. This series offers documentary and feature-style stories on computers and computer technology from such award-winning news shows as *Nightline*.

SuperSoftware (IBM PC and Apple IIe). SuperSoftware is a dual-purpose educational software package. It is equally effective as a stand-alone interactive software package for students or as a teaching tool to demonstrate interactively a myriad of computer-related concepts, such as computers (configuring a micro), information processing (airline reservations), software (mail merge with word processing), and programming (sorting). SuperSoftware, which contains 60 hands-on lab activities, is designed to instruct, intrigue, and motivate.

Author "Hotline." If you have questions about the text, its package, or course planning, call me on the hotline. The telephone number appears in the IRM portion of the AIE.

Microcomputer Software and Micro Software Support Materials. Prentice Hall is the largest publisher of computer texts in the world. In many instances, full-function and educational versions of commercial software are distributed with these books. For example, Prentice Hall's Software Kit for Introductory Computing, which contains educational versions of WordPerfect 4.2, The TWiN, and dBASE III Plus, is available with this text. Your PH representative will be happy to discuss the many options you have in the selection of lab manuals and support software.

Acknowledgments

This space is insufficient to thank all the people who have made contributions to this text and its support package. The key players, however, deserve special recognition because "Intro 3/E" is their book, too. At Prentice Hall, acquisitions editor Ted Werthman committed himself and the resources of the company to the success of the project; production editor Nancy DeWolfe has woven ten thousand multicolored threads into an exquisite tapestry; and Jenny Kletzin, Delores Kenny, Rob Dewey, Sue Behnke, Mary Ann Gloriande, Trudy Pisciotti, and Bob Anderson have proven once again that they are the best in the business. I would also like to extend my gratitude to a group of Prentice Hall managers for their continued support—Dennis Hogan, Alison Reeves, Jeanne Hoeting, Leah Jewel, Seth Reichlin, Rudy Lopes, and John Jones.

Twenty-plus books and two kids later, my wife, Nancy, remains the mainstay of the Long series of books. Joel Stauffer's artistic acumen and computer wizardry are evident in CAPS, the electronic transparencies that accompany the text. Both are to be congratulated.

Scores of people from a variety of companies have in some way participated in the preparation of this book and its supplements. I thank them, one and all. I would like to single out several of these people for their ongoing commitment to education: Jessie Kempter (IBM), Pete McLaughlin (EDS), Kathy Donahue (Dynatech), Carol Parcels (Hewlett-Packard), Vicki Hawthorne (NASA), Gail Jackson (Wang), Christie Campbell (TRW), Linda Morgan (Gannet), and Peter Van Avery (General Electric).

The insight of hundreds of instructors, administrators, and students who have used *Introduction to Computers and Information Processing* has been invaluable to the evolution of its third edition. I would like to extend my sincere appreciation to each of them and to a select group of professors who critiqued the manuscript.

- Sarah Rothenberg, Hartwick College
- Maribeth King, Kilgore College
- Larry Buch, Milwaukee Area Technical College
- Alex Ephrem, Monroe College

■ Don Cartlidge, New Mexico State University

■ Jeffery Corcoran, Nichols College

■ Vernon Case, Penn Valley Community College

■ Gary Nunn, Radford University

■ Paul Dietz, The University of Mary

■ Gary Hyslop, The University of Rhode Island

■ Deborah Martin, Virginia Western Community College

■ Elizabeth Rhodes, Virginia Western Community College

Finally, I would like to thank the pioneers of our industry profiled in the text for their cooperation.

LARRY LONG, Ph.D.

About the Author

Dr. Larry Long, of Long and Associates, is a lecturer, author, consultant, and educator in the computer and information services field. His many books cover a broad spectrum of computer/MIS-related topics from programming to MIS strategic planning. Dr. Long addresses a breadth of management, computer, and MIS issues in his executive seminars. Throughout the 1980s, his "Turnaround Time" column was a regular feature in *Computerworld.*

Dr. Long has served as a consultant to all levels of management in virtually every major type of industry. He has 20 years of classroom experience at the University of Oklahoma and at Lehigh University, where he continues to be an active lecturer. He received his Ph.D., M.S., and B.S. degrees in industrial engineering at the University of Oklahoma and holds certification as a C.D.P. and a Professional Engineer.

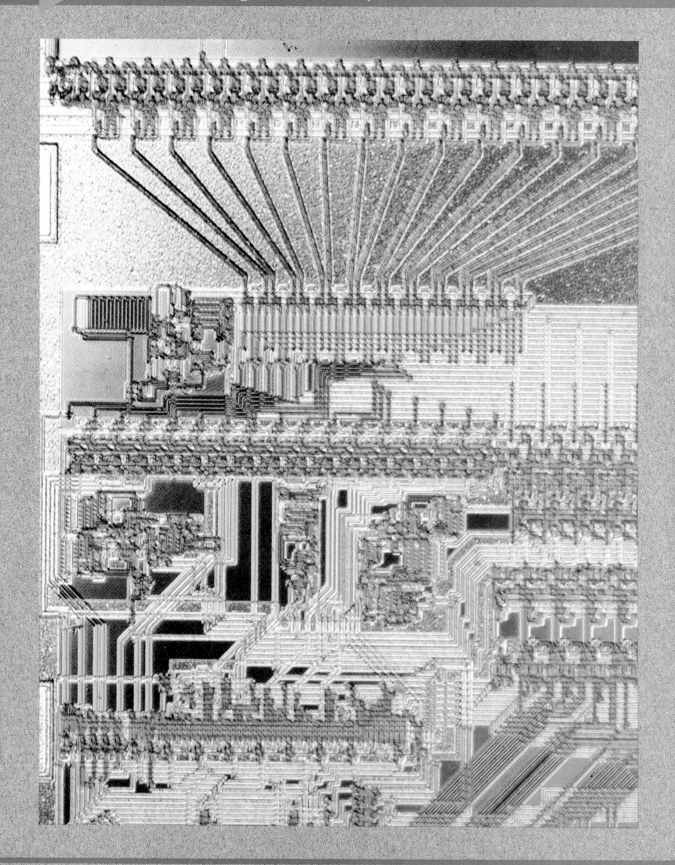

1

The World
of Computers

▶ To grasp the scope of computer understanding needed by someone living in an information society.

▶ To distinguish between data and information.

▶ To contrast the function and purpose of an information services department with those of an information center.

▶ To describe the fundamental components and the operational capabilities of a computer system.

▶ To identify and describe uses of the computer.

▶ To describe the general function of these microcomputer productivity software tools: word processing, desktop publishing, electronic spreadsheet, database, and presentation graphics.

1–1   THE INFORMATION SOCIETY

From Dirt to Data

Two centuries ago, 90 of every 100 people worked to produce food. As people became more efficient in food production, an *agrarian society* gave way to the growth of an *industrial society*. Our transition to an industrial society was slow and marked with social strife. Each new technological innovation had a profound impact. For example, the steam shovel did the work of 100 men.

We know now that the Industrial Revolution shortened the work week, provided greater opportunities for employment, and improved

This is the nerve center of EDSNET, Electronic Data Systems Corporation's global communications system. EDSNET facilitates data, voice, and video communication between a quarter of a million sites on five continents. Here in Plano, Texas, (near Dallas) more than 100 operators manage the system. Operators view 12-by-16-foot screens to keep abreast of system activity. Fourteen smaller screens provide detailed information for troubleshooting situations, and thirteen clocks display times from around the world.

A computer artist used a computer and 3D graphics software to create this remarkable collage of reflecting balls. Computer art emerged from the decade of the 1980s as a new art form.

the quality of life for all. But at the time nothing could convince the 100 men who lost their jobs to a steam shovel that the Industrial Revolution eventually would improve everyone's standard of living.

Today two people produce enough food for the remaining 98, and we are in the middle of a transition from an *industrial society* to an *information society*. The trend in today's offices and factories is paralleling that of the farm 200 years earlier. If history repeats itself—and most experts believe it will—automation will continue to reduce the number of workers needed to accomplish unskilled and semiskilled tasks. Automation also will provide workers with valuable information that will help them to better do their jobs.

In the information society, workers will focus their energies on providing a myriad of information services. Today it is a bit difficult to imagine a society that may become desperately dependent on certain information services. But let's put this concern in its proper perspective. Can you imagine our nineteenth-century forefathers becoming as desperately dependent on the speed of air travel or hair dryers as we are? Who among us would give up our hair dryer!

The Computer Revolution

The driving force behind our transition into an information society is the *computer*. The computer and the emerging information society are having a profound impact on the business community. Retailers are making it possible for us to do more shopping from the comfort of our own homes. Financial analysts are consulting their computer "partners" before advising clients on investment strategies. Some factories have no windows or lights—computer-controlled robots don't need to see!

The *computer revolution* is upon us. This unprecedented technical revolution has made computers a *part of life*. With the rapid growth in the number and variety of computer applications, they are rapidly becoming a *way of life*.

In our private lives, computers speed the checkout process at supermarkets, enable 24-hour banking, provide up-to-the-minute weather information, and, of course, entertain us with video games. If that is not enough, computers are the culprits behind our "conversations" with elevators, automobiles, and vending machines.

In our professional lives, the computer is an integral tool in the performance of many jobs. Retailers query their computer systems to determine which products are selling and which are not. Managers use word processing systems to compose memos and to check spelling, grammar, and style. Geologists rely on an "expert" computer system for guidance in the quest for minerals. Bankers examine up-to-the-minute securities information from their computer terminals.

The overwhelming majority of people believe that computers enhance the quality of life. People all over the world have become com-

The precise, untiring movement of computer-controlled industrial robots helps assure quality in the assembly of everything from electrical components to automobiles. Here in this Chrysler Motors Corporation plant, 66 industrial robots apply spot welds. About 300 robots weld, seal, train, paint, clean, and handle material at this plant.

mitted to a better way of life through computers, and it is unlikely that the momentum toward this goal will change. It is our responsibility to ensure that this inevitable evolution of computer technology is directed to the benefit of society.

1–2   LEARNING ABOUT COMPUTERS

Cyberphobia

Computers are synonymous with change, and any type of change is usually met with some resistance. We can attribute much of this resistance to a lack of knowledge about computers and, perhaps, to a fear of the unknown. People seem to perceive computers as something mystical. And it is human nature to fear what we don't understand, be it the Extra Terrestrial or computers. Less than 5% of the population is comfortable enough with computers to deem themselves computer-literate. And society will remain in transition from an industrial to an information society until the majority of workers are computer-literate. That may not happen until well into the 1990s.

Fear of the computer is so widespread that psychologists have created a name for it: **cyberphobia**. Cyberphobia is the irrational fear of, and aversion to, computers. In truth, computers are merely machines and don't merit being the focus of such fear. If you are a cyberphobic, you will soon see that your fears are unfounded.

Today we are rapidly becoming an information society where "knowledge workers" depend on computer-generated information to accomplish their jobs. These insurance adjusters use their personal computers to compile claims information.

The Computer Adventure

Fifteen years ago people who pursued a career in almost any facet of business, education, or government were content to leave computers to computer professionals. Well, things have changed. Computers are now an integral part of the learning experience in virtually any career. By the time you complete this course, you will have an understanding of computers that will enable you to be an active and effective participant in the emerging information society. You should:

1. Feel comfortable using and operating a computer system.
2. Be able to make the computer work for you through judicious development or use of **software**. (*Software* refers collectively to a set of machine-readable instructions, called **programs**, that cause the computer to perform desired functions.)
3. Be able to interact with the computer—that is, generate input to the computer and interpret output from it.
4. Understand the impact of computers on society, now and in the future.
5. Be an intelligent consumer of computer-related products and services.

You are about to embark on an emotional and intellectual journey that will stimulate your imagination, challenge your every resource—from physical dexterity to intellect—and perhaps alter your sense of perspective. Learning about computers is more than just education. It's an adventure!

1–3   COMPUTERS ARE FOR EVERYONE

Computer Systems in "the Old Days"

In "the old days" (that is, during the 1950s, 1960s, and even into the 1970s) business computer systems were designed so that a computer professional served as an intermediary between the **end user** and the computer system. End users, or simply **users**, are blue- and white-collar workers who use the computer to help them do their jobs better. In the past, plant supervisors, financial directors, and marketing managers would relate their information needs to computer professionals, such as *programmers* or *systems analysts*, who would then work with the computer system to generate the necessary information.

In "the old days," elapsed time between the submission of a request for information and the distribution of the results could be at least a week or as much as a month. The resulting information was often of little value by the time it reached the manager.

Computer Systems Today

The *timeliness of information* is critical in today's fast-paced business world. Managers cannot wait for the information they need. They want it now, not next week or next month. In response to managers' requests for more timely information, computer systems are now designed to be *interactive*. **Interactive computer systems** eliminate the need to go through an intermediary (the computer professional) and permit users to communicate directly with the computer system. This interactive

Timeliness is critical in the newspaper business. Here several of the 425 USA Today reporters, editors, and researchers are writing and editing copy at their computer terminals. Their late-breaking stories are entered directly into a central computer system. The system processes the copy and sends it to phototypesetters. Within minutes the stories are transmitted via satellite to 33 print sites across the U.S. A couple of hours later, you can pick up a copy of USA Today and read the stories.

mode of operation gives managers the flexibility to analyze the results of one query, then make subsequent queries based on more information.

Today computers and software are being designed to be **user-friendly**. Being user-friendly means that someone with a fundamental knowledge of and exposure to computers can make effective use of the computer and its software. Ten years ago this was not the case. If you didn't have a computer science degree and the mental agility of a wizard, you were out of luck.

1–4 SUPPORTING A COMPANY'S INFORMATION NEEDS

The Information Services Department

Most companies have a computer center and the personnel to support their **information systems**. An information system is a computer-based system that provides data processing capability and information for making decisions. This combination of computing equipment (called **hardware**), the software that tells the computers what to do, and the people who run the computers and develop the software is often referred to as the **information services department** or the **data processing (DP) department**.

The information services department handles the organization's information needs in the same way that the finance department handles the organization's money needs. The department provides data processing and information-related services to virtually every business area. For example, programmers and systems analysts might work with plant managers and engineers to develop a computer-based production and inventory-control system. Jobs and employment opportunities in an information services department are discussed in Chapter 14, "Career Opportunities and Applications of Tomorrow."

The hub of any information services department is the central computing facility that houses the mainframe computer system.

The Information Center

An **information center** is a "hands-on" facility in which computing resources are made available to various user groups. Users come to an information center because they know they can find the computing resources and technical support they need to help with their short-term business information and computing needs. The computing resources might include:

- *Terminals* that enable users to interact directly with the business's central computer system
- *Microcomputers* for "personal," or stand-alone, computing
- *Printers* for **hard copy**, or printed output
- *Plotters* for preparation of presentation graphics

The information center would also have a variety of software packages available for use, such as electronic spreadsheet, word processing, database, and presentation graphics. The center might also provide decision support software and the capability of writing programs. All these hardware and software tools are discussed in detail in later chapters.

Profile

Bill Gates
The First Software Billionaire

It all started around 1968 with two eager young boys entering commands to a computer in a Seattle school. They were so enthralled with this fantastic tool that they used $3000 worth of computing time in the first week—the school's entire allocation for the year! Bill Gates, then a seventh-grader, and Paul Allen, a ninth-grader, were teaching the computer to play Monopoly. They went on to teach it to play millions of games in order to discover gaming strategies.

Seven years later, in 1975, they were to set a course that would revolutionize the computer industry. While at Harvard, Gates and Allen developed a BASIC programming language for the first commercially available microcomputer, the MITS Altair. After successful completion of the project, the two formed Microsoft Corporation to develop and market software for the emerging microcomputer marketplace.

In the years that followed, Microsoft, currently the largest microcomputer software company, has set standards for the software industry in languages, operating systems, and applications software. Gates, now chairman of the board and CEO, provides the company's vision on new-product ideas and technologies. Paul Allen is currently owner of Assymetrics, a software startup company. Gates is frequently referred to as the most influential person in the $100 billion microcomputer industry.

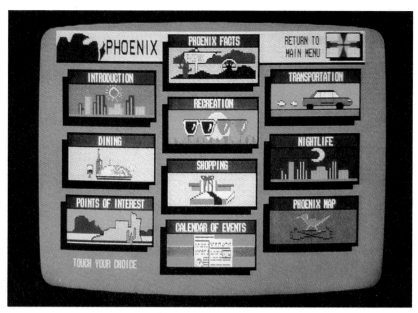

Computer-based information is being made readily available to the general public. For example, in Phoenix, Arizona, tourists need only locate the nearest InfoWindow (at tourist information centers, hotels, and so on) to learn about points of interest, transportation, upcoming events, and other tourist information. The tourist simply touches the appropriate box (for example, "Nightlife") for information. Similar interactive touch screen systems are installed in shopping centers, zoos, airports, grocery stores, and many other environments. By the mid-1990s the information you need will be at your fingertips wherever you go.

1–5   DATA: THE SOURCE OF INFORMATION

Up to now we have talked quite a bit about information, but little about the origin of information—data. **Data** (the plural of *datum*) are the raw material from which information is derived. **Information** is data that have been collected and processed into a meaningful form.

We routinely deal with the concepts of data and information in our everyday experiences. We use data to produce information that will help us make decisions. For example, when we wake up in the morning, we collect two pieces of data. We look at the clock, then recall from our memory the time our first class begins or when we are due at work. Then we subtract the current time from the starting time of class or work. This mental computation provides information on how much time we have to get ready and go. Based on this information, we make a decision to hurry up or to relax and take it easy.

We produce information from data to help us make decisions for thousands of situations each day. In many ways, the content of this book is just an extension of concepts with which you are already familiar.

1–6   UNCOVERING THE "MYSTERY" OF COMPUTERS

The Computer System

Technically speaking, the computer is any counting device. But in the context of modern technology, we will define the **computer** as *an electronic device capable of interpreting and executing programmed commands for input, output, computation, and logic operations.*

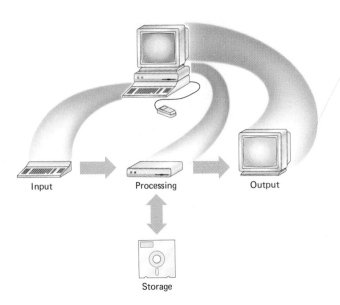

FIGURE 1–1   The Four Fundamental Components of a Microcomputer System
In a microcomputer system, the storage and processing components are often contained in the same physical unit. In the illustration, the diskette storage medium is inserted into the unit that contains the processor.

Computers may be technically complex, but they are conceptually simple. The computer, also called a **processor**, is the "intelligence" of a **computer system**. A computer system has only four fundamental components: *input*, *processing*, *output*, and *storage*. Note that a computer system (not a computer) is made up of the four components. The actual computer is the processing component; when combined with the other three components, it forms a *computer system* (see Figures 1–1 and 1–2).

The relationship of data to a computer system is best explained by showing an analogy to gasoline and an automobile. Data are to a computer system as gas is to a car. Data provide the fuel for a computer system.

FIGURE 1–2   The Four Fundamental Components of a Computer System
In larger computer systems, each of the four components is contained in a separate physical unit.

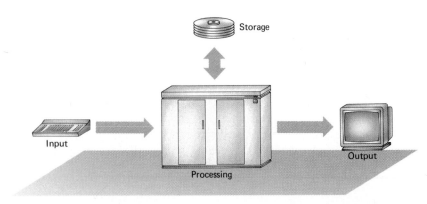

A computer system without data is like a car with an empty gas tank: No gas, no go; no data, no information.

How a Computer System Works

A computer system also can be likened to the biological system of the human body. Your brain is the processing component. Your eyes and ears are input components that send signals to the brain. If you see someone approaching, your brain matches the visual image of this person with others in your memory (storage component). If the visual image matches that of a friend, your brain sends signals to your vocal chords and right arm (output components) to greet your friend with a hello and a handshake. Computer system components interact in a similar way.

The payroll system in Figure 1–3 illustrates how data are entered and how the four computer system components interact to produce information (a year-to-date overtime report) and payroll checks. The hours-worked data are *input* to the system and are *stored* on the personnel **master file**. The master file is made up of **records**, each of which contains data about a particular employee (for example: name, hours worked). Files, records, and other data management concepts are discussed in detail in Chapter 10, "Software Concepts and Data Management."

The payroll checks are produced when the *processing* component, or the computer, executes a program. In this example, the employee records are recalled from storage, and the pay amounts are calculated. The *output* is the printed payroll checks. Other programs extract data from the personnel master file to produce a year-to-date overtime report and any other information that might help in the management decision-making process.

FIGURE 1–3   Payroll System

This microcomputer-based payroll system illustrates input, storage, processing, and output.

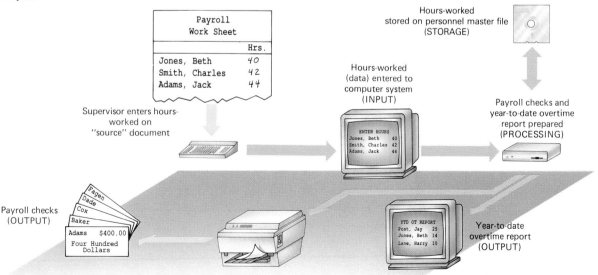

At the "Mac Fac" (Macintosh factory) in Fremont, California, Apple Macintosh microcomputers are rolled out the door at the rate of two per minute. In the spirit of keeping it in the family, Macintosh computers help test those in production.

The Hardware

In the payroll example, data are entered (input) on a **video display terminal**. A **video display terminal**, or simply **terminal**, has a typewriter-like **keyboard** for input and a televisionlike (video) screen, called a **monitor**, for output such as the year-to-date overtime report. The payroll checks are output on a device called a **printer**. Data are stored for later recall on **magnetic disk**. There are a wide variety of **input/output (I/O)** and storage devices. The variety of hardware devices that make up a computer system are discussed in detail in Part II, "Hardware."

The principles discussed here apply equally to **microcomputers** (Figure 1–1) and **mainframe computers** (Figures 1–2 and 1–3). Each has the four components and each uses data to produce information in a similar manner. The difference is that microcomputers, also called **personal computers**, are more limited in their capabilities and are designed primarily for use by *one person at a time*. Mainframe computers can service *many users*, perhaps every manager in the company, all at once. We discuss microcomputers and mainframe computers in more detail in Chapter 2, "Micros, Minis, Mainframes, and Supercomputers."

What Can a Computer Do?

Remember from our previous discussion that the *input/output* and *data storage* hardware components are *configured* with the *processing* component (the computer) to make a computer system (Figures 1–1 and 1–2). Let's discuss the operational capabilities of a computer system just a bit further.

Input /Output Operations.   The computer *reads* from input and storage devices. The computer *writes* to output and storage devices. Before data can be processed, they must be "read" from an input device or data storage device. Input data are usually entered by an operator on a video display terminal or retrieved from a data storage device such as a magnetic disk drive. Once data have been processed, they are "written" to an output device, such as a printer, or to a data storage device.

Input/output (I/O) operations are illustrated in the payroll system example in Figure 1–3. Hours-worked data are entered, or "read," into the computer system. These data are "written" to magnetic disk storage for recall at a later date.

Processing Operations.   The computer is totally objective. That is, any two computers instructed to perform the same operation will arrive at the same result. This is because the computer can perform only *computation* and *logic operations*.

The computational capabilities of the computer include adding, subtracting, multiplying, and dividing. Logic capability permits the computer to make comparisons between numbers and between words then, based on the result of the comparison, perform appropriate functions. In the payroll-system example of Figure 1–3, the computer calculates the gross pay in a computation operation (for example, 40 hours at $15/hour = $600). In a logic operation, the computer compares the the number of hours worked to 40 to determine the number of overtime hours that an employee has worked during a given week. If the hours-worked figure is greater than or equal to 40 (42, for example), the difference (2 hours) is credited as overtime and paid at time and a half.

Computer System Capabilities

In a nutshell, computers are fast, accurate, and reliable; they don't forget anything; and they don't complain. Now for the details.

Speed.   The smallest unit of time in the human experience is, realistically, the second. Computer operations (such as the execution of an instruction, such as adding two numbers) are measured in **milliseconds**, **microseconds**, **nanoseconds**, and **picoseconds** (one thousandth, one millionth, one billionth, and one trillionth of a second, respectively). A beam of light travels down the length of this page in about one nanosecond!

MEMORY BITS

COMPUTER OPERATIONS
- Input /output
  - Read
  - Write
- Processing
  - Computation
  - Logic

MEMORY BITS

FRACTIONS OF A SECOND

Millisecond = .001 seconds (one thousandth of a second)

Microsecond = .000001 seconds (one millionth of a second)

Nanosecond = .000000001 seconds (one billionth of a second)

Picosecond = .000000000001 seconds (one trillionth of a second)

Stockbrokers need more than up-to-the-second quotations on stocks, bonds, and commodities to properly service their clients. These brokers have ready access to market trends in all industries and financial information on hundreds of companies.

Accuracy. Errors do occur in computer-based information systems, but precious few can be directly attributed to the computer system itself. The vast majority can be traced to a program logic error, a procedural error, or erroneous data. These are *human errors*.

Reliability. Computer systems are particularly adept at repetitive tasks. They don't take sick days and coffee breaks, and they seldom complain. Anything below 99.9% *uptime* is usually unacceptable. For some companies, any *downtime* is unacceptable. These companies provide *backup* computers that take over if the main computers fail.

Memory Capability. Computer systems have total and instant recall of data and an almost unlimited capacity to store these data. A typical mainframe computer system will have many billions of characters stored and available for instant recall. To give you a benchmark for comparison, this book contains approximately a million characters.

1–7   HOW DO WE USE COMPUTERS?

For the purpose of this discussion, we will classify the uses of computers into six general categories: *information systems/data processing, personal computing, science and research, process control, education,* and *artificial intelligence*. Figure 1–4 shows how the sum total of existing computer capacity is apportioned to each of these general categories. In the years ahead, look for personal computing, process control, education, and artificial intelligence to grow rapidly and become larger shares of the computer "pie."

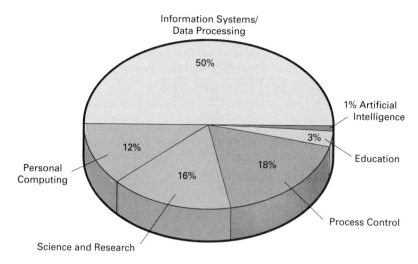

FIGURE 1–4   The Way We Use Computers
This pie chart is an estimate of how existing computer capacity is distributed among the general categories of computer usage.

Information Systems/Data Processing

The bulk of existing computer power is dedicated to *information systems* and *data processing*. This category includes all uses of computers that support the administrative aspects of an organization. Example applications include payroll systems, airline reservation systems, student registration systems, hospital-patient billing systems, and countless others.

Crowded skies have resulted in a rash of "near misses" in recent years. Airlines and the Federal Aviation Administration are counting on sophisticated computer and information systems to eliminate or minimize the risk of mid-air collisions.

Computer-based systems expedite materials movement in factories and warehouses. This automatic guided vehicle is delivering a completed computer system to the distribution center.

We combine *hardware*, *software*, *people*, *procedures*, and *data* to create an information system. A computer-based information system provides a manager's department with *data processing* capabilities and managers with the *information* they need to make better, more informed decisions.

To get a feeling for the widespread influence of computers, let's take a look at how the computer services the data processing and information needs of Zimco Enterprises (a fictional manufacturer of handy consumer products).

- In the *accounting* division, all financial/accounting systems are computerized.
- Zimco's *production* division uses information systems for such applications as inventory control and production scheduling.
- As competition becomes keener, the *marketing* division has turned to the information services division for assistance in fine-tuning the marketing effort.
- The *human resources development* division has automated the basic personnel functions of employment history and career planning.
- The *purchasing* division has replaced cumbersome manual systems with computer-based systems that extend its buying power through selective, time-phased purchasing.
- The *research and development* division relies on the information services division to support a variety of technical programs that include simulation and computer-aided design.
- Zimco's *headquarters staff* and top management routinely make "what if" inquiries, such as: "What if the advertising budget were increased by 20%? How might sales be affected?"

The influence of computer information systems is just as pervasive in hospitals, government agencies, and colleges. A wide variety of information systems for virtually every industry is described and discussed throughout the remainder of the book.

Personal Computing

Individuals and companies are purchasing small, inexpensive microcomputers, also called personal computers, or **PCs**, for a variety of business and domestic applications. A microcomputer system, or **micro** for short, easily sits on a desktop and can be controlled by one person. The growth of this general area, called **personal computing**, has surpassed even the most adventurous forecasts of a decade ago. Some companies actually have more personal computers than telephones. Personal computers far outnumber mainframe computers. But, of course, a single mainframe computer may have the processing capacity of 1000 personal computers.

Domestic Applications for Personal Computing.   A variety of domestic and business applications form the foundation of personal computing. Domestic applications include some of the following: maintaining an up-to-date inventory of household items; storing names and addresses for a personal mailing list; maintaining records for, preparing, and sending income tax returns; creating and monitoring a household budget; keeping an appointment and social calendar; handling household finances (for

HOW OFTEN DO YOU USE THE COMPUTER?

How would you respond to the question "How often do you use computers?" Many people who are just beginning to learn about computers might say, "I don't use them at all," and most of these people would be wrong. The computer and its applications have become so much a part of our everyday routine that we tend to take them for granted. Just about everyone uses and even programs computers, even people who have never sat in front of a personal computer or video display terminal.

- Have you set up your VCR to tape a couple of movies while you sleep? If you have, then you have programmed a computer. VCRs have one or more small computers that activate internal motors based on programmed commands. If you do not have a VCR, then you probably have a programmable microwave oven or answering machine.

- Have you ever called a mail-order merchandiser and been greeted by a recorded message like this: "Thank you for calling Zimco Enterprises Customer Service. If you wish to place an order, press one. If you wish to inquire about the status of an order, press two. To speak to a particular person, enter that person's four-digit extension, or hold and an operator will process your call momentarily." More and more companies are installing computer-controlled telephone systems to expedite calls. These systems permit customers to interact directly with a computer.

- Have you paid your latest electric bill? Sometimes we use the computer indirectly. Did you return a preprinted stub with your check? If you did, you were providing input into a computer system. The information on the stub, which is computer-readable, is entered directly into the computer system.

- Have you driven or ridden in a late-model automobile recently? Most of the newer cars have several on-board computer systems. A computerized warning device checks various systems and "tells" you which ones are not ready: "Please fasten your seat belt," or "A door is open." A computerized fuel-control system feeds the exact mixture of fuel and air to the engine. Another on-board computer provides travel information such as miles per gallon, average miles per hour, and so on.

- How's the temperature at home? Many homes are equipped with computer-controlled environmental systems. These systems permit you to program daily and weekly temperature settings to fit your lifestyle and your pocketbook.

- Did traffic flow smoothly this morning? If it did, then it probably was due to an automated traffic-control system. Sensors in the street feed data on your position, speed, and direction into a central computer. The system uses these data to synchronize traffic signals to optimize the flow of traffic.

- Have you ever been hungry and short of cash? It's lunchtime and you have only 47 cents in your pocket? No problem. Just stop at an automatic teller machine and ask for some lunch money.

So, as you see, computers are quietly playing an increasingly significant role in our lives. Each day technological innovations that will ultimately make life a little more convenient for all of us are being explored. For example, you may be doing your grocery shopping from the comfort of your kitchen counter (via a personal computer) within this very decade!

example, checkbook balancing, paying bills, coupon refunding); writing letters; education; and, of course, entertainment. You can purchase software for all these applications, and you can probably obtain software for your special interest, whether it be astrology, charting biorhythms, composing music, or dieting.

Business Applications for Personal Computing.   Of course, virtually any business application (for example, payroll and sales analysis) discussed

In years past, this executive would fill his attache case with reports, documents, and other work-related papers. Now he carries his portable personal computer and with it the information resources of his company. From his home (or anywhere there is a telephone) he can establish a communications link with his company and make inquiries to the company's central computer system, check on his electronic mail, enter data, or send a memo to the managers in his department.

in this book is supported on a personal computer, but the most popular business use of personal computers is with *productivity software*. Microcomputer-based productivity software is a series of commercially available programs that can help people in the business community save time and get information they need to make more informed decisions. *Productivity software* is the foundation of personal computing in the business world. These productivity tools include the following:

- *Word processing.* **Word processing** software permits users to enter, store, manipulate, and print text.
- *Desktop publishing.* **Desktop publishing** software allows users to produce near-typeset-quality copy for newsletters, advertisements, and many other printing needs, all from the confines of a desktop.
- *Electronic spreadsheet.* **Electronic spreadsheet** software permits users to work with the rows and columns of a matrix (or spreadsheet) of data.
- *Database.* **Database** software permits users to create and maintain a data base and to extract information from the data base.
- *Presentation graphics.* **Presentation graphics** software permits users to create charts and line drawings that graphically portray the data in an electronic spreadsheet or data base.

The function and concepts of these productivity tools are described in Chapter 7, "Productivity Software: Word Processing and Desktop Publishing," and Chapter 8, "Productivity Software: Electronic Spreadsheet and Database." Hands-on tutorials for the most popular word processing, electronic spreadsheet, and database software packages (WordPerfect®, Lotus® 1-2-3®, and dBASE III Plus®, respectively) are contained in Appendices E, F, and G.

Information Services.   Personal computers, or **PCs**, are normally used as stand-alone computer systems, but as we have seen from earlier discussions, they can also double as remote terminals. This dual-function capability provides you with the flexibility to work with the PC as a stand-alone system or to link it with a larger computer and take advantage of its increased capacity. With a PC, you have a world of information at your fingertips. The personal computer can be used in conjunction with the telephone system to transmit data to and receive data from an **information network**.

A growing trend among personal computer enthusiasts is to subscribe to the services of an information network. These information networks have one or several large computer systems that offer a variety of information services. These services include hotel reservations, home banking, shopping at home, daily horoscopes, financial information, games, up-to-the-minute news, and much more. Information networks are discussed in more detail in Chapter 6, "Data Communications."

The services provided by information networks, coupled with the capabilities of microcomputer productivity software, eventually should make personal computers a "must-have" item in every home and business.

Science and Research

Engineers and scientists routinely use the computer as a tool in experimentation and design. Aerospace engineers use computers to simulate the effects of a wind tunnel to analyze the aerodynamics of an airplane prototype. Political scientists collect and analyze demographic data, such as median income and housing starts, to predict voting trends. Chemists use computer graphics to create three-dimensional views of an experimental molecule. There are at least as many science and research applications for the computer as there are scientists and engineers.

An information service makes the full text of newspapers, wire services, magazines, newsletters, and government publications available for immediate on-line access. Subscribers to this service, such as this district attorney, use key words to enter the data base and select a particular topic (such as computer crime, real estate fraud). Eventually information services will make the full text of books available for perusal.

Traditional approaches to screening anticancer drugs and testing a patient's response to new cancer treatments can be time-consuming, costly, and prone to inaccuracies. The merging of optical and computer technologies has produced sophisticated image analysis capabilities that speed the evaluation of chemotherapeutic drugs. This analyzer automatically scans tumor-cell colonies and provides valuable information to doctors.

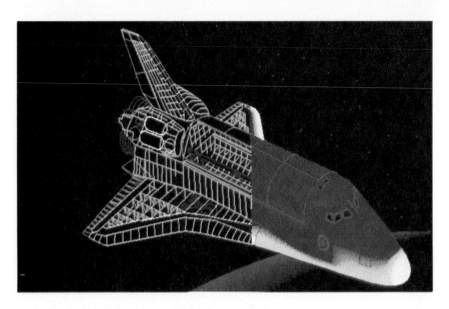

With the prospect of increased productivity, people in every discipline are rushing to install more and more computer applications. By using computer modeling techniques, engineers can test the effectiveness of the heat shield on NASA's space shuttle without burning an ounce of fuel. Upon reentry to the earth's atmosphere, the spacecraft is subjected to intense heat. The white area around the nose is the hottest.

Process Control

Computers used for **process control** accept data in a continuous *feedback loop*. In a feedback loop, the process itself generates data that become input to the computer. As the data are received and interpreted by the computer, the computer initiates action to control the ongoing process. For example, process-control computers monitor and control the environment (temperature, humidity, lighting, security) inside skyscrapers (see Figure 1–5). These computer-controlled skyscrapers are often referred to as "smart" buildings.

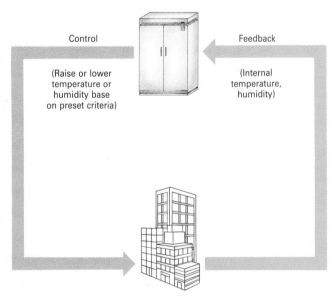

Control

(Raise or lower temperature or humidity base on preset criteria)

Feedback

(Internal temperature, humidity)

FIGURE 1–5 Process-Control Feedback Loop
Computer-based environmental control systems monitor and control the temperature and humidity in thousands of buildings.

This is the control room at a Texaco refinery. A computer system gathers data from remote sensors throughout the refinery to monitor all processes within the refinery.

Tiny "computers on a chip" are being embedded in artificial hearts and other organs. Once the organs are implanted in the body, the computer monitors critical inputs, such as blood pressure and flow, then takes corrective action to ensure stability of operation in a continuous feedback loop.

Education

Computers can interact with students to enhance the learning process. Relatively inexpensive hardware capable of multidimensional communication (sound, print, graphics, and color) has resulted in a phenomenal growth of the computer as an educational tool in the home, in the classroom, and in business. Computer-based education will not replace teachers and books, but educators are in agreement that *computer-based training* (CBT) is having a profound impact on traditional modes of education.

Computers have been used for drill and practice for over a decade. Only recently has sophisticated CBT been economically feasible. Now powerful personal computers have added a dimension that is not possible with books and the traditional classroom lectures. The student controls the pace of learning and can interact directly with the computer system. Through interactive computer graphics, a CBT system can demonstrate certain concepts more effectively than can books or even teachers. The teacher-book-CBT approach has spawned a new era in education. The software supplement to this text provides many examples of sophisticated CBT.

Computers can help us read and understand poetry. The photo shows how Robert Browning's poem "Meeting at Night" can be highlighted to demonstrate the concept of parenthetical rhyme. An aspiring poet can examine this and other attributes of Browning's classic as well, such as metrical accent.

Meeting At Night

The gray sea and the long black land
And the yellow half-moon large and low
And the startled little waves that leap
In fiery ringlets from their sleep
As I gain the cove with pushing prow
And quench its speed in the slushy sand.

Then a mile of warm sea-scented beach-
Three fields to cross till a farm appears-
A tap at the pane- the quick sharp scratch
And blue spurt of a lighted match
And a voice less loud- through its joys and fears
Than the two hearts beating each to each!

- Robert Browning

parenthetical rhyme

Computers are interactive—that is, in their own special way they can communicate with human beings. This capability makes them excellent educational tools. These computers are helping children learn to read and write. Computers also help adults learn about everything from auto mechanics to zoology.

Artificial Intelligence

Human Beings Are Born, Not Manufactured.   Today's computers can simulate many human capabilities such as reaching, grasping, calculating, speaking, remembering, comparing numbers, and drawing. Researchers are working to expand these capabilities and, therefore, the power of computers by developing hardware and software that can imitate intelligent human behavior. For example, researchers are working on systems that have the ability to reason, to learn or accumulate knowledge, to strive for self-improvement, and to simulate human sensory and mechanical capabilities. This general area of research is known as **artificial intelligence (AI)**.

Artificial intelligence? To some, the mere mention of artificial intelligence creates visions of electromechanical automatons replacing human beings. But as anyone involved in the area of artificial intelligence will tell you, there is a distinct difference between human beings and machines. Computers will never be capable of simulating the distinctly human qualities of creativity, humor, and emotions! However, computers can drive machines that mimic human movements (such as picking up objects and placing them at a prescribed location) and provide the "brains" for systems that simulate the human thought process within the domain of a particular area of expertise (tax preparation, medical diagnosis, and so on).

Categories of Artificial Intelligence.   Research in the field of artificial intelligence can be divided into categories (see Figure 1–6): knowledge-based and expert systems, natural languages, simulation of human sensory capabilities, and robotics.

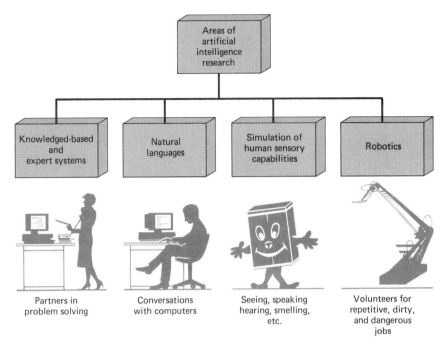

FIGURE 1–6   Categories of Artificial Intelligence

Knowledge-based and expert systems   A **knowledge-based system** relies on a **knowledge base** that is filled with "rules of thumb" (intuition, judgment, and inferences) about a specific application area, such as computer repair. Humans can use the knowledge-based system and the IF–THEN rules in the knowledge base to help them solve a particular problem. **Expert systems** are the most sophisticated implementation of a knowledge-based system. Once the knowledge of one or more human experts has been entered to an expert system's knowledge base, users can tap this knowledge by interacting with the system in much the same way they would interact with a human expert in that field. Both the user and the computer-based expert system ask and respond to one another's questions until a problem is resolved. Expert systems are discussed in more detail in Chapter 11, "Applications of Information Technology."

Natural languages   **Natural languages** refer to software that enables computer systems to accept, interpret, and execute instructions in the native, or "natural," language of the end user, typically English. For example, the end user uses a natural language when he or she enters brief English commands such as "Show me a pie chart for regional sales" to a computer system. There are, of course, limitations on the complexity of the commands that can be interpreted. The state of the art of natural languages is still somewhat primitive. Most commercial natural languages are designed to provide end users with a means of communicating with a corporate data base or an expert system.

Simulation of human sensory capabilities   One area of AI research involves computer simulation of human capabilities. This area focuses

Locomotive mechanics get troubleshooting help with a computer-based expert system. They simply key in responses to questions asked by the "expert" about the malfunction. Through interactive questioning, the expert system eventually identifies the cause of the malfunction and demonstrates repair procedures on the video monitor.

on equipping computer systems with the capabilities of seeing, hearing, speaking, and feeling (touching). These artificial intelligence capabilities are possible with current technology, to varying degrees. Several of them are discussed in Chapter 4, "Input/Output Devices."

Robotics   **Robotics** is the integration of computers and **industrial robots**. Industrial robots, which are usually equipped with an arm and a hand, can be "taught" to perform almost any repetitive manipulative task, such as painting a car, screwing on a bolt, moving material, and even such complex tasks as inspecting a manufactured part for defects. The topic of robotics is addressed in more detail in Chapter 11, "Applications of Information Technology."

Computers and Opportunity

Computers provide many opportunities for us to improve the quality of both our private and professional lives. Our challenge is to take advantage of the opportunities afforded by the computer revolution and our emergence as an information society. People like you who are willing to put forth the effort and accept the challenge will be the ones who benefit the most.

SUMMARY OUTLINE AND IMPORTANT TERMS_____

1–1   **THE INFORMATION SOCIETY.** After existing for millennia in an agrarian society, many countries progressed to industrial societies. Today we are being transformed into an information society. Each year computers, both in general and at a more personal level, are having a greater influence on our lives. It is our responsibility to direct their application to the benefit of society.

1–2   **LEARNING ABOUT COMPUTERS. Cyberphobia**, the irrational fear of, and aversion to, computers, is a result of people's fear of the unknown. They overcome cyberphobia by learning about computers. Computer-literate people know how to purchase, use, and operate a computer system, and how to make it work for them. The computer-literate person is also aware of the computer's impact on society.

Software refers collectively to a set of machine-readable instructions, called **programs**, that cause the computer to perform desired functions.

1–3   **COMPUTERS ARE FOR EVERYONE.** During the 1950s, 1960s, and 1970s, **end users**, or simply **users**, would relate their information needs to such computer professionals as programmers or systems analysts, who would then work with the computer system to generate the necessary information. In "the old days," information was often obsolete by the time it reached the manager. In response to managers' requests for more timely information, **interactive computer systems** were created to permit users to communicate directly with the computer system via **user-friendly** software.

Both white-collar and blue-collar workers will spend more and more of each working day interacting with some kind of computer-based system.

1–4   **SUPPORTING A COMPANY'S INFORMATION NEEDS.** Companies depend on **information systems** and the capabilities of computing **hardware** for their data processing and information needs. The organizational entity charged with supporting these needs is called the **information services department** or **data processing (DP) department**. An **information center** is a facility that includes a variety of computing resources: terminals, microcomputers, printers and plotters for **hardcopy** output, and a variety of user-oriented software packages.

1–5   **DATA: THE SOURCE OF INFORMATION. Data** are the raw material from which information is derived. **Information** consists of data that have been collected and processed into a meaningful form.

1–6   **UNCOVERING THE "MYSTERY" OF COMPUTERS.** The **computer**, or **processor**, is an electronic device capable of interpreting and executing programmed commands for input, output, computation, and logic operations. Computer system capabilities are defined as either input/output or processing. Processing capabilities are subdivided into computation and logic operations. A **computer system** is not as complex as we are sometimes led to believe. **Personal computers**, also called **microcomputers**, and **mainframe computers** are all computer systems, and each has only four fundamental components: **input** (for example, via the **keyboard** of a **video display terminal—VDT** or **terminal**), processing (executing a program), **output** (via a **monitor** or a **printer**), and storage. (For example, **master files** and **records** can be stored on **magnetic disk**.)

The computer is fast, accurate, reliable, and has an enormous memory capacity. Computer operations are measured in **milliseconds**, **microseconds**, **nanoseconds**, and **picoseconds**.

1–7   **HOW DO WE USE COMPUTERS?** The uses of computers can be classified into six general categories:

- *Information systems/data processing*. The computer is used to process data and produce business information. Hardware, software, people, procedures, and data are combined to create an information system.

- *Personal computing*. The single-user **micro** is used by individuals for a variety of business and domestic applications, including such productivity software tools as **word processing, desktop publishing, electronic spreadsheet, database,** and **presentation graphics**. This area of computing is often referred to as **personal computing**. The dual-function personal computers, or **PCs**, can be used in conjunction with the telephone system to transmit data to and receive data from an **information network**.

- *Science and research*. The computer is used as a tool in experimentation and design.

- *Process control*. The computer is used to control a process by accepting and evaluating data in a continuous feedback loop.

■ *Education.* The computer interacts with a student to enhance the learning process.

■ *Artificial intelligence.* **Artificial intelligence (AI)** is the area of research that involves creating computer systems with the ability to reason, to learn or accumulate knowledge, to strive for self-improvement, and to simulate human sensory and mechanical capabilities. There are four categories of AI research: **knowledge-based systems** and **expert systems**, **natural languages**, simulation of human sensory capabilities, and **robotics**.

A knowledge of computers opens the door to opportunity in many professions.

REVIEW EXERCISES

Concepts

1. What are the four fundamental components of a computer system?
2. Which component of a computer system executes the program?
3. Name the four categories of artificial intelligence research.
4. Associate the following with the appropriate category of computer usage: continuous feedback loop, experimentation, home use, CBT, synthesized speech, and business systems.
5. Light travels at 186,000 miles per second. How many milliseconds does it take for a beam of light to travel across the United States, a distance of about 3000 miles?
6. Compare the information-processing capabilities of human beings to those of computers with respect to speed, accuracy, reliability, and memory.
7. What term is used to describe the integration of computers and industrial robots?
8. What are the primary functions of an organization's information-services department?
9. Describe the relationship between data and information.
10. In computerese, what is meant by *read* and *write*?
11. Name the five microcomputer tools that are collectively referred to as productivity software.
12. Which microcomputer productivity tool would be most helpful in writing a term paper? Explain.
13. List at least six information network services.
14. What type of hardware and software would be appropriate for an information center?

Discussion

15. The computer has had far-reaching effects on our lives. How has the computer affected your life?
16. What is your concept of computer literacy? In what ways do you

think achieving computer literacy will affect your domestic life? Your business life?

17. Discuss how the complexion of jobs will change as we evolve from an industrial society into an information society. Give several examples.

18. The use of computers tends to stifle creativity. Argue for or against this statement.

SELF-TEST (by section)

1–1 To be computer-literate, you must be able to write computer programs. (T/F)

1–2 The irrational fear of, or aversion to, computers is called _____.

1–3 What type of system permits users to communicate directly with the computer: (a) a controlled-use system, (b) an interactive system, or (c) a loop system?

1–4 The information center is a company's primary resource for the development of full-scale information systems. (T/F)

1–5 _____ are the raw material from which _____ is derived.

1–6 **a.** A printer is an example of which of the four computer system components?

   b. The two types of processing operations performed by computers are _____ and _____ .

   c. A microsecond is 1000 times longer than a nanosecond. (T/F)

1–7 **a.** The greatest amount of available computing capacity is dedicated to the information systems/data processing category of computer usage. (T/F)

   b. The microcomputer productivity tool that manipulates data organized in a tabular structure of rows and columns is called an _____.

   c. Artificial intelligence refers to an area of research that uses computers to simulate human capabilities. (T/F)

Self-test answers.   **1–1** F. **1–2** cyberphobia. **1–3** b. **1–4** F. **1–5** data, information. **1–6 (a)** output; **(b)** computation, logic; **(c)** F. **1–7 (a)** T; **(b)** electronic spreadsheet; **(c)** T.

2

Micros, Minis, Mainframes, and Supercomputers

STUDENT LEARNING OBJECTIVES

▶ To distinguish between microcomputers, minicomputers, mainframes, and supercomputers.

▶ To illustrate typical hardware configurations for microcomputers, minicomputers, and mainframes.

▶ To distinguish between the different types of microcomputers.

▶ To demonstrate awareness of the relative size, scope, characteristics, and variety of available computer systems.

2–1   COMPUTER SYSTEMS COME IN ALL SHAPES AND SIZES

Categories of Computer Systems

The most distinguishing characteristic of any computer system is its size—not its physical size, but its computing capacity. Computers have been classified as *microcomputers, minicomputers, superminicomputers, midicomputers, maxicomputers,* and *supercomputers,* to mention a few. From this list you might think these terms were coined by fashion designers. This is not the case. The minicomputer preceded the miniskirt!

Now and even in the past, these computer classifications have defied definition. Although it is doubtful that any two computer specialists would describe a minicomputer or a supercomputer in the same way, these terms are still frequently used. Rapid advances in computer technology have blurred what used to be distinguishing characteristics (physical size, cost, memory capacity, and so on).

All computers, no matter how small or large, have the same fundamental capabilities—processing, storage, input, and output. Just as "a rose, is a rose, is a rose. . . ." (Gertrude Stein), "a computer, is a computer, is a computer. . . ." Keep this in mind as we discuss the four basic categories of computers. They are listed in ascending order of their processing capabilities:

- Microcomputer system
- Minicomputer system
- Mainframe computer system
- Supercomputer system

It should be emphasized that these are relative categories, and what people call a minicomputer system today may be called a microcomputer system at some time in the future.

Micros versus Minis, Mainframes, and Supercomputers

Micros are computer systems. Minicomputers, mainframes, and supercomputers are computer systems. Each offers many input and output alternatives, and each is supported by a wide variety of packaged software. There are, of course, obvious differences in size and capabilities. Everything associated with minicomputers, mainframes, and supercomputers is larger in scope than that associated with microcomputers: Execution of programs is faster; disk storage has more capacity; printer speeds are much faster. Computers in these three categories can service many terminals and, of course, they cost more. (Interestingly, the price-performance ratio of computers is inversely proportional to the size of the computer. That is, it costs less to execute a million instructions on a microcomputer than it does to execute the same number on a minicomputer.)

Besides size and capability, the single most distinguishing characteristic of minicomputers, mainframe computers, and supercomputers is the manner in which each type is used. The three larger computers, with their expanded processing capabilities, provide a computing resource that can be shared by many people. In contrast, most microcomputers

This architect is interacting with a member of the IBM Personal System/2 series, IBM's successor to the popular IBM PC series microcomputers. Most PS/2 models are designed to rest on a desktop. The component that houses the processing and disk storage capabilities of this high-end PS/2 model is designed to rest on the floor. It is sometimes difficult to distinguish the appearance and functionality of this system from some low-end minicomputers.

are used primarily by a single user at a time. It is common in a company for the finance, personnel, and accounting departments to share the resources of a mini, mainframe, or supercomputer, possibly all at the same time.

2–2   MICROCOMPUTERS: SMALL BUT POWERFUL

Microprocessors

Here is a tough one. What is smaller than a dime and found in wristwatches, sewing machines, and jukeboxes? The answer: a **microprocessor**. Microprocessors play a very important role in our lives. You probably have a dozen or more of them at home and may not know it. They are used in telephones, ovens, televisions, thermostats, greeting cards, automobiles, and of course, personal computers.

The microprocessor is a product of the microminiaturization of electronic circuitry; it is literally a "computer on a chip." The first fully operational microprocessor was demonstrated in March 1971. Since that time, these relatively inexpensive microprocessors have been integrated into thousands of mechanical and electronic devices—even elevators, band saws, and ski-boot bindings. In a few years virtually everything mechanical or electronic will incorporate microprocessor technology into its design.

Many automobile-engine functions are monitored and controlled by microprocessors. This one optimizes gear shifting in this five-speed automatic transmission by controlling the throttle and clutch.

Microcomputers

There is no commonly accepted definition of microcomputer or any other type of computer. A microcomputer is just a small computer. However, it is a safe bet that any computer you can pick up and carry is probably a micro. But don't be misled by the *prefix*. You can pick up and carry some very powerful computers!

The microprocessor is sometimes confused with its famous offspring, the microcomputer. A keyboard, video monitor, and memory were attached to the microprocessor and the microcomputer was born! Suddenly owning a computer became an economic reality for individuals and small businesses.

The Motherboard. In a microcomputer, the microprocessor—the electronic circuitry for handling input/output signals from the **peripheral devices** (keyboard, printer, and so on)—and the memory chips are mounted on a single circuit board, called a **motherboard**, or **system board**. Before being attached to the motherboard, the microprocessor and other chips are mounted onto a *carrier*. Carriers have standard-sized pin connectors that allow the chips to be attached to the motherboard.

The motherboard, the "guts" of a microcomputer, is what distinguishes one microcomputer from another. The central component of the motherboard, the microprocessor, is not made by the manufacturers of micros but by companies that specialize in development and manufacture of microprocessors, such as Motorola and Intel. All Apple's Macintosh-series micros use Motorola chips: the Motorola 68000 in earlier models, the Motorola 68020 in the Macintosh II, and the Motorola 68030 in recent models. The original IBM PC, the IBM PC/XT, and most of the IBM-PC–compatibles manufactured through 1986 used the Intel 8088 microprocessor chip. The IBM PC/AT and low-end models of the IBM PS/2 use the Intel 8086 chip. Although faster than the Intel 8088, the Intel 8086 is technologically similar to the Intel 8088. High-end models of the IBM PS/2 and their compatibles use the more advanced Intel 80286, 80386, and 80486 chips. When someone talks about a "286" or "386" machine, they are referring to a micro that uses an Intel 80286 or 80386.

After the microprocessor and other chips have been mounted on the motherboard, it is simply inserted into one of several slots designed for circuit boards. The processing components of most micros are sold with several empty **expansion slots** so that you can purchase and plug in optional capabilities in the form of **add-on boards**. Add-on boards are discussed in more detail later in this chapter.

Pocket, Laptop, and Desktop PCs. Personal computers come in three different physical sizes: *pocket PCs*, *laptop PCs*, and *desktop PCs*. The pocket and laptop PCs are light (a few ounces to eight pounds), compact, and can operate without an external power source, so they earn the "portable" label as well. There are also a number of "transportable" desktop PCs on the market, but they are more cumbersome to move. They fold up to about the size of a small suitcase, weigh about 25 pounds, and usually require an external power source. Desktop PCs

When searching for a personal computer, this medical sales representative identified portability as her primary criterion. She purchased a laptop PC because it gave her the flexibility to carry her files and the power of a computer wherever she goes. During a flight to Chicago, she decided to review physician profiles before making sales calls.

are not designed for frequent movement and therefore are not considered portable.

The power of a PC is not necessarily related directly to its size. A few laptop PCs can run circles around some of the desktop PCs. Some

This project manager spends at least three days a week away from the office. When he travels, his transportable PC is part of his luggage. He uses the PC in conjunction with project management software. To prepare the computer for movement, he fastens the keyboard in position to cover the monitor and attaches a handle to the top of the micro.

user conveniences, however, must be sacrificed to achieve portability. For instance, the miniature keyboards on pocket PCs, sometimes called *palmtop PCs*, make data entry to and interaction with the computer difficult and slow. The display screen on some laptop PCs is small and does not hold as much text as a display screen on a desktop PC.

Configuring a PC: Putting the Pieces Together

Normally computer professionals are called upon to select, configure, and install the hardware associated with minis, mainframes, and supercomputers. But the user typically selects, configures, and installs his or her own micro; therefore, it is important that you know what makes up a microcomputer system and how it fits together.

A Typical Microcomputer Configuration.   The computer and its peripheral devices are called the computer-system **configuration**. The configuration of a microcomputer can vary. The most typical micro configuration consists of the following:

1. A computer
2. A keyboard for input
3. A monitor for *soft-copy* (temporary) output
4. A printer for *hard-copy* (printed) output
5. One or two disk drives for permanent storage of data and programs

In some microcomputer systems these components are purchased as separate physical units, then linked together. Micros that give users the flexibility of configuring the system with a variety of peripheral devices (input/output and storage) are said to have an **open architecture**. A good analogy that illustrates the concept of open architecture is a component stereo system to which a record turntable, an equalizer, a tape

All or parts of many traditional office fixtures can be absorbed within a desktop PC: typewriters and opaquing fluid, calculators, notepads and worksheets, drawing equipment, telephone indices, calendars, tickler files, file cabinets, important reports and memos, and reference books such as a dictionary or thesaurus. The beverage glass and coffee cup, however, will continue to occupy their place on the desktop.

deck, a compact disk player, speakers, and so on can be attached. A microcomputer system with an open architecture is configured by linking any of the many peripheral devices discussed in Chapters 4 and 5 (I/O and data storage devices) to the processor component. In a **closed architecture**, the system is fully configured when it is sold. Except for a few pocket and laptop PCs, virtually all micros placed on the market during the past couple of years have an open architecture.

Linking Micro Components.   An open architecture, also called a **bus architecture**, is possible because all micro components are linked by a common electrical **bus**. In Chapter 1, we compared the processing component of a microcomputer to the human brain. Just as the brain sends and receives signals through the central nervous system, the processor sends and receives electrical signals through the bus. The bus is the path through which the processor sends and receives data and commands to and from **random-access memory** and all peripheral devices, such as printers and disk storage. Random-access memory, which is usually called **RAM** (rhymes with *Sam*), is made up of solid-state electronics components, specifically memory chips. All programs and data must reside in RAM before programs can be executed or data can be processed. (RAM is discussed in detail in Chapter 3, "Inside the Computer.") Data and commands are transmitted between the processor, RAM, and its peripheral devices in the form of electronic signals. In short, the bus is a vehicle for communication between the processor, RAM, and the various peripheral devices.

In an open architecture, external input/output devices (devices external to the processor cabinet) and some storage devices are plugged into the bus in much the same way you would plug a lamp into an electrical outlet. The receptacle, called a *port*, provides a direct link to the micro's common electrical bus.

External peripheral devices are linked, or *interfaced*, with the processor through either a **serial port** or a **parallel port**. Serial ports facilitate the *serial transmission* of data—the transmission of only one electronic signal at a time. Serial ports provide an interface for low-speed printers and other low-speed devices. The de facto standard for micro serial ports is the 25-pin (male or female) **RS-232C port**.

Parallel ports facilitate the *parallel transmission* of data: the simultaneous transmission of multiple electronic signals. Parallel ports provide the interface for such devices as high-speed printers (for example, laser printers), magnetic tape backup units, and other computers.

Also connected to the common electrical bus are *expansion slots*, which are usually housed in the processor cabinet. These slots enable a micro owner to enhance the functionality of a basic micro configuration with a wide variety of special-function *add-on boards*, also called **add-on cards**. These "add-ons" contain the electronic circuitry for a wide variety of computer-related functions. The number of available expansion slots varies from computer to computer. Some of the more popular add-on boards are listed below.

■ *RAM*. Expands random-access memory in increments ranging from 64,000 characters to four million characters.

The inside of this IBM PS/2 Model 50Z is representative of what you might see when you remove the cover of a desktop micro. The bottom right side is the front of the computer. Looking across the front from left to right, there is a speaker for audible output, a 3½-inch microdisk drive, space for another microdisk drive, and the on/off switch. The motherboard, which is directly behind the speaker component, contains an Intel 80286 microprocessor (the square chip). The black box in the center is a 3½-inch fixed disk that can store 60 million characters of data. Three expansion slots are positioned at the left rear of the micro. Serial and parallel ports (not shown) are positioned at the back of the unit.

- *Color and graphics adapter.* Permits the interfacing of video monitors that have graphics and/or color capabilities. These boards usually come with dedicated RAM that is not accessible to the user.
- *Modem.* Permits communication with remote computers via a telephone line link.
- *Internal battery-powered clock/calendar.* Provides continuous and/or on-demand display of or access to the date and time (for example: Monday, Dec. 18, 1992, 9:35 a.m.).
- *Serial port.* Installation of this board provides access to the bus through another serial port.
- *Parallel port.* Installation of this board provides access to the bus via another parallel port.
- *Printer spooler.* Enables data to be printed while the user continues with other processing activities. The data are transferred (spooled) at high speed from RAM to a *print buffer* (an intermediate storage area) and then routed to the printer from the buffer.
- *Hard disk.* Hard disks, sometimes called hard cards, with capacities of as much as 40 million characters, can be installed in expansion slots.
- *Coprocessor.* These "extra" processors, which are under the control of the main processor, help relieve the main processor of certain tasks, such as arithmetic functions. This sharing of duties helps increase the processing capability of the computer system.
- *VCR backup.* This board enables an ordinary Beta or VHS videocassette recorder to be used as a tape backup device. One ordinary videocassette tape can hold up to 80,000,000 characters of data.
- *FAX.* This board, when used in conjunction with appropriate input/output devices, enables the computer to perform the functions of a facsimile (FAX) machine.

Most of the add-on boards are *multifunctional*: In other words, they include two or more of these capabilities. For example, one popular **multifunction add-on board** comes with a serial port, a modem, and an internal battery-powered clock/calendar.

Expansion slots are at a premium. To make the most efficient use of them, circuit-board manufacturers have created half-size expansion boards that fit in a *short slot* (half an expansion slot). These half-size boards effectively double the number of expansion slots available for a given microcomputer.

Multiuser Micros

In the early 1960s, mainframe computer systems could service only one user at a time. By the mid-1960s, technological improvements had made it possible for computers to service several users simultaneously. Now, a quarter of a century later, some mainframes service thousands of users at the same time!

We can draw a parallel between what happened to the mainframe in the 1960s and what is happening to microcomputers today. Until recently micros were "personal" computers—for individual use only. But technological improvements have been so rapid that it has become difficult for a single user to tap the full potential of state-of-the-art micros. To tap this unused potential, hardware and software vendors are marketing products that permit several people to use the system at once.

These multiuser micros are configured with up to 12 VDTs. These terminals, often located in the same office, share the microcomputer's resources and its peripheral devices. With a multiuser micro, a secretary can transcribe dictation at one terminal while a manager does financial analysis at another terminal and a clerk enters data to a data base at yet another. All this can take place at the same time on the same multiuser micro.

Personal computers are everywhere and, as such, are particularly vulnerable to unauthorized use or malicious tampering. As an added layer of security, many companies are opting to use a magnetic card reader as part of the user sign-on procedure. The card reader comes with an add-on board that is inserted in one of the micro's expansion slots. The reader reads commonly carried credit cards, door-opener cards, telephone cards, and so on. When used in conjunction with authorization codes, a PC can have the same level of security as an automatic teller machine.

The Dual-Purpose Micro: Two for the Price of One

A terminal is the hardware that allows you to interact with a computer system, be it a mainframe or a multiuser micro. A microcomputer can also function as a terminal. With the installation of an optional data communications adapter, a micro has the flexibility to serve as a *stand-alone* computer system or as an "intelligent" terminal of a multiuser micro, a mini, a mainframe, or a supercomputer.

The term *intelligent* is applied to terminals that also can operate as stand-alone computer systems, independent of any other computer system. For example, you can dial up any one of a number of commercial information services on travel, securities, and consumer goods, link your micro to the telephone line and remote computer, then use your micro as a terminal to receive information. Both the micro and the VDT can transmit and receive data from a remote computer, but only the micro terminal can process and store the data independently.

BUYING MICROCOMPUTERS AND THEIR PERIPHERAL DEVICES

More than a million people a year go through the process of buying a microcomputer, micro peripheral devices, and related software. The information presented here will help those planning to purchase a microcomputer to spend their money wisely.

Retail Sales

Where to buy   Microcomputers and related hardware and software can be purchased at thousands of convenient locations. Retail chains, such as ComputerLand, ENTRE, and MicroAge, market and service a variety of small computer systems. Radio Shack stores carry and sell their own line of computers. Micros are also sold in the computer departments of most department stores. The demand for micros has encouraged major computer system manufacturers to open their own retail stores.

There is an alternative to buying a computer at a retail store. If you know what you want, you can call any of several mail-order services, give them a credit-card number, and your PC will be delivered to your doorstep.

The perks of employment   You might be able to acquire a micro through your employer. Many companies offer their employees a "computer perk." In cooperation with vendors, companies make volume purchases of PCs at discount rates, then offer them to employees at substantial savings. Many colleges sponsor similar programs to benefit students and professors.

Steps in Buying a Microcomputer

Buying a microcomputer can be a harrowing experience or it can be a thrilling and fulfilling one. If you approach the purchase of a micro haphazardly, expect the former. If you go about the acquisition methodically and with purpose, expect the latter. This section contains a nine-step procedure to help you evaluate and select a microcomputer system.

1. *Achieve computer literacy.* You do not buy an automobile before you learn how to drive, and you should not buy a microcomputer without a good understanding of its capabilities and how you intend to use it.

2. *Determine how much you are willing to spend.* Microcomputer systems can be purchased for as little as a few hundred dollars or as much as $40,000. Assess your circumstances and decide how much you are willing to commit to the purchase of a microcomputer system.

3. *Determine your information and computer-usage needs.* There is an adage: "If you don't know where you are going, any road will get you there." The statement is certainly true of choosing a PC. Knowing where you are going can be translated into: "How do you plan to use the PC?"

Do you want to develop your own software, purchase commercially available software packages, or perhaps do both? If you want to write your own programs, you must select the programming language best suited to your skills and application needs. If you plan on purchasing the software, determine which general application areas you wish to have supported on the proposed PC (spreadsheet, accounting, word processing, data communications, home banking, graphics, or others).

4. *Assess availability of software and information services.* Determine what software and information services are available to meet your needs. Good sources of this type of information include a wide variety of periodicals (*PC*, *Byte*, *Software*, *Computerworld*, and *Personal Computing*, to name a few), salespeople at computer stores, and acquaintances who have knowledge in the area.

Several hundred micro productivity software packages are available commercially and vary greatly in capabilities and price. Software with essentially the same capabilities may have price differences of several hundred dollars. Some graphics software creates displays of graphs in seconds, while others take minutes. Some software packages are easy to learn and are accompanied by good documentation, while others are not. Considering the amount of time you might spend using micro software, any extra time you devote to evaluating the software will be time well spent.

5. *Investigate microcomputer system options*. If you select a specific proprietary software product (for example, desktop publishing or a general accounting system for a clinical laboratory), your selection may dictate the general micro-computer-system configuration requirements and, in some cases, a specific microcomputer system. However, if you are like most people and want to take advantage of the wide variety of microcomputer productivity software, you will have up to a dozen micro alternatives available to you. Become familiar with the features and options of each system.

6. *Determine the processor features you desire*. You can go with a basic processor or, if your budget allows, you can select a more powerful processor and add a few "bells and whistles." Expect to pay for each increase in convenience, quality, and speed. For example, you may wish to enhance your processor's capability by increasing the size of the random-access memory (RAM) and including some add-on capabilities (for example, a modem for data communications or a fax board).

7. *Determine the peripheral devices you desire*. Generally speaking the only necessary peripheral devices are the disk drive, monitor, keyboard, and printer. However, these and other peripheral devices come in a wide variety of speeds, capacities, and qualities. The peripherals you select depend on your specific needs, volume of usage, and the amount you are willing to spend. Most people will pay a little extra for the added convenience of a two-disk system (usually a floppy and a hard disk), although one disk will suffice. On the other hand, a color monitor may be an unnecessary luxury for some applications. You can pay $150 or $10,000 for a desktop printer. This choice depends on the anticipated volume of hard-copy output; whether you need graphics output, letter-quality print, color output, and so on.

Other peripheral options such as a joystick, mouse, optical scanner, speech-recognition device, vision-input system, plotter, desktop film recorder, speech synthesizer, and tape drive are discussed in detail in Chapter 4, "Input/Output Devices," and Chapter 5, "Data Storage Devices and Media."

8. *"Test drive" several alternatives*. Once you have selected several software and hardware alternatives, spend enough time to gain some familiarity with them. Do you prefer one keyboard over another? Does a word processing system fully use the hardware features? Is one system easier to understand than another? Use these sessions to answer any questions you might have about the hardware or software. Salespeople at most retail stores are happy to give you a "test drive"—just ask.

9. *Select and buy*. Apply your criteria, select, and then buy your hardware and software.

Factors to Consider When Buying a Micro

- *Future computing needs*. What will your computer and information-processing needs be in the future? Make sure the system you select can grow with your needs.

- *Who will use the system?* Plan not only for yourself but for others in your home or office who will also use the system. Get their input and consider their needs along with yours.

- *Availability of software*. Software is developed for one or several microcomputers, but not for all of them. As you might expect, a more extensive array of software is available for the more popular micros. However, do not overlook some of the less visible vendors if you consider their products superior to the alternatives.

- *Service*. Computing hardware is very reliable. Even so, the possibility exists that one or several of the components will eventually malfunction and have to be repaired. Before purchasing a micro, identify a reliable source of hardware maintenance. Most retailers service what they sell. If a retailer says the hardware must be returned to the manufacturer for repair, choose another retailer or another system.

   Most retailers or vendors will offer a variety of maintenance contracts. Maintenance-contract options range from on-site repairs that cover all parts and service to a carry-in service that does not include parts. Most domestic users elect to treat their micros like their televisions and cars: When the warranty runs out, they pay for repairs as they are needed. Under normal circumstances, this strategy will prove the least expensive.

Service extends beyond hardware maintenance. Service is also an organization's willingness to respond to your inquiries before *and* after the sale. Some retailers and vendors offer classes in programming and in the use of the hardware and software they sell.

■ *Hardware obsolescence.* "I'm going to buy one as soon as the price goes down a little more." If you adopt this strategy, you may never purchase a computer. If you wait another six months, you probably will be able to get a more powerful micro for less money. But what about the lost opportunity?

There is, however, a danger in purchasing a micro that is near or at the end of its life cycle. If you are planning on using a micro frequently at school, home, or work, focus your search on micros with state-of-the-art technology. Although you may get a substantial discount on a micro with dated technology, you may be better off in the long run by choosing up-to-date technology.

■ *Software obsolescence.* Software can become obsolete as well. Software vendors are continually improving their software packages. Each package is assigned a *version number*. The first *release* might be identified as 1.0 (referred to as *one-point-zero*). Subsequent updates to Version 1.0 become Version 1.1, Version 1.2, and so on. The next major revision of the package is released as Version 2.0. Make sure you are buying the most recent release of a particular software package.

■ *Other costs.* The cost of the actual microcomputer system is the major expense, but there are many incidental expenses that can mount up and so influence your selection of a micro. If you have a spending limit, consider these costs when purchasing the hardware (the cost ranges listed are for a first-time user): software ($100–$1500); maintenance ($0–$500 a year); diskettes and tape cassettes ($50–$200); furniture ($0–$350); insurance ($0–$40); and printer ribbons or cartridges, paper, and other supplies ($40–$400).

2–3   MINICOMPUTERS: DEPARTMENT-SIZED COMPUTERS

Until the late 1960s all computers were mainframe computers, and they were expensive—too expensive for all but the larger companies. About that time vendors introduced smaller, slightly "watered down" computers that were more affordable for smaller companies. The industry dubbed these small computers **minicomputers**, or simply **minis**. The name has stuck, even though some of today's so-called minis are many times as powerful as the largest mainframes of the early 1970s (see Figure 2–1).

What Is a Mini and How Is It Used?

In the past the minicomputer has been described in terms of physical size, processing capability, the number of people that could be serviced simultaneously, memory capacity, the type of technology used in the processor, environmental requirements (temperature and humidity), and, yes, even weight. In truth, there is no generally accepted definition of a minicomputer. Creating a rigorous definition of a minicomputer is

Minicomputers are being designed to operate in a normal office environment. Most minicomputers, such as the one in this automobile dealership (on the floor by the desk at the left of the photo), do not require special accommodations for temperature and humidity control. More than a dozen terminals in sales, service, and administration are connected to this mini.

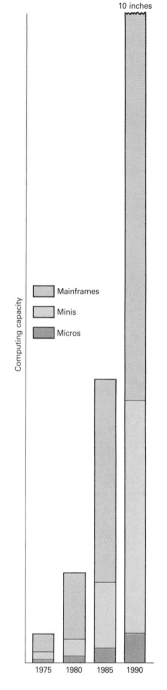

like trying to hit a moving target—one that technology has created. Each leap in technological innovation and the passage of time have obscured whatever clear-cut distinctions could be made between minis and mainframes. Minis are now accomplishing processing tasks that traditionally have been associated with mainframes. Minicomputers bridge the gap between micros and mainframes, but the way they are used makes them more like mainframes than micros. So, even though some of the more powerful micros service multiple users and look very much like small minis, we describe the minicomputer simply as the smallest computer *designed specifically* for the multiuser environment.

Minicomputers usually serve as stand-alone computer systems for small businesses (10 to 400 employees) and as remote **departmental computer systems**. In the latter case, these departmental systems are used both as stand-alone systems in support of a particular department and as part of a network of departmental minis, all linked to a large centralized computer. Minis are also common in research groups, engineering firms, and colleges.

Configuring a Minicomputer System

Minis have most of the operational capabilities of mainframe computers that may be 10 to 1000 times faster. They just perform their tasks more slowly. Minicomputer input, output, and storage devices are similar in appearance and function to those used on much larger systems. However, the printers are not quite as fast, the storage capacity is smaller, and fewer terminals can be serviced. Figure 2–2 illustrates a midsized minicomputer system configuration that provides information systems

FIGURE 2–1 Micro, Mini, and Mainframe Computing Capacities
The computing capacity of a micro, mini, and mainframe increases with advancing technology. As a rule of thumb, the computing capacity of supercomputers is 10 times that of a mainframe computer.

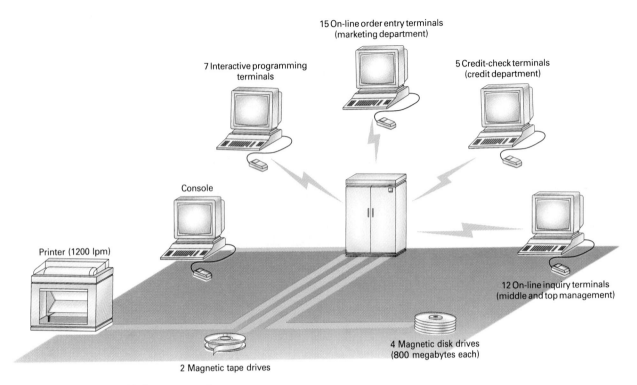

15 On-line order entry terminals
(marketing department)

7 Interactive programming
terminals

5 Credit-check terminals
(credit department)

Console

Printer (1200 lpm)

12 On-line inquiry terminals
(middle and top management)

4 Magnetic disk drives
(800 megabytes each)

2 Magnetic tape drives

FIGURE 2–2   A Minicomputer System
*This system supports a mail-order sporting goods retailer with $40 million in sales
and is representative of a midsized minicomputer.*

support for a mail-order sporting goods retailer with $40 million in
sales. The components illustrated in Figure 2–2 are described in the
following discussion.

■ *Processing.* It is premature to give you a technical description of processing
capabilities. That will be done in Chapter 3, "Inside the Computer." We
can, however, give you a feeling for the relative processing capabilities of
a minicomputer by comparing it to one with which most of us have at
least a casual familiarity—the microcomputer. The processor in the minicomputer system of Figure 2–2 has about 10 times the processing capability
of a state-of-the-art single-user micro.

■ *Storage.* An organization's storage-capacity requirements increase even faster
than its processing requirements. The minicomputer system in Figure 2–2
has four *disk drives* (discussed in Chapter 5, "Data Storage Devices and
Media"), each capable of storing 800 megabytes, for a total capacity of
3200 megabytes. The system also has two magnetic *tape drives*, each with
a capacity of 200 megabytes of on-line sequential storage. Disk data files
are periodically dumped, or loaded, to tape for backup. If, for some reason,
the data on the disks are destroyed, the data on the backup tapes could
be loaded to the disks so that processing could continue.

■ *Input.* The primary means of data input to the system are the 20 VDTs
installed in the marketing and credit departments. The **operator console**
in the machine room is also used to communicate instructions to the

system. Seven terminals are used by programmers to write and test their programs.

■ *Output.* A 1200-line-per-minute (lpm) printer provides hard-copy output. The VDTs in the marketing, credit, and programming departments and the console in the machine room provide soft-copy output. Twelve VDTs are available to middle and top management for on-line inquiry.

It is unlikely that you would find two minicomputers configured in exactly the same way. A company that prefers to use disk rather than tape backup would not need magnetic tape drives. Another may have a substantial volume of printed output and require a 2000-line-per-minute printer and a laser printer that prints two pages of output each second. Figure 2–2 is just an example of one possible configuration.

As the definition of a minicomputer becomes more obscure, the term *minicomputer* will take its place beside *electronic brain*, a name given to computers during the early 1950s. But, for now, it remains a commonly used term. The term *supermini* is often applied to a high-end minicomputer. Superminis typically have the capability of servicing one hundred or more users simultaneously. Such systems can be difficult to distinguish from mainframe computers.

2–4 MAINFRAME COMPUTERS: THE CORPORATE WORKHORSE

Aside from the obvious difference in the speeds at which they process data, the major difference between minicomputers and mainframe computers is in the number of remote terminals they can service. The category of computers that falls between minicomputers and supercomputers is sometimes referred to as **maxicomputers**; however, in "computerese," most people continue to refer to this category of computers simply as mainframes. As a rule of thumb, any computer that services more than 100 remote terminals should no longer be called a minicomputer. Some supercomputers, the fastest and most powerful of computers, provide service to over 10,000 remote terminals.

The speed at which medium-sized and large mainframe computers can perform operations allows more input, output, and storage devices with greater capabilities to be configured in the computer system. The computer system in Figure 2–3 is used by the municipal government of a city of about one million people. This example should give you an appreciation of the relative size and potential of a medium-sized mainframe computer system. The hardware devices illustrated will be explained in detail in subsequent chapters. The components are described briefly below.

■ *Processing.* Mainframe computer systems, including some minis, will normally be configured with the mainframe, or **host processor**, and several other processors. The host processor has direct control over all the other processors, storage devices, and input/output devices. The other processors relieve the host of certain routine processing requirements. For example, the **back-end processor** performs the task of locating a particular record

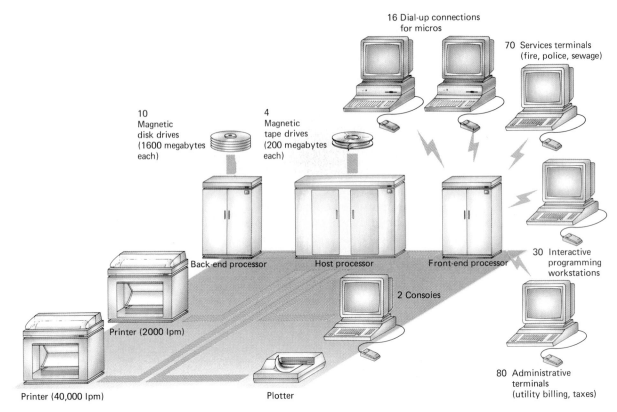

FIGURE 2–3   A Mainframe Computer System
This midsized mainframe computer system supports the administrative processing needs for the municipal government of a city with a population of about one million.

on a data storage device. The **front-end processor** relieves the host processor of communications-related processing duties—that is, the transmission of data to and from remote workstations and other computers. In this way, the host can concentrate on overall system control and the execution of applications software.

A typical configuration would have a host processor, a *front-end processor*, and perhaps a *back-end processor*. The host is the main computer and is substantially larger and more powerful than the other *subordinate* processors. The front-end and back-end processors control the data flow in and out of the host processor. Although the host could handle the entire system without the assistance of the front-end and back-end processors, overall system efficiency would be drastically reduced without them.

■ *Storage*. All mainframe computer systems use similar direct and sequential storage media. The larger ones simply have more of them, and they usually work faster. In Figure 2–3 there are four magnetic tape drives and 10 magnetic disk drives. The disk drives are *dual density* and can pack twice the data in the same amount of physical storage space as can the disks shown in Figure 2–2. The total data storage capacity in the example is 800 megabytes of sequential storage (tape) and 16,000 megabytes of direct-access storage (disk).

The activity in a mainframe machine room is fast and furious. However, most of the activity is electronic. It is not unusual for three or four operators to handle all the machine room duties for a multimillion-dollar computer system that services scores of programmers and hundreds of users.

■ *Input.* The primary means of entering data to the system is the same, no matter what the size of the computer system. The only difference between a large and a small system is in the number and location of the terminals. In the example of Figure 2–3, 150 terminals are dedicated to service and administrative functions, 30 are used for programming, and 16 *ports* are available for those who might wish to use their PCs to establish a link with the mainframe computer. A port on a mainframe is like the micro port discussed earlier in that it provides an access point in a computer system.

■ *Output.* As in the minicomputer system in Figure 2–2, the hard copy is produced on high-speed printers and the soft copy on terminals. In the Figure 2–3 example, there are two printers: a line printer with a speed of 2000 lines per minute and a page printer that uses laser-printing technology to achieve speeds of over 40,000 lines per minute. The plotter, also pictured in the configuration, is used by city engineers to produce hard copies of graphs, charts, and drawings.

2–5   SUPERCOMPUTERS: PROCESSING GIANTS

The Evolution of Supercomputers

During the early 1970s administrative data processing dominated computer applications. Bankers, college administrators, and advertising executives were amazed by the blinding speed at which these million-dollar mainframes processed data. Engineers and scientists were grateful for this tremendous technological achievement, but they were far from satisfied. When business executives talked about unlimited capability, engineers and scientists knew they would have to wait for future enhancements before they could use computers to address complex problems. Automotive engineers were yet to build three-dimensional prototypes of automobiles inside a computer. Physicists could not explore the activities of an atom during a nuclear explosion. The engineering and scientific communities had a desperate need for more powerful computers. In response to that need, computer designers began work on what are now known as supercomputers.

The large mainframe computers are oriented to **input/output-bound operation**; that is, the amount of work that can be performed by the computer system is limited primarily by the speeds of the I/O devices. Administrative data processing jobs, such as generating monthly statements for checking accounts at a bank, require relatively little calculation and a great deal of input and output. In I/O-bound operations, the computer is often waiting for data to be entered or for an output device to complete its current task. In contrast, the types of computer applications that are helpful to engineers and scientists are **processor-bound** and require relatively little in the way of input or output: The amount of work that can be performed by the computer system is limited primarily by the speed of the computer. A typical scientific job involves the manipulation of a complex mathematical model, often requiring trillions of operations to resolve. During the early 1970s some of the complex processor-bound scientific jobs would tie up large mainframe computers at major universities for days at a time. This, of course, was unacceptable.

Making Computers Faster

During the past two decades, computer designers have employed three basic strategies for increasing the speed of computers.

1. *Use faster components.* Essentially this means employing electronic circuitry that enables the fastest possible switching between the two electronic states, on and off.

2. *Reduce the distance that an electronic signal must travel.* This means increasing the density of the electronic circuitry.

The CRAY-2 supercomputer is one of the world's fastest computers. The circuitry of the compact CRAY-2 is immersed in an inert fluorocarbon liquid that dissipates the heat generated by the densely packed electronic components.

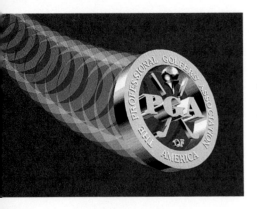

The graphics that introduce television newscasts, sports events, and movies are by-products of supercomputer technology. The processing power of supercomputers is needed to manipulate billions of picture elements into imaginative dynamic images.

3. *Improve the computer system architecture.* The architecture of a computer refers to the manner in which it handles data and performs logic operations and calculations. The architecture of supercomputers is substantially different from those of the other three categories of computers.

The greatest obstacle facing designers of supercomputers is heat buildup. Densely packed integrated circuits produce a tremendous amount of heat. For example, imagine burning 3000 sixty-watt light bulbs in a space the size of an average clothes closet. Without some type of cooling mechanism, densely packed integrated circuits literally would melt. The air-cooling systems traditionally used in mainframe computers proved inadequate, so designers have tried a variety of *supercooling* methods, from freon-based refrigeration to bathing the circuit elements in a liquid coolant. Computer designers are continually trying to increase the density of the integrated circuits while allowing for adequate cooling. At this point in the evolution of supercomputers, innovation in supercooling is just as important as innovation in electronic circuitry.

Supercomputers are known as much for their applications as they are for their speed or computing capacity, which is often an order of magnitude (10 times) that of the largest mainframe computers. Supercomputers sort through and analyze mountains of seismic data gathered during oil-seeking explorations. Supercomputers enable the simulation of airflow around an airplane at different speeds and altitudes. Auto manufacturers use supercomputers to simulate auto accidents on video screens. (It is less expensive, more revealing, and safer than crashing the real thing.) Physicists use supercomputers to study the results of explosions of nuclear weapons. Meteorologists employ supercomputers to study the formation of tornadoes. Even Hollywood has found an application for supercomputers. Studios use advanced graphics to create special effects for movies and TV commercials. All these applications are impractical, if not impossible, on mainframes.

Supercomputers are seldom called upon to do I/O-bound administrative processing, such as payroll processing or accounting. To do so would waste an expensive and relatively rare resource. (Only a few hundred supercomputers are currently installed in the world, and a supercomputer could not process the payroll any faster than a mainframe.) Because of their applications, supercomputers are more likely to be configured with sophisticated graphics workstations and plotters than with rows of high-speed printers.

SUMMARY OUTLINE AND IMPORTANT TERMS

2–1   COMPUTER SYSTEMS COME IN ALL SHAPES AND SIZES. Each of the computers in the four main categories (micros, minicomputers, mainframes, and supercomputers) is a computer system, but they differ greatly in processing capabilities and in how they are used. The three largest share functional similarities, including their ability to service many users. The microcomputer is designed primarily for the single-user environment.

2–2 **MICROCOMPUTERS: SMALL BUT POWERFUL. Microprocessors** not only set the stage for microcomputers, but they are found in dozens of devices around the home. The **motherboard**, also called the **system board**, in a microcomputer contains the electronic circuitry for processing (the microprocessor chip), input/output operations, and some memory. The processing components of most micros have several empty **expansion slots** so you can purchase and plug in optional capabilities in the form of **add-on boards**. The micro comes in pocket, laptop, and desktop sizes.

The computer and its **peripheral devices** are called the computer system **configuration**. A typical micro configuration would be a computer, a keyboard, a monitor, a printer, and one or two disk drives. Micros that give users the flexibility to configure the system with a variety of peripheral devices are said to have an **open architecture**, or **bus architecture**. In a **closed architecture**, the system is fully configured when it is sold.

The electrical **bus** is the path through which the processor sends and receives data and commands to **RAM** (**random-access memory**) and all peripheral devices. A port provides a direct link to the micro's bus. External peripheral devices are interfaced with the processor through either a **serial port** or a **parallel port**. The de facto standard for micro serial ports is the **RS-232C port**.

Expansion slots can house a wide variety of special-function add-on boards, or **add-on cards**. The add-ons can include one or more of the following functions: RAM, color/graphics adapter, modem, internal battery-powered clock/calendar, serial port, parallel port, printer spooler, hard disk, coprocessor, VCR backup, and FAX. Most are **multifunction add-on boards**.

Multiuser micros are configured with several terminals. Micros can be used as stand-alone computer systems, or they can serve as "intelligent" terminals to mainframe computers.

2–3 **MINICOMPUTERS: DEPARTMENT-SIZED COMPUTERS.** The term **minicomputer**, or **mini**, emerged about 20 years ago as a name for small computers. The name has stuck, even though some of today's minis are more powerful than any computer of the 1960s. Minis now accomplish processing tasks that traditionally have been associated with mainframe computers. Minicomputers usually serve as stand-alone computer systems for small businesses and as remote **departmental computer systems**.

2–4 **MAINFRAME COMPUTERS: THE CORPORATE WORKHORSE.** Mainframe computers, the computer category between minicomputers and supercomputers, are also called **maxicomputers**. Aside from the obvious differences in processing speed, the major difference between minicomputers and mainframes is the number of remote terminals that can be serviced. A computer servicing more than 100 terminals is no longer considered a minicomputer.

A typical mainframe configuration might have a **host processor**, a **front-end processor**, and perhaps a **back-end processor**. The special-function processors help improve overall system efficiency.

2–5 SUPERCOMPUTERS: PROCESSING GIANTS. Mainframe computers are oriented to **input/output-bound operation**. In contrast, supercomputers handle the types of computer applications that are helpful to engineers and scientists. These applications are typically **processor-bound** and require relatively little in the way of input or output. Supercomputers are more likely to be configured with sophisticated graphics workstations and plotters than with high-speed printers.

REVIEW EXERCISES

Concepts

1. Describe the capabilities of a multiuser micro.
2. What is the relationship between a microprocessor, a motherboard, and a microcomputer?
3. In terms of physical size, how are PCs categorized?
4. What is the name given to printed output? Output on a monitor?
5. Give two examples each of input hardware and output hardware.
6. What is the purpose of a mainframe computer's operator console?
7. Contrast the processing environment for mainframe computers with that of a microcomputer.
8. Describe an "intelligent" terminal.
9. Departmental computer systems are generally associated with which category of computer system?
10. Name three subordinate processors that might be configured with a mainframe computer system.
11. List five functional enhancements that can be added to a microcomputer by inserting one or more optional add-on boards into expansion slots.
12. Why are some microcomputers sold with empty expansion slots?

Discussion

13. The primary use of computers in the home is for job-related work done at home. Is there a contradiction when one speaks of "business" microcomputers and "home" microcomputers? Explain.
14. Is the use of terms such as *microcomputer*, *minicomputer*, *midicomputer*, *supercomputer*, and so on a help or a hindrance in distinguishing between the processing capabilities of computer systems? Explain.
15. List at least 10 products that are smaller than a breadbox and use microprocessors. Select one and describe the function of its microprocessor.
16. What options would you like to have on your own personal micro that are not included in a minimum configuration? Why?
17. Discuss at least five domestic applications for personal computers.
18. How might a microcomputer help in the day-to-day administration of an appliance store with 20 employees?

19. Ask two people who know and have worked with computers for at least three years to describe a minicomputer. What can you conclude from their responses?

SELF-TEST (by section)

2–1 **a.** The most distinguishing characteristic of any computer system is physical size. (T/F)
  b. The price-performance ratio of a computer is _____ (directly/inversely) proportional to its computing capacity.

2–2 **a.** The processing component of a motherboard is a _____.
  b. The three size categories of personal computers are miniature, portable, and business. (T/F)
  c. The computer and its peripheral devices are called the computer system _____.
  d. The RS-232C connector provides the interface to a port. (T/F)

2–3 **a.** A minicomputer is often referred to as a personal computer. (T/F)
  b. There is no commonly accepted definition of a minicomputer. (T/F)

2–4 **a.** Micros can be linked to a mainframe computer through a: (a) base, (b) port, or (c) plug.
  b. Mainframe computers are also called: (a) minicomputers, (b) midicomputers, or (c) maxicomputers.

2–5 **a.** Supercomputers are oriented to _____ -bound applications.
  b. One of the strategies employed by computer designers to increase the speed of computers involves reducing the distance that an electronic signal must travel. (T/F)

Self-test answers   **2–1 (a)** F; **(b)** inversely. **2–2 (a)** microprocessor; **(b)** F; **(c)** configuration; **(d)** T. **2–3 (a)** F; **(b)** T. **2–4 (a)** b; **(b)** c. **2–5 (a)** processor; **(b)** T.

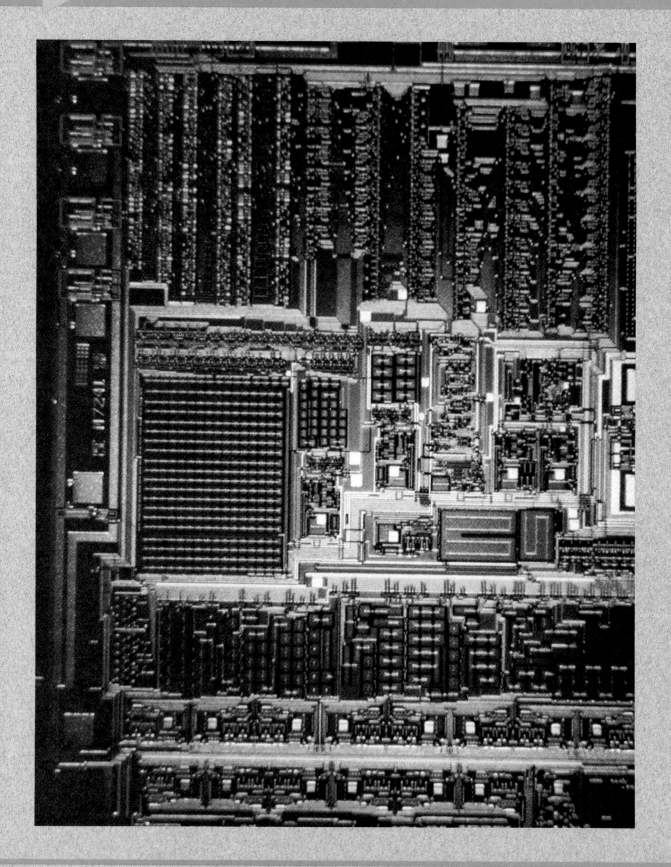

3

Inside the Computer

STUDENT LEARNING OBJECTIVES

▶ To describe how data are stored in a computer system.

▶ To demonstrate the relationships between bits, bytes, characters, and encoding systems.

▶ To understand the translation of alphanumeric data into a format for internal computer representation.

▶ To explain and illustrate the principles of computer operations.

▶ To identify and describe the relationships between the internal components of a computer.

▶ To distinguish processors by their speed, memory capacity, and word length.

3–1   DATA STORAGE: DATA IN THE COMPUTER_____

In Chapter 1 we learned that *data*, not *information*, are stored in a computer system. *Data are the raw material from which information is derived*, and *information is data that have been collected and manipulated into a meaningful form*. To manipulate data, we must have a way to store and retrieve this raw material.

It is easy to understand data storage in a manual system. For example, when a customer's address changes, we pull the folder, erase the old address, and write in the new one. We can see and easily interpret data that are kept manually. We cannot see or easily interpret data stored in a computer. Data are represented and stored in a computer system to take advantage of the physical characteristics of electronics and computer hardware, not human beings.

Data are stored *temporarily* during processing in a section of the computer system called **primary storage**. Primary storage is also called **main memory**, or random-access memory (RAM). If you will remember, RAM was introduced and discussed briefly in Chapter 2, "Micros, Minis, Mainframes, and Supercomputers." Data are stored *permanently* on **secondary storage** devices such as magnetic tape and disk drives. We discuss primary storage in detail later in this chapter. Secondary storage is covered in Chapter 5, "Data Storage Devices and Media." In this chapter we focus on the details of how data are represented electronically in a computer system and on the internal workings of a computer.

Programs and data are stored temporarily in these solid-state RAM chips (primary storage) during processing. The RAM chips on this 9-by-7-inch circuit board can store over 80 million characters. Permanent storage is on magnetic disk (secondary storage).

3–2 A BIT ABOUT THE BIT

The computer's seemingly endless potential is, in fact, based on only two electronic states—*on* and *off*. The physical characteristics of the computer make it possible to combine these two electronic states to represent letters and numbers. An "on" or "off" electronic state is represented by a **bit**. (*Bit* is short for *binary digit*.) The presence or absence of a bit is referred to as *on-bit* and *off-bit*, respectively. In the **binary** numbering system (base 2) and in written text, the on-bit is a 1 and the off-bit is a 0.

The vacuum tubes, transistors, and integrated circuits (see Appendix A, "An Abbreviated History of Computers") that characterize the generations of computers all enable them to distinguish between on and off and, therefore, to use binary logic.

Physically, these states are achieved in a variety of ways. In primary storage the two electronic states are represented by the direction of current flow. Another approach is to turn the circuit itself on or off. In secondary storage the two states are made possible by the magnetic arrangement of the surface coating on magnetic tapes and disks (see Chapter 5, "Data Storage Devices and Media").

Bits may be fine for computers, but human beings are more comfortable with letters and decimal numbers (the base-10 numerals 0 through 9). Therefore, the letters and decimal numbers that we input to a computer system must be translated into 1s and 0s for processing and storage. The computer translates the bits back into letters and decimal numbers on output. This translation is performed so we can recognize and understand the output. It is made possible by encoding systems.

In the first generation of computers (1951–59), each bit was represented by a vacuum tube. Today computers use fingernail-sized chips that can store over one million bits each.

3–3 ENCODING SYSTEMS: COMBINING BITS TO FORM BYTES

EBCDIC and ASCII

Computers do not talk to each other in English, Spanish, or French. They have their own languages, which are better suited to electronic communication. In these languages, bits are combined according to an **encoding system** to represent letters (**alpha** characters), numbers (**numeric** characters), and special characters (such as *, $, +, and &). For example, in the eight-bit **EBCDIC** encoding system (*Extended Binary-Coded Decimal Interchange Code*—pronounced *IB-see-dik*), which is used primarily in mainframe computers, 11000010 represents the letter B, and 11110011 represents a decimal number 3. In the seven-bit **ASCII** encoding system (*American Standard Code for Information Interchange*—pronounced *AS-key*), which is used primarily in micros and data communications, a *B* and a *3* are represented by 1000010 and 0110011, respectively. There is also an eight-bit version of ASCII called **ASCII-8**.

Letters, numbers, and special characters are collectively referred to as **alphanumeric** characters. Alphanumeric characters are *encoded* into a bit configuration on input so that the computer can interpret them.

When you press the letter B on a PC keyboard, the B is transmitted to the processor as a coded string of binary digits (for example, 1000010 in ASCII). The characters are *decoded* on output so we can interpret them. For example, a monitor's device controller will interpret an ASCII 0110011 as a 3 and display a 3 on the screen. This coding, which is based on a particular encoding system, equates a unique series of bits and no-bits with a specific character. Just as the words *mother* and *father* are arbitrary English-language character strings that refer to our parents,

FIGURE 3–1 ASCII Codes

This figure contains the binary and decimal values for commonly used ASCII characters.

Character	ASCII Code		
	Binary Value		Decimal Value
A	100	0001	65
B	100	0010	66
C	100	0011	67
D	100	0100	68
E	100	0101	69
F	100	0110	70
G	100	0111	71
H	100	1000	72
I	100	1001	73
J	100	1010	74
K	100	1011	75
L	100	1100	76
M	100	1101	77
N	100	1110	78
O	100	1111	79
P	101	0000	80
Q	101	0001	81
R	101	0010	82
S	101	0011	83
T	101	0100	84
U	101	0101	85
V	101	0110	86
W	101	0111	87
X	101	1000	88
Y	101	1001	89
Z	101	1010	90
a	110	0001	97
b	110	0010	98
c	110	0011	99
d	110	0100	100
e	110	0101	101
f	110	0110	102
g	110	0111	103
h	110	1000	104
i	110	1001	105
j	110	1010	106
k	110	1011	107
l	110	1100	108
m	110	1101	109
n	110	1110	110
o	110	1111	111
p	111	0000	112
q	111	0001	113
r	111	0010	114
s	111	0011	115
t	111	0100	116
u	111	0101	117
v	111	0110	118
w	111	0111	119
x	111	1000	120
y	111	1001	121
z	111	1010	122

Character	ASCII Code		
	Binary Value		Decimal Value
0	011	0000	48
1	011	0001	49
2	011	0010	50
3	011	0011	51
4	011	0100	52
5	011	0101	53
6	011	0110	54
7	011	0111	55
8	011	1000	56
9	011	1001	57
Space	010	0000	32
.	010	1110	46
<	011	1100	60
(	010	1000	40
+	010	1011	43
&	010	0110	38
!	010	0001	33
$	010	0100	36
*	010	1010	42
)	010	1001	41
;	011	1011	59
,	010	1100	44
%	010	0101	37
—	101	1111	95
>	011	1110	62
?	011	1111	63
:	011	1010	58
#	010	0011	35
@	100	0000	64
'	010	0111	39
=	011	1101	61
"	010	0010	34
½	1010	1011	171
¼	1010	1100	172
▓	1011	0010	178
■	1101	1011	219
▬	1101	1100	220
▮	1101	1101	221
◼	1101	1110	222
▬	1101	1111	223
√	1111	1011	251
n	1111	1100	252
2	1111	1101	253
▪	1111	1110	254
(blank)	1111	1111	255

11000010 is an arbitrary EBCDIC code that refers to the letter B. The combination of bits used to represent a character is called a **byte** (pronounced *bite*). Figure 3–1 shows the binary value (the actual bit configuration) and the decimal equivalent of commonly used characters in both EBCDIC and ASCII.

The seven-bit ASCII can represent up to 128 characters (2^7). EBCDIC and ASCII-8 can represent up to 256 characters (2^8). Although the English language has considerably fewer than 128 *printable* characters, the extra bit configurations are needed to represent noncharacter images (for example, a bullet point or paragraph symbol) and to communicate a variety of activities (such as ringing a bell, signaling the computer to accept a piece of datum).

The Nibble

The eight-bit EBCDIC and ASCII-8 encoding systems are endowed with an interesting and useful quality. Only four bit positions are needed to represent the 10 decimal digits. Therefore, a single numeric digit can be stored in a half-byte, or a **nibble**, as it is sometimes called. This enables us to store data more efficiently by "packing" *two* decimal digits into one eight-bit byte (see Figure 3–2).

Because two decimal digits can be packed into one byte, a byte is not always the same as a character. Even so, the terms *byte* and *character* are often used interchangeably, with an implied understanding that some bytes may contain two numeric characters.

Parity Checking

Within a computer system, data in the form of coded characters are continuously transferred at high rates of speed between the computer, the input/output (I/O) and storage devices, and the remote workstations. Each device uses a built-in checking procedure to help ensure that the transmission is complete and accurate. This procedure is called **parity checking**.

Logically, an ASCII character may have seven bits, but physically there are actually *eight* bits transmitted between hardware devices. Confused? Don't be. The extra **parity bit**, which is not part of the character code, is used in the parity-checking procedure to detect whether a bit has been accidentally changed, or "dropped," during transmission. A dropped bit results in a **parity error**.

FIGURE 3–2   Decimal 29 in EBCDIC

Because all numeric codes in EBCDIC have 1111 in the first four positions, the 1s can be eliminated and two numeric digits can be "packed" into one byte. Of course, the programmer must tell the computer that a particular set of data is to be stored and retrieved in packed decimal format.

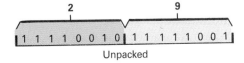

Unpacked

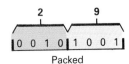

Packed

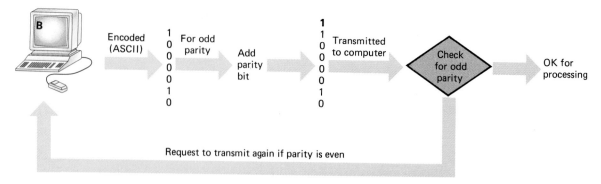

FIGURE 3–3   Parity Checking
*The letter B is entered and transmitted to the computer for processing. Because the
ASCII B has an even number of bits, an on-bit must be added to maintain odd
parity.*

To maintain *odd parity* (see Figure 3–3), the extra parity bit is turned
on when the seven-bit ASCII byte has an *even* number of on-bits. When
the ASCII byte has an *odd* number of on-bits, the parity bit is turned
off. The receiving device checks for this condition. A parity error occurs
when an even number of on-bits is encountered. Some computer systems
are designed to maintain *even parity*, but odd and even parity work in
a similar manner.

3–4   NUMBERING SYSTEMS AND COMPUTERS

We humans use a **decimal**, or base-10, numbering system, presumably
because people have 10 fingers. If we had three fingers and a thumb
on each hand, as does the Extra Terrestrial (E.T.) from the popular
movie, then in all probability we would be using the **octal** numbering
system, which has a base of 8.

Early computers were designed around the decimal numbering system.
This approach made the creation of computer logic capabilities unnecessarily complex and did not make efficient use of resources. (For example,
10 vacuum tubes were needed to represent one decimal digit.) In 1945,
as computer pioneers were struggling to improve this cumbersome approach, John von Neumann suggested that the numbering system used
by computers should take advantage of the physical characteristics of
electronic circuitry. To deal with the basic electronic states of on and
off, von Neumann suggested using the *binary* numbering system. His
insight has vastly simplified the way computers handle data.

Computers *operate* in binary and *communicate* to us in decimal. A
special program translates decimal into binary on input, and binary
into decimal on output. Under normal circumstances, a programmer
would see only decimal input and output. On occasion, though, he or
she must deal with long and confusing strings of 1s and 0s in the form
of a **memory dump**. A memory dump is like a snapshot of the contents
of primary storage (on-bits and off-bits) at a given moment in time.
To reduce at least part of the confusion of seeing only 1s and 0s on

```
38C070  29306294 4580623F D20DD0AA 62A29640  8CECCC04 88F00010 80000004 88100010  41110003 5010D064 94FCD067 D703D06C
38C0A0  D06E0610 12114770 6202D203 D09F629D  4120D121 45B06236 5820D120 413062C4  477061A6 4810D06E 41110001 4010D06E
38C0D0  1A2C44E0 60701A1E 41818001 44F06076  9640D112 455062DA 94BFD112 4810D06C  02FF1302 FFC3C9D5 C5E240E2 C1D4C540
38C100  FF0098E0 D08012EE 47806310 D27CF000  48A0D06A 4BA0D06C 88A00002 45B0623E  D12094FC D1235B00 D1201A10 5800D120
```

FIGURE 3–4 A Hexadecimal Dump
Each of the lines contains a hexadecimal representation of the contents of primary storage. The column of numbers farthest to the left consists of storage addresses. Each pair of hexadecimal digits represents the eight bits of an EBCDIC byte. The address of the first byte (29) in the memory dump is 0038C070 in hexadecimal (or 00000000001110001100000001110000 in binary). You can see how much space is saved by displaying dumps in "hex" rather than binary.

the output, the **hexadecimal** (base-16) numbering system is used as a shorthand to display the binary contents of both primary and secondary storage (see Figure 3–4).

The decimal equivalents for binary, decimal, and hexadecimal numbers are shown in Figure 3–5. We know that in decimal, any number greater than 9 is represented by a sequence of digits. When you count in decimal, you "carry" to the next position in groups of 10. As you examine Figure 3–5, notice that you carry in groups of 2 in binary and in groups of 16 in hexadecimal. Also note that any combination of *four* binary digits can be represented by one "hex" digit.

The hexadecimal numbering system is used only for the convenience of the programmer when reading and reviewing the binary output of a dump (see Figure 3–4). Computers *do not operate or process in hex.* During the 1960s and early 1970s, programmers often had to examine the contents of primary storage to debug their programs (that is, to eliminate program errors). Today's programming languages have sophisticated **diagnostics** (*error messages*) and computer-assisted tools that help programmers during program development. These diagnostics and development aids have minimized the need for applications programmers to convert binary and hexadecimal numbers into their more familiar decimal equivalents. However, if you become familiar with these numbering systems, you should achieve a better overall understanding of computers.

Appendix B, "Working with Numbering Systems," presents the principles of numbering systems, discusses numbering-system arithmetic, and illustrates how to convert a value in one numbering system into its equivalent in another.

FIGURE 3–5 Numbering-System Equivalence Table

Binary (base 2)	Decimal (base 10)	Hexadecimal (base 16)
0	0	0
1	1	1
10	2	2
11	3	3
100	4	4
101	5	5
110	6	6
111	7	7
1000	8	8
1001	9	9
1010	10	A
1011	11	B
1100	12	C
1101	13	D
1110	14	E
1111	15	F
10000	16	10

3–5 COMPONENTS OF A COMPUTER SYSTEM: A CLOSER LOOK AT THE PROCESSOR AND PRIMARY STORAGE

Let's review. We have learned that all computers have similar capabilities and perform essentially the same functions, although some might be faster than others. We have also learned that a computer system has input, output, storage, and processing components; that the *processor* is the "intelligence" of a computer system; and that a single computer

PROFILE

Since his tenure at the International Business Machines Corporation (IBM) in the 1960s, Dr. Gene Amdahl has demonstrated great skill and creativity in developing new systems. At IBM, Amdahl was involved in simulation studies and machine design for character recognition. He also worked on the development of the early jumbo computers and was the chief architect of the innovative IBM System/360 series of computers, the system that ushered in the third generation of computers. At the time the System/360 project was the largest private venture ever undertaken.

In 1970 Dr. Amdahl established his own company, Amdahl Corporation, which successfully developed plug-compatible machines capable of duplicating IBM performances at lower costs.

Dr. Amdahl retired from the company that bears his name in 1980 and established two other computer system companies, Trilogy Systems Corporation and, in 1987, Andor International, Ltd.

system may have several processors. We have discussed how data are represented inside a computer system in electronic states called bits. We are now ready to expose the inner workings of the nucleus of the computer system—the processor.

The internal operation of a computer is interesting, but there really is no mystery to it. The mystery is in the minds of those who listen to hearsay and believe science-fiction writers. The computer is a nonthinking electronic device that has to be plugged into an electrical power source, just like a toaster or a lamp.

Literally hundreds of different types of computers are marketed by scores of manufacturers. The complexity of each type may vary considerably, but in the end each processor, sometimes called the **central processing unit** or **CPU**, has only two fundamental sections: the *control unit* and the *arithmetic and logic unit*. *Primary storage* also plays an integral part in the internal operation of a processor. These three—primary storage, the control unit, and the arithmetic and logic unit—work together. Let's look at their functions and the relationships between them.

Primary Storage

The Technology.   Unlike magnetic secondary storage devices, such as tape and disk, primary storage has no moving parts. With no mechanical movement, data can be accessed from primary storage at electronic speeds, or close to the speed of light. Most of today's computers use CMOS (Complementary Metal-Oxide Semiconductor) technology for primary storage. A state-of-the-art CMOS memory chip about one eighth the size of a postage stamp can store about 4,000,000 bits, or over 400,000 characters of data!

Modern technology has taken away some of the romance associated with the computer mystique. Today's computers don't have hundreds of multicolored blinking lights and swirling tapes. The processing component of this mainframe computer system (behind the operators) has only one switch—on/off.

But there is one major problem with semiconductor storage. When the electrical current is turned off or interrupted, the data are lost. Researchers are working to perfect a primary storage that will retain its contents after an electrical interruption. Several "nonvolatile" technologies, such as **bubble memory**, have emerged, but none has exhibited the qualities necessary for widespread application. However, bubble memory is superior to CMOS for use in certain computers. It is highly reliable, it is not susceptible to environmental fluctuations, and it can operate on battery power for a considerable length of time. These qualities make bubble memory well suited for use with industrial robots and in portable computers.

Function. Primary storage, or main memory, provides the processor with *temporary* storage for programs and data. *All programs and data must be transferred to primary storage from an input device (such as a VDT) or from secondary storage (such as a disk) before programs can be executed or data can be processed.* Primary storage space is always at a premium; therefore, after a program has been executed, the storage space it occupied is reallocated to another program awaiting execution.

Figure 3–6 illustrates how all input/output (I/O) is "read to" or "written from" primary storage. In the figure, an inquiry (input) is made on a VDT. The inquiry, in the form of a message, is routed to primary storage over a **channel** (such as a coaxial cable). The message is interpreted, and the processor initiates action to retrieve the appropriate

Bubble memory is magnified 5000 times so that we can see its physical structure.

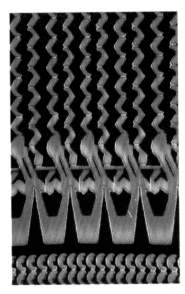

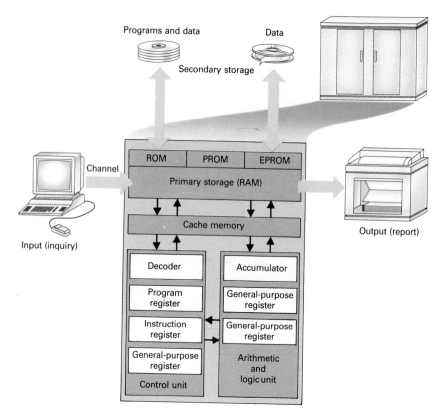

FIGURE 3–6   Interaction Between Primary Storage and Computer System Components
All programs and data must be transferred from an input device or from secondary storage before programs can be executed and data can be processed. During processing, instructions and data are passed between the various types of internal memories, the control unit, and the arithmetic and logic unit. Output is transferred to the printer from primary storage.

program and data from secondary storage. The program and data are "loaded," or moved, to primary storage from secondary storage. This is a *nondestructive read* process. That is, the program and data that are read reside in both primary storage (temporarily) and secondary storage (permanently). The data are manipulated according to program instructions, and a report is written from primary storage to a printer.

A program instruction or a piece of data is stored in a specific primary storage location called an **address**. Addresses permit program instructions and data to be located, accessed, and processed. The content of each address is constantly changing as different programs are executed and new data are processed.

RAM, ROM, PROM, and EPROM.   Another name for primary storage is random-access memory, or RAM. A special type of primary storage, called **read-only memory (ROM)**, cannot be altered by the programmer. The contents of ROM are "hard-wired" (designed into the logic of the memory chip) by the manufacturer and can be "read only." When you turn on a microcomputer system, a program in ROM automatically readies the computer system for use. Then the ROM program produces the initial display screen prompt.

A variation of ROM is **programmable read-only memory (PROM)**. PROM is ROM into which you, the user, can load "read-only" programs and data. Some microcomputer software packages, such as electronic spreadsheets, are available as PROM units as well as on diskette. Once a program is loaded to PROM, it is seldom, if ever, changed. However, if you need to be able to revise the contents of PROM, there is **EPROM**, erasable PROM.

Cache Memory. Programs and data are loaded to primary storage, or RAM, from secondary storage because the time required to access a program instruction or piece of data from primary storage is significantly less than from secondary storage. Thousands of instructions or pieces of data can be accessed from primary storage in the time it would take to access a single piece of data from disk storage. RAM is essentially a high-speed holding area for data and programs. In fact, nothing really happens in a computer system until the program instructions and data are moved to the processor. This transfer of instructions and data to the processor can be time-consuming, even at microsecond speeds. To facilitate an even faster transfer of instructions and data to the processor, some computers are designed with **cache memory** (see Figure 3–6). Cache memory is employed by computer designers to increase the computer system **throughput** (the rate at which work is performed).

Like RAM, cache is a high-speed holding area for program instructions and data. However, cache memory uses a technology that is about 10 times faster than RAM and about 100 times more expensive. With only a fraction of the capacity of RAM, cache memory holds only those instructions and data that are likely to be needed next by the processor.

The Control Unit

Just as the processor is the nucleus of a computer system, the **control unit** is the nucleus of the processor. If you will recall from an earlier discussion, the control unit and the arithmetic and logic unit are the two fundamental sections of a processor. The control unit has three primary functions:

1. To read and interpret program instructions
2. To direct the operation of internal processor components
3. To control the flow of programs and data in and out of primary storage

A program must first be loaded to primary storage before it can be executed. During execution, the first in a sequence of program instructions is moved from primary storage to the control unit, where it is decoded and interpreted by the **decoder**. The control unit then directs other processor components to carry out the operations necessary to execute the instruction.

THE COMPUTER ON A CHIP

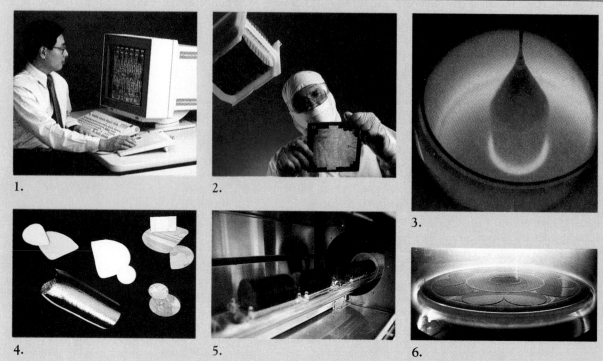

1.

2.

3.

4.

5.

6.

The 1879 invention of the light bulb symbolized the beginning of electronics. Electronics then evolved into the use of vacuum tubes, then into transistors, and now integrated circuits. Today's microminiaturization of electronic circuitry is continuing to have a profound effect on the way we live and work.

These relatively inexpensive "computers on a chip" have thousands of uses, many of which we now take for granted. They are found in almost every type of modern machine from computers to robots, from "smart" home appliances to "talking" cash registers, from automobile dashboards to high-flying spaceships.

Current technology permits the placement of hundreds of thousands of transistors and electronic switches on a single chip. Chips already fit into wristwatches and credit cards, but electrical and computer engineers want them even smaller. In electronics, smaller is better. The ENIAC, the first full-scale digital electronic computer, weighed 50 tons and occupied an entire room. Today a complete computer is fabricated within a single piece of silicon the size of a child's fingernail.

Chip designers think in terms of nanoseconds (1/1,000,000,000 of a second) and microns (1/1,000,000 of a meter). They want to pack as many circuit elements as they can into the structure of a chip. High-density packing reduces the time required for an electrical signal to travel from one circuit element to the next—resulting in faster computers. Current research indicates that chips eventually will be produced that contain millions of circuit elements!

The fabrication of integrated circuits involves a multistep process using various photochemical etching and metallurgical techniques. This complex and interesting process is illustrated here with photos, from silicon to the finished product.

Design

1. Chips are designed and manufactured to perform a particular function. One chip might be a microprocessor for a personal computer. Another might be primary storage. Another might be the logic for a talking vending machine. Chip designers use computer-aided design (CAD) systems to create the logic for individual circuits. A chip contains from one to 30 layers of circuits. In this multilayer circuit design, each layer is color-coded so the designer can distinguish between the various layers.

2. An electron-beam exposure system etches the circuitry into a glass stencil called a *mask*. A mask such as this one is produced for each circuit layer. The number of layers depends on the complexity of the chip's logic.

Fabrication

3. Molten silicon is spun into cylindrical ingots. Because silicon, the second most abundant sub-

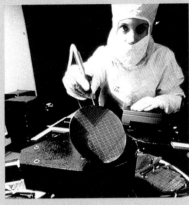
7.

8.

9.

10.

11.

12.

stance, is used in the fabrication of integrated circuits, chips are sometimes referred to as "intelligent grains of sand."

4. The ingot is shaped and prepared prior to being cut into silicon wafers. Once the wafers are cut, they are polished to a perfect finish.

5. Silicon wafers that eventually will contain several hundred chips are placed in an oxygen furnace at 1200 degrees Centigrade. In the furnace the wafer is coated with other minerals to create the physical properties needed to produce transistors and electronic switches on the surface of the wafer.

6. The mask is placed over the wafer and both are exposed to ultraviolet light. In this way the circuit pattern is transferred onto the wafer. Plasma (superhot gases) technology is used to etch the circuit pattern permanently into the wafer. This is one of several techniques used in the etching process. The wafer is returned to the furnace and given another coating on which to etch another circuit layer. The procedure is repeated for each circuit layer until the wafer is complete.

7. The result of the coating/etching process is a silicon wafer that contains from 100 to 400 integrated circuits.

8. It takes only a second for this instrument to drill 1440 tiny holes in a wafer. The holes enable the interconnection of the layers of circuits.

Each layer must be perfectly aligned (within a millionth of a meter) with the others.

Testing

9. The chips are tested while they are still part of the wafer. Each integrated circuit on the wafer is powered up and given a series of tests. Fine needles make the connection for these computer-controlled tests. The precision demands are so great that as many as half the chips are found to be defective. A drop of ink is deposited on defective chips.

Packaging

10. A diamond saw separates the wafer into individual chips in a process called *dicing*.

11. The chips are packaged in protective ceramic or metal carriers. The carriers have standard-sized electrical pin connectors that allow the chip to be plugged conveniently into circuit boards. Because the pins tend to corrode, the pin connectors are the most vulnerable part of a computer system. To avoid corrosion and a bad connection, the pins on some carriers are made of gold.

12. The completed circuit boards are installed in computers and thousands of other computer-controlled devices.

MEMORY BITS

INTERNAL STORAGE
- Primary storage (or main memory, RAM)
- ROM, PROM, and EPROM
- Cache
- Registers

The control unit contains high-speed working storage areas called **registers** that can store no more than a few bytes (see Figure 3–6). The speed at which registers handle instructions and data is about 10 times faster than that of cache memory. They are used for a variety of processing functions. One register, called the **instruction register**, contains the instruction being executed. Other general-purpose registers store data needed for immediate processing. Registers also store status information. For example, the **program register** contains the address of the next instruction to be executed. Registers facilitate the movement of data and instructions between primary storage, the control unit, and the arithmetic and logic unit.

The Arithmetic and Logic Unit

The **arithmetic and logic unit** performs all computations (addition, subtraction, multiplication, and division) and all logic operations (comparisons).

Examples of *computations* include the payroll deduction for Social Security, the day-end inventory, the balance on a bank statement, and the like. A *logic* operation compares two pieces of data. Then, based on the result of the comparison, the program "branches" to one of several alternative sets of program instructions. Let's use an inventory system to illustrate the logic operation. At the end of each day the inventory level of each item in stock is compared to a reorder point. For each comparison indicating an inventory level that falls below (<) the reorder point, a sequence of program instructions is executed that produces a purchase order. For each comparison indicating an inventory level at or above (= or >) the reorder point, another sequence of instructions is executed.

The arithmetic and logic unit also does alphabetic comparisons. For example, when comparing Smyth and Smith, Smyth is evaluated as being greater alphabetically, so it is positioned after Smith.

The Machine Cycle

You have probably heard of computer programming languages such as COBOL, BASIC, and RPG. There are dozens of programming languages in common usage. However, in the end, COBOL, BASIC, and the other languages are translated into the only language that a computer understands—machine language. Machine-language instructions are represented inside the computer as strings of binary digits, up to 64 digits in length. An overview of machine languages and of some of the more popular higher level programming languages is provided in Chapter 9, "Programming Concepts."

Every machine language has a predefined format for each type of instruction. The relative position within the instruction designates whether a sequence of characters is an **operation code**, an **operand**, or irrelevant. The typical machine language will have from 50 to 200 separate operation codes. The operation code, or **op-code**, is that portion of the fundamental computer instruction that designates the operation to be performed (add, compare, retrieve data from RAM, and so on).

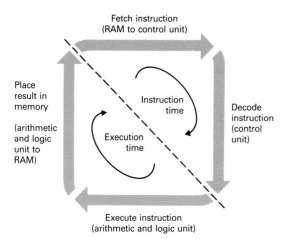

Fetch instruction
(RAM to control unit)

Place
result in
memory

(arithmetic
and logic
unit to
RAM)

Instruction
time

Execution
time

Decode
instruction
(control
unit)

Execute instruction
(arithmetic and logic unit)

FIGURE 3–7
The Machine Cycle

The operand is that portion of the instruction that designates data or refers to one or more addresses in RAM in which data can be found or placed. The op-code determines whether the operand contains data, addresses, or both.

Every computer has a **machine cycle**. The following actions take place during the machine cycle (see Figure 3–7):

- *Fetch instruction.* The next instruction to be executed (op-code and operand) is retrieved, or "fetched," from RAM or cache memory and loaded to the instruction register in the control unit (see Figure 3–6).
- *Decode instruction.* The instruction is decoded and interpreted.
- *Execute instruction.* Using whatever processor resources are needed (primarily the arithmetic and logic unit), the instruction is executed.
- *Place result in memory.* The results are placed in the appropriate memory position (usually RAM or a register in the arithmetic and logic unit called the **accumulator**). (See Figure 3–6.)

The speed of a processor is sometimes measured by how long it takes to complete a machine cycle. The timed interval that comprises the machine cycle is the total of the **instruction time**, or **I-time**, and the **execution time**, or **E-time** (see Figure 3–7). The I-time is made up of the first two activities of the machine cycle—fetch and decode the instruction. The E-time comprises the last two activities of the machine cycle—execute the instruction and store the results.

Parallel Processing: An Alternative Design Architecture

Computer manufacturers have relied on the single processor design architecture since the late 1940s. In this environment, the processor addresses the programming problem sequentially, from beginning to end. Today designers are doing research on computers that will be able to break a programming problem into pieces. Work on each of these pieces will then be executed simultaneously in separate processors, all of which are part of the same computer. The concept of using multiple processors in the same computer system is known as **parallel processing**.

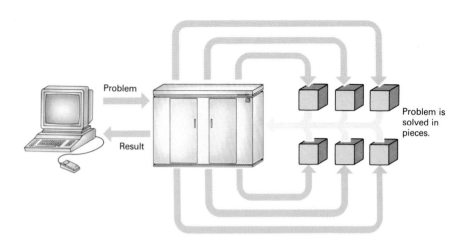

FIGURE 3–8 Parallel Processing
In parallel processing, auxiliary processors solve pieces of a problem to enhance system throughput.

In Chapter 2, "Micros, Minis, Mainframes, and Supercomputers," the point was made that a computer system may be made up of several special-function processors. For example, a single computer system may have a host, a front-end processor, and a back-end processor. By dividing the workload among several special-function processors, the system throughput is increased. Computer designers began asking themselves, "If three or four processors can enhance throughput, what could be accomplished with 20, or even a thousand, processors?"

In parallel processing, one main processor (for example, a mini or a host mainframe) examines the programming problem and determines what portions, if any, of the problem can be solved in pieces (see Figure 3–8). Those pieces that can be addressed separately are routed to other processors and solved. The individual pieces are then reassembled in the main processor for further computation, output, or storage. The net result of parallel processing is better throughput. Many people feel that parallel processing may be the wave of the future. However, much is yet to be done. Research and design in this area, which some say characterizes a fifth generation of computers, is still in the formative stages. (The first four generations of computers are discussed in Appendix A, "An Abbreviated History of Computers.")

3–6 DESCRIBING THE PROCESSOR: DISTINGUISHING CHARACTERISTICS

People are people, and computers are computers, but how do we distinguish one computer from another? We describe people in terms of height, build, age, and so on. We describe computers or processors in terms of *word length*, *speed*, and the *capacity* of their associated primary storage. For example, a computer might be described as a 32-bit, 20 MHz, 4 Mb micro. Let's see what this means.

Word Length

A **word** is the number of bits that are handled as a unit for a particular computer system. The word length of modern microcomputers is normally 16 bits or 32 bits. Supercomputers have 64-bit words. Other common word lengths are eight and 36 bits.

Processor Speed: Minis, Mainframes, and Supercomputers

Processor speed is often measured in **MIPS**, or millions of instructions per second. The processing speed of today's minis, mainframes, and supercomputers is in the range of 20 to 1000 MIPS.

The timed intervals of the machine cycle also provide a measure of processor speed (see Section 3–5). The shorter the machine cycle, the faster the processor. Machine cycles are measured in milliseconds, microseconds, and nanoseconds—or thousandths, millionths, and billionths of a second. As technology advances, machine cycles eventually will be measured in picoseconds—or trillionths of a second.

Processor Speed: Micros

A *crystal oscillator* paces the execution of instructions within the processor of a microcomputer. A micro's processor speed is rated by its frequency of oscillation, or the number of clock cycles per second. Most personal computers are rated between five and 50 megahertz or MHz (clock cycles). The elapsed time for one clock cycle is 1/frequency (one divided by the frequency). For example, the time it takes to complete one cycle on a 20 MHz processor is 1/20,000,000, or 0.00000005 seconds, or 50 nanoseconds. Normally, several clock cycles are required to retrieve, decode, and execute a single program instruction. The shorter the clock cycle, the faster the processor.

This supercomputer, which looks something like a space-age sofa, helps an oil company process mountains of data into pictures of the underground. It has a machine cycle of 4.1 nanoseconds (4.1 billionths of a second), a word size of 64 bits, and 2048 megabytes of primary storage.

The transportable microcomputer being used by this financial planner is based on the Intel 80386 chip. It has a processor speed of 16 Mhz, a RAM capacity of 10 megabytes, and a word length of 32 bits.

To properly evaluate the processing capability of a micro, you must consider both the processor speed and the word length. A 32-bit micro with a 20 MHz processor has more processing capability than a 16-bit micro with a 20 MHz processor.

We seldom think in time units smaller than a second; consequently, it is almost impossible for us to think in terms of computer speeds. Imagine, today's microcomputers can execute more instructions in a minute than you have had heartbeats since the day you were born!

Capacity of Primary Storage

The capacity of primary storage, or RAM, is stated in terms of the number of bytes it can store. As we learned in this chapter, a byte is roughly equivalent to a character (such as A, 1, &).

Memory capacity is usually stated in terms of **kilobytes (Kb)**, a convenient designation for 1024 (2^{10}) bytes of storage, and in terms of **megabytes (Mb)**, approximately a million bytes of storage. Memory

---

MEMORY BITS

PROCESSOR DESCRIPTION

Speed (mainframes): MIPS and machine cycle

Speed (micros): MHz (clock cycles)

RAM Capacity: Kb or Mb

Word length: Bits handled as a unit

capacities range from 640 Kb to 16 Mb in micros. In the multiuser environment, memory capacities vary widely from 4 Mb in low-end minis to 8000 Mb in supercomputers.

Now if anyone ever asks you what a 32-bit, 20 MHz, 4 Mb, micro is, you've got the answer!

SUMMARY OUTLINE AND IMPORTANT TERMS

3-1 **DATA STORAGE: DATA IN THE COMPUTER.** Data, not information, are stored in a computer system. Data are stored temporarily during processing in **primary storage**, or **main memory**, and permanently on **secondary storage** devices, such as magnetic tape and disk drives.

3-2 **A BIT ABOUT THE BIT.** The two electronic states of the computer are represented by a **bit**, short for *binary digit*. These electronic states are compatible with the **binary** numbering system. Letters and decimal numbers are translated into bits for storage and processing on computer systems.

3-3 **ENCODING SYSTEMS: COMBINING BITS TO FORM BYTES. Alphanumeric** characters are represented in computer storage by combining strings of bits to form unique bit configurations for each character. Characters are translated into these bit configurations, also called **bytes**, according to a particular coding scheme, called an **encoding system**. Popular encoding systems include **EBCDIC**, **ASCII**, and **ASCII-8**.

Parity-checking procedures ensure that data transmission between hardware devices is complete and accurate.

3-4 **NUMBERING SYSTEMS AND COMPUTERS.** The two primary numbering systems used in conjunction with computers are binary and **decimal**. Decimal is translated into binary on input and binary is translated into decimal on output. The **hexadecimal** numbering system is used primarily as a programmer convenience in reading and reviewing binary output in the form of a **memory dump**.

3-5 **COMPONENTS OF A COMPUTER SYSTEM: A CLOSER LOOK AT THE PROCESSOR AND PRIMARY STORAGE.** The processor is the "intelligence" of a computer system. A processor, which is also called the **central processing unit** or **CPU**, has only two fundamental sections, the **control unit** and the **arithmetic and logic unit**, which work together with primary storage to execute programs. The control unit interprets instructions and directs the arithmetic and logic unit to perform computation and logic operations.

Primary storage, or **RAM** (random-access memory), provides the processor with temporary storage for programs and data. Most of today's computers use CMOS technology for primary storage. However, with CMOS, the data are lost when the electrical current is turned off or interrupted. In contrast, **bubble memory** provides nonvolatile memory. All input/output, including programs, must enter and exit primary storage. Other variations of internal storage are **ROM**, **PROM**, and **EPROM**.

Some computers employ **cache memory** to increase **throughput**. Like RAM, cache is a high-speed holding area for program instructions and data. However, cache memory holds only those instructions and data likely to be needed next by the processor. During execution, instructions and data are passed between very high-speed **registers** (for example, the **instruction register** and the **accumulator**) in the control unit and the arithmetic and logic unit.

Every machine language has a predefined format for each type of instruction. Each instruction has an **operation code** and an **operand**. During one **machine cycle**, an instruction is "fetched" from RAM, decoded in the control unit, executed, and the results are placed in memory. The machine cycle time is the total of the **instruction time** and the **execution time**.

In **parallel processing**, one main processor examines the programming problem and determines what portions, if any, of the problem can be solved in pieces. Those pieces that can be addressed separately are routed to other processors, solved, then recombined in the main processor to produce the result.

3–6 DESCRIBING THE PROCESSOR: DISTINGUISHING CHARACTERISTICS. A processor is described in terms of its word length, speed, and primary storage capacity. The **word** (the number of bits handled as a unit) length of computers ranges from 16 bits for the smaller micros to 64 bits for supercomputers. Mainframe speed is measured in **MIPS** and by the timed intervals that make up the machine cycle. Microcomputer speed is measured in megahertz (MHz). Memory capacity is measured in **kilobytes (Kb)** or **megabytes (Mb)**.

REVIEW EXERCISES

Concepts

1. Distinguish between RAM, ROM, PROM, and EPROM.
2. How many EBCDIC bytes can be stored in a 32-bit word?
3. Which two functions are performed by the arithmetic and logic unit?
4. List examples of alpha, numeric, and alphanumeric characters.
5. Write your first name as an ASCII bit configuration.
6. What are the functions of the control unit?
7. What advantage does the use of a nibble offer when using the ASCII-8 or EBCDIC encoding system?
8. We describe computers in terms of what three characteristics?
9. What are the binary and hexadecimal equivalents of a decimal 12?
10. What is the basic difference between CMOS technology and nonvolatile technology, such as bubble memory?
11. For a given computer, which type of memory would have the greatest capacity to store data and programs: cache or RAM? RAM or registers? Registers or cache?
12. Name three types of registers.
13. Which portion of the fundamental computer instruction designates the operation to be performed?

Discussion

14. *Kb* is used to represent 1024 bytes of storage. Would it not have been much easier to let *Kb* represent 1000 bytes? Explain.

15. Millions of bytes of data are transferred routinely between computing hardware devices without any errors in transmission. Very seldom is a parity error detected. In your opinion, is it worth all the trouble to add and check parity bits every time a byte is transmitted from one device to another? Why?

16. Create a five-bit encoding system to be used for storing uppercase alpha characters, punctuation symbols, and the apostrophe. Discuss the advantages and disadvantages of your encoding system in relation to the ASCII encoding system.

SELF-TEST (by section)

3–1 Data are stored permanently on secondary storage devices, such as magnetic tape. (T/F)

3–2 **a.** *Bit* is the singular of *byte*. (T/F)
b. The base of the binary number system is: (a) 2, (b) 8, or (c) 16.

3–3 **a.** The combination of bits used to represent a character is called a _____.
b. The procedure that ensures complete and accurate transmission of data is called ASCII checking. (T/F)

3–4 **a.** A _____ is a "snapshot" of the contents of primary storage at a given moment in time.
b. When you count in hexadecimal, you carry to the next position in groups of _____.

3–5 **a.** Data are loaded from secondary to primary storage in a nondestructive read process. (T/F)
b. The _____ is that part of the processor that reads and interprets program instructions.
c. The arithmetic and logic unit controls the flow of programs and data in and out of main memory. (T/F)
d. Put the following memories in order based on speed: cache, registers, and RAM.
e. The timed interval that comprises the machine cycle is the total of the _____ time and the _____ time.

3–6 **a.** The word length of most microcomputers is 64 bits. (T/F)
b. MIPS is an acronym for "millions of instructions per second." (T/F)
c. The time it takes to complete one cycle on a 10 MHz processor is _____ nanoseconds.

Self-test answers   **3–1** T. **3–2** (a) F; (b) a. **3–3** (a) byte; (b) F. **3–4** (a) memory dump; (b) 16. **3–5** (a) T; (b) control unit; (c) F; (d) from the slowest memory: RAM, cache, registers; (e) instruction, execution. **3–6** (a) F; (b) T; (c) 100.

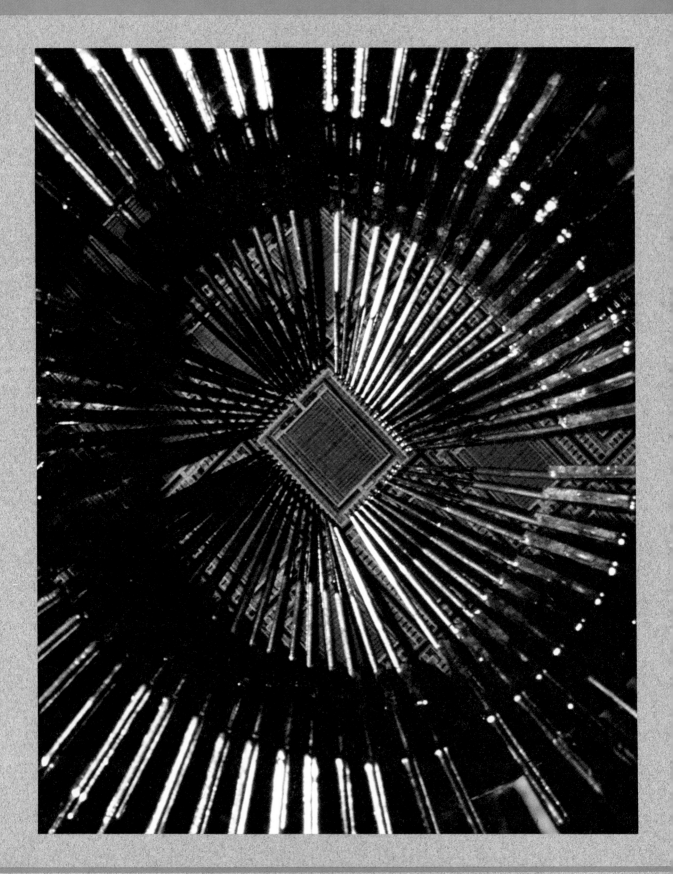

Input/Output Devices

STUDENT LEARNING OBJECTIVES

▶ To describe the use and characteristics of the different types of terminals.

▶ To explain alternative approaches to and devices for data entry.

▶ To describe the operation and application of common output devices.

4–1 I/O DEVICES: OUR INTERFACE WITH THE COMPUTER

Data are created in many places and in many ways. Before data can be processed and stored, they must be translated into a form the computer can interpret. For this, we need *input* devices. Once the data have been processed, they must be translated back into a form that *we* can understand. For this, we need *output* devices. These input/output (I/O) devices, also referred to as peripheral devices, enable communication between us and the computer.

The diversity of computer applications has encouraged manufacturers to develop and market a variety of I/O methods and hardware. Innovative I/O devices are being introduced continuously into the marketplace. For example, voice recognition devices accept data (input) from human speech. Speech synthesizers produce simulated human speech as output.

This chapter is divided into three parts. The first part focuses on the variety of terminals available, most of which are used for both input and output. The second part presents devices for entering data using *source-data automation*—in other words, data are entered into the computer directly from the source, without the need for manual data entry. The last part describes devices used strictly for output.

The people in this department provide administrative support to three regional insurance claims offices. Because each of these knowledge workers routinely deals with computer-generated information, each person needs a terminal to interact with the computer.

4–2   TERMINALS AND WORKSTATIONS

A *video display terminal*, or *VDT*, is a device that allows us to interact with a computer from just about anywhere. VDTs, or simply *terminals*, were first introduced in Chapter 1. A VDT's primary input mechanism is usually a *keyboard*, and the output is usually displayed on a televisionlike screen called a *monitor*. Terminals come in all shapes and sizes and have a variety of input/output capabilities.

Although the telephone, with its touch-tone keypad and computer-generated voice output, is the terminal with which we are most familiar, the VDT and the microcomputer are those most commonly used for remote interaction with a computer system. The VDT is affectionately known as "the tube," short for **cathode-ray tube**. From our past discussions (Chapter 2, "Micros, Minis, Mainframes, and Supercomputers"), we know that a microcomputer can serve as a stand-alone computer or as a terminal linked to a mainframe.

The Keyboard

Just about all terminals and micros come equipped with a keyboard for input. The typical one will have a standard *alphanumeric keyboard* with an optional numeric keyboard called a *10-key pad*. A **text cursor**, or blinking character (often an underline character or a solid rectangle), always indicates the location of the next keyed-in character on the screen. When you press a character key, it is displayed at the cursor position and the cursor advances to the next position, usually one character to the right. Some keyboards will also have *special-function keys*, which can be used to instruct the computer to perform a specific operation that may otherwise require several keystrokes. Keyboards are described in detail in Appendix C, "Using a Microcomputer."

Some keyboards are designed for specific applications. The cash-register-like terminals at most fast-food restaurants have special-purpose keyboards. Rather than type in the name and price of an order of french fries, attendants need only press the key marked "french fries" to record the sale.

Other Input Devices

The keyboard is too cumbersome for some applications. A computer artist may want to enter curved lines to create an image. An engineer might need to "draw" a line to connect two points on a graph. A physician may have to outline the exact shape of a tumor. Such applications call for devices that go beyond the capabilities of keyboards. These devices move a **graphics cursor** to create the image. The graphics cursor, which can be positioned anywhere on the screen, is often displayed as a small arrow or crosshair. Depending on the application, the character and graphics cursors may be displayed on the screen at the same time. The light pen, joy stick, track ball, digitizing tablet and pen, and mouse are among the most popular input devices that move graphics cursors.

When it is moved close to the screen, the *light pen* detects light from the cathode-ray tube. The graphics cursor automatically locks onto

Terminals are an increasingly familiar sight in modern hospitals. Immediate access to patient data is critical to quality health care. This lab technician and doctor are using a keyboard to request the results of a patient's blood test.

An engineer uses a crosshair device along with a digitizing tablet to design the intricate circuitry for a special-purpose computer.

the position of the pen and tracks its movement over the screen. An engineer may create or modify images directly on the screen with a light pen. A city planner can select from a menu of possible computer functions by simply pointing the light pen to the desired function.

Video arcade wizards are no doubt familiar with the *joy stick* and *track ball*. The joy stick is a vertical stick that moves the graphics cursor in the direction the stick is pushed. The track ball is a ball inset in the work table in front of the screen or in the keyboard of some portable computers. The ball is "rolled" to move the graphics cursor. The *digitizing tablet and pen* are a pen and a pressure-sensitive tablet with the same X–Y coordinates as the screen. The outline of an image drawn on a tablet is reproduced on the display screen. The digitizing tablet is also used in conjunction with a *crosshair* device.

The *mouse*, sometimes called the "pet peripheral," is now standard equipment for some terminals and many micros. Attached to the computer by a cable, the mouse is a small device that, when moved across a desktop, moves the graphics cursor accordingly. The movement begins when a button on the mouse is pushed. You can also move objects on the screen by holding down the button and moving the mouse. The mouse is commonly used for quick positioning of the graphics cursor over the desired menu item. It is discussed further in Appendix C, "Using a Microcomputer."

Once an image has been entered to a computer system, it can be stored and, if needed, modified during subsequent sessions.

Interactive in-store information systems use graphic user interfaces, sometimes called GUIs, to help take the frustration out of grocery shopping. This color monitor is sensitive to the touch. Suppose you are shopping at your favorite supermarket and can't find the nachos. You go to the monitor and touch the letter N on a display of the alphabet to view a list of all products that begin with N. Then you would scroll through the alphabetical list and touch the nacho chips entry. A screen of the store's layout appears with a flashing signal showing the product's precise location (the green rectangle on left side of store).

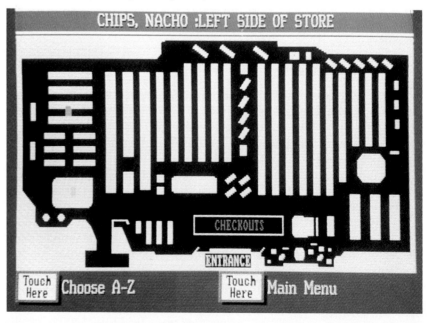

The Monitor

Alphanumeric and graphic output are displayed on the terminal's monitor. The three primary attributes of monitors are the *size* of the display screen; whether the display is *color* or *monochrome*; and the *resolution*, or detail, of the display. The diagonal dimension of the display screen varies from 5 to 25 inches. Output on a monitor is *soft copy*; that is, it is temporary and is available to the end user only until another display is requested, as opposed to the permanent *hard-copy* output of printers.

Monitors are either monochrome or color. Monochrome monitors display images in a single color, usually white, green, blue, red, or amber. A monochrome monitor can, however, display shades of its one color. The industry uses the term **gray scales** to refer to the number of shades of a color that can be shown on a monochrome monitor's screen. Color monitors add another dimension to the display. Their use of colors can focus attention on different aspects of the output. For example, an engineer designing pipelines for an oil refinery can use colors to highlight such things as the direction and type of fluid flow, the size of the pipes, and so on.

Some monitors have a much higher **resolution**, or quality of output. Resolution refers to the number of addressable points on the screen: the number of points to which light can be directed under program control. These points are sometimes called **pixels**, short for *picture elements*. Each pixel can be assigned a shade of gray or a color. A low resolution monitor has about 65,000 addressable points. A monitor used primarily for computer graphics and computer-aided design may have over 16 million addressable points. The high-resolution monitors project extremely clear images that almost look like photographs.

Some space-saving monitors are flat. Most **flat-panel monitors** are used in conjunction with portable microcomputers. Flat-panel monitors

These mechanical engineers at GE Research and Development Center use a sophisticated solid-state modeling program in conjunction with a high-resolution monitor to design injection molds for the manufacture of plastic parts such as a lawn tractor hood. Engineers optimize a plastic product's design by computer rather than by actually building and testing numerous prototypes.

Two common complaints among users of portable computers are that flat-panel monitors are difficult to see and that the mouse must be carried separately. This Macintosh portable addresses these concerns. It is configured with an easy-to-read backlit liquid crystal display (LCD) and a permanently installed track ball instead of a mouse.

use three basic types of technology: *LCD* (liquid crystal display), the technology commonly used in digital wristwatches; *gas plasma*; and *EL* (electroluminescent). Up until the late 1980s, all flat-panel monitors were monochrome. With the recent introduction of color LCD monitors, portable PC buyers now have a choice.

Graphics Workstations

Video display terminals of every size and shape are used by secretaries for word processing, by programmers for interactive program development, by clerks for recording transactions, by commercial artists for creating ad pieces, by management for making decisions, by computer operators for communicating with the computer (via the operator console), by shop supervisors for line scheduling, and by thousands of other people for hundreds of applications.

This graphics workstation is used for CAD applications. The engineer is designing an enclosure that will hold interchangeable circuit boards. Graphics workstations are often configured with auxiliary keypads to expand the number of function keys (front left) available to the user.

The class of video display terminals designed especially for the sophisticated user is the **graphics workstation**. All graphics workstations are **intelligent workstations**; that is, they are endowed with their own processing capability as well as the ability to interface with a mainframe. Typically, a minimum configuration for a graphics workstation would include a medium-sized high-resolution graphics monitor, a keyboard, and at least two more modes of input (for example, a mouse, joystick, track ball, and/or digitizing tablet). Some graphics workstations have two monitors, a large one for graphics output and a small one for alphanumeric output. The graphics monitor may be monochrome or color. Often users elect to configure their graphics workstations with some kind of hard-copy device, such as a printer/plotter (discussed later in this chapter).

The applications for these sophisticated workstations are endless. For the most part, graphics workstations help in the design process. Different types of engineers use them for computer-aided design (CAD) applications. For example, electrical engineers use them to design the logic for silicon chips. Industrial engineers use them to design the layout of manufacturing plants. Civil engineers use them to design bridges. Of course, people other than engineers use graphics workstations. Architects use them to design buildings. Systems analysts rely on graphics workstations to show the work and information flow within an information system.

YOUR TELEPHONE IS ALSO A TERMINAL

Traditionally, the telephone has been an instrument for interactive voice communication between two or more people. Recently, however, the common Touch-Tone telephone also is being used as a terminal for interactive communication between a person and a computer. A telephone terminal has both input and output capabilities. You can input alphanumeric data on the Touch-Tone keypad of a telephone (keyboard), and you can speak into the receiver (voice input). Output consists of computer-generated sounds, primarily voice, heard on the speaker portion of the hand set.

A number of organizations are looking for ways to provide their customers, clients, suppliers, distributors, alumni, and so on with the convenience of direct access to their computer system. Many of these organizations have opted for the telephone terminal, rather than a video display terminal or a microcomputer, as the basis for their computer network. Telephones are everywhere and everyone knows how to use them. A computer network integrates a computer system, terminals, and the communication links. A computer network designed within the input/output limitations of telephone terminals can be accessed by anyone with a Touch-Tone telephone. All that is needed for such a network is the central computer. The terminals (telephones) and the communications links (telephone lines) are already in place.

The TouchLine service offered by the USAA Investment Management Company is a good example of a telephone-based computer network. TouchLine provides USAA customers with a direct line into their computer via telephone. The USAA TouchLine service enables investors to call a toll-free number (24 hours a day, seven days a week) and perform any of these functions:

- Request price quotes on any of USAA's 15 funds (for example, Income Stock Fund, Gold Fund, Money Market Fund).

- Request the balance in a given account.
- Request information on the last transaction for a given account.
- Make exchanges between accounts (for example, transfer money from a Gold Fund account to a Money Market Fund account).
- Redeem part or all of an account.
- Change a security code.

Here is how the USAA TouchLine service works. The first time the customer uses the service, the computer asks, via a voice-response unit, for a security code. The security code, known only to the customer, must be entered to receive information on a customer account. During subsequent interactive sessions, the customer is prompted each step of the way. For example, he or she is presented with a main menu at the onset of the session. The voice-response unit presents the options: "If at any time you need to talk to a service representative, press the star [asterisk] key followed by the zero key"; "For current fund prices, push one"; "For account information, push 2"; and so on. Depending on what the customer wishes to do, the system may prompt him or her to key in a USAA member number, a security code, codes for one or more of the various funds, one or more personal account numbers, or an amount to be transferred or redeemed.

While using the TouchLine service, the customer can issue commands from the keypad, such as the following:

∗	To pause temporarily.
∗ G	To begin after a pause.
∗ B	To return to the beginning of the call.
∗ R	To repeat the last message or prompt.
∗ D	To cancel the last command.
∗ W	To change a security code.
# #	To skip over information being presented.

Terminal and Workstation Summary

The trend in terminals and workstations is to provide processing as well as I/O capability. In the not-too-distant future, virtually all terminals will be microcomputers with stand-alone processing capability. Microcomputers are becoming so powerful that users are no longer completely dependent on mainframe capabilities for complex processing jobs. With

MEMORY BITS

TERMINALS

- Also called
    Video display terminal
    VDT
    Cathode-ray tube
    The tube
- Input
    Keyboard
    Light pen
    Joystick
    Track ball
    Digitizing tablet and pen
    Mouse
- Output
    Monitor
        Diagonal size of 5 to 25
            inches
        Monochrome or color
        Low or high resolution

these intelligent terminals and workstations, users can interact with mainframe computers or download data for stand-alone processing. Data processed in a stand-alone mode can also be uploaded to the mainframe so that the data can be shared with users at other terminals.

The computer is playing an ever-increasing role in how we do our jobs. Because it is the means by which we communicate with the computer, it is fast becoming a companion to workers in most fields of endeavor.

4–3   SOURCE-DATA AUTOMATION: GETTING DATA INTO THE COMPUTER SYSTEM

Trends in Data Entry

The trend in data entry has been toward decreasing the number of transcription steps. This is accomplished by entering the data as close to the source as possible. For example, in sales departments, salespeople input orders directly to the system. In accounting departments, bookkeepers and accountants record and enter financial transactions into the system. However, whenever possible, the need for key entry transcription of data is eliminated altogether. This is known as **source-data automation**.

Until recently, data entry has been synonymous with *keystrokes*. The keystroke will continue to be the basic mode of data entry for the foreseeable future, but recent innovations have eliminated the need for key-driven data entry in many applications. For example, you have

This law enforcement officer is using a portable computer with handwriting recognition capability to record pertinent data at the scene of an accident. The 9-by-12-by-1¼-inch GRiDPad, made by GRiD Systems Corporation, can also accept and store a detailed drawing that shows how the accident happened. The violator uses the tethered electronic pen to sign the "ticket."

Overnight mail couriers are leaders in source data automation. Federal Express couriers use portable radio data terminals to transmit delivery information and receive customer requests to pick up packages. Linked to a host computer, their terminals help in tracking shipments and keeping customer information up-to-date.

probably noticed the preprinted **bar codes** on grocery products. At some supermarket checkout counters these bar codes have eliminated the need for most key entry. Checkers need only pass the product over the *laser scanner*, the price is entered, and the shelf inventory is updated as well.

Data entry is an area in which enormous potential exists for increases in productivity. The technology of data entry devices is constantly changing. New and improved methods of transcribing raw data are being invented and put on the market each month. These data entry methods and associated devices are discussed next.

Optical Character Recognition

Optical character recognition (OCR) is a way to encode (write) certain data in machine-readable format on the original source document. For example, the International Standard Book Number (ISBN) on the back cover of this book is printed in machine-readable OCR. This eliminates the need for publishers and bookstore clerks to key these data manually. OCR equipment consists of a family of devices that encode and read OCR data.

OCR Scanners.   OCR characters are identified by light-sensitive devices called **OCR scanners**. Both scanner technologies, *contact* and *laser*, bounce a beam of light off an image, then measure the reflected light to determine the value of the image. Hand-held *wand scanners* make

Supermarket checkout systems are now an established cost-saving technology. The automated systems use stationary laser scanners to read the bar codes that identify each item (left). Price and product descriptions are retrieved from a data base and recorded on the sales slip. The scanner incorporates a spinning disk of 21 holographic films that function as glass prisms and lenses (right). A laser beam passing through the disk creates a complex light pattern that strikes the Universal Product Code on the item. The light reflected by the UPC stripes is converted into digital signals for processing.

contact as they are brushed over the printed matter to be read. Stationary *laser scanners* are more versatile and can read data passed near the scanning area. Both can recognize printed characters and various types of codes.

OCR devices can "learn" to read almost any typeface, including the one used for this book! The "learning" takes place when the structure of the character set is described to the OCR device. Special OCR devices can even read hand-printed letters if they are recorded on a standard form and written according to specific rules.

OCR scanners can be classified into the following five categories:

■ *Label scanners.* These devices read data on price tags, shipping labels, and the like. A hand-held wand scanner is a label scanner.

■ *Page scanners.* These devices scan and interpret the alphanumeric characters on regular typewritten pages.

■ *Document scanners.* Document scanners are capable of scanning documents of varying sizes (for example, utility-bill invoice stubs and sales slips from credit-card transactions).

■ *Continuous-form scanners.* These devices read data printed on continuous forms, such as cash register tapes.

■ *Optical-mark scanners.* Optical mark scanners scan preprinted forms, such as multiple-choice test answer forms. The position of the "sense mark" indicates a particular response or character.

Applications of Optical Scanners

Bar codes   Stationary scanners, such as those in supermarkets, use lasers to interpret the bar codes printed on products. Bar codes represent alphanumeric data by varying the width and combination of adjacent vertical lines. Just as there are a variety of internal bit encoding systems, there are a variety of bar-coding systems (see Figure 4–1). One of the most visible of these systems is the Universal Product Code (UPC). The UPC, originally used for supermarket items, is gaining popularity and is now being printed on other consumer goods. The advantage of bar codes over characters is that the position or orientation of the code being read is not as critical to the scanner. In a supermarket, for example, the data can be recorded even if a bottle of ketchup is rolled over the laser scanner.

Wand scanners   The hand-held wand scanner is now common in point-of-sale (POS) systems in retail stores throughout the world. Clerks need only brush the wand over the price tag to record the sale. Because the POS terminal is on-line, the inventory also is updated as each item is sold.

Wand scanners also are used to read package labels in shipping and receiving and in inventory management. Passport inspection is even being automated with the use of wand scanners. Customs officials enter passport numbers via wand scanners to help speed the processing of international travelers.

OCR turnaround documents   OCR devices are custom-made for situations where data can be encoded by the computer system on a **turnaround document** when visual recognition is important. A turnaround document is *computer-produced output* that is ultimately returned to a computer system as *machine-readable input*. The billing system of an electric utility company is a good example of this OCR application. Data on the invoice

FIGURE 4–1   Various Codes That Can Be Interpreted by OCR Scanners

are printed in a format that can be read by an OCR document scanner. The customers return the OCR-readable invoice stubs (turnaround documents) with the payment. An OCR scanner reads the original turnaround document, and the customer's account is credited by the amount of the payment.

Original-source data collection   Optical character recognition is also used for original-source data collection. An example is data collection for gasoline credit-card purchases. When you make a credit-card purchase, your card, a multicopy form, and a portable imprint device are used to record the sales data in machine-readable OCR format. The data recorded on the form for most gasoline credit-card purchases include the *account number of the buyer* (imprinted from the customer's credit card), the *account number of the service station* (imprinted from a permanently installed merchant card in the portable imprint device), and the *amount of the purchase* (entered by the attendant). The customer is given one copy of the form as a record of purchase, one copy is retained by the service station, and the third copy, a stiffer card, is sent to the oil company that issued the credit card. With the data already in OCR format, no further data entry is required. During processing, the amount charged is recorded as a debit to the buyer's account and as a credit to the service station's account.

This personal reader allows visually impaired people to "hear" books and typewritten material. An optical scanner reads the words into the computer system, where they are converted into English speech using a speech synthesizer (a device that produces electronic speech). Users can request any of nine different voices (including male, female, and child).

Image Scanners

In recent years, source-data automation has expanded to allow the direct entry of pictorial information as well as test-based information via OCR scanners. An **image scanner** employs laser technology to scan and **digitize** an image. That is, the hard-copy image is translated into an electronic format that can be interpreted by and stored on computers. The digitized image is then stored on magnetic disk. The image to be scanned can be handwritten notes, a photograph, a drawing, an insurance form—anything that can be digitized. Once an image has been digitized and entered to the computer system, it can be retrieved, displayed, altered, merged with text, stored, and sent via data communications to one or several remote locations.

An image scanner can be purchased with optional hardware and software that provide it with the capability of performing the function of an OCR page scanner. That is, the image scanner can read and interpret the characters from most typewritten or typeset documents, such as a typewritten letter or a page from this book.

Magnetic-Ink Character Recognition

Magnetic-ink character recognition (MICR) is similar to optical character recognition and is used exclusively by the banking industry. MICR readers are used to read and sort checks and deposits. You probably have noticed the *account number* and *bank number* encoded on all your checks and personalized deposit slips. The *date* of the transaction is automatically recorded for all checks processed that day; therefore, only the *amount* must be keyed in (see Figure 4–2) on a **MICR inscriber**. A **MICR reader-sorter** reads the data on the checks and sorts the checks for distribution to other banks and customers or for further processing.

Magnetic-ink character-recognition devices are used instead of OCR scanners because of MICR's increased speed and accuracy. The special magnetic characters permit the speeds that banks need to sort and process over 500 million checks each day.

FIGURE 4–2   A Magnetic-Ink Character-Recognition (MICR) Encoded Check
Notice that the amount is entered on the check when it is received by the bank.

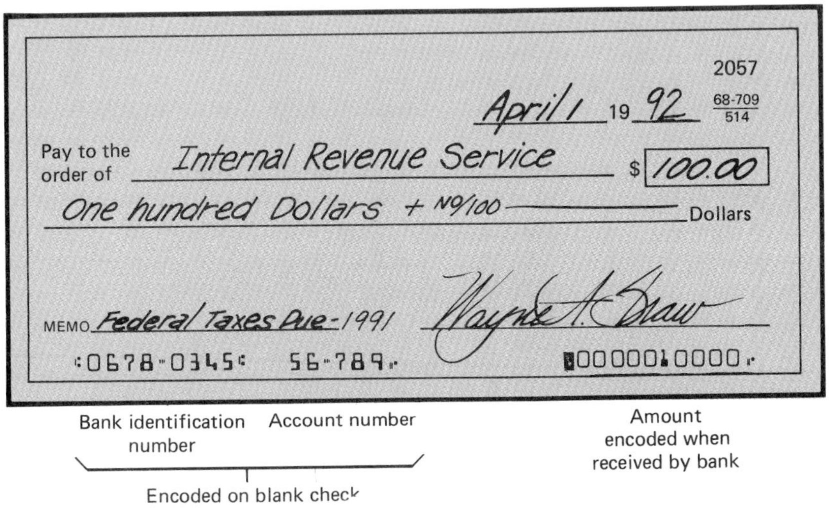

This check-processing machine can sort up to 100,000 MICR-encoded checks or deposit slips each hour.

Magnetic Stripes and Smart Cards

Very few jobs will be unchanged in the information society. Restaurants are going high-tech, too. Waiters enter orders on terminals like this by pressing keys corresponding to the appropriate menu item (New York strip) and options (medium) at terminals located throughout the restaurant. The order is routed to the kitchen staff, inventory is updated, and upon request, the customer's check is tallied and printed. Here the waiter scans the magnetic stripe on the customer's credit card to obtain a charge authorization number.

The **magnetic stripes** on the back of charge cards and badges offer another means of data entry. The magnetic stripes are encoded with data appropriate for the application. For example, your account number and privacy code are encoded on a card for automatic teller machines.

Magnetic stripes contain much more data per unit of space than do printed characters or bar codes. Moreover, because they cannot be read visually, they are perfect for storing confidential data such as the privacy code. Employee cards and security badges often contain authorization data for access to physically secured areas, such as the computer center. To gain access, an employee inserts a card or badge into a **badge reader**. This device reads and checks the authorization code before permitting the individual to enter a secured area. The badge reader may also be on-line to the computer. On-line badge readers maintain a chronological log of people entering or leaving secured areas.

The enhanced version of cards with a magnetic stripe is called the **smart card**. The smart card, similar in appearance to other cards, contains a microprocessor that retains certain security and personal data in its memory at all times. Because the smart card can hold more information, has some processing capability, and is almost impossible to duplicate, smart cards may replace cards with magnetic stripes in the future.

Voice Data Entry

Computers are great talkers, but they are not very good listeners. It is not uncommon for a **speech-recognition** device to misinterpret a slamming door for a spoken word. Nevertheless, speech-recognition systems can be used to enter limited kinds and quantities of information. Despite its limitations, speech recognition has a number of applications. Salespeople in the field can enter an order simply by calling the computer and stating the customer number, item number, and quantity. Quality-control personnel who must use their hands call out defects as they are detected.

Baggage handlers at airports simply state the three-letter destination identifier ("L-A-X" for Los Angeles International), and luggage is routed to the appropriate conveyer system. Physicians in the operating room can request certain information about a patient while operating. A computer-based audio response unit or a speech synthesizer makes the conversation two-way.

Figure 4–3 illustrates how it works. When you speak into a microphone, each sound is broken down and examined in several frequencies. The sounds in each frequency are digitized and are matched against similarly formed *templates* in the computer's electronic dictionary. The digitized template is a form that can be stored and interpreted by computers (in 1s and 0s). When a match is found, the word (*Move* in Figure 4–3) is displayed on a VDT or, in some cases, repeated by a speech synthesizer for confirmation. If no match is found, the speaker is asked to repeat the word.

In speech recognition, the creation of the data base is called *training*. Most speech-recognition systems are *speaker-dependent*; that is, they respond to the speech of a particular individual. Therefore, a data base of words must be created for each person using the system. To create

FIGURE 4–3   Speech Recognition
The sound waves created by the spoken word Move *are digitized by the computer. The digitized template is matched against templates of other words in the electronic dictionary. When the computer finds a match, it displays a written version of the word.*

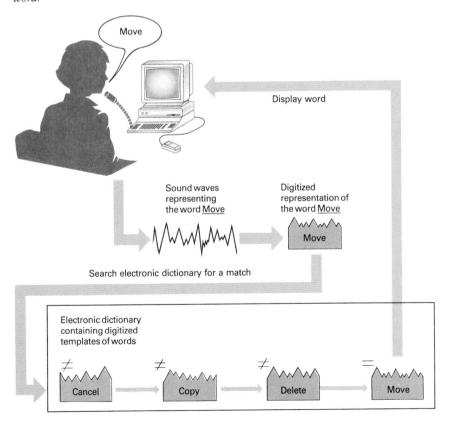

Quality-control inspectors in this circuit-board assembly plant record defects through voice data entry. The system enables interactive communication with the computer and frees the inspector's hands for other activities.

this data base, each person using the system must repeat—as many as 20 times—each word to be interpreted by the system. This "training" is necessary because we seldom say a word the same way each time. Even if we say the word twice in succession, it will probably have a different inflection or nasal quality.

State-of-the-art *speaker-independent* systems have a limited vocabulary: perhaps *yes, no,* and the 10 numeric digits. Although the vocabulary is limited, speaker-independent systems do not require training and can be used by anyone. However, they do require a very large data base to accommodate anyone's voice pattern.

Today we must see and touch our workstations to interact with a computer, but in a few years we may be talking with computers as we move about our offices and homes.

Vision-Input Systems

The simulation of human senses, especially vision, is extremely complex. A computer does not actually see and interpret an image the way a human being does. A camera is needed to give computers "eyesight." To create the data base, a vision system, via a camera, digitizes the images of all objects to be identified, then stores the digitized form of each image in the data base. When the system is placed in operation, the camera enters the image into a digitizer. The system then compares the digitized image to be interpreted to the prerecorded digitized images in the computer's data base. The computer identifies the image by matching the structure of the input image with those images in the data base. This process is illustrated by the digital vision-inspection system in Figure 4–4.

FIGURE 4–4 Digital-Vision Inspection System

In this digital-vision inspection system, the system examines parts for defects. If the digitized image of the part does not match a standard digital image, the defective part is placed in a reject bin.

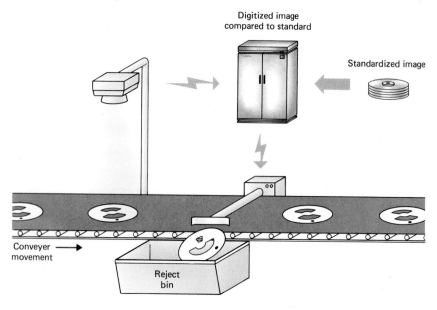

As you can imagine, **vision-input systems** are best suited to very specialized tasks in which only a few images will be encountered. These tasks are usually simple, monotonous ones, such as inspection. For example, in Figure 4–4 a digital vision-inspection system on an assembly line rejects those parts that do not meet certain quality-control specifications. The vision system performs rudimentary gauging inspections, and then signals the computer to take appropriate action.

Portable Data Entry

Portable data-entry devices are hand-held and usually *off-line*; that is, the portable device is not linked to the main computer during data collection activities. The typical portable data-entry device would have a limited keyboard and some kind of storage capability for the data, usually random-access memory or magnetic cassette tape. After the data have been entered, the data-entry device is linked with the host computer so that data can be *uploaded* (transmitted from the data-entry device to host) for processing.

One portable data-entry device combines a hand-held optical wand with a keyboard. Stock clerks in department stores routinely use such devices to collect and enter reorder data. As clerks visually check the inventory level, they identify the items that need to be restocked. First they scan the price tag with the wand, then they enter the number to be ordered on the keyboard.

Another portable data-entry device contains a pressure-sensitive writing pad that recognizes hand-printed alphanumeric characters.

This hand-held industrial computer is designed for remote data collection in manufacturing environments. The stock clerk is using a keyboard and an OCR wand scanner to enter data to the device. At the end of the day, he transmits the data to the company's host computer via a telephone hookup.

4–4 OUTPUT DEVICES: COMPUTERS COMMUNICATE WITH US

Output devices translate bits and bytes into a form we can understand. Terminals are both input and output devices. The monitors of terminals and workstations provide soft copy, or temporary output. The most common "output only" devices are discussed in this section. These include printers, desktop film recorders, screen-image projectors, computer-output microform, plotters, and voice-response units.

Printers

Printers produce hard-copy output, such as management reports, memos, payroll checks, and program listings. Printers are generally classified as **serial printers**, **line printers**, or **page printers**. Printers are rated by their print speed. Print speeds are measured in *characters per second* (*cps*), for serial printers, in *lines per minute* (*lpm*) for line printers, and in *pages per minute* (*ppm*) for page printers. The print-speed ranges for the three types of printers are 40–450 cps, 1000–5000 lpm, and 4–800 ppm, respectively.

Printers are further categorized as *impact* or *nonimpact*. An impact printer uses some type of hammer or hammers to hit the ribbon and the paper, much as a typewriter does. Nonimpact printers use chemicals, lasers, and heat to form the images on the paper. Only nonimpact printers can achieve print speeds in excess of 5000 lpm.

Small businesses, such as this retail sporting goods store, need the flexibility of dot matrix printers (foreground). This woman routinely adjusts the feed mechanism on the printer to accommodate a variety of print jobs. The mailing labels are printed on four-inch-wide peel-off paper, and inventory reports (shown here) are printed on 15-inch continuous-feed stock paper.

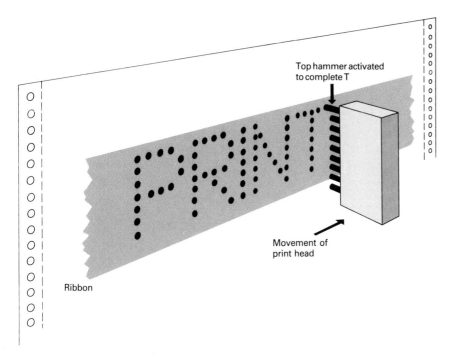

FIGURE 4–5   Dot-Matrix-Printer Character Formation
Each character is formed in a 7 × 5 matrix as the nine-pin print head moves across the paper. The two bottom pins are used for lowercase letters that extend below the line (for example, g and p).

Serial Printers. Most serial printers are configured with one or more microcomputer systems. They are also used in support of terminal clusters to give users the flexibility to obtain hard-copy output. Impact serial printers rely on **dot-matrix** and **daisy-wheel** technology. Nonimpact serial printers employ **ink-jet** and **thermal** technology. Regardless of the technology, the images are formed *one character at a time* as the print head moves across the paper. Virtually all serial printers are *bidirectional*; that is, they print whether the print head is moving left to right or right to left.

The dot-matrix printer   The dot-matrix printer arranges printed dots to form characters and all kinds of images in much the same way as lights display time and temperature on bank signs. One or several vertical columns of small print hammers, referred to as *pins*, are contained in a rectangular print head. The hammers are activated independently to form a dotted character image as the print head moves horizontally across the paper. The characters in Figure 4–5 are formed by a nine-pin print head within a matrix that is nine dots high and five dots wide (9 × 5). The number of dots within the matrix varies from one printer to the next.

The quality of the printed output is directly proportional to the density of the dots in the matrix. The 18-pin and 24-pin dot-matrix printers form characters that appear solid, and they can be used for business letters as well as for routine data processing output. Figure 4–6 illustrates how the dots can be overlapped with an 18-pin print head

FIGURE 4–6   Near-Letter-Quality Dot-Matrix Character Formation
The 18-pin print head permits dots to overlap to increase the density and, therefore, the quality of the image.

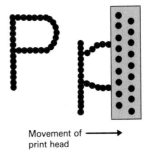

to create a *near-letter-quality* (NLQ) appearance. These printers are called *dual-mode* because of their dual-function capabilities (draft and NLQ).

Dot-matrix printers are further categorized as *monochrome* and *color*. The monochrome printer prints in the color of the ribbon, usually black. Color dot-matrix printers can select and print any of the colors on a multicolored ribbon (usually bands of black, yellow, red, and blue), or the printer can mix these colors via multiple passes and overstrikes to create the appearance of other colors in the rainbow. As you might imagine, you have to wait a little longer for a color graph than you would a monochrome graph.

Dot-matrix printers are more flexible than printers of fully formed characters (printers that use an embossed rendering of a character to reproduce the image on paper). Depending on the model, dot-matrix printers can print a variety of sizes and types of characters (even old English and script characters), graphics, and bar codes.

Features common to most dot-matrix printers include boldface, underline, subscript and superscript, and compressed print (narrower letters). Optional features include proportional spacing (using more or less space, depending on the width of the character) and italics.

The daisy-wheel printer   The daisy-wheel printer produces *letter-quality* (LQ) output for word processing applications. An interchangeable daisy wheel containing a set of fully formed characters spins to the desired character. A print hammer strikes the character embossed on the print wheel to form the image on the paper. Although daisy-wheel printers have the highest quality text output of serial printers, they are the slowest and cannot produce graphic output. These disadvantages and the emergence of high-quality dot-matrix printers have driven the once-popular daisy-wheel printer from the market during the past few years.

Cash registers use special-purpose dot-matrix printers to print receipts and itemized charge slips. This quality engineer is examining the magnified image of a sample output to determine if the dots are within acceptable limits.

The ink-jet printer   Monochrome and color ink-jet printers squirt dots of ink on paper to form images in much the same way dot-matrix printers do. The big advantage that ink-jet printers have over impact dot-matrix printers is the quality of the output, especially color output. Sales of color ink-jet printers are expected to increase substantially as users, accustomed to color output on their video monitors, come to want color hard-copy outputs.

The thermal printer   The thermal printer is an alternative to the other serial printers. Heat elements produce dot-matrix images on heat-sensitive paper. The major disadvantage is the cost of the heat-sensitive paper. The advantages include compact size, limited noise, and low purchase price.

Line Printers.   Line printers are impact printers that print *one line at a time*. The most popular types of line printers are the band printer, chain printer, and matrix line printer.

Band and chain printers   Both band and chain printers have a print hammer for each character position in the line of print (usually 132). On a band printer, several similar sets of fully formed characters are embossed on a horizontal band that is continuously moving in front of the print hammers. On a chain printer, the characters are embossed on each link of the print chain. With both types, the paper is momentarily stopped and, as the desired character passes over a given column, the hammer activates, pressing the ribbon against the paper to form the image.

Band and chain printers are capable of printing on continuous-feed paper as well as on cards and on documents of varying sizes (even mailing labels). Interchangeable bands and chains make it easy for operators to change the style of print (typeface).

This line printer (left) uses 132 printer hammers, one of which is shown in the photo, in conjunction with an operator-changeable steel band to achieve print speeds in excess of 2000 lines per minute. To load the continuous-feed paper, an acoustical enclosure is raised, and the "gate" containing the band and ribbon is swung open.

Inside a high-speed page printer, laser beams scan across the print drum to create text and graphics at speeds up to 800 pages per minute.

The matrix line printer Matrix line printers print one line of *dots* at a time. Needlelike hammers are lined up across the width of the paper. Like serial matrix printers, the characters are formed in rectangular dot configurations as the paper passes the line of print hammers. Matrix printers are much more flexible than band printers, and they can perform the same types of print operations as serial matrix printers (see above), including graphic output and machine-readable bar codes.

Page Printers. Page printers are of the nonimpact type and use a variety of technologies to achieve high-speed hard-copy output by printing *a page at a time.* Most very high-speed page printers employ laser technology. Operating at peak capacity during an eight-hour shift, the fastest page printer can produce almost a quarter of a million pages—that's 50 miles of output. This enormous output capability is normally directed to people outside an organization. For example, large banks use page printers to produce statements for checking and savings accounts; insurance companies print policies on page printers; and electric utility companies use them to bill their customers.

Very high-speed laser printers used in the mainframe environment have the capability of superimposing preprinted forms on continuous-feed stock paper. This eliminates a company's need to purchase expensive preprinted forms. Page printers have the capability of printing graphs and charts, and they offer considerable flexibility in the size and style of print.

Until the mid-1980s, virtually all printers configured with microcomputers were serial printers. Now economically priced **desktop page printers** are becoming the standard for office microcomputer systems. These printers, capable of print speeds up to 22 pages per minute, have redefined the hard-copy output potential of micros. Although most employ laser technology, other page-printer technologies include ink-jet, thermal-transfer, LED (light-emitting diode), and LCS (liquid crystal shutter).

Desktop page printers are capable of producing *near-typeset-quality* (*NTQ*) text and graphics. The resolution (quality of output) of the typical desktop page printer is *300 dpi* (dots per inch). Commercial typesetting quality is a minimum of 1200 dpi. Contrast the desktop page printer output in Figure 4–7 with the typeset print in this book.

Desktop page printers are also quiet (an important consideration in an office setting), and they can combine type styles and sizes with graphics on the same page. The emergence of desktop page printers has fueled the explosion of *desktop publishing* (discussed in detail in Chapter 7, "Productivity Software: Word Processing and Desktop Publishing").

FIGURE 4–7   Printer Output Comparison

```
This sentence was printed in draft mode on a 24-pin dot matrix printer.

This sentence was printed in NLQ mode on a 24-pin dot matrix printer.

This sentence was printed on a daisy-wheel printer.

This sentence was printed on a desktop page printer.
```

This graphics and text output shows the versatility of a desktop page printer. A page printer can produce hard copies of graphic images (as they would appear on a screen) just as easily as it prints letters and reports.

Figure 4–7 contrasts the output of a dot-matrix printer, in both draft and near-letter-quality (NLQ) modes, a daisy-wheel printer (letter quality), and a desktop page printer (near-typeset-quality).

Printer Summary.   Hundreds of printers are produced by dozens of manufacturers. There is a printer manufactured to meet the hard-copy output requirements of any company or individual, and almost any combination of features can be obtained. You can specify its speed, quality of output, color requirements, flexibility requirements, and even noise level. Printers sell for as little as a good pair of shoes or for as much as a small office building.

Plotters

Dot-matrix, ink-jet, thermal, and page printers are capable of producing graphic output, but they are limited in its quality and size. **Pen plotters** are devices that convert computer-generated graphs, charts, and line drawings into high-precision hard-copy output. The two basic types of pen plotters are the *drum plotter* and the *flatbed plotter*. Both types have one or more pens that move over the paper under computer control to produce an image. Several pens are required to vary the width and color of the line, and the computer selects and manipulates them. On the drum plotter, the pens and the drum move concurrently in different

MEMORY BITS

PRINTER OUTPUT QUALITY
- Near-letter quality (NQL)
- Dual mode (draft and NQL)
- Letter-quality (LQ)
- Near-typeset-quality (NTQ)

axes to produce the image. Drum plotters are used to produce continuous output, such as plotting earthquake activity, or for long graphic output, such as the structural view of a skyscraper.

On some flatbed plotters, the pen moves in both axes while the paper remains stationary. This is always true of very large flatbed plotters, some of which are larger than regulation pool tables. On smaller ones, especially small desktop plotters, both paper and pen move concurrently in much the same way as drum plotters.

Electrostatic plotter/printers produce a "quick-and-dirty" hard copy of graphic images for previewing. The final image is produced on the high-precision drum or flatbed plotter.

Presentation Graphics: Desktop Film Recorders and Screen Image Projectors

Businesspeople have found that sophisticated and colorful graphics add an aura of professionalism to any report or presentation. This demand for *presentation graphics* has created a need for corresponding output devices. Computer-generated graphic images can be recreated on paper and transparency acetates with printers and plotters. Graphic images also can be captured on 35-mm slides, or they can be displayed on a monitor or projected onto a large screen.

Desktop film recorders reproduce a high-resolution graphic image on 35-mm film in either black and white or color. Some models allow users to process and mount their own slides. Others require outside processing. **Screen-image projectors** project the graphic image onto a large screen, similar to the way television programs are projected onto a large TV screen. Another device transfers the graphic image displayed on the monitor onto a large screen with the use of an ordinary overhead projector.

Computer Output Microform

Computer output microform (COM) devices prepare microfiche that can be read on microform viewers. Microfiche is hard-copy output that becomes a permanent record that can be referenced over and over. Each COM device contains an image-to-film recorder and a duplicator for making multiple copies of a microfiche.

A market research analyst uses a flatbed pen plotter to portray the results of surveys in the form of pie and bar graphs.

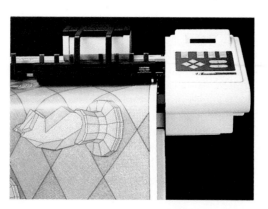

This drum pen plotter is capable of a mechanical resolution of 0.0005 inch; that is, the output is accurate to within five thousandths of an inch.

In the COM process (see Figure 4–8), the images (output) to be miniaturized are prepared, as if to be printed, on a computer system. This output is then sent to the COM device. Here the images are miniaturized for microform viewers.

In the miniaturization process, images are displayed on a small high-resolution video display. A camera exposes a segment of the microfilm for each display, thereby creating a grid pattern of images, or frames. The microfilm is then developed and cut into 4- by 6-inch sheets of microfiche, each containing up to 270 frames. The duplicator section makes multiple copies of the microfiche. Each sheet of microfiche is titled and indexed so the appropriate frame, or "page," can be retrieved quickly on a viewer.

COM is an alternative to an on-line computer-based system when up-to-the-minute information is not critical. COM is also used extensively instead of hard copy for archival storage (old income tax records, for example).

COM equipment can produce in minutes what may take hours to produce on a printer. But the real advantage of COM is the elimination of cumbersome volumes of printed output. Nevertheless, these advantages are overshadowed by the potential of on-line systems. As terminals and on-line systems become commonplace, a trend will be to replace COM with on-line systems. On-line systems offer the added advantages of direct access to and immediate update of the data base.

Computer centers produce output in a variety of formats, including 35 mm slides.

Voice-Response Units

If you have ever called directory assistance, you probably have heard something like: "The number is eight-six-one-four-zero-three-eight." You may have driven a car that advised you to "fasten your seat belt." These are examples of talking machines, output from voice-response units. There are two types of **voice-response units**: One uses a *reproduction* of a human voice and other sounds, and the other uses a *speech synthesizer*. Like monitors, voice-response units provide a temporary, soft-copy output.

The first type of voice-response unit selects output from user-recorded words, phrases, music, alarms, or anything you might record on tape, just as a printer would select characters. In these recorded voice response units, the actual analog recordings of sounds are converted into digital data, then permanently stored in a memory chip. When output, a particular sound is converted back into analog before being routed to a speaker.

FIGURE 4–8   The Computer Output Microform (COM) Process
In the on-line COM process, data are routed directly from the computer to the COM system.

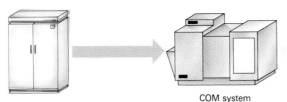

COM system

4" X 6"
Microfiche

Microform viewer

These young men are using a hand-held speaking dictionary to "look up" the spelling of a word. First they enter a phonetic spelling of the word, then the computer-based dictionary interprets the input and finds the word in its memory. The speaking dictionary, made by Franklin Electronic Publishers, uses a speech synthesizer to actually pronounce the word in plain English. The definition is then displayed.

These chips are mass-produced for specific applications, such as output for automatic teller machines, microwave ovens, smoke detectors, elevators, alarm clocks, automobile warning systems, video games, and vending machines, to mention only a few.

Speech synthesizers convert raw data into electronically produced speech. To do this, these devices combine sounds resembling the phonemes (basic sound units) that make up speech. A speech synthesizer is capable of producing at least 64 unique sounds. The existing technology produces synthesized speech with only limited vocal inflections and phrasing. Still, the number of applications is growing. In one application, an optical character reader scans books to retrieve the raw data. The speech synthesizer then translates the printed matter into spoken words for blind people. In another application, the use of speech synthesizers is opening a new world to speech-impaired children who were once placed in institutions because they could not communicate verbally. Speech synthesizers are also used in grocery checkout systems, alarm systems, and computer-based training. As the quality of the output improves, speech synthesizers will enjoy a broader base of applications. They are relatively inexpensive and are becoming increasingly popular with many personal computer owners.

SUMMARY OUTLINE AND IMPORTANT TERMS _____

4–1   **I/O DEVICES: OUR INTERFACE WITH THE COMPUTER.** A variety of input/output peripheral devices provide the interface between us and the computer system.

4–2   **TERMINALS AND WORKSTATIONS.** We interact with a computer system through a video display terminal (*VDT* or simply *terminal*). The VDT is affectionately known as "the tube," short for **cathode-ray tube**. VDTs and micros are the most common terminals. The input mechanism is usually a keyboard, and the output is normally a display screen called a *monitor*. A **text cursor** indicates the location of the next keyed-in character on the monitor's screen. Other input devices used with terminals include the light pen, the joy stick, the track ball, the digitizing tablet and pen or crosshair, and the mouse. These devices permit movement of a **graphics cursor** to create an image or select a menu item.

A soft copy (as opposed to hard copy) of alphanumeric and graphic output is displayed on the monitor. The three attributes of monitors are size (diagonal dimension 5 to 25 inches), color (monochrome or color), and **resolution**. A monochrome monitor can display shades of one color, called **gray scales**. A monitor's resolution is determined by the number of **pixels** it has. Space-saving monochrome and color **flat-panel monitors** use LCD, gas plasma, and EL technologies.

Graphics workstations are **intelligent workstations** for sophisticated users. Typically, a minimum configuration for a graphics workstation would include a medium-sized high-resolution graphics monitor, a keyboard, and at least two more modes of input.

4–3   **SOURCE-DATA AUTOMATION: GETTING DATA INTO THE COMPUTER SYSTEM.** The trend in data entry has been toward **source-data automation**, where the need for the key entry transcription of data is eliminated altogether.

Optical character recognition reduces the need for manual data entry by encoding certain data in machine-readable format. **OCR scanners** (label, page, document, continuous-form, and optical mark) recognize printed characters and certain coded symbols, such as **bar codes**. OCR scanners are used for original-source data collection and with **turnaround documents**. An **image scanner** enables **digitized** images of photos, drawings, and other images to be stored on magnetic disk. **Magnetic-ink character recognition** (**MICR**) devices, which are used almost exclusively in banking, are similar to OCR scanners in function but are faster and more accurate.

Magnetic stripes and **smart cards** provide input to **badge readers**. **Speech-recognition** devices can be used to enter limited kinds and quantities of data. They do this by comparing digitized representations of words to similarly formed templates in the computer's electronic dictionary. **Vision-input systems** are best suited for tasks that involve only a few images. **Portable data-entry** devices are hand-held and normally are used to collect data off-line.

4–4   **OUTPUT DEVICES: COMPUTERS COMMUNICATE WITH US.** Output devices translate data stored in binary into a form that can be interpreted by the end user. Terminals and workstations are both input and output devices. Printers prepare hard-copy output at speeds of 40 characters per second to 800 pages per minute. **Serial printers** are both impact (**dot-matrix** and **daisy-wheel**) and nonimpact (**ink-jet** and **thermal**). **Line printers** are impact only, and **page printers** are nonimpact only. The emergence of **desktop page printers** has fueled the explosion of desktop publishing. The technologies used to produce the printed image vary widely from one printer to the next. **Pen plotters** and **electrostatic plotter/printers** convert stored data into hard-copy graphs, charts, and line drawings.

Desktop film recorders reproduce a high-resolution graphic image on 35-mm film in either black and white or color. **Screen-image projectors** project the graphic image onto a large screen.

Computer output microform (COM) devices prepare microfiche as a space- and time-saving alternative to printed output. **Voice-response units** provide recorded or synthesized voice output.

REVIEW EXERCISES

Concepts

1. Which has greater precision, a pen plotter or an electrostatic plotter?
2. What is meant when someone says that speech-recognition devices are "speaker-dependent"?
3. List devices, other than key-driven, that are used to input data into a computer system.
4. Which types of printers print fully formed characters?
5. What is a turnaround document? Give two examples.
6. Identify all input and output methods used by an automatic teller machine.
7. What is a smart card?
8. What is the relationship between a light pen and a graphics cursor?
9. Give two applications for bar codes.
10. Why do banks use MICR rather than OCR for data entry?
11. What output device reproduces high-resolution graphic images on 35-mm film?
12. Name a device other than a monitor that produces soft-copy output.
13. What kind of printer can produce near-typeset-quality output?

Discussion

14. Give three examples of how a police department would use computer output.
15. Describe the input/output characteristics of a workstation that would be used by engineers for computer-aided design.
16. Department stores use hand-held wands to interpret the bar codes printed on the price tags of merchandise. Why do they not use slot scanners as supermarkets do?

17. What input/output capabilities are available at your college?

18. Compare today's vision-input systems with those portrayed in such films as *2001* and *2010*. Do you believe we will have a comparable vision technology by the year 2001?

SELF-TEST (by section) ⎯⎯⎯⎯⎯⎯⎯⎯⎯⎯⎯⎯⎯⎯

4–1 **a.** Input devices translate data into a form that can be interpreted by a computer. (T/F)

  b. The primary function of I/O peripherals is to facilitate computer-to-computer data transmission. (T/F)

4–2 **a.** The terminal that is familiar to most people is the: (a) VDT, (b) telephone, or (c) graphics workstation?

  b. The quality of output on a terminal's monitor is determined by its _____.

  c. A _____ is a blinking character that indicates the location of the next keyed-in character on the screen.

  d. Most flat-panel monitors are used in conjunction with minicomputer consoles. (T/F)

  e. VDTs designed especially for the sophisticated user are called _____.

4–3 **a.** Optical character recognition is a means of source-data automation. (T/F)

  b. The Universal Product Code (UPC) was originally used by which industry: (a) supermarket, (b) hardware, or (c) mail-order merchandising?

  c. In speech recognition, words are _____ and matched against similarly formed _____ in the computer's electronic dictionary.

  d. Vision-input systems are best suited to generalized tasks in which a wide variety of images will be encountered. (T/F)

4–4 **a.** Ink-jet printers are classified as impact printers. (T/F)

  b. Dot-matrix printing technology is available in serial and line printers. (T/F)

  c. What type of printers are becoming the standard for office microcomputer systems: (a) desktop page printers, (b) daisy-wheel printers, or (c) thermal printers?

  d. _____convert raw data into electronically produced speech.

Self-test answers **4–1 (a)** T; **(b)** F. **4–2 (a)** b; **(b)** resolution; **(c)** text cursor; **(d)** F; **(e)** graphics workstations. **4–3 (a)** T; **(b)** a; **(c)** digitized, templates; **(d)** F. **4–4 (a)** F; **(b)** T; **(c)** a; **(d)** Speech synthesizers.

5

Data Storage Devices and Media

STUDENT LEARNING OBJECTIVES

- ▶ To distinguish between primary and secondary storage.
- ▶ To distinguish between secondary storage devices and secondary storage media.
- ▶ To describe the principles of operation, methods of data storage, and use of magnetic disk drives.
- ▶ To describe the principles of operation, methods of data storage, and use of magnetic tape drives.
- ▶ To discuss the applications and use of optical laser disk storage.

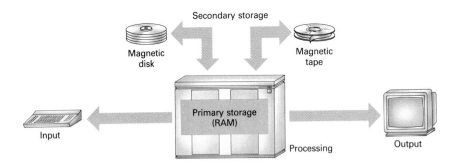

FIGURE 5–1   Primary and Secondary Storage
Programs and data are stored permanently in secondary storage and temporarily in primary storage.

5–1   SECONDARY STORAGE: PERMANENT DATA STORAGE

Within a computer system, programs and data are stored in *primary storage* and in *secondary storage* (see Figure 5–1). Programs and data are stored *permanently* for periodic retrieval in **secondary storage**, also called **auxiliary storage**. Programs and data are retrieved from secondary storage and stored *temporarily* in high-speed primary storage, also called random-access memory, or RAM, for processing (see Chapter 3, "Inside the Computer").

"Why two types of storage?" you might ask. Remember from Chapter 3 that most primary storage is semiconductor memory, and the data are lost when the electricity is interrupted. Primary storage is also expensive and has a limited capacity. The RAM capacity of a large mainframe computer would not come close to meeting the data and program storage needs of even a small company. Secondary storage, however, is relatively inexpensive and has an enormous capacity.

Data are stored temporarily in primary storage (left) during processing and permanently on secondary storage, such as magnetic disk (right).

Over the years manufacturers have developed a variety of devices and media for the permanent storage of data and programs. *Paper tape*, *punched cards*, the *data cell*, and a variety of others have become obsolete. Today the various types of **magnetic disk drives** and their respective storage media are the state of the art for on-line storage of programs and data. **Magnetic tape drives** complement magnetic disk storage by providing inexpensive backup capability and off-line archival storage. In this chapter we focus on the terminology, principles, operation, and trade-offs of these secondary storage devices. We will also discuss the potential and applications of **optical laser disk** technology, a rapidly emerging alternative to magnetic-disk and magnetic-tape storage.

5–2   SEQUENTIAL AND DIRECT ACCESS: NEW TERMS FOR OLD CONCEPTS

An important consideration both in the design of an information system and the purchase of a computer system is the way that data are accessed. Magnetic tape can be used for **sequential access** only. Magnetic disks have **random-,** or **direct-access** capabilities as well as sequential-access capabilities. You are quite familiar with these concepts, but you may not realize it. Operationally, the magnetic tape is the same as the one in home and automobile tape decks. The magnetic disk can be compared to a phonograph record.

Suppose you have the Beatles' classic record album *Sgt. Pepper's Lonely Hearts Club Band*. The first four songs on this album are: (1) "Sgt. Pepper's Lonely Hearts Club Band," (2) "With a Little Help from My Friends," (3) "Lucy in the Sky with Diamonds," and (4) "Getting Better." Now suppose you also have this Beatles album on a tape cassette. To play the third song on the cassette, "Lucy in the Sky with Diamonds," you would have to wind the tape forward and search for it *sequentially*. To play "Lucy in the Sky with Diamonds" on the phonograph record, all you would have to do is move the needle directly to the track containing the third song. This simple analogy demonstrates the two fundamental methods of storing and accessing data—*sequential* and *random*. Both methods are discussed in detail in the pages that follow.

5–3   MAGNETIC DISKS: ROTATING STORAGE MEDIA

Hardware and Storage Media

Magnetic disk drives are secondary storage devices that provide a computer system with **random-** *and* **sequential-processing** capabilities. In random processing, the desired programs and data are accessed *directly* from the storage medium. In sequential processing, the computer system must search the storage medium to find the desired programs or data.

Because magnetic-disk storage is used almost exclusively for direct access, random processing is discussed with magnetic disks in this section. Sequential processing is discussed with magnetic tape in the next section.

Because of its random- and sequential-processing capabilities, magnetic-disk storage is the overwhelming choice of computer users, whether on micros or on supercomputers. A variety of magnetic disk drives (the hardware device) and magnetic disks (the media) are manufactured for different business requirements. There are two fundamental types of magnetic disks: those that are interchangeable, and those that are permanently installed, or fixed. **Interchangeable magnetic disks** can be stored **off-line** (that is, not accessible to the computer system) and loaded to the magnetic disk drives as they are needed. Once inserted in the disk drives, the disks are said to be **on-line**; that is, the data and programs on the disks are accessible to the computer system.

The trend in magnetic-storage media is to **fixed disks**, also called *hard disks*. All fixed disks are rigid and are usually made of aluminum with a surface coating of easily magnetized elements, such as iron, cobalt, chromium, and nickel. In the past, interchangeable disks containing certain files and programs were taken from the shelf and loaded to the disk drives as needed. This is still true today, but to a much lesser extent. Today's integrated software and data bases require all data and programs to be on-line at all times.

The different types of interchangeable magnetic disks and fixed disks are shown in the accompanying photographs. As you can see, magnetic disks are available in a wide variety of shapes and storage capacities. The type used would depend on the volume of data you have and the frequency with which those data are accessed.

The trend in disk storage is toward permanently installed storage media. Fixed disks are manufactured in rooms that are 1000 times cleaner than operating rooms in hospitals. When completed, these fixed disks will be installed in microcomputers. Here workers are installing the motors in the disk drive chassis.

Magnetic Disks: The Microcomputer Environment

Microcomputer Disk Media.   The two most popular types of interchangeable magnetic disks for micros are the **diskette** and the **microdisk**.

- *Diskette*. The diskette is a thin, flexible disk that is permanently enclosed in a soft, 5¼-inch-square jacket. Because the magnetic-coated mylar diskette and its jacket are flexible like a page in this book, the diskette is also called a **flexible disk** or a **floppy disk**. The storage capacity of a diskette ranges from about 360 Kb to 1.2 Mb.

- *Microdisk*. The 3½-inch **microdisk**, also called a **microfloppy**, is enclosed in a rigid plastic jacket. The storage capacity of microdisks ranges from about 400 Kb to 1.4 Mb.

The microcomputer hard disk is called the **Winchester disk**. The Winchester disk got its nickname from the 30-30 Winchester rifle. Early disk drives had two 30-megabyte disks—thus the nickname "Winchester." Most of the newer personal computers are configured with at least one diskette or microdisk drive and one hard disk. Having two disks increases system throughput. The storage capacity of these 3½- and 5¼-inch hard disks ranges from about 20 Mb to 760 Mb, which is as much as 2300 times the capacity of a diskette.

A Winchester hard disk, which may contain several disk platters, spins continuously at a high speed within a sealed enclosure. The enclosure keeps the disk-face surfaces free from contaminants such as dust and cigarette smoke. This contaminant-free environment allows Winchester disks to have greater density of data storage than the interchangeable diskettes. In contrast to the Winchester disk, the floppy disk is set in motion only when a command is issued to read from or write to the disk. An indicator light near the disk drive is illuminated only when the diskette is spinning.

The rotational movement of a magnetic disk passes all data under or over a **read/write head**, thereby making all data available for access on each revolution of the disk.

Micro Disk Organization.   The way in which data and programs are stored and accessed is similar for both hard and floppy disks. The disk-storage medium has a thin film coating of one of the easily magnetized elements (cobalt, for example). The thin film coating on the disk can be magnetized electronically by the read/write head to represent the absence or presence of a bit (0 or 1). Data are stored in concentric circles called **tracks** by magnetizing the surface to represent bit configurations (see Figure 5-2). Bits are recorded using **serial representation**. The number of tracks varies greatly between disks, from as few as 40 on some 5¼-inch diskettes to over 1000 on high-capacity Winchester disks.

Microcomputer disk-storage devices use **sector organization** to store and retrieve data. In sector organization, the recording surface is divided into from nine to 33 pie-shaped **sectors**. The surface of the diskette in Figure 5-2 is logically divided into 15 sectors. Typically, the storage capacity of each sector on a particular track is 512 bytes, regardless of the number of sectors per track. Each sector is assigned a unique number;

Interchangeable diskettes come in two sizes, 5¼- and 8-inch. The 8-inch diskettes, however, are seldom used in conjunction with microcomputers. The trend in interchangeable storage media for microcomputers is to the 3½-inch microdisk (foreground). Data are stored on both sides of the diskettes and microdisks.

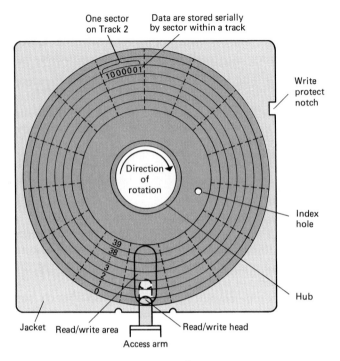

FIGURE 5–2   Cutaway of a 5¼-Inch Diskette
Photoelectric cells sense light as it passes through the index hole. This feedback enables the computer to monitor which sector is under or over the read/write head at any given time. Data are read or written serially in tracks within a given sector.

therefore, the *sector number* and *track number* are all that are needed for a **disk address**. The disk address represents the physical location of a particular set of data or a program. To read from or write to a disk, an **access arm** containing the read/write head is moved, under program control, to the appropriate *track* (see Figure 5–2). When the sector containing the desired data passes under or over the read/write head, the data are read or written.

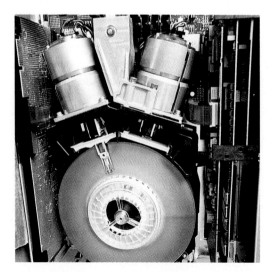

This Winchester disk has two read/write heads for each recording surface that are mounted on two access arms. The access arms move the read/write heads to the appropriate track to retrieve the data. Having two access arms saves precious milliseconds because a head will never have to transverse more than half the width of the disk's recording surface. The access arm that is extended in the photo services the inside half of the disk.

Magnetic Disks: The Mainframe Environment

Mainframe Disk Media.   Magnetic disks are used for all information systems where the data must be on-line and accessed directly. An airline reservation system provides a good mainframe-oriented example of this need. Direct-access capability is required to retrieve the record for any flight at any time from any reservations office. The data must be current, or flights may be overbooked or underbooked. Because of the random nature of the reservations data, sequential-only magnetic tape cannot be used as a storage medium for this or any other system that requires random processing. File and data base organization for random processing, also called **direct processing**, and sequential processing are discussed in detail in Chapter 9, "Software Concepts and Data Management."

In the mainframe environment, the most popular interchangeable disk-storage media are the **disk cartridge** and the **disk pack** (see accompanying photos). Most disk cartridges have a single platter and are entirely encased in a hard plastic cover. When inserted into a disk drive, the disk-face surfaces are exposed to accommodate the movement of the read/write head. The 14-inch disk pack has been the disk-media mainstay in the mainframe environment for the past three decades. Although its size has remained relatively stable, the density at which data can be written on the disk-face surfaces has increased dramatically. The larger disk packs contain up to 12 platters stacked around a hollow core. Each of the finely machined aluminum platters has a magnetized coating about 40 millionths of an inch thick. Most mainframe computers and supercomputers use 14-inch disk packs with 11 platters and 20 usable disk-face surfaces. The current technology enables a single disk pack to store several *gigabytes* of data. Each gigabyte consists of a billion bytes. To mount a disk pack onto a disk drive, it is slipped over a shaft in the disk drive and the protective plastic cover is removed. The procedure is reversed to remove the disk pack for off-line storage.

Minis, mainframes, and supercomputers use a wide variety of fixed-disk media, also capable of storing several gigabytes of data. Fixed-disk media come in 5¼-inch, 8-inch, and 14-inch formats. Generally speaking,

Sitting atop rows of disk drives are interchangeable magnetic disk packs that provide billions of characters of direct-access storage for this supermini-computer system.

the density at which data can be stored is greater for fixed than for interchangeable disks because the environment can be more carefully controlled. Some very high-density fixed disks can store over 30 million characters on one square inch of recording surface. That's the text of this and 20 other books in a space the size of a postage stamp!

Mainframe Disk Organization.   The way data are organized on mainframe disk systems is similar to that on microcomputer disk systems. Like microcomputer disks, data are recorded serially in concentric circles called **tracks**. The hard disks on mainframes spin continuously at a high speed, typically 3600 revolutions per minute.

To illustrate mainframe disk organization, we will use a fixed magnetic disk with four platters (see Figure 5–3). Data are stored on all *recording surfaces*. For a disk with four platters, there are eight recording surfaces on which data can be stored. A disk drive will have at least one read/write head for each recording surface. The heads are mounted on *access arms* that move together and literally float on a cushion of air over (or under) the spinning recording surfaces. The tolerance is so close that a particle of smoke from a cigarette will not fit between these "flying" heads and the recording surface. This is primary reason why computer operators display "No Smoking" signs in the machine room.

Mainframe disk systems use either *sector* or **cylinder organization**. Sector organization is same as that described earlier in the section on micro disk systems. In the mainframe environment, each of the high-density disk-face surfaces can have up to 1600 tracks per inch; therefore, any disk-face surface may have several thousand tracks, numbered consecutively from outside to inside. A particular **cylinder** refers to every

FIGURE 5–3   Fixed Hard Disk with Four Platters and Eight Recording Surfaces
In the illustration, the read/write heads are positioned over Cylinder 0012. At this position, the data on any one of the eight tracks numbered 0012 are accessible to the computer on each revolution of the disk. The read/write head must be moved to another cylinder to access other data on the disk.

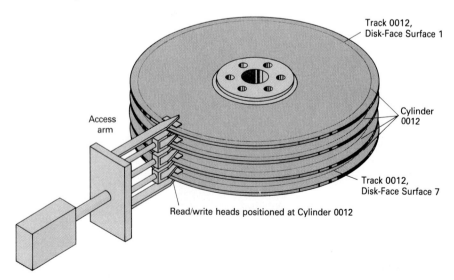

This highly magnified area of a magnetic disk-face surface shows elongated information bits recorded serially along eight of the disk's 1774 concentric tracks. One square inch of this disk's surface can hold 22 million bits of information.

track with the same number on all recording surfaces. To read from or write to a disk, the access arms are moved, under program control, to the appropriate *cylinder*. For example, each recording surface has a track numbered 0012, so the disk has a cylinder numbered 0012. If the data to be accessed are on Recording Surface 01, Track 0012, then the access arm and the read/write heads for all eight recording surfaces are moved to Cylinder 0012.

In Figure 5–3 the access arm is positioned over Cylinder 0012. In this position, any data on any of the tracks in Cylinder 0012 can be accessed without further movement of the access arm. If data on Surface 5, Track 0145, are to be read, the access arm must be positioned over Cylinder 0145 until the desired record passes under the read/write head.

Fortunately, software automatically monitors the location, or address, of our files and programs. We need only enter someone's name to retrieve his or her personnel record. The computer system locates the record and loads it to primary storage for processing. Although the addressing schemes vary considerably between disks, the address will normally include the *cylinder*, the *recording surface*, and the *relative position* of a record on a track (for example, the fourth record).

Disk Access Time

Access time is the interval between the instant a computer makes a request for transfer of data from a secondary storage device to primary storage and the instant this operation is completed. The access of data from primary storage is performed at electronic speeds, or approximately the speed of light. But the access of data from secondary storage depends

---

MEMORY BITS

CHARACTERISTICS OF MAGNETIC DISK

Permanent media	Fixed ($5\frac{1}{4}''$, $8''$, and $14''$)
Interchangeable media	For micros: diskette and microdisk
	For mainframes: disk cartridge and disk pack
Type access	Direct (random) or sequential
Data representation	Serial
Storage scheme	Cylinder, sector

on mechanical apparatus. Any mechanical movement significantly increases the access time. The access time for hard disks is significantly less than for floppy disks because the hard disk is in continuous motion.

The *seek time*, the largest portion of the total access time, consists of how long it takes the mechanical access arm to move the read/write head to the desired track or cylinder. Some disk drives have two access arms, one for reading and writing on the inside tracks and another for the outside tracks. Two access arms significantly reduce the average seek time because they have a shorter distance to move and one can move while the other is reading or writing.

The *rotational delay time* is the time it takes for the appropriate data to be positioned under the read/write head. On the average, it would be half the time it takes for one revolution of the disk, or about 8 milliseconds for a hard disk spinning at 3600 rpm. The rotational delay time for a diskette spinning at 400 rpm is 75 milliseconds, almost 10 times that of a hard disk. The *transmission time*, or the time it takes to transmit the data to primary storage, is negligible. The average access time for most hard-disk drives is less than 20 milliseconds—still very slow when compared with the microsecond-to-nanosecond processing speeds of computers.

PROFILE

Seymour Cray
The Superman of Supercomputers

In 1972 Seymour Cray founded Cray Research, Inc., (CRI) to design and build the world's highest performance general-purpose computer system. The CRAY computers, the first to be dubbed "supercomputers," have set the standard for high-end computers for two decades. The people at CRI and Cray Computer Corporation (CCC), a new supercomputer company of which Cray is chairman of the board, are said to be motivated not so much by a business philosophy as by a belief in creativity. You have to be very creative to deal with the problems that confront those who want to make computers that execute billions of instructions per second. The Seymour Cray style is apparent in CRI's written corporate philosophy: "At Cray Research, we take what we do very seriously, but don't take ourselves very seriously."

Cray has spent his entire career designing large-

scale computer equipment. Very much a hands-on man, he is the principal designer of the CRAY-3 and CRAY-4 computer systems at CCC. He made significant contributions to the CRAY-1 and CRAY-2 supercomputers at CRI, especially in the critical area of system cooling. He was one of the founders of Control Data Corporation in 1957 and was

responsible for the design of the company's highly successful CDC 7600. Prior to 1957 he had design responsibility for a major portion of the first commercially successful scientific computer.

5–4   MAGNETIC TAPE: RIBBONS OF DATA

Magnetic-tape storage is used primarily as a backup medium for magnetic-disk storage. A magnetic tape may be used in an occasional application that involves only *sequential processing*. A magnetic-tape medium, such as the **reel** or the **cartridge**, can be mounted conveniently onto a tape drive (the hardware device) for processing, then removed for off-line storage. For backup, a tape is taken from off-line storage, mounted onto a tape drive, and the contents of a disk file are "dumped" from the disk to the tape. The tape is removed and placed in off-line storage as a backup to the content of the operational magnetic disk. Details of backup procedures are discussed and illustrated in Chapter 9, "Software Concepts and Data Management."

Hardware and Storage Media

The mechanical operation of a magnetic tape drive is similar to that of a reel-to-reel or audiocassette tape deck. The tape, a thin polyester ribbon coated with a magnetic material on one side, passes under a *read/write head*, and the data are either (1) read and transmitted to primary storage or (2) transmitted from primary storage and written to the tape.

The $\frac{1}{2}$-inch tape reel has been around since the mid-1950s. This form of "mag" tape was the main type of secondary storage medium until the advent of economically priced and reliable magnetic-disk storage (the mid-1960s). Thousands of reel-to-reel mag-tape drives are still in service today, but they are used almost exclusively as a backup for disk storage. They are being replaced by the more convenient, less costly, and space-saving tape cartridges, also called **data cartridges**.

Two types of tape cartridges are in common use, the $\frac{1}{4}$-inch and the $\frac{1}{2}$-inch versions. Both are self-contained and are inserted into and removed from the tape drive in much the same way you would load or remove a videotape from a VCR. Like the videotape, the supply and the take-up reels for the $\frac{1}{4}$-inch cartridges are encased in a plastic shell. However, the shell for the $\frac{1}{2}$-inch tape cartridge contains only the supply reel. The take-up reel is permanently installed in the tape drive unit.

The mag-tape reel and the $\frac{1}{2}$-inch cartridge are used exclusively in the mini, mainframe, and supercomputer environments. The $\frac{1}{4}$-inch cartridges, popular with micros and minis, are being used more frequently in the mainframe environment.

A tape drive is rated by the **density** at which the data can be stored on a magnetic tape as well as by the speed of the tape as it passes under the read/write head. Combined, these determine the **transfer rate**, or the number of characters per second that can be transmitted to primary storage. Tape density is measured in **bytes per inch (bpi)**, or the number of bytes (characters) that can be stored per linear inch of tape. Tape density varies from 800 to 20,000 bpi. A 6250-bpi tape, a common-density mag-tape reel, traveling under the read/write head at 300 inches per second is capable of a transfer rate of 1,875,000 characters per second. Some high-speed tape drives move the tape under the read/write head at speeds in excess of 50 miles per hour.

TAPE PRODUCTS INCLUDING 3480 CARTRIDGES

During the 1960s and 1970s machine rooms were alive with the motion of rows of spinning magnetic tapes. Magnetic tape reels (left), however, are being replaced by tape cartridges. The much smaller high-density ½-inch tape cartridges (top right), which are used primarily in mini and mainframe computer environments, can store one billion characters each, about five times the capacity of a ½-inch tape reel. The ¼-inch tape cartridges, shown here in two sizes, are used with microcomputers to back up disk-based files.

The most common lengths of magnetic tape reels are 600, 1200, and 2400 feet. The capacity of a tape is equal to the tape density (bpi) times the length of the tape in inches. A 6250-bpi, 2400-foot (28,800-inch) tape has a capacity of approximately 180 Mb (million bytes). Very high-density mag-tape reels, which are not in common usage, can store up to 800 Mb. Magnetic tape cartridges are available in a variety of lengths, from 150 to 600 feet, and are capable of storing up to 200 Mb.

One hundred and eighty megabytes sounds like ample storage for just about anything, but this is not the case. For example, over 100 such tapes would be required to store just the names and addresses of people living in the United States. The tape library at the U.S. Internal Revenue Service contains over 500,000 reels!

Principles of Operation: Mag-Tape Reels

Because of the physical nature of magnetic-tape reels, files must be processed sequentially from beginning to end for each computer run. On any given run, a *single* tape is either input or output, not both. Sequential processing with magnetic tape is discussed in detail in Chapter 9, "Software Concepts and Data Management."

The principles of mag-tape data storage are illustrated in Figure 5–4. The film coating on the tape is electronically magnetized by the read/write head to form bit configurations. In EBCDIC, eight bits (the

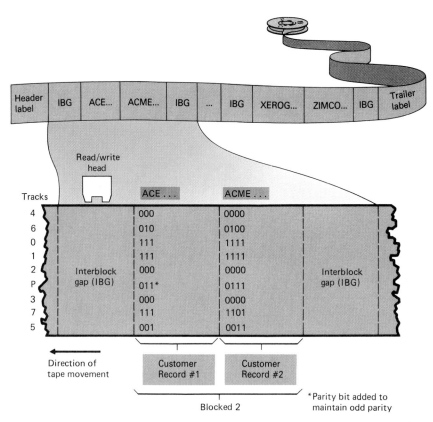

FIGURE 5–4   Cross-Section of a Magnetic Tape: Parallel Representation
Parallel representation is used to store the customer master file on this nine-track magnetic tape. This cross-section of mag tape contains two records from a customer master file. Those tracks in which an "on" bit appears most often (0, 1, 2, P, 3) are clustered in the center of the tape. Those tracks that are least likely to be magnetized to an "on" bit (4, 6, 7, 5) are placed toward the outside so the data on a tape with damaged edges are less likely to be affected. The tape travels past the write head, then the read head. This enables the computer to read and check the data immediately after they are written to the tape.

EBCDIC code) plus the *parity bit* are needed to represent a character. The parity bit is used to ensure the accuracy of the data transmission to and from the tape drive. Each of the nine bits is stored in one of nine *tracks* that run the length of the tape. In the *nine-track mag-tape reel* of Figure 5–4, characters are represented by parallel EBCDIC bit configurations. This method of storing data in adjacent bit configurations is known as **parallel representation**. In parallel representation, data are read or written a byte at a time. Compare this parallel representation with the serial representation of magnetic disks in Figure 5–2.

Figure 5–4 portrays a cross-section of a magnetic tape that contains a *customer master file*. The data relating to each customer are grouped and stored in a *customer record*. The records are stored *alphabetically by customer name* (from ACE, ACME . . . to ZEROG, ZIMCO).

Records are usually grouped in blocks of two or more, separated by an **interblock gap (IBG)**. The IBGs not only signal a stop in the reading

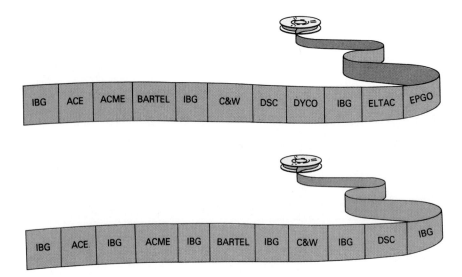

FIGURE 5–5   Customer Records Blocked Three (top) and Unblocked (bottom)

process but also provide some margin for error in the rapid *start/stop* operation of the tape drive.

Blocking permits additional records to be transmitted with each "read" or "write." Each time the computer is instructed to read from a magnetic tape, all data between adjacent interblock gaps are transmitted to primary storage for processing. The next "read" transmits the next **block** of records to primary storage. When the computer is instructed to write to a tape, the data are transmitted from primary storage to the tape drive. Then a block of data and an IBG are written to the tape.

In Figure 5–4, the records have a blocking factor of 2 and are said to be "blocked two." Figure 5–5 shows how the same file would appear blocked three and unblocked. Notice how the tape blocked three contains more records than the unblocked tape.

To signal the beginning and end of a particular tape file, the computer adds a **header label** and a **trailer label**, respectively (see Figure 5–4). The header label contains the name of the file and the date it was created. The trailer label is written at the end of the data file and shows the number of records in the file.

Principles of Operation: Tape Cartridges

The ½-Inch Tape Cartridge.   The operation of the ½-inch tape cartridge is more like that of the ½-inch mag-tape reel than the ¼-inch tape cartridge so popular with micro and mini users. Aside from the obvious differences in mechanical operation, the main difference lies in the number of tracks each contains. The ½-inch tape cartridge has 18 tracks, as opposed to nine for most mag-tape reels. Like the nine-track mag-tape reel, the *18-track tape cartridge* stores data using parallel representation; however, it stacks two bytes of data across the width of the tape. This enables more bytes of data to be stored on the same length of tape. Both ½-inch tapes block records for processing.

Up to 16 half-inch tape cartridges can be mounted to this magnetic tape subsystem for processing. Up to six cartridges can be mounted in a stacker for each of the 16 tape drives. Stacked tapes are automatically loaded and unloaded in the order in which they are stacked.

In most data centers, magnetic tape cartridges are manually mounted or stacked for processing. The alternative is an automated tape library. Under computer control, the automated tape library retrieves the appropriate tape cartridge from the library and mounts it on a tape drive for processing. The tape is returned automatically to the library at the end of the job. This automated system holds up to 6000 cartridges. A tape cartridge is not considered on-line (accessible to the computer) until it is mounted to a tape drive. Those in the automated library are said to be near-line, or almost on-line.

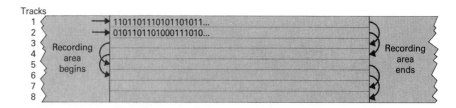

FIGURE 5–6   Cross-Section of a Magnetic Tape: Serial Representation
Data are recorded serially on this eight-track tape in a serpentine manner, two tracks at a time.

The ¼-Inch Tape Cartridge.   In the past the simplicity and lower cost of magnetic tape processing often made it preferable to magnetic disk processing. This is no longer true, and today magnetic tape is used primarily for backup. During backup or recovery runs, backup tapes are processed continuously from beginning to end. Because there is seldom a need for selective access of records from magnetic tape, there is no reason to start and stop the tapes.

Most ¼-inch tape cartridges record data in a continuous stream, thereby eliminating the need for the start/stop operation of traditional tape drives. Drives for ¼-inch tape cartridges, often called **streamer tape**

An alternative to disk and tape storage is the mass storage device. Mass storage devices are used when on-line access is required for very large data bases. Half a trillion characters of data can be stored in this mass storage device. Inside, data cartridges are retrieved from honeycomblike storage bins and loaded to the read/ write station for processing. A modern magnetic disk pack can store about 5 billion characters of data, but the access time, about 16 milliseconds, is much faster. As the density of magnetic disks increases, look for the relatively slow mass storage devices to be replaced by magnetic disks.

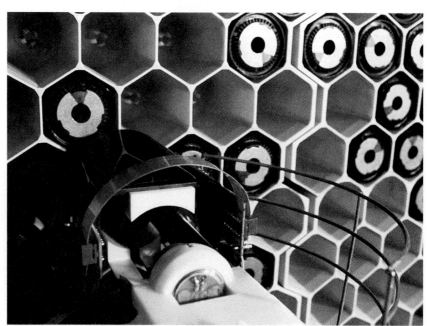

MEMORY BITS

CHARACTERISTICS OF MAGNETIC TAPE

	1/2" Reel	*1/2" Cartridge*	*1/4" Cartridge*
Tracks	9	18	4 to 15
Type access	Sequential	Sequential	Sequential
Data representation	Parallel	Parallel	Serial
Storage scheme	IBG separation	IBG separation	Serpentine

drives, store data in a **serpentine** manner (Figure 5–6). That is, data are recorded serially in tracks, as they are on mag disks. A data cartridge can have from four to 15 tracks, depending on the tape drive. The read/write head reads or writes data to one, two, or four tracks at a time. Figure 5–6 illustrates how data are written two tracks at a time. Data are written serially on the top two tracks for the entire length of the tape or until the data are exhausted. The tape is reversed, the read/write head is positioned over the next two tracks, and writing continues in a similar manner. If more backup capacity is needed, the computer operator is informed. He or she inserts a clean tape and writing continues.

Having no start/stop mechanisms, streamer tape drives can store data much more efficiently than the traditional tape drives that stop, then start the tape's movement over the read/write head at each IBG. Because streamer tape drives store IBGs "on the fly" (without stopping), an IBG occupies only $\frac{1}{100}$ inch, as compared to over $\frac{1}{2}$ inch for start/stop tape drives. Streamer tape drives use that "extra" $\frac{1}{2}$ inch to store as many as 10,000 more characters of data. Streamer tape drives use 97% of the tape for data storage, whereas traditional start/stop tapes use only 35% to 70%, depending on the blocking factors.

5–5   OPTICAL LASER DISKS: HIGH-DENSITY STORAGE

Some industry analysts have predicted that **optical laser disk** technology, now in its infant stage of use and development, eventually may make magnetic-disk and -tape storage obsolete. With this technology, the read/write head used in magnetic storage is replaced by two lasers. One laser beam writes to the recording surface by scoring microscopic pits in the disk, and another laser reads the data from the light-sensitive recording surface. A light beam is easily deflected to the desired place on the optical disk, so an access arm is not needed.

Optical laser disks are becoming a very inviting option for users. They are less sensitive to environmental fluctuations, and they provide more direct-access storage at a cost that is much less per megabyte of storage than the magnetic-disk alternative. Optical laser disk technology is still emerging and has yet to stabilize; however, at present there are three main categories of optical laser disks. They are *CD-ROM*, *WORM disk*, and *magneto-optical disk*.

WHO KNOWS WHAT ABOUT YOU?

Each day your name and personal information is passed from computer to computer. Depending on your level of activity, this could happen 20 or more times a day. Thousands of public- and private-sector organizations maintain data on individuals. The data collection begins before you are born and does not end until all your affairs are settled and those maintaining records on you are informed of your parting.

Tax Data.   The Internal Revenue Service is the most visible stockpile of personal information. It, of course, keeps records of our whereabouts, earnings, taxes, deductions, employment, and so on. Now the IRS is supplementing basic tax information with external information to create personal profiles to tell if a person's tax return is consistent with his or her lifestyle. By law, all IRS data must be made available to about 40 different government agencies.

Education Data.   What you've accomplished during your years in school, such as grades and awards, is recorded in computer-based data bases. Included in these data bases is a variety of information such as your scores on college entrance exams, data on loan applications that include details of your family's financial status, roommate preferences, disciplinary actions, and so on. In one instance, a Chicago woman was turned down for several government jobs because of a note her third-grade teacher entered in her file. In the note the teacher stated that in her view the girl's mother was crazy.

Medical Data.   Medical files, which contain a mountain of sensitive personal data, are not always treated with the respect they deserve. In many hospitals, hundreds of employees, most of whom do not have a need-to-know, have ready access to patient information. Your medical records list all your visits to clinics and hospitals, your medical history (and often that of your family), allergies, and diseases you have or have had. They also may include assessments of your mental and physical health.

Driver and Crime Data.   State motor vehicle bureaus maintain detailed records on over 150 million licensed drivers. This information includes personal descriptive data (sex, age, height, weight, color of eyes and hair) as well as arrests, fines, traffic offenses, and whether your license has been revoked. Some states sell descriptive information to retailers on the open market. The FBI's National Crime Information Center (NCIC) and local police offices maintain data bases that contain rap sheet information on 20 million people. This information is readily available to thousands of law-enforcement personnel.

Census Data.   With the 1990 census still fresh in our minds, we are reminded that the U.S. Bureau of the Census maintains some very personal data: names, racial heritage, income, the number of bathrooms in our home, and persons of the opposite sex who share our living quarters. Statistics, however, are released without names.

CD-ROM

Introduced in 1980, the extraordinarily successful CD, or compact disk, is an optical laser disk designed to enhance the recorded reproduction of music. To make a CD recording, the analog sounds of music are translated into their digital equivalents and stored on a 4.72-inch optical laser disk. Seventy-four minutes of music can be recorded on each disk in digital format by 2 billion digital bits. With its tremendous storage capacity, computer-industry entrepreneurs immediately recognized the potential of optical laser disk technology. In effect, anything that can be digitized can be stored on optical laser disk: data, text, voice, still pictures, music, graphics, and video.

Insurance Data. Insurance companies have formed a cooperative to maintain a single data base containing medical information on millions of people. This revealing data base includes claims, doctors' reports, whether or not you have been refused insurance, how risky you would be as an insuree, and so on.

Lifestyle Data. A number of cities are installing two-way cable TV that allows the accumulation of information on people's personal viewing habits. When you watch an X-rated movie, or any other movie, your choice is recorded in the family's viewing data base. As interactive cable TV matures, you will be able to use it to pay bills, respond to opinion polls, and make dinner reservations. This, of course, will add a greater variety of information to your personal file.

Credit Data. Credit bureaus routinely release intimate details of our financial well being. We, of course, hope that the information about us is up-to-date and accurate. However, this is not always the case. About one third of those who ask to review their records (you have the right to do this at any time) challenge their accuracy. Credit bureaus are bound by law to correct inaccuracies within two weeks of being notified of them.

Miscellaneous Data. Every time you make a long-distance telephone call, the number is recorded. When you make a credit-card purchase, your location at the time and the type of item you buy is recorded. Job-related information is maintained at current and past employers, including the results of performance reports and disciplinary actions. Local and state governments maintain records of property transactions that involve homes, automobiles, boats, guns, and so on. Banks not only keep track of your money, but some monitor the volume and type of transactions you make.

Summary. The social security number, now assigned to all citizens, is the link that ties all our personal information together. It doubles as a military serial number, and in many states it serves as your driver's license number. It is the one item, along with your name, that appears on almost all personal forms. For example, your social security number is a permanent entry in hospital, tax, insurance, bank, employment, school, and scores of other types of records.

The few organizations discussed here represent the tip of the iceberg, so to speak. For the most part, these and thousands of other organizations are making a genuine attempt to handle personal data in a responsible manner. However, instances of abuse are widespread and give us cause for concern. Computers are now the primary vehicle for processing and storing personal information, and they will store even more information about us in the future. However, it's not computers that abuse the privacy of our personal information, it's the people who run them. We as a society must be prepared to meet the challenge with a system of laws that deals realistically with the problem.

CD-ROM (pronounced *cee-dee*-ROM) is a spinoff of audio CD technology. CD-ROM stands for *compact disk-read only memory*. The name implies its application. CD-ROM disks, like long-playing record albums, are "pressed" at the factory and distributed with their prerecorded contents (for example, the complete works of Shakespeare or the first 30 minutes of *Gone With the Wind*). Once inserted into the disk drive, the text, video images, and so on can be read into primary storage for processing or display; however, the data on the disk are fixed—they cannot be altered. This is in contrast, of course, to the read/write capability of magnetic disks.

The tremendous amount of low-cost direct-access storage made possible by optical laser disks has opened the door to many new applications.

A single CD-ROM disk can hold the equivalent of 13,000 images, 250,000 pages of text, or 1500 floppy disks. This tremendous storage capacity has opened the door to interactive video applications. In the photo, a high school student is learning about careers in nursing via interactive video. Unlike a videotape, CD-ROM gives the student instant random access to any sequence of images on the disk.

The capacity of a single CD-ROM is over 550 Mb. To put this in perspective, the words in every book ever written could be stored on a hypothetical CD-ROM that is 7 feet in diameter. Currently, most of the 100 or so commercially produced CD-ROM disks contain reference material. A sampling of these disks follows: *The Groliers Electronic Encyclopedia; The Oxford English Dictionary; The Daily Oklahoman* (1981–86); the 1980 U.S. Census (county level); maps at the national, state, regional, and metropolitan levels; a world history tutorial; and scientific writings for the Apple Macintosh. The cost of commercially produced CD-ROMs varies considerably from as little as $50 to several thousand dollars.

WORM Disks

Write once, read many, or **WORM,** optical laser disks are used by end user companies to store their own, proprietary information. Once the

The most common secondary storage devices are the magnetic disk drive and magnetic tape drive. However, for certain applications, optical laser disk storage technology (shown here) is emerging as a viable alternative to disk and tape storage.

data have been written to the medium, they only can be read, not updated or changed.

WORM disks are a feasible alternative to magnetic tape for archival storage. For example, a company might wish to keep a permanent record of all financial transactions during the last year. Another popular application of WORM disks is in information systems that require the merging of text and images that do not change for a period of time. A good example is an "electronic catalog." A customer can peruse a retailer's electronic catalog on a VDT, or perhaps a PC, and see the item while he or she reads about it. And, with a few keystrokes the customer can order the item as well. The Library of Congress is using WORM technology to alleviate a serious shelf-space problem.

Magneto-Optical Disk

A new technology called **magneto-optical disk** offers promise that optical laser disks will become commercially viable as a read-*and*-write storage technology. The 5¼-inch disks can store up to 1000 Mb. However, the technology must be improved before the disks can experience widespread acceptance. At present, magneto-optical disks are too expensive and do not offer anywhere near the kind of reliability that users have come to expect of magnetic media. In addition, the access times are relatively slow, about the same as a low-end Winchester disk.

As optical laser disk technology matures to reliable, cost-effective, read/write operation, it eventually may dominate secondary storage in the future as magnetic disks and tape do today.

SUMMARY OUTLINE AND IMPORTANT TERMS

5–1 **SECONDARY STORAGE: PERMANENT DATA STORAGE.** Data and programs are stored on **secondary**, or **auxiliary**, **storage** for permanent storage. **Magnetic disk drives** and **magnetic tape drives** are the state of the art for both on-line and off-line storage. **Optical laser disk** technology is emerging as an alternative to magnetic disks and magnetic tapes.

5–2 **SEQUENTIAL AND DIRECT ACCESS: NEW TERMS FOR OLD CONCEPTS.** Data are stored sequentially on magnetic tape; they are stored randomly on magnetic disks. **Sequential access** requires that the file be searched record by record until the desired record is found. **Random access** enables the desired record to be retrieved directly from its storage location.

5–3 **MAGNETIC DISKS: ROTATING STORAGE MEDIA.** Magnetic disk drives provide the computer system with direct-access and **random-processing** capabilities. Magnetic disks also support **sequential processing**.

Interchangeable magnetic disks can be removed from the drive and stored **off-line**; **fixed disks** are permanently installed in the drive. When spinning in the drive, the disks are said to be **on-line**.

In the microcomputer environment, the two most popular types of interchangeable magnetic disks are the **diskette** (also called a **flexible disk** or a **floppy disk**) and the **microdisk** (also called a **microfloppy**). The microcomputer hard disk is called the **Winchester disk**. In the mainframe environment, the most popular interchangeable disk storage media are the **disk cartridge** and the **disk pack**.

Data are stored via **serial representation** within **tracks** on each recording surface. A particular set of data stored on a disk is assigned a **disk address** that designates its physical location. An **access arm**, with at least one **read/write head** for each recording surface, is moved to the appropriate track to retrieve the data.

The two types of disk organization are **sector organization** and **cylinder organization**. In sector organization, the recording surface is divided into pie-shaped **sectors**, and each sector is assigned a number. In cylinder organization, a particular **cylinder** number refers to every track with the same number on all recording surfaces. To read from or write to a disk, the access arms are moved, under program control, to the appropriate cylinder. The **disk address** points to the physical location of a particular set of data on a disk.

The **access time** for a magnetic disk is the sum of the seek time, the rotational delay time, and the transmission time.

5–4   MAGNETIC TAPE: RIBBONS OF DATA. A thin polyester tape is spun on a **reel** or encased in a **cartridge**. This magnetic tape is loaded onto a tape drive, where data are read or written as the tape is passed under a read/write head. The physical nature of the magnetic tape results in data being stored and accessed sequentially. On $\frac{1}{2}$-inch magnetic tape, data are stored using **parallel representation**, and they are **blocked** between **interblock gaps** (**IBGs**) to minimize the start/ stop movement of the tape. The standard nine-track, 2400-foot tape reel stores data at a **density** of 6250 **bytes per inch** (**bpi**). Magnetic-tape density and its speed over the read/write head combine to determine the **transfer rate**.

The operation of the 18-track, $\frac{1}{2}$-inch **data cartridge** (tape cartridge) is more like that of the $\frac{1}{2}$-inch mag-tape reel than the $\frac{1}{4}$-inch tape cartridge. Most $\frac{1}{4}$-inch tape cartridges record data serially in a continuous stream, eliminating the need for the start/stop operation of traditional tape drives. These cartridges use **streamer tape drives**, which store data in a **serpentine** manner.

5–5   OPTICAL LASER DISKS: HIGH-DENSITY STORAGE. Optical laser disk storage, now in its infant stage of use and development, is capable of storing vast amounts of data. The three main categories of optical laser disks are **CD-ROM**, **WORM**, and **magneto-optical**. Most of the commercially produced read-only CD-ROM disks contain reference material. The write once, read many (WORM) optical laser disks are used by end user companies to store their own, proprietary information. The new magneto-optical disk offers promise that optical laser disks will become commercially viable as a read-and-write storage technology.

REVIEW EXERCISES

Concepts

1. What are other names for flexible disks, auxiliary storage, and direct processing?
2. CD-ROM is a spinoff of what technology?
3. What is the purpose of the interblock gap?
4. What information is contained on a magnetic-tape header label?
5. How many megabytes are there in a gigabyte?
6. A program issues a "read" command for data to be retrieved from a magnetic tape. Describe the resulting movement of the data.
7. Use the initials of your name and the ASCII encoding system to graphically contrast parallel and serial data representation.
8. A company's employee master file contains 120,000 employee records. Each record is 1800 bytes in length. How many 2400-foot, 6250-bpi magnetic tapes (interblock gap = 0.6 inch) will be required to store

the file? Assume records are blocked five. Next, assume records are unblocked, and perform the same calculations.

9. A disk pack contains 20 recording surfaces and 400 cylinders. If a track can store 10,000 bytes of data, how much data can be stored on eight such disk packs?

10. What are the three main categories of optical laser disks?

11. What is the nickname of the hard disk used with microcomputers?

12. What are the most popular interchangeable disk-storage media in the mainframe environment?

Discussion

13. If increasing the blocking factor for a magnetic-tape file improves tape utilization, why not eliminate all IBGs and put all the records in one big block? Explain.

14. A floppy disk does not move until a read or write command is issued. Once it is issued, the floppy begins to spin. It stops spinning after the command is executed. Why is a disk pack not set in motion in the same manner? Why is a floppy not made to spin continuously?

15. Every Friday night a company makes backup copies of all master files and programs. Why is this necessary? The company has both tape and disk drives. What storage medium would you suggest for the backup? Why?

16. Describe the potential impact of optical laser disk technology on public and university libraries. On home libraries.

SELF TEST (by section) —————————————————————————————

5–1 Data are retrieved from temporary auxiliary storage and stored permanently in RAM. (T/F)

5–2 Magnetic disks have both _____ - and _____ -access capabilities.

5–3 a. In a disk drive, the read/write heads are mounted on an access arm. (T/F)
     b. Fixed disks cannot be removed and stored off-line. (T/F)
     c. The diskette is _____ inches in diameter, and the microfloppy is _____ inches in diameter.
     d. What percentage of the data on a magnetic disk is available to the system with each complete revolution of the disk: (a) 10%, (b) 50%, or (c) 100%?
     e. The _____ denotes the physical location of a particular set of data or a program on a magnetic disk.

5–4 a. Tape density is based on the linear distance between IBGs. (T/F)
     b. The $\frac{1}{2}$-inch tape cartridge has more in common with the magnetic-tape reel than it does the $\frac{1}{4}$-inch tape cartridge. (T/F)
     c. Streamer tape drives store data in a _____ manner.

5–5   **a.** _____ technology permits on-line direct access of both still
pictures and video.
   b. All optical laser disk technology is read-only. (T/F)

Self-test answers.   **5–1** F. **5–2** direct *or* random; sequential. **5–3** (a) T; **(b)**
T; **(c)** $5\frac{1}{4}$, $3\frac{1}{2}$; **(d)** c; **(e)** disk address. **5–4** **(a)** F; **(b)** T; **(c)** serpentine. **5–5** **(a)** Optical
laser disk; **(b)** F.

6

Data Communications

STUDENT LEARNING OBJECTIVES

▶ To describe the concept of connectivity.
▶ To demonstrate an understanding of data communications terminology and applications.
▶ To detail the function and operation of data communications hardware.
▶ To describe the types of data transmission services.
▶ To illustrate the various kinds of computer networks.

6–1   DATA COMMUNICATIONS: FROM ONE ROOM TO THE WORLD

In the 1960s computers numbered in the tens of thousands. Today computers number in the tens of millions. Information is everywhere. The challenge of the next decade is to make this information more accessible to a greater number of people. To do this, the business and computer communities are seeking ways to interface, or connect, a diverse set of hardware, software, and data bases. **Connectivity**, as it is called, is necessary to facilitate the electronic communication between companies, end user computing, and the free flow of information within an enterprise. This chapter focuses on connectivity concepts and the base technology of connectivity—data communications.

Data communications is, very simply, the collection and distribution of the electronic representation of information from and to remote facilities. The information can appear in a variety of formats: data, text, voice, still pictures, graphics, and video. Prior to transmission, the raw information must be digitized. (For example, data and text might be translated into their corresponding ASCII codes.) Ultimately all forms of information are sent over the transmission media as a series of binary bits (1s and 0s). Information is transmitted from computers to terminals

This office is one of 12 regional customer support centers, each of which is part of a computer network. The terminals at this office are linked to a local minicomputer that is connected via a high-speed communications line to the company's headquarters in Columbus, Ohio. The regional minis also are used for local processing.

and other computers over land via optical fiber, through the air by satellites, and under the sea through coaxial cable. The technical aspects of data communications are discussed later in this chapter.

Several other terms describe the general area of data communications. **Telecommunications** encompasses not only data communications but any type of remote communication, such as transmitting a television signal. **Teleprocessing**, or **TP**, is the combination of *tele*communications and data *processing*; it often is used interchangeably with the term *data communications*. The integration of computer systems, terminals, and communication links is referred to as a **computer network**.

Through the mid-1960s, a company's computing hardware was located in a single room called the machine room. The only people who had direct access to the computer were those who worked in the machine room. Since that time, microcomputers, terminals, and data communications have made it possible to move hardware and information systems "closer to the source"—to the people who use them. Before long, terminals will be as much a part of our work environment as desks and telephones are now.

6–2   THE BEGINNING OF AN ERA: COOPERATIVE COMPUTING

Intracompany Networking

This is the era of **cooperative computing**. Information is the password to success in today's business environment. To get meaningful, accurate, and timely information, businesses have decided they must cooperate internally and externally to take full advantage of what is available. To promote internal cooperation, they are moving in the direction of *intracompany networking* (see Figure 6–1). For example, information main-

FIGURE 6–1   Intracompany and Intercompany Networking

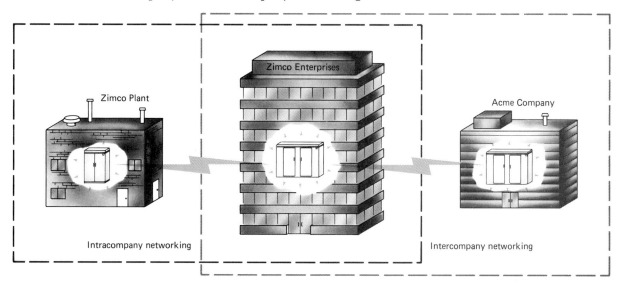

tained in the personnel department is readily accessible to people throughout the company on a *need-to-know* basis. The same is true of information maintained by purchasing, engineering, or any other department. At the individual level, managers or knowledge workers create microcomputer-based systems and data bases to help them do their jobs. When these personalized systems and data bases have the potential of benefiting other people in the company, they can be made a part of the company's computer network to permit the sharing of these information resources.

Intercompany Networking

Companies have recognized that they must cooperate with one another to compete effectively in a world market. They are doing this via *intercompany networking* (Figure 6–1) or, more specifically, **electronic data interchange (EDI)**. EDI uses computers and data communications to transmit data electronically between companies. Invoices, orders, and many other intercompany transactions, including the exchange of information, can be transmitted from the computer of one company to the computer of another. For example, at General Foods, over 50% of all shipments result from computer-to-computer order processing—customers submitting their orders to General Foods via EDI. Figure 6–2 contrasts the traditional interaction between a customer and supplier company with interactions via EDI. EDI is a strategic advantage that some companies

FIGURE 6–2   Interactions Between Customer and Supplier
In the figure, the traditional interaction between a customer company and a supplier company is contrasted with similar interactions via electronic data interchange.

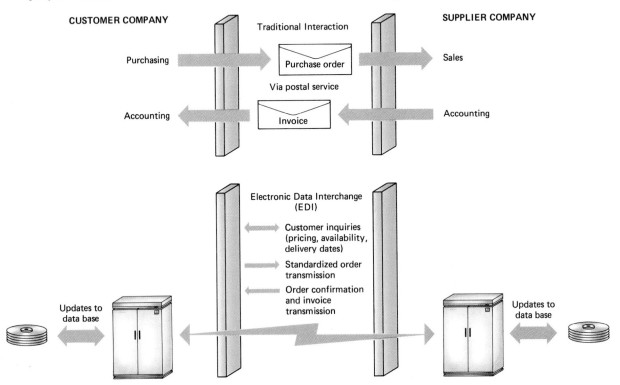

have over their competitors. It reduces paper-processing costs and delays, it reduces errors and correction costs, it minimizes receivables and inventory disputes, and it improves relations between trading partners.

Executives are no longer debating whether or not to implement EDI; they are more concerned about the speed at which it can be put to work in their companies. Essentially, they have two choices. They can elect to create the hardware- and software-based EDI system in-house, or they can use a **third-party provider** of EDI services. A third-party provider is an intermediary who helps facilitate EDI between trading partners with incompatible hardware and software. By far the fastest way to take advantage of EDI is to contract for the services of a third-party provider. However, in-house development of EDI capabilities is less expensive than using an intermediary, even though it may take longer.

External Computing Support: Service via Computer

The phenomenal growth of the use of micros in the home is causing companies to expand their information system capabilities to permit linkages with home and portable PCs. This form of cooperative computing increases system efficiency while lowering costs. For example, in over 100 banks, services have been extended to home micro owners in the form of home banking systems. Subscribers to a home banking service use their personal computers as terminals linked to the bank's mainframe computer system to pay bills, transfer funds, and inquire about account status.

The Internal Revenue Service (IRS) now permits tax returns to be filed by professional preparers from their PCs. This service saves both the taxpayer and the IRS time and money. For the taxpayer and the preparer, the on-line system performs all the necessary table searches and computations, and it even cross-checks the accuracy and consistency of the input data. For the IRS, no further data entry or personal assistance is required. Brokerage firms now permit customers to access up-to-the-minute stock market quotations and to issue buy/sell orders directly through their personal computers. Several supermarkets are experimenting with electronic shopping. In the 1990s virtually every type of industry will provide the facility for external links to their mainframe computer systems.

As oil companies automate the distribution of gasoline and the handling of credit transactions, service-station owners, attendants, and customers are learning to use computers. This customer is linked via data communications to Phillips Petroleum mainframe computers in Bartlesville, Ok.

Connectivity: Linking Hardware, Software, and Data Bases

Connectivity refers to the degree to which hardware devices can be linked functionally to one another. Some people expand the scope of connectivity to include software and data bases. It has become such an important consideration that virtually all future decisions involving hardware, software, and data base management must be evaluated with respect to connectivity.

Connectivity is implemented in degrees. To achieve almost any level, technical specialists must juggle communication protocols (rules), official and de facto standards, different approaches to data base design, different computer system architectures, and user information requirements. Each of these considerations poses formidable technological hurdles.

The ideal implementation of intracompany connectivity would be to make all corporate computer and information resources accessible from each worker's terminal. This ideal is referred to as **total connectivity**. Realistically, industry analysts are predicting that total connectivity is still a decade or more away. Nevertheless, almost every company has made a commitment to strive for a higher level of connectivity.

PROFILE

Philippe Kahn
The Software Industry's Contrarian

In 1983 a French mathematics teacher came to the United States to find a job in Silicon Valley. Philippe Kahn said, "I was looking for a job, not trying to start a company." Now Kahn is chairman, president, and CEO of Borland International, a microcomputer software company whose corporate philosophy frequently ruffles the feathers of its competitors.

The flamboyant Kahn is sometimes referred to as software's "bad boy" because, among other things, Borland offers, through mail order, inexpensive, high-performance software that is not copy-protected. Kahn says, "If I had played the game by their rules, obviously I would have lost. For Borland, the idea was to create new rules." Industry analysts point to his marketing philosophy as the major contributor to the significant drop in the cost of microcomputer applications software during the late 1980s.

Kahn studied under Niklaus Wirth, the creator of Pascal. He introduced Turbo Pascal as Borland's first product, and today Turbo Pascal is the worldwide de facto Pascal programming standard.

An avid sailor, Kahn holds a trans-Pacific sailing record. He speaks French, English, Spanish, and German. He also likes to jam on his saxophone with the Borland Turbo Jazz Band in a room next to his office.

6–3   DATA COMMUNICATIONS HARDWARE

Data communications hardware is used to transmit data between terminals and computers and between computers in a computer network. This hardware includes modems, down-line processors, front-end processors, and PBXs. The integration of these devices (except the PBX) with terminals and computer systems is illustrated in Figure 6–3 and discussed in the paragraphs that follow.

The Modem

If you have a micro, you have the capability of establishing a communications link between your microcomputer and any remote computer system in the world. However, to do this you must have ready access to a telephone line and your micro must be equipped with a *modem*. Telephone lines were designed for voice communication, not data communication. The **modem** (*modulator-dem*odulator) converts terminal-to-computer and micro-to-computer electrical *digital* signals into *analog* signals so that the data can be transmitted over telephone lines (see Figure 6–4). The digital electrical signals are modulated to make sounds similar to those you hear on a touch-tone telephone. Upon reaching their destination, these analog signals are demodulated by another modem into computer-compatible electrical signals for processing. The procedure is reversed

FIGURE 6–3   Hardware Components in Data Communications
Devices that handle the movement of data in a computer network are the modem, down-line processor, front-end processor, and host processor.

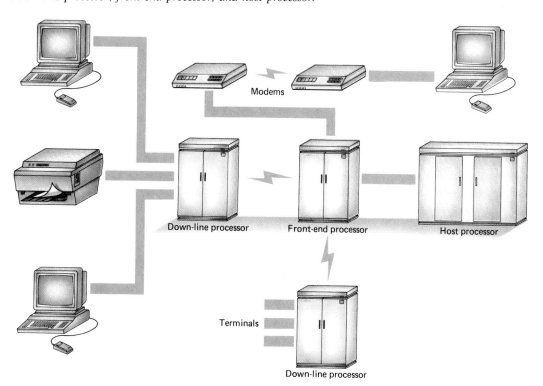

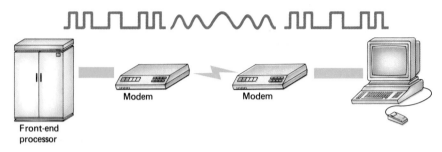

FIGURE 6–4   The Modulation/Demodulation Process
Electrical digital signals are modulated into analog signals for transmission over telephone lines and then demodulated for processing at the destination.

for computer-to-terminal or computer-to-micro communication. A modem is always required when you dial up the computer on a telephone line. The modulation-demodulation process is not needed for transmission media other than telephone lines, so they do not require modems.

Internal and External Modems.   There are two types of modems for micros and terminals: *internal* and *external*. Most micros and terminals have internal modems; that is, the modem is on an optional add-on circuit board that is simply plugged into an empty expansion slot in the micro's processor unit or the terminal's housing. The external modem is a separate component, as illustrated in Figure 6–4, and is connected

At the end of each month, this plant manager uses an external modem (under the telephone) to download cost data from the company's mainframe computer to the plant's minicomputer. He then compares the expenditures of the Boston plant with those of the Phoenix and Indianapolis plants.

via a serial interface port (see Chapter 3, "Microcomputers"). To make the connection with a telephone line and either type of modem, you simply plug the telephone line into the modem just as you would when connecting the line to a telephone.

Smart Modems. Modems have varying degrees of "intelligence" produced by embedded microprocessors. For instance, some modems can automatically dial up the computer (*auto-dial*), establish a link (*log on*), and even answer incoming calls from other computers (*auto-answer*). **Smart modems** also have made it possible to increase the rate at which data can be transmitted and received.

Acoustical Couplers. If you need a telephone hookup for voice conversations on the same telephone line used for data communication and do not want to disconnect the phone each time, you can purchase a modem with an **acoustical coupler**. To make the connection, you mount the telephone handset directly on the acoustical coupler. Acoustical couplers are essential items for travelers who routinely make micro–mainframe connections from public telephones.

The Down-Line Processor

The **down-line processor**, also called a **cluster controller**, is remote from the *host processor*. It collects data from a number of low-speed devices, such as terminals and serial printers. The down-line processor then "concentrates" the data—sending the data over a single communications channel (see Figure 6–5).

FIGURE 6–5 "Concentrating" Data for Remote Transmission
The down-line processor "concentrates" the data from several low-speed devices for transmission over a single high-speed line. At the host site, the front-end processor separates the data for processing. Data received from a front-end processor are interpreted by the down-line processor and routed to the appropriate device.

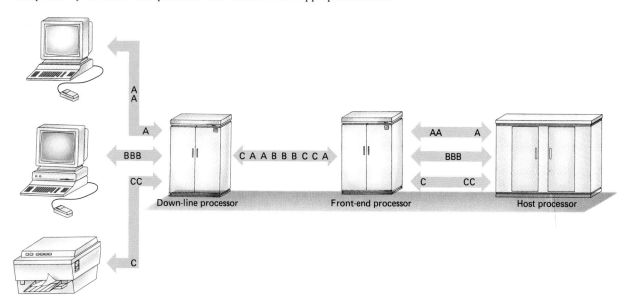

The down-line processor, also called a **concentrator** or **multiplexor**, is an economic necessity when several low-speed terminals are located at one remote site. One high-speed line connecting the down-line processor to the host is considerably less expensive than several low-speed lines connecting each terminal to the host. An airline reservations counter might have 10 terminals. Each terminal is connected to a common down-line processor, which in turn is connected to a central host computer. An airline might have one or several down-line processors at a given airport, depending on the volume of passenger traffic.

A microcomputer can be made to emulate the function of a down-line processor. This often occurs when a network of micros is linked to a mainframe computer.

The Front-End Processor

The terminal or computer sending a **message** is the *source*. The terminal or computer receiving the message is the *destination*. The **front-end**

FIGURE 6–6   Message Routing
In the illustration, the president sends a message to two vice presidents and the plant manager. The front-end processor accepts the president's message for processing and routes it to the appropriate addresses.

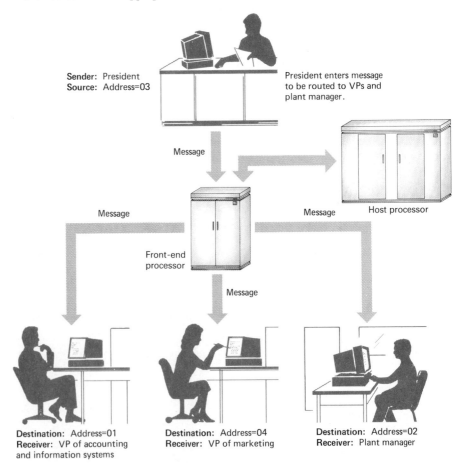

Sender: President
Source: Address=03

President enters message to be routed to VPs and plant manager.

Message

Message

Host processor

Message

Front-end processor

Message

Destination: Address=01
Receiver: VP of accounting and information systems

Destination: Address=04
Receiver: VP of marketing

Destination: Address=02
Receiver: Plant manager

processor establishes the link between the source and destination in a process called **handshaking**.

If you think of messages as mail to be delivered to various points in a computer network, the front-end processor is the post office. Each computer system and terminal is assigned an **address**. The front-end processor uses these addresses to route messages to their destinations. The content of a message could be a prompt to the user, a user inquiry, a program instruction, an "electronic memo," or any type of information that can be transmitted electronically—even the image of a handwritten report. Figure 6–6 illustrates how a memo would be sent from the president of a company to two vice presidents and the plant manager. It is not uncommon for a front-end processor to control communications between a dozen down-line processors and 100 or more terminals.

The front-end processor relieves the host processor of communications-related tasks, such as message routing, parity checking, code translation, editing, and cryptography (the encryption/decryption of data). This processor specialization permits the host to operate more efficiently and to devote more of its resources to processing applications programs.

The PBX

The old-time telephone **PBX** (private branch exchange) switchboard has evolved into a sophisticated device capable of switching not only voice but also digital electronic signals. The PBX is actually a computer that electronically connects computers and terminals much as telephone operators manually connected telephone lines on the old PBX switchboards. Approximately 70% of the traffic handled by a modern PBX is voice; the remainder consists of digital electronic signals.

A PBX connects computing devices for data communications in much the same way operators used to connect telephones for voice communication. However, with the modern voice and data PBX, it's all automatic.

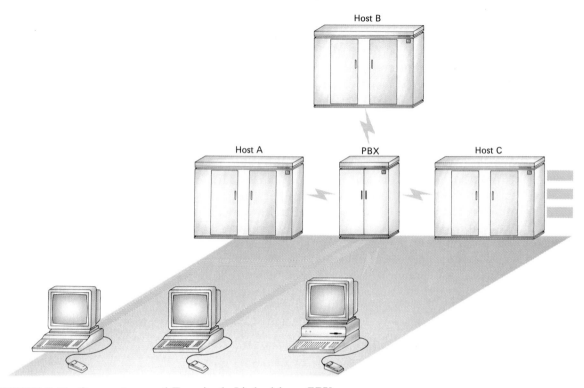

FIGURE 6–7   Computers and Terminals Linked by a PBX
Any two of the host computers or terminals can be linked together for data transmission
by the PBX.

As discussed earlier, there is definitely a trend toward making information systems more responsive to end users by "distributing" processing capabilities closer to the people who use them. Because of this trend, a single organization is likely to have at least one mainframe computer, several minis, and many micros and terminals. The PBX, serving as the hub of data activity, permits these computers and terminals to "talk" to one another. Figure 6–7 illustrates how several computer systems can be linked via a PBX.

6–4   THE DATA COMMUNICATIONS CHANNEL: DATA HIGHWAYS

Transmission Media

A **communications channel** is the facility through which electronic signals are transmitted between locations in a computer network. Data, text, and digitized images are transmitted as combinations of bits (0s and 1s). A *channel's capacity* is rated by the number of bits it can transmit per second. A regular telephone line can transmit up to 9600 **bits per second (bps)**, or 9.6 K bps (thousands of bits per second). Under normal circumstances, a 9.6 K-bps line would fill the screen of a typical video monitor with text in one or two seconds.

In practice, the word **baud** is often used interchangeably with bits per second. But, in reality, they are quite different. Baud is a measure of the maximum number of electronic signals that can be transmitted via a communications channel. It is true that a 300-bps modem operates at 300 baud, but both 1200-bps and 2400-bps modems operate at 600 baud. A technical differentiation between baud and bits per second is beyond the scope of this book. Suffice it to say that when someone says *baud* and he or she is talking about computer-based communications, that person probably means bits per second. The erroneous use of *baud* is so common that some software packages that facilitate data communication ask you to specify baud when they actually want bits per second.

Data rates of 1500 K bps are available through common carriers such as American Telephone & Telegraph (AT&T). The channel, also called a **line** or a **data link**, may comprise one or a combination of the transmission media discussed next.

Telephone Lines. The same transmission facilities we use for voice communication via telephones can also be used to transmit data. This capability is provided by communications companies throughout the country and the world.

Optical Fiber. Very thin transparent fibers have been developed that will eventually replace the copper wire traditionally used in the telephone system. These hairlike **optical fibers** carry data faster and are lighter and less expensive than their copper-wire counterparts.

The differences between the data transmission rates of copper wire and optical fiber are tremendous. In the time it takes to transmit a single page of *Webster's Unabridged Dictionary* over copper wire (about 6 seconds), the entire dictionary could be transmitted over a single optical fiber.

Another of the many advantages of optical fiber is its contribution to data security. It is much more difficult for a computer criminal to intercept a signal sent over optical fiber (via a beam of light) than it is over copper wire (an electrical signal).

Coaxial Cable. **Coaxial cable** contains electrical wire and is constructed to permit high-speed data transmission with a minimum of signal distortion. Coaxial cable is laid along the ocean floor for intercontinental voice and data transmission. It is also used to connect terminals and computers in a "local" area (from a few feet to a few miles).

Microwave. Communications channels do not have to be wires or fibers. Data can also be transmitted via **microwave radio signals**. Transmission of these signals is *line-of-sight*; that is, the radio signal travels in a direct line from one repeater station to the next until it reaches its destination. Because of the curvature of the earth, microwave repeater stations are placed on the tops of mountains and towers, usually about 30 miles apart.

Satellites have made it possible to minimize the line-of-sight limitation. Satellites routinely are launched into orbit for the sole purpose of relaying data communications signals to and from earth stations. A satellite, which is essentially a repeater station, is launched and set in

Copper wire in the telephone network is being replaced by the more versatile optical fiber. Laser-generated light pulses are transmitted through thin glass fibers. A pair of optical fibers can carry simultaneously 1344 voice conversations and interactive data communications sessions.

The view above the floor in a computer machine room is quite different from the view below the raised floor. A spaghetti-like arrangement of coaxial cables link computers, storage devices, I/O devices, and remote terminals.

Microwave repeater stations relay voice, data, and television signals to transceivers or other repeater stations.

a **geosynchronous orbit** 22,300 miles above the earth. A geosynchronous orbit permits the communications satellite to maintain a fixed position relative to the surface of the earth. Each satellite can receive and retransmit signals to slightly less than half of the earth's surface; therefore, three satellites are required to cover the earth effectively (see Figure 6–8). The big advantage of satellites is that data can be transmitted from one location to any number of other locations anywhere on (or near) our planet.

Data Transmission in Practice

A communications channel from Computer A in Seattle, Washington, to Computer B in Orlando, Florida, (see Figure 6–9) usually would consist of several different transmission media. The connection between Computer A and a terminal in the same building is probably coaxial cable. The Seattle company might use a communications company such as AT&T to transmit the data. AT&T would then send the data through a combination of transmission facilities that might include copper wire, optical fiber, and microwave radio signals.

FIGURE 6–8   Satellite Data Transmission
Three satellites in geosynchronous orbit provide worldwide data transmission service.

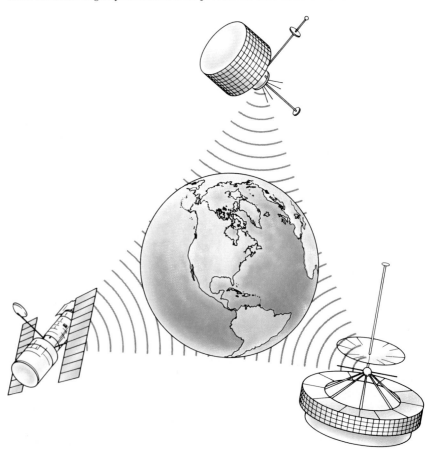

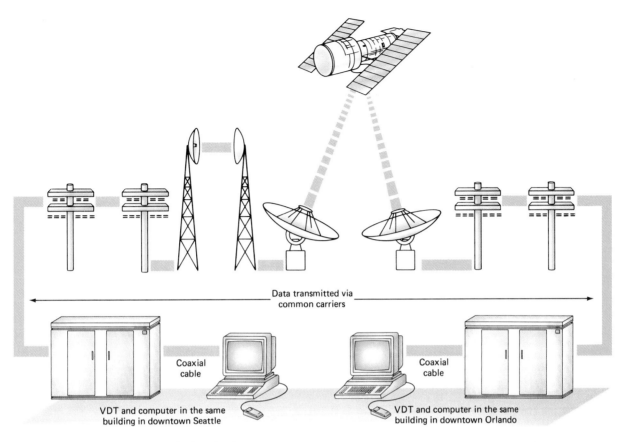

Data transmitted via
common carriers

Coaxial
cable

Coaxial
cable

VDT and computer in the same
building in downtown Seattle

VDT and computer in the same
building in downtown Orlando

FIGURE 6–9   Data Transmission Path
*It's more the rule than the exception that data are carried over several transmission
media between source and destination.*

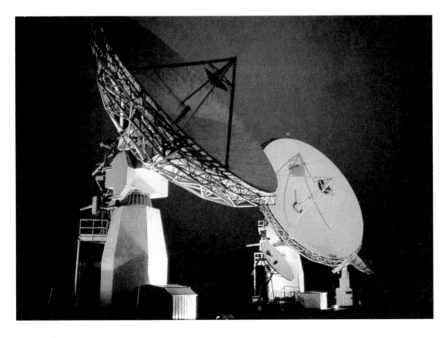

*In satellite communications, data
are transmitted first to an earth
station where giant antennae route
signals to another earth station via
a communications satellite. The
signals are then transmitted to their
destination over another type of
communications channel.*

This communications satellite is being released from the space shuttle over the Gulf of Mexico. The state of Florida is visible just below the horizon.

6–5   DATA TRANSMISSION SERVICES

Common Carriers

It is impractical, not to mention illegal, for companies to string their own coaxial cables between two locations, such as Philadelphia and New York City. It is also impractical for them to set their own satellites in orbit. Therefore, companies turn to **common carriers**, such as AT&T and Western Union to provide communications channels. Communications common carriers, which are regulated by the Federal Communications Commission (FCC), offer two basic types of service: private lines and switched lines.

A **private line** (or **leased line**) provides a dedicated data communications channel between any two points in a computer network. The charge for a private line is based on channel capacity (bps) and distance (air miles).

A **switched line** (or **dial-up line**) is available strictly on a time-and-distance charge, similar to a long-distance telephone call. You make a connection by "dialing up" the computer, then a modem sends and receives data.

As a rule of thumb, a private line is the least expensive alternative if you expect to use the channel more than three hours a day and you do not need the flexibility to connect with several different computers.

This is the fax room at USA Today, where pages of the newspaper are faxed via common carriers to over 30 print sites. It takes $3\frac{1}{2}$ minutes to transmit a black-and-white page to the satellite and then to all print sites. A full-color editorial page is transmitted in 26 minutes.

Specialized Common Carriers

A **specialized common carrier**, such as a **value-added network (VAN)**, may or may not use the transmission facilities of a common carrier, but in each case it "adds value" to the transmission service. The value added over and above the standard services of the common carriers may include electronic mail, data encryption/decryption, access to commercial data bases, and code conversion for communication between incompatible computers. Not only do VANs such as Tymshares's Tymnet and GTE's Telenet offer expanded services but the basic communications service provided by the VAN also may be less expensive than the same service from a common carrier.

6–6   NETWORKS: LINKING COMPUTERS AND PEOPLE

Network Topologies

Each time you use the telephone, you use the world's largest computer network—the telephone system. A telephone is an end point, or a **node**, connected to a network of computers that route your voice signals to any one of the 500 million telephones (other nodes) in the world.

In a computer network the node can be a terminal or another computer. Computer networks are configured to meet the specific requirements of an organization. The basic computer **network topologies**—star, ring, and bus—are illustrated in Figure 6–10. A network topology is a description of the possible physical connections within a network. The topology is the configuration of the hardware and indicates which pairs of nodes are able to communicate.

FIGURE 6–10   Network Topologies
(a) star (b) ring (c) bus

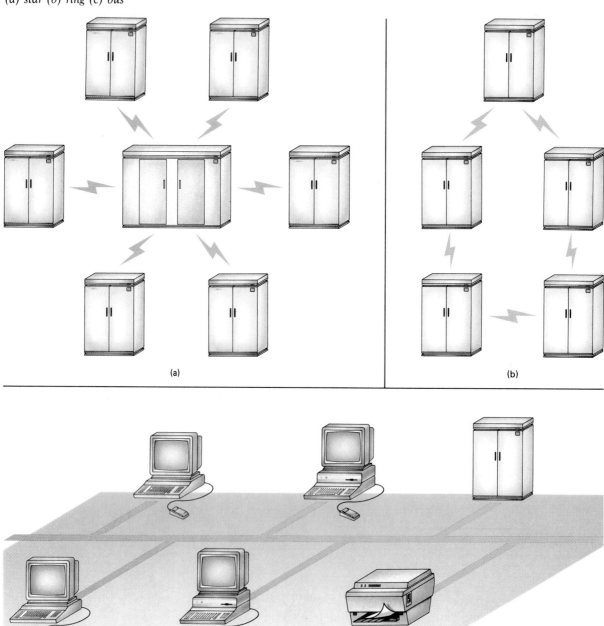

(a)

(b)

(c)

The **star topology** involves a centralized host computer connected to a number of smaller computer systems. The smaller computer systems communicate with one another through the host and usually share the host computer's data base. Both the central computer and the distributed computer systems are connected to terminals (micros or video display terminals). Any terminal can communicate with any other terminal in the network. Banks usually have a large home-office computer system with a star network of minicomputer systems in the branch banks.

The **ring topology** involves computer systems that are approximately the same size, with no one computer system as the focal point of the network. When one system routes a message to another system, it is passed around the ring until it reaches its destination address.

The **bus topology** permits the connection of terminals, peripheral devices, and microcomputers along a central cable called a **transmission medium**. It is easy to add devices or delete them from the network. Bus topologies are most appropriate when the linked devices are physically close to one another. (See the discussion of local area networks that follows.)

A pure form of any of these three topologies is seldom found in practice. Most computer networks are *hybrids*—combinations of topologies.

One of the most sophisticated computer networks is the one used by thousands of air traffic controllers. Each controller has a display that shows the relative position, altitude, and flight path of all aircraft in his or her area of responsibility. The system gives controllers a visual and audible warning when adequate aircraft separation is violated.

Three-Tier and Two-Tier Networks

The different types of networks are sometimes classified as **three-tier** or **two-tier networks**, referring to the number of layers of computers in the network. A three-tier network contains three layers of computers. At the top is the host mainframe that is linked to multiple minicomputers. Each mini is linked to multiple micros. The three-tier concept was the norm until the capabilities of micros began to approach those of the multiuser minis of the mid-1980s. The increased power of the microcomputer made three-tier networks redundant at the bottom level, thus prompting the concept of the two-tier network. A two-tier network has only two layers of computers, usually a mainframe computer that is linked directly to multiple minicomputers and/or microcomputers. The tier concept is most often associated with the star topology or a hybrid based on the star topology.

The Micro/Mainframe Link

Micros, initially designed for use by a single individual, have even greater potential when linked to mainframe computers. To give micros this dual-function capability, vendors have developed the necessary hardware and software to enable some **micro/mainframe links**. There are three types of micro/mainframe links:

1. The microcomputer serves as a "dumb" terminal (that is, I/O only with no processing) linked to the mainframe.
2. Microcomputer users request that data be **downloaded** (mainframe-to-micro transmission of data) from the mainframe to their micros for processing. Upon completion of processing, user data may be **uploaded** from their microcomputers to the mainframe.
3. Both microcomputer and mainframe work together to process data and produce information.

Micro/mainframe links of the first two types are well within the state of the art, but achieving the third is more involved. The tremendous differences in the way computers and software are designed make complete integration of micro/mainframe activities difficult and, for some combinations of micros and mainframes, impossible.

Local Area Networks

A **local area network (LAN)**, or **local net**, is a system of hardware, software, and communications channels that connects devices in close proximity, such as in a suite of offices. A local net permits the movement of data (including text, voice, and graphic images) between mainframe computers, personal computers, terminals, I/O devices, and PBXs. For example, your micro can be connected to another micro, to mainframes, and to shared resources, such as printers and disk storage. The distance separating devices in the local net may vary from a few feet to a few miles.

A local area network links microcomputers at this company so that managers and administrative staff can share hardware, software, and data base resources.

The unique feature of a local net is that a common carrier is not necessary for transmitting data between computers, terminals, and shared resources. Because of the proximity of devices in local nets, a company can install its own communications channels (such as coaxial cable or optical fiber).

Like computers, automobiles, and just about everything else, local nets can be built at various levels of sophistication. At the most basic level, they permit the interconnection of PCs in a department so that users can send messages to one another and share files and printers. The more sophisticated local nets permit the interconnection of mainframes, micros, and the gamut of peripheral devices throughout a large but geographically constrained area, such as a cluster of buildings.

In the near future you will be able to plug a terminal into a communications channel just as you would plug a telephone line into a telephone jack. This type of data communications capability is being installed in the new "smart" office buildings and even in some hotel rooms.

Local nets are often integrated into "long-haul" networks. For example, a bank will link home-office teller terminals to the central computer via a local net. But for long-haul data communication, the bank's branch offices must rely on common carriers.

MEMORY BITS

NETWORKING
- Network topologies
    Star
    Ring
    Bus
- Multiple tier
    Three-tier
    Two-tier
- Micro-mainframe link
- Local area network
    Also called local net
    Also called LAN

A WORLD OF INFORMATION
AT YOUR FINGERTIPS

Today's microcomputer is much more than a small stand-alone computer. Connect it to any telephone line via a modem and you can interact with other computers at your college, at work, or in other countries. The capability of micros to communicate with other computers has resulted in an explosion of interest in information networks, bulletin boards, telecommuting, and the "electronic cottage."

Information Networks

A growing trend among microcomputer users is to subscribe to the services of an information network. A few of the more popular commercial information networks are CompuServe, The Source, Dow Jones,

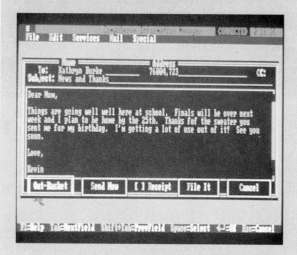

An information network includes such services as electronic mail, electronic shopping, and news.

Western Union, and NewsNet. These information networks consist of one or several large computer systems that offer a variety of information services, from hotel reservations to daily horoscopes. The user normally pays a one-time fee for an account number that will permit him or her to establish a link with the network. Billing is based on usage of network services.

The following list summarizes the types of entertainment, information, and other services available through information networks:

Home Banking.   Check account balances, transfer money, and pay bills in the comfort of the office or home.

News, Weather, and Sports.   Get the latest releases directly from the wire services.

Games.   Access hundreds of single and multiplayer games. Users can even play games with friends in other states!

Financial Information.   Get up-to-the-minute quotes on stocks, bonds, options, and commodities.

Bulletin Boards.   Use special-interest electronic bulletin boards as a forum for the exchange of ideas and information. The largest information network, CompuServe, now has over 200,000 subscribers. Its closest rival is The Source. CompuServe has over 100 bulletin boards to choose from on topics ranging from graphics showing the FBI's most wanted fugitives, to gardening, to astrology, to IBM personal

6–7   LINE CONTROL: RULES
FOR DATA TRANSMISSION

Polling and Contention

When a terminal or a microcomputer is connected to a computer over a single communications channel, this is a **point-to-point connection**. When more than one terminal or micro is connected via a single communications channel, the channel is called a **multidrop line**. Terminals on a multidrop line must share the data communications channel. Because

computers. There are thousands of privately spon-sored *bulletin-board systems* (BBSs). One in Denver is devoted to parapsychology. Some senators sponsor BBSs to communicate with their constituents. Other BBSs are devoted to religion.

Electronic Mail.   Send and receive mail to and from other network users. Each subscriber is assigned an ID and an electronic mailbox. To retrieve mail, the subscriber must enter a secret password.

Shop at Home.   Select what you want from a list of thousands of items offered at discount prices. Payment is made via electronic funds transfer (EFT), and orders are delivered to your doorstep.

Reference.   Look up items of interest in an elec-

tronic encyclopedia. Scan through various govern-ment publications. Recall articles on a particular subject.

Education.   Choose from a variety of educational packages, from learning arithmetic to preparing for the Scholastic Aptitude Test. A user can even deter-mine his or her IQ!

Real Estate.   Check out available real estate by scanning the listings for the city to which you may be moving.

Travel.   Plan your own vacation or business trip by checking airline schedules and making your own reservations. You can even charter a yacht in the Caribbean or rent a lodge in the Rockies.

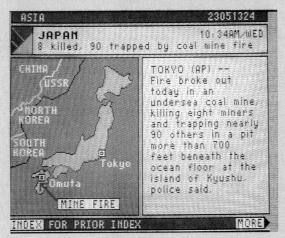

all terminals cannot use the same channel at once, line-control procedures are needed. The most common line-control procedures are **polling** and **contention**.

In polling, the front-end processor "polls" each terminal in rotation to determine whether a message is ready to be sent (see Figure 6–11). If a particular terminal has a message ready to be sent and the line is available, the front-end processor accepts the message and polls the next terminal.

Programmers can adjust the polling procedure so that some terminals are polled more often than others. For example, tellers in a bank are

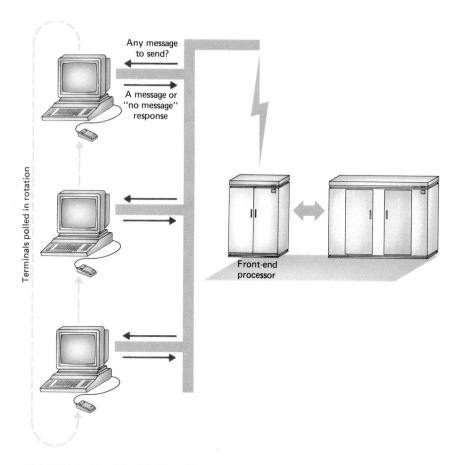

FIGURE 6–11   The Polling Process
Each terminal is polled in rotation to determine if a message is ready to be sent.

continuously interacting with the system. A loan officer, however, may average only two inquiries in an hour. In this case, the teller terminals might be polled four times for each poll of a loan officer's terminal.

In the contention line-control procedure, a terminal with a message to be sent automatically requests service from the host processor. The request might result in a "Line busy" signal, in which case the terminal waits a fraction of a second and tries again, and again, until the line is free. Upon assuming control of the line, the terminal sends the message and then relinquishes control of the line to another terminal.

Communications Protocols

Communications protocols are rules established to govern the way data are transmitted in a computer network. A number of different protocols are in common use. For example, X12 is the standard for electronic data interchange (EDI); X.25 is used for packet switching; X.75 is used for interconnections between networks of different countries; XON/XOFF is the de facto standard for microcomputer data communications; and XMODEM is used for uploading and downloading files. Protocols fall

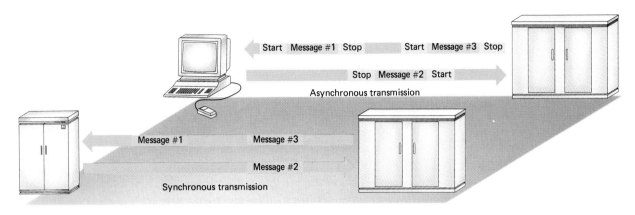

FIGURE 6–12   Asynchronous and Synchronous Transmission of Data
Asynchronous data transmission takes place at irregular intervals. In asynchronous transmission, the message is typically a single character. Synchronous data transmission requires timed synchronization between sending and receiving devices. The message is typically a block of characters.

into two general classifications, **asynchronous** and **synchronous** (see Figure 6–12).

In asynchronous data transmission, data are transmitted at irregular intervals on an as-needed basis. *Start/stop bits* are appended to the beginning and end of each message. The start/stop bits signal the receiving terminal/computer at the beginning and end of the message. A message could be a single character or a short string of characters, depending on the communications protocol. Asynchronous transmission, sometimes called *start/stop transmission*, is best suited for data communication involving low-speed I/O devices, such as terminals and serial printers.

In synchronous transmission, the source and destination operate in timed synchronization to enable high-speed data transfer. Start/stop bits are not required in synchronous transmission. Data transmission between computers and between down-line processors and front-end processors is normally synchronous.

SUMMARY OUTLINE AND IMPORTANT TERMS_____

6–1   **DATA COMMUNICATIONS: FROM ONE ROOM TO THE WORLD.**
Connectivity facilitates the electronic communication between companies, end user computing, and the free flow of information within an enterprise. Modern businesses use **data communications** to transmit data and information at high speeds from one location to the next. Data communications, or **teleprocessing (TP)**, makes an information system more accessible to the people who use it. The integration of computer systems via data communications is referred to as a **computer network**.

6–2   **THE BEGINNING OF AN ERA: COOPERATIVE COMPUTING.** This is the era of **cooperative computing**. To obtain meaningful, accurate, and timely information, businesses have decided they must cooperate internally and externally to take full advantage of available information. To encourage internal cooperation, they are promoting intracompany networking. To compete in a world market, they are encouraging intercompany networking, or **electronic data interchange (EDI)**.

Connectivity refers to the degree to which hardware devices can be functionally linked to one another. Some people expand the scope of connectivity to include other aspects of information systems, such as software and data bases. The ideal implementation of connectivity is referred to as **total connectivity**.

6–3   **DATA COMMUNICATIONS HARDWARE.** The data communications hardware used to facilitate the transmission of data from one remote location to another includes **modems, down-line processors** (also called **cluster controllers, concentrators,** or **multiplexors**), **front-end processors,** and **PBXs**. Modems modulate and demodulate signals so that data can be transmitted over telephone lines. Down-line processors, front-end processors, and PBXs are special-function processors; they not only convert the signal to a format compatible with the transmission facility but also relieve the host processor of a number of processing tasks associated with data communications. One of the duties of the front-end processor is to establish the link between source and destination for sending and receiving messages in a process called **handshaking**.

6–4   **THE DATA COMMUNICATIONS CHANNEL: DATA HIGHWAYS.** A **communications channel (line,** or **data link)** is the facility through which data are transmitted between locations in a computer network. A channel may consist of one or more of the following transmission media: telephone lines, **optical fiber, coaxial cable,** and **microwave radio signals.** Satellites are essentially microwave repeater stations that maintain a **geosynchronous orbit** around the earth.

A channel's capacity is rated by the number of bits it can transmit per second (**bits per second,** or **bps**). In practice, the word **baud** is often used interchangeably with bits per second; in reality, they are quite different.

6–5   **DATA TRANSMISSION SERVICES. Common carriers** provide communications channels to the public, and lines can be arranged to suit a particular application. A **private,** or **leased, line** provides a dedicated communications channel. A **switched,** or **dial-up, line** is available on a time-and-distance-charge basis. **Specialized common carriers,** such as **value-added networks (VANs),** offer expanded transmission services.

6–6   **NETWORKS: LINKING COMPUTERS AND PEOPLE.** Computer systems are linked together to form a computer network. The basic patterns for configuring computer systems within a computer network are **star topology, ring topology,** and **bus topology.** In practice, most networks are actually *hybrids* of these **network topologies.** Networks are sometimes classified as **three-tier** or **two-tier.**

The connection of microcomputers to a mainframe computer is called a **micro/mainframe link**. With this link, microcomputer users **download/upload** data from/to the mainframe as needed.

A **local area network (LAN),** or **local net,** is a system of hardware, software, and communications channels that connects devices in close proximity and does not involve a common carrier. A local net permits the movement of data between mainframe computers, personal computers, terminals, I/O devices, and PBXs.

6–7 **LINE CONTROL: RULES FOR DATA TRANSMISSION.** A communications channel servicing a single workstation is a **point-to-point connection.** A communications channel servicing more than one workstation is called a **multidrop line.** The most common line-control procedures are called **polling** and **contention**.

Communications protocols are rules for transmitting data. The **asynchronous** protocol begins and ends each message with start/stop bits and is used primarily for low-speed data transmission. The **synchronous** protocol permits the source and destination to communicate in timed synchronization for high-speed data transmission.

REVIEW EXERCISES

Concepts

1. Would EDI be more closely associated with intercompany networking or intracompany networking?

2. What is meant by *geosynchronous orbit*, and how does it relate to data transmission via satellite?

3. What is the unit of measure for the capacity of a data communications channel?

4. Expand the following acronyms: TP, bps, VAN, and LAN.

5. What is the purpose of a multiplexor?

6. What is the relationship between teleprocessing and a computer network?

7. At what channel capacity is the bits per second equal to the baud?

8. What computerese term refers to the degree to which hardware devices can be functionally linked to one another?

9. What device converts digital signals into analog signals for transmission over telephone lines? Why is it necessary?

10. Why is it not advisable to increase the distance between microwave relay stations to 200 miles?

11. What is the ideal implementation of connectivity called?

12. Briefly describe the function of a PBX.

13. What is the purpose of the X12 communications protocol?

14. Describe circumstances in which a leased line would be preferable to a dial-up line.

15. Consider this situation: A remote line printer is capable of printing 800 lines per minute (70 characters per line average). Line capacity options are 2.4 K, 4.8 K, or 9.6 K bps. Data are transmitted according to the ASCII encoding system (seven bits per character). What capacity would you recommend for a communications channel to permit the printer to operate at capacity?

Discussion

16. What is the relationship between EDI and connectivity?

17. Discuss connectivity from the perspective of any non-IBM hardware vendor. From the perspective of IBM.

18. Describe how information can be made readily accessible, but only on a need-to-know basis.

19. List and discuss those characteristics that would typify a knowledge worker.

20. Corporate management is evaluating a proposal to allow employees to telecommute one day each week—that is, to work at home with a direct link to the company via a microcomputer. Argue for or against this proposal.

21. The five PCs in the purchasing department of a large consumer goods manufacturer are used primarily for word processing and database applications. What would be the benefits and burdens associated with connecting the PCs in a local area network?

SELF-TEST (by section)

6–1 **a.** The general area of data communications encompasses telecommunications. (T/F)

b. The integration of computer systems, terminals, and communication links is referred to as a _____.

6–2 **a.** Using computers and data communications to transmit data electronically between companies is called: (a) EDI, (b) DIE, or (c) DEI.

b. A company either has total connectivity or it has no connectivity. (T/F)

6–3 **a.** The modem converts computer-to-terminal electrical _____ (digital *or* analog) signals into _____ (digital *or* analog) signals so that the data can be transmitted over telephone lines.

b. The terminal sending a message is the source, and the computer receiving the message is the destination. (T/F)

c. Another name for a front-end processor is multiplexor. (T/F)

6–4 **a.** It is more difficult for a computer criminal to tap into an optical fiber than a copper telephone line. (T/F)

b. A 9600-bits-per-second channel is the same as a: (a) 9.6 kps line, (b) 9.6 K bps line, or (c) dual 4800X2 K bps line.

6–5 **a.** The two basic types of service offered by common carriers are a private line and a leased line. (T/F)

b. A value-added network will always use the transmission facilities of a common carrier. (T/F)

6–6 **a.** A LAN is designed for "long-haul" data communications. (T/F)

b. An end point in a network of computers is called a _____.

c. The central cable called a transmission medium is most closely associated with which network topology: (a) ring, (b) star, or (c) bus?

6–7   **a.** In asynchronous data transmission, start/stop bits are appended to the beginning and end of each message. (T/F)

b. The _____ communications protocol is the standard for electronic data interchange.

Self-test answers   **6–1 (a)** F; **(b)** computer network. **6–2 (a)** a; **(b)** F. **6–3 (a)** digital, analog; **(b)** T; **(c)** F. **6–4 (a)** T; **(b)** b. **6–5 (a)** F; **(b)** F. **6–6 (a)** F; **(b)** node; **(c)** c. **6–7 (a)** T; **(b)** X12.

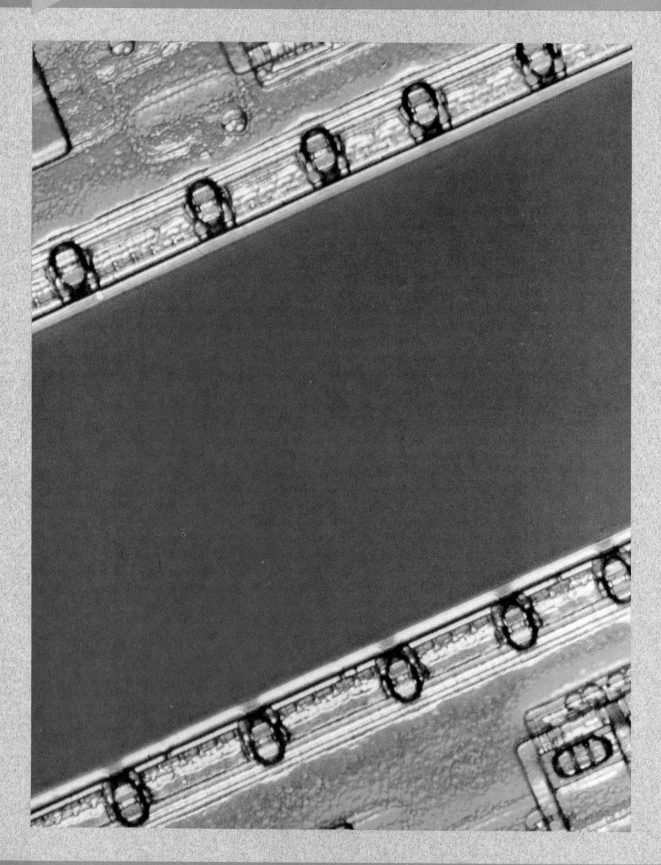

7

Productivity Software: Word Processing and Desktop Publishing

STUDENT LEARNING OBJECTIVES

▶ To distinguish between the three categories of software: general-purpose, applications, and systems software.

▶ To describe the function and applications of word processing software.

▶ To discuss word processing concepts.

▶ To identify and describe add-on capabilities for word processing software packages.

▶ To describe the function and applications of desktop publishing software.

▶ To discuss desktop publishing concepts.

7–1 CATEGORIES OF SOFTWARE

We use the term *software* to refer to programs that direct the activities of the computer system. Software falls into three major categories: general-purpose, applications, and systems.

General-purpose software provides the framework for a great number of business and personal applications. Word processing and electronic spreadsheet software fall into this category. Most general-purpose software is sold as a package—that is, with more specific software and documentation (manuals, keyboard templates, and so on). It is then up to the user of the software to create the application (for example, a letter, report, or sales summary). This chapter and Chapter 8, "Productivity Software: Electronic Spreadsheet and Database," address a subcategory of general-purpose software called *personal productivity software.*

Applications software is designed and written to perform specific personal, business, or scientific processing tasks, such as payroll processing, order entry, or financial analysis. The creation of applications software is discussed in Chapter 9, "Programming Concepts."

Systems software is usually independent of any general-purpose software package or any specific application area. The operating system, discussed in Chapter 10, "Software Concepts and Data Management," is classified as systems software. The operating system controls all activities within a computer system.

Microcomputers and productivity software have become fixtures in every business, educational, and government environment. On board the space shuttle Columbia, astronaut Bonnie Dunbar relies on her laptop computer to help her analyze and document the results of a fluids experiment.

7–2   THE MICROCOMPUTER FAMILY
OF PRODUCTIVITY SOFTWARE

Thousands of commercially available software packages run on microcomputers, but the most popular business software is the family of productivity software packages. The most widely used productivity packages are illustrated in Figure 7–1. They are characterized as productivity tools because they help relieve the tedium of many time-consuming manual tasks, such as retyping and summarizing numerical data. Each package is briefly described below.

- *Word processing.* **Word processing** software permits users to enter, store, manipulate, and print text.
- *Desktop publishing.* **Desktop publishing** software allows users to produce near-typeset-quality copy from the confines of a desktop.
- *Electronic spreadsheet.* **Electronic spreadsheet** software permits users to work with rows and columns of a matrix (or spreadsheet) of data.

FIGURE 7–1   Microcomputer Productivity Software
Popular microcomputer productivity software packages include (clockwise from top left) database, electronic spreadsheet, word processing, presentation graphics, and desktop publishing.

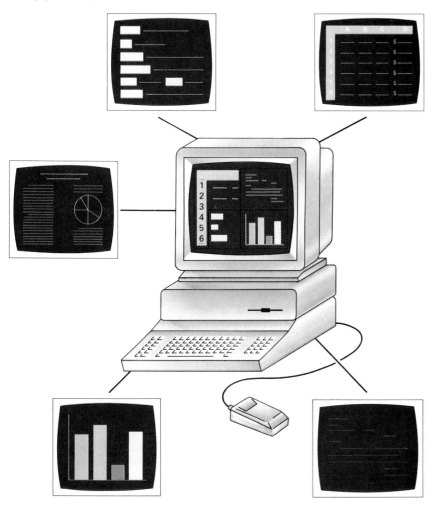

MEMORY BITS

**MICROCOMPUTER
PRODUCTIVITY TOOLS**

■ Word processing
■ Desktop publishing
■ Electronic spreadsheet
■ Database
■ Presentation graphics

■ *Database.* **Database** software enables users to create and maintain a data base and to extract information from the data base.

■ *Presentation graphics.* **Presentation graphics** software allows users to create charts and line drawings that graphically portray the data in an electronic spreadsheet or data base.

The *function*, *concepts*, and *use* of each of these productivity tools are the focus of the first two chapters in Part III, "Software." This chapter covers word processing and desktop publishing. Electronic spreadsheet, database, and presentation graphics are covered in Chapter 8. Appendices E, F, and G contain keystroke tutorials for WordPerfect (word processing), Lotus 1-2-3 (electronic spreadsheet), and dBASE III Plus (database), the most widely used productivity software packages in their respective categories.

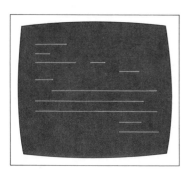

7-3   WORD PROCESSING

Function

Word processing is using the computer to enter, store, manipulate, and print text in letters, reports, books, and so on. Once you have used word processing, you will probably wonder (like a million others before you) how in the world you ever survived without it!

Word processing has virtually eliminated the need for opaque correction fluid and the need to rekey revised letters and reports. Revising a hard copy is time-consuming and cumbersome, but revising the same

At many companies all office workers, including executives, are trained to use word processing. Workers at this company save time and money by using word processing to edit their reports. They find this approach more effective than having a secretary key in their red-pencil revisions from a hard copy.

text in electronic format is quick and easy. You simply make corrections and revisions to the text on the computer before the document is displayed or printed in final form.

Concepts

Creating a document

Formatting a document   Before you begin keying in the text of a word processing document, you may need to *format* the document to meet your application needs. However, if you are satisfied with the software's preset format specifications, you can begin keying in text right away. Typically, the preset format, or *default settings*, fit most word processing applications. For example, the size of the output document is set at $8\frac{1}{2}$ by 11 inches; the left, right, top, and bottom margins are set at 1 inch; tabs are set every $\frac{1}{2}$ inch; and line spacing is set at 6 lines per inch. However, if you are planning to print your document on legal-size paper, then you would need to reset the size of the output document to $8\frac{1}{2}$ by 14 inches.

Depending on the software package, some or all of these specifications are made in a *layout line*. You can have as many layout lines as you want in a single document. Text is printed according to specifications in the most recent layout line in the running text of the document.

Entering text   Text is entered in either **typeover mode** or **insert mode**. On most word processing systems you **toggle**, or switch, between typeover and insert modes by pressing a key, often the insert (or INS) key.

Let's use the draft copy of a memo written by Pat Kline (see Figure 7–2), the national sales manager for a manufacturer of high-tech products, to illustrate the two modes of data entry. When in typeover mode,

FIGURE 7–2   Word Processing: Memorandum
This first-draft memo is revised for illustrative purposes in Figures 7–3 through 7–7.

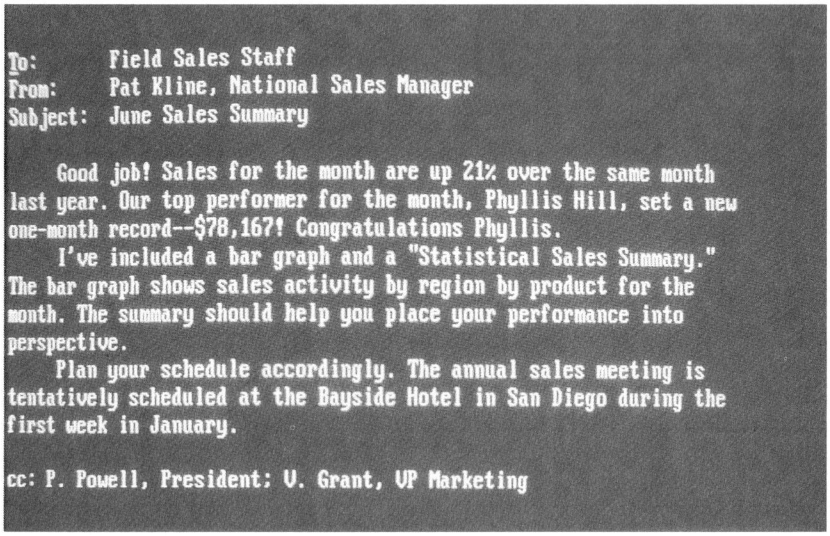

To: Field Sales Staff
From: Pat Kline, National Sales Manager
Subject: June Sales Summary

   Good job! Sales for the month are up 21% over the same month last year. Our top performer for the month, Phyllis Hill, set a new one-month record--$78,167! Congratulations Phyllis.
   I've included a bar graph and a "Statistical Sales Summary." The bar graph shows sales activity by region by product for the month. The summary should help you place your performance into perspective.
   Plan your schedule accordingly. The annual sales meeting is tentatively scheduled at the Bayside Hotel in San Diego during the first week in January.

cc: P. Powell, President; V. Grant, VP Marketing

the character you enter *types over* the character at the cursor position. For example, in the last sentence of the memo, Pat began with *The* and realized that *Our* is a better word. To make the correction in typeover mode, Pat positioned the cursor at the *T* and typed *O-u-r*, thereby replacing *The* with *Our*. When in insert mode, any text entered is *additional* text. Pat forgot to enter the full name of the hotel in the last sentence. To complete the name, Pat selected the insert mode, placed the cursor at the *i* in *in*, and entered *and Marina* followed by a space (see Figure 7–3).

On most word processing packages, text that extends past the defined margins is automatically *wrapped* to the next line. That is, the words that are pushed past the right margin are automatically moved down to the next line, and so on, to the end of the paragraph. In Figures 7–2 and 7–3, notice how the word *during* (in the last sentence) is wrapped to the next line when *and Marina* is inserted.

Word processing permits *full-screen editing*. In other words, you can move the text cursor to any position in the document to insert or type over text. You can browse through a multiscreen document by *scrolling* a line at a time or a "page" (a screen) at a time. You can edit any part of any screen.

When you enter text, you press the ENTER key only when you wish to begin a new line of text. In the memo of Figure 7–2, Pat pressed ENTER after each of the three information lines, after each paragraph in the body of the memo, and after the "copy to" (cc) line. Pat also pressed ENTER to insert each of the blank lines. The TAB key was pressed at the beginning of each paragraph to indent the first line of the paragraph.

FIGURE 7–3   Word Processing: Typeover and Insert Mode
This memo is the result of two revisions of the first sentence of the last paragraph. The The *is replaced with* Our *in typeover mode. The phrase* and Marina *and a space are added in insert mode. Notice how the text wraps around to make room for the additional text.*

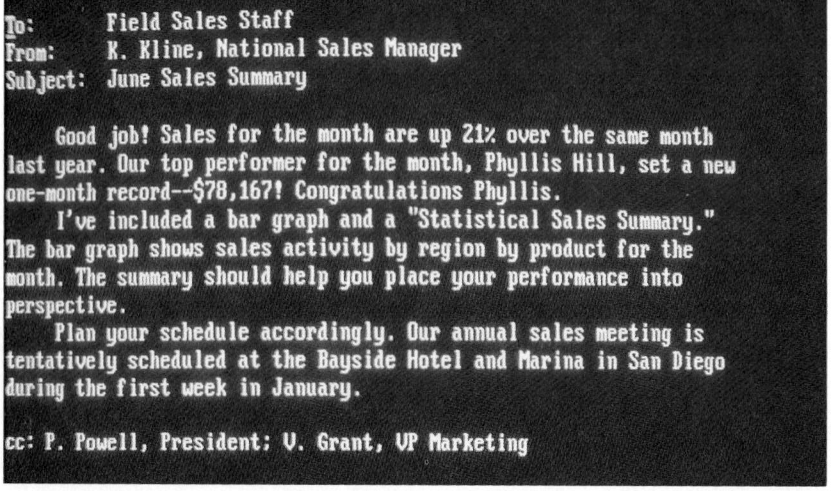

```
To:       Field Sales Staff
From:     K. Kline, National Sales Manager
Subject:  June Sales Summary

    Good job! Sales for the month are up 21% over the same month
last year. Our top performer for the month, Phyllis Hill, set a new
one-month record--$78,167! Congratulations Phyllis.
    I've included a bar graph and a "Statistical Sales Summary."
The bar graph shows sales activity by region by product for the
month. The summary should help you place your performance into
perspective.
    Plan your schedule accordingly. Our annual sales meeting is
tentatively scheduled at the Bayside Hotel and Marina in San Diego
during the first week in January.

cc: P. Powell, President; V. Grant, VP Marketing
```

With a line of over 500 products, this clothing sales representative keeps product information handy in the form of word processing documents. He uses on-screen displays of product information during customer presentations.

As you enter text in typeover mode, the cursor automatically moves to the next line when you reach the right-hand margin. In insert mode, the computer manipulates the text so that it wraps around. This type of text movement is called **word wrap**.

Block Operations.   Features common to most word processing software packages are mentioned and discussed briefly in this section. *Block* operations are among the handiest word processing features. They are the block-*move*, the block-*copy*, and the block-*delete* commands. These commands are the electronic equivalent of a "cut and paste" job.

Let's discuss the move command first. With this feature, you can select a block of text (for example, a word, a sentence, a paragraph, a section of a report, or as much contiguous text as you desire) and move it to another portion of the document. To do this, follow these steps:

1. Indicate the start and ending positions of the block of text to be moved (*mark* the text).

2. Issue the move command (a main-menu option or a function key).

3. Move the cursor to the beginning of the destination location (where you wish the text to be moved).

4. Press ENTER (or the appropriate function key) to complete the move operation.

At the end of the move procedure, the entire block of text you selected is moved to the location you designated, and the text is adjusted accordingly.

The following example demonstrates the procedure for marking and moving a block of text. After reading over the memo to the field staff (Figure 7–3), Pat decided to edit the memo to make it more readable. This is done by moving the first sentence in the last paragraph to the end of the memo. To perform this operation, Pat marked the beginning (*P* in *Plan*) and end (the position following the period at the end of the sentence) of the block. On most word processing systems, the portions of text marked for a block operation are usually displayed in **reverse video** (see Figure 7–4a). To complete the operation (see Figure 7–4b), Pat selected the move option, then positioned the cursor at the destination location (after a space following the end of the paragraph) and pressed the appropriate key. Notice that the text in the last paragraph is reformatted (wrapped) to accommodate the move operation.

The copy command works in a similar manner, except that the text block you select is copied to the location you designate. When the operation is completed, the text block in question appears twice in the document. To delete a block of text, you mark the block in the same manner, then select the delete-block option. The meeting at the Bayside Hotel and Marina was confirmed while Pat was composing the memo in Figure 7–2. To reflect the confirmation, Pat used the

FIGURE 7–4   Word Processing: Marking and Moving Text
(a) *The first sentence of the last paragraph of the memo is marked to be moved.*
(b) *The marked sentence is moved to the end of the paragraph.*

(a)

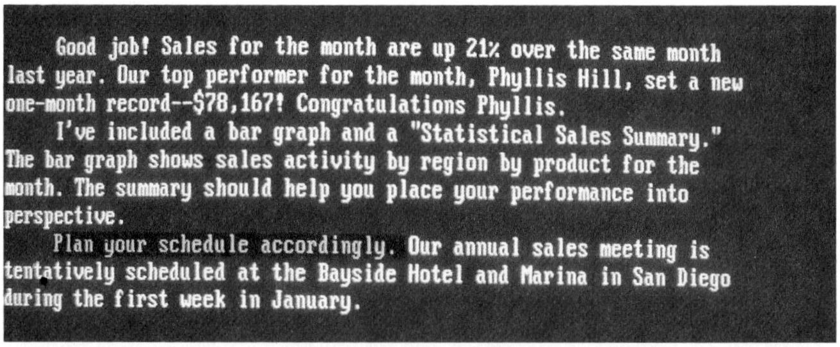

(b)

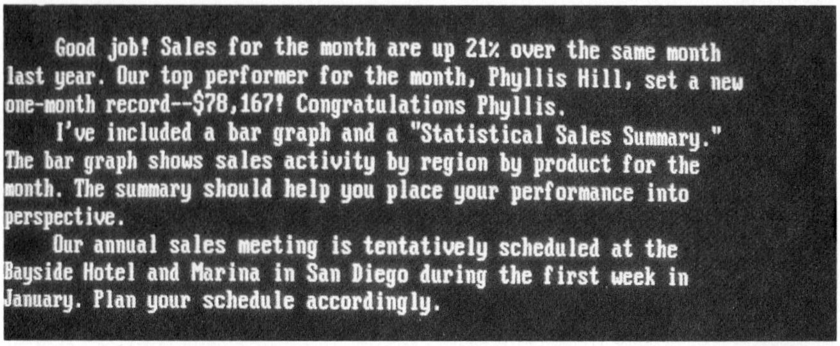

block-delete command to drop the phrase *tentatively scheduled*, then inserted the word *set*. This operation is illustrated in sequence in Figure 7–5.

The Search Feature.   While looking over the memo, Pat Kline decided that it would read better if all generic references to *the month* were replaced by the name of the month, *June*. The necessary revisions in the memo can be made by using any of several word processing features.

FIGURE 7–5   Word Processing: Marking and Deleting Text
(a) The phrase tentatively scheduled *in the first sentence of last paragraph is marked to be deleted. (b) The phrase is deleted. (c) The word* set *is inserted at the cursor position.*

(a)

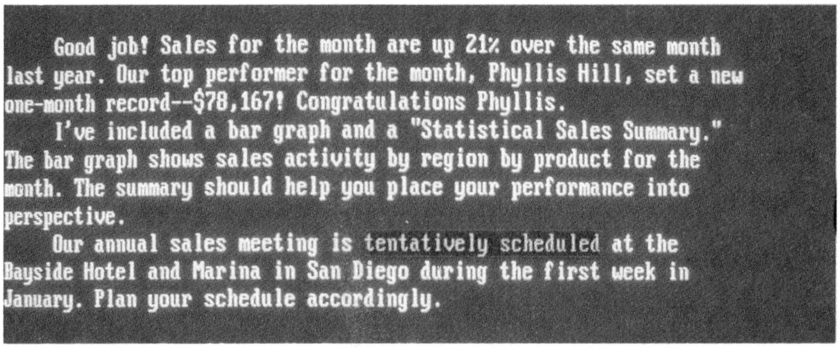

> Good job! Sales for the month are up 21% over the same month last year. Our top performer for the month, Phyllis Hill, set a new one-month record--$78,167! Congratulations Phyllis.
>
> I've included a bar graph and a "Statistical Sales Summary." The bar graph shows sales activity by region by product for the month. The summary should help you place your performance into perspective.
>
> Our annual sales meeting is tentatively scheduled at the Bayside Hotel and Marina in San Diego during the first week in January. Plan your schedule accordingly.

(b)

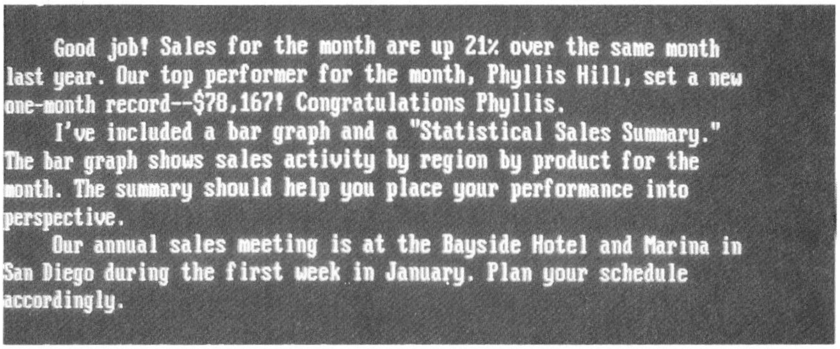

> Good job! Sales for the month are up 21% over the same month last year. Our top performer for the month, Phyllis Hill, set a new one-month record--$78,167! Congratulations Phyllis.
>
> I've included a bar graph and a "Statistical Sales Summary." The bar graph shows sales activity by region by product for the month. The summary should help you place your performance into perspective.
>
> Our annual sales meeting is at the Bayside Hotel and Marina in San Diego during the first week in January. Plan your schedule accordingly.

(c)

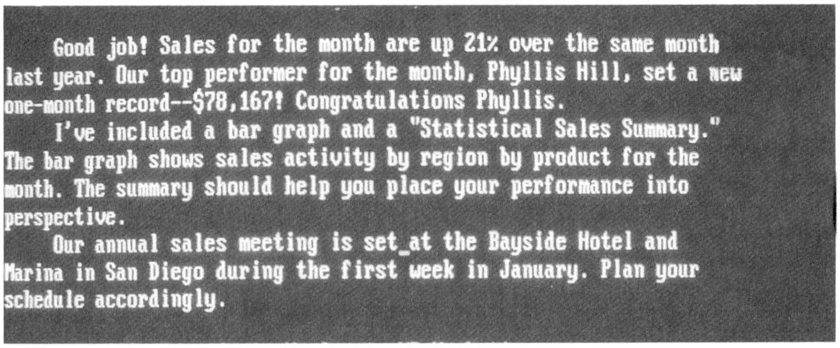

> Good job! Sales for the month are up 21% over the same month last year. Our top performer for the month, Phyllis Hill, set a new one-month record--$78,167! Congratulations Phyllis.
>
> I've included a bar graph and a "Statistical Sales Summary." The bar graph shows sales activity by region by product for the month. The summary should help you place your performance into perspective.
>
> Our annual sales meeting is set at the Bayside Hotel and Marina in San Diego during the first week in January. Plan your schedule accordingly.

One option is to use the *search*, or *find*, feature. This feature allows Pat to search the entire document and identify all occurrences of a particular character string. For example, if Pat wanted to search for all occurrences of *the month* in the memo, the manager simply would initiate the search command and type in the desired *search string—the month*, in this example. Immediately, the cursor is positioned at the first occurrence of the character string *the month* so Pat can easily edit the text to reflect the new meeting day. From there, other occurrences of *the month* can be located by pressing the appropriate search key.

An alternative to changing each occurrence of *the month* to *June* involves using the *search-and-replace* feature. This feature enables *selective* replacement of *the month* with *June*. Issuing the *global search-and-replace* command causes *all* occurrences of *the month* to be replaced with *June*. Opting for the global search-and-replace command, Pat wanted all three occurrences of *the month* to be replaced with *June* (see Figure 7–6).

FIGURE 7–6   Word Processing: Search and Replace
(a) The memo contains three occurrences of the string the month. *(b) The search-and-replace command is used to replace all occurrences of* the month *with* June.

(a)

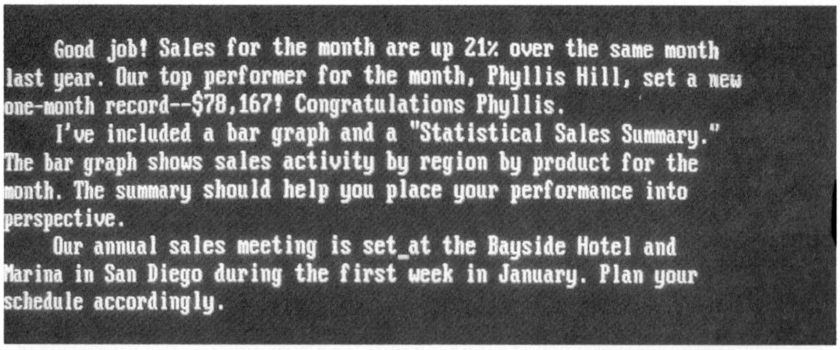

> Good job! Sales for the month are up 21% over the same month last year. Our top performer for the month, Phyllis Hill, set a new one-month record--$78,167! Congratulations Phyllis.
> I've included a bar graph and a "Statistical Sales Summary." The bar graph shows sales activity by region by product for the month. The summary should help you place your performance into perspective.
> Our annual sales meeting is set at the Bayside Hotel and Marina in San Diego during the first week in January. Plan your schedule accordingly.

(b)

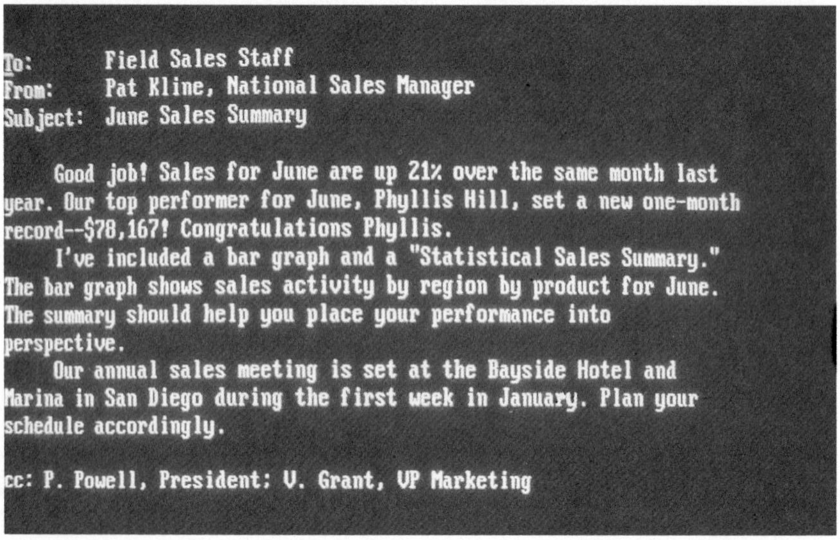

> To: Field Sales Staff
> From: Pat Kline, National Sales Manager
> Subject: June Sales Summary
>
> Good job! Sales for June are up 21% over the same month last year. Our top performer for June, Phyllis Hill, set a new one-month record--$78,167! Congratulations Phyllis.
> I've included a bar graph and a "Statistical Sales Summary." The bar graph shows sales activity by region by product for June. The summary should help you place your performance into perspective.
> Our annual sales meeting is set at the Bayside Hotel and Marina in San Diego during the first week in January. Plan your schedule accordingly.
>
> cc: P. Powell, President; V. Grant, VP Marketing

Features That Enhance Appearance and Readability.   Pat used several other valuable word processing features to enhance the appearance and readability of the memo before distributing it to the field sales staff. First, the manager decided to enter the current date at the top of the memo and use the automatic *centering* feature to position it in the middle of the page. On most word processing systems, centering a particular line is as easy as moving the cursor to the desired line and pressing the *center* function key. The rest is automatic (see Figure 7–7a).

Word processing provides the facility to *boldface* and/or *underline* parts of the text for emphasis. In the memo, Pat decided to highlight

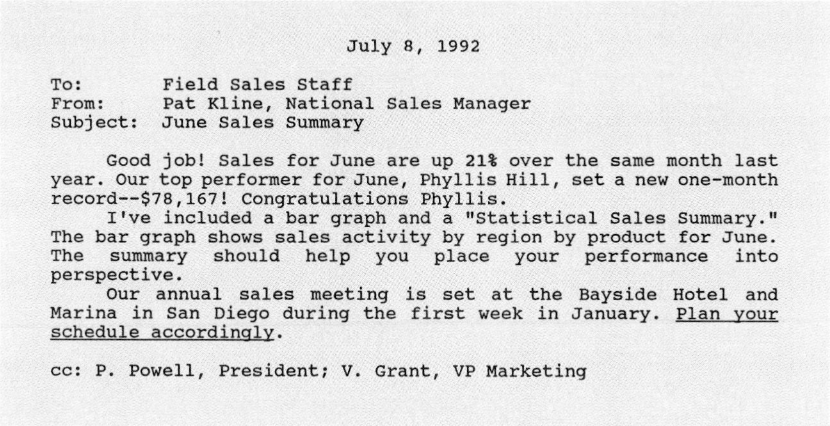

FIGURE 7–7   Word Processing: Centering, Boldface, and Underlined
(a) The date is centered at the top of the memo. On a color monitor, text to be in printed in boldface type or underlined is displayed in different colors. (b) The memo is printed on a desktop page printer.

(a)

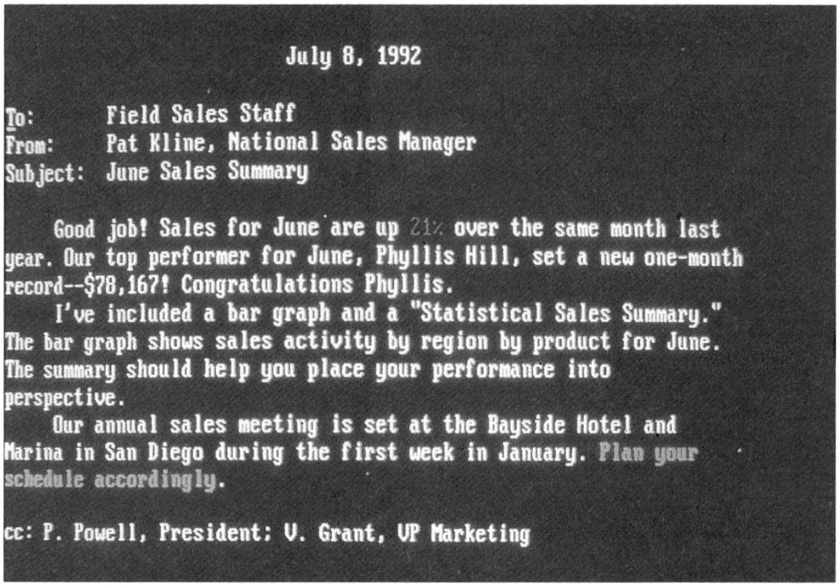

(b)

the remarkable 21% increase in sales by requesting that it be printed in boldface type (see Figure 7–7b). To do so, the manager marked 21% and issued the boldface command. To make the point that sales representatives should plan now for the January meeting, Pat followed a similar procedure to make sure the last sentence is underlined on output (see Figure 7–7b).

On color monitors, highlighted words usually appear on the screen in a different color (Figure 7–7a). Some word processing systems display text that is to be in boldface type or underlined on output in reverse video

FIGURE 7–8   Word Processing: Displaying Boldface and Underlined Text
(a) Boldface and underline are displayed in reverse video on some monitors. (b) High-resolution monitors can display boldface and underlined text.

(a)

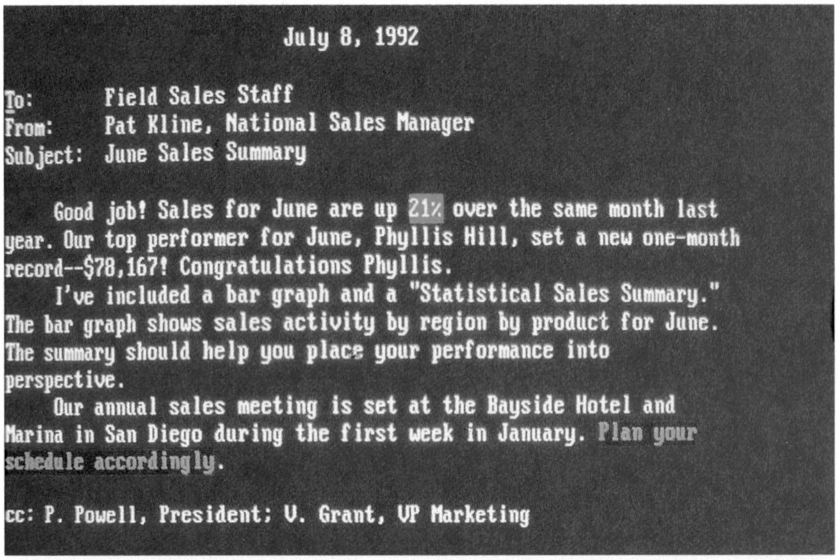

```
                        July 8, 1992

To:      Field Sales Staff
From:    Pat Kline, National Sales Manager
Subject: June Sales Summary

    Good job! Sales for June are up 21% over the same month last
year. Our top performer for June, Phyllis Hill, set a new one-month
record--$78,167! Congratulations Phyllis.
    I've included a bar graph and a "Statistical Sales Summary."
The bar graph shows sales activity by region by product for June.
The summary should help you place your performance into
perspective.
    Our annual sales meeting is set at the Bayside Hotel and
Marina in San Diego during the first week in January. Plan your
schedule accordingly.

cc: P. Powell, President; V. Grant, VP Marketing
```

(b)

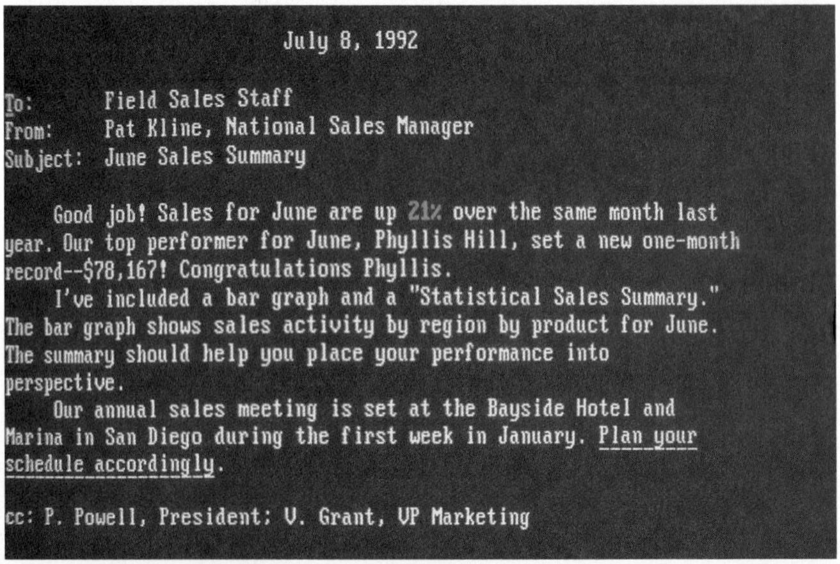

```
                        July 8, 1992

To:      Field Sales Staff
From:    Pat Kline, National Sales Manager
Subject: June Sales Summary

    Good job! Sales for June are up 21% over the same month last
year. Our top performer for June, Phyllis Hill, set a new one-month
record--$78,167! Congratulations Phyllis.
    I've included a bar graph and a "Statistical Sales Summary."
The bar graph shows sales activity by region by product for June.
The summary should help you place your performance into
perspective.
    Our annual sales meeting is set at the Bayside Hotel and
Marina in San Diego during the first week in January. Plan your
schedule accordingly.

cc: P. Powell, President; V. Grant, VP Marketing
```

(Figure 7–8a). Systems with high-resolution monitors allow text to appear in boldface and underlined right on the display screen (Figure 7–8b).

To enhance the appearance of a document, some people like to *justify* (align) text on the left or the right margin, or on both margins, like the print in newspapers and in this book. Word processing software is able to produce "clean" margins on both sides by adding small spaces between characters and words in a line as it is output. The right and left margins of the memo in Figure 7–7b are justified. However, Pat prefers the more traditional *ragged right* margin on personal letters. The first paragraph in Figure 7–9 is printed as ragged right.

FIGURE 7–9   Word Processing: Features Overview
Many of the more common capabilities of word processing software are illustrated in this printout.

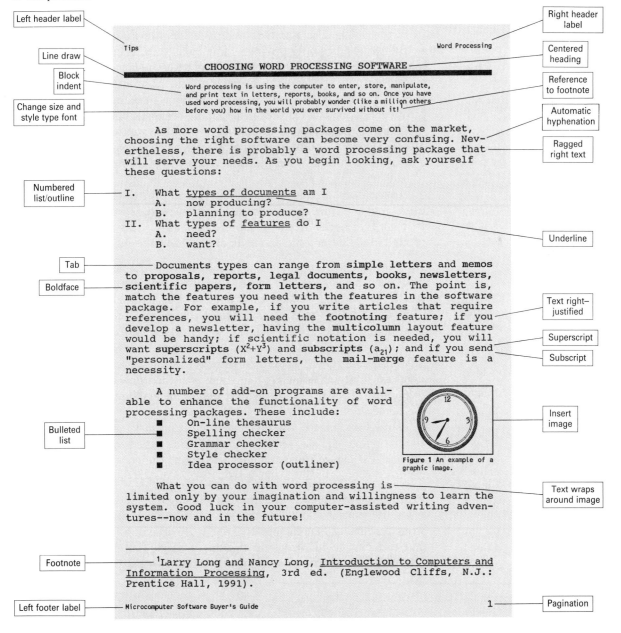

In creating the memo of Figure 7–7, Pat used many but not all the word processing features available to enhance its appearance and readability. Other such features are illustrated in Figure 7–9. Users can *indent* a block of text, cause *header* and *footer labels* to be printed on each page, and request that pages be numbered (*pagination* feature). On long reports, Pat usually repeats the report title at the top of each page (header label) and numbers each page at the bottom (pagination).

The example in Figure 7–9 also illustrates hyphenation, footnotes, numbered list/outline, bulleted list, line draw, superscripts and subscripts, and the insertion of an image into the running text. The *hyphenation* feature automatically breaks and hyphenates words to create a smoother appearing right margin. One of the most tedious typing chores, *footnoting*, is done automatically. Footnote spacing is resolved electronically before anything is printed. The *numbered list* and *outline* features enable descriptive items to be presented in a numbered list or in outline format (shown in Figure 7–9). The numbers and/or letters are inserted automatically by the word processing program. The *bulleted list* is created in a similar manner. Users can create special effects with the *line-draw* feature. This feature permits the drawing of vertical and horizontal lines of varying widths. *Superscripts* and *subscripts* are common in technical writing. One of the most popular features of the more sophisticated word processing programs is the ability to *insert images* into the running text. In Figure 7–9, notice how the text wraps around the image. Not shown in Figure 7–9 is the feature that permits *multicolumn output*, one or more columns of text on a single page.

Depending on the type of software and printer you have, you may even be able to mix the size and style of type fonts in a single document. In Figure 7–9, the headers, footer, quotation, and figure caption are printed in a different size and style of type than the rest of the document.

File Features. Certainly one of the most important features of a word processing package is the ability to store a document on disk for later recall. The stored version of a document is referred to as a *text file*. The *file* feature permits you to save, retrieve, and delete a text file. At a minimum, most word processing systems provide users with the save-, retrieve-, and delete-file options. No matter which option you choose, you are asked by the system to identify the file (document). You then enter an arbitrary name that in some way identifies the document (for example, MEMO). To retrieve or delete an existing file, you enter its file name.

Pat Kline "saved" the memo (stored it on disk) of Figure 7–7 under the file name MEMO. Because the memo is stored in electronic format on disk, Pat can retrieve and edit it to report the sales results for another month.

Printing a Document. To print a document, all you have to do is ready the printer and select the print option on the main menu. Some word processing systems present you with other options. For example, you can choose to print the document single- or double-spaced; you also could be given the option of printing specific pages or the whole document.

PROFILE

The idea for the Apple computer began in 1976 when two young engineers collaborated on a small computing board for their personal use. Steven Jobs and Stephen Wozniak (then 21 and 26 years of age, respectively) took six months to design the prototype. They built it in only 40 hours and soon had orders for 50 of their computers. After raising $1300 by selling Jobs's Volkswagen van and Wozniak's programmable calculator, they opened a makeshift production line in Jobs's garage. Seven year later, Apple Computer, Inc., earned a spot on the Fortune 500, a list of the 500 largest corporations in the United States.

So why the name Apple? They say it was because the apple represents the simplicity they were trying to achieve in the design and use of their computer.

Jobs, former chairman of the board of Apple Computer, Inc., oversaw Apple's growth to a $2 billion company. He is currently chairman and president of NeXT, Inc., whose mission is to collaborate with institutions of higher

education to develop innovative, personal, and affordable workstation solutions for the 1990s and beyond. In recognition of his pioneering work, he was awarded the National Technology Medal by President Reagan in 1985.

Most word processing packages are considered **WYSIWYG** (pro-nounced *WIZ-e-wig*), short for "What you see is what you get." What you see on the screen is essentially what the document will look like when it is printed. WYSIWYG is slightly misleading in that what you see while editing a document is *not exactly* what you get. For example, the text you see on the screen may not be right-justified. However, most of the new word processing packages have a *preview* feature that permits you to see *exactly* what the document will look like when it is printed.

Add-on Capabilities.   A number of programs are designed to enhance the functionality of word processing programs. These add-on capabilities are usually separate programs that can interface with a word processing package. They can be purchased separately or as part of the word process-ing package.

Have you ever been writing a letter or memo and been unable to put your finger on the right word? Some word processing packages have an **on-line thesaurus**! Suppose you have just written: *The Grand Canyon certainly is beautiful.* But *beautiful* is not quite the right word. Your elec-tronic thesaurus is always ready with suggestions: *pretty, gorgeous, exquisite, angelic, pulchritudinous, ravishing,* and so on.

If spelling is a problem, then word processing is the answer. Once you have entered the text and formatted the document the way you want it, you can call on the **spelling checker** capability. The spelling checker checks every word in the text against an **electronic dictionary** (usually from 75,000 to 150,000 words) and alerts you if a word is not in the dictionary. Upon finding an unidentified word, the spell function normally will give you several options:

1. You can correct the spelling.

2. You can ignore the word and continue scanning the text. Normally you do this when a word is spelled correctly but is not in the dictionary (for example, a company name such as Zimco).

3. You can ask for possible spellings. The spell function then gives you a list of words of similar spelling from which to choose. For example, assume that Pat left out the *o* in *month*. Upon finding the nonword *mnth*, the spelling checker might suggest the following alternatives: *math, month, moth, myth,* and *nth.*

4. You can add the word to the dictionary and continue scanning.

Grammar and style checkers are the electronic version of a copy editor. A **grammar checker** highlights grammatical concerns and deviations from conventions. For example, it highlights split infinitives, phrases with redundant words (*very highest*), misuse of capital letters (*JOhn or MarY*), subject and verb mismatches (*they was*), double words (*and and*), and punctuation errors. When applied to the memo in Figure 7–7, the grammar checker noted the incomplete sentence at the end. of the first paragraph ("Congratulations Phyllis"). A **style checker** alerts users to such writing concerns as sexist words or phrases (*chairman*), long or complex sentence structures, clichés (*the bottom line*), and sentences written in the passive rather than the active voice.

Like word processing software, an **idea processor** permits the manipulation of text, but with a different twist. It deals with one-line explanations of items: ideas, points, notes, and so on. Idea processors, which are also called **outliners**, can be used to organize these single-line items into an outline format. Some people have referred to the idea processor as an electronic version of the yellow notepad. When you use it, you can focus your attention on the thought process by letting the computer help document your ideas.

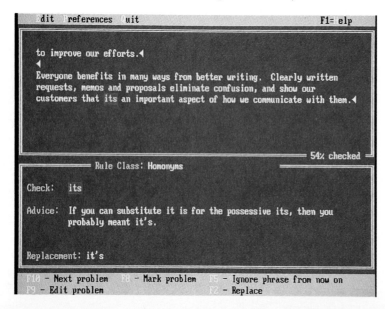

This screen illustrates how Grammatik IV handles a problem encountered while scanning a word processing document for grammar, style, usage, punctuation, and spelling errors. In the example, the program advises the user to replace *its* with the homonym *it's.* The user has the option of taking no action and going on to the next problem; editing the problem; marking it for later examination; ignoring similar problems for the rest of the scan; or replacing *its* with *it's.*

The more sophisticated word processing packages provide users with the capability of doing rudimentary *desktop publishing*. Desktop publishing is discussed in detail in Section 7–4.

Use

Mail Merge.   You can create just about any kind of text-based document with word processing: letters, reports, books, articles, forms, memos, tables, and so on. The features of some word processing packages go beyond the generation of text documents, however. For example, some word processing systems provide the capability of merging parts of a data base with the text of a document. An example of this *mail-merge* application is illustrated in Figure 7–10. In the example, Zimco Enter-

FIGURE 7–10   Merging Data with Word Processing
The names and addresses from a customer master file are retrieved from secondary storage and are merged with the text of a letter. In the actual letter, the appropriate data items are inserted for *First Name*, *Company*, *Address*, *City*, and so on. In this way, a "personalized" letter can be sent to each customer.

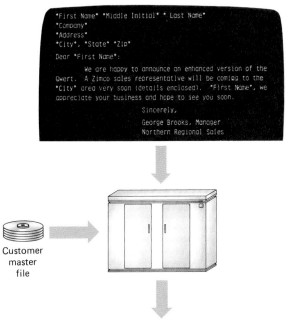

Customer
master
file

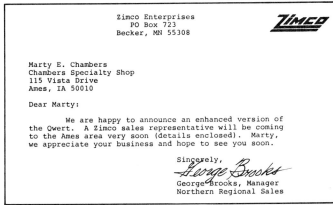

Many executives have become so accustomed to writing memos, preparing meeting agendas, and documenting ideas with word processing software that they take a portable computer along when they travel.

prises announced the enhanced version of its Qwert, one of its hottest selling items. Each regional sales manager sent a "personal" letter to every one of the thousands of Zimco customers in his or her respective region. Using word processing, a secretary enters the letter once, stores it on the disk, then simply merges the customer name-and-address file (also stored on the disk) with the letter. The letters then can be printed with the proper addresses and salutations. Figure 7–10 illustrates how the Qwert announcement letter could be merged with the customer name-and-address file to produce a "personalized" letter.

Boilerplate. The mail-merge example is a good illustration of the use of **boilerplate**. Boilerplate is existing text that can in some way be customized to be used in a variety of word processing applications. One of the beauties of word processing is that you can accumulate text on

FIGURE 7–11   Integrating Text with Graphics
The bar graph and the "Statistical Sales Summary" referred to in the memo of Figure 7–7 are combined in the same word processing document and printed on a desktop page printer. The bar graph and summary were produced using electronic spreadsheet software.

July 8, 1992

To: Field Sales Staff
From: Pat Kline, National Sales Manager
Subject: June Sales Summary

Good job! Sales for June are up 21% over the same month last year. Our top performer for June, Phyllis Hill, set a new one-month record--$78,167! Congratulations Phyllis.

I've included a bar graph and a "Statistical Sales Summary." The bar graph shows sales activity by region by product for June. The summary should help you place your performance into perspective.

Our annual sales meeting is set at the Bayside Hotel and Marina in San Diego during the first week in January. Plan your schedule accordingly.

cc: P. Powell, President; V. Grant, VP Marketing

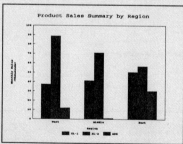

Figure 1   Region/Product Graph

***** STATISTICAL SALES SUMMARY *****				
SALES BY REP.	XL-1	XL-2	MPX	TOTAL
LOW	$15,570	$24,660	$0	$48,305
AVG.	$21,551	$36,069	$7,250	$64,869
HIGH	$28,067	$58,388	$25,440	$78,167
RANGE	$12,497	$33,728	$25,440	$29,862

Figure 2   Sales Stats

disk storage that eventually will help you meet other word processing needs. You can even *buy* boilerplate.

The legal profession offers some of the best examples of the use of boilerplate. Simple wills, uncontested divorces, individual bankruptcies, real estate transfers, and other straightforward legal documents may be as much as 95% boilerplate. Even more complex legal documents may be as much as 80% boilerplate. Once the appropriate boilerplate has been merged into a document, the lawyer edits the document to add transition sentences and the variables, such as the names of the litigants. Besides the obvious improvement in productivity, lawyers can be relatively confident that their documents are accurate and complete. Lawyers, of course, do not have a monopoly on boilerplate. Its use is common in all areas of business, education, government, and personal endeavor.

Integration of Text and Graphics.   Most state-of-the-art word processing packages enable the integration of text and graphic images. For example, the text in Figure 7–11 refers to a "bar graph" and a "Statistical Sales Summary." Figure 7–11 shows how the memo, the bar graph (produced with electronic spreadsheet software), and the sales summary (from an electronic spreadsheet file) can be integrated into a single word processing document.

Summary.   Word processing is the perfect example of how automation can be used to increase productivity and foster creativity. It minimizes the effort you must devote to the routine aspects of writing so you can focus your attention on its creative aspects. Most word processing users will agree that their writing styles have improved measurably. The finished product is less verbose, better organized, devoid of spelling errors, and, of course, more visually appealing.

7–4   DESKTOP PUBLISHING

Function

The ultimate extension of word processing is *desktop publishing*, sometimes abbreviated as **DTP**. Desktop publishing refers to the capability of producing *near-typeset-quality copy* from the confines of a desktop. The concept of desktop publishing is changing the way companies, government agencies, and individuals approach printing newsletters, brochures, user manuals, pamphlets, restaurant menus, periodicals, greeting cards, and thousands of other items.

Concepts

Traditionally, drafts of documents to be printed are delivered to commercial typographers to be typeset. The typeset text is physically pasted together with photos, artwork, ruled lines, and so on to achieve the final layout. Desktop publishing has made it possible to eliminate this typesetting and pasteup process for those documents that require only near-typeset quality (for example, those documents produced by desktop page printers with 300 to 600 dots per inch). In practice, near-typeset-quality copy is acceptable for most printed documents. Relatively few

THE PLOT THICKENS: WILL IT BE MCA, EISA, OR NUBUS?

Since the emergence of microcomputers in the mid-1970s, the dominant PCs have been the Apple II series, the Apple Macintosh series, the IBM PC series (and its compatibles), and the IBM PS/2 series. Dozens of manufacturers make clones of the IBM PC and the low-end PS/2 micros; however, the cloning may end with the next generation of microcomputers. The new micros permit concurrent processing, that is, more than one computer can compete for the resources linked to the common 32-bit electrical bus. In effect, this means that the user can assign one processor to one job (word processing) and another to a different job (printing invoices).

A group of prominent manufacturers of IBM-PC–compatible computers, known as the Gang of Nine (Compaq Computer Corporation, Hewlett Packard Company, AST Research Inc., Zenith Data Systems, Tandy Corporation, and others), has decided to break away from IBM design architectures. The Gang of Nine is banking on their collective strength being great enough to offset the market dominance that IBM has enjoyed for decades. Now, we as users are being asked to make a choice that may affect our computing environment for years. For the overwhelming majority of micro users, the choice used to be between IBM and Apple. Now the Gang of Nine is proposing a third alternative.

The concurrent processing environment being pursued by IBM is called Micro Channel Architecture, or MCA for short. MCA is found on the high-end PS/2 line of computers. Apple's state-of-the-art architecture, called Nubus, is being installed on high-end Macintosh computers. The Gang of Nine created and adopted the Extended Industry Standard Architecture, or EISA (rhymes with *visa*). These maverick manufacturers are using EISA architecture as the basis for micros powered by the Intel 80386 and 80486 microprocessors.

The MCA and EISA architectures enable processors to take greater advantage of computing resources, especially random-access memory (RAM). The IBM PC and compatible computers limit the applications software to 640 Kb of RAM. This limits the size and, therefore, the potential of applications software developed for IBM-PC–compatible computers. The RAM limit for applications software on MCA- and EISA-based micros is 16 Mb. Unlike the MCA, EISA is compatible with the millions of 8-bit and 16-bit add-on boards that users have been combining with IBM PC and compatible computers.

Many power users of IBM-PC–compatible microcomputers are ready to make the transition to the next generation of micros. Corporate decision makers also are aware that a transition to the next level is inevitable. The question remains: "Which architecture will emerge as the industry standard—MCA, EISA, or Nubus?" Most will agree that Apple has an established niche in the marketplace and enough loyal followers to maintain its position. The real question is whether IBM with MCA or the Gang of Nine (and others) with EISA will emerge as the architecture of choice for the next generation of micros.

The vast majority of the IBM-PC–compatible users has yet to exploit the potential of the Intel 8088, 8086, 80286, and 80386 microprocessors. These people will not be directly affected by the resolution of the MCA versus EISA debate until well into the 1990s. However, anyone needing the power of the Intel 80486 microprocessor (roughly equivalent to an average minicomputer), may have to make a big decision.

need to be prepared using the expensive commercial phototypesetting process (which uses 1200 dpi or greater). The output of the desktop publishing process is called *camera-ready copy*. Duplicates of the camera-ready copy are reproduced by a variety of means, from duplicating machines to commercial offset printing.

The Components of Desktop Publishing.   The components required for desktop publishing include:

■ *Document-composition software.* The document-composition software enables users to design and make up the page or pages of a document. When people talk of desktop publishing software, they are actually talking about document-composition software. Two of the most popular document-composition packages are Xerox's Ventura Publisher and Aldus Corporation's PageMaker.

■ *Font software/ROM.* Most DTP-produced documents use a variety of typefaces, called **fonts.** A font is described by its letter style (Helvetica, Courier, Times Roman, and so on), its height in points (8, 10, 14, 24, and so on; 72 points to the inch), and its presentation attribute (medium, bold, italic, and so on). Each font (such as 24 point Helvetica Bold) is stored on disk or in ROM (read-only memory). When needed to print a document, the fontware (font software) for a particular font is either retrieved from disk storage and downloaded to the page printer's memory, or the ROM cartridge containing the desired font is inserted in the page printer. People engaged in DTP typically will have a minimum of a dozen fonts available for use. The more sophisticated user will have access to hundreds of fonts.

■ *Microcomputer.* Of all of the microcomputer productivity tools, DTP is the most technologically demanding. A high-end microcomputer is a prerequisite for effective desktop publishing. The typical micro used for DTP will be fast (16 MHz or faster) and will be configured with a high-resolution monitor, a mouse, at least 640 Kb of RAM, and a hard disk with a capacity of at least 40 Mb.

■ *Desktop page printer.* The overwhelming majority of desktop page printers configured with DTP systems are laser printers that print at 300 dpi. How-

Desktop publishing software certainly has captured the attention of the business community. Not only can users bypass the expense of professional typesetting and page layout, they also can drastically reduce the time needed to prepare a camera-ready document. Here a designer is creating an ad piece for an amateur photographers' convention. To do this, she is using a microcomputer with a keyboard and mouse for input.

ever, affordable desktop page printers with 1000 dpi resolution recently have been introduced to the marketplace.

■ *Image scanners.* Image scanners (see Chapter 4, "Input/Output Devices"), found on high-end DTP systems, are used to digitize images, such as photographs. Image scanners re-create a electronic version of text or an image (photograph or line drawing) that can be manipulated and reproduced under computer control.

Desktop Publishing Files.   Typically, a DTP-produced document such as a newsletter consists of several files. A long report or a book may be made up of hundreds of files. During the document composition process, each file is assigned to a rectangular **frame**. A frame holds the text or an image of a particular file. Each page is a frame. There also can be frames within a page (figures, photos, logos, columns, and so on).

A DTP document will involve one or more text files, perhaps one or more picture files, a style-sheet file, and a print file. The *text files* are created by a word processing program, such as WordPerfect. Although DTP software provides the facility to create and edit text, it is much easier to do these tasks with a word processing program.

Picture files are made up of **clip art**, line art, scanned-in graphics and photos, and renderings of screen displays (for example, the summary at the bottom of Figure 7–11). Clip art refers to prepackaged electronic images that are stored on disk to be used as needed. (For example, the clock in Figure 7–9 is clip art.)

In the traditional approach to publishing, the designer of a print job (a book or a restaurant menu) creates a style sheet that provides the information needed by the typesetter (for example, size and typeface for first-level headings). In DTP, the user creates a *style-sheet file* that tells the document-composition software what to do with the text. To create the style-sheet file, the user must go into the document and *tag* each paragraph with the appropriate typographical attributes (type style, size, italics or bold, and so on). The *print file* contains all the information

This personnel manager has just received one of the most important components of her desktop publishing system—a desktop page printer. The printer enables her to generate near-typeset-quality copy for the personnel department's monthly employee benefits newsletter.

needed to combine the text and picture files with the style sheet and print the document.

The Document-Composition Process.   The document-composition process involves integrating graphics, photos, text, and other elements into a visually appealing *document layout*. With DTP, you can produce finished, professional-looking documents in four steps (see Figure 7–12).

FIGURE 7–12   Preparing a Document with Desktop Publishing Software
Desktop publishing software combines text prepared with word processing software with images from a variety of sources and loads each into prepositioned frames. The graph and spreadsheet frames appear within the frame of the word processing text. The style sheet combines the elements, and the document is printed.

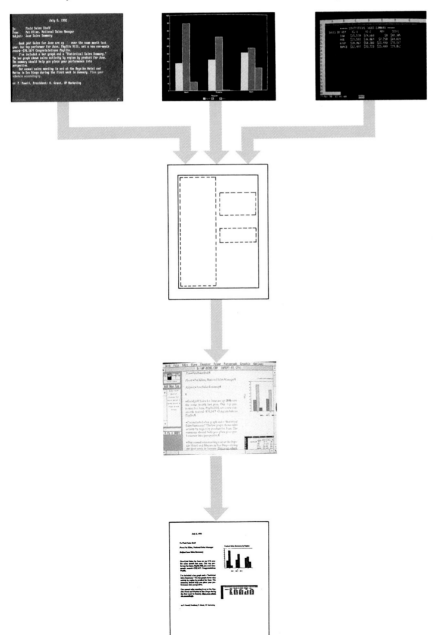

1. *Prepare text and graphics.* Use your word processing software to create and edit the text of your document. For illustrations you can use clip art, computer-created graphics (such as a pie graph), or scanned images (photos).

2. *Create the style sheet.* Define the document format (for example, margins and number of columns) and text attributes. Once a style-sheet file for a particular job is created, it can be applied to similar text files (for example, monthly newsletters).

3. *Combine text and picture files.* Create and position needed frames, then insert text and picture files to fit your needs. The DTP display is WYSIWYG—that is, "What you see is what you get"—when the document is printed. If what you see is not what you want, then you can use the mouse to reposition text and graphics to the desired locations.

4. *Print the document.* Once the WYSIWYG display shows what you want, use a desktop page printer to produce the finished camera-ready copy.

Use

Desktop publishing software is being used to produce the copy for every conceivable type of printed matter, from graduation certificates to full-length books. One problem with desktop publishing is that the capability of producing camera-ready documents is now available to a large number of people, many of whom do not have the artistic skills needed to produce aesthetically pleasing and functionally readable copy. Recognizing this, many companies are adopting standards and policies that apply to all copy printed with the company logo that is released to the public.

SUMMARY OUTLINE AND IMPORTANT TERMS

7–1 **CATEGORIES OF SOFTWARE.** Software directs the activities of the computer system. Software falls into three general categories: general-purpose, applications, and systems. **General-purpose software** provides the framework for a great number of business and personal applications, such as word processing and electronic spreadsheet. Personal productivity software is a subcategory of general-purpose software. **Applications software** is designed and written to perform specific personal, business, or scientific processing tasks, such as payroll processing or order entry. **Systems software**, such as the operating system, is usually independent of any general-purpose software package or any specific application area.

7–2 **THE MICROCOMPUTER FAMILY OF PRODUCTIVITY SOFTWARE.** The primary microcomputer productivity software tools include: **word processing**, **desktop publishing**, **electronic spreadsheet**, **database** software, and **presentation graphics**.

7–3 **WORD PROCESSING.** Word processing is using the computer to enter, store, manipulate, and print text in letters, reports, books, and so on.

When you format a document, you are describing the size of the page to be printed and how you want the document to look when it is printed. To enter and edit text, you **toggle** between **typeover mode** and **insert mode**. **Word wrap** occurs when text that extends past the defined margins automatically wraps around to the next line. Word processing permits full-screen editing.

The block-move, the block-copy, and the block-delete commands are known collectively as *block operations*, the electronic equivalent of "cut and paste." The search, or find, feature permits the user to search the entire word processing document and identify all occurrences of a particular search string.

Word processing has several features that enable users to enhance the appearance and readability of their documents. These include automatic centering, boldface, underlining, right and/or left justification, indentation, header and footer labels, pagination, hyphenation, footnotes, numbered-list/outline format, bulleted-list format, line draw, superscripts and subscripts, the insertion of an image into the running text, and multicolumn text.

All word processing packages allow users to save, retrieve, and delete files that contain word processing documents. The print function transforms your electronic document into a hard-copy document.

Most word processing packages are considered **WYSIWYG**, short for "What you see is what you get."

Several add-on programs are designed to enhance the functionality of word processing programs. An **on-line thesaurus** is always ready with synonyms for any word in a document. The **spelling checker** program checks every word in the text against an **electronic dictionary** and alerts the user when a word is not in the dictionary. A **grammar checker** highlights grammatical concerns and deviations from conventions. A **style checker** alerts users to such writing concerns as sexist words and hackneyed clichés. **Idea processors**, or **outliners**, can be used to organize single-line items into an outline format. Some word processing packages have desktop publishing capabilities.

Any kind of text-based document can be created with word processing software. **Boilerplate** is existing text that can in some way be customized so it can be used in a variety of word processing applications (for example, mail merge). Most state-of-the-art word processing packages enable the integration of text and graphic images.

7–3 **DESKTOP PUBLISHING.** Desktop publishing **(DTP)** refers to the capability of producing near-typeset-quality copy from the confines of a desktop. The components required for desktop publishing include: document-composition software, font software/ROM (the typefaces, or **fonts**), a high-end microcomputer, desktop page printer, and image scanners (optional).

Typically, a DTP-produced document consists of several (often many) files. During the document composition process, each file is assigned to a rectangular **frame**. A frame holds the text or an image of a particular file.

A DTP document will involve one or more text files, perhaps one or more picture files, a style-sheet file, and a print file. Text files are created by a word processing program. *Picture files* are made up of **clip art** and other images. The *style-sheet file* tells the document-composition software what do do with the text. The *print file* contains all the information needed to combine the text and picture files with the style sheet and print the document.

The document composition process involves integrating graphics, photos, text, and other elements into a visually appealing layout. The steps are: (1) prepare text and graphics, (2) create the style sheet, (3) combine text and picture files, and (4) print the document.

REVIEW EXERCISES

Concepts

1. What is the function of word processing software?
2. What must be specified when formatting a document?
3. What is meant when a document is formatted to be justified on the right and on the left?
4. Text is entered in either of what two modes? What mode would you select to change *the table* to *the long table*? What mode would you select to change *pick the choose* to *pick and choose*?
5. What causes text to wrap around?
6. Give an example of when you might issue a global search-and-replace command.
7. Name four popular microcomputer productivity software tools.
8. When running the spelling checker, what options does the system present when it encounters an unidentified word?
9. What productivity software package provides the capability of producing near-typeset-quality copy for printing jobs?
10. Name two software components and two hardware components of a desktop publishing system.
11. What is the shape of a desktop publishing frame?
12. What term is used to refer to prepackaged electronic images?
13. Which DTP file tells the document-composition software what to do with the text?

Discussion

14. Most word processing packages have a default document size. Discuss other defaults you might expect a word processing package to have.
15. Customer-service representatives at Zimco Enterprises spend almost 70% of their day interacting directly with customers. Approximately one hour each day is spent preparing courtesy follow-up letters, primarily to enhance goodwill between Zimco and its customers. Do you think the "personalized" letters are a worthwhile effort? Why or why not?
16. Describe the relationship between word processing, electronic images, and desktop publishing software.
17. With the advent of desktop publishing, the number of printed items bearing the company logo has increased dramatically. Many companies

require that all such documents be approved by a central DTP review board prior to distribution. What concerns prompted these managers to establish the review board?

SELF-TEST (by section)

7–1 Microcomputer personal productivity software is a subcategory of _____ software.

7–2 Presentation graphics software allows users to create charts and line drawings. (T/F)

7–3 a. Preset format specifications are referred to as _____.

b. To add a word in the middle of an existing sentence in a word processing document, you would use the insert mode. (T/F)

c. Which word processing feature enables the automatic numbering of pages of a document: (a) pagination, (b) page breaking, or (c) footers?

d. The word processing feature that automatically breaks long words that fall at the end of a line is called _____.

e. An on-line thesaurus can be used to suggest synonyms for a word in a word processing document. (T/F)

7–4 a. The type of printer normally associated with desktop publishing is the daisy-wheel printer. (T/F)

b. The output of the desktop publishing process is _____ copy.

c. What device re-creates a black-and-white version of an image in an electronic format: (a) image scanner, (b) image-reduction aid, or (c) vision-entry device?

d. Fontware is that component of the document-composition software that enable WYSIWYG display of DTP documents. (T/F)

Self-test answers **7–1** general-purpose. **7–2** T. **7–3** (a) default settings; (b) T; (c) a; (d) hyphenation; (e) T. **7–4** (a) F; (b) camera-ready; (c) a; (d) F.

8

Productivity Software: Electronic Spreadsheet and Database

STUDENT LEARNING OBJECTIVES

▶ To describe the function, purpose, and applications of electronic spreadsheet software.

▶ To discuss common electronic spreadsheet concepts.

▶ To describe how presentation graphics can be created from electronic spreadsheet data.

▶ To describe the function, purpose, and applications of database software.

▶ To discuss common database software concepts.

8–1   THE ELECTRONIC SPREADSHEET

Function

The name *electronic spreadsheet* describes this software's fundamental application. The spreadsheet has been a common business tool for centuries. Before computers, the ledger (a book of spreadsheets) was the accountant's primary tool for keeping a record of financial transactions. A professor's grade book is also set up in spreadsheet format.

Electronic spreadsheets are simply an electronic alternative to thousands of traditionally manual tasks. No longer are we confined to using pencils, erasers, and hand calculators to deal with rows and columns of data. Think of anything that has rows and columns of data and you have identified an application for spreadsheet software: income (profit-and-loss) statements, personnel profiles, demographic data, and budget summaries, just to mention a few. Because electronic spreadsheets parallel so many of our manual tasks, they are enjoying widespread acceptance.

All commercially available electronic spreadsheet packages provide the facility for manipulating rows and columns of data. However, the *user interface*, or the manner in which the user enters data and commands, differs from one package to the next. The conceptual coverage that follows is generic; it is applicable to all electronic spreadsheets.

Concepts

Pat Kline, the national sales manager for a manufacturer of high-tech products, uses electronic spreadsheet software to compile a monthly

As this radiologist interprets X-rays, a nurse enters his verbal comments into an electronic spreadsheet.

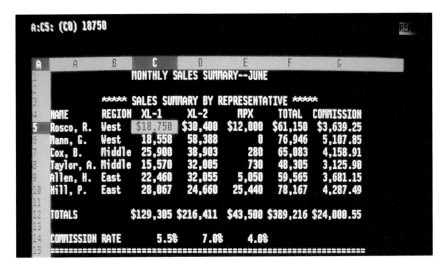

FIGURE 8–1   Electronic Spreadsheet: A Monthly Sales Summary Template
This electronic spreadsheet template is the basis for the explanation and demonstration of spreadsheet concepts.

sales summary. We will use Pat's June sales summary, shown in Figure 8–1, to demonstrate electronic spreadsheet concepts. Pat uses a monthly sales **template** each month. The template, simply a spreadsheet model, contains the layout and formulas needed to produce the summary in Figure 8–1. Pat need only enter the data for the current month (June in the example).

Viewing Data in a Spreadsheet.   Scrolling through a spreadsheet is much like looking through a magnifying glass as you move it around a newspaper page. You scroll left and right (horizontal scrolling) and/or up and down (vertical scrolling) to see different portions of a large spreadsheet. In Figure 8–1 the entire sales summary can be displayed on a single screen. However, if five more products or 20 more salespeople were added, Pat would have to scroll horizontally and vertically to view the entire spreadsheet.

Organization.   Electronic spreadsheets are organized in a *tabular structure* with **rows** and **columns**. The intersection of a particular row and column designates a **cell**. As you can see in Figure 8–1, the rows are *numbered* and the columns are *lettered*. Single letters identify the first 26 columns; double letters are used thereafter (A, B, . . . Z; AA, AB, . . . AZ; BA, BB, . . . BZ). The number of rows or columns available to you depends on the size of your micro's RAM (random-access memory). Most spreadsheets permit hundreds of columns and thousands of rows.

Data are entered and stored in a cell at the intersection of a column and a row. During operations, data are referred to by their **cell address**. A cell address identifies the location of a cell in the spreadsheet by its column and row, with the column designator first. For example, in the monthly sales summary of Figure 8–1, C4 is the address of the column heading for product XL-1, and D5 is the address of the total amount of XL-2 sales for R. Rosco ($30,400).

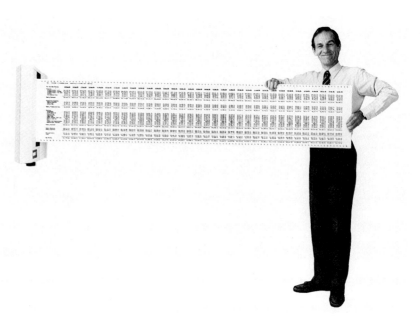

Sometimes an electronic spreadsheet output is too wide for the printer. When this happens, it can be printed sideways. Shown is a 30-year financial projection.

In the spreadsheet work area (the rows and columns), a movable highlighted area "points" to the *current cell*. This highlighted area, called the **pointer**, can be moved around the spreadsheet with the cursor-control keys to any cell address. To add or edit an entry at a particular cell, the pointer must be moved to that cell. The address and content of the current cell (the location of the pointer) are displayed in the user-interface portion of the spreadsheet, the area above and/or below the spreadsheet work area (above in Figure 8–1). Specifically, the information for a particular cell (Cell C5 in Figure 8–1) is displayed in a *cell status line*. The content, or resulting value (for example, from a formula), of each cell is shown in the spreadsheet work area. The current cell is displayed in reverse video (black on white or, for color monitors, black on a color). Also notice in Figure 8–1 that when the pointer is positioned at C5, the actual numeric value (18750) is displayed as the cell contents in the user interface, and an optional *edited* version ($18,750) is displayed in C5.

Cell Entries.   To make an entry in the spreadsheet, simply move the pointer with the cursor-control keys to the appropriate cell, and key in the data. To *edit* or replace an existing entry, you also move the pointer to the appropriate cell. Key in the new or revised entry in the user-interface panel beside the cell address (see Figure 8–1). Once you have completed work on a particular entry, press the ENTER key or a cursor-control key to insert the entry in the actual spreadsheet.

Spreadsheet packages allow the user to vary the column width to improve readability. The width for Column A in Figure 8–1 is set at 11 positions; the width for Column B is set at six positions.

Ranges. Many electronic spreadsheet operations ask you to designate a **range** of cells. The four types of ranges are highlighted in Figure 8–2:

1. A single cell. (Example range is G12.)
2. All or part of a column of adjacent cells. (Example range is A5..A10.)
3. All or part of a row of adjacent cells. (Example range is C14..E14.)
4. A rectangular block of cells. (Example range is C5..E10.)

A particular range is indicated by the addresses of the endpoint cells separated by two periods. (Some packages use only one period or a colon, for example: C5.E10 or C5:E10.) Any cell can comprise a single-cell range. The range for the commission percentages in Figure 8–2 is C14..E14, and the range for the row labels (salesperson names) is A5..A10. The range of sales amounts for the three products is indicated by any two opposite-corner cell addresses (for example, C5..E10 or E5..C10).

When you want to copy, move, or erase a portion of the spreadsheet, you must first define the range you wish to copy, move, or erase.

FIGURE 8–2 Electronic Spreadsheet: Ranges
The highlighted cells in these spreadsheet displays illustrate the four types of ranges: (a) cell (G12), (b) column (A5..A10), (c) row (C14..E14), and (d) block (C5..E10).

(a)

11							
12	TOTALS		$129,305	$216,411	$43,500	$389,216	$24,000.55
13							
14	COMMISSION RATE		5.5%	7.0%	4.0%		

(b)

3		***** SALES SUMMARY BY REPRESENTATIVE *****					
4	NAME	REGION	XL-1	XL-2	MPX	TOTAL	COMMISSION
5	Rosco, R.	West	$18,750	$30,400	$12,000	$61,150	$3,639.25
6	Mann, G.	West	18,558	58,388	0	76,946	5,107.85
7	Cox, B.	Middle	25,900	38,903	280	65,083	4,158.91
8	Taylor, A.	Middle	15,570	32,005	730	48,305	3,125.90
9	Allen, H.	East	22,460	32,055	5,050	59,565	3,681.15
10	Hill, P.	East	28,067	24,660	25,440	78,167	4,287.49
11							

(c)

11							
12	TOTALS		$129,305	$216,411	$43,500	$389,216	$24,000.55
13							
14	COMMISSION RATE		5.5%	7.0%	4.0%		

(d)

3		***** SALES SUMMARY BY REPRESENTATIVE *****					
4	NAME	REGION	XL-1	XL-2	MPX	TOTAL	COMMISSION
5	Rosco, R.	West	$18,750	$30,400	$12,000	$61,150	$3,639.25
6	Mann, G.	West	18,558	58,388	0	76,946	5,107.85
7	Cox, B.	Middle	25,900	38,903	280	65,083	4,158.91
8	Taylor, A.	Middle	15,570	32,005	730	48,305	3,125.90
9	Allen, H.	East	22,460	32,055	5,050	59,565	3,681.15
10	Hill, P.	East	28,067	24,660	25,440	78,167	4,287.49
11							

Text, Numeric, and Formula Entries. An entry to a cell is classified as either a *text* (also called *label*) entry, a *numeric* entry, or a *formula* entry. (Strictly *numeric* entries fall into the formula category in some spreadsheet programs.) In Figure 8–1, the dollar sales values in the range C5..E10 are numeric. A text entry, or a label, is a word, phrase, or any string of alphanumeric text (spaces included) that occupies a particular cell. In Figure 8–1, "NAME" in Cell A4 is a text entry, as is "COMMISSION" in G4 and "MONTHLY SALES SUMMARY-- JUNE" in C1. Notice that the label in C1 extends across Columns C, D, and E. This is possible when the adjacent cells (D1 and E1) are blank. If an entry were made in D1, only the first nine positions (the width of column C) of the entry in Cell C1 would be visible on the spreadsheet (that is, "MONTHLY S").

Unless otherwise specified, numeric entries are right-justified (lined up on the right edge of the column), and text entries are left-justified. However, you can specify that entries be left- or right-justified or centered in the column. In Figure 8–1 all column headings except "NAME" are centered.

Cell F5 contains a formula, but it is the numeric result (for example, $61,150) that is displayed in the spreadsheet work area. With the pointer positioned at F5, the formula appears in the cell contents line in the user-interface panel, and the actual numeric value appears in the spreadsheet work area (see Figure 8–3). The formula value in F5 (see Figure 8–3) computes the total sales made by the salesperson in Row 5 for all three products (that is, total sales is +C5+D5+E5).

Spreadsheet formulas use standard notation for **arithmetic operators**: + (add), − (subtract), * (multiply), / (divide), ∧ (raising to a power, or exponentiation). The formula in F5 (top of Figure 8–3) computes the total sales for R. Rosco. The range F6..F10 contains similar formulas that apply to their respective rows (+C6+D6+E6, +C7+D7+E7, and so on). For example, the formula in F6 computes the total sales for G. Mann.

Relative and absolute cell addressing The formulas in the range G5..G10 (see Figure 8–4) compute the commission for the salespeople based on the commission rates listed in Row 14. The commission rates

FIGURE 8–3   Electronic Spreadsheet: Formulas
The actual content of F5 is the formula in the user-interface panel in the upper left-hand part of the screen. The result of the formula appears in the spreadsheet at F5.

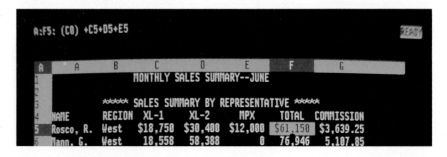

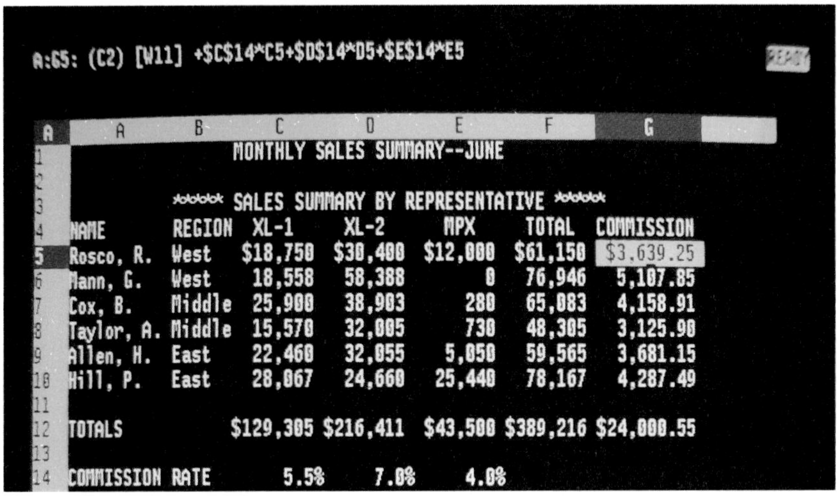

A:G5: (C2) [W11] +$C$14*C5+$D$14*D5+$E$14*E5 READY

	A	B	C	D	E	F	G
1			MONTHLY SALES SUMMARY--JUNE				
2							
3		***** SALES SUMMARY BY REPRESENTATIVE *****					
4	NAME	REGION	XL-1	XL-2	MPX	TOTAL	COMMISSION
5	Rosco, R.	West	$18,750	$30,400	$12,000	$61,150	$3,639.25
6	Mann, G.	West	18,558	58,388	0	76,946	5,107.85
7	Cox, B.	Middle	25,900	38,903	280	65,083	4,158.91
8	Taylor, A.	Middle	15,570	32,005	730	48,305	3,125.90
9	Allen, H.	East	22,460	32,055	5,050	59,565	3,681.15
10	Hill, P.	East	28,067	24,660	25,440	78,167	4,287.49
11							
12	TOTALS		$129,305	$216,411	$43,500	$389,216	$24,000.55
13							
14	COMMISSION RATE		5.5%	7.0%	4.0%		

FIGURE 8–4 Electronic Spreadsheet: Formulas with Relative and Absolute Cell Addresses
Each of the commission computation formulas in the range G5..G10 has the same multipliers—the commission rates in the range C14..E14. Because the relative positions between the commission formulas in G5..G10 and the commission rates in C14..E14 vary from row to row, the commission rates are entered as absolute cell addresses.

vary from month to month. The percentages in Row 14 reflect the rates for June. The commission for R. Rosco is computed by the following formula.

G5: +$C$14*C5+$D$14*D5+$E$14*E5

The distinction between the way the sales amounts and the commission-rate variables are represented in the formula highlights a very important concept in electronic spreadsheets, that of **relative cell addressing** and **absolute cell addressing**. The dollar signs ($), which preface both the column and row in an absolute cell address ($C$14), distinguish it from a relative cell address (C5). *The relative cell address is based on its position relative to the cell containing the formula.* If the contents of a cell containing a formula is copied to another cell, the relative cell addresses in the copied formula are revised to reflect its new position, but the absolute cell addresses are unchanged.

The two types of cell addressing are illustrated in the spreadsheet in Figure 8–5. Suppose the formula B3*$E$1 is in Cell A1. B3 is a relative cell address that is one column to the right of and two rows down from A1. If this formula is copied to C2, the formula in C2 is D4*$E$1. Notice that D4 has the same relative position to the formula in Cell C2 as B3 has to the formula in Cell A1: one column to the right and two rows down. The absolute cell address ($E$1) remains the same in both formulas.

Copying formulas In creating the spreadsheet template for the monthly sales summary, Pat Kline entered only one formula to compute

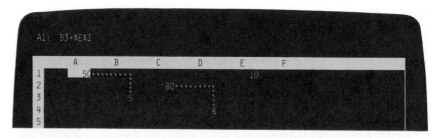

FIGURE 8–5   Electronic Spreadsheet: Relative and Absolute Cell Addressing
When the formula in A1 is copied to C2, the formula in C2 becomes D4∗$E$1.

salesperson commission—in G5 (see Figure 8–4). Then spreadsheet commands were selected that *copied*, or *replicated*, the formula into each cell in the range G6..G10. Notice in the following copied formulas for G. Mann and B. Cox how the absolute addresses ($C14, $D$14, and $E$14) remained the same in each formula and the relative addresses were revised to reflect the applicable row.

> G6:   +$C$14•C6+$D$14•D6+$E$14•E6
> G7:   +$C$14•C7+$D$14•D7+$E$14•E7

The formula in G6 (above) applies to the sales data in the cells adjacent to G. Mann, not R. Rosco (as in the formula in G5). The same is true of other formulas in the range G5..G10.

Creating Spreadsheet Formulas.   This section expands on the use and application of formulas—the essence of spreadsheet operations. A formula enables the spreadsheet software to perform numeric and/or string calculations and/or logic operations that result in a numeric value (for example, 18750) or an alphanumeric character string (for example, *ABOVE QUOTA* or *BELOW QUOTA*). A formula may include one or all of the following: *arithmetic operations*, *functions*, *string operations*, and *logic operations*. The first two are discussed here in more detail. String operations (for example, joining, or concatenating, character strings) and logic operations (formulas that involve relational operators, such as < and >, and logic operators, such as *AND* and *OR*) are beyond the scope of this presentation.

When you design the spreadsheet, keep in mind where you want to place the formulas and what you want them to accomplish. Because formulas are based on relative position, you will need a knowledge of the layout and organization of the data in the spreadsheet. When you define a formula, you must first determine what you wish to achieve (for example, to calculate total sales for the first salesperson). Then select a cell location for the formula (for example, F5), and create the formula by connecting relative cell addresses, absolute cell addresses, and/or numbers with operators, as appropriate. In many instances, you will copy the formula to other locations (for example, in Figure 8–4, F5 was copied to each cell in F6..F10).

Profile

Mitchell Kapor was one of the major forces behind the microcomputer boom in the 1980s. In 1982 Kapor founded Lotus Development Company, now the largest applications software company in the world. The company introduced an electronic spreadsheet product that gave IBM's previously introduced (1981) IBM PC credibility in the business marketplace. Sales of the IBM PC and the electronic spreadsheet Lotus 1-2-3 soared.

Kapor designed Lotus 1-2-3, which is now the industry standard for spreadsheet programs. Over four million copies have been sold.

Kapor has a B.A. in cybernetics from Yale University, a degree held by relatively few individuals. Cybernetics is the study of human control functions and the mechanical and electrical systems designed to replace them.

Currently Mr. Kapor is chairman and chief executive officer of ON Technology, Inc., a developer and publisher of applications software for the Macintosh computer.

Spreadsheet applications begin with a blank screen and an idea. The spreadsheet you create is a product of skill and imagination. What you get from a spreadsheet depends on how effectively you use formulas.

Arithmetic operations   Formulas containing arithmetic operators are resolved according to a hierarchy of operations. That is, when more than one operator is included in a single formula, the spreadsheet software uses a set of rules to determine which operation to do first, second, and so on. In the hierarchy of operations illustrated in Figure 8–6, exponentiation has the highest priority, followed by multiplication-division and addition-subtraction. In the case of a tie (for example, * and /, or + and −), the formula is evaluated *from left to right. Parentheses*, however, override the priority rules. Expressions placed in parentheses have priority and are evaluated innermost first and left to right.

The formula that results in the value in G5 (3639.25) of Figure 8–4 is shown below:

G5:   +$C$14·C5+$D$14·D5+$E$14·E5

FIGURE 8–6   Hierarchy of Operations

The Hierarchy of Operations	
OPERATION	**OPERATOR**
Exponentiation	∧
Multiplication-Division	* /
Addition-Subtraction	+ −

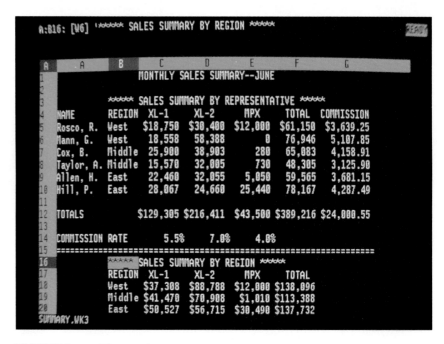

FIGURE 8–7   Electronic Spreadsheet: Adding a Regional Sales Summary
The "Sales Summary by Region" portion of the template is extrapolated from the data in the "Sales Summary by Representative" portion.

Following the hierarchy of operations, the three multiplications are performed first. The products are then added to arrive at the result in G5.

Pat Kline's monthly sales summary template also includes a "Sales Summary by Region" in Rows 16 through 20 (see Figure 8–7). All the formulas in the spreadsheet of Figure 8–7 are listed in Figure 8–8.

FIGURE 8–8   Electronic Spreadsheet: Actual Content of Formula Cells
This figure illustrates the actual content of the cells in Figure 8–7 that contain formulas. In an actual spreadsheet display, the formulas would be resolved when displayed (F5 would appear as $61,150).

```
         A        B         C             D            E          F              G          H        I
 1                          MONTHLY SALES SUMMARY--JUNE
 2
 3                ***** SALES SUMMARY BY REPRESENTATIVE *****
 4     NAME      REGION     XL-1          XL-2          MPX        TOTAL                   COMMISSION
 5     Rosco, R. West      $18,750       $30,400       $12,000    +C5+D5+E5      +$C$14*C5+$D$14*D5+$E$14*E5
 6     Mann, G.  West       18,558        58,388            0     +C6+D6+E6      +$C$14*C6+$D$14*D6+$E$14*E6
 7     Cox, B.   Middle     25,900        38,903          280     +C7+D7+E7      +$C$14*C7+$D$14*D7+$E$14*E7
 8     Taylor, A.Middle     15,570        32,005          730     +C8+D8+E8      +$C$14*C8+$D$14*D8+$E$14*E8
 9     Allen, H. East       22,460        32,055        5,050     +C9+D9+E9      +$C$14*C9+$D$14*D9+$E$14*E9
10     Hill, P.  East       28,067        24,660       25,440     +C10+D10+E10   +$C$14*C10+$D$14*D10+$E$14*E10
11
12     TOTALS             @SUM(C5..C10) @SUM(D5..D10) @SUM(E5..E10) @SUM(F5..F10) @SUM(G5..G10)
13
14     COMMISSION RATE      5.5%          7.0%          4.0%
15     ==================================================================================================
16                ***** SALES SUMMARY BY REGION *****
17               REGION     XL-1          XL-2          MPX        TOTAL
18               West      +C5+C6        +D5+D6        +E5+E6     +C18+D18+E18
19               Middle    +C7+C8        +D7+D8        +E7+E8     +C19+D19+E19
20               East      +C9+C10       +D9+D10       +E9+E10    +C20+D20+E20
```

Functions   Electronic spreadsheets offer users a wide variety of predefined operations called **functions**. These functions can be used to create formulas that perform mathematical, logical, statistical, financial, and character-string operations on spreadsheet data. To use a function, simply enter the desired function name (for example, SUM for "Compute the sum") and enter the **argument**. Some spreadsheet programs require the user to prefix the function with a symbol such as @. (The symbol may vary from one software package to the next). The argument, which is placed in parentheses, identifies the data to be operated on. The argument can be one or several numbers, character strings, or ranges that represent data.

In the spreadsheet in Figure 8–7, the "TOTALS" for each column (C12..G12) are determined by adding the amounts in the respective columns. For example, the total sales for the XL-1 is determined with the following formula.

$$\text{C12:} \quad +C5+C6+C7+C8+C9+C10$$

Or the total sales for the XL-1 can be computed with a function and its argument:

$$\text{C10:} \quad @SUM(C5..C10)$$

The use of predefined functions can save a lot of time. What if the range to be added was C5..C100? Other spreadsheet functions include trigonometric functions, square root, comparisons of values, manipulations of strings of data, computation of Julian dates, computation of net present value and internal rate of return, and a variety of techniques for statistical analysis.

Pat Kline has included a "Statistical Sales Summary" on the second screen of the spreadsheet template in Rows 21 through 27 (see Figure 8–9). The summary uses three common statistical functions: minimum (MIN), average (AVG), and maximum (MAX). The actual formulas

FIGURE 8–9   Electronic Spreadsheet: Functions
The "Statistical Sales Summary" portion of the template is extrapolated from the data in the "Sales Summary by Representative" portion (see Figure 8–7). The statistical summary employs the MIN (minimum), AVG (average), and MAX (maximum) functions (see Figure 8–10).

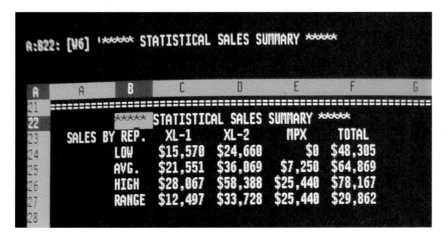

SALES BY REP.	XL-1	XL-2	MPX	TOTAL
LOW	$15,570	$24,660	$0	$48,305
AVG.	$21,551	$36,069	$7,250	$64,869
HIGH	$28,067	$58,388	$25,440	$78,167
RANGE	$12,497	$33,728	$25,440	$29,862

```
         A       B         C           D         E             F
21  ==========================================================================
22              ***** STATISTICAL SALES SUMMARY *****
23  SALES BY REP.  XL-1      XL-2        MPX         TOTAL
24          LOW   @MIN(C5..C10) @MIN(D5..D10) @MIN(E5..E10) @MIN(F5..F10)
25          AVG.  @AVG(C5..C10) @AVG(D5..D10) @AVG(E5..E10) @AVG(F5..F10)
26          HIGH  @MAX(C5..C10) @MAX(D5..D10) @MAX(E5..E10) @MAX(F5..F10)
27          RANGE +C26-C24   +D26-D24    +E26-E24    +F26-F24
```

FIGURE 8–10   Electronic Spreadsheet: Actual Content of Formula Cells
This figure illustrates the actual content of the cells in Figure 8–9 that contain formulas.

in Rows 21 through 27 are shown in Figure 8–10. Vendors of spreadsheet software create slightly different names for their functions.

Formatting Data for Readability.   The spreadsheet of Figures 8–7 and 8–9 has been modified to enhance readability. For example, .055 was entered as the rate of commission for the XL-1 in C14 (Figure 8–7), but it appears in the spreadsheet display as a percent (5.5%). This is because the range C14..E14 was *formatted* so the values are automatically displayed as percentages with one decimal place rather than as decimals.

The monthly sales summary example in the text is presented on a two-dimensional worksheet in rows and columns. Some electronic spreadsheet packages permit three-dimensional spreadsheets. A 3-D spreadsheet has multiple worksheets. This 3-D example contains a monthly sales summary for the current month (June) and the previous two months (May and April). The cell references in 3-D spreadsheets are prefaced with the letter of the worksheet. In the photo, the pointer is on Cell C:C1, the title of the report. The titles of the other two reports are in Cells A:C1 and B:C1. A quarterly sales summary can be compiled in a fourth worksheet (D) by adding like cells in Worksheets A, B, and C. For example, the XL-1 sales by R. Rosco for the quarter would be computed in Cell D:C5 by the formula A:C5+B:C5+C:C5.

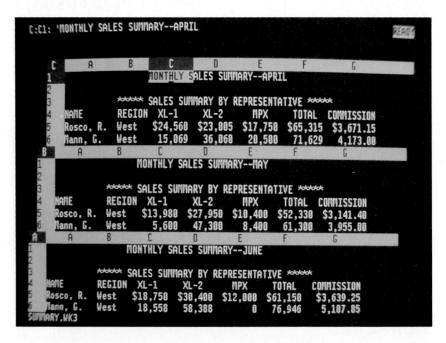

All currency amounts entered in the spreadsheet template of Figure 8–7 were entered without commas or dollar signs. The currency amounts are formatted so that commas and a dollar sign (first row and totals) are inserted. For example, in Figure 8–7 the value for R. Rosco's XL-1 sales was entered as 18750 in C4, which is formatted for currency. Notice that it is displayed as $18,750.

Numeric data can be defined so they are displayed with a fixed number of places to the right of the decimal point. In Figure 8–7, the format of the sales data in the range C5..F10 is currency with the number of decimal places fixed at zero. Numbers with more decimal digits than specified in the format are rounded when displayed. The amounts in the "COMMISSION" column of the spreadsheet of Figure 8–7 are formatted to be displayed as currency with two decimal places.

Use

The possibilities of what Pat Kline, you, and others can do with electronic spreadsheet software and micros are endless. Find any set of numbers and you have identified a potential application for electronic spreadsheet software.

Spreadsheet Templates.   The electronic spreadsheet in Figures 8–7 and 8–9 is a *template*, or a model, for Pat Kline's monthly sales summary. All Pat has to do is enter the sales data for the current month in the range C4.. E10. All other data are calculated with formulas.

Most electronic spreadsheet applications eventually take the form of a spreadsheet template. Once created, the template becomes the basis for handling a certain type of data (for example, monthly sales data).

Modifying a Spreadsheet Template.   Electronic spreadsheet templates are modified easily. For example, any of these modifications of Figures 8–7 and 8–9 would require only a few minutes: Add another column to accommodate a new product; delete a row to accommodate one less salesperson; compute the standard deviation for XL-1 sales data; and change the rate of commission for the XL-1 to 6.0%.

"What If" Analysis.   The real beauty of an electronic spreadsheet is that if you change the value of a cell, all other affected cells are revised accordingly. This capability makes spreadsheet software the perfect tool for "what if" analysis. For example, Pat Kline used the current data to assess how commissions might be affected if each of the rates of commission were increased by 0.5% (for example, from 5.5% to 6.0% for the XL-1). The resulting spreadsheet in Figure 8–11 indicates that the salesperson earning the highest commission (G. Mann) would have earned almost $400 more under the proposed commission rates.

Spreadsheet Summary.   All major electronic spreadsheet software packages are *integrated packages* that offer spreadsheet, graphics, and database capabilities. The presentation graphics capability, which is discussed in the next section, enables graphs to be produced from spreadsheet data. When used as a database tool, electronic spreadsheet software organizes data elements, records, and files into columns, rows, and tables,

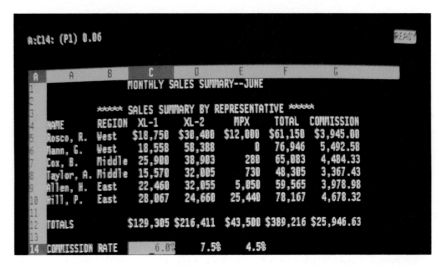

FIGURE 8–11   Electronic Spreadsheet: "What If" Analysis
"What if" each of the commission rates were increased by 0.5%? This spreadsheet reflects the commissions that would have been earned had the increase been in effect.

respectively. For example, in a name-and-address file, each row in the spreadsheet would contain the data items for each individual record (for example, Jeffrey Bates, 1401 Oak St., Framingham, MA 01710). All the records are combined in a table of rows (records) and columns (data elements) to make a file. Many of the capabilities of specialized database software (discussed later in this chapter) are also capabilities of electronic spreadsheet software. These include sorting records, extracting records that meet certain conditions (for example, STATE="MA"), and generating reports.

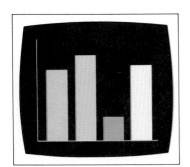

8–2   PRESENTATION GRAPHICS

Function

With presentation graphics software, you can create a variety of graphics from data in an electronic spreadsheet or a data base. Among the most popular presentation graphics are **bar graphs**, **pie graphs**, and **line graphs** (as seen in Figures 8–13, 8–15, and 8–16, respectively). It is also possible to produce other types of graphs. Each of these graphs can be annotated with graph *titles*, *labels*, and *legends*.

The graphics component of an electronic spreadsheet package is usually limited to producing bar, pie, and line graphs from the data in the associated spreadsheet. However, dedicated, or stand-alone, presentation graphics packages offer an extensive array of features. For example, dedicated graphics packages provide the ability to prepare *text charts* (such as lists of key points) and *organization charts* (such as block charts showing the hierarchical structure of an organization), and they provide users with the flexibility of customizing graphs. The functionality of

The information contained in a page full of numbers is seldom obvious and, consequently, may not be apparent to the reader. However, trends, extraordinary efforts, and problem areas become easy to perceive when the same data are summarized in the form of a graph.

graphs prepared by electronic spreadsheet packages and dedicated graphics packages is about the same, but graphs produced by dedicated graphics packages are usually more visually appealing. (For example, pie and bar graphs are three-dimensional).

Graphic representations of data have proved to be a very effective means of communication. It is easier to recognize problem areas and trends in a graph than it is in a tabular summary of the same data. For many years the tabular presentation of data was the preferred approach to communicating such information because it was simply too expensive and time-consuming to produce presentation graphics manually. Prior to the introduction of graphics software, the turnaround time was at least a day and often a week. Today you can use graphics software to produce perfectly proportioned, accurate, and visually appealing graphs in a matter of seconds.

Concepts

Usually the data needed to produce a graph already exist in a spreadsheet or data base. The graphics software leads you through a series of prompts, the first of which asks you what type of graph is to be produced—a bar graph, pie graph, line graph, and so on. You then select the data to be plotted. You can also enter names for the labels. Once you have identified the source of the data (one or more spreadsheet ranges), have entered the labels, and perhaps have added a title, you can plot, display, and print the graph. Any changes made to data in a spreadsheet or data base are reflected in the graphs as well.

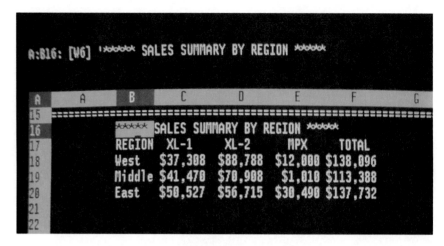

FIGURE 8–12   Electronic Spreadsheet: Sales Data for Graphs
*The bar, pie, and line graphs of Figures 8–13 through 8–16 are derived from
these sales figures.*

Use

Pat Kline, the national sales manager who produced the monthly sales
summary spreadsheet in the last section, is an avid user of spreadsheet
and presentation graphics software. The spreadsheet segment in Figure
8–12 consists of Rows 15 through 20 of the monthly sales summary
spreadsheet in Figure 8–7. The spreadsheet in Figure 8–12 is the basis
for the preparation of bar, pie, and line graphs in the following sections.

Bar Graphs.   To prepare the bar graph in Figure 8–13, Pat had to
specify appropriate ranges; that is, the values in the "TOTAL" column

FIGURE 8–13   Presentation Graphics: Bar Graph
The total sales for each region in Figure 8–12 are represented in this bar graph.

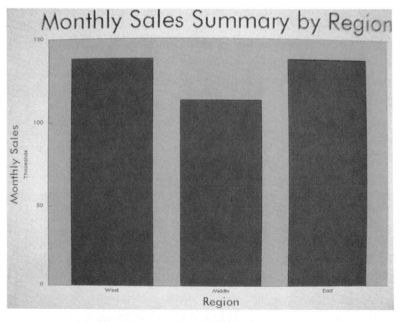

(Range F18..F20 of Figure 8–12) are to be plotted, and the region names (Range B18..B20 in Figure 8–12) are to be inserted as labels along the horizontal, or *x*, axis. Pat also added a title for the graph ("Monthly Sales Summary by Region"), and titles for the *x* axis ("Region"), and the vertical, or *y*, axis ("Monthly Sales").

The sales figures for each region in Figure 8–12 (Range C18..E20) can be plotted in a *stacked-bar graph*. The resulting graph, shown in Figure 8–14, permits Pat Kline to better understand the regional distribution of sales. The *clustered-bar graph* is an alternative to the stacked-bar graph in Figure 8–14. These graphs visually highlight the relative contribution each product has made to the total sales for each region.

Pie Graphs.   Pie graphs are the most basic of presentation graphics. A pie graph illustrates each "piece" of data in its proper relationship to the whole "pie." To illustrate how a pie graph is constructed and used, refer again to the monthly sales spreadsheet in Figure 8–12. Pat Kline produced the sales-by-region pie graph in Figure 8–15 by specifying that the values in the "TOTAL" column become the "pieces" of the pie. To emphasize the region with the greatest contribution to total sales, Pat decided to *explode* (or separate) the western region's piece of the pie.

Line Graphs.   A line graph connects similar points on a graph with one or several lines. Pat Kline used the same data in the spreadsheet of Figure 8–12 to generate the line graph in Figure 8–16. The line graph makes it easy to compare sales between regions for a particular product.

FIGURE 8–14   Presentation Graphics: Stacked-Bar Graph
Regional sales for each of the three products in Figure 8–12 are represented in this stacked-bar graph.

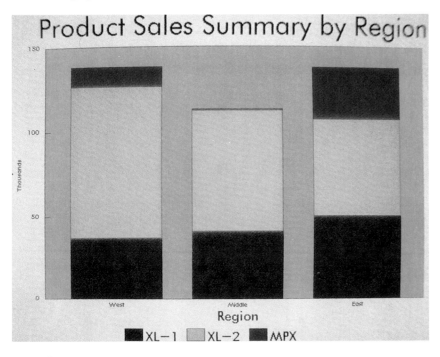

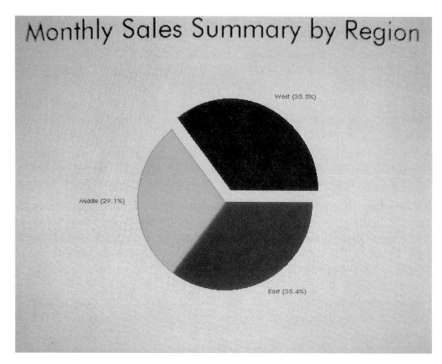

FIGURE 8–15   Presentation Graphics: Pie Graph
*The total sales for each region in Figure 8–12 are represented in this pie graph.
The western region's piece of the pie is exploded for emphasis.*

FIGURE 8–16   Presentation Graphics: Line Graph
*This line graph shows a plot of the data in Figure 8–12. A line connects the sales
for each product by region.*

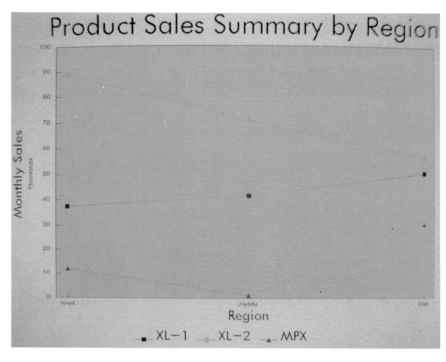

8–3   DATABASE SOFTWARE

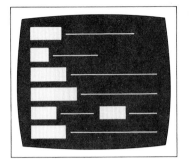

Function

With database software, you can create and maintain a data base and extract information from it. To use database software, you first identify the format of the data, then design a display format that will permit interactive entry and revision of the data base. Once the data base is created, its *records* (related data about a particular event or thing) can be deleted or revised, and other records can be added. Notice that *database* is one word when it refers to the software that manages the data base. *Data base* is two words when the term refers to the highest level of the hierarchy of data organization (bit, character, data element or field, record, file, and data base).

All database software packages have these fundamental capabilities:

1. To create and maintain (add, delete, and revise records) a data base

2. To extract and list all records or only those records that meet certain conditions

3. To make an inquiry (for example, "What is the total amount owed by all customers?")

4. To sort records in ascending or descending sequence by primary, secondary, and tertiary fields

5. To generate formatted reports with subtotals and totals

In the construction business, the accuracy of cost estimates may mean the difference between making or losing money. The historical and current cost data in a data base makes it possible for this engineer to produce reliable estimates of project costs.

The more sophisticated packages include a variety of other features, such as spreadsheet-type computations, graphics, and programming.

Concepts

Many similarities exist between commercially available word processing packages and commercially available electronic spreadsheet packages. With word processing, you see and manipulate lines of text. With electronic spreadsheets, you see and manipulate data in numbered rows and lettered columns. This is not the case with database packages. All commercial software packages permit the creation and manipulation of data bases, but what you see on the screen may be vastly different from one package to the next. However, the concepts behind these database packages are very similar. The conceptual coverage that follows is generic and can be applied to all database packages. The example displays are taken from Paradox (a product of Borland International).

The organization of the data in a microcomputer data base is similar to the traditional hierarchy of data organization. Related fields, such as company name, region, and representative name, are grouped to form records (for example, the customer record in the KEY_ACCT data base in Figure 8–17). A collection of related records make up a data file or a data base. (In database software terminology, *file* and *data base* are often used interchangeably.)

The best way to illustrate and demonstrate the concepts of database software is by example. Pat Kline, the national sales manager from previous examples in Chapters 7 and 8, uses a micro-based database software package to track product sales of important accounts. To do this, Pat created a KEY_ACCT data base (see Figure 8–17) that contains a record for each of the company's nine key accounts. Almost 30% of the company's worldwide sales comes from these key accounts. Each record in the KEY_ACCT data base contains the following fields:

- COMPANY (the name of a key account company)
- REGION (sales region: west, middle, or east)
- REP_NAME (name of field representative who services account)

FIGURE 8–17   Database: The KEY_ACCT Data Base
The KEY_ACCT data base contains a record for each of a company's nine key accounts. The fields for each account (customer company) are described in the text.

COMPANY	REGION	REP. NAME	PRODUCTS			
			XL1 NO.	XL2 NO.	MPX NO.	LAST ORDER
Hi-Tech	West	Rosco	22	35	5	01/11/91
Electronic	East	Allen	48	21	15	02/06/91
Compufast	Middle	Taylor	103	67	42	02/07/92
Zapp. Inc.	West	Rosco	71	85	40	01/16/92
Whizzard	East	Hill	35	45	20	10/12/91
SuperGood	Middle	Cox	24	55	4	12/24/91
Bigco	East	Hill	38	50	21	09/09/91
Actionpak	Middle	Cox	24	37	14	11/01/91
Zimco	West	Mann	77	113	40	01/13/91

Salespeople at computer retail stores usually are happy to give you an overview of the most popular micro productivity software packages. Available in most retail stores are "demo disks" that, when loaded to a PC, demonstrate the features of a software package.

- XL1_NO (the number of XL1s installed at the account)
- XL2_NO (the number of XL2s installed at the account)
- MPX_NO (the number of MPXs installed at the account)
- LAST_ORDER (the date of the last order for one or more XL1s, XL2s, or MPXs)

Creating a Data Base.   To create a data base, the first thing you do is to set up a *screen format* that enables you to enter the data for a record. The data-entry screen format is analogous to a hard-copy form that contains labels and blank lines (for example, a medical questionnaire or an employment application). Data are entered and edited (deleted or revised) one record at a time with database software as they are on hard-copy forms.

The structure of the data base   To set up a data-entry screen format, you must first specify the *structure* of the data base by identifying the characteristics of each field in the data base. This is done interactively, with the system prompting you to enter the field name, field type, and so on (see Figure 8–18). The *field name* is "COMPANY," the *field length* is 10 positions, and the *field type* is alphanumeric, or character. An alphanumeric field type can be a single word or any alphanumeric (numbers, letters, and special characters) phrase up to several hundred positions in length. For numeric field types, you must specify the maximum number of digits (field length) and the number of decimal positions you wish to have displayed. Because the product sales are all defined in whole hours, the number of decimal positions for the XL1_NO, XL2_NO, and MPX_NO fields is set at zero.

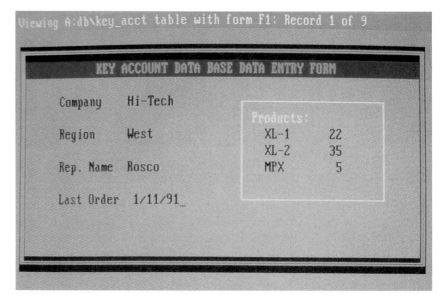

```
Restructuring A:db\key_acct table

STRUCT━━━━━━━━Field Name━━━━━━━━━━┐Field Type┐
        1_   Company                    A10
        2    Region                     A6
        3    Rep_name                   A8
        4    Xl1_no                     N
        5    Xl2_no                     N
        6    Mpx_no                     N
        7    Last_order                 D
```

FIGURE 8–18   Database: Structure of the KEY_ACCT Data Base
This display shows the structure of the KEY_ACCT data base for Paradox, a popular database software package. The KEY_ACCT record has three alphanumeric (A) fields, three numeric (N) fields, and a data (D) field.

Entering and editing a data base   The screen format for entering, editing, and adding records to the KEY_ACCT data base is shown in Figure 8–19. To create the KEY_ACCT data base, the sales manager issued a command that called up the data entry screen in Figure 8–19, entered the data for first record, then entered the second record, and so on. On most database systems, the records are automatically assigned a number as they are entered. Records can, of course, be added to the data base and edited (deleted or revised).

FIGURE 8–19   Database: Data Entry Screen Format
The screen format for entering, editing, and adding records to the KEY_ACCT data base is illustrated.

```
Viewing A:db\key_acct table with form F1: Record 1 of 9


        ╔══════ KEY ACCOUNT DATA BASE DATA ENTRY FORM ══════╗

          Company    Hi-Tech
                                    ┌─────────────────┐
          Region     West          │ Products:       │
                                    │   XL-1     22   │
                                    │   XL-2     35   │
          Rep. Name  Rosco         │   MPX      5    │
                                    │                 │
          Last Order 1/11/91_      └─────────────────┘
```

Query by Example. Database software also permits you to retrieve, view, and print records based on **query by example**. In query by example, you set conditions for the selection of records by composing one or more example *relational expressions*. A relational expression normally compares one or more field names to numbers or character strings using the **relational operators** (= [equal to], > [greater than], < [less than], and combinations of these operators). Several conditions can be combined with **logical operators** (*AND, OR,* and *NOT*). Commonly used relational and logical operators are summarized in Figure 8–20.

Pat Kline wanted a listing of all key accounts in the eastern region, so the sales manager requested a list of all key accounts that meet the condition Region = East in the KEY_ACCT data base (see Figure 8–17). The result is shown in Figure 8–21. To produce the output in Figure 8–22, Pat Kline asks for the names of accounts in the eastern region that have not posted an order since July 1, 1991 (REGION = East AND LAST_ORDER < 7/1/91). Of course, the output can be routed to a display screen or to a printer. In addition, the sales manager can select which fields are to be displayed as a result of a query. For example, in Figure 8–22, Pat may have wanted to display only the COMPANY and LAST_ORDER fields.

The following relational expressions establish conditions that will select or extract records (noted to the right of the expression) from the KEY_ACCT data base in Figure 8–17.

COMPANY = Hi-Tech	(Hi-Tech)
XL1_NO > 40 AND XL2_NO > 30	(Compufast, Zapp, Zimco)
LAST_ORDER > 10*1*91 AND LAST_ORDER < 1/1/92	(Actionpak, SuperGood, Whizzard)
REGION = West OR Middle; MPX_NO < 5	(Hi-Tech, SuperGood)
REP_NAME NOT Rosco	(All but Hi-Tech and Compufast)

FIGURE 8–20 Relational and Logical Operators

Relational Operators	
COMPARISON	**OPERATOR**
Equal to	=
Less than	<
Greater than	>
Less than or equal to	< =
Greater than or equal to	> =
Not equal to	<>

Logical Operators AND and OR	
OPERATION	**OPERATOR**
For the condition to be true: Both subconditions must be true	AND
At least one subcondition must be true	OR

```
Viewing Answer table: Record 1 of 3
```

Company	Region	Rep_name	X11_no	X11_no
	East			

Company	Region	Rep_name	X11_no	X12_no	Mpx_no	Last_order
Hi-Tech	West	Rosco	22	35	5	1/11/91
Electronic	East	Allen	48	21	15	2/06/91
Compufast	Middle	Taylor	103	67	42	2/07/92
Zapp, Inc.	West	Rosco	71	85	40	1/16/92
Whizzard	East	Hill	35	45	20	10/12/91
SuperGood	Middle	Cox	24	55	4	12/24/91
Bigco	East	Hill	30	50	21	9/09/91
Actionpak	Middle	Cox	24	37	14	11/01/91
Zimco	West	Mann	77	113	40	1/13/91

Company	Region	Rep_name	X11_no	X12_no	Mpx_no	Last_order
Bigco_	East	Hill	30	50	21	9/09/91
Electronic	East	Allen	48	21	15	2/06/91
Whizzard	East	Hill	35	45	20	10/12/91

FIGURE 8–21   Database: Query by Example, One Condition
All records in Figure 8–17 that meet the condition REGION = East are displayed.

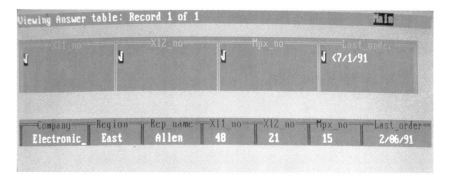

FIGURE 8–22   Database: Query by Example, Two Conditions
All records in Figure 8–17 that meet the condition REGION = East and LAST_ORDER < (is prior to) 7/1/91 are displayed.

The process of selecting records by setting conditions is sometimes called *filtering*; those records or fields that you don't want are "filtered" out of the display.

Sorting Records.   Data can also be sorted for display in a variety of formats. For example, the records in Figure 8–17 can be sorted by company, representative's name, or date of last order. Figure 8–23 illustrates how the KEY_ACCT data base in Figure 8–17 has been sorted by REP_NAME within REGION. This involves the selection of a *primary* and a *secondary key field*. The sales manager selected REGION as the primary key field but wanted the account records to be listed in ascending

Company	Region	Rep_name	X11_no	X12_no	Mpx_no	Last_order
Electronic_	East	Allen	48	21	15	2/06/91
Bigco	East	Hill	38	50	21	9/09/91
Whizzard	East	Hill	35	45	20	10/12/91
Actionpak	Middle	Cox	24	37	14	11/01/91
SuperGood	Middle	Cox	24	55	4	12/24/91
Compufast	Middle	Taylor	103	67	42	2/07/92
Zimco	West	Mann	77	113	40	1/13/91
Hi-Tech	West	Rosco	22	35	5	1/11/91
Zapp, Inc.	West	Rosco	71	85	40	1/16/92

Viewing Key_sort table: Record 1 of 9

FIGURE 8–23   Database: KEY_ACCT Data Base Sorted by REP_NAME within REGION
This display is the result of a sort operation on the KEY_ACCT data base (Figure 8–17) with the REGION field as the primary key field and the REP_NAME field as the secondary key field.

order by REP_NAME within REGION. To achieve this record sequence, Pat selected REP_NAME as the secondary key field. In most database packages, issuing a sort command results in the creation of a temporary data base. After the sort operation, the temporary data base contains the records in the order described in the sort command.

Customized Reports.   Database software provides the capability of creating customized, or formatted, reports. This capability allows you to

Engineers monitor subjects while they learn and use software packages that may someday be released as commercial software products. The objective of this phase of testing is to gather feedback that enables system designers to fine-tune the user interface before the software is released for beta testing (prerelease testing by potential users of the software product).

```
                    KEY ACCOUNT SALES SUMMARY


   Company        Rep Name      XL-1      XL-2      MPX    Last Order
   ==================================================================
          *** Key Acounts for Region:  East
   Bigco          Hill            38        50        21    9/09/91
   Electronic     Allen           48        21        15    2/06/91
   Whizzard       Hill            35        45        20   10/12/91
                                ------    ------    ------
             Region Totals       121       116        56

          *** Key Acounts for Region:  Middle
   Actionpak      Cox             24        37        14   11/01/91
   Compufast      Taylor         103        67        42    2/07/92
   SuperGood      Cox             24        55         4   12/24/91
                                ------    ------    ------
             Region Totals       151       159        60

          *** Key Acounts for Region:  West
   Hi-Tech        Rosco           22        35         5    1/11/91
   Zapp, Inc.     Rosco           71        85        40    1/16/92
   Zimco          Mann            77       113        40    1/13/91
                                ------    ------    ------
             Region Totals       170       233        85

                                ======    ======    ======
             Overall Totals      442       508       201
```

FIGURE 8–24   Database: Formatted Report

This formatted report was compiled by merging a predefined report format with the KEY_ACCT data base (Figure 8–17). The records are printed in alphabetical order by COMPANY within REGION.

design the *layout* of the report. This means that you have some flexibility in spacing and can include titles, subtitles, column headings, separation lines, and other elements that make a report more readable. You describe the layout of the *customized* report interactively, then store it for later recall. The result of the description, called a *report form*, is recalled from disk storage and merged with a data base to create the customized report. Managers often use this capability to generate periodic reports (for example, monthly sales summary reports).

Once a month, Pat Kline generates several summary reports, one of which groups the key accounts by region and provides product subtotals and an overall total for each product (see Figure 8–24). This customized report was compiled by merging a predefined report format with the KEY_ACCT data base.

Use

Database software earns the "productivity tool" label by providing users with the capability of organizing data into an electronic data base that can be maintained and queried (can permit user inquiries) easily. The examples illustrated and discussed in the "Concepts" section merely "scratch the surface" of the potential of database software. With relative ease, you can generate some rather sophisticated reports that involve subtotals, calculations, and programming. In addition, data can be presented in the form of a graph (see Figure 8–25). You can even change

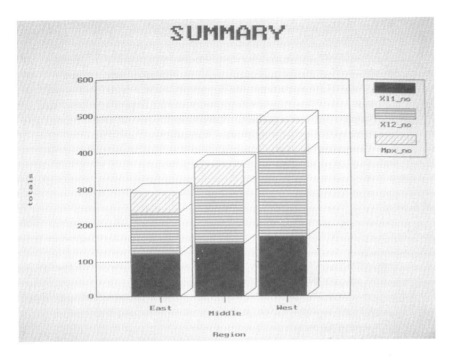

FIGURE 8–25   Database: Presentation Graphics
Like electronic spreadsheet packages, most database packages have the capability of preparing presentation graphics. This stacked-bar graph, which is derived from the data in Figure 8–17, shows the contribution of each product to regional sales.

the structure of a data base (for example, add another field). The programming capability enables users to create their own microcomputer-based information systems.

SUMMARY OUTLINE AND IMPORTANT TERMS

8–1   **THE ELECTRONIC SPREADSHEET.** Electronic spreadsheets are simply an electronic alternative to thousands of manual tasks that involve rows and columns of data. The primary example used in this chapter to illustrate and demonstrate electronic spreadsheet concepts is an electronic spreadsheet **template** of a monthly sales summary.

Electronic spreadsheets are organized in a tabular structure with **rows** and **columns**. The intersection of a particular row and column designates a **cell**. During operations, data are referred to by their **cell addresses**. The **pointer** can be moved around the spreadsheet to any cell with the cursor-control keys.

To make an entry, edit, or replace an entry in a spreadsheet, move the pointer to the appropriate cell. When in edit mode, revise the entry in much the same way you would revise the text in a word processing document.

The four types of **ranges** are a single-cell, all or part of a column of adjacent cells, all or part of a row of adjacent cells, and a rectangular block of cells. A particular range is depicted by the addresses of the endpoint cells (for example, C5..E10).

An entry to a cell is classified as text (or label), numeric, or formula. A text entry is any string of alphanumeric text (spaces included) that occupies a particular cell. A numeric entry is any number. A cell may contain a formula, but it is the numeric results that are displayed in the spreadsheet. Spreadsheet formulas use standard programming notation for **arithmetic operators**.

The **relative cell address** is based on its position in relation to the cell containing the formula. When you copy, or replicate, a formula to another cell, the relative cell addresses in the formula are revised so they retain the same position in relation to the new location of the formula. When a formula is copied, the **absolute cell addresses** in the formula remain unchanged.

Predefined **functions** can be used to create formulas that perform mathematical, logical, statistical, financial, and character-string operations on spreadsheet data.

The appearance of data in a spreadsheet can be modified to enhance readability by adjusting the column width and formatting the individual numeric entries.

An electronic spreadsheet template can be used over and over for different purposes by different people. If you change the value of a cell in a spreadsheet, all other affected cells are revised accordingly. This capability makes spreadsheet software the perfect tool for "what if" analysis.

8–2 PRESENTATION GRAPHICS. With presentation graphics software, you can create a variety of graphics from data in an electronic spreadsheet or a data base. Among the most popular presentation graphics are **bar graphs** (including the stacked-bar and clustered-bar graphs), **pie graphs**, and **line graphs**. Each of these graphs can be annotated with titles, labels, and legends.

The variety of graphs that can be produced by an electronic spreadsheet or database software package is limited. However, dedicated, or stand-alone, graphics packages offer the user the capability of creating a more extensive array of graphs, such as text charts, organization charts, customized graphs, and even original drawings.

8–3 DATABASE SOFTWARE. Database software permits users to create and maintain a data base and extract information from it. Once the data base is created, its records can be deleted or revised, and other records can be added to it.

In database software, the user-defined structure of a data base identifies the characteristics of each field in the data base. The screen format for entering, editing, and adding records to a data base is generated automatically from the specifications outlined in the structure of the data base.

Database software also permits you to retrieve, view, and print records based on **query by example**. To do this, users set conditions for the selection of records by composing a relational expression containing **relational operators** that reflects the desired conditions. Several expressions can be combined into a single condition with **logical operators**.

Records in a data base can be sorted for display in a variety of formats. To sort the records in a data base, select a primary key field and, if needed, secondary and tertiary key fields. In most database packages, issuing a sort command results in the compilation of another data base.

Database software provides the capability of creating customized, or formatted, reports. The user describes the layout of the customized report interactively, then stores it for later recall.

REVIEW EXERCISES

Concepts

1. Describe the layout of an electronic spreadsheet.
2. Give an example of a cell address. Which portion of the address depicts the row and which portion depicts the column?
3. Give an example of each of the four types of ranges.
4. Give examples of the three types of entries that can be made in an electronic spreadsheet.
5. Write the equivalent formula for @AVG(A1..D1) without the use of functions.
6. If the formula B2•$B$1 is copied from C1 to E3, what is the formula in E3? If the formula in E3 is copied to D45, what is the formula in D45?
7. List three different descriptors for the range A4..P12.
8. What formula would be entered in A5 to add all numbers in the range A1..A4?
9. Name three types of graphs commonly used for presentation graphics.
10. Name two sources of data for generating pie graphs and bar graphs.
11. Name and graphically illustrate (by hand) two variations of the bar graph.
12. What is shown when a portion of a pie chart is "exploded"?
13. What characteristics describe a field in a data base record?
14. What is the purpose of setting conditions for a data base?
15. What is the relationship between a field, a record, and the structure of a data base?
16. Give examples and descriptions of at least two other fields that might be added to the record for the KEY_ACCT data base.
17. If the KEY_ACCT data base (Figure 8–17) were sorted so that the primary and secondary key fields were REGION and LAST_ORDER, respectively, what is the company name for the third record?

18. What records would be displayed if the selection condition for the KEY_ACCT data base (Figure 8–17) were XL1_NO > 20 AND MPX_NO < = 5?

Discussion

19. All commercial electronic spreadsheet packages manipulate rows and columns of data in a similar manner. What makes one spreadsheet package more desirable than another?

20. If you were asked to create a micro-based inventory management system for a privately owned retail shoe store, would you use electronic spreadsheet software, database software, or both? Why?

21. In data base terminology, what is meant by *filtering*?

22. Describe two types of inquiries to a data base that involve calculations.

23. Under what circumstances is a graphic representation of data more effective than a tabular presentation of the same data?

24. Is it possible to present the same information in a stacked-bar and a line graph? How about stacked-bar and pie graphs?

SELF-TEST (by section)

8–1 a. The term *spreadsheet* was coined at the beginning of the personal computer boom. (T/F)

b. Data in an electronic spreadsheet are referred to by their cell _____.

c. The electronic spreadsheet pointer highlights the: (a) relative cell, (b) status cell, or (c) current cell.

d. D20..Z40 and Z20..D40 define the same electronic spreadsheet range. (T/F)

e. When the electronic spreadsheet formula +H4·$Z$18 is copied from A1 to A3, the formula in A3 is _____.

f. The electronic spreadsheet formula @SUM(A1..A20) results in the computation of the sum of the values in the range A20..A1. (T/F)

g. A model of a spreadsheet designed for a particular application is sometimes called a _____.

8–2 a. Among the most popular presentation graphics are bar graphs, pie graphs, and _____ graphs.

b. An alternative to the clustered-bar graph is the _____ graph.

c. Charts that contain a list of key points are called: (a) text charts, (b) organization charts, or (c) sequence charts.

8–3 a. If the KEY_ACCT data base in Figure 8–17 is sorted in descending order by XL1_NO, the third record would be Zapp, Inc. (T/F)

b. The definition of the structure of a data base would not include which of the following: (a) field names, (b) selection conditions for fields, (c) field lengths.

c. The relational operator for greater than or equal to would be _____.

d. What record(s) would be selected from the KEY_ACCT data base in Figure 8–17 for the condition REGION = West and MPX_NO>15: (a) Zapp, Inc., Zimco; (b) Compufast; or (c) no records are selected?

Self-test answers   **8–1 (a)** F; **(b)** addresses; **(c)** c; **(d)** T; **(e)** +H6·$Z$18; **(f)** T; **(g)** template. **8–2 (a)** line; **(b)** stacked-bar; **(c)** a. **8–3 (a)** F; **(b)** b; **(c)** >=; **(d)** a.

Programming Concepts

STUDENT LEARNING OBJECTIVES

▶ To discuss the terminology and concepts associated with programming languages and software.

▶ To identify approaches to solving a programming problem.

▶ To describe the concept of structured programming.

▶ To demonstrate an understanding of the principles and use of flowcharting and other program design techniques.

▶ To classify the various types of program instructions.

▶ To describe the steps and approaches to program development.

▶ To categorize programming languages by generation.

▶ To describe the function of compilers and interpreters.

9–1 PROGRAMMING IN PERSPECTIVE

The operation and application of computer hardware were discussed in Chapters 2 through 6. But computer *hardware* is useless without *software*, and software is useless without hardware.

A computer system does nothing until directed to do so by a human. A **program**, which consists of instructions to the computer, is how we tell a computer to perform certain operations. These instructions are logically sequenced and assembled through the act of **programming**. **Programmers** use a variety of **programming languages**, such as COBOL and BASIC, to communicate instructions to the computer.

9–2 PROBLEM SOLVING AND PROGRAMMING LOGIC

Computer Programs: The Power of Logic

A computer is not capable of performing calculations or manipulating data without exact, step-by-step instructions. These instructions take the form of a computer program. An information system may require five, fifty, or even several hundred programs. Electronic spreadsheet software is made up of dozens of programs that work together so that you can perform spreadsheet tasks. The same is true of word processing software.

A single program addresses a particular problem: to compute and assign grades, to permit an update of a data base, to monitor a patient's

Programming is no longer limited to technical specialists. These product marketing managers have their own computer and have learned to program. In the case of short programs, it may take less time for end users to write their own than to describe the problem to a professional programmer.

heart rate, to analyze marketing data, and so on. In effect, when you write a program, you are solving a *problem*. To solve a problem you must use your powers of *logic* to develop an **algorithm**, or procedure, for solving the problem.

Creating a program is like constructing a building. Much of the brainwork involved in the construction goes into the blueprint. The location, appearance, and function of a building are determined long before the first brick is laid. And so it is with programming. The design of a program, or its *programming logic* (the blueprint), is completed before the program is written (the building is constructed). This section and the next discuss approaches to designing the logic for a programming task. Later in this chapter we discuss the program and the different types of program instructions.

Structured Program Design: Divide and Conquer

Figure 9–1 illustrates a *structure chart* for a program to print weekly payroll checks. Hourly and commission employees are processed weekly. A structure chart for a program to print monthly payroll checks for salaried employees would look similar, except that Task 1.2, Compute gross earnings, would not be required. The salary amount can be retrieved directly from the employee data base.

The structure chart permits a programming problem to be broken into a hierarchy of tasks. (Any task can be broken into subtasks if a finer level of detail is desired.) The most effective programs are designed to be written in **modules**, or independent tasks. It is much easier to address a complex programming problem in small, more manageable

FIGURE 9–1   Program Structure Chart
The logic of a payroll program to print weekly payroll checks can be broken down into modules for ease of understanding, coding, and maintenance.

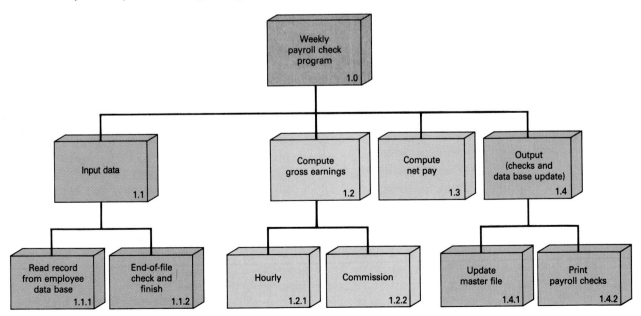

modules than as one big task. This is done using the principles of **structured programming**.

In structured programming, the logic of the program is addressed hierarchically in logical modules (see Figure 9–1). In the end, the logic of each module is translated into a sequence of program instructions that can be executed independently. By dividing the program into modules, the structured approach to programming reduces the complexity of the programming task. Some programs are so complex that if taken as a single task, they would be almost impossible to conceptualize, design, and code. We must "divide and conquer."

9–3   PROGRAM DESIGN TECHNIQUES

A number of techniques are available to help programmers analyze a problem and design the program. Two popular techniques are *flowcharting* and *pseudocode*. These techniques also can be used as system design tools.

Flowcharting

In **flowcharting**, **flowcharts** are used to illustrate data, information, and work flow by the interconnection of *specialized symbols* with *flow lines*. The combination of symbols and flow lines portrays the logic of the program or system. The more commonly used flowchart symbols are shown in Figure 9–2.

Flowcharting Symbols.   Each symbol indicates the *type* of operation to be performed, and the flowchart graphically illustrates the *sequence* in which the operations are to be performed. *Flow lines* ⟶ depict the sequential flow of the program logic. A rectangle ▭ signifies some type of *computer process*. The process could be as specific as "Compute an individual's grade average" (in a program flowchart) or as general as "Prepare class schedules for the fall semester" (in a system flowchart). The *predefined process* ⫐, a special case of the process symbol, is represented by a rectangle with extra vertical lines. The predefined process refers to a group of operations that may be detailed in a separate flowchart. The parallelogram ▱ is a generalized *input/output* symbol that denotes any type of input to or output from the program or system. The diamond-shaped symbol ◇ marks the point at which a *decision* is to be made. In a program flowchart, a particular set of instructions is executed based on the outcome of a decision. For example, in a payroll program, gross pay is computed differently for hourly and commission employees; therefore, for each employee processed, a decision is made as to which set of instructions is to be executed.

Each flowchart must begin and end with the oval *terminal point* symbol ⬭. A small circle ○ is a *connector* and is used to break and then link flow lines. The connector symbol often is used to avoid having to cross lines. The trapezoid ⬭ indicates that a *manual process* is to be performed. Contrast this with a computer process represented by a

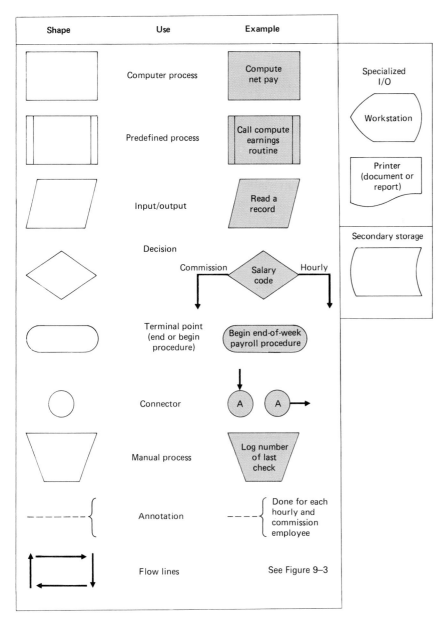

FIGURE 9–2   Flowchart Symbols

rectangle. The bracket ---{ permits descriptive notations to be added to flowcharts.

The *on-line data storage symbol* ▭ represents a file or data base. The most common *specialized input/output* symbols are the *workstation* ◯ and the *printer* (hard copy) ▱ symbols.

These symbols are equally applicable to system and program flow-charting and can be used to develop and represent the logic for each. The program flowchart of Figure 9–3 portrays the logic for the structure chart of Figure 9–1. The instructions adjacent to the flowchart symbols will be discussed in the next section. The company in the example of Figure 9–1 processes hourly and commission employee checks each week.

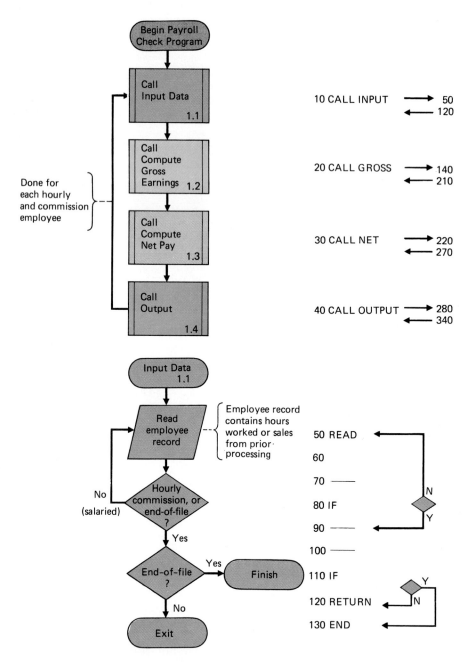

FIGURE 9–3   Program Flowchart with Language-Independent Instructions

The flowchart presents the logic of a payroll program to compute and print payroll checks for commission and hourly employees. (See the structure chart of Figure 9–1.) The logic is designed so that a driver module calls subroutines as they are needed to process each employee. The accompanying "program" has a few language-independent instructions to help illustrate the concepts and principles of programming. This figure is discussed in detail in the text.

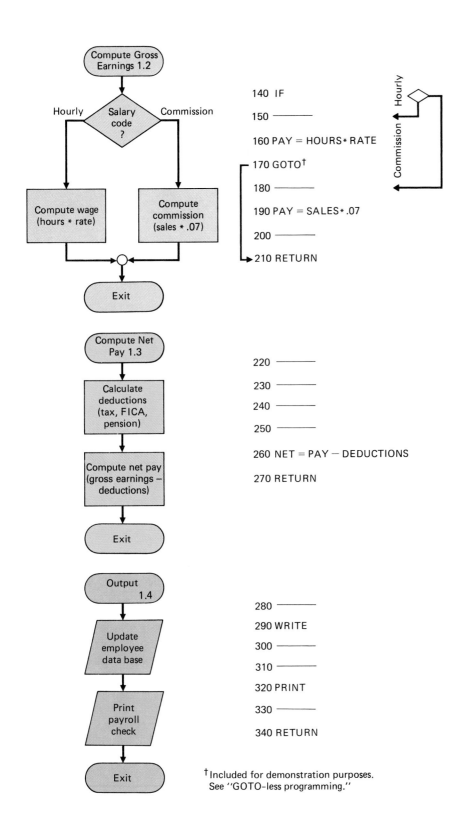

Compute Gross Earnings 1.2

| Salary code ? |
| Hourly — Commission |

Compute wage (hours * rate)

Compute commission (sales * .07)

Exit

140 IF
150 ———
160 PAY = HOURS * RATE
170 GOTO†
180 ———
190 PAY = SALES * .07
200 ———
210 RETURN

Commission ← ◇ → Hourly

Commission

Compute Net Pay 1.3

Calculate deductions (tax, FICA, pension)

Compute net pay (gross earnings − deductions)

Exit

220 ———
230 ———
240 ———
250 ———
260 NET = PAY − DEDUCTIONS
270 RETURN

Output 1.4

Update employee data base

Print payroll check

Exit

280 ———
290 WRITE
300 ———
310 ———
320 PRINT
330 ———
340 RETURN

† Included for demonstration purposes. See "GOTO-less programming."

229

These insurance claims agents interact with mainframe-based information systems.
A number of them also work with micro-based information systems. The techniques
used in designing the computer programs for these systems are the same for both
mainframes and micros.

(Salary employee checks are processed monthly.) Gross earnings for hourly employees are computed by multiplying hours worked times the rate of pay. For salespeople on commission, gross earnings are computed as a percentage of sales.

The Driver Module.   In structured programming, each program has a **driver module**, which is sometimes called the **main program**, that causes other program modules to be executed as they are needed. The driver module in the payroll program (see Figure 9–3) is a **loop** that "calls" each of the subordinate modules, or **subroutines**, as needed for the processing of each employee. The program is designed so that when the payroll program is initiated, the "input data" module (1.1) is executed, or "performed," first. After execution, control is then returned to the driver module unless there are no more employees to be processed, in which case execution is terminated (the "Finish" terminal point). For each hourly or commission employee, Modules 1.2, 1.3, and 1.4 are performed, and at the completion of each subroutine, control is passed back to the driver module.

Programming Control Structures.   Through the 1970s, many programmers unknowingly wrote what is now referred to as "spaghetti code."

It was so named because their program flowcharts appeared more like a plate of spaghetti than like logical analyses of programming problems. The unnecessary branching (jumps from one portion of the program to another) of a spaghetti-style program resulted in confusing logic, even to the person who wrote it.

Computer scientists overcame this dead-end approach to developing program logic by identifying three basic *control structures* into which any program or subroutine can be segmented. By conceptualizing the logic of a program in these three structures—*sequence*, *selection*, and *loop*—programmers can avoid writing spaghetti code and produce programs that can be understood and maintained more easily. The use of these three basic control structures has paved the way for a more rigorous and scientific approach to solving a programming problem. These control structures are illustrated in Figures 9–4, 9–5, and 9–6, and their use is demonstrated in the payroll example of Figure 9–3.

Sequence structure   In the sequence structure (Figure 9–4), the processing steps are performed in sequence, one after another. Modules 1.3 and 1.4 in Figure 9–3 are good examples of sequence structures.

Selection structure   The selection structure (Figure 9–5) depicts the logic for selecting the appropriate sequence of statements. In Figure 9–3, our payroll program, the selection structure is used to illustrate the logic for the computation of gross pay for hourly and commission employees (Module 1.2). In the selection structure, a decision is made as to which sequence of instructions is to be executed next.

The selection structure of Module 1.2 presents two options: hourly or commission. Other circumstances might call for three or more options.

Loop structure   The loop structure (Figure 9–6) is used to represent the program logic when a portion of the program is to be executed repeatedly until a particular condition is met. There are two variations of the loop structure (see Figure 9–6): (1) When the decision, or *test-*

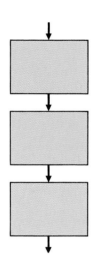

FIGURE 9–4   Sequence Control Structures

FIGURE 9–5   Selection Control Structures
Any number of options can result from a decision in a selection control structure.

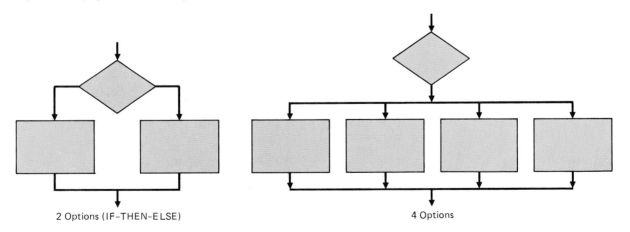

2 Options (IF-THEN-ELSE)   4 Options

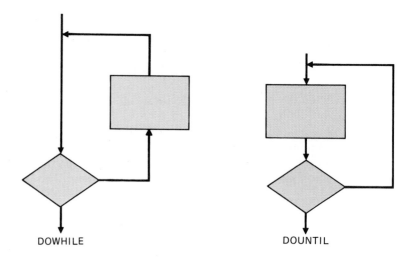

FIGURE 9–6   Loop Control Structures
The two types of loop structures are DOWHILE and DOUNTIL.

on-condition, is placed at the beginning of the statement sequence, it becomes a *DOWHILE loop*; (2) when placed at the end, it becomes a *DOUNTIL loop* (pronounced *doo-while* and *doo-until*). In the payroll flowchart of Figure 9–3, that portion of the input data module (1.1) that reads an employee record is illustrated in a DOUNTIL loop.

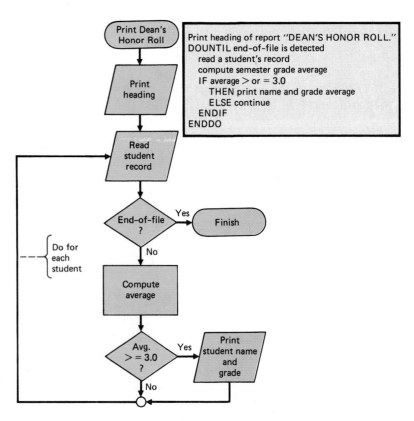

FIGURE 9–7   Pseudocode with Flowchart
This pseudocode program depicts the logic of a program to compile a list of students who have qualified for the dean's honor roll. The same logic is shown in a flowchart.

Pseudocode

Another design technique used almost exclusively for program design is called **pseudocode**. While the other techniques graphically represent the logic of the program, pseudocode represents the logic in programlike statements written in plain English. Because pseudocode does not have any syntax guidelines (rules for formulating instructions), you can concentrate solely on developing the logic of your program. Once you feel that the logic is sound, the pseudocode is easily translated into a procedure-oriented language such as COBOL or BASIC that can be run on a computer. In Figure 9–7 the logic of a simple program is represented both in pseudocode and by a flowchart.

There is no substitute for good, sound logic in programming. If you follow the guidelines of structured programming and make judicious use of these and other program design techniques, your program will be easier to write, use, and maintain.

9–4   SO WHAT'S A PROGRAM? CONCEPTS AND PRINCIPLES OF PROGRAMMING _____

A computer program consists of a sequence of instructions that are executed one after another. These instructions, also called **statements**, are executed in sequence unless their order is altered by a "test-on-condition" instruction or a "branch" instruction.

The flowchart of our payroll program (Figure 9–3) is accompanied by a sequence of language-independent instructions. Except for the computation of gross earnings, the processing steps are similar for both types of employees. Two sequences of instructions are needed to compute gross earnings for *hourly* and *commission* employees. We can also see from the flowchart that the sequence in which the instructions are executed may be altered at three places (decision symbols), depending on the results of the test-on-condition. In Module 1.2, for example, the sequence of instructions to be executed depends on whether the test-on-condition detects an hourly or a commission employee.

To the right of the flowchart in Figure 9–3 is a representation of a sequence of language-independent instructions and the order in which they are executed. *Statement numbers* are included, as they are in most program listings. This program could be written in any procedure-oriented language. The purpose of the discussion that follows is to familiarize you with general types of programming instructions, not those of any particular programming language. Each language has an instruction set with at least one instruction in each of the following *instruction classifications:* input/output, computation, control, data transfer and assignment, and format.

Input/Output.   Input/output instructions direct the computer to "read from" or "write to" a peripheral device (for example, printer or disk drive). *Statement 50* of Figure 9–3 requests that an employee record, including pay data, be read from the data base.

Computation.   Computation instructions perform arithmetic operations (add, subtract, multiply, divide, and raise a number to a power). *Statement 160* (PAY = HOURS · RATE) computes gross earnings for hourly employees.

Control (Decision and/or Branch).   Control instructions can alter the sequence of the program's execution or terminate execution. In Figure 9–3, *Statements 10 through 40, 80, 110, 130, 140, 210, 270, and 340* are control instructions. The two types of control instructions are *unconditional branch* and *conditional branch* instructions.

Statements *10 through 40* are unconditional branch instructions. An unconditional branch instruction disrupts the normal sequence of execution by causing an unconditional branch to another part of the program or to a subroutine. In *Statements 10 through 40*, the branch is from the driver module to a subroutine. The CALL statement works in conjunction with the RETURN statement to branch to another location, then RETURN control back to the statement following the CALL.

Statements *80 and 110* are conditional branch instructions and are generally referred to as IF statements: If certain conditions are met, then a branch is made to a certain part of the program. The conditional branch at *Statement 80* causes the program to "loop" until the employee record read is for either an hourly or a commission employee, or the end-of-file marker is reached. The sequence of instructions, *Statements 50 through 80*, comprise a DOUNTIL loop.

Data Transfer and Assignment.   Data can be transferred internally from one primary storage location to another. In procedure-oriented languages, data are transferred, or "moved," by *assignment instructions*. These instructions permit a *string constant*, also called a *literal value*, such as "The net pay is" or a *numeric value* such as 234 to be assigned to a named primary storage location.

In a program, a primary storage location is represented by a **variable name** (for example, PAY, HOURS, NET). A variable name in a program statement refers to the *contents* of a particular primary storage location. For example, a programmer may use the variable name HOURS in a computation statement to refer to the numeric value of the *hours worked* by a particular employee.

Format.   Format instructions are used in conjunction with input and output instructions; they describe how the data are to be entered or outputted from primary storage. On output, format instructions print headings on reports and present data in a readable format.

With these few types of instructions, you can model almost any business or scientific procedure, whether it be sales forecasting or guiding rockets to the moon.

9–5   WRITING PROGRAMS

Each program is a project. The following steps are followed for each programming project.

Step 1. Describe the problem.
Step 2. Analyze the problem.
Step 3. Design the general logic of the program.
Step 4. Design the detailed logic of the program.
Step 5. Code the program.
Step 6. Test and debug the program.
Step 7. Document the program.

Step 1. Describe the Problem.   Identify exactly what needs to be done.

Step 2. Analyze the Problem.   In this step you break the problem into its basic components for analysis. Remember to "divide and conquer." Although different programs have different components, a good starting place for most is to analyze the *output, input, processing,* and *file-interaction.*

Steps 3 and 4. Design the General and Detailed Logic of the Program. Now you need to put the pieces together in the form of a logical program design. A program is designed in a hierarchical manner—that is, from general to the specific.

The general design (Step 3)   The *general* design of the program is oriented primarily to the major processing activities and the relationships between these activities. The structure chart of Figure 9–1 and the flowchart of Figure 9–3, both discussed earlier in this chapter, illustrate the general design of a weekly payroll program to compute and print paychecks. By first completing a general program design, you make it easier to investigate alternative design approaches. Once you are confident of which approach is best, you may complete a more detailed design.

Programmers often work as a team on big projects. This programming team meets as a group at least once a week to coordinate efforts, discuss problems, and report on individual and team progress.

The detailed design (Step 4)   The *detailed* design results in a graphic representation of the program logic that includes *all* processing activities and their relationships, calculations, data manipulations, logic operations, and all input/output.

Step 5. Code the Program.   Whether you "write" or "code" the program is a matter of personal preference. In this context, the terms are the

COMPUTERS HAVE VIRUSES, TOO

In a manner of speaking, computers get sick, too. A variety of highly contagious "diseases" can spread from computer to computer, much the way biological viruses do among human beings. A *computer virus* is a program that literally "infects" other programs and data bases upon contact. It can hide duplicates of itself within legitimate programs, such as an operating system or word processing program.

Virus programs are written with malicious intent and are loaded to the computer system of an unsuspecting victim. Viruses have been found at all levels of computing, from microcomputers to supercomputers; however, the microcomputer environment is particularly susceptible to virus infiltration because of the lack of system controls exercised by individual users.

There are many types of viruses. Some act quickly by erasing user programs and data bases. Others grow like a cancer, destroying small parts of a data base each day. Some act like a time bomb. They lay dormant for days or months, but eventually are activated and wreak havoc on any software on the system. Many companies warn their micro users to back up all software prior to every Friday the thirteenth, a favorite date of those who write virus programs. Some viruses attack the hardware and have been known to throw the mechanical components of a computer system, such as disk-access arms, into costly spasms.

The most common source of viral infection is the public electronic bulletin board on which users exchange software. Typically, a user logs onto the bulletin board and downloads what he or she thinks is a game, a utility program, or some other enticing piece of freeware, but gets a virus instead. One virus frequently distributed via electronic bulletin boards displayed "Gotcha" on the user's monitor, then erased all programs and data from accessible disk storage.

Viruses are also spread from one system to another via common diskettes. For example, a student with an infected applications disk might infect several other laboratory computers with a virus which, in turn, infects the applications software of other students. Software companies have unknowingly distributed viruses with their proprietary software products.

In the minicomputer and mainframe environment, viruses generally are spread from one computer network to another. In late 1988 a Cornell graduate student wrote a costly virus (causing over $20 million in damages) that infiltrated 6000 computers on six continents via a worldwide computer network.

Since first appearing in the mid-1980s, viruses have erased bank records, damaged hospital records, destroyed the programs in thousands of microcomputers, and even infected part of the systems at NORAD (strategic defense) and NASA. Disgruntled employees have inserted viruses in disks that were distributed to customers. The motives of those who would infect a system with a virus run from electronic vandalism to revenge to terrorism. There is no monetary reward, only the "satisfaction" of knowing that their efforts have been very costly to individuals, companies, and governments.

Viruses are a serious problem. They have the potential of affecting an individual's career and even destroying companies. (A company that loses its accounts receivables records could be a candidate for bankruptcy.) Antiviral programs, also called *vaccines*, exist, but they can be circumvented by a persistent (and malicious) programmer. The best way to cope with viruses is to recognize that they exist and to take precautionary measures. For example, one company requires micro users to turn off their micros and reload their personal copies of the operating system before each use. In the mainframe environment, systems programmers must search continually for suspicious-looking programs and be particularly wary of downloading programs from computer systems outside the company.

same. In Step 5, the graphic and narrative design of program development Steps 1 through 4 are translated into machine-readable instructions, or programs. If the logic is sound and the design documentation (flowcharts, pseudocode, and so on) is thorough, the coding process is relatively straightforward.

Step 6. Test and Debug the Program. Once the program has been entered into the system, it is likely that you will encounter at least one of those cantankerous **bugs**. A bug is either a *syntax error* (violation of one of the rules for writing instructions) or a *logic error*. Ridding a program of bugs is the process of **debugging**.

A good programmer lives by Murphy's Law, which assumes that if anything can go wrong, it will! Don't assume that whoever uses your program will not make certain errors in data entry.

Step 7. Document the Program. Procedures and information requirements change over the life of a system. For example, because the social security tax rate is revised each year, certain payroll programs must be modified. To keep up with these changes, programs must be updated periodically, or *maintained*. Program maintenance can be difficult if the program documentation is not complete and up-to-date.

The programs you write in college are not put into production and therefore are not maintained. You may ask, "Why document them?" The reason is simple. Good documentation now helps to develop good programming habits that undoubtedly will be carried on in your future programming efforts. *Documentation* is part of the *programming process*. It's not something you do after the program is written.

All the example programs in the BASIC supplement to this text, *BASIC for Introductory Computing*, provide good examples of program documentation. Each program is documented with a *program description*, *structure chart*, *flowchart*, *program listing* (with internal comments), and *interactive session*.

9–6 GENERATIONS OF PROGRAMMING LANGUAGES

We "talk" to computers within the framework of a particular programming language. There are many different programming languages, most of which have highly structured sets of rules. The selection of a programming language depends on who is involved and the nature of "conversation."

Programming languages have evolved in generations. With each new generation, fewer instructions are needed to tell the computer to perform a particular task. A program written in a first-generation language that computes the total sales for each sales representative, then lists those over quota may require 100 or more instructions; the same program in a fourth-generation language may have fewer than 10 instructions.

The hierarchy in Figure 9–8 illustrates the relationships between the various generations of programming languages. The later generations do not necessarily provide us with greater programming capabilities, but they do provide a *more sophisticated programmer/computer interaction*.

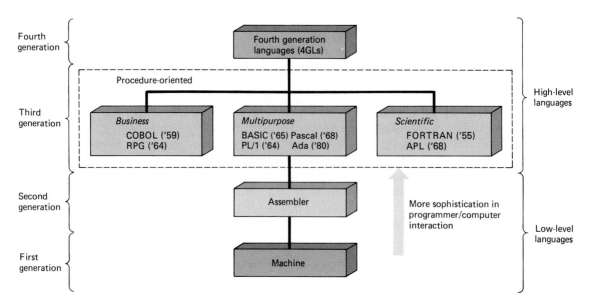

FIGURE 9–8   The Hierarchy of Programming Languages
As you progress from one generation of programming language to the next, fewer instructions are required to perform a particular programming task.

In short, each new generation is easier to understand and use. For example, in a fourth-generation language you need only instruct the computer system *what to do*, not necessarily *how to do it*. When programming in one of the first three generations of languages, you have to tell the computer what to do *and* how to do it.

The ease with which the later generations can be used is certainly appealing, but the earlier languages also have their advantages. All generations of languages are in use today.

The First and Second Generations: "Low-Level"

Machine Language.   Each computer has only *one* programming language that can be executed—the **machine language**. We talk of programming in COBOL, Pascal, and BASIC, but all these languages must be translated into the machine language of the computer on which the program is to be executed. These and other high-level languages are simply a convenience for the programmer.

Not all programming is administrative or scientific in nature. The development of computer-controlled systems such as the U.S. Navy submarine sonar systems involve substantial programming efforts. The programs that run the sonar system have over five million lines of code. The sonar system, however, is just one of dozens of computer-controlled systems on board a submarine.

Machine-language programs, the *first generation*, are written at the most basic level of computer operation. Because their instructions are directed at this basic level of operation, machine language and assembler language (see discussion that follows) are called, collectively, **low-level languages**. In machine language, instructions are coded as a series of 1s and 0s. As you might expect, machine-language programs are cumbersome and difficult to write. Early programmers had no alternative. Fortunately, we do.

Assembler Language.   A set of instructions for an **assembler language** essentially essentially correspond on a one-to-one basis with those of a machine language. Like machine languages, assembler languages are

```
COMP$PAY        PROC PUBLIC
;
;        COMP$PAY - procedure to compute gross pay (PAY = HOURS * RATE)
;
         MOV     AX,HOURS                ;multiplicand
         MUL     RATE+2                  ;  times second word of multiplier
         MOV     PAY+2,AX                ;store the product in PAY
;
         MOV     AX,HOURS                ;multiplicand
         MUL     RATE                    ;  times first word of multiplier
         ADD     PAY+2,AX                ;add the product to PAY
         ADC     PAY,DX                  ;add the carry, if any
         RET                             ;end procedure
COMP$PAY        ENDP
```

FIGURE 9–9   An Assembler Program Procedure
These assembler instructions compute PAY by multiplying the number of HOURS times the RATE.

unique to a particular computer. The big difference between the two is the way the instructions are represented by the programmer. Rather than a cumbersome series of 1s and 0s, assembler languages use easily recognized symbols, called **mnemonics**, to represent instructions (see Figure 9–9). For example, most assembler languages use the mnemonic *MUL* to represent a "Multiply" instruction. The assembler languages ushered in the *second generation* of programming languages.

The Third Generation: For Programmer Convenience

Compilers and Interpreters: Programs for Programs.   No matter which **high-level language** (third and later generations) a program is written in, it must be translated into machine language before it can be executed. This conversion of high-level instructions into machine-level instructions is done by systems software programs called *compilers* and *interpreters*.

Compilers   The **compiler** program translates the instructions of a high-level language such as COBOL into machine-language instructions that the computer can interpret and execute. A separate compiler (or an interpreter, discussed in the next section) is required for each programming language intended for use on a particular computer system. That is, to execute both COBOL and Pascal programs, you must have a COBOL compiler and a Pascal compiler. High-level programming languages are simply a programmer convenience; they cannot be executed in their source, or original, form.

The actual high-level programming-language instructions, called the **source program**, are translated, or **compiled**, into machine-language instructions called an **object program** by a compiler. It is the object program—the output of the compilation process—that actually is executed by the computer. Object programs to be executed again at another time typically are stored on secondary storage, such as magnetic disk, for later recall.

Interpreters   An **interpreter** is a systems software program that ultimately performs the same function as a compiler, but in a different manner. Instead of translating the entire source program in a single pass, an interpreter translates *and* executes each source-program instruction before translating and executing the next.

PROFILE

Grace Hopper
Amazing Grace

Navy Rear Admiral Grace Hopper was the oldest active-duty military officer when she retired in 1986 at the age of 79. Nicknamed "the Grand Old Lady of Software," Admiral Hopper continues to be an active speaker on and advocate of computers. She likes to introduce herself at speaking engagements by saying that she was the third programmer on the first large-scale digital computer in the United States, and she's been coping with it ever since.

Dr. Hopper was a professor of mathematics when she joined the Navy in 1943 and began her distinguished career in computers. She was assigned to the Bureau of Ordinance Computation Project at Harvard University, helping program the first large-scale digital computer, the Mark I. After the war she continued her work on the Mark II and Mark III.

In 1949 she moved to the Eckert-Mauchly Computer Corporation in Philadelphia where she helped build the UNIVAC I, the first commercial large-scale electronic digital computer. In 1959 Dr. Hopper led an effort that laid the foundation for the development of COBOL, the most popular programming language. She also created a compiler that enabled COBOL to run on many types of computers. Her reason for developing the business compiler was: "Why start from scratch with every program you write when a compiler could be developed to do a lot of the basic work for you over and over again?"

To Admiral Hopper's long list of honors, awards, and accomplishments, add the fact that she found the first "bug" in a computer—a real one. She repaired the computer by removing a moth that

had gotten caught in Relay Number 70 of the Mark II. From that day on programmers have *debugged* software by removing *bugs*. Of course, today's "bugs" are not insects, but errors in programming syntax or logic.

Procedure-Oriented Languages. The introduction of the *third generation* of programming languages, most of which would be classified as **procedure-oriented languages**, resulted in a quantum leap in programmer convenience. The flexibility of procedure-oriented languages permits programmers to model almost any scientific or business procedure. Instructions are **coded**, or written, sequentially and processed according to program specifications.

Procedure-oriented languages are classified as *business*, *scientific*, or *multipurpose*.

Business languages   Business programming languages are designed to be effective tools for developing business information systems. The strength of business-oriented languages lies in their ability to store, retrieve, and manipulate alphanumeric data.

COBOL, the first business programming language, was introduced in 1959. It remains the most popular. The original intent of the developers of COBOL (*Common Business Oriented Language*) was to make its instructions approximate the English language. Here is a typical COBOL *sentence*: "IF SALARY-CODE IS EQUAL TO 'H' MULTIPLY SALARY

The minicomputer system at this tractor assembly plant helps production personnel keep track of inventory, orders, and shipping information. The software for this system was written in COBOL.

BY HOURLY-RATE GIVING GROSS-PAY ELSE PERFORM SALA-RIED-EMPLOYEE-ROUTINE." Note that the sentence contains several instructions and even a period.

Figure 9–10 illustrates a COBOL program that computes gross pay for hourly wage earners. Notice that the program is divided into four divisions: identification, environment, data, and procedure.

For purposes of comparison, the COBOL program in Figure 9–10 and the other examples of third-generation programs (Figures 9–11 through 9–13) are written to perform the same input, processing, and output activities: Compute gross pay for hourly wage earners. The interactive session (see Figure 9–10) is the same for all four programs.

Another popular business programming language is **RPG** (*Report Program Generator*). RPG has always differed somewhat from other procedure-oriented languages in that the programmer specifies certain processing requirements by selecting the desired programming options.

Scientific languages   Scientific languages are algebraic formula–type languages. They are specifically designed to meet typical scientific processing requirements, such as matrix manipulation, precision calculations, iterative processing, the expression and resolution of mathematical equations, and so on.

```
0100 IDENTIFICATION DIVISION.
0200 PROGRAM-ID.              PAYPROG.
0300 REMARKS.                 PROGRAM TO COMPUTE GROSS PAY.
0400 ENVIRONMENT DIVISION.
0500 DATA DIVISION.
0600 WORKING-STORAGE SECTION.
0700 01 PAY-DATA.
0800        05 HOURS          PIC 99V99.
0900        05 RATE           PIC 99V99.
1000        05 PAY            PIC 9999V99.
1100 01 LINE-1.
1200        03 FILLER         PIC X(5)       VALUE SPACES.
1300        03 FILLER         PIC X(12)      VALUE "GROSS PAY IS  ".
1400        03 GROSS-PAY      PIC $$$$9.99.
1500 01 PRINT-LINE.           PIC X(27).
1600 PROCEDURE DIVISION.
1700 MAINLINE-PROCEDURE.
1800        PERFORM ENTER-PAY.
1900        PERFORM COMPUTE-PAY.
2000        PERFORM PRINT-PAY.
2100        STOP RUN.
2200 ENTER-PAY.
2300        DISPLAY "ENTER HOURS AND RATE OF PAY".
2400        ACCEPT HOURS, RATE.
2500 COMPUTE-PAY.
2600        MULTIPLY HOURS BY RATE GIVING PAY ROUNDED.
2700 PRINT-PAY.
2800        MOVE PAY TO GROSS-PAY.
2900        MOVE LINE-1 TO PRINT-LINE.
3000        DISPLAY PRINT-LINE.
```

```
Enter hours and rate of pay
43, 8.25
    Gross pay is $354.75
```

FIGURE 9–10   A COBOL Program
This COBOL program accepts the number of hours worked and the pay rate for an hourly wage earner, then computes and displays the gross pay amount. The interactive session shows the input prompt, the values entered by the user, and the result.

FORTRAN (*Formula Translator*), the first procedure-oriented language, was developed in 1955. It was and remains the most popular scientific language. The FORTRAN program in Figure 9–11 performs the same processing functions as the COBOL program in Figure 9–10.

Multipurpose languages   Multipurpose languages are equally effective for both business and scientific applications. They are an outgrowth of the need to simplify the programming environment by providing program-

FIGURE 9–11   A FORTRAN Program
This FORTRAN program accepts the number of hours worked and the pay rate for an hourly wage earner, then computes and displays the gross pay amount. The resulting interactive session is the same as that of Figure 9–10.

```
        program payprog
c
c       payprog        - Program to compute the pay for an employee,
c                        given hours worked and the employee's pay rate.
c
        real hours, rate, pay                        !define the variables
c
        write(6,1)                                   !input prompt
1       format(1H,'Enter hours and rate of pay')
        read(5,*) hours, rate                        !accept hours & pay rate
        pay = hours * rate                           !compute pay
        write(6,2) pay                               !display gross pay
2       format(1H,5X,'Gross pay is $',F7.2)
        end
```

The computer systems on board the space shuttle collect flight data that are relayed to earth and analyzed by programs written in FORTRAN.

mers with one language capable of addressing all the programming needs of a company.

The results of a recent employment survey showed C programmers to be in the greatest demand. Developers of proprietary packaged software are very interested in C because it is considered more transportable than other languages. That is, it is relatively machine-independent: A C program written for one type of computer (see Figure 9–12) can be run on another type with little or no modification.

FIGURE 9–12   A C-Language Program

This C program accepts the number of hours worked and the pay rate for an hourly wage earner, then computes and displays the gross pay amount. The resulting interactive session is the same as that of Figure 9–10.

```
/*      payprog.c      - Program to compute the pay for an employee,
                         given hours worked and the employee's pay rate. */

main()
{
        float hours, rate, pay;                 /* define the
                                                   variables used */
        printf("Enter hours and rate of pay\n");    /* input prompt */
        scanf("%f %f", &hours, &rate);          /* accept hours
                                                   and pay rate */

        pay = hours * rate;                     /* compute pay */
        printf("\tGross pay is $%.2f\n",pay);   /* print gross pay */
}
```

```
100 REM payprog          Program to compute the pay for an employee,
110 REM                  given hours worked and the employee's pay rate.
120 REM
130 PRINT "Enter hours and rate of pay"        'input prompt
140 INPUT HOURS, RATE                          'accept hours & pay rate
150 LET PAY = HOURS * RATE                     'compute pay
160 PRINT TAB(5);"Gross pay is $";PAY          'display gross pay
170 END
```

FIGURE 9–13   A BASIC Program
This BASIC program accepts the number of hours worked and the pay rate for an hourly wage earner, then computes and displays the gross pay amount. The resulting interactive session is the same as that of Figure 9–10.

BASIC, developed in 1964, is the primary language supported by millions of personal computers. BASIC is also used extensively on mainframe computer systems, primarily for one-time "quick-and-dirty" programs. It is perhaps the easiest language to learn and use (see Figure 9–13). It is common in both scientific and business applications—and even in developing video games. The widespread use of BASIC attests to the versatility of its features. In fact, it is the only programming language supported on virtually every computer.

Three other multipurpose languages are widely used. **Pascal** (1968), a powerful, self-documenting language, has become the language of choice in many computer science curriculums. **PL/I**, short for *Programming Language/I* (1964), eliminates the need for programmers to learn both a business and a scientific language, specifically COBOL and FORTRAN.

Pascal, a multipurpose programming language, often is used to develop software for computer image generation.

Ada (1980) has been adopted as the standard language by the U.S. Department of Defense.

Other Third-Generation Languages.   The foregoing coverage of third-generation languages is not intended to be exhaustive. The languages were selected to provide an overview of some you might encounter in practice. A dozen other third-generation languages are commonly used in business and taught in academic institutions. These include the following:

- *APL* (1968). A symbolic interactive programming language popular with engineers, mathematicians, and scientists. It requires a special keyboard.
- *LISP* (1959). A list-processing language better at manipulating symbols than numbers (used in artificial intelligence).
- *LOGO* (1967). Uses a "turtle" to teach children geometry, mathematics, and programming.
- *FORTH* (1971). Used for device control applications.
- *Prolog* (1972). Can manipulate relationships between facts (used in artificial intelligence).
- *Modula-2* (1981). Enables self-contained modules to be combined in a program.

The Fourth Generation: 4GLs

Types of 4GLs.   The trend in software development is toward using high-level, user-friendly, **fourth-generation languages (4GLs)**. There are two types of 4GLs.

These managers are being taught the use and application of fourth-generation query languages. After completing a one-day seminar, they will be able to make inquiries to the corporate data base without the assistance of a computer specialist.

- *Production-oriented 4GLs.* Production-oriented 4GLs are designed primarily for computer professionals. They use 4GLs such as ADR's Ideal, Software AG's Natural 2, and Cincom's Mantis to create information systems. Professional programmers who use 4GLs claim productivity improvements over third-generation, procedure-oriented languages (COBOL, FORTRAN, BASIC, and so on) of 200% to 1000%.
- *User-oriented 4GLs.* This type of 4GL is designed primarily for end users. Users write 4GL programs to query (extract information from) a data base and to create personal or departmental information systems. User-oriented 4GLs include Mathematica Products Group's RAMIS II and Information Builders' FOCUS.

Over the years most companies have accumulated large quantities of computer-based data. Prior to fourth-generation languages (the mid-1970s), these data were not directly accessible to users. They had to describe their information needs to a professional programmer, who would then write a program in a procedure-oriented language like COBOL to produce the desired results. Fulfilling a typical user request would take at least a couple of days and as long as two weeks. By then the desired information might no longer be needed. With fourth-generation languages, these same ad hoc requests, or queries, can be completed in minutes. When 4GLs are available, many users elect to handle their own information needs without involving computer professionals at all!

Principles and Use.   Fourth-generation languages use high-level English-like instructions to retrieve and format data for inquiries and reporting. Most of the procedure portion of a 4GL program is generated automatically by the computer and the language software. That is, for the most part the programmer specifies what to do, *not* how to do it. In contrast, a COBOL or FORTRAN programmer writes instructions for what to do *and* how to do it.

The features of a 4GL include English-like instructions, limited mathematical manipulation of data, automatic report formatting, sequencing (sorting), and record selection by criteria.

Using 4GLs   The 4GL example presented here gives you a sense of the difference between a procedure-oriented language such as COBOL and a 4GL. About 20 4GLs are commercially available. The example that follows shows how a 4GL program can be used to generate a management report. Suppose, for example, that a personnel manager wants to make the following request for information:

> List the employee ID, sex, net pay, and gross pay for all employees in Departments 911 and 914.

To obtain the report, the manager wrote the query-language program in Figure 9–14; the report generated by this program is shown in Figure 9–15.

- *Instruction 1* specifies that the payroll data are stored on a FILE called PAYROLL. The payroll file contains a record for each employee. Although the data of only one file are needed in this example, requests requiring data from several files are no more difficult.

```
1.  FILE IS PAYROLL
2.  LIST BY DEPARTMENT:    NAME ID SEX NET GROSS
3.  SELECT DEPARTMENT = 911, 914
4.  SUBTOTALS BY DEPARTMENT
5.  TITLE: "PAYROLL FOR DEPARTMENTS 911, 914"
6.  COLUMN HEADINGS:   "DEPARTMENT", "EMPLOYEE, NAME";
    "EMPLOYEE, NUMBER"; "SEX"; "NET, PAY"; "GROSS, PAY"
```

FIGURE 9–14   A 4GL Program
This representative 4GL program generates the report shown in Figure 9–15. Each instruction is discussed in detail in the text.

- *Instruction 2* specifies the basic format of the report. Employee records are *sorted* and LISTed BY DEPARTMENT. It also specifies which data elements within the file (NAME and ID, for example) are to be included in the report of Figure 9–15. If the instruction had been LIST BY DEPARTMENT BY NAME, then the employee names would be listed in alphabetical order for each department.

- *Instruction 3* specifies the criterion by which records are SELECTed. The personnel manager is interested in only those employees from Departments 911 and 914. Other criteria could be included for further record selections. For example, the criterion "GROSS > 400.00" could be added to select only those people (from Departments 911 and 914) whose gross pay is greater than $400.00.

- *Instruction 4* causes SUBTOTALS to be computed and displayed BY DE-PARTMENT.

FIGURE 9–15   A Payroll Report
This payroll report is the result of the execution of the 4GL program of Figure 9–14.

PAYROLL FOR DEPARTMENTS 911, 914

DEPARTMENT	EMPLOYEE NAME	EMPLOYEE NUMBER	SEX	NET PAY	GROSS PAY
911	ARNOLD	01963	1	356.87	445.50
911	LARSON	11357	2	215.47	283.92
911	POWELL	11710	1	167.96	243.20
911	POST	00445	1	206.60	292.00
911	KRUSE	03571	2	182.09	242.40
911	SMOTH	01730	1	202.43	315.20
911	GREEN	12829	1	238.04	365.60
911	ISAAC	12641	1	219.91	313.60
911	STRIDE	03890	1	272.53	386.40
911	REYNOLDS	05805	2	134.03	174.15
911	YOUNG	04589	1	229.69	313.60
911	HAFER	09764	2	96.64	121.95
DEPARTMENT TOTAL				2,522.26	3,497.52
914	MANHART	11602	1	250.89	344.80
914	VETTER	01895	1	189.06	279.36
914	GRECO	07231	1	685.23	1,004.00
914	CROCI	08262	1	215.95	376.00
914	RYAN	10961	1	291.70	399.20
DEPARTMENT TOTAL				1,632.83	2,403.36
FINAL TOTAL 17 RECORDS TOTALED				4,155.09	5,900.88

By drawing on artificial intelligence techniques, a GE research team has taught a computer the rudiments of how to read and digest a variety of printed material. In a demonstration, the system was fed a day's worth of stories from a financial news service (500 in all). At the user's request, it selected stories on mergers and acquisition and was then able to answer basic questions about them. The questions and the computer's answers are phrased in plain English, not in a specialized computer language. In the future, much of our interaction with the computer will be via a natural language; that is, we will communicate with computers in much the same way that we talk with one another.

- *Instructions 5 and 6* allow the personnel manager to improve the appearance and readability of the report by including a title and labeling the columns. Instruction 5 produces the report title, and Instruction 6 specifies descriptive column headings.

The COBOL equivalent of this request would require over 150 lines of code!

Fourth-generation languages are effective tools for generating responses to a variety of requests for information. Short programs, similar to the one in Figure 9–14, are all that are needed to respond to the following typical management requests:

- Which employees have accumulated over 20 sick days since May 1?
- Are there going to be any deluxe single hospital rooms vacated by the end of the day?
- What is a particular student's average in all English courses?
- List departments that have exceeded their budgets alphabetically by the department head's name.

Strengths and weaknesses   The problem with 4GLs is that they are less efficient than third-generation languages. That is, 4GLs require more computer capacity to perform a particular operation. Proponents of 4GLs claim that the added cost of the hardware is more than offset by the time saved in creating the programs. Critics claim that 4GL capabilities are limited (when compared to third-generation languages) and that users end up fitting their problems to the capabilities of the software.

MEMORY BITS

PROGRAMMING LANGUAGES

- 1st generation (machine)
- 2nd generation (assembler)
- 3rd generation (procedure-oriented)
    Business
    Scientific
    Multipurpose
- 4th generation (4GLs)
    Production-oriented
    User-oriented

248

SUMMARY OUTLINE AND IMPORTANT TERMS_____

9–1   **PROGRAMMING IN PERSPECTIVE.** A **program** directs a computer to perform certain operations. The program is produced by a **programmer**, who uses any of a variety of **programming languages** to communicate with the computer.

9–2   **PROBLEM SOLVING AND PROGRAMMING LOGIC.** We direct computers to perform calculations and manipulate data by describing step-by-step instructions in the form of a program. Programs can provide solutions to particular problems. The creativity in programming is in the application of logic, or the creation of the **algorithm**, to problem solving.

The most effective programs are designed so that they can be written in **modules**. Addressing a programming problem in logical modules is known as **structured programming**.

9–3   **PROGRAM DESIGN TECHNIQUES.** Design techniques such as **flowcharting** and **pseudocode** are commonly used to represent systems and programming logic.

Flowcharts illustrate data, information, and work flow by the interconnection of specialized symbols with flow lines. In structured programming, each program is designed with a **driver module**, or **main program**, that calls **subroutines** as they are needed.

Program logic can be conceptualized in three basic control structures: sequence, selection, and **loop**. There are two variations on the loop structure: DOWHILE and DOUNTIL.

Pseudocode represents program logic in programlike statements that are written in plain English. There are no syntax guidelines for formulating pseudocode statements.

9–4   **SO WHAT'S A PROGRAM? CONCEPTS AND PRINCIPLES OF PROGRAMMING.** A computer program is made up of a sequence of instructions, or **statements**. There are five classifications of instructions.

■ Input/output instructions direct the computer to read from or write to a peripheral device.

■ Computation instructions perform arithmetic operations.

■ Control instructions can alter the sequence of a program's execution.

■ Data transfer and assignment instructions permit data to be transferred internally.

■ Format instructions describe how data are to be entered or outputted from primary storage.

9–5   **WRITING PROGRAMS.** Writing a program is a project in itself and follows these seven steps:

Step 1. Describe the problem.

Step 2. Analyze the problem. Examine the output, input, processing, and file-interaction components.

Step 3. Design the general logic of the program.

Step 4. Design the detailed logic of the program.

Step 5. Code the program.

Step 6. Test and debug the program. Programs are **debugged** to eliminate syntax and logic errors and to clean up the input/output.

Step 7. Document the program.

9–6   **GENERATIONS OF PROGRAMMING LANGUAGES.** Like computers, programming languages have evolved in generations. Each new generation permits a more sophisticated programmer/computer interaction.

The first two generations of programming languages are **low-level languages**; that is, the programmer must identify each fundamental operation the computer is to perform. The **machine language** is the only language that can be executed on a particular computer. **High-level languages** have surpassed machine language and **assembler language** in terms of human efficiency.

High-level languages must be translated into machine language to be executed. High-level languages are a programmer convenience and facilitate the programmer/computer interaction. A **compiler** is needed to translate a **source program** in a high-level language into an **object program** in machine language for execution. An **interpreter** performs a function similar to a compiler, but it translates one instruction at a time.

Third-generation languages are **procedure-oriented languages** and are generally classified as business (**COBOL** and **RPG**), scientific (**FORTRAN**), or multipurpose (**C, BASIC, Pascal, PL/I,** and **Ada**). Other third-generation languages include APL, LISP, LOGO, FORTH, Prolog, and Modula-2.

In **fourth-generation languages**, the programmer need only specify *what* to do, not *how* to do it. The features of **4GLs** include English-like instructions, limited mathematical manipulation of data, automatic report formatting, sequencing (sorting), and record selection by criteria.

REVIEW EXERCISES _____

Concepts

1. Draw the flowcharting symbols for manual process, terminal point, workstation, and decision.

2. Where is the test-on-condition placed in a DOWHILE loop? In a DOUNTIL loop?

3. Assign meaningful variable names to at least six data elements you might expect to find in a personnel record.

4. Write a pseudocode program that represents the logic of Module 1.1 (Input Data) in Figure 9–3.

5. Give an original example of a computation instruction.

6. Name and illustrate the three basic program control structures.

7. What is the purpose of a test-on-condition instruction?

8. What are the benefits of structured programming?

9. Associate each of the following with a particular generation of language: 4GLs, mnemonics, and Ada.

10. Name two types of program errors.

11. Name a procedure-oriented programming language in each of the three classifications—business, scientific, and multipurpose.

12. What are the programs called that translate source programs into machine language? Which one does the translation on a single pass? Which one does it one statement at a time?

Discussion

13. Discuss the rationale for the "divide and conquer" approach to programming.

14. What is the rationale for completing the general design of a program's logic before completing a detailed design?

15. Discuss the justification for the extra effort required to document a program fully.

16. Discuss the difference between a program and a programming language.

17. If each new generation of language enhances interaction between programmers and the computer, why not write programs using the most recent generation of language?

18. Which generation of language would a public relations manager be most likely to use? Why?

SELF-TEST (by section)

9–1 Programmers use a variety of _____ to communicate instructions to the computer.

9–2 **a.** The software for an electronic spreadsheet package is contained in a single program. (T/F)
b. Computer programs direct the computer to perform calculations and manipulate data. (T/F)
c. Programs are written in _____ , or independent tasks.
d. The effectiveness of structured programming is still a matter of debate. (T/F)

9–3 Flowcharting is used primarily for program design, rarely for systems design. (T/F)

9–4 In programming, "Subtotal Amount" is not a: (a) numeric value, (b) string constant, or (c) literal value.

9–5 Once all the syntax errors have been removed from a program, no further testing is required. (T/F)

9–6 **a.** When programming in a procedure-oriented language, you tell the computer what to do and how to do it. (T/F)
b. Assembler-level languages use mnemonics to represent instructions. (T/F)
c. A fourth-generation program normally will have fewer instructions than the same program written in a third-generation language. (T/F)

Self-test answers. **9–1** programming languages. **9–2** **(a)** F; **(b)** T; **(c)** modules; **(d)** F. **9–3** F. **9–4** a. **9–5** F. **9–6** **(a)** T; **(b)** T; **(c)** T.

10

Software Concepts and Data Management

STUDENT LEARNING OBJECTIVES

▶ To detail the purpose and objectives of an operating system.

▶ To describe and illustrate the relationships between the levels of the hierarchy of data organization.

▶ To describe how data are stored, retrieved, and manipulated in computer systems.

▶ To demonstrate an understanding of the principles and use of sequential processing and random, or direct-access, processing.

▶ To demonstrate an understanding of the principles and use of database management systems.

▶ To discuss the differences between file-oriented and data base organization.

10–1   THE OPERATING SYSTEM: THE BOSS

Just as the processor is the nucleus of the computer system, the **operating system** is the nucleus of all software activity. The operating system is a family of *systems software* programs that are usually, although not always, supplied by the computer system vendor.

Mainframe Operating Systems

Because minicomputer, mainframe, and supercomputer operating systems are similar, all are discussed under this heading.

Design Objectives.   All hardware and software, both systems and applications, are controlled by the operating system. You might even call the operating system "the boss." Some of the more popular mainframe operating systems include IBM's *MVS*® and *VM/370*®, DEC's *VMS*®, and AT&T's *UNIX*®. The logic, structure, and nomenclature of these and other operating systems vary considerably. However, each is designed with the same four objectives in mind:

1. To minimize **turnaround time** (elapsed time between submittal of a job—for example, print payroll checks—and receipt of output).

2. To maximize **throughput** (amount of processing per unit of time).

3. To optimize the use of the computer system resources (processor, primary storage, and peripheral devices).

4. To facilitate communication between the computer system and the people who run it.

Most duties of an operating system are automatic; however, activities such as the loading of preprinted forms to a line printer require operator intervention. The operating system warns machine-room operators that intervention is needed via audible and visual warnings.

The Supervisor.   One of the operating system programs is always *resident* in primary storage (see Figure 10–1). This program, called the **supervisor**, loads other operating system and applications programs to primary storage as they are needed. For example, when you request a COBOL program compilation, the supervisor loads the COBOL compiler to primary storage and links your source program to the compiler to create an object program. In preparing for execution, another program—the **linkage editor**—assigns a primary storage address to each byte of the object program.

Allocating Computer Resources.   In a typical computer system, several jobs will be executing at the same time. The operating system determines which computer system resources are allocated to which programs. As an example, suppose that a computer system with only one printer has three jobs whose output is ready to be printed. Obviously, two must wait. The operating system continuously resolves this type of resource conflict to optimize the allocation of computer resources.

Operator Interaction.   The operating system is in continuous interaction with computer operators. The incredible speed of a computer system

FIGURE 10–1   Software, Storage, and Execution
The supervisor program is always resident in primary storage and calls other programs, as needed, from secondary storage. For example, applications programs rely on database management system software to assist in the retrieval of data from secondary storage. Software in the front-end processor handles data-communications-related tasks.

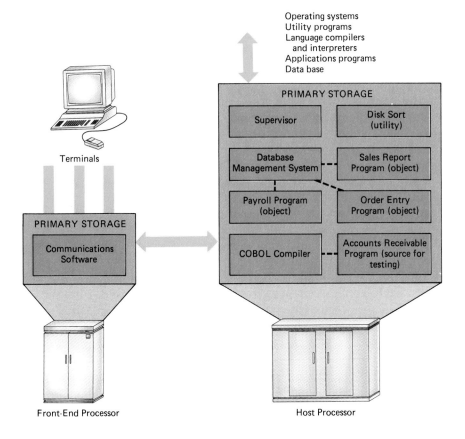

dictates that resource-allocation decisions be made at computer speeds. Most are decided automatically by the operating system. For decisions requiring human input, the operating system interrogates the operators through the operator console (a VDT in the machine room). The operating system also sends messages to the operator. A common message is: "Printer No. 1 is out of paper."

Operators enter commands to direct the operating system to perform specific tasks. For example, operators request the execution of certain programs, reallocate computing resources, and perform system shutdowns.

Programmer Interaction.   Programmers can interact with the operating system within the context of their individual programs, or they can use **job-control language (JCL)**. Programmers often use JCL to specify the **job stream**, the sequence in which their programs are to be executed. They also use JCL to tell the operating system what programming language they are using and where to find the data (for example, which disk drive).

Compatibility Considerations.   There are usually several operating system alternatives available for minis, mainframes, and supercomputers. The choice of an operating system depends on the processing orientation of the company. Some operating systems are better for *timesharing* (servicing multiple end users), others for *processor-intensive jobs* (for example, jobs that involve complex mathematical operations), and still others for *distributed processing* (linking a central computer system with several smaller computer systems).

An information system is designed and coded for a specific *compiler*, *computer*, and *operating system*. This is true for both micros and mainframes. Therefore, programs that work well under one operating system may not be compatible with a different operating system. To minimize compatibility problems, some mainframe operating systems create a **virtual machine (VM)** environment. A VM-type operating system enables a single mainframe computer to emulate other computers and their operating systems while executing programs in its own computing environment. That is, the specifications of a program may designate that it is to be run on Computer A using Operating System X. Upon interpreting the specifications, a VM computer loads the program to that portion of main memory that contains the emulation software for Computer A and Operating System X. Another portion of memory might contain the emulation software for Computer B and Operating System Y.

Virtual machine operating systems are especially valuable when a company is in transition from one computing environment to another. Typically, the new VM computer emulates the old computing environment while applications programs are being modified to run in the new environment. Virtual machine operating systems provide the best of both worlds by using working programs from the past and by taking advantage of the improved price–performance ratio of new technology.

Microcomputer Operating Systems

Objectives and Functions.   The objectives and functions of microcomputer operating systems are similar to those of mainframe operating systems. However, they differ markedly in orientation. In the mainframe environment, specially trained operators and programmers interact with the operating system so that end users can focus on their applications. In contrast, all micro users need a working knowledge of their micro's operating system because they must use it to interface their applications programs with the microcomputer hardware.

The four most popular micro operating systems based on number of installations are:

1. *MS-DOS* (Microsoft Corporation). MS-DOS is the operating system used with IBM-PC–compatible computers. The version of MS-DOS used with the IBM PC is called *PC-DOS*. In practice, MS-DOS is referred to simply as DOS (rhymes with *boss*), an acronym for *disk operating system* (the operating system is stored on disk). Appendix D, "MS-DOS Tutorial and Exercises," contains details on the use and application of this popular operating system.

2. *Macintosh DOS* (Apple Computer, Inc.). Macintosh DOS is the operating system for the Macintosh line of computers.

3. *Operating System/2* or *OS/2* (Microsoft/IBM). OS/2 is the operating system designed for IBM's Personal System/2 (PS/2) line of microcomputers.

4. *UNIX* (AT&T). Originally a mainframe operating system, UNIX and its spinoffs, such as *XENIX*, are frequently used with multiuser microcomputers.

Because these operating systems are so widely used, hundreds of software vendors have developed systems and applications software with which they are compatible.

Although some personal computers can service several workstations, the operating systems for most personal computers are oriented to servicing a single user. This architect has arranged his computer system so that all components are within arm's reach.

Besides controlling the ongoing operation of the microcomputer systems, the micro operating system has two other important functions.

- *Input/output control.* DOS facilitates the movement of data between peripheral devices, the processor, RAM, and programs.
- *File and disk management.* The microcomputer operating system and its file and disk management utility programs enable users to perform such tasks as making backup copies of work disks, erasing disk files that are no longer needed, making inquiries about the number and type of files on a particular diskette, and preparing new diskettes for use. It also handles many file- and disk-oriented tasks that do not involve the end user. For example, the operating system keeps track of the physical location of disk files so we, as users, need only refer to them by name (for example, MYFILE) when loading them from disk to RAM for processing.

Booting the System.   Before you can use a microcomputer, you must load the operating system, or **boot** the system. When you do this, the computer "pulls itself up by its own bootstraps" (without the assistance of humans). The procedure for booting the system on most micros is simply to load the operating system from disk storage into random-access memory. In most micros this is no more difficult than inserting an operating system disk in a disk drive, closing the disk-drive door, and flipping on the switch. On micros with hard disks, all you have to do is turn on the system and the operating system is automatically loaded from the hard disk to RAM.

Operating Environments.   Most micro applications-software packages would be considered more user-friendly than the operating system. There are, however, programs that make micro operating systems as user-friendly as any applications program. These programs are sometimes called *DOS shells* or *DOS helpers* and provide a user-friendly interface between the operating system, applications software, and user files. The term **operating environment** is sometimes used to describe this graphics-oriented, user-friendly DOS interface. Instead of entering sometimes-cryptic operating system commands, you interact with DOS by selecting options from a **pop-up menu** (a boxed display of user options temporarily superimposed over whatever is currently on the screen) or by identifying the appropriate symbolic icon (a pictograph of a file cabinet representing file operations, for example).

For occasional users, operating system commands can be difficult to learn and use. Designers of the OS/2 operating system address this concern by providing a user-friendly interface between the operating system, applications software, and user files. The term operating environment *is sometimes used to describe such an interface. The photo shows one of OS/2's many help screens.*

These RAM-resident interface software packages are accompanied by a variety of helpful RAM-resident programs, including an on-line calendar, scratch pad, calculator, and clock. Because these programs remain in RAM with the operating system, they can be called up at any time, even in the middle of a word processing session.

User-friendly operating system interfaces have effectively eliminated the need for users to memorize and enter cumbersome commands. This user-friendly concept is being applied to future enhancements of personal computer operating systems.

Other System Software Categories

So far we have discussed two system software categories: *programming-language compiler/interpreters* (in Chapter 9, "Programming Languages") and *operating systems*. Other system software categories are *utility programs*, *performance-monitoring software*, *communications software*, and *database management system software*.

- **Utility programs** are service routines that make life easier for us. They eliminate the need for us to write a program every time we need to perform certain computer operations. For example, with the help of utility programs, an employee master file can be easily "dumped" (copied from magnetic disk to magnetic tape for backup), or the employee master file can be sorted by social security number.

- **Performance-monitoring software** is used to monitor, analyze, and report on the performance of the overall computer system and the computer system components. This software provides such information as the percentage of processor utilization and the number of disk accesses during any given period of time. This type of information enables the scheduler to make the most efficient use of hardware resources, and it helps management plan for future hardware upgrades.

- **Communications software** controls the flow of traffic (data) to and from remote locations. Functions performed by communications software include: preparing data for transmission (inserting start/stop bits in messages), polling remote terminals for input, establishing the connection between two terminals, encoding and decoding data, and parity checking. In the mainframe environment, communications software is executed on the front-end processor, the down-line processor, and the host processor.

- **Database management system (DBMS) software** provides the interface between application programs and the data base. DBMS concepts are discussed in greater detail in Section 10–5.

MEMORY BITS

SYSTEM SOFTWARE CATEGORIES
- Programming-language compiler/interpreters
- Operating systems
- Utility programs
- Performance monitoring software
- Communications software
- Database management system (DBMS) software

10–2 SOFTWARE CONCEPTS

Multiprogramming

All computers except small micros have **multiprogramming** capability. Multiprogramming is the *concurrent execution* of more than one program at a time. Actually, a computer can execute only one program at a time. But its internal processing speed is so fast that several programs

The operating system of this supercomputer system is the nerve center of a network of computer systems. The system services hundreds of on-line users in a multiprogramming environment.

can be allocated "slices" of computer time in rotation; this makes it appear that several programs are being executed at once.

The great difference in processor speed and the speeds of the peripheral devices makes multiprogramming possible. An 800-page-per-minute printer cannot even challenge the speed of an average mainframe processor. The processor is continually waiting for the peripheral devices to complete such tasks as retrieving a record from disk storage, printing a report, or copying a backup file onto magnetic tape. During these waiting periods, the processor just continues processing other programs. In this way, computer system resources are used efficiently.

In a multiprogramming environment, it is not unusual for several programs to require the same I/O device. For example, two or more programs may be competing for the printer. Rather than hold up the processing of a program by waiting for the printer to become available, both programs are executed and the printer output for one is temporarily loaded to magnetic disk. As the printer becomes available, the output is called from magnetic disk and printed. This process is called **spooling**.

Virtual Memory

We learned in Chapter 3, "Inside the Computer," that all data and programs must be resident in primary storage in order to be processed. Therefore, primary storage is a critical factor in determining the throughput—how much work can be done by a computer system per unit of time. Once primary storage is full, no more programs can be executed until a portion of primary storage is made available.

COMPUTERS ARE NOT COMPATIBLE WITH EARTHQUAKES

At the peak of the evening rush hour on October 17, 1989, San Francisco and the surrounding area experienced a severe earthquake that registered 7.1 on the Richter scale. The rest of the country watched fires, fallen bridges, and evacuation efforts on television, and became deeply concerned about the people of northern California. Some were also concerned about the fate of the 1989 World Series. Those in San Francisco and the Silicon Valley were worried about their family, friends, property, and their computer systems—yes, their computer systems. PCs were jumping off desks. Mainframes and minis were rocking and literally rolling on the floor. Racks filled with communications hardware and data-storage media tipped over. A data center director at a San Francisco hospital compared his machine room to the aftermath of a bomb explosion.

The Hewlett Packard Company reacted to the earthquake as many other companies did. Executives gave all of Hewlett Packard's 18,000 employees the day off—all except its data processing staff. When a company's computer system goes down, its survival is at stake. A University of Minnesota study examined corporate victims of disasters and concluded that the probability of long-term survival is low if they are unable to recover critical computer system operations within 30 hours.

The earthquake forced many companies to test their disaster recovery plans. The first order of business was to get the computer system up and running as soon as possible. If the computer system is intact, the company's only concern is power. Power was cut off for hours and even days throughout northern California. As power went out in much of San Francisco, companies switched to their UPS (uninterruptible power supply) system, at least those that worked. Backup batteries, connections, and generators also had fallen to the earthquake.

Companies with damaged computers either transferred critical systems to a backup site, repaired damaged hardware, or ordered new hardware. Companies with undamaged hardware pitched in and provided limited backup support to less-fortunate companies. Computer manufacturers such as IBM and Digital Equipment Company made every resource available to their customers. Disaster recovery firms, which are set up to handle one disaster at a time, did everything possible to accommodate subscribers.

People cooperated, and disaster plans worked. Computer centers in northern California experienced minimal damage, and operations at all but a few companies were restored by the next day, a truly amazing recovery from a major disaster.

Virtual memory is a systems software addition to the operating system that effectively expands the capacity of primary storage through the use of software and secondary storage. This allows more data and programs to be resident in primary storage at any given time.

The principle behind virtual memory is quite simple. Remember, a program is executed sequentially—one instruction after another. Programs are segmented into **pages**, so only that portion of the program being executed (one or more pages) is resident in primary storage. The rest of the program is on disk storage. Appropriate pages are *rolled* (moved) into primary storage from disk storage as they are needed to continue execution of the program. The paging process and use of virtual memory are illustrated in Figure 10–2.

The advantage of virtual memory is that primary storage is effectively enlarged, giving programmers greater flexibility in what they can do. For example, some applications require several large programs to reside in primary storage at the same time. (See the order-processing and

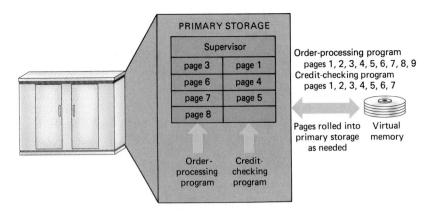

FIGURE 10–2   Virtual Memory
Pages of the order-processing and credit-checking programs are rolled from virtual memory on magnetic disk into "real" memory (primary storage) as they are needed.

credit-checking programs illustrated in Figure 10–2.) If the size of these programs exceeds the capacity of primary storage, then virtual memory can be used as a supplement to complete the processing.

The disadvantage of virtual memory is the cost in efficiency during program execution. If the logic of a program causes frequent branching between pages, the program will execute more slowly because of the time required to roll pages from secondary to primary storage. Excessive page movement results in too much of the computer's time devoted to page handling and not enough to processing. This excessive data movement is appropriately named *thrashing* and actually can be counterproductive.

10–3   THE HIERARCHY OF DATA ORGANIZATION: BITS TO DATA BASES

The six levels of the *hierarchy of data organization* are illustrated in Figure 10–3. They are *bit*, *character*, *data element* or *field*, *record*, *file*, and *data base*. You are already familiar with several levels of the hierarchy. Bits and characters are discussed in some detail in Chapter 3, "Inside the Computer." Records and files are introduced in Chapter 1, "The World of Computers," and Chapter 5, "Data Storage Devices and Media."

Each information system has a hierarchy of data organization, and each succeeding level in the hierarchy is the result of combining the elements of the preceding level (see Figure 10–3). Data are logically combined in this fashion until a data base is achieved. Bits—the first level—are handled automatically, without action on the part of either the programmer or the end user. The other five levels are important design considerations for any information-processing activity. The following paragraphs explain each level of the hierarchy and how it relates to the succeeding level.

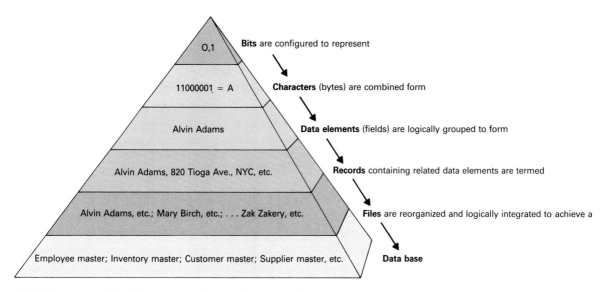

FIGURE 10–3 The Hierarchy of Data Organization

Bits and Characters

A **character** is represented by a group of *bits* that are configured according to an encoding system, such as ASCII or EBCDIC. Whereas the bit is the basic unit of primary and secondary storage, the character is the basic unit for human perception. When we enter a program instruction on a terminal, each character is automatically encoded into a bit configuration. The bit configurations are decoded on output so we can read and understand the output. In terms of data storage, a character is usually the same as a *byte*. (See Chapter 3 for more on bits, bytes, and encoding systems.)

Data Elements, or Fields

The **data element**, or **field**, is the lowest level *logical* unit in the data hierarchy. For example, a single character (such as A) has little meaning out of context. But when characters are combined to form a name (for example, *Alicia* or *Alvin*), they form a logical unit. A data element is best described by example: social security number, first name, street address, marital status. These are all data elements.

An address is not one, but four data elements: street address, city, state, and ZIP code. If we treated the entire address as one data element, it would be cumbersome to print because the street address is normally placed on a separate line from the city, state, and ZIP code. Because name-and-address files are often sorted by ZIP code, it is also a good idea to store the ZIP code as a separate data element.

When it is stored in secondary storage, a data element is allocated a certain number of character positions. The number of these positions is called the *field length*. The field length of a telephone area code is 3. The field length of a telephone number is 7.

When you travel by air and check your luggage through to your destination, a
three-character destination tag is attached to each piece of luggage. The destination
code is one of several data elements in the luggage handling data base. If your
destination is Oklahoma City, the data item associated with your luggage is OKC,
the designator of Will Rogers World Airport. At this airport, the destination code
on the luggage tag is read by an optical scanner and your luggage is automatically
routed, via conveyor, to the appropriate pickup station.

Pharmacists check prescriptions against a drug-interaction data base to prevent
dispensing drug combinations that might prove harmful.

Data Elements	Data Items
Employee/social security number	445447279
Last name	SMITH
First name	ALVIN
Middle initial	E
Department (coded)	ACT
Sex (coded)	M
Marital status (coded)	S
Salary (per week)	800.00

FIGURE 10–4   A Portion of an Employee Record
The data elements listed are commonly found in employee records. Data items appear next to each data element.

Whereas the data element, or field, is the general (or generic) reference, the specific content of a data element is called the **data item**. For example, a social security number is a data element, but *445487279* and *440214158* are data items. A street address is a data element, but *1701 El Camino* and *134 East Himes Street* are data items.

Records

A *record* is a description of an event (a sale, a hotel reservation) or an item (a customer, a part). Related data elements describing an event or item are logically grouped to form a record. For example, Figure 10–4 contains a partial list of data elements for a typical employee record. It also shows the data items for an *occurrence* of a particular employee record (Alvin E. Smith): "Department," "Sex," and "Marital status" are *coded* for ease of data entry and to save storage space.

In general, the record is the lowest level logical unit that can be accessed from a file. For instance, if the personnel manager needs to know only the marital status of Alvin E. Smith, he will have to retrieve Smith's entire record from secondary storage and transmit it to primary storage for processing.

Files

A **file** is a collection of related records. The employee file contains a record for each employee. An inventory file contains a record for each inventory item. The accounts receivable file contains a record for each customer. The term *file* is also used to refer to a named area on a secondary storage device that contains a *program*, *textual material* (such as a letter), or even an *image*.

Data Bases

The **data base** is the data resource for every computer-based information system. In essence, a data base is a collection of files that are in some way logically related to one another. In a data base, the data are integrated and related so that data redundancy is minimized. For example, if records are kept in a traditional file environment and an employee moves, his or her address must be changed in all files that maintain address data. In a data base, employee-address data are stored only once and are made available to all departments. Therefore, only one update is needed.

Database management system software, discussed later in this chapter, has enabled many organizations to move from traditional file organization to data base organization, thereby enjoying the benefits of a higher level of data management sophistication.

MEMORY BITS

HIERARCHY OF DATA ORGANIZATION
- Bit
- Character (byte)
- Data element, or field
- Record
- File
- Data base

10–4   TRADITIONAL APPROACHES TO DATA MANIPULATION AND RETRIEVAL

Data Management

Data management encompasses the storage, retrieval, and manipulation of data. In the remainder of this chapter we will discuss the concepts and methods involved in computer-based data management. We first discuss the traditional methods of data organization, then database management systems.

Your present or future employer will probably use both the traditional and the data base approaches to data management. Many existing information systems were designed using traditional approaches to data management, but the trend now is to use the data base approach to develop new information systems.

In traditional file processing, files are sorted, merged, and processed by a **key data element**. For example, in a payroll file the key might be "social security number," and in an inventory file the key might be "part number."

When you write programs based on the traditional approaches, data are manipulated and retrieved either *sequentially* or *randomly*. You might recall that sequential and random (or direct) access were discussed briefly in Chapter 5, "Data Storage Devices and Media." An analogy was made between sequential processing and cassette tapes, and between random processing and phonograph records. Sequential and random processing are presented in detail in the sections that follow.

Sequential Processing: One after Another

Sequential files, used for **sequential processing**, contain records ordered according to a key data element. The key, also called a **control field**, in an employee record might be social security number or employee name. If the key is social security number, the employee records are ordered and processed *numerically* by social security number. If the key is employee name, the records are ordered and processed *alphabetically* by last name. A *sequential file is processed from start to finish. The entire file must be processed, even if only one record is to be updated.*

The principal storage medium for sequential files is magnetic tape. Direct-access storage devices (DASD), such as magnetic disks, also can be used for sequential processing.

Principles of Sequential Processing.   Sequential processing procedures for updating an inventory file are illustrated in Figures 10–5, 10–6, and 10–7. Figure 10–5 lists the contents of an inventory *master file*, which is the permanent source of inventory data, and a *transaction file*, which reflects the daily inventory activity.

Prior to processing, the records on both files are sorted and arranged in ascending sequence by part number (the key). A utility sort program takes a file of unsequenced records and creates a new file with the records sorted according to the values of the key. The sort process is illustrated in Figure 10–6.

Inventory master file (sorted by part number)

Part no.	Price	No. used to date	No. in stock
2	25	40	200
4	1.40	100 [106] *	100 [94]
8	.80	500	450
•	•	•	•
•	•	•	•
•	•	•	•
20	4.60	60 [72]	14 [2]
21	2.20	50	18

One record ➡ (record for part no. 2)

*[ ] reflects updated values

Transaction file (sorted by part number)

Part no.	No. used today
4	6
20	12

FIGURE 10–5   Inventory Master and Transaction Files
Both files are sorted by part number. The numbers in brackets [ ] reflect the inventory master file after the update. Figures 10–7 and 10–8 illustrate the update process.

Figure 10–7 shows both the inventory master and transaction files as input and the *new inventory master file* as output. Because the technology does not permit records to be "rewritten" on the magnetic-tape master file, a new master file tape is created to reflect the updates to the master file. *A new master file is always created for master file updates in tape*

FIGURE 10–6   Sorting
Unsequenced inventory master and transaction files are sorted prior to sequential processing. Normally, the master file would have been sorted as a result of prior processing.

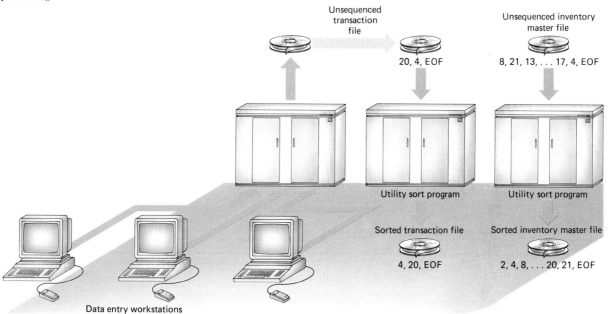

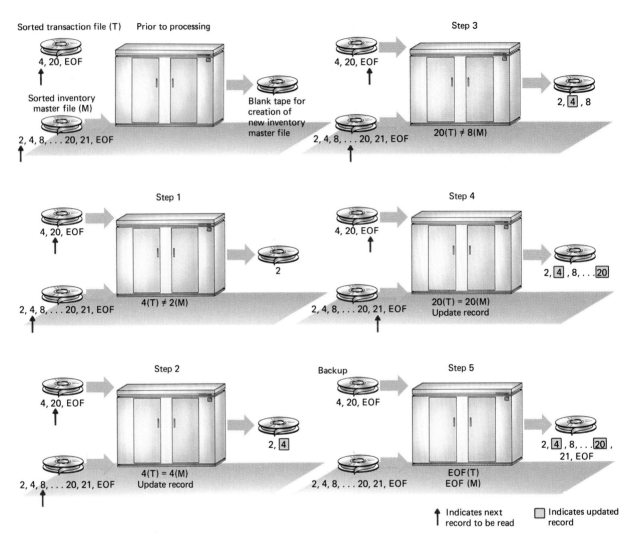

FIGURE 10–7   Sequential Processing
An inventory master file is updated using sequential processing and magnetic tapes.
Processing steps are discussed in the text. Notice in Step 5 that the backup is a
by-product of sequential processing.

sequential processing. The processing steps are illustrated in Figure 10–7
and explained as follows:

- *Prior to processing.* If the two input tapes are *not sorted* by part number,
  they must be sorted as shown in Figure 10–6. The sorted tapes are then
  mounted on the tape drives. A blank tape, mounted on a third tape drive,
  will ultimately contain the updated master file. The arrows under the
  part numbers in Figure 10–7 indicate which records are positioned at the
  read/write heads on the respective tape drives. These records are the *next*
  to be read. Each file has an **end-of-file marker (EOF)** that signals the
  end of the file.

- *Step 1.* The first record (4) on the transaction file (T) is read and loaded
  to primary storage. Then the first record (2) on the master file (M) is

loaded to primary storage. A comparison is made of the two keys. Because there is no match (4 ≠ [is not equal to] 2), the first record on the master file is written to the new master file tape without being changed.

■ *Step 2.* The next record (4) on the master file is read and loaded to primary storage. After a positive comparison (4 = 4), the record of Part Number 4 is updated (see Figure 10–5) to reflect the use of six items and then written to the new master file. In Figure 10–5 note that the Number in Stock data item is reduced from 100 to 94 and the Number Used to Date is increased from 100 to 106. Updated records in Figure 10–7 are enclosed in boxes.

■ *Step 3.* The next record from the transaction file (20) and the next record from the master file (8) are read and loaded to primary storage. A comparison is made. Because the comparison is negative (20 ≠ 8), the record for Part Number 8 is written to the new master file without being changed.

■ *Step 4.* Records from the master file are individually read and loaded, and the part number is compared to that of the transaction record (20). With each negative comparison (for example, 20 ≠ 17), the record from the old master file is written, without change, to the new master file. The read-and-compare process continues until a match is made (20 = 20). Record 20 is then updated and written to the new master file.

■ *Step 5.* A "read" is issued to the transaction file and an end-of-file marker is found. All records on the master file following the record for Part Number 20 are written to the new master file, and the end-of-file marker is recorded on the new master file. All tapes are then automatically rewound and removed from the tape drives for off-line storage and processing at a later time.

This is one of 10 aisles in a large magnetic-tape library. Most of the ½-inch tape cartridges in this library are used for archival storage and backup. Those used for processing are organized by key data element. The entire library is secured in a fireproof vault to protect the data stored on the tapes from theft and environmental disasters.

Backup.   The transaction file and old master file are retained as *backup* to the new master file. Fortunately, *backup is a by-product of sequential processing*. After the new master file is created, the old master file and the transaction file become the backup. If the new master is destroyed, the transaction file can simply be run against the old master file to recreate the new master file.

Backup files are handled and maintained by *generation*, the up-to-date master file being the current generation. This tape cycling procedure is called the **grandfather-father-son method** of file backup. The "son" file is the up-to-date master file. The "father" generation is noted in Step 5 of Figure 10–7. Most computer centers maintain a grandfather file (from the last update run) as a backup to the backup.

Random, or Direct-Access, Processing: Pick and Choose

A **direct-access file**, or a **random file**, is a collection of records that can be processed randomly (in any order). This is called **random processing**, or **direct-access processing**. Only the value of the record's key field is needed in order to retrieve or update a record. More often than not magnetic disks are the storage medium for random processing.

You can access records on a direct-access file by more than one key. For example, a salesperson inquiring about the availability of a particular product could inquire by *product number* and, if the product number is not known, by *product name*. The file, however, must be created with the intent of having multiple keys.

This real estate company subscribes to a regional on-line multilist service. The record of any listed property can be retrieved from a direct-access file by keying in the property's listing code, which is the key data element.

Random-Access Methods. The procedures and mechanics of the way a particular record is accessed directly are, for the most part, transparent (not a concern) to users and even to programmers. However, some familiarity will help you understand the capabilities and limitations of direct-access methods. **Indexed-sequential organization** is a popular method that permits both sequential and random processing.

In indexed-sequential organization there are actually two files: The *data file* contains the records (for each student, for each inventory item, and so on); the smaller *index file* contains the key and disk address of each record on the data file. A request for a particular record is first directed to the smaller, more accessible index file which, in turn, "points" to the physical location of the desired record on magnetic disk (see Chapter 5, "Data Storage Devices and Media").

Principles of Random Processing. In Figure 10–8, the inventory master file of Figure 10–5 is updated from an *on-line* terminal to illustrate the principles of random processing. The following activities take place during the update:

- *Step 1.* The first transaction (for Part Number 20) is entered into primary storage from an on-line terminal. The computer issues a read for the record of Part Number 20 on the inventory master file. The record is retrieved and transmitted to primary storage for processing. The record is updated and written back to the *same* location on the master file. The updated record is simply written over the old record.

- *Step 2.* A second transaction (for Part Number 4) is entered into primary storage. The computer issues a read for the record of Part Number 4 on the inventory master file. The record is retrieved and transmitted to primary storage for processing. The record is then updated.

FIGURE 10–8   Random Processing
An inventory master file is updated using random processing and magnetic disks. Processing steps are discussed in the text.

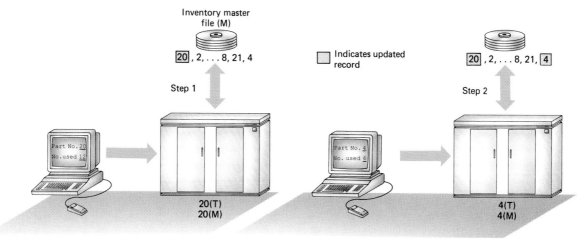

In 1968 John Cullinane, now president of the Cullinane Group, Inc., founded Cullinet Software, the first company to specialize exclusively in software products. It went on to become the first software company to be listed on the New York Stock Exchange.

Being at the forefront of a new industry poses such special challenges as: How do you meet an $8500 payroll with only $500? Fortunately, an $8500 check was in the mail, but the incident prompted Cullinane to downsize from nine employees to five. He later said, "It turned out that we were much more efficient with five than we were with nine."

In the 1960s companies purchased computers, then created their applications software from scratch. Reflecting on the computer industry during that era, Cullinane said, "It just didn't make good sense to re-invent the software 'wheel.' Others recognized the opportunity as well and, as a result, the software industry has grown to such an extent that software, once dominated by hardware, now often drives hardware sales."

Because only two updates are to be made to the inventory master file, processing is complete. However, unlike sequential processing where the backup is built in, random processing requires a special run to provide backup to the inventory master file. In the backup activity illustrated in Figure 10–9, the master file is "dumped" from disk to tape at frequent intervals, usually daily. If the inventory master file is destroyed, it can be recreated by dumping the backup file (on tape) to disk (the reverse of Figure 10–9).

As you can see, random processing is more straightforward than sequential processing, and it has those advantages associated with on-line, interactive processing. Figure 10–10 summarizes the differences between sequential and random processing.

FIGURE 10–9   Backup Procedure for Random Processing
Unlike sequential processing, a separate run is required to create the backup for random processing.

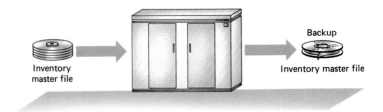

Inventory
master file

Backup

Inventory master file

	Sequential Processing	Random Processing
Primary storage medium	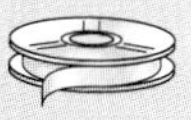	
Preprocessing	Files must be sorted	None required
File updating	Requires complete processing of file and creation of new master file	Only active records are processed, then rewritten to the same storage area
Data currency	Batch (at best, data are a day old)	On-line (up-to-the-minute)
Backup	Built-in (old master file and transaction file)	Requires special provisions

FIGURE 10–10   Differences Between Sequential and Random Processing

10–5   DATABASE MANAGEMENT SYSTEMS: SOLVING THE DATA PUZZLE

Our discussion thus far has focused on traditional file processing. Usually these files are designed to meet the specific requirements of a particular functional-area department, such as accounting, sales, or production. Consequently, different but similar files are created to support these functions. Many of the data elements on each of these files are common. For example, each functional area needs to maintain such data as customer name, customer address, and the contact person at the customer location. When the name of the contact person changes in a traditional file environment, each file must be updated separately.

Data redundancy is costly, but it can be minimized by designing an *integrated data base* to serve the organization as a whole, not just one specific department. The integrated data base is made possible by *database management system (DBMS)* software. Some of the DBMS software packages on the market include IMS, DB2, dBASE III®, TOTAL, IDMS, IDMS/R, DL1, System 2000, RAMIS, ADABAS, Ingress, SQL/DS, and Encompass. Notice that *database* is one word when it refers to the software that manages the data base. *Data base* is two words when it refers to the highest level of the hierarchy of data organization (see Figure 10–3).

What's to Be Gained from a Data Base Environment?

Greater Access to Information.   Most organizations have accumulated a wealth of data, but translating these data into meaningful information has, at times, proved difficult, especially in a traditional file environment. The structure of an integrated data base provides enormous *flexibility* in the types of reports that can be generated and the types of on-line inquiries that can be made.

Less Data Redundancy.   A database management system minimizes data redundancy through advanced *data structures*, or the manner in which the data elements and records are related to each other.

Software Development Made Easier.   The programming task is simplified with a database management system because data are more readily available. In a data base, data are *independent* of the applications programs. That is, data elements can be added, changed, and deleted from the data base, and this does not affect existing programs. In addition, the processing constraints of traditional files are overcome by database management systems software.

DBMS versus Traditional File Processing

In contrast to the traditional approaches to file management, a DBMS accesses data by *content* rather than by *address*. That is, the DBMS approach uses the computer to search the data base for the desired data rather than accessing data through a series of indices and physical addresses. In the example DBMS that follows, the data structures, or relationships between data, are defined in *logical* rather than *physical* terms. That is, the data base has no predetermined relationship between the data, such as records in the traditional file environment (see Figure 10–11). In this way, data can be accessed at the *data element* level. In traditional file processing, the entire record must be retrieved to examine a single data element.

A Database Management Systems Example

The following DBMS example should help you better understand the principles and advantages of database management systems. The example focuses on the book circulation activity in a library. The objective of a circulation system is to keep track of who borrows which books, then monitor their timely return. In the traditional file environment, the record layout might be as shown in Figure 10–11. In this record, a library patron can borrow from one to four books. Precious storage space is wasted for patrons who borrow infrequently, and the four-book limit may force prolific readers to make more frequent trips to the library.

The *relational* DBMS organization shown in Figure 10–12 is the basis for this example. The relational DBMS is one of three types of database management systems commonly found in practice. The data base in Figure 10–12 contains two *tables*, each containing rows and columns of data. A row is roughly equivalent to a record in a traditional file environment. The column headings, called *attributes*, are analogous to data elements.

The first table contains patron data and the second table contains data relating to books out on loan. Each new patron is issued a library

FIGURE 10–11   Record Layout
This record layout is for a traditional book circulation file in a library.

Card No.	First Name	Last Name	Address				Book #1 (ISBN)	Due Date	Book #2 (ISBN)	Due Date	Book #3 (ISBN)	Due Date	Book #4 (ISBN)	Due Date
			Street	City	ST	ZIP								

Patron Data

Card No.	First Name	Last Name	Address				Books-on-Loan Data

Card No.	First Name	Last Name	Street	City	ST	ZIP
1243	Jason	Jones	18 W. Oak	Ponca City	OK	74601
1618	Kay	Smith	108 10th St.	Newkirk	OK	74647
2380	Heather	Hall	2215 Pine Dr.	Ponca City	OK	74604
2644	Brett	Brown	1700 Sunset	Ponca City	OK	74604
3012	Melody	Beck	145 N. Brook	Ark. City	KS	67005
3376	Butch	Danner	RD#7	Tonkawa	OK	74653
3859	Abe	Michaels	333 Paul Ave.	Kaw City	OK	74641

Books-on-Loan Data

Card No.	Book No. (ISBN)	Due Date
1618	89303-530	4/7
1243	12-201702	4/20
3859	13-48049	4/9
2644	18-23614	4/14
2644	71606-214	4/14
2644	22-68111	4/3
1618	27-21675	4/12

FIGURE 10–12   A Relational Data Base Organization
The record layout of the traditional book circulation file of Figure 10–11 is reorganized and integrated into a relational data base with a Patron Data table and a Books-on-Loan Data table.

card with a number that can be read with an optical wand scanner. The patron's card number, name, and address are added to the data base. When the patron borrows a book, the librarian at the circulation desk uses a wand scanner to enter the card number and the book's ISBN (International Standard Book Number). These data and the due date, which are entered on a keyboard, become a row in the Books on Loan Data table. Notice that by using a relational DBMS there is no limit to the number of borrowed books the system can handle for a particular patron.

Suppose the circulation librarian wanted a report of overdue books as of April 8 (4/8). The query would be: "List all books overdue" (query date is 4/8). The search criterion of "due date < (before) 4/8" is applied to the Due Date column in the Books on Loan Data table (see Figure 10–13). The search reveals two overdue books; then the system uses the card numbers to cross-reference delinquent patrons in the Patron Data table to obtain their names and addresses. The report at the bottom of Figure 10–13 is produced in response to the librarian's query. Data on each book, including publisher, author, and ISBN, might be maintained in another table in the relational data base.

FIGURE 10–13   Queries to a Relational Data Base
The figure illustrates the resolution and output of an April 8 query to the data base: "List all books overdue." The card numbers in the "yes" response rows are cross-referenced to the Patron Data table in Figure 10–12 to produce the report.

Card No.	Book No. (ISBN)	Due Date	Overdue? (Due Date < 4/8)
1618	89303-530-0	4/7	⟶ Yes
1243	13-201702-5	4/20	⟶ No
3859	13-48049-8	4/9	⟶ No
2644	18-23614-1	4/14	⟶ No
2644	71606-214-0	4/14	⟶ No
2644	22-68111-7	4/3	⟶ Yes
1618	27-21675-2	4/12	⟶ No

Overdue Books (4/8)			
Card No.	Name	Due Date	ISBN
1618	Kay Smith	4/7	89303-530-0
2644	Brett Brown	4/3	22-68111-7

Companies are converting their sequential and direct-access files to data base systems. Data base systems almost eliminate data redundancy, and they provide knowledge workers with immediate on-line access to the information necessary to do their jobs efficiently and effectively.

We all keep data, both at our place of business and at home. DBMS software and the availability of computing hardware make it easier for us to extract meaningful information from these data. In time, working with data bases will be as familiar to us as reaching in a desk drawer for a file folder.

SUMMARY OUTLINE AND IMPORTANT TERMS

10–1   **THE OPERATING SYSTEM: THE BOSS.** The design objectives of an **operating system**, the nucleus of all software activity, are to minimize **turnaround time**, maximize throughput, optimize the use of computer resources, and facilitate communication with computer operators.

Mainframe operating systems are oriented to a particular type of processing environment, such as timesharing, processor-intensive jobs, or distributed processing. The memory-resident **supervisor** program loads other operating-system and applications programs to primary storage as they are needed. The **linkage editor** assigns a primary storage address to each byte of the object program.

Programmers can interact with the operating system within the context of their individual programs, or they can use the **job-control language (JCL)**. Programmers often use JCL to specify the **job stream**.

A **virtual machine (VM)** operating system enables a single mainframe computer to emulate other computers and their operating systems while executing programs in its own computing environment.

MS-DOS®, Macintosh DOS, OS/2, and UNIX® are popular operating systems for microcomputers. Until recently micro operating systems were oriented to servicing a single user. Today the more sophisticated micro operating systems support the multiuser environment. Besides controlling the ongoing operation of a microcomputer system, the micro operating system controls all input/output and handles file and disk management duties.

MEMORY BITS

APPROACHES TO DATA MANAGEMENT
- Sequential processing
- Random (or direct) processing
    Indexed-sequential organization
    Direct access
- Database management systems (DBMS)

Before you can use a microcomputer, you must **boot** the system—that is, load the operating system from disk storage into RAM.

DOS shells, or *DOS helpers*, provide a user-friendly interface between the operating system, applications software, and user files. The term **operating environment** describes the user-friendly operating system interface.

Systems software categories include programming-language compilers/interpreters, operating systems, **utility programs, performance-monitoring software, communications software**, and **database management system (DBMS) software.**

10–2 SOFTWARE CONCEPTS. **Multiprogramming** is the seemingly simultaneous execution of more than one program at a time on a single computer. **Virtual memory** effectively expands the capacity of primary storage through the use of software, the **paging** process, and secondary storage.

10–3 THE HIERARCHY OF DATA ORGANIZATION: BITS TO DATA BASES. The six levels of the hierarchy of data organization are bit, **character** (or byte), **data element** (or **field**), record, **file**, and **data base**. The first level is transparent to the programmer and end user, but the other five are integral to the design of any information processing activity. A string of bits is combined to form a character. Characters are combined to represent the content of data elements—**data items**. Related data elements are combined to form records. Records with the same data elements combine to form a file. The data base is the company's data resource for all information systems.

10–4 TRADITIONAL APPROACHES TO DATA MANIPULATION AND RETRIEVAL. Most organizations use both the traditional and data base approaches to data management. The trend is to the data base approach.

In traditional file processing, files are sorted, merged, and processed by a **key data element**. Data are retrieved and manipulated either sequentially or randomly.

Sequential files, used for **sequential processing**, contain records ordered according to a key, also called a **control field**. A sequential file is processed from start to finish, and a particular record cannot be updated without processing the entire file.

In tape sequential processing, the records on both the transaction and the master file must be sorted prior to processing. A new master file is created for each computer run in which records are added or changed.

The **direct-access**, or **random, file** permits **random processing** of records. The primary storage medium for direct-access files is magnetic disk.

Indexed-sequential organization is one of several access methods that permit a programmer random access to any record on a file. In indexed-sequential organization, access to any given record begins with a search through an index file. This search results in the disk address of the record in question.

In random processing, the unsorted transaction file is run against a random master file. Only the records needed to complete the transaction are retrieved from secondary storage.

10–5   DATABASE MANAGEMENT SYSTEMS: SOLVING THE DATA PUZZLE. A traditional file usually is designed to meet the specific requirements of a particular functional-area department. This approach to file design results in the same data being stored and maintained in several separate files. Data redundancy is costly and can be minimized by designing an integrated data base to serve the organization as a whole, rather than any specific department. The integrated data base is made possible by database management system (DBMS) software.

The benefits of a data base environment have encouraged many organizations to convert information systems that use traditional file organization into an integrated data base. Database management systems permit greater access to information, minimize data redundancy, and provide programmers more flexibility in the design and maintenance of information systems.

In relational DBMSs, data are accessed by content rather than by address. There is no predetermined relationship between the data; therefore, the data can be accessed at the data element level. Data are organized in tables in which each row is roughly equivalent to a record in a traditional file environment.

REVIEW EXERCISES

Concepts

1. Why is it necessary to spool output in a multiprogramming environment?

2. Name the systems software category associated with: (a) a company's data base, (b) file backup, and (c) overall software and hardware control.

3. What is meant by "booting the system"?

4. What are the six levels of the hierarchy of data organization?

5. What is the lowest level logical unit in the hierarchy of data organization?

6. Name two possible key data elements for a personnel file. Name two for an inventory file.

7. In the grandfather-father-son method of file backup, which of the three files is the most current?

8. What is the purpose of an end-of-file marker?

9. Under what circumstances is a new master file created in sequential processing?

10. What is meant when someone says that data are program-independent?

11. Use the technique of Figure 10–7 to illustrate graphically the sequential-processing steps required to update the inventory master file of Figure 10–5. The transaction file contains activity for Part Numbers 8 and 21. Assume that the transaction file is unsequenced.

12. Use the technique of Figure 10–8 to illustrate graphically the random-processing steps required to update the inventory master file of Figure 10–5. The transaction file contains activity for Part Numbers 8 and 21. Provide for backup.

13. The attribute of a relational DBMS is analogous to which level of the hierarchy of data organization?

Discussion

14. Contrast the advantages and disadvantages of sequential and random processing. Do you feel there will be a place for sequential processing in 1995? If so, where?

15. Assume that the registrar, housing office, and placement service at your college all have computer-based information systems that rely on traditional file organization. Identify possible redundant data elements.

16. The author contends that a fundamental knowledge of the capabilities and limitations of indexed-sequential organization is important, even though storage and search procedures are transparent to the programmer. Do you agree or disagree? Why?

17. What do you feel is the most significant advantage of using a database management system? Why?

SELF-TEST (by section)

10–1 **a.** The operating system program that is always resident in main memory is called the supervisor. (T/F)
  b. A micro user must "kick the system" to load the operating system to RAM prior to processing. (T/F)
  c. A user-friendly interface between the operating system, the applications program, and user files is called an operating environment. (T/F)
  d. Programmers often use JCL to specify the _____, or the sequence in which their programs are to be executed.
  e. What type of systems software provides information on processor utilization: (a) utility programs, (b) performance-monitoring software, or (c) communications software?

10–2 **a.** Programs are segmented into pages before they are spooled. (T/F)
  b. Virtual memory effectively expands the capacity of primary storage through the use of software and secondary storage. (T/F)

10–3 The specific value of a data element is called the _____.

10–4 **a.** A key data element is not needed for sequential processing. (T/F)
  b. The entire magnetic tape master file must be processed even if only one record is to be updated. (T/F)
  c. In indexed-sequential organization, the data file contains the key and disk address. (T/F)

10–5 **a.** Integrated data bases are made possible by DBMS software. (T/F)
  b. One of the disadvantages of DBMS software is that data are independent of the applications programs. (T/F)
  c. In relational DBMSs, the data structures are defined in logical rather than physical terms. (T/F)

Self-test answers   **10–1** (a) T; (b) F; (c) T; (d) job stream; (e) b. **10–2** (a) F; (b) T. **10–3** data item. **10–4** (a) F; (b) T; (c) F. **10–5** (a) T; (b) F; (c) T.

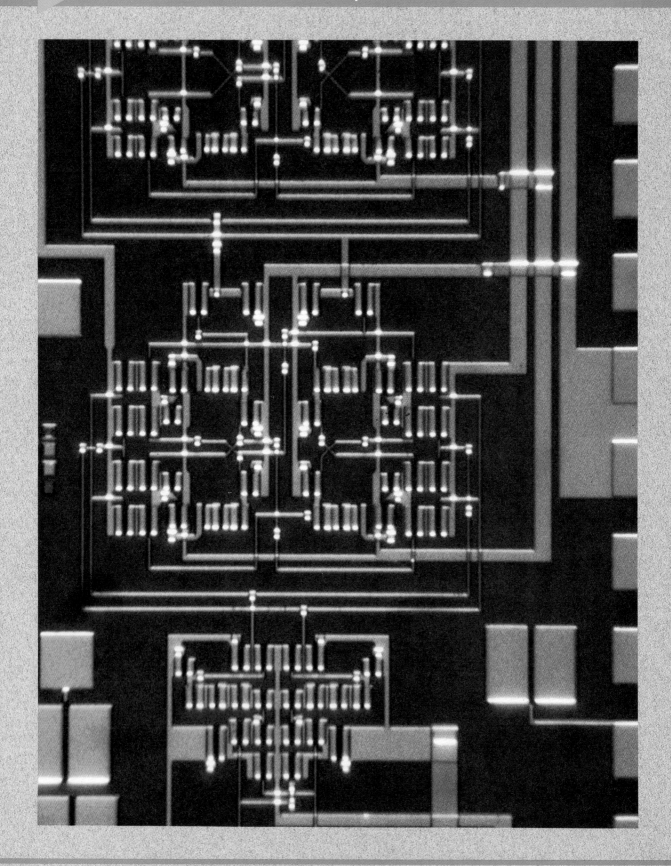

11

Applications of Information Technology

STUDENT LEARNING OBJECTIVES

▶ To identify the elements and scope of a management information system.

▶ To discuss the principles and use of expert systems

▶ To discuss computer and information system applications common to most organizations.

▶ To describe applications of office automation.

▶ To discuss computer and information system applications unique to a specific type of industry.

11–1   MANAGEMENT'S THIRST FOR INFORMATION

Managers have become adept at taking full advantage of the resources of *money*, *materials*, and *people*; but only recently have managers begun to make effective use of the fourth major resource—*information*. In fact, corporate management everywhere is adopting this new concept called **information resource management (IRM)**. Information resource management treats information as a valuable resource that should be managed accordingly, just like money, materials, and people. In an all-out effort to meet the "productivity" challenge, managers are turning to the information resource. IRM has whetted every manager's appetite for more and better information.

Information Systems

We combine *hardware*, *software*, *people*, *procedures*, and *data* to create an *information system* (see Figure 11–1). A computer-based information system provides a manager's department with *data processing* capabilities and managers with the *information* they need to make better, more informed decisions. The data processing capability, or the handling and

FIGURE 11–1   Information System Ingredients and Capabilities

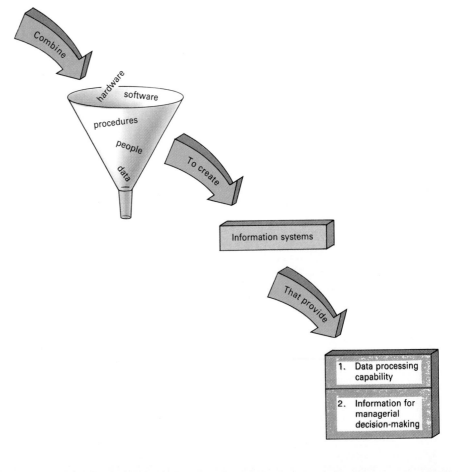

The need for information exists in all fields of endeavor, not just business. These astrophysicists rely on computer-generated information to help them in their study of the formation and growth of galaxies.

processing of data, is only one facet of an information system. A complete information system provides decision makers with on-demand reports and inquiry capabilities as well as routine periodic reports. Because an information system helps management make business decisions, it is sometimes called a **management information system (MIS)**. In practice, the terms *information system*, *management information system*, and *MIS* are used interchangeably.

Decision Support Systems

The term **decision support system (DSS)** generally refers to user-friendly software that produces and presents information to help management in the decision-making process. DSS software often involves the latest technological innovations (for example, color graphics and database management systems), planning and forecasting models, and user-oriented 4GLs (discussed in Chapter 9, "Programming Concepts"). Managers spend much of their day requesting and analyzing information before making a decision. Decision support systems help close the information gap so managers can improve the quality of their decisions.

Decision support systems help remove the tedium of gathering, analyzing, and presenting data. No longer are managers strapped with such laborious tasks as manually entering and extending numbers (adding rows and columns of numbers) on spreadsheet paper. Graphics software enables managers to generate illustrative bar and pie graphs in minutes. And now, with the availability of a variety of DSSs, managers can get the information they need without having to depend on direct technical assistance from a computer professional.

Decision-support systems provide these product marketing managers with direct access to the information necessary to make critical decisions about the timing of promotional campaigns. A DSS can supply the information when they want it and in the form they want it.

Expert Systems

Perhaps the ultimate decision support system is the **expert system**. Expert systems are part of the general area of research known as **artificial intelligence (AI)**. Other areas of artificial intelligence research are summarized in Chapter 14, "Career Opportunities and Applications of Tomorrow." Expert systems provide "expert" advice and guidance for a wide range of activities, from locomotive maintenance to surgery. An expert system is an interactive system that responds to questions, asks for clarification, makes recommendations, and generally helps in the decision-making process. At the heart of an expert system is a **knowledge base**.

A knowledge base is *not* a data base. The library-book circulation data base illustrated in Figure 10-12 in Chapter 10, "Software Concepts and Data Management," deals with data that have a static relationship between the elements. That is, the patron name and card number fields have a fixed relationship with the library patron record. A knowledge base is created by *knowledge engineers*, who translate the knowledge of real live human experts into rules and strategies. A knowledge base is heuristic; that is, it provides the expert system with the capability of recommending directions for user inquiry. It also encourages further investigation into areas that may be important to a certain line of questioning but not apparent to the user.

A knowledge base grows because it "learns" from user feedback. An expert system learns by "remembering": It stores past occurrences in its knowledge base. For example, a recommendation that sends a user on a "wild goose chase" is thereafter deleted as a workable strategy for similar future inquiries. Expert systems simulate the human thought

These financial analysts rely on historical and predictive data as well as up-to-the-second stock-trading information. They sometimes request a second opinion from an expert system before advising their clients.

process. To varying degrees they can reason, draw inferences, and make judgments.

Computer-based expert systems have fared well against expert human physicians in the accuracy of their diagnoses of illnesses. Other expert systems help crews repair telephone lines, financial analysts counsel their clients, computer vendors configure computer systems, and geologists explore for minerals.

11–2   THE USES OF INFORMATION TECHNOLOGY

New and innovative uses of computers and information systems are being implemented every day in every type of organization. Even so, organizations are still in the early stages of automation. Each company has a seemingly endless number of opportunities to use information technology to operate more efficiently and, perhaps, to use it to achieve a *competitive edge*.

This chapter contains an overview of the applications of computers and information systems, sometimes referred to as **information technology**. This overview is not intended to be an exhaustive treatment of information technology applications. However, it can acquaint you with a few of the ways information technology is contributing to and, in many instances, changing society.

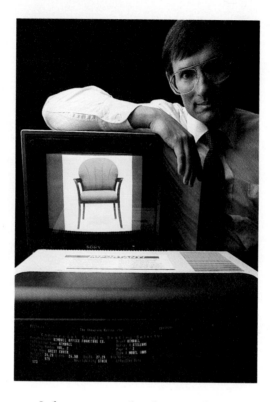

This furniture retailer can recall the images of thousands of items from optical laser disk storage. The images are then displayed on high-resolution color monitors. This capability enables his company to maintain a lower inventory and offer better service to its customers. This company gains a distinct competitive advantage by being able to show the same chair in a wide variety of fabrics.

Information technology applications are covered in two sections.

- *Common systems.* Section 11–3 addresses those applications *common to most organizations* that employ people to produce goods and services (payroll processing, for example).
- *Industry-specific applications.* Section 11–4 presents applications *unique to a particular type of industry or organization* (for example, the point-of-sale systems used in the retail industry).

11–3   APPLICATIONS OF INFORMATION TECHNOLOGY COMMON TO MOST ORGANIZATIONS

Certain computer applications and information systems are universal and equally appropriate for a manufacturing company, a university, a hospital, or even a cottage industry (where people work out of their homes). These applications normally involve *personnel* and *monetary accounting*, but they also include several other common application areas, such as inventory control. Each of these areas can be, and usually is, integrated to some extent with one or more of the other application areas.

Payroll

Having already read several payroll-related examples earlier in the text, you should be somewhat familiar with payroll systems. The two primary outputs of a payroll system are the payroll checks and stubs distributed to the employees and the payroll register, which is a summary report of payroll transactions.

Accounts Receivable

The accounts receivable system keeps track of money owed the company on charges for goods sold or services rendered. When a customer purchases goods or services, the customer record is updated to reflect the charge. An invoice, bill, or statement reflecting the balance due is periodically sent to active customers. Upon receipt of payment, the amount due is decreased by the amount of the payment.

Management relies on the accounts receivable system to identify overdue accounts. Reports are generated that "age" accounts to identify those customers whose accounts are overdue by more than 30, 60, or 90 days.

Accounts Payable

Organizations purchase everything from paper clips to bulldozers on credit. So the accounts payable system is the other side of the accounts receivable system. An invoice from a creditor company's accounts receivable system is input to the accounts payable system. When a company receives an invoice, the system generates a check and adjusts the balance. Most companies design their accounts payable system to take advantage of discounts for prompt payment.

These accountants spend much of their time interacting with a financial information system. The system has accounts receivable, accounts payable, budgeting, and general ledger subsystems.

General Ledger

Every monetary transaction that occurs within an organization must be properly recorded. Both the payment of a bill and an interdepartmental transfer of funds are examples of monetary transactions. The general ledger system keeps track of these transactions and provides the input necessary to produce an organization's financial statement. A financial statement includes the *profit-and-loss statement* and the *balance sheet.*

The Securities & Exchange Commission (SEC) requires publicly held companies to file quarterly financial statements. In the past this requirement resulted in 6 million pages of reports being sent to the SEC every three months. Now each report is transmitted to the SEC electronically via data communications. With the current system, stock-brokers and investors can look through thousands of financial statements from their terminals, whereas in the past they had to wait several weeks before they could see reports.

In the not-too-distant past, accountants manually posted debits and credits for each account in a ledger book—thus the name *general ledger* for today's electronic system. Other "account" systems (accounts receivable, accounts payable, payroll, and so on) are sources of financial transactions and feed data into the general ledger system.

Inventory Management and Control

Walk into most organizations and you see desks, file cabinets, and even computers. These items are called *fixed assets.* A fixed-asset inventory record is maintained for each item and includes such data as date purchased, cost, and inventory item number. These records are maintained for asset-control and tax purposes.

Manufacturing companies must also manage in-process and finished-goods inventories. These inventory systems monitor the quantity on hand and the location of each inventory item. Figure 11–2 illustrates a few of the menus and input/output displays in a typical on-line inventory system.

Human Resource Development

Human resource development systems are essentially personnel accounting systems that maintain pertinent data on employees. Besides routine historical data (educational background, salary history, and so on), the system includes data on performance reviews, skills, and professional development.

Budgeting

Each year managers spend months preparing their departmental budgets for the coming fiscal year. To help in this task, the budget system provides each manager with information on past line-item expenditures (salaries, office equipment, office supplies, and so on). Based on this information and projected budget requirements, each manager can make requests for the next fiscal year. The budget system matches these requests against projected revenues and generates an exception report showing

FIGURE 11–2 Interactive Session with an On-Line Inventory System

(a) The main menu presents the user with six processing options. The user enters Option 5 to obtain an inventory exception report. (b) This exception report is produced when Main Menu Option 5 is selected. Only those inventory items whose quantity on hand is too high or too low are listed. (c) From the main menu, the user selects Option 1 to get the transaction menu. (d) This screen is produced when Main Menu Option 1 is selected. To update quantity on hand, the user selects Transaction Option 1. (e) From this transaction display screen, the user enters item number (1015), number received (2000), and number used (300) to update quantity on hand for Farkle valves.

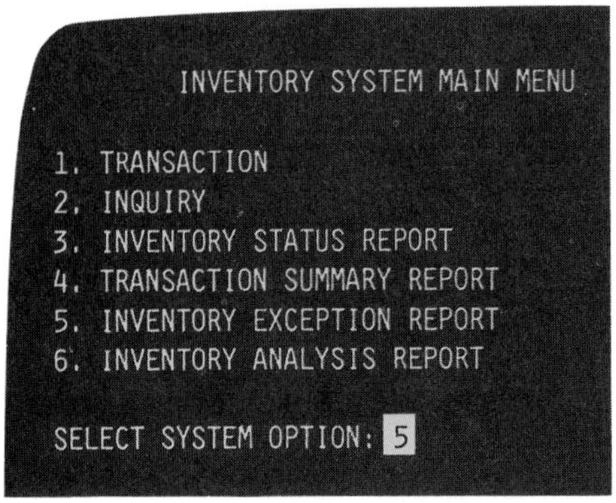

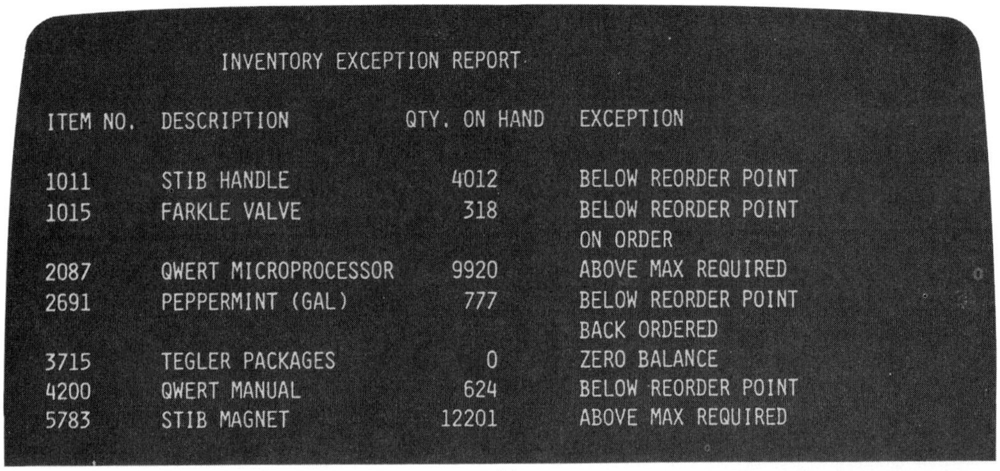

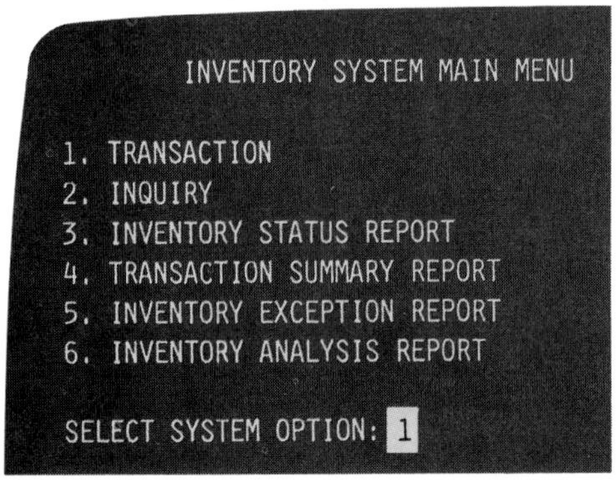

The more sophisticated point-of-sale (POS) systems do much more than record sales and generate receipts. Because this chain store's POS system is integrated with the inventory control system, buyers can obtain up-to-the-minute information that enables them to react quickly to the buying trends of their customers.

those line items that exceed projected funding levels. The budget items are reviewed and the process is repeated until the coming year's budget is established.

Office Automation

Office automation, which is sometimes abbreviated as **OA**, refers collectively to those computer-based applications associated with general office work. OA encompasses all the personal productivity software tools discussed in Chapters 7 and 8 (word processing, desktop publishing, electronic spreadsheet, database, and presentation graphics), plus electronic mail, image processing, voice processing, and office information systems.

Electronic Mail.   Computer networks enable us to route messages to each other. A message can be a note, letter, report, chart, or even the manuscript for a book. Each person in a company can be assigned an *electronic mailbox* in which messages are received and held in secondary storage, usually magnetic disk. To "open" and "read" **electronic mail**, or **E-mail**, the user simply goes to the nearest terminal and recalls the message from storage.

Image Processing.   Image processing involves the creation, storage, and distribution of pictorial information. There are two levels of image-processing sophistication. At the first level, **facsimile** equipment, which has been around since the 1960s, transfers images of hard-copy documents

PROFILE

Dr. An Wang was a man whom friends, customers, and employees referred to as "the Doctor." Dr. Wang, former chairman of the board and CEO of Wang Laboratories, Inc., came to the United States from China in 1945 to pursue a Ph.D. in physics at Harvard University. In 1951 "the Doctor" founded what is now Wang Laboratories with an investment of $600.

In the early 1950s Dr. Wang invented magnetic core memory, a major breakthrough in the development of computers. IBM bought his core memory patent. In 1965 he introduced a desktop computer named LOCI. Dr. Wang is credited with the creation of computer-based word processors and minicomputers in the 1970s. Since then his company has continued with a steady

progression of innovations in the field of office automation.

During Dr. Wang's memorial service at Harvard University, his son, Frederick Wang, shared a few notes that his father, a philosophical man, had compiled in his last few days. "Always be humble." "Remember—the world does not need us, but we need the world." "I have always tried to do my best." And indeed he did.

via telephone lines to another office. The process is similar to using a copying machine except that the original is inserted in a facsimile ("fax") machine at one office and a hard copy is produced on another fax machine in another office.

Recent technological innovations have expanded the scope of image processing. Image scanners, discussed in Chapter 4, "Input/Output Devices," enable any kind of image (for example, a photo, a drawing) to be digitized and the digitized image stored on a disk. Once on disk, the image can be manipulated in much the same way you would text. Image scanners frequently are used in conjunction with desktop publishing software (see Chapter 7).

Image processing has come a long way in the last few years. Some companies are beginning to digitize handwritten documents and store them on disk to facilitate their storage and recall. In this era of sophisticated information processing, it is just too inefficient to make frequent trips to the file cabinet.

Companies that operate on a global scale, like Hewlett-Packard, rely on information and communications systems such as teleconferencing to enable their widely scattered employees to work together more effectively.

Voice Processing.   Voice processing includes **voice message switching** and **teleconferencing**. The terminal for voice message switching (a store-and-forward "voice mailbox" system) is a touch-tone telephone. Voice message switching accomplishes the same function as electronic mail, except the hard copy is not available. When you send a message, your voice is digitized and stored on a magnetic disk for later retrieval. The message is routed to the destination(s) you designate using the telephone's keyboard; then it is heard upon request by the intended receiver(s). A voice store-and-forward system permits you to send one or many messages with just one telephone call.

   Teleconferencing enables people in different locations to see and talk to each other and to share charts and other visual meeting materials. The voice and video of teleconferencing are supported by the telephone network. People who are geographically scattered can meet without the need for time-consuming and expensive travel.

Office Information Systems.   Several small information systems address traditional office tasks. For example, one system allows people to keep their *personal calendars* on-line. As workers schedule activities, they block out times on their electronic calendars.

There are definite advantages to having a central data base of personal calendars. Let's say that a public relations manager wants to schedule a meeting to review the impact of some unexpected favorable publicity. To do this, the manager enters the names of the participants and the expected duration of the meeting. The *conference scheduling system* searches the calendars of people affected and suggests possible meeting times. The manager then selects a meeting time, and the participants are notified by electronic mail. Of course, their calendars are automatically updated to reflect the meeting time.

Another common office application is the company *directory*. The directory contains basic personnel data: name, title, department, location, and phone number. To look up someone's telephone number, all you have to do is enter that person's name on your terminal and the number is displayed. The beauty of the directory data base is that it is always up-to-date, unlike hard-copy directories, which never seem to have all the current titles or phone numbers.

Other systems permit users to organize *personal notes*, keep *diaries*, document ideas in a *preformatted outline*, and keep a *tickler file*. When users log on in the morning, the tickler file automatically reminds them of things to do for that day.

11-4   INDUSTRY-SPECIFIC APPLICATIONS OF INFORMATION TECHNOLOGY

Many applications of information technology are unique to a particular type of industry or organization. For example, fire incident-reporting systems are unique to local governments. The use of automatic teller machines is unique to the banking industry. These and other industry-specific applications are briefly discussed in the remainder of this section.

Manufacturing

Traditional Manufacturing Information Systems.   In a manufacturing company, the *order entry and processing system* accepts and processes customer orders. The system then feeds data to the warehouse or plant,

> **MEMORY BITS**
>
> **COMMON INFORMATION SYSTEMS**
> - Payroll
> - Accounts receivable
> - Accounts payable
> - General ledger
> - Inventory management and control
> - Human resource development
> - Budgeting
> - Office automation
>   Micro productivity software
>   Electronic mail
>   Image processing
>   Voice processing
>   Office information systems

Terminals in the factory are becoming as common as steel-toed shoes. This one is designed to withstand the heat, humidity, and dust that accompany shop activity.

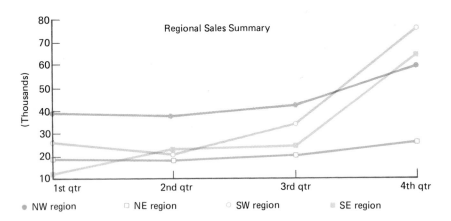

FIGURE 11–3   Scatter Plot of Regional Sales
Quarterly sales figures from four regions are plotted to help in market analysis.

depending on whether the order is for stock items or is a special order, and to the *accounts receivable system* for billing. The order entry and processing system also tracks orders and provides status information from the time the order is received until the product is delivered to the customer.

Production scheduling systems allocate manufacturing resources in an optimal manner. A well-designed system will minimize idle time for both workers and machines and ensure that materials are at the right place at the right time.

Market analysis systems rely on historical and current data to identify fast- and slow-moving products, to pinpoint areas with high sales potential, to make forecasts of production requirements, and to plan marketing strategy. For example, in Figure 11–3, the scatter plot of regional sales over the last four quarters demonstrates clearly that fourth-quarter sales in the northeast region did not keep pace with the others. Based on this finding, management might elect to focus more attention on the northeast region during the coming quarter.

Project management and control systems provide management with the information necessary to keep projects within budget and on time. Periodic reports present actual versus anticipated project costs and the number of days ahead of or behind schedule.

Other information systems commonly found in manufacturing companies include *standard costing* and *manufacturing resource planning* (MRP).

Robotics

Rudimentary robotics   **Robotics,** the integration of computers and **industrial robots,** is more often than not associated with manufacturing. This "steel-collar" workforce is made up of over 250,000 industrial robots throughout the world. The most common industrial robot is a single mechanical arm controlled by a computer. The arm, called a *manipulator*, has a shoulder, forearm, and wrist and is capable of performing the motions of a human arm. The manipulator is fitted with a hand designed to accomplish a specific task, such as painting, welding, picking and placing, and so on.

With the prospect of increased productivity, manufacturing companies have been rushing to install more and more applications of robotics. In the photo, an industrial robot positions materials for assembly in a pick-and-place application.

An industrial robot is best at tasks that are repetitive and those that require precision movements, moving heavy loads, and working in hazardous areas. Such tasks are not unique to manufacturing; they exist in virtually every kind of industry, from hospitals to cannery row. The automotive industry is the largest user of robots (painting, welding), and the electronics industry is second (circuit testing, connecting chips to circuit boards). Even surgeons are using robots to help in brain surgery. They can be set up to manipulate the surgical drill and biopsy needle with great accuracy, thereby making brain surgery faster, more accurate, and safer.

Teaching robots to do their jobs   A computer program is written to control the robot just as one is written to print payroll checks. It includes such commands as when to reach, in which direction to reach, how far to reach, when to grasp, and so on. Once programmed, robots do not need much attention. One plant manufactures vacuum cleaners 24 hours a day, seven days a week, in total darkness!

Outfitting robots with intelligence and human sensory capabilities   Most robots are programmed to reach to a particular location, find a particular item, and then place it somewhere else. This simple application of robotics is called *pick and place*. Instead of a grasping mechanism, other robots are equipped with a variety of industrial tools such as drills, paint guns, welding torches, and so on. Of course, it will be a very long time before our companions and workmates are robots. However, industrial robots are being equipped with rudimentary sensory capabilities such as vision that enable them to simulate human behavior. A robot with the added dimension of vision can be given some intelligence. (Robots without intelligence simply repeat preprogrammed motions.) Even though the state of the art of vision systems is embryonic, a robot can be "taught" to distinguish between dissimilar objects under controlled conditions. With the addition of this sensory subsystem, the robot has the capability of making crude but important decisions. For example, a robot equipped with a vision subsystem can distinguish between two boxes approaching on the conveyor. It can be programmed to place a box of particular dimensions on an adjacent conveyer and let all other boxes pass.

If vision-system technology continues to improve, more and more robots will have navigational capabilities. Now most robots are stationary; those that are not are programmed only to detect the presence of an object in their path or to operate within a well-defined work area where the positions of all obstacles are known. Within the decade of the 1990s, robots will be able to move about the work area just as people do.

Computer-Integrated Manufacturing.   Manufacturing companies are using information technologies to streamline their operations. The integration of computers and manufacturing is called **computer-integrated manu-**

Computer-aided design (CAD) systems are used to design consumer goods, such as this 35-mm camera. In the design process, engineers create a framework (left), then the CAD software fills in between the lines to create the three-dimensional solid model (right).

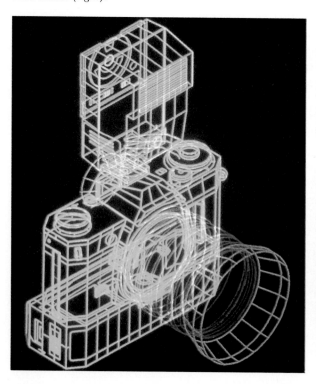 

facturing (CIM). The computer is used at every stage of the manufacturing process, from the time a part is conceived until it is shipped. In computer-integrated manufacturing, the various computer systems are linked together via data communications, and they feed data to one another. CIM uses an integrated network of computers to design the product, to operate and monitor production equipment, to facilitate communication and information flow throughout the plant and the company, and to interface with the company's administrative information systems.

An engineer uses a **computer-aided design (CAD)** system to design the part. The design specifications are stored on a magnetic disk. The specifications, now in an electronic data base, become input to another computer system that generates programs to control the robots and machine tools that handle and make the part. These computer-driven tools are even linked to the company's MIS computers to provide data for order processing, inventory management, shop-floor scheduling, and general accounting. Some CIM systems go one step further and provide a link between the manufacturer and the customer via electronic data interchange (EDI). EDI is discussed in Chapter 6, "Data Communications."

Several companies in each industry are working feverishly toward the implementation of total CIM. Few, if any, have accomplished it yet, but many are on their way.

Financial Services

The financial services industries, which include banking, savings and loan institutions, and brokerage firms, are entering an exciting era. The computer is the impetus for some radical and progressive changes in the way these money brokers do business. For example, financial services organizations serve as a "money buffer" between buyer and seller. The traditional approach to money exchange has been for the seller to bill the buyer, the buyer to write a check for the amount of the bill, the seller to deposit the check, and the bank to transfer the funds from the buyer's to the seller's account. This approach is not only time-consuming but expensive for all concerned. Throughout the remainder of the 1990s we can expect to see this traditional approach give way more and more to **electronic funds transfer (EFT)**.

In electronic funds transfer, the amount owed is transferred electronically from one account to another in a bank, savings and loan, or brokerage firm. For example, rather than sending out thousands of statements that require each customer to pay the bill in his or her own way, some utility companies are cooperating with customers and banks so that payments are transferred electronically at the end of each billing period. As another example, some employers are bypassing printing payroll checks. Based on data supplied to the banks, pay is electronically transferred from employer to employee accounts.

The ever-present **automatic teller machines (ATMs)** are the most visible symbol of EFT. ATMs enable bank customers to deposit, withdraw, and transfer funds from or to their various accounts. As each money transaction is completed, the customer's record is updated and he or

This grocery store has an automated checkout system with the capability of operating without cash transfers. The customer slides her bank card (containing account number and authorization data) through a badge reader and enters a personal identification number on the keyboard, both of which are connected to a network of banking computers. The customer then enters the amount of the purchase. This amount is deducted from her bank account and credited to that of the grocery store.

The banking industry would prefer that its customers use ATMs for banking transactions rather than tellers. This bank gives customers the option of selecting a teller or an ATM. The average ATM transaction takes less time, but most important, it costs less than half that of a teller-aided transaction. The more that customers use ATMs, the more banks can reduce the cost of their services.

she is provided with a printed receipt (see Figure 11–4). In over 100 banks, EFT has been extended to the home in the form of *home banking systems*. Subscribers to a home banking system use their personal computers as terminals to pay bills, transfer funds, and inquire about account status. Some systems also provide subscribers with other services, such as "electronic shopping," electronic mail, and up-to-the-minute stock market quotations.

All financial institutions offer *financial planning services*. Part of the service involves a computer-based analysis of a customer's investment portfolio. Input to the system includes current and anticipated income, amount and type of investments, assets and liabilities, financial objectives (such as: minimize taxes, desired pension at age 65), and willingness to take risks. The output from the analysis consists of recommendations aimed at optimizing the effectiveness of a particular person's investment portfolio.

Futurists are predicting that the current system of currency exchange will be replaced gradually by EFT. More and more point-of-sale systems are being integrated with EFT systems so that what is now a *credit* transaction will be a *cash-transfer* transaction. That is, when a customer purchases an item, the amount of the sale is debited, via EFT, from the customer's checking account and credited to the account of the retail store. No further funds transfer is needed. Of course, the option of making a credit purchase will remain.

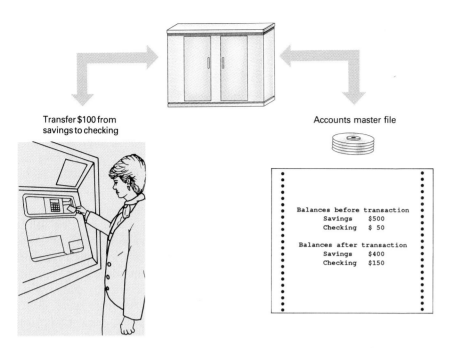

FIGURE 11–4   Banking Transactions at an Automatic Teller Machine
The electronic funds transfer (EFT) of $100 from savings to checking updates the accounts master file.

Publishing

Word processing, computerized *typesetting*, computer-aided *graphics design*, and *page formatting* have revolutionized the way newspapers, books, and magazines are produced. Newspaper reporters and writers enter and edit their stories on their portable micros or on-line terminals. Once all copy is on-line, pages are automatically formatted according to type and spacing specifications. Traditionally a manually produced document prepared with pencils, paper, and typewriters went on to editing, retyping, composing, proofreading, cutting, pasting, and photographing of the final page format before plates could be made for the presswork.

Several magazines are mailed in electronic format. These *magazines on a disk* are distributed on diskettes for display on microcomputers. Dictionaries, encyclopedias, and other reference materials already are being sold in the form of high-density optical laser disks.

Airlines

An airline *reservation system* is a classic example of an information system that reflects an up-to-the-minute status. An airline reservations agent communicates with a centralized computer via a remote terminal to update the data base the moment a seat on any flight is filled or becomes available.

An airline reservation system does much more than keep track of flight reservations. Departure and arrival times are closely monitored so that ground crew activities can be coordinated. The system offers many kinds of management information needs: the number of passenger miles flown, profit per passenger on a particular flight, percent of arrivals on time, average number of empty seats on each flight for each day of the week, and so on. To give you an idea of the size and scope of these systems, the American Airlines Sabre System involves more than 100,000 terminals and printers and can process 1450 transactions per second!

You may be interested to know that airlines routinely overbook flights; that is, they book seats they do not have. The number of extra seats sold is based on historical "no-show" statistics compiled from the reservation system data base. Although these statistics provide good guidelines, occasionally everyone does show up!

Insurance

The information systems of an insurance company have more external interaction, or communication with people outside the company, than most other businesses. Most of this external communication is with customers. The volume of such transactions makes computer-based *policy administration* and *claims processing systems* a necessity. Insurance agents hook up to computers at headquarters so they can quote, write, and deliver insurance policies while customers wait.

An insurance company makes or loses money according to the accuracy of its *actuarial accounting system*. This system maintains countless statistics that serve as the basis for the rate structure. An actuarial system provides the following kinds of information: the probability that a 20-year-old Kansas City resident with no automobile accident history will have an accident or the life expectancy of a 68-year-old female whose parents died of natural causes.

Many insurance companies say that they are quick to process claims, but some are more effective than others. This insurance claims adjuster brings a cellular laptop, which is capable of transmitting voice, data, and images, plus a video camera to the site of an accident or a natural disaster. While writing up the claim, he transmits videos, frame by frame, to the company's home office. Normally, electronic approval for issuing a check is sent to him via his laptop. He then issues a check on the spot to the policyholder.

Entertainment

The computer is now an integral part of the entertainment industry. *Pro football* coaches rely heavily on feedback from their computer systems to call plays and set defenses during a game. The system predicts what the opposing team is expected to do, based on statistics of what they have done in the past. In fact, the computer is becoming the deciding factor between evenly matched opponents in many sports.

Computers have had quite an impact on the *film industry*. Many *special effects* and even the sets for some movies are generated with computer graphics. *Animation* for cartoons and movies is no longer drawn one frame at a time. The scenes and characters are drawn, by hand or with a computer, then manipulated with computer graphics to create the illusion of motion.

During professional tennis matches, a scorer who is familiar with tennis uses a microcomputer to enter data on each point played. After or during the match, information is summarized and displayed for coaches or television commentators. The statistics highlight a player's strengths, weaknesses, and patterns of play.

Laurel and Hardy in living color! This photo shows a colorized version of a black-and-white Laurel and Hardy movie.

Computer graphics has even made it possible to revive old black-and-white movies—in color! Imagine Laurel and Hardy in living color! Now, through an innovative use of computer technology called *colorization*, it is possible to change the old black-and-white films to color.

At this television station, a newsroom automation system controls programming flow, monitors the electronic teleprompter display, and operates studio camera movement through robotics.

In the *theater*, playwrights use word processing systems especially designed for the theater environment. Besides the obvious value of word processing, there are additional benefits to having the script on-line. Actors can learn their lines by interacting with a computer that "reads" the lines of other actors; that is, only the lines of other actors are displayed on the screen unless the actor requests that all lines be displayed.

Health Care

Hospitals. The computer is a constant companion to both patients and medical personnel. This is especially so in hospitals where, at the beginning of each day, the status of each room is updated in the *room-census* data base. The *patient accounting system* updates patient records to reflect lab tests, drugs administered, and visits by a physician. This system also handles patient billing.

In the *operating room*, surgeons have on-line access to the patient's medical records. Some of these interactive systems are even voice-activated to free the surgeon's hands for more critical tasks. Computers have taken some of the risk out of complex surgical procedures by warning surgeons of life-threatening situations: During brain surgery, for example, a computer monitors the patient's blood flow to the brain. Once a patient is moved to an *intensive care unit*, computers continue to monitor vital signs and alert attending personnel to dangerous situations. Most life-support systems (such as artificial lungs) are also computer-controlled.

Computer-controlled devices provide physicians and surgeons with information that simply was not available a few years ago. Because surgeons can "see" more clearly into a person's body with CT, or CAT

Computers have enabled medical doctors to make a quantum leap in the quality of health care. This system allows doctors to electronically examine enhanced images, such as X-rays, from the next room or from across the country.

(computer tomography), *scanners* and MR (magnetic resonance) *scanners*, medical procedures may be less drastic because better information is available. For example, a surgeon may not have to amputate an entire limb to stop the spread of bone cancer if an MR scan detects the cancer only in a limb's extremities. CAT scanners permit the results of several scans to be combined and forged into three-dimensional images. MR scanners, the most recent technology for viewing inside the body, combine computers and a large doughnut-shaped magnet to produce video images of a cross-section of a body. Before MR scanners, exploratory surgery was necessary to produce such internal "pictures." Physicians see and analyze the images from CAT and MR scanners on color graphics monitors.

Expert diagnosis systems help physicians identify diseases and isolate problems. The physician enters the patient's symptoms, and the system queries an expert system's knowledge base to match the symptoms with possible illnesses. If the illness cannot be diagnosed with existing information, the expert system requests more information.

In recent years the cost of a hospital room has soared, and some hospitals still operate in the red. To get back in the black, they are implementing procedures to help control costs. For the first time, they are using systems that optimize their resources while maximizing revenue.

This unusual view of the hand—showing all of its major blood vessels—was made without X-rays. The experimental computer-based technique, which is called phase contrast magnetic resonance angiography, is noninvasive and painless. It enables physicians to see flowing blood and thereby delineate the veins and arteries through which the fluid is traveling. If a disease that narrows the passages is present, the blood vessels do not show up as brightly as they otherwise would.

A *physician's accounting system* provides hospital administrators with information about how each physician is using hospital facilities. For example, such systems identify physicians who tend to admit patients who could just as well be treated on an outpatient basis. These patients typically generate less revenue for the hospital and take up beds that could best be used by seriously ill patients.

Medical Research. The microprocessor has opened new vistas for *medical research.* Our body is an electrical system that is very compatible with these tiny computers. Researchers have made it possible for paraplegics to pedal bicycles and take crude steps under the control of external computers: Various muscle groups are electronically stimulated to move the legs in a walking motion. The system has given new hope to paraplegics who thought they would never walk again. Much remains to be done, but researchers insist that someday computer implants will enable paraplegics to walk.

Government

Local Government. Local governments use a wide variety of information systems. Most cities supply and bill citizens for at least one of the three major utility services—water, refuse, and electricity. Besides these *utility billing systems,* a *tax-collection system* periodically assesses citizens for income, school, and real estate taxes.

Cities also have *police systems* used for incident reporting, inquiry, and dispatching. Many police departments even have terminals mounted in their cruisers. On these terminals officers can see the arrest record of an individual, request a "rundown" on an auto's license number, or check on what other officers are doing. Police detectives can search

The local fire and police departments fight crime and fires and attend to other emergencies with the help of an information system. In seconds, dispatchers can select which squad car or fire station would be the most responsive to a given emergency.

data bases for suspects by matching *modi operandi*, nicknames, body marks, physical deformities, locations, times of day, and even footwear.

Some fire departments are informed electronically of the location of a fire by a *fire incident-reporting system*. Here's how it works: Someone at the site of the fire calls a three-digit fire-reporting number. In a split second a computer system searches its data base for the address of the phone (and the location of the fire), then automatically dispatches vehicles from the nearest fire station.

Have you ever driven an automobile through a city with an *automated traffic-control system*? If so, you would soon notice how the traffic signals are coordinated to minimize delays and optimize traffic flow. Traffic sensors are strategically placed throughout the city to feed data continuously to the computer on the volume and direction of traffic flow (see Figure 11–5). The computer system that activates the traffic signals is programmed to plan ahead: If the sensors locate a group of cars traveling together, traffic signals are timed accordingly.

State Government.   At the state level of government, each major agency has its own information services department. *Welfare, employment security, highway patrol, revenue,* and *education* are only a few of the many state agencies that have such departments. In some states one of the most visible systems is the *lottery* agency. A bet is registered immediately at any of thousands of on-line terminals located in stores and restaurants throughout the state. The on-line lottery systems have made it possible for people to be "instant winners" (or losers).

FIGURE 11–5 An Automated Traffic Control System
In a continuous feedback loop, street sensors provide input to a process-control computer system about the direction and volume of traffic flow. Based on their feedback, the system controls the traffic lights to optimize the flow of traffic.

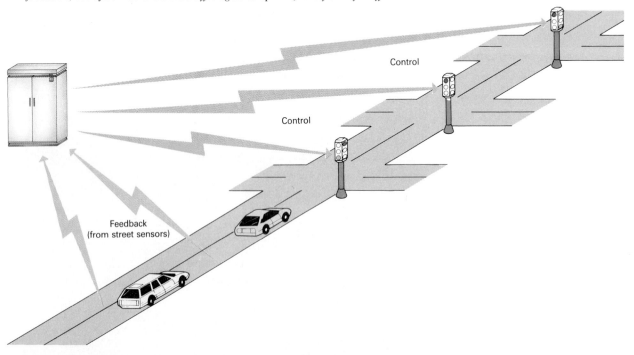

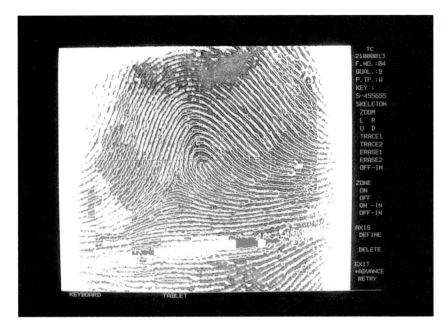

In the past, a manual search through a fingerprint file could take a detective months—often without success. Today, computers take only a few minutes to check fingerprints from the scene of a crime against a large data base of fingerprints—often with great success.

Several state *crime bureaus* are using computers for fingerprint identification. Once the millions of fingerprints have been converted into digital data and stored on magnetic disk, the system can check up to 650 prints per second. In a manual search, an investigator would take hours to do what a computer can do in a single second. This new technology doesn't give criminals much of a head start!

Federal Government.   The federal government has thousands of computer systems scattered throughout the world. The Federal Bureau of Investigation (FBI) uses its *national crime information system (NCIS)* to help track down criminals. The Internal Revenue Service (IRS) now permits qualified accountants to *file tax returns* on-line. This service saves us and the IRS a lot of time and money. The on-line system performs all the necessary table searches and computations, and it even cross-checks the accuracy and consistency of the input data. For the IRS, no further data entry or personal assistance is required.

Computer technology has given Congress a new look. Senators and representatives have terminals in their offices that allow them to scan proposed legislation, send electronic mail, vote on legislation from their offices, do research, and correspond with constituents. The system also allows lobbyists, reporters, and other interested people to monitor voting records, session attendance, and other matters of public interest. Another benefit of the *congressional computer network* is that it lets congressional committees poll members of Congress for their feedback while legislation is still in draft form instead of waiting until the legislation is put to a vote.

MEMORY BITS

INDUSTRY-SPECIFIC INFORMATION SYSTEMS

- Manufacturing
  Order-entry and processing
  Production scheduling
  Market analysis
  Project management and
    control
  Standard costing
  Manufacturing resource
    planning (MRP)
  Robotics
  Computer-integrated
    manufacturing (CIM)
  Computer-aided design
    (CAD)

- Financial services
  Electronic funds transfer
    (EFT)
  Automatic teller machines
    (ATM)
  Home banking
  Financial planning

- Publishing
  Word processing
  Typesetting
  Graphics design
  Page formatting
  Magazines on a disk

- Airlines
  Reservations

- Insurance
  Policy administration
  Claims processing
  Actuarial accounting

- Entertainment
  Professional sports systems
  Film industry
    Special effects
    Animation
    Colorization
  Theater (on-line scripts)

- Health care
  Hospitals
    Room census
    Patient accounting
    Operating room
    Intensive care unit
    Diagnostic equipment
    Expert diagnosis systems
    Physician accounting
    Source data automation
  Medical research (*cont.*)

- Government
    - Local
        - Utility billings
        - Tax collection
        - Police systems
        - Fire incident reporting
        - Traffic control
    - State
        - Welfare
        - Employment security
        - Highway patrol
        - Revenue
        - Education
        - Lottery
        - Crime bureau
    - Federal
        - National crime information system
        - Filing taxes
        - Congressional computer network
        - Space programs (NASA)

Not all federal computer systems are massive in scope. This forest ranger routinely enters data, such as rainfall and humidity, to a program that alerts him when the potential for forest fires is high.

The most sophisticated government computer systems are associated with *NASA* and the space program. A mind-boggling network of ground and on-board computers must work together, without malfunction, to shuttle people between the earth and orbit around the earth.

Johnson Space Center's mission-control center tracks space shuttle flights with the help of two large mainframe computers. Tracking stations around the world gather data directly from the computers onboard the space shuttle. These data are transmitted via satellite to the mission control center where a host mainframe computer provides position reports and makes trajectory predictions.

SUMMARY OUTLINE AND IMPORTANT TERMS

11–1   **MANAGEMENT'S THIRST FOR INFORMATION.** The attitude of management toward the use of computers has evolved from basic data processing to **information resource management (IRM)**. The need for more timely and meaningful information prompted this change of attitude.

An information system is a computer-based system that provides both a data processing capability and information to help managers make decisions. An information system is also called a **management information system (MIS)** because of its orientation to management. A **decision support system (DSS)** is user-friendly software that employs the latest hardware and software technologies to provide better, more timely information to support the decision-making process.

Expert systems are part of the general area of research known as **artificial intelligence (AI)**. An expert system is an interactive system that responds to questions, asks for clarification, makes recommendations, and generally helps in the decision-making process. At the heart of an expert system is a **knowledge base**. In effect, expert systems simulate the human thought process.

11–2   **THE USES OF INFORMATION TECHNOLOGY.** New uses of computers and information systems are being implemented every day in every type of organization. The general area of computers and information systems is sometimes referred to as **information technology**.

11–3   **APPLICATIONS OF INFORMATION TECHNOLOGY COMMON TO MOST ORGANIZATIONS.** Certain computer applications and information systems are universal and equally appropriate in any business environment. Computer applications found in most organizations include payroll, accounts receivable, accounts payable, general ledger, inventory management and control, human resource development, budgeting, and **office automation (OA)**.

Office automation refers collectively to computer-based applications associated with general office work. These include personal productivity software tools (word processing, desktop publishing, electronic spreadsheet, database, and presentation graphics), plus **electronic mail (E-mail)**, image processing (**facsimile** and image scanner), voice processing (**voice message switching** and **teleconferencing**), and office information systems.

11–4   **INDUSTRY-SPECIFIC APPLICATIONS OF INFORMATION TECHNOLOGY.** Some computer applications are unique to a particular type of business, such as production scheduling (manufacturing), **electronic funds transfer** (financial services), typesetting (publishing), reservation system (airlines), actuarial accounting (insurance), and special effects in movies and on-line theater scripts (entertainment).

Robotics (the integration of computers and **industrial robots**), **computer-integrated manufacturing (CIM)**, and **computer-aided design (CAD)** are three of the more prominent applications of information technology commonly found in manufacturing.

In health care, computers help hospital administrative personnel with billing and help doctors diagnose illnesses. The computer has enabled medical research to advance by leaps and bounds.

Some of the computer applications found in local government include utility billing, tax collection, police and fire incident reporting, and traffic control. State governments use computers for everything from fingerprint analysis to running statewide lotteries. The federal government has thousands of computer systems throughout the world that are used in a wide variety of applications.

REVIEW EXERCISES

Concepts

1. What elements are combined to create an information system?
2. What is IRM, and how does it relate to money, materials, and people?
3. What differentiates a decision support system from an information system?
4. Electronic funds transfer is associated with what industry?
5. Information systems common to most businesses usually involve accounting for what two corporate resources?
6. Name four applications of the computer in a municipal government.
7. CAD and robotics are usually associated with what industry?
8. What computer-based applications are unique to hospitals?
9. Which common information system produces invoices? Purchase orders? Balance sheets?
10. Name three office information systems.
11. Briefly describe the concept of CIM.
12. Expand the following acronyms: MIS, OA, EDI, and ATM.

Discussion

13. Movie purists abhor the thought of great black-and-white classics such as *Casablanca* being changed to color with the help of computer technology. What do you think?
14. Has the application of computer technology in the theater in any way stifled artistic creativity? Has it enhanced creativity? Explain.
15. Discuss the emerging role of personal computers in electronic funds transfer.
16. Physicians' accounting systems have been implemented under a cloud of controversy. Why?
17. Would you buy a "magazine on a disk"? Why or why not?
18. Describe MIS strategies that companies in the construction industry could employ to achieve a competitive advantage.

SELF-TEST (by section) ━━━━━━━━━━━━━━━

11–1   **a.** The four major corporate resources are money, materials, information, and _____.

   b. We combine hardware, software, people, procedures, and data to create an _____ .

   c. Expert systems are part of the general area of research known as _____.

11–2   The general area of computers and information systems is sometimes referred to as _____.

11–3   **a.** The balance sheet is a by-product of a general ledger system. (T/F)

   b. Accounts payable is generally associated with office automation applications. (T/F)

   c. Management relies on which common information system to identify overdue customer accounts: (a) accounts receivable, (b) accounts payable, or (c) budgeting?

   d. Voice message switching is associated with the office automation application of _____.

11–4   **a.** The integration of the computer with manufacturing is called CIM, or _____ .

   b. Automatic teller machines are an implementation of EFT. (T/F)

   c. Actuarial accounting systems are associated with the _____ industry.

   d. Computer-based traffic-control systems are implemented at what level of government: (a) local, (b) state, or (c) federal?

   e. Among financial institutions, only brokerage firms offer computer-based financial planning services. (T/F)

   f. The Internal Revenue Service is investigating the feasibility of allowing preparers to file tax returns from their personal computers, but such a service is not yet available. (T/F)

Self-test answers   **11–1** **(a)** people; **(b)** information system; **(c)** artificial intelligence. **11–2** information technology. **11–3** **(a)** T; **(b)** F; **(c)** a; **(d)** voice processing. **11–4** **(a)** computer-integrated manufacturing; **(b)** T; **(c)** insurance; **(d)** a; **(e)** F; **(f)** F.

12

Developing Information Systems

STUDENT LEARNING OBJECTIVES

▶ To describe how information needs vary at each level of organizational activity.

▶ To contrast the concepts of on-line and off-line.

▶ To describe the circumstances appropriate for batch and transaction-oriented data entry.

▶ To describe the four stages of the system life cycle.

▶ To describe and order the major activities that take place during each phase of system development.

▶ To distinguish between the different approaches to system conversion.

▶ To explain the concept of prototyping.

▶ To identify points of security vulnerability for the computer center and for information systems.

12–1   INFORMATION SYSTEM CONCEPTS

Filtering Information

A company has four levels of activity—*clerical, operational, tactical,* and *strategic*. Information systems process data at the clerical level and provide information for managerial decision-making at the other three levels.

Programmers, systems analysts, and users must determine the specific information needs at each level of organizational activity during the system design process. The key to developing quality information systems is to *filter* information so that people at the various levels of activity receive the information they need to do their jobs—no more, no less. The quality of an information system depends very much on getting the *right information* to the *right people* at the *right time*.

Clerical Level. Clerical-level personnel, those involved in repetitive tasks, are concerned primarily with transaction handling (for example, entering customer orders on their terminals).

Operational Level. Personnel at the operational level have well-defined tasks that might span a day, a week, or as much as three months, but their tasks are essentially short-term. Their information requirements are directed at operational feedback (such as an end-of-quarter sales summary report).

Tactical Level. At the tactical level, managers concentrate on achieving that series of goals required to meet the objectives set at the strategic level. The information requirements are usually periodic (for example, a corporate sales report by region), but on occasion managers require "what if" reports.

Strategic Level. Managers at the strategic level are objective-minded. Their information system requirements are often one-time reports, "what if" reports, and trend analyses. For example, the president of the company might ask for a report that shows the four-year sales trend for each of the company's products and overall (Figure 12–1). Knowing that it is easier to detect trends in a graphic format than in a tabular listing, the president requested that the trends be summarized in a bar graph (Figure 12–1).

Not all information systems are developed in cooperation with the information-services department. Some systems, especially micro-based systems, are developed entirely by users.

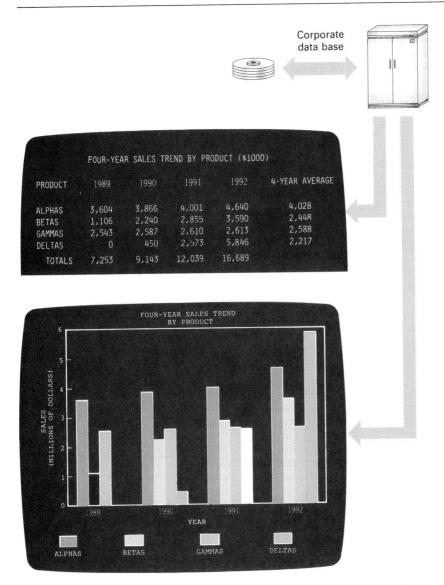

FIGURE 12–1   A Strategic-Level Sales-Trend-by-Product Report Shown in Tabular and Graphic Formats
The sales-trend report and bar graph are prepared in response to inquiries from a strategic-level manager.

On-Line versus Off-Line

In a computer system the input, output, and data storage components receive data from and transmit data to the processor over electrical cables, or "lines." These hardware components are said to be **on-line** to the processor. Hardware devices that are not accessible to or under the control of a processor are said to be **off-line**. The concepts of on-line and off-line also apply to data. Data are said to be *on-line* if they can be accessed and manipulated by the processor. All other data are *off-line*.

On-line and off-line are important information system concepts. Consider the payroll example in Figure 12–2. In an *off-line* operation, all supervisors complete the weekly time sheets. The time sheets are then collected and *batched* for input to the computer system. When transactions are grouped together for processing, it is called **batch processing**.

Before the data can be entered and the payroll checks printed, the payroll master file must be placed on-line. To do this, the master file is retrieved manually from a library of disk files and loaded to a storage component called a disk drive. Once loaded, the payroll master file is on-line. The process is analogous to selecting a compact disk (CD) that you wish to play from your CD library and loading it to the CD player.

An operator at a terminal enters the data contained on the time sheets directly into the computer system in an *on-line* operation. Employee data, such as name, social security number, pay rate, and deductions, are retrieved from the payroll master file and combined with the number of hours worked to produce the payroll checks. The payroll checks are produced on a printer, which is an output device.

Because the payroll checks are printed on continuous, preprinted forms, they must be separated before they can be distributed to the employees. In an *off-line* operation, a machine called a burster separates and stacks the payroll checks.

FIGURE 12–2   On-Line and Off-Line Operations
Those processing activities, hardware, and files that are not controlled by or accessible to the computer are referred to as off-line.

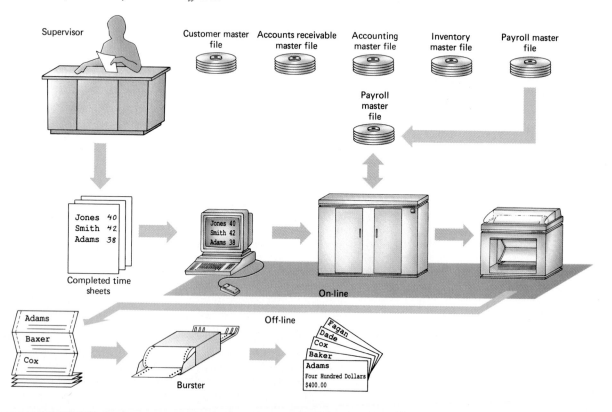

Data Entry

Most data do not exist in a form that can be "read" by the computer. In the example of Figure 12–2, the supervisor uses a pencil and paper to record manually on the time sheet the hours worked by the staff. Before the payroll checks can be computed and printed, the data on these time sheets must be *transcribed* (converted) into a *machine-readable format* that can be interpreted by a computer. This is done as an *on-line* operation by someone at a terminal. The time sheet is known as the **source document** and, as you might expect, the data on the time sheet are the **source data**.

Data can be entered on a terminal in the following ways:

- *Batch*. Transactions are grouped, or *batched*, and entered consecutively, one after the other.
- *Transaction-oriented*. Transactions are recorded and entered as they occur.

To illustrate the difference between batch and transaction-oriented data entry, consider an order processing system for a mail-order merchandiser. The system accepts orders by both mail and phone. The orders received by mail are accumulated, or batched, for data entry—usually at night. There are no handwritten source documents for phone orders; people taking the phone orders interact with the computer via terminals to enter the order on-line while talking with the customer.

All airline reservation systems are transaction-oriented. The workstations at ticket counters in airports are on-line to a centralized computer facility. Each time an agent writes a ticket and assigns a passenger a seat, the master record for that flight is immediately updated to reflect the addition of one more passenger.

Information System Capabilities

Not surprisingly, an information system has the same four capabilities as a computer system: *input, processing, storage,* and *output.*

Input.   The information system input capability can accept:

- *Source data*: Usually recording a transaction or documenting an event or item.
- *An inquiry*: A request for information.
- *A response to a prompt*: For example, a Y or N.
- *An instruction*: For example, "Store file" or "Print record."
- *A message to another user on the system.*
- *A change*: For instance, editing a word processing document.

Processing.   The information system processing capability encompasses:

- *Sorting*: Arranging data or records in some order (for example, alphabetizing a customer file by last name).
- *Accessing, recording, and updating data in storage*: For example, retrieving a customer record from a data base for processing, entering expense data into an accounting system's data base, and changing a customer's address on a marketing data base, respectively.
- *Summarizing*: Presenting information in a condensed format, often to reflect totals and subtotals.
- *Selecting*: Selecting records by criteria. (For example, "Select all employees with 25 or more years of service in the company.")
- *Manipulating*: Performing arithmetic operations (addition, multiplication, and so on) and logic operations (comparing an employee's years of service to 25 to determine if they are greater than, equal to, or less than 25).

Storage.   The information system storage capability permits it to store *data, text, images* (graphs, pictures), and *other digital information* (voice messages) so they can be recalled easily for further processing.

Output.   The information system output capability allows it to produce output in a variety of formats.

- *Hard copy*: For example, printed reports, documents, and messages.
- *Soft copy*: Temporary displays on terminal screens, for instance.
- *Control*: For example, instructions to industrial robots or automated processes.

12–2   THE SYSTEM LIFE CYCLE

An information system is analogous to the human life. It is born, it grows, it matures, and it eventually dies. The **system life cycle** has four stages, as shown in Figure 12–3.

Birth Stage.   In the *birth stage* of the system life cycle, someone has an idea about how the computer can help provide better and more timely information.

FIGURE 12–3   The System Life Cycle

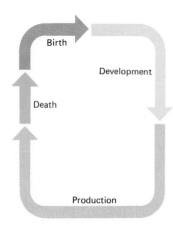

Birth

Development

Death

Production

Development Stage.   The idea becomes a reality during the *development stage* of the system life cycle. During this stage systems analysts, programmers, and users work together to analyze a company's information processing needs and design an information system. The design specifications are then translated into programs, and the system is implemented.

Production Stage.   Upon implementation, the information system enters the *production stage* and becomes operational, serving the information needs of the company. The production stage is the longest of the four stages and normally will last from four to seven years. During this stage, information systems are continuously modified, or maintained, to keep up with the changing needs of the company.

Death Stage.   The accumulation of modifications to a dynamic information system eventually takes its toll on system efficiency. The *death stage* arrives when an information system becomes so cumbersome to maintain that it is no longer economically or operationally effective. At this time it is discarded, and the system life cycle is repeated.

12–3   THE SYSTEMS DEVELOPMENT PROCESS

The systems development process is a cooperative effort of users and computer professionals. On one hand, computer professionals are familiar with the technology and how it can be applied to meet a business's information processing needs. On the other, users have in-depth familiarity with their respective functional areas and information processing

At the start of a project, it is always a good idea for the project team leader to assemble the team, go over the system development methodology, and make sure responsibility areas are clearly understood.

needs. The skills and knowledge of these two groups complement each other and can be combined to create any type of information system during the systems development process.

Because systems development is a team effort, most companies have adopted a standardized **systems development methodology** that provides a framework for cooperation. This step-by-step approach to systems development is essentially the same, be it for an airline reservation system or an inventory management system. As members of a **project team** progress through the procedures outlined in a systems development methodology, the results of one step provide the input for the next step and/or subsequent steps. The project team typically is made up of both users and computer professionals.

The methodological approach to systems development is a tool that information services and user-managers can employ to coordinate the efforts of a variety of people engaged in a complex process. The activities of the systems development process typically are grouped in phases, often labeled *systems analysis, systems design, programming, conversion,* and *implementation.* Each phase is examined in the following discussions.

Systems Analysis: Understanding the System

The systems analysis phase of the systems development process produces the following results:

- Existing system review
- System objectives
- Design constraints
- Requirements definition

Each of these results defines an activity that is to take place.

Existing System Review.   Before designing a new or enhanced information system, the members of the project team must have a good grasp of the existing work and information flow, be it manual or computer-based. To do this, the project team conducts interviews with users and observes the present system in operation. Then the team documents the work and information flow of the system by reducing it to its basic components—*input, processing,* and *output.* A variety of design techniques can be used to depict graphically the logical relationships between these parts. Perhaps the most popular, although not necessarily the best for all situations, is *flowcharting* (see Chapter 9, "Programming Concepts"). A more structured technique, **data flow diagrams**, is introduced later in this chapter.

System Objectives.   Once the existing system is documented, the project team can begin to identify the obvious and not-so-obvious problem areas, including procedural bottlenecks, inefficiencies in information flow and storage, duplication of effort, deficiencies in information dissemination, worker discontent, problems with customer interaction, inaccuracy of operational data, and so on. Once these are identified, project team members can concentrate their energies on identifying opportunities for the coordination of effort, the integration of systems, and the use of information. This knowledge is formalized as system objectives.

Design Constraints.   The target system will be developed subject to specific constraints. The purpose of this activity is to detail, at the onset of the systems development process, any costs, hardware, schedule, procedural, software, data base, and operating constraints that may limit the definition and design of the target system. For example, cost constraints include any limits on developmental, operational, or maintenance costs.

Requirements Definition.   In this activity the project team completes a *needs analysis* that results in a definition of the data processing and information requirements for the target system. To accomplish this task, the project team begins by gathering information. User feedback from interviews is the basis for the project team's **functional specifications** for system input, processing, and output requirements (information

The prespecification approach to systems development requires the user to sign off on the design specifications at various stages of the process. This programmer/analyst is demonstrating the proposed layouts of the input/output screens for an inventory-management subsystem to the plant manager. The plant manager is encouraged to make recommendations to improve the layouts and other aspects of the system design until she signs off, after which time the specs are frozen.

MEMORY BITS

**RESULTS OF SYSTEMS
ANALYSIS PHASE**

- Existing system review
- System objectives
- Design constraints
- Requirements definition

needs). The functional specifications describe the logic of the system (input/output, work, and information flow) from the perspective of the user.

At this point the emphasis turns toward *output requirements*. In the systems development process, the project team begins with the desired output and works backward to determine input and processing requirements. Outputs are typically printed reports, terminal displays, or some kind of transaction (for example, purchase order, payroll check). At this time, outputs are described functionally. The actual **layout** (spacing on the screen or page) and detailed content of a display screen or report is specified during the system design phase.

Systems Design: A Science or an Art?

The systems design stage of the systems development process produces the following results:

- General system design
- Data base design
- Detailed system design

Each of these results defines an activity that is to take place.

General System Design

System design: The creative process   The design of an information system is more of a challenge to the human intellect than it is a procedural challenge. Just as an author begins with a blank page and an idea, the members of the project team begin with empty RAM (random-access memory) and the information requirements definitions. From here they must create what can sometimes be a very complex information system. The number of ways in which a particular information system can be designed is limited only by the imaginations of the project team members.

Completing the general system design   The project team analyzes the existing system, assesses information processing requirements, and then develops a **general system design** for the target system. The general system design, and later the detailed design, involve continuous communication between members of the project team and all levels of users (clerical through strategic), as appropriate. After evaluating several alternative approaches, the project team translates the system specifications into a general system design.

At a minimum, the documentation of the general design of the target system includes the following:

- A graphic illustration that depicts the fundamental operation of the target system (for example, data flow diagrams).
- A written explanation of the graphic illustration.
- General descriptions of the outputs to be produced by the system, including display screens and hard-copy reports and documents. (The actual layout— for example, spacing on the page or screen—is not completed until the detailed system design.)

Software packages are available that enable project team members to design systems interactively at their workstations. Automated design tools, such as Teamwork/SA from Cadre Technologies, have helped programmers and systems analysts make significant strides in productivity improvement. With Teamwork/SA, systems analysts can depict the work and information flow in a system that uses any of a variety of structured design techniques.

Data Base Design.   The data base is the common denominator of any system. It contains the raw material (data) necessary to produce the output (information). In manufacturing, for example, you decide what you are going to make, then you order the raw material. In the process of developing an information system, you decide what your output requirements are, then you determine which data are needed to produce the output. In a sense, output requirements can be thought of as input to data base design. Data bases and data base design are discussed in Chapter 10, "Software Concepts and Data Management."

Detailed System Design.   The **detailed system design**—the detailed input/output, processing, and control requirements—is the result of the analysis of user feedback on the general system design. The general system design depicts the relationship between major processing activities and is detailed enough for users to determine whether or not that is what they want. The detailed design includes *all* processing activities and the input/output associated with them.

The screen layout for this accounts-receivable system makes good use of color to help the user distinguish between input prompts, user-supplied input, system-supplied customer data, and messages to the user.

The detailed design is the cornerstone of the systems development process. It is here that the relationships between the various components of the system are defined. The system specifications are transformed with the project team's imagination and skill into an information system. The detailed system design is the culmination of all previous work. Moreover, it is the *blueprint* for all project-team activities that follow.

A number of techniques help programmers and analysts in the design process. Each of these techniques permits the system design to be illustrated graphically. One of these techniques, data flow diagrams, is briefly discussed here.

Structured system design   It is much easier to address a complex design problem in small, manageable modules than as one big task. This is done using the principles of **structured system design**. The structured approach to system design encourages the top-down design technique:

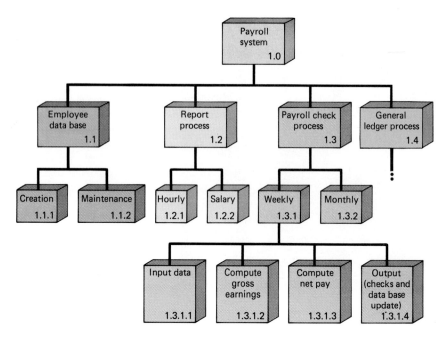

FIGURE 12–4   Structure Chart

This structure chart breaks a payroll system down into a hierarchy of modules.

That is, the project team divides the system into independent modules for ease of understanding and design. The **structure chart** in Figure 12–4 illustrates how a payroll system can be conceptualized as a hierarchy of modules. Eventually the logic for the modules is represented in detail in step-by-step diagrams that illustrate the interactions between input, processing, output, and storage activities for a particular module.

Data flow diagrams   **Data flow diagrams**, or **DFD**s, enable analysts to design and document systems using the structured approach to systems development. Only four symbols are needed for data flow diagrams: entity, process, flow line, and data store. The symbols are summarized in Figure 12–5 and their use is illustrated in Figure 12–6.

- *Entity symbol.* The entity symbol, a square with a darkened "shadow," is the source or destination of data or information flow. An entity can be a person, a group of people (for example, customers or employees), a department, or even a place (such as a warehouse).

- *Process symbol.* Each process symbol, a rectangle with rounded corners,

FIGURE 12–5   Data Flow Diagram Symbols

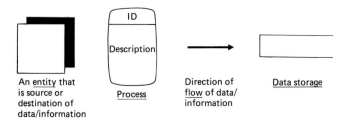

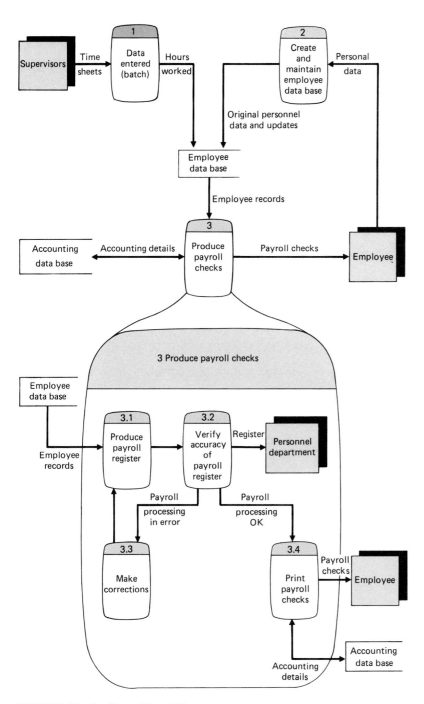

FIGURE 12–6   Data Flow Diagram
In this diagram of a payroll system, Process 3 is exploded to show greater detail.

contains a description of a function to be performed. Process symbols also can be depicted as circles. Typical processes include *enter data, calculate, store, create, produce,* and *verify.* Process-symbol identification numbers are assigned in levels. (For example, Processes 1.1 and 1.2 are subordinate to Process 1.)

■ *Flow line*. The flow lines indicate the flow and direction of data or information.

■ *Data store*. These symbols, open-ended rectangles, identify storage locations for data, which could be a file drawer, a shelf, a data base on magnetic disk, and so on.

In Figure 12–6, a data flow diagram documents that portion of a personnel system that produces payroll checks. Processes 1 and 2 deal with the employee data base, but in Process 3 the actual payroll checks are produced. In the bottom portion of Figure 12–5, Process 3 is *exploded* to show greater detail. Notice that the second-level processes within the explosion of Process 3 are numbered 3.1, 3.2, 3.3, and 3.4. Process 3.1 could be exploded to a third level of processes to show even greater detail (for example, 3.1.1, 3.1.2, and so on).

CASE: AUTOMATING THE DESIGN PROCESS

For years most people thought the best way to improve productivity in systems development was to make it easier for programmers to create programs. In the early 1980s people began asking the question "Why can't the power of the computer be applied to analysis and design work as well?" Now we know that it can. Many time-consuming manual tasks, such as creating a data dictionary and documenting information flow, can be automated. This general family of software development productivity tools falls under the umbrella of computer-aided software engineering, or CASE, tools.

CASE tools, which are also referred to as workbench technologies, provide automated support throughout the entire system life cycle. The CASE tool kit consists of the following:

■ *Design Tools*. Prior to the introduction of CASE technologies, the tool kit for the systems analyst and programmer consisted of flowcharting and data flow diagram templates, lettering templates, rulers, scissors, glue, pencils, pens, and plenty of erasers and correction fluid. The CASE design tool provides an automated alternative. It helps analysts and programmers prepare the schematics that graphically depict the logic of a system or program (for example, data flow diagrams and structure charts). They do this in much the same way word processing software helps a writer prepare an article for

publication. They also help designers prepare screen and report layouts.

Automated design tools enable an analyst or programmer to select and position symbols, such as the DFD process and entity symbols, and to connect these symbols with flow lines. Both symbols and flow lines can be labeled. Because all the design techniques supported by CASE products are structured design techniques, systems ultimately are depicted in several levels of generality.

■ *Prototyping Tools*. CASE prototyping tools are used by project team members to create a physical representation of a target system at one of the three levels of sophistication—a nonfunctional, partially functional, or fully functional prototype system. Prototyping tools enable project team members to create a mockup of a system's user interface (essentially a hierarchy of menus) and its screens layout (data entry forms, reports, inquiries, and so on) in a few days as opposed to a few months if they had to be programmed.

■ *Information Repository Tools*. The information repository is a central computer-based storage facility for all design information. For example, in an information repository, each data element is cross-referenced to all other components in the system. That is, the data element *customer*

There is no one best analytical or design technique. Design techniques are just tools. It's your skill and imagination that make an information system a reality.

The presentation of information   Within the context of an information system, information can be presented in many ways. During the systems design process, members of the project team work in close cooperation with users to describe each output that will be generated from the target system. An output could be a hard-copy report, a display of information, or a transaction document (an invoice). Transaction documents are typically periodic (monthly invoices). Reports (generally, the presentation of information in either hard-copy or soft-copy format) can be either *periodic* or *ad hoc*.

Of course, not all reports contain numbers and text. Some of the most effective ways of presenting information involve the use of graphics.

number would be cross-referenced to every screen, report, graph, record/file, data base, program, or any other design element in which it occurred. Cross-references are also made to processes in data flow diagrams. Once the company has had the information repository in place for a while, cross-references can be extended between information systems. In addition, any part of the system—layouts, data dictionary, notes, pseudocode (nonexecutable program code), project schedules, and so on—can be recalled and displayed for review or modification. In effect, the information repository is the "data base" for the system development project.

- *Program Development Tools.* Program development tools focus on the back-end, or the latter stages, of the systems development effort. CASE program development tools fall into four categories:

  1. *Program structure charts* enable programmers to create a graphic, hierarchical representation of all the programs in a system.
  2. *Code generators* actually generate program instructions (code) based on program design specifications.
  3. *Program preprocessors* preprocesses programmer-written programs in high-level languages, such as COBOL and PL/I, to point

out potential problems in the program logic and syntax and to generate the documentation for the program.

  4. *Test data generators* compile test data for programmers. The programmer describes the parameters of the desired data (format, range, distribution, and so on), and the test data generator does the rest.

- *Methodology Tools.* The *methodology tool* is a computer-based version of the traditional systems-development methodology manual. Both describe phased procedures and responsibilities, and both provide forms and formats for documenting the system.

CASE tools are in their infancy. To some extent each tool is available commercially. While no comprehensive CASE tool kit to date integrates all the various tools, some companies offer packages that integrate two or three. Software engineers are working overtime to develop products that will bridge the gap between design and executable program code. In a two-step process, these tool kits would enable project teams to use automated software packages to help them complete the logic design (information flow, I/O), then the CASE software would translate the design into the physical implementation of the system (executable program code). In fact, several existing CASE products are bordering on this level of sophistication.

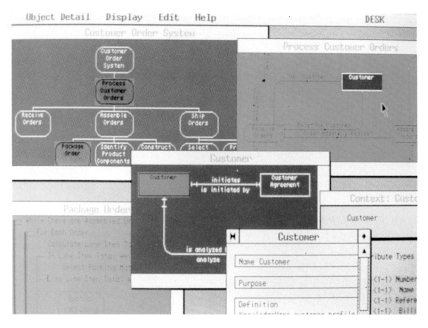

KnowledgeWare, Inc., provides an integrated CASE environment for the planning, analysis, design, and construction of information systems. The KnowledgeWare tools function as an integrated set and independently as stand-alone products. The windows in the screen illustrate the capabilities of the Analysis Workstation, an integrated set of diagrammatic tools for requirements analysis. The techniques incorporated into the software include decomposition diagrams (top left), data flow diagrams (top right), entity relationship diagrams (middle), and action diagrams (bottom left).

Programming: Ideas Become Reality

The next challenge is to translate the system design and specifications into instructions that can be interpreted and executed by the computer. This, of course, is the programming phase of the systems development process.

The programming phase of the systems development process produces the following results:

- System specifications review
- Program identification and description
- Program coding, testing, and documentation

Each of these results defines an activity that is to be accomplished. With detailed specifications in hand, programmers are now ready to write the programs needed to make the target system operational.

System Specifications Review.   During the programming phase, programming becomes the dominant activity. The system specifications completed during the system analysis and design phase are all that is necessary for programmers to write, or *code*, the programs to implement the information system. But before getting started, programmers should review the system specifications (layouts, design, and so on) created during system analysis and design.

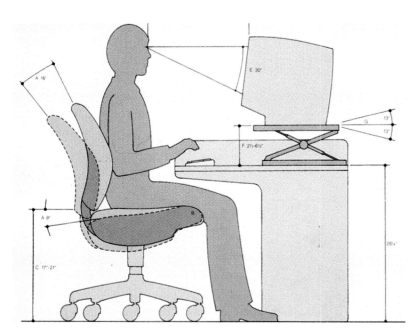

Because programmers may spend four or more hours each day at a workstation, vendors are paying more attention to the ergonomics (efficiency of the person-machine interface) of the programmer terminal. Features of an ergonomically designed terminal include a high-resolution and non-glare display, tilt and swivel adjustments for the display, tilt adjustment for the keyboard, and noise level adjustments for prompting alarms.

Program Identification and Description. An information system needs an array of programs to create and update the data base, print reports, permit on-line inquiry, and so on. Depending on the scope of the system and how many programs can be generated using application development tools, as few as three or four or as many as several hundred programs may need to be written before the system can be implemented. At this point, all programs necessary to make the system operational are identified and described. A typical program description would include:

- Type of programming language (COBOL, BASIC, FOCUS, Ideal, and so on)
- A narrative of the program, describing the tasks to be performed
- Frequency of processing (for example, daily, weekly, on-line)
- Input to the program (data and their source)
- Output produced by the program
- Limitations and restrictions (for example, sequence of input data, response-time maximums, and so on)
- Detailed specifications (for example, specific computations and logical manipulations, tables)

Program Coding, Testing, and Documentation. Armed with system specifications and program descriptions, programmers can begin the actual coding of programs. The development of a program is actually a project within a project. Just as there are certain steps the project team takes

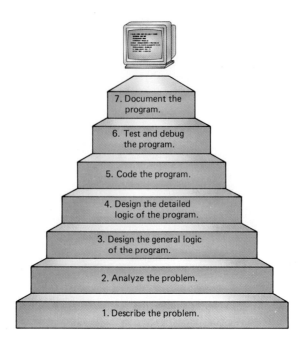

FIGURE 12–7   Steps in Writing a Program

to develop an information system, there are certain steps a programmer takes to write a program. These seven steps are discussed in Chapter 9, "Programming Concepts" and are summarized in Figure 12–7.

System Conversion and Implementation

System Testing.   The first step of the system conversion and implementation phase of the system development process is system testing. This testing encompasses everything that makes up the information system—the hardware, the software, the end users, the procedures (for example, user manuals), and the data. If needed, the interfaces between the system and other systems are tested as well.

During the programming phase of systems development, programs are written according to system specifications and are individually tested. Although the programs that comprise the software for the system have undergone **unit testing** (individual testing) and have been debugged, there is no guarantee that the programs will work as a system. To ensure that the software can be combined into an operational information system, the project team performs integrated **systems testing**.

To conduct the system test, the project team compiles and thoroughly tests the system with test data. In this first stage, tests are run for each subsystem (one of the functional aspects of the system) or cycle (weekly or monthly activities). The test data are judiciously compiled so all program and system options and all error and validation routines are tested. The tests are repeated and modifications are made until all subsystems or cycles function properly. At this point the entire system is tested as a unit. Testing and modifications continue until the components of the system work as they should and all input/output is validated.

The second stage of system testing is done with *live data* by several of the people who will eventually use the system. Live data have already been processed through the existing system. Testing with live data provides an extra level of assurance that the system will work properly when implemented.

Approaches to System Conversion.   Once systems testing is complete, the project team can begin to integrate people, software, hardware, procedures, and data into an operational information system. This normally involves a conversion from the existing system to the new one. An organization's approach to system conversion depends on its *willingness to accept risk* and the *amount of time available* for the conversion. Four common approaches are parallel conversion, direct conversion, phased conversion, and pilot conversion. These approaches are illustrated in Figure 12–8 and discussed in the paragraphs that follow.

Parallel conversion   In **parallel conversion**, the existing system and the new system operate simultaneously, or in parallel, until the project team is confident that the new system is working properly. Parallel conversion has two important advantages. First, the existing system serves as a backup if the new system fails to operate as expected. Second, the results of the new system can be compared to the results of the existing system.

There is less risk with this strategy because not only does the present system provide backup but it also doubles the workload of personnel and hardware resources during the conversion. Parallel conversion usually takes one month or a major system cycle. For a public utility company, this might be one complete billing cycle, which is usually a month.

Direct conversion   As companies improve their system testing procedures, they begin to gain confidence in their ability to implement a working system. Some companies forego parallel conversion in favor of

PLEASE TAKE YOUR
CARD AND CASH
THANK YOU

Systems analysts are relying more and more on the graphical user interface, sometimes referred to as the GUI. Computer graphics are being used to enhance the user interface and, therefore, the user friendliness of all kinds of computer-based systems. The display on this automatic teller machine (ATM) provides the user with both visual cues and written instructions.

FIGURE 12–8   Common Approaches to System Conversion

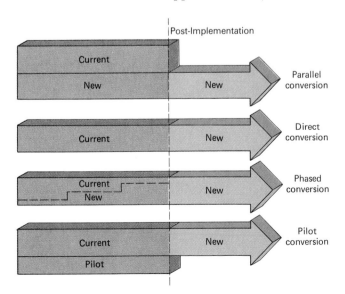

a **direct conversion.** Direct conversion involves a greater risk because there is no backup in case the system fails.

Companies select this "cold-turkey" approach when there is no existing system or when the existing system is substantially different. For example, all on-line hotel reservations systems are implemented "cold turkey."

Phased conversion   In **phased conversion,** an information system is implemented one module at a time by either parallel or direct conversion. For example, in a point-of-sale system, the first phase might be to convert the sales-accounting module. The second phase could involve the inventory-management module. The third might be the credit-check module.

Phased conversion has the advantage of spreading the demand for resources to avoid an intense demand. The disadvantages are that the conversion takes longer and an interface must be developed between the existing system and the new one.

Pilot conversion   In **pilot conversion,** the new system is implemented by parallel, direct, or phased conversion as a pilot system in only one of the areas for which it is targeted. Suppose a company wants to implement a manufacturing resources planning system in its eight plants. One plant would be selected as a pilot, and the new information system would be implemented there first.

The advantage of pilot conversion is that the inevitable bugs in a system can be removed before the system is implemented at the other locations. The disadvantage is that the implementation time for the total system takes longer than if the entire system were implemented at one time.

The System Becomes Operational.   Once the conversion has been completed, the information system enters the production stage of the system life cycle (see Figure 12–3). During the production stage the system becomes operational and is turned over to the users. The operations function of the information services division provides operational support for the system. This function encompasses everything associated with running an information system including all interaction with the hardware that supports the system.

Post-Implementation Activities

Just as a new automobile will need some screws tightened after a few hundred miles, an information system will need some fine-tuning just after implementation. Thereafter and throughout the production stage of the system life cycle, the system will be modified many times to meet the changing needs of the company.

Post-Implementation Review.   The **post-implementation review** is a critical examination of the system three to six months after it has been put into production. This waiting period allows several factors to stabilize: the resistance to change, the anxieties associated with change, and the learning curve. It also allows time for unanticipated problems to surface.

The post-implementation review focuses on the following:

- A comparison of the system's actual performance versus the anticipated performance objectives
- An assessment of each facet of the system with respect to preset criteria
- Mistakes made during system development
- Unexpected benefits and problems

System Maintenance. Once an information system is implemented and goes on-line, the emphasis switches from *development* to *operations*. In a payroll system, supervisors begin to enter hours worked on their terminals, and the computer center produces and issues payroll checks. Once operational, an information system becomes a cooperative effort between the users and the information services division.

An information system is dynamic and must be responsive to the changing needs of the company and those who use it. The process of modifying an information system to meet changing needs is known as **system maintenance**.

Three to six months after the hardware, software, people, procedures, and data have been integrated into an operational information system, key members of the project team are conducting a post-implementation evaluation to assess the overall effectiveness of an aircraft maintenance system.

An information system cannot live forever. The accumulation of modifications and enhancements eventually will make any information system cumbersome and inefficient. Minor modifications are known as **patches**. Depending on the number of patches and enhancements, an information system will remain operational—that is, be in the production stage—from four to seven years.

Toward the end of the useful life of an information system, it is more trouble to continue patching the system than it is to redesign the system completely. The end of the production stage signals the death stage of the information system life cycle (see Figure 12–3). A new system is then "born" of need, and the system development process is repeated.

12–4   PROTOTYPING: CREATING A MODEL OF THE TARGET SYSTEM

Throughout the twentieth century manufacturers have built prototypes of everything from toasters to airplanes. Automobile manufacturers routinely build prototypes according to design specifications. Scaled-down clay models are made to evaluate aesthetics and aerodynamics. Ultimately a full-size, fully functional prototype is created that enables the driver and passengers to test all aspects of the car's functionality. If engineers see possibilities for improvement, the prototypes are modified and retested until they meet or exceed all specifications. The prototype approach to development is now being embraced by the computer and information system communities. Prototyping is emerging as an enhancement of or an alternative to the methodological approach to system development discussed in Section 12–3.

The Prototype System

The three objectives of **prototyping** are:

1. To analyze the current situation
2. To identify information needs
3. To develop a scaled-down model of the target system

The scaled-down model, called a **prototype system**, normally would handle the main transaction-oriented procedures, produce the critical reports, and permit rudimentary inquiries. The prototype system gives users an opportunity to actually work with the functional aspect of the target system long before the system is implemented. Once users gain hands-on familiarity with the prototype system, they are in a position to be more precise when they relate their information processing needs to the project team.

A prototype system can be anything from a nonfunctional demonstration of the input/output of a target information system to a full-scale operational system. These models are tested and refined until the users are confident that what they see is what they want. In some cases, the software that was developed to create an initial prototype

PROFILE

James Martin, chairman of James Martin Associates, is described in *Computerworld* as "the computer industry's most widely read author, best attended lecturer, and foremost authority on the social and commercial impact of computers." He has written over 70 best-selling books on computer and communication technology, many of which are influential works that continue to change perceptions in the industry. Among Martin's numerous video-based courses are the world's first educational course on videodisk and the first interactive educational laser disk.

Martin is a man whose predictions have been accurate. In 1960 he predicted the growth of teleprocessing, on-line storage, and real-time systems. In 1968 he predicted that hobby computing would boom in 10 years. He also has forecast markets in communication satellites, optical fibers, and value-added carriers. Martin foresaw the growth of

application development tools and originated the term *fourth-generation languages*. He created the discipline of *information engineering*. He may well be the most frequently quoted person in the computer industry.

According to Martin, "The challenge of today's technology is not to automate what already exists but to change it into fundamentally better forms. Corporations everywhere need drastic retooling and restructuring because of global networks and computer power."

system is expanded to create a fully operational information system. However, in most cases, the prototype system provides an alternate vehicle for completing the functional specifications activity of a systems development methodology. Incomplete and/or inaccurate user specifications have been the curse of systems development methodologies. Many companies have exorcised this curse by the integration of prototyping into their methodologies.

Creating the Prototype System.   To create a prototype system, project team members rough out the logic of the system and how the elements fit together with an automated design tool. Then they work with the user to define the I/O interfaces (the system interaction with the user). During interactive sessions, project team members and users create whatever interactive display screens are required to meet the user's information processing needs. To do this, project team members use the applications development tools such as fourth-generation languages, or 4GLs, (discussed in Chapter 9, "Programming Concepts") to create the screen images (menus, reports, inquiries, and so on) and to generate much of the programming code.

Users actually can sit down at a terminal and evaluate portions of, then, eventually all of the prototype system. Invariably they have suggestions for improving the user interfaces and/or the format of the I/O. And without fail their examination reveals new needs for information.

In effect, the prototype system is the beginning. From here the system is expanded and refined to meet the users' total information needs. Prototyping software tools are limited in what they can do, so the typical system may require a considerable amount of custom coding, probably written in third- and fourth-generation languages.

12–5   COMPUTER-CENTER AND SYSTEM SECURITY

One of the most important considerations in the development and ongoing operation of an information system is security. As more and more systems go on-line, more people have access to the system. A company must be extremely careful not to compromise the integrity of the system. The company must be equally careful with the "engine" for the information system—the computer.

An information system has many points of vulnerability and too much is at stake to overlook the threats to the security of an information system and a computer center. These threats take many forms: white-collar crime, natural disasters (such as earthquakes, floods), vandalism, and carelessness.

This section is devoted to discussing the security considerations for a computer center or an information system.

Computer-Center Security. A company's computer center has a number of points of vulnerability; they are *hardware*, *software*, *files/data bases*, *data communications*, and *personnel*. These are summarized in Figure 12–9 and briefly discussed here.

- *Hardware.* If the hardware fails, the MIS fails. The threat of failure can be minimized by implementing security precautions that prevent access by unauthorized personnel and by taking steps to keep all hardware operational.
- *Software.* Unless properly controlled, the software for an MIS can be modified for personal gain. Thus, close control over software development and the documentation of an MIS is needed to minimize the opportunity for computer crime. Operational control procedures that are built into the design of an MIS will constantly monitor processing accuracy.
- *Files/data bases.* The data base contains the raw material for information. In some cases, the files/data bases are the life blood of a company and must be protected.
- *Data communications.* The mere existence of data communications capabilities, where data are transmitted via communications links from one computer to another, poses a threat to security. Some companies use *cryptography— encryption/decryption* hardware that scrambles and unscrambles messages.
- *Personnel.* Managers are paying close attention to who gets hired for positions with access to computer-based information systems and sensitive data.

Information Systems Security. Information systems security is classified as physical or logical. *Physical security* refers to hardware, facilities, mag-

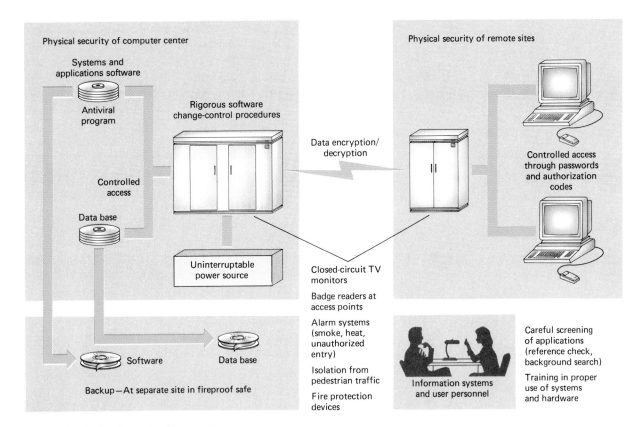

FIGURE 12–9   Security Precautions
Some or all of the security measures noted in the figure are in force in most computer centers. Each precaution helps minimize the risk of an information system's or a computer system's vulnerability to crime, disasters, and failure.

netic disks, and other things that could be illegally accessed, stolen, or destroyed.

Logical security is built into the software by permitting only authorized persons to access and use the system. Logical security for on-line systems is achieved primarily by **passwords** and **authorization codes**. Only those persons with a "need to know" are told the password and given authorization codes.

Level of Risk.   No amount of security measures will completely remove the vulnerability of a computer center or an information system. Each company must determine the level of risk it is willing to accept.

SUMMARY OUTLINE AND IMPORTANT TERMS

12–1   **INFORMATION SYSTEM CONCEPTS.** The four levels of organizational activity are clerical, operational, tactical, and strategic. Information must be filtered at the various levels of activity to ensure that the intended end user receives only information necessary to accomplish his or her job function.

Data or hardware devices are said to be **on-line** if they are directly accessible to and under the control of the computer. Other data and hardware are said to be **off-line**. In **batch processing**, transactions are grouped before they are processed.

In batch data entry, **source data** are entered consecutively as a group. In transaction-oriented data entry, the operator interacts directly with the data base and updates the data base as the transaction occurs.

An information system has the same four capabilities as a computer system: input, processing, storage, and output. The processing capabilities include sorting; accessing, recording, and updating data in storage; summarizing; selecting; and manipulating.

12–2   **THE SYSTEM LIFE CYCLE.** The four stages of a computer-based information system comprise the **system life cycle**. They are birth, development, production, and death.

12–3   **THE SYSTEMS DEVELOPMENT PROCESS.** The systems development process is a cooperative undertaking by users who know the functional areas and computer professionals who know the technology. The step-by-step **systems development methodology** provides the framework for system development.

During the systems analysis phase of the systems development process, the following activities take place.

■ *Existing system review.* The work and information flow of the present system is documented by reducing the system to its basic components—input, processing, and output. System design techniques include flowcharting and other more structured techniques such as **data flow diagrams**.

■ *System objectives.* The **project team** arrives at general system objectives by engaging in discussions with all end user managers ultimately affected by the target system.

■ *Design constraints.* The target information system must be developed within the boundaries of any applicable hardware, cost, schedule, procedural, software, data base, and operating constraints.

■ *Requirements definition.* User feedback provides the basis for the **functional specifications** for system input, processing, and output requirements. These specifications describe the logic of the system from the perspective of the user.

During the systems design phase of the systems development process, the following activities are completed.

■ *General system design.* At a minimum, the documentation of the **general system design** includes a graphic illustration and explanation of the fundamental operation of the target system and general descriptions of the outputs to be produced by the system.

■ *Data base design.* During systems development, designers describe the output requirements and determine which data are needed to produce the output.

■ *Detailed system design.* The **detailed system design** includes all processing activities and the input/output associated with them. When adhering to **structured system design**, designers divide the system into independent modules for ease of understanding and design. **Data flow diagrams** enable analysts to design and document systems using the structured approach to systems development. The four symbols used in **DFDs** are entity, process, flow line, and data store. Reports, or the general presentation of information, can be either periodic or ad hoc.

During the programming phase of the systems development process, programs are written to create the software necessary to make the information system operational. The following activities take place.

- *System specifications review.* Programmers review the system specifications created during system analysis and design.
- *Program identification and description.* A typical program description would include the type of programming language, a narrative description, frequency of processing, input/output, limitations and restrictions, and detailed specifications.
- *Program coding, testing, and documentation.* For each program, the programmer describes the problem; analyzes the problem; designs the general, then the detailed logic; and codes, tests, and documents the program.

Although the programs that make up an information system have been debugged on an individual basis (**unit testing**), they must be combined and subjected to integrated **systems testing** prior to implementation.

The four common approaches to system conversion are **parallel conversion**, **direct conversion**, **phased conversion**, and **pilot conversion**. The approach that an organization selects depends on its willingness to accept risk and the amount of time available for the conversion.

Once the conversion has been completed, the information system enters the production stage of the system life cycle and is turned over to the users.

The **post-implementation review**, which is a critical examination of the system after it has been put into production, is conducted three to six months after implementation.

An information system is dynamic and must be responsive to the changing needs of the company and those who use it. The process of modifying, or **patching**, an information system to meet changing needs is known as **system maintenance**.

12-4   PROTOTYPING: CREATING A MODEL OF THE TARGET SYSTEM. The three objectives of prototyping are to analyze the current situation, to identify information needs, and to develop a scaled-down model of the target system. A **prototype system** normally would handle the main transaction-oriented procedures, produce the critical reports, and permit rudimentary inquiries.

Ideally, users should experiment and familiarize themselves with the operation of a target system as early in the development process as possible. The prototyping process enables users to relate accurate information processing needs to the project team from the early phases of the project and on.

12–5 **COMPUTER-CENTER AND SYSTEM SECURITY.** The threats to the security of computer centers and information systems call for precautionary measures. A computer center can be vulnerable in its hardware, software, files/data bases, data communications, and personnel. Information systems security is classified as physical security or logical security.

REVIEW EXERCISES

Concepts

1. What are the levels of organizational activity, from specific to general?
2. Distinguish between on-line operation and off-line operation.
3. What advantages does transaction-oriented data entry have over batch data entry?
4. In which stage of the information system life cycle are systems "conceived"? "Maintained"?
5. Name the four symbols used in data flow diagrams.
6. The functional specifications describe the logic of a proposed system from whose perspective?
7. What is the design philosophy called that enables complex design problems to be addressed in small, manageable modules?
8. Name two system design techniques.
9. What are the objectives of prototyping?
10. Which comes first during system testing, testing with live data or testing with test data?
11. List three areas addressed during a post-implementation review.
12. The mere fact that a system uses data communications poses a threat to security. Why?
13. What advantage does direct conversion have over parallel conversion? Parallel over direct?

Discussion

14. It is often said that time is money. Would you say that information is money? Discuss.
15. Suppose the company you work for batches all sales data for data entry each night. You have been asked to present a convincing argument to top management for why funds should be allocated to convert the current system to transaction-oriented data entry. What would you say?
16. Give examples of reports that might be requested by an operational-level manager in an insurance company. A tactical-level manager. A strategic-level manager.
17. How does adhering to a systems development methodology help a project team "do it right the first time"?
18. Would it be easier for one person or five people to do a relatively simple program? Draw a parallel to the size of a project team.

19. Evaluate your college's (or your company's) computer center with respect to security. Identify areas where you think it is vulnerable and discuss ways to improve its security.

SELF-TEST (by section)

12–1 **a.** Operational-level personnel are concerned primarily with transaction handling. (T/F)
  b. A device is said to be _____ when it is accessible to or under the control of the processor.
  c. The summarizing activity would be associated with which capability of an information system: (a) input, (b) output, or (c) processing?

12–2 The system becomes operational in the _____ stage of the system life cycle.

12–3 **a.** A standardized _____ provides the framework for cooperation during the systems development process.
  b. Which of the following is not a design technique: (a) flowcharting, (b) data flow diagrams, or (c) SAD?
  c. Functional specifications include system input, _____, and processing requirements.
  d. The _____ (general/detailed) system design includes all processing activities and the input/output associated with them.
  e. A typical program description would *not* include which of the following: (a) the type of programming language, (b) the output produced by the program, or (c) the data base design?
  f. Individual program testing is known as: (a) unit testing, (b) module testing, or (c) hierarchical testing.
  g. In the _____ approach to system conversion, the existing system and the new system operate simultaneously until the project team is confident the new system is working properly.
  h. The post-implementation evaluation is normally conducted one year after system implementation. (T/F)

12–4 **a.** A prototype system is essentially a complete information system without the data base. (T/F)
  b. A prototype system normally would permit rudimentary inquiries. (T/F)

12–5 Logical security for on-line systems is achieved primarily by _____ and authorization codes.

Self-test answers   **12–1** **(a)** F; **(b)** on-line; **(c)** c. **12–2** production. **12–3** **(a)** systems development methodology; **(b)** c; **(c)** output; **(d)** detailed; **(e)** c; **(f)** a; **(g)** parallel; **(h)** F. **12–4** **(a)** F; **(b)** T. **12–5** passwords.

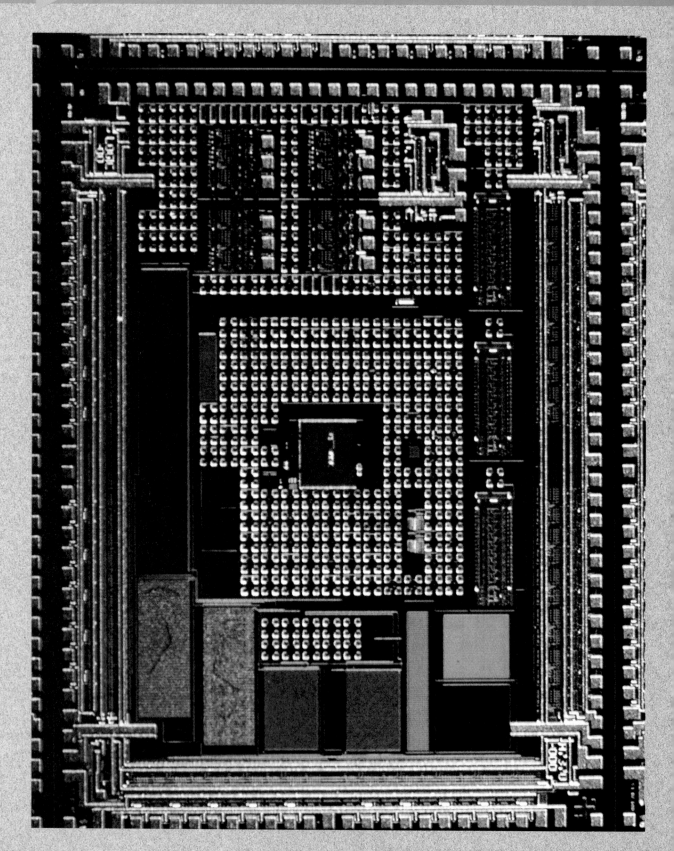

13

Computers in Society: Today and Tomorrow

STUDENT LEARNING OBJECTIVES

▶ To put society's dependence on computers in perspective.
▶ To identify and discuss controversial computer-related issues.
▶ To appreciate the scope and influence of computers in society.
▶ To identify causes of illegal information processing activity.
▶ To explore ethical questions concerning the use of computers.

13–1   COMPUTERS: CAN WE LIVE WITHOUT THEM?

Reaching the Point of No Return

There are those who believe that a rapidly advancing computer technology exhibits little regard for the future of the human race. They contend that computers are overused, misused, and generally detrimental to society. This group argues that the computer is dehumanizing and is slowly forcing society into a pattern of mass conformity. To be sure, the computer revolution is presenting society with complex problems, but they can be overcome.

Computers and information systems have enhanced our lifestyles to the point that most of us take them for granted. There is nothing wrong with this attitude, but we must recognize that society has made a very real commitment to computers. Whether it is good or bad, society has reached the point of no return in its dependence on computers. And stiff business competition means their use will continue to grow. On the more personal level, we are reluctant to forfeit the everyday conveniences made possible by computers. More and more of us find that our personal computers are an integral part of our daily activities.

Society's dependence on computers is not always apparent. For example, today's automobile assembly line is as computer-dependent as it is people-dependent: An inventory-management system makes sure that parts are delivered to the right assembly point at the right time; computer-controlled robots do the welding and painting; and a process-control computer directs the movement of the assembly line.

The number of monetary transactions handled by banks and other financial institutions is growing rapidly as society continues to move in the direction of electronic funds transfer. The financial community is depending on sophisticated computer systems to help it keep pace with the demand.

Some knowledge workers blame headaches, depression, anxiety, nausea, fatigue, and irritability on interacting with a visual display terminal. These and other problems often associated with prolonged use of a VDT are collectively referred to as Video Operator's Distress Syndrome, or VODS. However, there is little evidence to link these problems with using VDTs. The same problems occur in work environments without VDTs, from the executive suite to the assembly line.

Turn off the computer system for a day in almost any company, and observe the consequences. Most companies would cease to function. Turn off the computer system for several days, and many companies would cease to exist. A company that helps other companies recover from disasters, Sunguard Recovery Services, estimates that a large bank would be out of business in two days if its computer systems went down. It estimated that a distribution company would last three days, a manufacturing company would last five days, and an insurance company would last six days. A University of Minnesota study examined victims of disasters that disabled computing capabilities. The study concluded that the probability of a victim company's long-term survival was low if it was unable to recover critical operations within 30 hours. Recognizing their dependence on computers, most companies have made contingency plans that provide for backup computers in case of disaster.

Give Up My Computer? Never!

Ask a secretary to trade a word processing system for a typewriter. Ask a physician for an alternative to a computer-controlled intensive care unit. Ask an airline executive how long the organization could continue to operate without its on-line reservation system. Ask yourself if you would give up the convenience of remote banking at automatic teller machines.

Our dependence on food has evolved into the joy of eating gourmet food—and so it is or can be with computers. Dependence is not necessarily bad as long as we keep it in perspective. We can't passively assume that computers will continue to enhance the quality of our lives. It is our obligation to learn to understand them so we can better direct their application for society's benefit. Only through understanding can we control the misuse of computer technology. We, as a society, have a responsibility to weigh the benefits, burdens, and consequences of each successive level of automation.

13–2   CONTROVERSY: ANOTHER WORD FOR COMPUTER

Intense controversy is a by-product of the computer revolution. The emotions of both the general public and the computer community run high on computer-related issues. Some of the more heated issues are discussed here.

The Misuse of Personal Information

Sources of Personal Data.   The issue of greatest concern to the general public is the privacy of personal information. Some people fear that computer-based record-keeping offers too much of an opportunity for the invasion of an individual's privacy. There is indeed reason for concern. For example, credit-card users unknowingly leave a "trail" of activities and interests that, when examined and evaluated, can provide a rather comprehensive personal profile.

The date and location of all credit-card transactions are recorded. In effect, when you charge a lunch, gasoline, or clothing, you are creating a chronological record of where you have been and your spending habits. From this information, a good analyst could compile a very accurate

The accumulation of personal data has become a matter of concern in our information society. Whether you realize it or not, you are continuously contributing data about yourself to some computer systems. For example, when you request a long-distance telephone number from an operator, your number and the requested number are recorded in a computer system. In this and most instances, personal data are collected as a matter of record, not for the purpose of abuse.

picture of your lifestyle. For example, the analyst could predict how you dress by knowing the type of clothing stores you patronize. On a more personal level, records are kept that detail the duration, time, and numbers of all your telephone calls. With computers, these numbers are easy to match to people. So each time you make a phone call, you also leave a record of whom you call. Enormous amounts of personal data are maintained on everyone by the IRS, your college, your employer, your creditors, your hospital, your insurance company, your broker, and on and on.

It is hoped that information about us is up-to-date and accurate. Unfortunately, much of it is not. Laws permit us to examine our records, but first we must find them. You cannot just write to the federal government and request to see your files. To be completely sure that you examine all your federal records for completeness and accuracy, you would have to write and probably visit each of the approximately 5800 agencies that maintain computer-based files on individuals. The same is true of computer-based personal data maintained in the private sector.

Violating the Privacy of Personal Information.   Most will agree that the potential exists for abuse, but are these data being misused? Some say yes. Consider the states that sell lists of the addresses of and data on their licensed drivers. At the request of a manager of several petite women's clothing stores, a state agency provided the manager with a list of all licensed drivers in the state who were women between the ages of 21 and 40, less than 5 feet 3 inches tall, and under 120 pounds. You be the judge. Is the sale of such a list an abuse of personal information?

Personal information has become the product of a growing industry. Companies have been formed that do nothing but sell information about people. Not only are the people involved not asked for permission to use their data, they are seldom even told that their personal information is being sold! A great deal of personal data can be extracted from public records. For example, one company sends people to county courthouses all over the United States to gather publicly accessible data about people who have recently filed papers to purchase a home. Mailing lists are

Personal information is a byproduct of credit-card businesses. These companies have an obligation to deal with this information in a responsible manner.

then sold to insurance companies, landscape companies, members of Congress seeking new votes, lawyers seeking new clients, and so on. Those placed on the mailing list eventually become targets of commerce and special-interest groups.

The use of personal information for profit and other purposes is growing at such a rapid rate that for all practical purposes the abuse of this information has slipped out from under the legislative umbrella. Antiquated laws, combined with judicial unfamiliarity with computers, make policing and prosecuting abuses of the privacy of personal information difficult and, in many cases, impossible. (See Section 13–3, "Computers and the Law.")

Computer Matching.   Computer matching is a procedure whereby separate data bases are examined and individuals common to both are identified. Computer matching has been referred to as Orwellian by some, while auditors think it is a great help in their jobs.

The focus of most computer-matching applications is to identify people engaged in wrongdoing. Federal employees are being matched with those having delinquent student loans. Wages are then garnisheed to repay the loan. In another computer-matching case, a $30 million fraud was uncovered when questionable financial transactions were traced to common participants. The Internal Revenue Service also uses computer matching to identify tax cheaters. The IRS gathers descriptive data, such as neighborhood and automobile type, then uses sophisticated models to create lifestyle profiles. These profiles are matched against reported income on tax returns to predict whether people seem to be underpaying taxes. When the income and projected lifestyle do not match, the return is audited.

Securing the Integrity of Personal Information.   Computer experts feel that the integrity of personal data can be more secure in computer data bases than in file cabinets. They contend that we can continue to be masters and not victims if we implement proper safeguards for the maintenance and release of this information and enact effective legislation to cope with the abuse of it.

The federal government is very active in applications of computer matching. For example, various agencies are using computer matching to identify those who cheat on their taxes and on welfare entitlement programs.

Computer Monitoring

One of the newest and most controversial applications of information technology is computer monitoring. In computer monitoring, computers continuously gather and assimilate data on job activities to measure worker performance. Today computers monitor the job performance of over 7 million American workers. Most of these workers interact with a mainframe computer system via terminals or work on a micro that is part of a local area network. Others work with electronic or mechanical equipment that can be linked to a computer system.

Many clerical workers who use VDTs are evaluated by the number of documents they process per unit of time. At insurance companies, computer-monitoring systems provide supervisors with information on the rate at which clerks process claims. Supervisors can request other information, such as time spent at the terminal and keying-error rate.

Computers monitor the activities of many jobs that demand frequent or constant use of the telephone. The number of inquiries handled by directory-assistance operators is logged by a computer. Some companies employ computers to monitor the use of telephones by all employees.

Although most computer monitoring is done at the clerical level, it is also being applied to higher level positions such as commodities brokers, programmers, loan officers, and plant managers. For example, CIM (computer integrated manufacturing) enables corporate executives to monitor the effectiveness of a plant manager on a real-time basis. At any given time executives can tap the system for productivity information, such as the rate of production for a particular assembly.

Most computer-monitoring applications are implemented in offices in which workers spend much of their day interacting with a computer system. However, the growing use of automation in the plant has made computer monitoring feasible for shop-floor employees. Here, a paint-shop employee at a Chrysler Motors assembly plant communicates paint-quality status to the plant's Factory Information System.

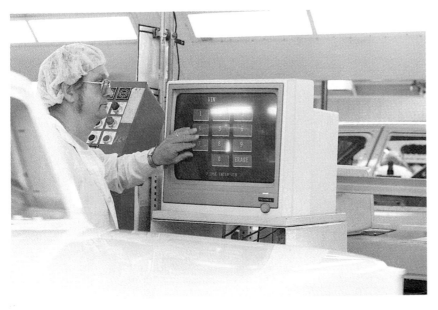

COMPUTER CRIMES: CATEGORIES AND TECHNIQUES

Computer crimes can be grouped into seven categories.

- *Crimes that create havoc inside a computer.* Trojan horses, computer viruses, and logic bombs fall into this category. A *Trojan horse* is a set of unauthorized instructions hidden in a legitimate program, such as an operating system. The intent of Trojan horse programmers is, by definition, malicious or criminal. The Trojan horse is a carrier of computer viruses and logic bombs. A *virus* is a Trojan horse that propagates versions of itself into other computer systems. A virus can result in the display of a harmless political message or in the devastating loss of all programs and data. A *logic bomb* is a Trojan horse that is executed when a certain set of conditions are met. For example, a disgruntled employee might plant a logic bomb to be "exploded" on the first Friday the thirteenth after his or her record is deleted from the personnel data base.

- *Crimes that involve the manipulation of computer systems and their data.* Embezzlement and fraud fall into this category. Embezzlement concerns the misappropriation of funds, and fraud involves obtaining illegal access to a computer system for the purpose of personal gain.

  The *salami technique* for embezzlement requires that a Trojan horse (unauthorized code in a legitimate program) be planted in the program code of a financial system that processes a large number of accounts. These covert instructions cause a small amount of money, usually less than a penny, to be debited periodically from each account and credited to one or more dummy accounts. A number of less sophisticated computer-manipulation crimes are the result of *data diddling.* Data diddling is changing the data, perhaps the "ship to" address, on manually prepared source documents or during entry to the system.

- *Crimes that involve telecommunications.* Illegal bulletin boards (for example, one that distributes confidential access codes and passwords), misuse of the telephone system, and any unauthorized access to a computer system, including eavesdropping (tapping into communications channels), fall into this category.

  Unauthorized entry to a computer system is achieved in a variety of ways. The most common approach is *masquerading.* People acquire authorization codes and personal information that will enable them to masquerade as an authorized user. The *tailgating* technique is used by vendors and company outsiders to gain access to sensitive information. The perpetrator simply begins using the terminal or computer of an authorized user who has left the room without terminating his or her session.

  The more sophisticated user might prefer building a trap door, scanning, or superzapping. A *trap door* is a Trojan horse that permits unauthorized and undetected access to a computer system. *Scanning* involves the use of a computer to test different combinations of access information until access is permitted (for example, stepping through a four-digit access code from 0000 to 9999). *Superzapping* involves using a program that enables someone to bypass all security controls.

- *Crimes that involve the abuse of personal information.* The willful release or distribution of personal information that is inaccurate would fall into this category.

- *Crimes that involve negligence.* Companies that employ computers to process data must do so in a responsible manner. Irresponsible actions that result in the deletion of a bank account or the premature discontinuation of electrical service would fall into this category. Lax controls and the availability of sensitive information invites scavenging. *Scavenging* is searching for discarded information that may be of some value on the black market, such as a printout containing credit-card numbers.

- *Crimes that support criminal enterprises.* Money laundering and data bases that support drug distribution would fall into this category.

- *Crimes that involve the theft of hardware or software.* Software piracy, theft of computers or computer components, and the theft of trade secrets belong in this category.

Workers complain that being constantly observed and analyzed by a computer adds unnecessary stress to their jobs. However, management is reluctant to give up computer monitoring because it has proved itself as a tool for increasing worker productivity. In general, affected workers are opposing any further intrusion into their professional privacy. On the other hand, management is equally vigilant in its quest for better information on worker performance.

Computer Crime

Computer crime is on the rise. There are many types of computer crimes, ranging from the use of an unauthorized password by a student to a billion-dollar insurance fraud. It is estimated that each year the total money lost from computer crime is greater than the sum total of that taken in all robberies. In fact, no one really knows the extent of computer crime because much of it is either undetected or unreported (most often the latter). In those cases involving banks, officers may elect to write off the loss rather than announce the crime and risk losing the goodwill of their customers.

Computer crime requires the cooperation of an experienced computer specialist. A common street thug does not have the knowledge or the opportunity to be successful at computer crime. The sophistication of the crime, however, makes it no less criminal.

Computer crime is a relatively recent phenomenon. Legislation, the criminal justice system, and industry are not yet adequately prepared to cope with it. Only a few police and FBI agents in the entire country have been trained to handle cases involving computer crime. And when a case comes to court, few judges have the background necessary to understand the testimony.

Recognizing the potential impact of computer crime, the legal system and industry are trying to speed up precautionary measures. Some say we are still moving too slowly and that a Three-Mile-Island–level catastrophe is the only thing that will make industry and government believe how severe computer crime can be.

There is a growing concern that the media is glorifying the illegal entry and use of computer systems by overzealous hackers. These "electronic vandals" have tapped into everything from local credit agencies to top-secret defense systems. The evidence of unlawful entry, perhaps a revised record or access during nonoperating hours, is called a **footprint**. Some malicious hackers leave much more than a footprint—they infect the computer system with a *virus*.

A **virus** is a program that literally "infects" other programs and data bases. Viral programs are written with malicious intent and are loaded to the computer system of an unsuspecting victim. The virus is so named because it can spread from one system to another like a biological virus. There are many types of viruses. Some act quickly by erasing user programs and data bases. Others grow like a cancer, destroying small parts of a data base each day. Some viruses act like a time bomb: They lay dormant for days or months but eventually are activated and wreak havoc on any software in the system. Some viruses attack hardware

The academic environment is conducive to the origination and propagation of viruses. One virus wreaked havoc at several universities. It infected the operating systems of IBM-compatible microcomputers, specifically the DOS COMMAND.COM file. When booted, the infected disk would replicate itself to an uninfected COMMAND.COM file. After repeating the replication four times, the original software virus would destroy itself—and all the files on its diskette. The other infected disks would continue to reproduce.

and have been known to throw the mechanical components of a computer system, such as disk access arms, into costly spasms. Viruses can spread from one computer network to another through data communications. Viruses also spread from one system to another via common diskettes. The motives of those who would infect a system with a virus run from electronic vandalism to revenge to terrorism. There is no monetary reward, only the "satisfaction" of knowing that their efforts have been very costly to individuals, companies, or governments.

A few hackers and computer professionals have chosen computer crime as a profession. But the threat of computer crime may be even greater from managers and consultants because they are in the best position to commit it successfully. They know how the systems operate, and they know the passwords needed to gain access to the systems.

The Cashless Society

The growing number of *automatic teller machines* (ATMs) have made *electronic funds transfer* (EFT) very visible to the public. In EFT, money is transferred electronically from bank to bank and from account to account via computers. Each weekday the financial institutions of the world use EFT to transfer over one trillion dollars—that's $1,000,000,000,000! Applications of EFT are being implemented all around us. Automatic teller machines and automatic payroll transfer systems have become commonplace. Some banks offer *home banking* services that permit customers to pay bills and perform banking transactions via their personal computers without leaving home.

The debate rages on as we move closer to a cashless society: Is this a reasonable and prudent manner in which to handle financial transactions? It is well within the state of the art to just about eliminate money and make the transition to a cashless society.

At some time in the future, the scope of EFT may be expanded because the buyer will be able to use a universal *smart card* ("smart" because of the tiny embedded microprocessor) and perhaps a password to buy everything from candy bars to automobiles. Upon purchasing an item, the buyer would give the card, called a *debit card*, to the seller. The seller would use the purchaser's card to log the sale on a

After we use our credit card to make a purchase at a retail store, we pay the credit-card company by check who, in turn, pays the retailer by check. In the next generation of EFT, the checks will be eliminated. In fact, the credit-card companies will not be needed for those who pay their bills promptly. When the purchase is made, the amount of the purchase will be transferred via EFT from the buyer's bank account to the retailer's bank account.

point-of-sale (POS) terminal linked to a network of banking computers. The amount of the sale would then be transferred from the buyer's account to the seller's account.

The advantages of an expanded use of EFT are noteworthy. EFT would eliminate the cumbersome administrative work associated with handling money and checks. It also would eliminate the need to carry money, eliminate rubber checks and counterfeit money, and minimize the possibility of error. It would provide a detailed record of all transactions. EFT would also eliminate the expense of making money. The cost of manufacturing a penny now exceeds the value of the coin!

The disadvantages are equally noteworthy. The critical issue is EFT's potential for the misuse of personal information. EFT generates a chronological record of all purchases. (See the discussion in the earlier section entitled "The Misuse of Personal Information.") In effect, this type of system permits everything about an individual to be monitored, from lifestyle to location. Opponents of EFT are also concerned about its vulnerability to crime.

Although there is a trend toward more electronic funds transfer, some experts feel that EFT is about to reach its peak of acceptance. Others think that total EFT is inevitable by the turn of the century.

The Effects of Automation on Jobs

Concern about the effects of automation began 200 years ago with the Industrial Revolution, and the public is still apprehensive. To many people, computers mean automation, and automation means loss of jobs. Just as the Industrial Revolution created hundreds of new job opportunities, so will the "Information Revolution."

At some banks you can take out a loan without talking to a loan officer. Loan information is entered at an interactive terminal and credit is checked automatically. This approach may be impersonal, but it is efficient and saves money. Moreover, customers can apply for loans at their convenience rather than the bank's.

Twenty years ago, college curricula in architecture included little or no study in the area of computers. Today, architects rely on computers for everything from design to cost analysis. The computer has dramatically changed the way architects do their jobs. The same is true of hundreds of other professions.

There is no doubt that the emergence of computer technology has resulted in the elimination of jobs involving routine, monotonous, and sometimes hazardous tasks. However, the loss of these jobs has been offset by the creation of more challenging ones. Many people whose jobs have been eliminated have been displaced to jobs carrying greater responsibilities and offering more opportunities. It is common for book-keepers to become systems analysts, for draftpersons to advance to computer-aided design, and for secretaries to become specialists in a myriad of computer applications from word processing to data management. This pattern is repeated thousands of times each month.

Automation will continue to eliminate and create jobs. Historically, any advancement in technology has increased overall productivity in certain areas, thereby cutting the number of workers needed. But this also produces a wave of new jobs in the wake of cutbacks in traditional areas. With the cost of labor increasing and the cost of computers decreasing, the trend toward the automation of routine activities probably will continue. However, to realize a smooth transition to an automated environment, industry and government must recognize that they have a social responsibility to retrain those who will be displaced by the loss of their jobs.

The National Data Base

Like EFT, the technology is available to establish a national data base. Many have proposed a national data base as a central repository for all personal data. An individual would be assigned a unique identification number at birth. This ID number would replace the social security number, driver's license number, student identification number, and dozens of others.

A national data base would consolidate the personal data now stored on tens of thousands of manual and computer-based files. It could contain an individual's name, past and present addresses, dependent data, work history, medical history, marital history, tax data, criminal records, military history, credit rating and history, and so on. Proponents of the national data base recognize that the aforementioned data are currently available, but they are redundant and often inaccurate or out of date because they are maintained in many different data bases. Proponents' contention is that at least the national data base would be accurate and up-to-date.

Those who are in favor of a national data base list certain advantages. It could provide the capability of monitoring the activities of criminal suspects; of virtually eliminating welfare fraud; of quickly identifying illegal aliens; of making an individual's medical history available at any hospital in the country; of taking the 10-year census almost automatically; and of generating valuable information. Medical researchers could isolate geographical areas with inordinately high incidences of certain illnesses. The Bureau of Labor Statistics could monitor real as opposed to reported employment levels on a daily basis. The information possibilities are endless.

Those who oppose the national data base call it impersonal and an invasion of privacy. Their feelings are that any advantages are more than offset by the potential for abuse.

The creation of a national data base is an extremely complex undertaking, the social implications notwithstanding. It is unlikely that we will see such a data base in this century. However, with the growing concern about welfare fraud, tax evasion, crime, and the influx of illegal aliens, the national data base may be an increasingly appealing alternative.

We are an increasingly mobile society. We routinely travel around the country and around the world, but we leave our medical records at hospitals, clinics, and doctors' offices. A strong case can be made for a national medical data base. When a national data base is implemented, probably before the end of the century, doctors and nurses at this hospital will be able to access the medical records of someone from out of state as quickly as the records of a local patient.

13-3   COMPUTERS AND THE LAW

Companies try to develop information systems and use the computer within the boundaries of the law. Unfortunately, the laws are not always clear because many legal questions involving computers and information processing are being debated for the first time. To no one's surprise, computer law is the fastest growing type of law practice.

Laws governing computer and information processing are few, and those that do exist are subject to a variety of interpretations. At present, two federal laws address computer crime. They are limited, however, because they apply only to those computer systems that in some way reflect a federal interest. These laws make it a felony to gain unauthorized access to any computer system with a federal interest with the intent to obtain anything of value, to defraud the system, or to cause more than $1000 in damages. Although most states have adopted computer-crime laws, they are only the skeleton of what is needed to direct an orderly and controlled growth of automation. Only now are lawmakers beginning to recognize the impact of computers, and legislation is slow in coming. Critics say that the bottleneck stems from our lawmakers' reluctance to become computer-literate.

Once we have definitive legislation, prosecution of computer crimes becomes another issue. Even when a computer crime is brought to the attention of the authorities, prosecutors lack sufficient technical knowledge to prepare a case. A judge and jury understand the concept of armed robbery and have a sense of the appropriate punishment, but what about computer crimes? Sophisticated computer crimes can be

Computers are revolutionizing legal practices. Rather than spending days researching related cases in legal casebooks, these attorneys use key words to search a massive full-text data base containing more cases than any law office's library. A search of applicable "computer negligence" cases was completed in 20 minutes.

extremely complex and may be well beyond the understanding of most prosecutors, judges, and jurors. Legislation must be enacted and prosecution issues resolved before the criminal justice system can begin to cope with computer crime.

Illegal Information Processing

Negligence.   The two main causes of illegal information processing are negligence and fraud. Negligence causes someone outside the organization to be unnecessarily inconvenienced, and it is usually the result of poor input/output control. For example, after she paid in full, a woman continually was sent dunning notices and visited by collection agencies for not making payments on her automobile. Although the records and procedures were in error, the company forcibly repossessed the automobile without thoroughly checking its procedures and the legal implications. The woman had to sue the company for the return of her automobile. The court ordered the automobile returned and the company to pay her a substantial sum as a penalty.

This is a clear case of a misinterpretation of a computer maxim— GIGO ("garbage in, garbage out"). GIGO does *not* stand for "garbage in, gospel out," as some people, who take the accuracy of computer output for granted, seem to think. The company blamed the incident on a mistake by the computer. The court stated that people enter data and interpret output and that the people affected should be treated differently from punched cards. *Trust in the infallibility of a computer does not constitute a defense in a court of law.* This incident points out the importance of careful system design and exhaustive testing.

Fraud.   The other area of illegal information processing is a premeditated or conscious effort to defraud the system. For example, a U.S. Customs official modified a program to print $160,000 worth of unauthorized federal payroll checks payable to himself and his co-conspirators. A 13-year-old high school student tapped into an AT&T computer and stole over $1 million worth of software. These are examples of fraud. Any illegal entry into a computer system for the purpose of personal gain is considered fraud. Over 50% of all computer frauds are internal; that is, they are committed by employees of the organization being defrauded. About 30% of those defrauding employees are computer specialists who work in an information services department.

The Privacy of Personal Information

More media and legislative attention has been focused on the issue of an individual's privacy than on computer crimes involving negligence or fraud. The individual must be afforded certain rights regarding the privacy of data or of information relating to him or her. However, these rights have yet to be uniformly defined by our lawmakers. In the absence of definitive legislative guidelines, the following principles are offered for consideration:

1. People should be made aware that data are being collected about them and made aware of how these data are to be used.

When asked what she does, Amy Wohl responds by saying that she "comments on the computer industry." Specifically, Wohl has been office automation's leading spokesperson and advocate, lecturing frequently in the United States, Europe, Africa, Japan, and Australia.

In her *Computerworld* column, other writings, and public speaking, Wohl advocates that every office worker should have a computer. The fact that we are moving in that direction is due, in part, to her persistent and convincing arguments.

Wohl, president of Wohl Associates, is the person that manufacturers of office automation (OA) products and services turn to when they want to tap the heartbeat of the OA industry. As a result, many of the office automation products that we see in computer stores are a reflection of Wohl's vision.

Much has been said and written about the emergence of the paperless office. For years many have speculated that the widespread use and acceptance of computers may make it possible for all office communications to be in soft-copy form, thus eliminating the need for paper. Wohl, however, expresses a different view in her now-famous statement on the paperless office. She said, "The paperless office is as practical today as the paperless toilet."

2. A person should be permitted to inspect his or her personal data and information.

3. A person should be permitted to supplement or clarify personal data and information.

4. Data and information found erroneous or irrelevant must be removed.

5. Disclosure of personal information should be limited to those with a need to know.

6. A log should be maintained of all people inspecting any individual's personal information.

7. Adequate safeguards must be in place to ensure the security of personal data and information (for example, locked doors, passwords).

13–4   ETHICS AND COMPUTERS

One of the largest computer-professional societies adopted a code of ethics over 15 years ago. The code warns members that they can be expelled or censured if they violate it. To date, not one of the society's tens of thousands of members has been expelled or censured for violating the code. Other professional societies publish a code of ethics as well, and they too rarely or never take action against delinquent members. Does this mean there are no violations? Of course not. A carefully

Professional societies meet each month to discuss computer-related topics, issues, and trends. At this Data Processing Management Association meeting, the topic was "The Impact of Artificial Intelligence on Information Systems Development."

drafted code of ethics provides some guidelines for conduct, but professional societies cannot be expected to police the misdoings of their membership. In many instances, a code violation is also a violation of the law.

A code of ethics provides direction for computer professionals and users so that they act responsibly in their application of computer technology. The following code of ethics is in keeping with the spirit of those encouraged by computer societies.

It is more the rule than the exception that a computer professional will have ready access to a broad range of sensitive information, both personal and corporate. Because of the potential for the abuse of this information, some professional societies have adopted a code of ethics.

1. Maintain the highest standard of professional behavior.
2. Avoid situations that create a conflict of interest.
3. Do not violate the confidentiality of your employer or those you service.
4. Continue to learn so your knowledge keeps pace with the technology.
5. Use information judiciously and maintain system integrity at all times.
6. Do not violate the rights or privacy of others.
7. Accomplish each task to the best of your ability.
8. Do not break the law.

If you follow this eight-point code, it is unlikely that anyone will question your ethics. Nevertheless, well-meaning people routinely violate this simple code because they are unaware of the tremendous detrimental impact of their actions. With the speed and power of computers, a minor code infraction easily can be magnified into a costly catastrophe. For this reason the use of computers is raising new ethical questions. The three case studies that follow illustrate the ethical implications of the application of information technology.

Ethics Case 1: Computerized Dialers

Let's take as an example the case of computerized dialers, a system that automatically dials a telephone number and plays a prerecorded message. Telephone numbers are entered into the system, then dialed one after another. If there is no answer, the number is redialed at a later time. Such systems are used for telemarketing a variety of products, not to mention politicians and ideologies. Is this an invasion of an individual's privacy?

Consider the company that for a fee will use its computerized dialing system to do telemarketing for local merchants. The system contains every telephone number in the city telephone directory. A message announcing a sale, a new service, or whatever is recorded for each client. Each day the system is activated and "the computer" makes calls from 8 A.M. to 10 P.M. During the course of a single day, the system can interrupt the lives of thousands of people. How many of us would welcome the opportunity to listen to a prerecorded commercial when we answer the phone? Is telemarketing in violation of the code of ethics just outlined? How about Item 6?

There are, of course, legitimate uses of computerized dialing systems. For example, the IRS uses them to notify taxpayers they are delinquent; school districts use them to notify parents of truant children; and retailers alert customers that they can pick up the items they ordered.

Ethics Case 2: Copyrighted Software

The vice president of a sporting-goods chain purchased a $500 electronic spreadsheet software package. The purchase agreement permits the use of the software on any micro at the office or at his home. However, the purchase agreement strictly prohibits the reproduction of this copyrighted software for purposes other than as a backup. The vice president convinced a colleague that it was the best spreadsheet package on the market, and the colleague asked the VP to make her a copy. Reluctantly, he accommodated her. The VP knew that this act was in violation of the purchase agreement, but he rationalized his actions, thinking that maybe she just wanted to test the package before purchasing her own copy. Did he violate the code of ethics? What about Items 1 and 8?

Ethics Case 3: Franking Privileges

Members of the U.S. Congress have franking privileges, or free mail. Before computers, most letters were sent in response to constituent inquiries. Computers and high-speed printers have made it possible to crank out 30,000 "individualized" letters per hour. Some members of Congress have been known to send out millions of letters a year.

Is this massive amount of correspondence an attempt to better inform the constituents, or is it politically motivated and an abuse of the power of the computer? Is this application a violation of our code of ethics? How about Items 2 and 5?

13–5 OVERSIGHTS: ARE WE KEEPING PACE WITH THE TECHNOLOGY?

For whatever reasons, business, government, and education have elected not to implement computer applications that are well within the state of the art of computer technology. Many cost-effective systems are working in the laboratory but have not been implemented in practice. The implementation of these potentially beneficial systems has lagged behind the state of the art of computer technology by five to 10 years. Some "oversights" are presented below.

Several experimental homes feature computer-controlled lighting, temperature, and security systems. Such "smart home" systems would start the coffee maker so we could awaken to the aroma of freshly brewed coffee. They would even help with paying the bills. This technology is available today and is relatively inexpensive if properly designed and installed during construction. In any case, such a system would pay for itself in a couple of years through energy savings alone.

Although some sophisticated computer-controlled medical equipment is now being used, relatively few physicians take advantage of the information-producing potential of the computer to improve patient care. They have expert systems that can help them diagnose diseases, drug-interaction data bases that can help them prescribe the right drug, and computer-assisted searches that can call up literature pertinent to a particular patient's illness. All the applications have the potential of saving lives.

A cashless society is technologically and economically possible. In a cashless society, the amount of a purchase would be transferred automatically from the purchaser's bank account to the vendor's bank account. Thus billing, payment, and collection problems would be eliminated, along with the need to write checks and to remember to mail them.

There are many reasons why these cost-effective and potentially beneficial computer applications have not been implemented. Among

Some say that we are not tapping the full potential of computers in our system of education—these students being the exception rather than the rule. While doing research for a term paper, they are saving time by entering appropriate comments and citations directly into a word processing document.

them are historical momentum, resistance to change, limited education, and lack of available resources. In the case of "smart home" systems, it is probably a matter of education, both of the builder and the home-owner. In the case of computer diagnosis of illness, some physicians are reluctant to admit that the computer is a valuable diagnostic aid. In the case of the cashless society, the question of invasion of privacy is yet to be resolved.

These and hundreds of other "oversights" will not be implemented until enough people have enough knowledge to appreciate their potential. This is where you come in!

SUMMARY OUTLINE AND IMPORTANT TERMS

13–1   **COMPUTERS: CAN WE LIVE WITHOUT THEM?** Society has reached a point of no return with regard to dependence on computers. Business competition demands their use. Individuals are also reluctant to give up those personal conveniences made possible by the computer. Only through understanding can we control the misuse or abuse of computer technology.

13–2   **CONTROVERSY: ANOTHER WORD FOR COMPUTER.** The emotions of both the general public and the computer community run high on computer-related issues. The abuse of personal information is perhaps the issue of greatest concern. Other issues include the merits of computer monitoring, coping with computer crime, the growing use of electronic funds transfer, the effect of automation on jobs, and the implementation of a national data base.

13–3   COMPUTERS AND THE LAW. An information system should be developed to comply with the law. At present the laws that govern the privacy of personal data and illegal computer-based activity are inadequate, but they are being revised and expanded. Therefore, the privacy of data and the possibility of fraud or negligence should be a consideration in the design of every information system.

13–4   ETHICS AND COMPUTERS. People whose jobs put them in contact with sensitive data actually can control events. This places even greater pressure on these people to conduct themselves as professionals. A code of ethics provides direction for computer professionals and users so they act responsibly in their application of computer technology.

13–5   OVERSIGHTS: ARE WE KEEPING PACE WITH THE TECHNOLOGY? Although society has been the beneficiary of a wide variety of computer applications, much more can be done with existing technology. Historical momentum, resistance to change, limited education, and lack of resources have slowed the implementation of technologically feasible computer applications.

REVIEW EXERCISES

Concepts

1. Has society reached the point of no return with regard to its dependence on computers?

2. Most computer monitoring takes place at which level of activity: clerical, operational, tactical, or strategic?

3. What is the objective of computer matching?

4. What are the two main causes of illegal processing?

5. What are the uses of a computerized dialing system?

6. Identify the hurdles that must be overcome to prosecute computer criminals effectively in a court of law.

7. Name two types of companies that might be interested in acquiring a list of names of people who have recently purchased a home.

8. Give examples of the type of descriptive data the IRS gathers to create lifestyle profiles of taxpayers.

9. Why are managers and consultants in a good position to commit computer crimes?

Discussion

10. Why would a judge sentence one person to 10 years in jail for an unarmed robbery of $25 from a convenience store and another to 18 months for computer fraud involving millions of dollars?

11. Some companies are experimenting with placing small microprocessors in charge cards as a means of thwarting theft and fraud. Describe how you think the computer would be used during the processing of a charge transaction. Speculate on the data that are input to, output from, permanently stored in, and processed by the charge-card computer.

12. List and discuss applications, other than those mentioned in the text, of a national data base.

13. Do you feel society's dependence on computers is good or bad? What would you suggest be done to improve the situation?

14. Describe what yesterday would have been like if you had not used the capabilities of computers. Keep in mind that businesses with which you deal rely on computers and that many of your appliances are computer-based.

15. Argue for or against a cashless society.

16. Discuss the kinds of personal information that can be obtained by analyzing a person's credit-card transactions during the past year.

17. Describe ways in which you feel the privacy of your personal information has been abused.

18. Relatively few computer professionals have any kind of certification. Is it really necessary?

SELF-TEST (by section)

13–1 **a.** It would take at least a month to retool a typical automobile assembly line so it could function without computers. (T/F)
   b. If the number of computer applications continues to grow at the present rate, our computer-independent society will be dependent on computers by the year 2000. (T/F)

13–2 **a.** It is estimated that each year the total monetary loss from computer crime is greater than the sum total of all robberies. (T/F)
   b. In the _____ application, computers continuously gather and assimilate data on worker activities for the purpose of measuring worker performance.
   c. The number of federal government agencies that maintain computer-based files on individuals is between: (a) 50 and 100, (b) 500 and 1000, or (c) more than 5000.
   d. The evidence of unlawful entry to a computer system is called a _____.

13–3 **a.** Gaining unauthorized access to any computer system with a federal interest with the intent of defrauding the system is a: (a) violation of public ethics, (b) misdemeanor, or (c) felony.
   b. Many legal questions involving computers and information processing are yet to be incorporated into the federal laws. (T/F)
   c. Trust in the infallibility of a computer does not constitute a defense in a court of law. (T/F)

13–4 Computer and MIS professional societies are expected to police the unethical and criminal misdoings of their membership. (T/F)

13–5 A cashless society is technologically and economically possible. (T/F)

Self-test answers **13–1** **(a)** F; **(b)** F. **13–2** **(a)** T; **(b)** computer monitoring; **(c)** c; **(d)** footprint. **13–3** **(a)** c; **(b)** T; **(c)** T. **13–4** F. **13–5** T.

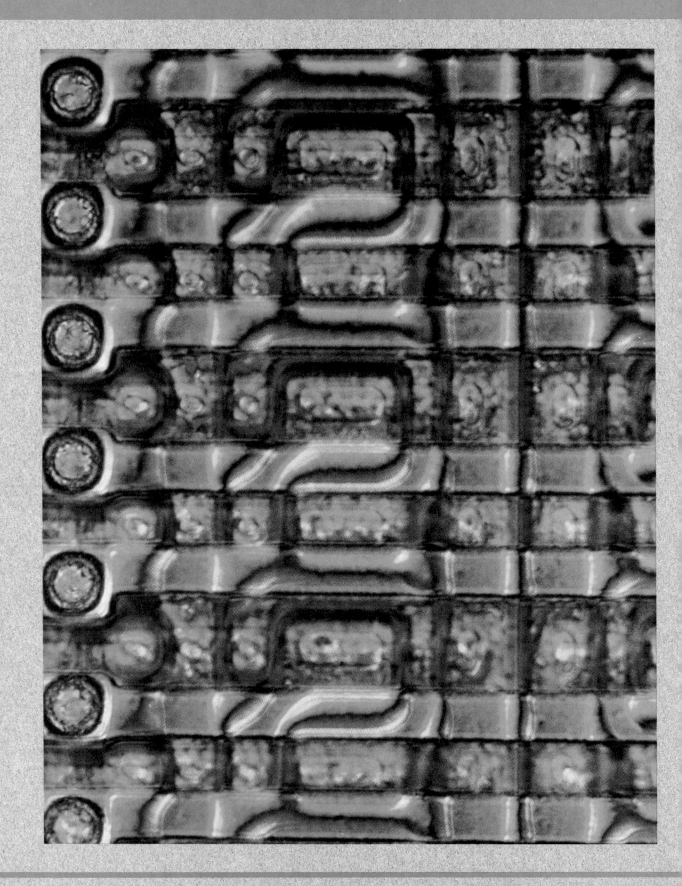

14

Career Opportunities and Applications of Tomorrow

STUDENT LEARNING OBJECTIVES

▶ To identify computer specialist positions in information services departments and in user departments.

▶ To identify job opportunities in organizations that provide computer-related products or services.

▶ To become aware of the relationship between career mobility and computer knowledge.

▶ To identify possible computer applications of the future.

14-1   THE JOB OUTLOOK

Opportunities for Users with Computer Knowledge

Those people seeking employment (or perhaps a promotion) in any of literally hundreds of jobs are often asked: "What do you know about computers?" Already well over half of all white-collar workers routinely work with computers. Soon virtually all white-collar workers and a good portion of the blue-collar workforce will spend a significant portion of their day interacting with computers.

Upon completion of this course, you will be part of the computer-literate minority and thus be able to respond confidently and positively to inquiries about your computer knowledge. But what about that 95% of our society that must answer: "Nothing" or "Very little"? These people will find themselves at a disadvantage.

Opportunities for Computer Specialists

If you are planning a career as a computer specialist, opportunity abounds. Almost every company, no matter how small or large, employs computer specialists. And most of those companies are always looking for qualified people.

These programmer/analysts are in one of the top-rated professions. The Jobs Rated Almanac *(1988) rated 250 common occupations based on six criteria: salary, stress, work environment, outlook, security, and physical demands. According to the rankings, the best occupation is actuary. (Actuaries compile and interpret statistics upon which insurance companies base their rate structures.) Job numbers two and three are computer programmer and computer systems analyst. Indeed, the future looks bright for the two mainstay computer-related occupations. As a basis for comparison, accountants are ranked 15; electrical engineers, 32; economists, 50; historians, 67; attorneys, 83; book authors, 137; mayors, 201; and NFL football players are 241!*

The computer revolution has had a dramatic impact on people in hundreds of professions—the way they train and ultimately what they do in the work place. For example, automobile and truck mechanics rely on automated diagnostic systems to help them service increasingly sophisticated vehicles. The typical automobile or truck will have at least one computer for controlling fuel flow, ignition, security, braking, and other systems.

For the last decade, people with computer/information systems education have been at or near the top of the "most wanted" list. With millions (yes, millions!) of new computers being purchased and installed each year, it is a good bet that this trend will continue. Of course, the number of people being attracted to the booming computer fields is also increasing.

According to U.S. Department of Labor employment projections, the future is bright for computer specialists. For example, during the decade of the 1990s the number of computer programmers is expected to increase from an estimated 575,000 to over 800,000. The number of computer systems analysts is expected to increase from an estimated 400,000 to over 580,000. The computer operator's career path is expected to follow a similar growth pattern.

Career Opportunities in an Information Services Department. If you are pursuing a career as a computer specialist, the material in this section will familiarize you with some of the opportunities in an organization's information services department. If you are pursuing a noncomputer career, this section will give you some insight as to whom to contact when you have a computer-related question or request. It is not uncommon for computer users to have daily contact with people in the information services department. In addition to helping in the development of information systems, computer specialists in an information services department routinely respond to user inquiries about micro/mainframe links, hardware evaluation, and use of software packages, to mention only a few subjects.

The information services department is the data and information "nerve center" of an organization. Most organizations—hospitals, insurance companies, universities, and so on—have an information services department. The *data* are supplied by the various user groups. In return, the information services department provides the software and operational support needed to produce *information*. The basic responsibility of an information services department is to be responsive to the organization's information processing needs.

Most of the career fields in an information services department can be divided into seven groups. These are *management, systems analysis, programming, data communications, technical support, operations,* and *education*. Figure 14–1 gives a brief explanation of each group.

Position descriptions in each of these seven major groups are presented in the sections that follow.

Management   The **director of information services** is the chief information officer (CIO) and has responsibility for all computer and information systems activity in the organization. At least half of the director's time is spent interacting with user managers and executives. In this capacity, the director coordinates the integration of data and information

FIGURE 14–1   Computer Specialist Positions by Group in an Information Services Department

The Information Services Department	
MANAGEMENT Director Group managers	Managers in each of the groups that follow perform the traditional management functions: planning, organizing, staffing, directing, and controlling.
SYSTEMS ANALYSIS Systems analyst	The systems analysis group analyzes, designs and implements computer-based information systems.
PROGRAMMING Applications programmer Programmer/analyst	The programming group translates system design specifications produced by systems analysts into programs.
DATA COMMUNICATIONS Data communications specialist	The data communications group designs computer networks and implements hardware and software that permits data transmission between computers and workstations.
TECHNICAL SUPPORT Data base administrator Systems programmer	The technical support group designs, develops, maintains, and implements systems software (i.e., generalized software, such as the operating system and database management system).
OPERATIONS Computer operator Control clerk Data entry operator Librarian	The operations group performs those machine room activities associated with the running of operational information systems (e.g., loading tapes, scheduling, and running jobs). Operations also includes control functions and data entry. The trend to on-line data entry is causing the data entry function to be "distributed" to the user areas.
EDUCATION Education coordinator	The education group is reponsible for the continuing education of computer specialists and for traininig users in the operation of hardware and information systems.

Systems analysts work with users to ensure that they get the information they need in an understandable format. This analyst recommended that printed sales data be made more accessible via on-line inquiry and, when appropriate, presented in the form of color-coded bar graphs.

systems and serves as the catalyst for new systems development. The remainder of the director's time is devoted to managing the information services department. In medium-sized and large information services departments, each group has a manager. The managers of systems analysis, programming, operations, and the other groups would normally report to the director of information services.

Systems analysis group The function of a **systems analyst**, or simply analyst, is the analysis, design, and implementation of information systems. Systems analysts work closely with users to design information systems that meet their data processing and information needs. Specific development tasks associated with these problem solvers are discussed in detail in Chapter 12, "Developing Information Systems."

Systems analysts are also assigned a variety of other tasks. These might include feasibility studies, system reviews, security assessments, MIS long-range planning, or perhaps serving on a hardware selection committee.

Programming group The **applications programmer**, or simply programmer, translates analyst-prepared system and input/output specifications into programs. Programmers design the logic, then code, debug, test, and document the programs as described in Chapter 9, "Programming Concepts." The programs written by an applications programmer are designed for a certain application, such as market analysis or inventory management. Sometimes called "implementors" or "miracle workers," programmers are charged with turning specifications into an information system.

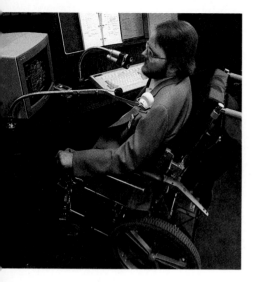

The nature of the work and the availability of specially designed workstations have made computer careers particularly inviting to the physically disabled. The man in the photo works as a data base administrator at a computer-services company.

A person holding a **programmer/analyst** position performs the functions of both a programmer and a systems analyst. In some companies, you are either a programmer or an analyst. In others, you are both and are part of a combined systems analysis and programming group.

Data communications group   The **data communications specialist** designs and maintains computer networks that link computers and terminals for data communications. This involves selecting and installing appropriate hardware, such as modems, data PBXs, and front-end processors as well as selecting the transmission media (see Chapter 6, "Data Communications"). Data communications specialists also develop and implement the software that controls the flow of data between computing devices.

Technical support group   **Systems programmers** develop and maintain systems software. Systems software is fundamental to the general operation of the computer; that is, it does not address a specific business or scientific problem. Systems software includes operating systems, database management systems, and language compilers.

The **data base administrator** position evolved with database management systems software and the need to integrate information systems. The data base administrator designs, creates, and maintains the organization's data base. The DBA coordinates discussions between user groups to determine the content and format of the data base so that data redundancy is kept to a minimum.

Operations group   The **computer operator** performs those hardware-based activities necessary to keep production information systems operational. An operator works in the machine room initiating software routines; mounting the appropriate tapes, disks, and preprinted forms; and troubleshooting.

The **librarian** selects the magnetic tapes and disks from off-line storage and delivers them to the operator. It is not unusual for a computer center to have hundreds, and even thousands, of tapes and disks. The librarian maintains a status log on each one.

The **control clerk** accounts for all input to and output from the computer center. He or she follows standard procedures to validate the accuracy of the output before it is distributed to the user departments.

Education coordinators plan and conduct seminars to acquaint both users and computer specialists with the latest software and hardware products. They also provide instruction on the organization's information systems. Here, a supervisor is learning the use of the company's new personnel systems.

The **data entry operator**, sometimes called the key operator, uses key entry devices to transcribe data into machine-readable format.

Education group   The **education coordinator** coordinates all computer-related educational activities. He or she schedules computer specialists for technical update seminars, video training programs, computer-assisted instruction, and others, as needed. The education coordinator often conducts the training sessions.

Organization of an information services department   In some information services departments, one person is the "chief cook and bottle washer." Other departments are made up of several thousand people. Both small and large "shops" (a slang term for information services departments) must accomplish the functions of systems analysis, programming, technical support, data communications, operations, and education. Differences in the way they are organized are due primarily to their degree of specialization.

Figure 14–2 illustrates how an information services department in a medium-sized and large corporation might be organized. This chart illustrates a traditional organizational structure that could vary, depending on circumstances.

FIGURE 14–2   Organization Chart—Medium-Sized and Large Information Services Departments
No two information services departments are organized in the same way, but the example is, in general, representative.

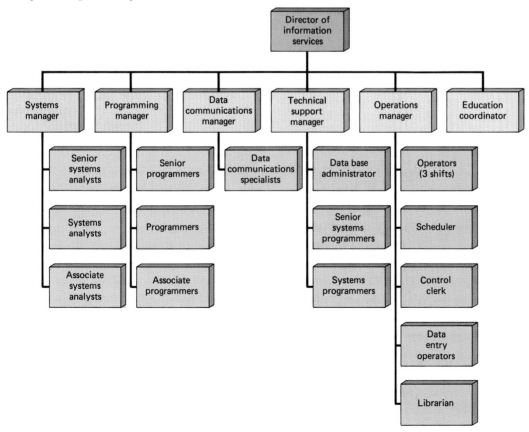

"Distributed" Career Opportunities.   The trend to distributed processing has prompted a movement of computer specialists to the user departments. At some point during the 1990s, more computer specialists will be working in the user groups than in the information services department. Even now virtually every type of user group, from R&D to distribution, is vigorously recruiting people with computer expertise.

Today it is not just the information services department that has computers. They are found in every area. In addition to computer specialists in the traditional areas (for example, programming and systems analysis), a new breed of computer specialists is emerging in the user areas. These include *office-automation specialists*, *microcomputer specialists*, *information-center specialists*, and *user liaisons*.

Office-automation specialists   Office automation encompasses those computer-based applications generally associated with office work (for details, see the discussion of office automation in Chapter 11, "Applications of Information Technology"). **Office-automation specialists** are being hired to help with the growing demand for automating office activities. They help users to implement, then make effective use of office systems.

Microcomputer specialists   From the popularity of microcomputers has emerged a new career path, sometimes referred to as **microcomputer specialist**. Users do not always have the time to learn the details of using microcomputers and their software. Rather than have each person in an office learn micros and micro software packages such as electronic spreadsheet from the inside out, a firm can employ a micro specialist to help users over the rough spots as well as develop new systems.

Information-center specialists   An information center is a facility in which computing resources are made available to various user groups. (The information center is introduced and explained in Chapter 1, "The World of Computers.") **Information-center specialists** conduct training sessions, answer questions, and help users to help themselves.

This microcomputer specialist specializes in desktop publishing applications.

PROFILE

During the first generation of computers, vendors such as IBM and UNIVAC worked in cooperation with clients to install and maintain computer systems. In 1962 Ross Perot, currently chairman of Perot Systems Corporation, offered an alternative when he founded Electronic Data Systems Corporation. Perot and EDS pioneered the concept of performing data processing and telecommunications management functions for clients under long-term contracts. Today thousands of companies provide computer services, from one-person contract programmers to the $5 billion EDS Corporation.

One of Perot's many honors is the Winston Churchill Award, given to those who best exemplify the imagination, boldness, and vigor of the late British prime minister. In 1979 Perot directed a team of EDS employees that successfully rescued two EDS employees being held hostage in Iran.

While a member of the board of directors of General Motors Corporation, he not only refused to rubber-stamp management's policies, he became an outspoken advocate of the need for major changes at GM.

Perot, often called a superpatriot, worked closely with the U.S. government to improve the treatment

of U.S. prisoners of war in North Vietnam. He also chaired the Texan's War on Drugs Committee that resulted in laws that made Texas the least desirable state for illegal drug operations.

User liaisons   **User liaisons** serve as the technical interface between the information services department and the user group. The user liaison coordinates system conversions and is the catalyst for new systems development.

Other Career Opportunities: Services, Hardware, Software, and Education.   There are a host of computer-specialist career opportunities in organizations that provide computer-related products or services. These organizations can be divided into four groups: services, hardware vendors, software vendors, and education.

Service vendors   The computer revolution is creating a tremendous demand for computer-related services. In response to this demand, a number of service organizations have emerged. These include *service bureaus, consulting firms,* and *computer repair stores,* to mention a few. Service bureaus provide almost any kind of information processing services. These services include but are not limited to developing and implementing information systems, providing computer time (timesharing), and transcribing source data. A service bureau is essentially a public computer center. Therefore, it needs people in most of the traditional computer career specialities. Consulting firms provide advice about the use of computers and the information resource. One of the fastest growing service groups consists of computer repair stores.

Hardware vendors   The most visible hardware vendors are the computer system manufacturers, such as Digital Equipment Corporation, Apple, IBM, and Hewlett-Packard (HP). These companies manufacture the processor and usually some or all of the peripheral equipment (disk drives, printers, terminals, and so on). Plug-compatible manufacturers, or *PCMs*, make peripheral devices that can be attached directly to another manufacturer's computer. **Value-added resellers**, or **VARs**, integrate the hardware and software of several vendors with their own hardware and/or software, then sell the entire package. They are called "value-added resellers" because they "add value" to each component of the system.

Hardware vendors market and service hardware. To do so, they need *marketing representatives* to sell the products and *systems engineers* to support them once they have been installed. Marketing representatives hold a technical sales position that requires a broad knowledge of the company's products and their capabilities. The systems engineer is the technical "expert" and is often called on by customers for advice on technical matters.

Software vendors   Companies that produce and market software are called *software vendors* or *software houses*. What you buy from a software house is a proprietary **software package** for a particular computer-based system or application. When a company purchases or leases a software package, the company receives a *license agreement* to use the copyrighted software.

Education   The computer explosion in the last few years has created an insatiable demand for computer-related education. This demand is

This medical specialist works for Hewlett-Packard, a vendor of hardware and software. HP maintains seven Medical Response Centers worldwide that are dedicated to supporting their medical customers and products.

Manufacturers "burn in" microcomputers for several days before shipment to lower the probability that a system will fail on delivery.

taxing the resources of our educational institutions and has given rise to a tremendous demand for *professors* and *instructors*. Instructors are needed in industry as well. Programmers, analysts, and users are forever facing the announcement of a new technological innovation or the installation of a new system. In-house education is focused on the specific educational needs of the organization.

Career Mobility and Computer Knowledge

Computer literacy is already a prerequisite to employment in some professions, such as business and engineering. Within a few years, computer literacy may well be a prerequisite for success in most professions. Career mobility is becoming forever intertwined with an individual's current and future knowledge of computers.

Just as advancing technology is creating new jobs, it is changing old ones. Some traditional jobs will change or even disappear. For example, office automation is radically changing the function and role of secretaries and office managers. With computer-aided design (CAD), draftspersons are learning new ways to do their jobs.

Career advancement, of course, ultimately depends on your abilities, imagination, and performance. But your understanding of computers can only enhance your opportunities. If you cultivate your talents and you aspire to leave your mark on your chosen profession, the possibilities are limitless.

14–2   COMPUTER APPLICATIONS OF THE FUTURE

It seems as if the computer is everywhere—yet we are only "scratching the surface" of possible computer applications. The outlook for innovative, exciting, and beneficial computer applications is bright.

Expectations and Reality

The short-term expectations of the general public for computer technology are probably unrealistic. Intense media coverage has given the computer novice the impression that bedmaking, dishwashing, and domestic robots are just around the corner; that computer-controlled organ transplants are almost perfected; and that computers have all the answers! To be sure, we are making progress in leaps and bounds, but we have a long way to go before such applications are feasible. Nevertheless, these rising expectations are a challenge to computer professionals to deliver.

Of course, no one can see into the future, but we can extrapolate from trends and our knowledge of current research. This section paints a picture of some computer applications that are sociologically, economically, and technologically feasible by the year 2000.

Information Networks

As the percentage of homes with micros increases, so does the potential for *information networks*. Information networks, a number of which exist today, provide certain services to an end user through a communications

This supercomputer is one of the most powerful computers in the world, but it's not effective enough for some people. It can simulate the wing or the fuselage of an airplane in flight but not the entire aircraft. Of course, aerospace engineers want it all. Their expectations are representative of people in other professions who already have plans for computers that have not even been developed.

A micro user can take advantage of many information services, such as electronic shopping, by establishing a communications link with a large computer system. Once on-line, the user has access to a random-access file that contains descriptions of thousands of items. The user shops by selecting an item from a "video catalog."

link to a microcomputer. Several currently available services provided by information networks are described in the special-interest sidebar in Chapter 6, "Data Communications." The two-way system provides the end user with information (for example, airline flight schedules) and permits the end user to enter data (such as reservations for airline flights).

The four components of an information network are the central computer, the data base, the network, and the microcomputers. The central computer system is accessed by end users who desire a particular service. The data base contains data and screens of information (perhaps a graphic display of a refrigerator with price and delivery information) that are presented to users. As microcomputers proliferate, a greater variety of information networks will be made available to more and more people. Even now, microcomputers that can access these networks are available in many airplanes and hotel rooms.

Hotel guests can communicate with their homes, companies, or virtually anyone else through the use of the computers in their rooms. They can obtain theater or airline tickets, shop or order gifts, scan restaurant menus, and even play video games. In a few years, all major hotels will provide their guests with access to microcomputers and information networks.

Commercially available information networks have an endless number of applications. Let's take real estate as an example. Suppose you live in Tuscon, Arizona, and have been transferred to Salt Lake City, Utah. It is only a matter of time before you will be able to gain access to a nationwide information network that maintains an up-to-date listing of every home in the country that is for sale. Here is how it will work. You will enter your purchase criteria: Salt Lake City, Utah; $150,000 to $210,000; no more than one mile from an elementary school; double garage; and so on. The system will then present pictures and specifications of those homes that meet your criteria.

Communications

The telephone as we know it will probably disappear and be replaced by a multifunction communications workstation. The workstation will integrate the functions of a personal computer, telephone, and fax (fac-

Computers and data communications have turned our world into a "global village." An astronaut in a manned maneuvering unit is preparing to dock with a Westar VI communications satellite. The astronaut later docked with the satellite and moved it near the end of the remote manipulator system so it could be loaded in the bay of the space shuttle and brought back to earth for repair.

simile) machine. Moreover, the workstation will enable us to see the person on the other end of the line. In addition, we will be able to pass data and information, both electronic and hard-copy, back and forth as if we were sitting at the same table.

Most of us will have ready access to microcomputers, whether at the office or on the road. From virtually anywhere, we will be able to use our microcomputers to read 50 different newspapers, turn on the heat at home, call a cab, order groceries, buy shares of stock, or make hotel reservations.

The television of the not-too-distant future will function as a terminal and enable limited two-way communication via a keyboard. You will be able to request that the stock market reports be subtitled across the screen while you continue to watch your favorite program. Newscasters will be able to sample the thinking of tens of thousands of people in a matter of minutes. After they ask the questions, we at home will respond on our keyboards. Our responses will be sent immediately to a central computer for analysis, and the results reported almost instantaneously. In this way, television news programs will keep us abreast of public opinion on critical issues and the feeling toward political candidates on a day-to-day basis.

BEAT THE TRAFFIC BY TELECOMMUTING

Traditionally, people get up in the morning, get dressed, and fight through rush hour to go to the office because that is where the work is. However, for many knowledge workers, work is really at a micro or terminal, whether it is at the office or at home. More and more employees are beginning to question the wisdom of going to the office in the traditional sense. Many would prefer to telecommute and work in the more comfortable surroundings of home. Telecommuting is "commuting" to work via a data communications link between home and office.

In theory, millions of people could telecommute to work at least a few days a week. People whose jobs involve considerable interaction with a computer system are perfect candidates (such as those who process insurance claims and programmers). Managers who need a few hours, or perhaps a few days, of uninterrupted time to accomplish tasks that do not require direct personal interaction are beginning to consider the merits of telecommuting.

At present, telecommuting is seldom an employee option. Most companies that permit telecommuting are restricting it to management and computer professionals. However, it is only a matter of time before self-motivated individuals at all levels and in a variety of disciplines are given the option of telecommuting at least part of the time. Most workers would view telecommuting and the accompanying flexible work hours as "perks" of employment. The company that does not offer them may be at a disadvantage in recruiting quality workers.

The trend is definitely to an increased level of telecommuting, especially with the proliferation of facsimile (fax) machines and sophisticated telephone systems that include voice mail and call forwarding. In effect, a knowledge worker's home office could function much like his or her "at work" office. In some cases, the "at work" office could be eliminated.

Everyone has a different reason for wanting to telecommute. A programmer with two school-age children says, "I want to say good-bye when the kids leave for school and greet them when they return." A writer goes into the office once a week, the day before the magazine goes to press. He says, "I write all my stories from the comfort of my home. An office that puts out a weekly magazine is not conducive to creative thinking." A financial analyst telecommutes to prepare quarterly financial statements. He says, "All the information I need is at my fingertips, and I finish in one day at home what used to take me a week at the office." The president of the same company stated emphatically, "I got sick and tired of spending nights up in my office. By telecommuting, I'm at least within earshot of my wife and kids. Also, I like to get into more comfortable clothes." The director of an MIS department describes one of many telecommuting applications: "Every Monday evening I write out the agenda for my Tuesday-morning staff meeting. I then send a summary of the agenda via electronic mail to my managers so they will see it first thing Tuesday morning when they log in."

Of course, there are differing opinions. One sales manager says, "I'm more productive working at the office, where household and family distractions fade into the distance."

Telecommuting may never catch on as a general alternative to working in the office, but for some applications it has proved to be a boon to productivity. As a personnel director observed: "With the elimination of travel time, coffee breaks, idle conversations, and numerous office distractions, we have found that conscientious, self-motivated employees can be more productive at home when working on certain projects." However, management at this company encourages workers to select their telecommuting activities carefully. Telecommuting is fine for interaction with the computer and the data base, but for interaction with other people, it has its limitations. Telecommuting does not permit "pressing of the flesh" and the transmittal of the nonverbal cues that are so essential to personal interaction.

In the Office

The traditional letter may never become obsolete, but electronic mail will become an increasingly popular alternative, especially because most of us will have our own microcomputers at home and at work. To

Integrated imaging is already beginning to change the face of offices with the use of the monitor's display. Knowledge workers can request to view the image of an original document, such as a letter, and the result of a data base inquiry on the same screen.

prepare and send a letter, an executive will dictate—not to a secretary, but to a computer! The executive's words will be transcribed directly into text, without key entry. The letter then will be routed to appropriate destinations via electronic mail. The recipient of the letter can request that it be displayed on a monitor or read aloud using synthesized speech.

With professionals spending a greater percentage of their working day interacting with the computer, look for the telecommuting and the electronic cottage concepts to gain momentum. At least a part of the work of most professionals will be done at home. For many, their work is at their fingertips, whether at home or the office. Look for the emergence of telecommuting and cottage industries to alter the demographics of cities. Less frequent trips to the office will surely encourage urban spread.

A Peek at the Crystal Ball

Manufacturing. Manufacturing companies, especially those that are labor-intensive, are faced with growing competition from international markets. In response to this challenge, executive James Baker noted that American industry is confronted with three choices: "automate, migrate, or evaporate." Companies can *automate*, thereby lowering costs and increasing productivity. They can *migrate* (move) to countries that offer less expensive labor. Or they can *evaporate*. Most have elected to automate, with the blessing of even organized labor. As one labor leader put it: "If we don't do it, I'm convinced we'll lose the jobs anyway."

With the trend toward greater automation, we can anticipate an increase in the number of industrial robots (see Chapter 11, "Applications of Information Technology"). As the smokestack industries become more "high-tech," the complexion of their workforce will change. There will be a shift of emphasis from brawn to brains. A few unmanned plants already exist, and this number will grow. These radical changes are a by-product of our transition from an industrial society to an information society. Traditional jobs will change or be lost forever, but new and, it is hoped, more challenging jobs will emerge to replace them.

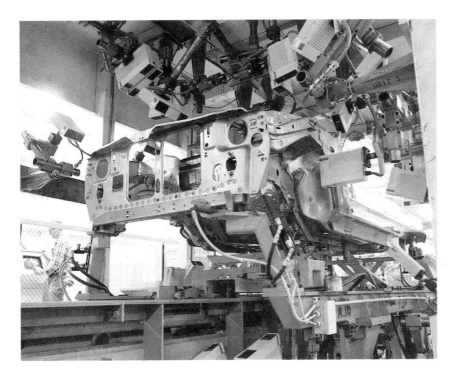

In manufacturing, those tasks that can be done better and at less cost by computers are being automated. In a world economy, this trend is irreversible. This optical gauging system at a Chrysler Motors plant automatically verifies complete underbody dimensional specifications. The system uses lasers, sensors, and cameras to ensure correct alignment of all sheet-metal body components.

Retail.   Information networks will enable us to do our shopping electronically. Instead of walking down the aisle of a grocery store or thumbing through stacks of shirts, we will be able to use our personal computer in conjunction with an information network to select and purchase almost any retail item. The items selected automatically will be picked, packaged, and possibly delivered to our doorstep. This information service will help speed the completion of routine activities such as grocery shopping and leave us more time for leisure, travel, and the things we enjoy.

Financial Services.   The overwhelming acceptance of automatic teller machines has spurred the trend toward more electronic funds transfer (EFT). Over the next decade, transaction documents such as checks and credit-card purchase slips will begin to disappear. Monies will be electronically transferred at the time of the purchase from the seller's account to the buyer's account. Total EFT will require an enormously complex communications network that links the computers of all financial institutions with virtually all businesses. Such a network is technologically and economically feasible today, but we are a few years away, sociologically.

Publishing.   Certainly books, magazines, newspapers, and the printed word in general will prevail for casual reading and study. However, it

First there was the automatic teller machine (ATM) and now there is the automated checkout machine (ACM). The move to self-checkout in supermarkets is gaining momentum. Shoppers scan their own groceries and receive visual and verbal confirmation of each purchase from the monitor. With ACMs, checkout is faster and less expensive. To pay, the customer takes a printed itemized receipt to the cashier.

Computer "showrooms" have made it easier for retailers to buy fashions for the next season. Rather than thumb through thousands of garments, buyers enter their fashion needs (for example, type, style, cost, fabric, and so on) into the apparel selection system and garments that meet their specification are displayed, along with the location and seller for each garment.

is not unreasonable to expect that publishers will offer *soft-copy* publishing as an alternative to *hard-copy* publishing. We will be able to receive books, magazines, and newspapers in electronic format, perhaps via data communications on our home computer or on a disk. A few specialized computer trade magazines are available now on disks, but in a few years a wide variety of magazines will be distributed via data communications or disks.

Can you imagine a bookstore without books? It's possible! With customized printing on demand, you will be able to browse through virtually any current book from a terminal. Then, if you wish to purchase the book, it will be printed (figures and all) and bound while you wait! This approach will provide a greater selection for the customer and vastly reduce costly inventory for both bookstore and publisher.

In the short term, CD-ROM (see Chapter 5, "Data Storage Devices and Media") is expected have the greatest influence on the publishing industry. Publishers can offer over 250,000 pages of text in the form of a single CD-ROM disk. Libraries, already cramped for space, are considering the possibility of providing many reference materials, such as encyclopedias and journals, in the form of CD-ROM.

Transportation. Someday soon computer-based automobile navigation systems will be standard equipment on cars. There already are enough satellites in the sky for an on-board automobile navigation system to obtain a fix establishing the location of the car. You will be able to call up appropriate regional or city maps from on-board optical laser

Relatively few aircraft are equipped with the Airshow Video Information System at this time, but this is changing rapidly. Airshow answers many questions frequently asked by travelers regarding the aircraft's flight path, estimated time of arrival, and related information in a real time, graphically exciting video format. In the photo, the display shows the aircraft flying over York, Pennsylvania, enroute to New York City.

disk storage. The car's location will be noted on a video display of a road map, and you will be able to plot your course and track your progress.

By now you are probably saying that this Buck-Rogers–type application is a bit farfetched. Well, prototypes of automobile navigation systems are now being tested—and they work!

Entertainment and the Arts. How about interactive soap operas? Yes, because of the two-way communication capabilities of your television/terminal, you can be an active participant in how a story unfolds. The soaps will be shot so they can be pieced together in a variety of ways. Imagine—you can decide whether Michelle marries Clifton or Patrick!

It won't be long before the rough drafts of television scripts are written by computers. Many weekly television shows have a formula plot. For instance, heroes are presented with a problem situation. They confront the problem, they get in trouble, they get out of trouble, they stick the bad guys, and they live to do it again next week. Formula plots lend themselves nicely to computer-produced rough-draft scripts. The computer system already will have the names of the key characters on file. The systems also will have dialogues on hand for a variety of situations. The names of nonregulars (such as the bad guys) will be generated randomly by the computer. The scriptwriters will enter a story-line sketch, then the computer will piece together dialogues and scenes within the restrictions of the show's formula plot and the story line. The scriptwriters will then refine the draft script.

Sculptors may someday become more productive with the help of computers. For example, a sculptor will be able to create three-dimensional "sketches" on a computer, much the same way an engineer designs a part using computer-aided design (CAD). The computer will activate a robotlike sculpting tool that will rough out the general shape of the figure. The sculptor will then add the creative touches that turn a piece of clay into a work of art.

Health Care. Expert systems have already benefited physicians by helping them diagnose physical illnesses (see Chapter 11, "Applications of Information Technology"). In the near future we can anticipate expert systems that help diagnose and treat mental illnesses and emotional problems as well. Psychologists and psychiatrists will continue to work with patients in the classical manner, but with the added advantage of a "partner." This "partner" will be able to tap a vast storehouse of knowledge and recommend everything from lines of questioning to diagnosis and treatment.

Encouraging research leads us to believe that the computer will play a vital role in tomorrow's medical miracles. We are still a few steps away, but lifesaving computer implants are inevitable. These tiny computers will control mechanical devices that can replace organs that have ceased to function. Other medical research has given paraplegics renewed hope that they may someday walk again with the assistance of a computerized nervous system. Handicapped people can look forward to improved mobility and independence. Sophisticated prostheses will

This image was created by a computer artist. Just as a writer can edit a manuscript by using word processing software, an artist can make changes easily to computer art pieces. For example, the artist could change the color of the silver chess pieces to gold. Whether the artist uses a palette and easel or a computer, it still takes a creative mind and a keen eye to produce good art.

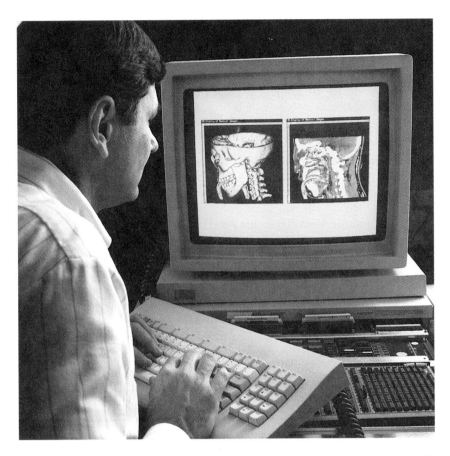

In the past, doctors have had to perform exploratory surgery to isolate and identify internal maladies. Computers are giving doctors better internal views, thereby eliminating the need for exploratory surgery. This man and his colleagues at the GE Research and Development Center have created a software package that converts raw data from computed tomography X-ray scans into exceptionally sharp three-dimensional images of a patient's head or body in just minutes.

be activated by voice, motion, muscle activity, breathing, and even the blinking of an eye.

Medical and technical researchers have dared to contemplate integrating computers and the brain. That is, eventually we may electronically connect tiny computer implants to the brain to enhance its computational and factual-recall capabilities.

Government.   Computer-enhanced photography will enable us to break out the finer details in photographs. With computer-enhanced photography, the headlines in a newspaper can be read from a photograph taken 150 miles above the earth. Its immediate application is in the area of military intelligence.

Local, state, and federal elections might not require an army of volunteers. Politicians might not have to worry about rain on Election Day. We eventually will record our votes through home or business microcomputers. Such a system will encourage greater voter participation although, of course, security and voter authenticity will be a concern.

One possible solution would be to ask voters to identify themselves with their social security numbers and voter registration security codes known only to the voters. A few years later we won't need to carry cards or remember numbers; each voter's identity will be validated when the system reads our fingerprint and our voiceprint. All we will have to do to identify ourselves will be to enter our voiceprint by speaking a few words and our fingerprint by placing our finger near an optical laser scanner.

Education.   Computer systems are revolutionizing the education process. For example, as students learn via computer-based instruction (CBT), they can request visual reinforcement from hundreds of still and moving pictures stored on optical laser disks. There is truth to the old saying that "one picture is worth a thousand words."

Computers are beginning to play a more active role in the education of learning-disabled children. Current human-resource limitations do not permit the luxury of constant one-on-one attention for these children. However, in between group and one-on-one sessions, a computer system capable of responding to a wide variety of inputs can be dedicated to each child. For example, computers complement the kinesthetic (touch and feel) approach to dyslexia (impaired reading ability). Children with dyslexia can engage in interactive reading that offers immediate feedback and reinforcement. At present, we are only beginning to tap the computer as an educational tool.

Computers have the potential of enabling nationwide uniform testing for elementary and secondary students. With uniform learning standards

Companies are beginning to use interactive videodisc systems to train their employees. Computer-based training (CBT) offers many advantages: It gives individual attention. It is interactive and quick to respond to student input. CBT systems can explain and demonstrate concepts then test for understanding. CBT is self-paced so that the student controls the pace of learning.

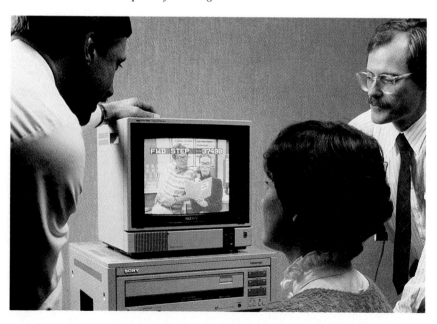

for each subject at each level, it will be possible to advance students from one grade to the next on the basis of achievement rather than age.

Artificial Intelligence

Artificial intelligence, or AI, was introduced in Chapter 1 and described as the ability of a computer to reason, to learn, to strive for self-improvement, and to simulate human sensory capabilities. We have access to artificial sweeteners, artificial grass, artificial flowers—why not artificial intelligence? To some extent, we do! Significant strides have been made in all four areas of artificial-intelligence research: natural languages (discussed in Chapter 1); simulation of human sensory capabilities (discussed in Chapter 4); knowledge-based and expert systems (discussed in Chapter 11); and robotics (discussed in Chapter 11).

The Future of Artificial Intelligence.   Natural-language software enables computer systems to accept, interpret, and execute instructions in the native language of the end user, typically English. At present, some relatively primitive natural languages enable a user-friendly interface of corporate data bases and expert systems. But with most other software, we must use programming and the selection of menu options to tell the computer what to do. In the future, look for natural-language interfaces to accompany virtually all user-oriented software, from word processing to inventory modeling packages. Instead of working through a series of menus to specify the layout of a word processing document, the user might enter, "Set the left and right margins at $1\frac{1}{2}$ inches and 1 inch and double-space the document."

Scientists in the field of artificial intelligence hope to make it possible for humans to communicate with computers in plain English—instead of a stilted and precise computer language. One unique approach simulates the way humans acquire a second language. The AI software analyzes a sentence by forming hypotheses about its possible meaning and eliminating the less likely candidates. At the same time, based on clarifications entered by the user, it is engaged in learning. When tested on idioms, the program figured out that "bury the hatchet" means to "terminate a conflict." But the meaning of less obvious idioms like "kick the bucket" still elude it.

The area of AI research that involves computer simulation of human sensory capabilities focuses on equipping computer systems with the capabilities of seeing, hearing, speaking, and feeling (touching). These artificial-intelligence capabilities already are possible with current technology to varying degrees. "Intelligent" machines that can simulate human sensory capabilities have the ability to establish a link with their environments. This link has opened the door to a number of real-world applications. Today most data are keyed in from a keyboard. Within the next decade, much of the data will be entered verbally. For example, mail-order customers will be able to verbalize order information over the telephone. The verbal information will be interpreted by a speech-recognition system and entered directly to the computer for processing. AI research is continually enhancing the abilities of computers to simulate human sensory capabilities. In the near future, we will be able to have meaningful verbal conversations with computers. These computers will be able to talk, listen, and even "smell the roses"!

Expert systems already have begun to make a major impact on the way people in the business community make decisions. Today there are hundreds of expert systems, most of which were developed at great expense to service a particular company. In a few years, there will be thousands of expert systems. In the professional environment, physicians in every specialty will have at least one expert system at their disposal. During the 1990s it is not unreasonable to expect that some doctors

The industrial robot shown here can be programmed to "pick and place" an item from anywhere to anywhere within the reach of the telescopic manipulator arm. Before robots, workers in assembly plants were primarily involved with manual tasks; now they work on tasks that tap their cognitive resources. These tasks include production scheduling, quality control, and the design and programming of robots.

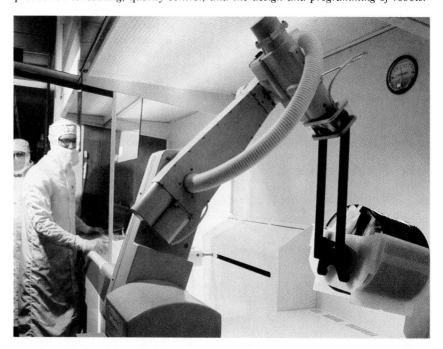

will accept expert systems as critical medical instruments and bring them into the examining room. Any person who routinely does some type of screening, such as a bank loan officer or a recruiter, will do so with the help of an expert system. At home we will be able to check an expert system that will help us to decorate our homes out of the local library.

Industrial robots can be "taught" to perform almost any repetitive manipulative task, such as painting a car, screwing on a bolt, moving material, and even complex tasks such as inspecting a manufactured part for defects. However, most existing robots are stationary—they are programmed to operate within a well-defined work area. The inevitable advances in vision systems will enable robots to move about the work area just as people do, probably during the 1990s.

14–3   YOUR CHALLENGE

Having mastered the contents of this book and this course, you are now poised to exploit the benefits of the computer in your personal and business lives. This course, however, is only the beginning. The computer learning process is ongoing. The dynamics of a rapidly advancing computer technology demand a constant updating of skills and expertise. Perhaps the excitement of technological innovation and the ever-changing opportunities for application are part of the lure of computers.

By their very nature, computers bring about change. With the total amount of computing capacity in the world doubling every two years, we can expect even more dramatic change in the future. The cumulative effects of these changes are altering the basic constructs of society and the way we conduct business.

Never before has such opportunity presented itself so vividly. This generation, *your generation*, has the technological foundation and capability to change dreams into reality.

SUMMARY OUTLINE AND IMPORTANT TERMS

14–1   THE JOB OUTLOOK. People who can claim computer knowledge on their resumes will have an advantage over those who cannot. This is true in a great many professional disciplines.

Virtually every company employs or is considering employing computer specialists. Some of the most visible career paths are found in a company's information systems department. These include **systems analysts**, **applications programmers**, **programmer/analysts**, **systems programmers**, **data communications specialists**, **data base administrators**, **computer operators**, **control clerks**, **data entry operators**, **librarians**, **education coordinators**, and of course, the managers of the various groups.

A new breed of computer specialist is emerging in the user areas. **Office-automation specialists** help users effectively apply office systems. The **microcomputer specialist** stays abreast of the latest micro hardware

Computer pioneer Grace Hopper is fond of comparing the evolution of computers to that of automobiles. She says if computers were automobiles, we would be at about the Model T Ford stage of development.

and software technology and helps implement this technology in a user area. **Information-center specialists** work in an information center and help users to help themselves. The **user liaison** serves as the technical interface between the information services department and the user groups.

There are a host of career opportunities that are not in an information services department or a user group. These opportunities are found with vendors of computer services, of hardware, and of software and in the area of computer education.

14–2 **COMPUTER APPLICATIONS OF THE FUTURE.** The number and variety of computer applications is expected to grow rapidly in the coming years. In the near future we can anticipate an even greater variety of services becoming available through information networks; integrated communications workstations; the widespread acceptance and use of electronic mail; unmanned manufacturing facilities; electronic shopping; diminished use of cash; soft-copy publishing; automobile navigation systems; create-your-own-story "soaps" on television; robot sculptors; computer-controlled artificial limbs; voting at home via microcomputers; nationwide uniform student testing; and AI (artificial intelligence), which encompasses natural languages, simulation of human sensory capabilities, expert systems, and robotics.

14–3 **YOUR CHALLENGE.** The computer offers us the opportunity to improve the quality of our lives. It is our challenge to harness the power of the computer and direct it to the benefit of society.

REVIEW EXERCISES

Concepts

1. What is the function of a user liaison?
2. Name six computer specialist positions commonly represented in a company's information services department.
3. Name four positions in the operations area.
4. People of what job function would be involved in the selection and implementation of PBXs and front-end processors?
5. Describe the business of VARs.
6. What is the product of a software house?
7. Contrast the jobs of systems engineer and marketing representative. How do they complement each other?
8. The use of automatic teller machines (ATMs) is an example of what computer application?
9. Briefly describe two applications for expert systems.
10. What are the four categories of artificial intelligence research?
11. What type of programmer is usually associated with the technical support group? With the programming group?
12. Which job function accounts for all input to and output from a computer center?

Discussion

13. Based on your knowledge of the capabilities of computers now and in the future, speculate on at least three futuristic applications that we can expect within the next five years.

14. Of the job functions described in this chapter, which would you prefer? Why?

15. Discuss the advantages of distributed processing from the standpoint of career mobility.

16. Some companies will have only one level of programmer or systems analyst, where other companies will have two, three, and even four levels. Discuss the advantages of having several levels for a particular position (such as Programmer I, Programmer II, and so on).

17. "Automate, migrate, or evaporate." Discuss this statement from the points of view of manufacturing management and of labor.

18. During the implementation of computer applications, managers have traditionally focused on hardware and software. Now they realize they must pay more attention to human needs as well. What are these needs?

19. Compare your perspective on computers today with what it was four months ago. How have your feelings and attitudes changed?

SELF-TEST (by section) _____

14–1 **a.** The trend to distributed processing is causing more and more computer specialists to move to the user departments. (T/F)
  b. The librarian handles most of the training in an information services department. (T/F)
  c. Office-automation specialist is a fancy name for a word processor. (T/F)
  d. PCM stands for _____.

14–2 **a.** The magazine-on-a-disk has been discussed but is beyond the state of the art. (T/F)
  b. Prototypes for on-board automobile navigation systems will be ready for testing by the turn of the century. (T/F)
  c. The acronym for artificial intelligence is: (a) ARTELL, (b) AI, or (c) AIG.
  d. Most existing industrial robots are stationary or they are programmed to operate within a well-defined work area. (T/F)

14–3 The total computing capacity in the world is increasing at slightly less than 25% per year. (T/F)

Self-test answers   **14–1 (a)** T; **(b)** F; **(c)** F; **(d)** plug-compatible manufacturer.
14–2 (a) F; **(b)** F; **(c)** b; **(d)** T. **14–3** F.

Appendix A

THE PASCALINE Pascal's invention, the Pascaline, used gear-driven counting wheels to do addition. He built the Pascaline to help his father, a tax collector, calculate tax revenues. The numbers for each digit position were arranged on wheels so that a single revolution of one wheel resulted in one tenth of a revolution of the wheel to its immediate left.

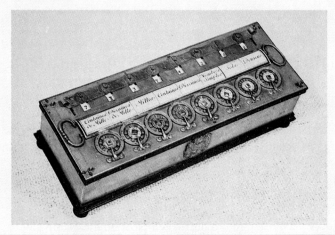

THE ABACUS The abacus was probably the original mechanical counting device, and its effectiveness has withstood the test of time. It is still used to illustrate the principles of counting.

500 B.C.

1642

BLAISE PASCAL French philosopher and mathematician Blaise Pascal (1623–62) invented and built the first mechanical adding machine. Pascal's early work with mechanical calculators is recognized today by the popular computer programming language that bears his name.

An Abbreviated History of Computers

JACQUARD'S LOOM The Jacquard weaving loom was invented by the Frenchman Joseph-Marie Jacquard (1753–1834) and is still in use today. It is controlled by cards in which holes are strategically punched. The punched cards are sequenced to indicate a particular weaving design.

CHARLES BABBAGE Concepts used in today's general-purpose computer were introduced over a century ago by Charles Babbage (1793–1871), an English visionary and Cambridge professor.

1805

1822–33

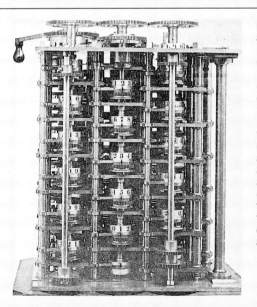

DIFFERENCE ENGINE Charles Babbage advanced the state of computational hardware by inventing a "difference engine" that was capable of computing mathematical tables. Unfortunately, he completed only a part of his difference engine (shown here). While working on it, Babbage conceived the idea of an "analytical engine." In essence, this was a general-purpose computer. As designed, his analytical engine would add, subtract, multiply, and divide in automatic sequence at a rate of 60 additions per minute. His 1833 design called for thousands of gears and drives that would cover the area of a football field and be powered by a locomotive engine. Babbage worked on his analytical engine until his death.

LADY ADA LOVELACE Lady Ada Augusta Lovelace suggested that punch cards could be prepared that would instruct Babbage's engine to repeat certain operations. Because of her suggestion, some people call Lady Lovelace the first programmer.

PUNCHED-CARD TABULATING MACHINE The U.S. Bureau of the Census did not complete the 1880 census until almost 1888. Bureau management concluded that before long, the 10-year census would take more than 10 years to complete! The Census Bureau commissioned Herman Hollerith to apply his expertise in the use of punched cards to the 1890 census. With punched-card processing and Hollerith's *punched-card tabulating machine* the census was completed in just three years and his process saved the bureau over $5,000,000. Thus began the emergence of automated data processing.

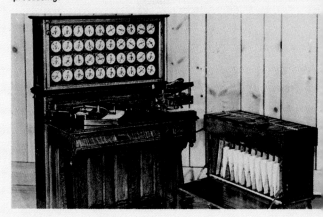

1843	1884	1890

DR. HERMAN HOLLERITH Herman Hollerith, a statistician, applied for a patent for a punched-card tabulating machine. Hollerith's idea for the punched card came not from Jacquard or Babbage but from "punch photography." Railroads of the day issued tickets with physical descriptions of the passengers. A conductor would punch holes in a ticket that noted a passenger's hair and eye color and the nose shape. Hollerith's daughter later said, "This gave him the idea for making a punch photograph of every person to be tabulated," which he later applied to taking the 1890 census. The patent was issued in 1889.

THE EAM ERA   For decades through the mid-1950s, punched-card technology improved with the addition of more punched-card devices and more sophisticated capabilities. The *electromechanical accounting machine* (*EAM*) family of punched-card devices includes the card punch, verifier, reproducer, summary punch, interpreter, sorter, collator, calculator, and the accounting machine. Most of the devices in this 1940s machine room were "programmed" to perform a particular operation by the insertion of a prewired control panel. A machine-room operator in a punched-card installation had a physically demanding job. Punched cards and printed output were moved from one device to the next on hand trucks.

IBM'S FIRST HEADQUARTERS BUILDING   In 1896 Herman Hollerith founded the Tabulating Machine Company which, in 1911, merged with several other companies to form the Computing-Tabulating-Recording Company. In 1924 the company's general manager, Thomas J. Watson, changed its name to International Business Machines Corporation and moved into this building.

DR. JOHN V. ATANASOFF During the years 1935 to 1938, Dr. John V. Atanasoff, a professor at Iowa State University, had begun to think about a machine that could reduce the time it took for him and his physics students to make long, complicated mathematical calculations. The decisions he made about such concepts as an electronic medium with vacuum tubes, the base-2 numbering system, memory, and logic circuits set the direction for the development of the modern computer.

THE MARK I The first electromechanical computer, called the *Mark I*, was the result of IBM-sponsored research. Howard Aiken, a Harvard University professor, completed the Mark I in 1944. It was essentially a serial collection of electromechanical calculators and had many similarities to Babbage's analytical engine. (Aiken was unaware of Babbage's work.) The Mark I was a significant improvement in the state of the art, but IBM's management still felt that electromechanical computers would not replace punched-card equipment.

1935   **1942**   **1944**

THE ABC In 1939 Dr. Atanasoff and one of his graduate students, Clifford E. Berry, assembled a prototype of the *ABC* (Atanasoff Berry Computer), which by 1942 evolved into the working model shown here. However, Iowa State, the business world, and the scientific community showed little interest in the ABC. For example, when Dr. Atanasoff contacted IBM about what he called his "computing machine proper," the company responded that "IBM never will be interested in an electronic computing machine." A 1973 federal court ruling officially credited Atanasoff with the invention of the automatic electronic digital computer.

THE UNIVAC I AND THE FIRST GENERATION OF COMPUTERS

The first generation of computers (1951–59), which is characterized by vacuum tubes, is generally thought to have started with the introduction of the first commercially viable electronic digital computer. The Universal Automatic Computer (*UNIVAC I* for short), developed by Mauchly and Eckert for the Remington-Rand Corporation, was installed in the U.S. Bureau of the Census in 1951. Later that year, CBS news gave the UNIVAC I national exposure when it correctly predicted Dwight Eisenhower's victory over Adlai Stevenson in the presidential election with only 5% of the votes counted. Shown here is Mr. Eckert instructing news anchor Walter Cronkite in the use of the UNIVAC I.

THE ENIAC Dr. John W. Mauchly (middle) collaborated with J. Presper Eckert, Jr.,(foreground) to develop a machine that would compute trajectory tables for the U.S. Army. The end product, a large-scale, fully operational electronic computer, was completed in 1946 and called the *ENIAC* (Electronic Numerical Integrator and Computer). The ENIAC (shown here), a thousand times faster than its electromechanical predecessors, signaled a major breakthrough in computer technology. It weighed 30 tons and occupied 1500 square feet of floor space. With over 18,000 vacuum tubes, the ENIAC needed a huge amount of electricity. Legend has it that the ENIAC, built at the University of Pennsylvania, dimmed the lights of Philadelphia whenever it was activated. Because of its imposing scale, electronic components, and wide applicability, the ENIAC is generally considered the first functional electronic digital computer.

1946   1951   1954

THE IBM 650 Not until the success of the UNIVAC I did IBM make the decision and the commitment to develop and market computers. IBM's first entry into the commercial computer market was the *IBM 701* in 1953. However, the *IBM 650* (shown here), introduced in 1954, is probably the reason that IBM enjoys such a healthy share of today's computer market. Unlike some of its competitors, the IBM 650 was designed as a logical upgrade to existing punched-card machines. IBM management went out on a limb and estimated sales of 50, a figure that was greater than the number of installed computers in the United States at that time. IBM actually installed more than 1000. The rest is history.

THE IBM SYSTEM 360 AND THE THIRD GENERATION OF COMPUTERS What some computer historians consider the single most important event in the history of computers occurred when IBM announced its *System 360* line of computers on April 7, 1964. The System 360 ushered in the third generation of computers (1964–71). Integrated circuits did for the third generation of computers what transistors did for the second generation. *Business Week* reported IBM's announcement of its System 360 line of computers, saying that "In the annals of major product changes it is like Ford's switch from the Model T to the Model A." The System 360s and the third-generation computers of other manufacturers made all previously installed computers obsolete.

1959　　　**1963**　　　**1964**

THE HONEYWELL 400 AND THE SECOND GENERATION OF COMPUTERS The invention of the transistor signaled the start of the second generation of computers (1959–64). The transistor meant more powerful, more reliable, and less expensive computers that would occupy less space and give off less heat than vacuum-tube-powered computers did. Honeywell (the *Honeywell 400* is shown here) established itself as a major player in the second generation of computers. Burroughs, Univac, NCR, CDC, and Honeywell—IBM's biggest competitors during the 1960s and early 1970s—became known as the BUNCH (the first initial of each name).

THE PDP-8 During the 1950s and early 1960s, only the largest companies could afford the six- and seven-digit price tags of mainframe computers. In 1963 Digital Equipment Corporation introduced the *PDP-8* (shown here). It is generally regarded as the first successful minicomputer. At $18,000, the transistor-based PDP-8 was an instant hit. It confirmed the tremendous demand for small computers for business and scientific applications. By 1971 over 25 firms were manufacturing minicomputers. Digital and Data General Corporation took an early lead in the sale and manufacture of minis.

INTEGRATED CIRCUITS AND THE FOURTH GENERATION OF COMPUTERS Most computer vendors classify their computers as fourth generation. Some people prefer to pinpoint 1971 as the start of the fourth generation of computers, with the introduction of large-scale integration (more circuits per unit space) of electronic circuitry. The base technology of today's computers is still the integrated circuit. This is not to say that two decades have passed without any significant innovations. In truth, the computer industry has experienced a mind-boggling succession of advances in the further miniaturization of circuitry, data communications, the design of computer hardware and software, and input/output devices.

1971

1977

THE APPLE II Not until 1975 and the introduction of the *Altair 8800* personal computer was computing made available to individuals and very small companies. This event has forever changed how society perceives computers. Certainly the most prominent entrepreneurial venture during the early years of personal computers was the *Apple II* computer (shown here). Two young computer enthusiasts, Steven Jobs and Steve Wozniak (then 21 and 26 years of age, respectively), collaborated to create and build their Apple II computer on a makeshift production line in Jobs' garage. Seven years later, Apple Computer earned a spot on the Fortune 500, a list of the 500 largest corporations in the United States.

1981

THE IBM PC In 1981 IBM tossed its hat into the personal computer ring with the announcement of the *IBM PC*. In the first year, 35,000 were sold. In 1982, 800,000 were sold, and the IBM PC was well on its way to becoming the standard for the micro industry. When software vendors began to orient their products to the IBM PC, many microcomputer manufacturers created and sold *clones* of the IBM PC. These clones, called *IBM-PC compatibles*, run most or all the software designed for the IBM PC.

Year	Historic Event	Processing	Input	Output	Storage (secondary)	Software	Systems Concepts	Information Systems Organization	Information Systems Personnel
1940	World War II begins	Electro-mechanical accounting machines ABC computer	Punched card Paper tape Mark sense	Punched card Paper tape Printer	Punched card Paper tape	Wired panels Switches	Data processing (DP)	Centralized punched card departments	
	And ends	1st generation (vacuum tubes) ENIAC							Programmer
						Machine language Stored program Assembler language			
1950		UNIVAC I (1st commercial)							
	Ike elected President			High-speed printers	Magnetic tape	Compilers	Artificial intelligence		Operator Data entry
	Sputnik launched	IBM 650	Magnetic ink character recognition (MICR)	Plotters MICR	Magnetic disk Interchange-able disk	FORTRAN APT Virtual memory COBOL LISP			Systems analyst Proprietary software introduced
		2nd generation (transistors)							
1960		PDP=8 Minicomputer 3rd generation (integrated circuits) IBM 360 family Computer networks	Optical character recognition (OCR) Keyboard (on-line) Light pen	OCR Voice (recorded) Soft copy (VDT) Computer output microfilm (COM)	Mass storage devices	Propietary software introduced Multiprogram-ming RPG PL/I BASIC APL LOGO	Management information systems (MIS)	Trend to large centralized information systems departments	Librarian Programmer (systems and applications) Control clerk
	J.F. Kennedy assassinated								
	Apollo II lands on moon								
1970	Watergate burglary	4th generation (large-scale integration) Microprocessors Microcomputers	Mouse Hand print	Graphics (VDT) Color graphics High-speed laser printers	IK RAM chip Floppy disk Winchester disk	Pascal Word processing Fourth-generation languages UNIX operating system	Information resource management (IRM)	Trend to decentra-lization and distributed processing	Data base administrator Project leader Education coordinator Documentalist Office automation specialist
	USA's 200th birthday	Personal computers Supercomputers Word processors Distributed processing IBM PC Pocket computers Multiuser micros Apple	Voice Vision input systems	Voice (synthesized) Desktop laser printers	Video disk Optical laser disk	Application generators Electronic spreadsheet Ada Integrated micro software Desktop publishing	Decision support systems (DDS) Expert systems	Information centers	Data communications specialist MIS long-range planner User-analyst Information center specialist User liaison
1980	Mt. St. Helens erupts								
	E.T. lands								
	Reagan begins second term								
	XXII Olympiad	Macintosh IBM PS/2			1 megabit RAM chip Magneto-optical disk	User-friendly interfaces		Departmental company	Microcomputer specialist
1990					4 megabit RAM chip				

FIGURE A–1   Chronology of Computer History

This chart summarizes important events in the history of computers and information processing. These events are discussed in this appendix and throughout the book.

1. John V. Atanasoff invented the electronic digital computer in 1931. (T/F)

2. Herman Hollerith used his tabulating machine for automated data processing at the U.S. Bureau of the Census. (T/F)

3. The first patent for an electronic digital computer was awarded to John V. Atanasoff for the: (a) ABC, (b) ENIAC, or (c) UNIVAC I.

4. The _____ was developed to compute trajectory tables for the U.S. Army.

5. The Mark I was IBM's first electronic digital computer. (T/F)

6. The _____ is considered the original mechanical computing device.

7. The devices used for data processing just prior to the emergence of electronic computers are known collectively as: (a) Pascal devices, (b) EAM equipment, or (c) micros.

8. The minicomputer was first introduced in the early 1970s. (T/F)

9. Electronic accounting machines used _____ as a storage medium.

10. The electrical component usually associated with the second generation of computers is the: (a) vacuum tube, (b) integrated circuit, or (c) transistor.

11. Jacquard's Loom was invented before the punched-card tabulating machine and after the: (a) ENIAC, (b) Pascaline, or (c) ABC.

12. The inventors of the ENIAC are _____ and _____.

13. Which of the following is not a microcomputer: (a) Apple II, (b) IBM PC, or (c) PDP-8?

14. Which came first: (a) UNIVAC I, (b) transistors in computers, or (c) personal computers?

15. In the early nineteenth century, a difference engine capable of computing mathematical tables was invented by J. Presper Eckert, Jr. (T/F)

Self-test answers. **1.** F. **2.** T. **3.** a. **4.** ENIAC. **5.** F. **6.** abacus. **7.** b. **8.** F. **9.** punched card **10.** c. **11.** b. **12.** Mauchly, Eckert. **13.** c. **14.** F. **15.** F.

B

Working with Numbering Systems

This appendix presents the principles of numbering systems, discusses numbering-system arithmetic, and illustrates how to convert a value in one numbering system to its equivalent in another. After studying this appendix you will be able to perform rudimentary arithmetic operations in the binary and hexadecimal numbering systems. The relationship between computers and the various numbering systems is discussed in Chapter 3, "Inside the Computer."

PRINCIPLES OF NUMBERING SYSTEMS

Binary

The binary, or base-2, numbering system is based on the same principles as the decimal, or base-10, numbering system, with which we are already familiar. The only difference between the two numbering systems is that binary uses only two digits, 0 and 1, and the decimal numbering system uses 10 digits, 0 through 9. The equivalents for binary, decimal, and hexadecimal numbers are shown in Figure B–1.

The value of a given digit is determined by its relative position in a sequence of digits. Consider the example in Figure B–2. If we want to write the number 124 in decimal, the interpretation is almost automatic because of our familiarity with the decimal numbering system. To illustrate the underlying concepts, let's give Ralph, a little green two-fingered Martian, a bag of 124 (decimal) marbles and ask him to express the number of marbles in decimal. Ralph, who is more familiar with binary, would go through the following thought process (see Figure B–2).

Step 1. Ralph knows that the relative position of a digit within a string of digits determines its value, whether the numbering system is binary or decimal. Therefore, the first thing to do is determine the value represented by each digit position.

Step 2. Ralph knows that as in any numbering system, the rightmost position has a value of the base to the zero power, or 1 ($10^0 = 1$). The second position is the base to the first power, or 10 ($10^1 = 10$). The third position is the base squared, or 100, and so on.

Binary (base 2)	Decimal (base 10)	Hexadecimal (base 16)
0	0	0
1	1	1
10	2	2
11	3	3
100	4	4
101	5	5
110	6	6
111	7	7
1000	8	8
1001	9	9
1010	10	A
1011	11	B
1100	12	C
1101	13	D
1110	14	E
1111	15	F
10000	16	10

FIGURE B–1   Numbering-System Equivalence Table

FIGURE B–2   Numbering-System Fundamentals
Ralph, our two-fingered Martian who is used to counting in binary, might go through the thought process illustrated here when counting 124 marbles in decimal. Ralph's steps are discussed in the text.

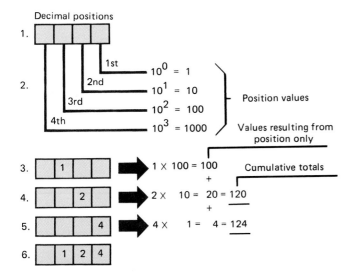

Step 3. Because the largest of the decimal system's 10 digits is 9, the greatest number that can be represented in the *rightmost position* is 9 (9 × 1). The greatest number that can be represented in the *second position*, then, is 90 (9 × 10). In the *third position*, the greatest number is 900, and so on. Having placed the marbles in stacks of 10, Ralph knows immediately that there will be no need for a fourth-position digit (the thousands position). It is apparent, however, that a digit must be placed in the third position. Because placing a 2 in the third position would be too much (200 > 124), Ralph places a 1 in the third position to represent 100 marbles.

Step 4. Ralph must continue to the second position to represent the remaining 24 marbles. In each successive position, Ralph wants to represent as many marbles as possible. In this case, a 2 placed in the second position would represent 20 of the remaining marbles ($2 \times 10^1 = 20$).

Step 5. There are still four marbles left to be represented. This can be done by inserting a 4 in the rightmost, or ones, position.

Step 6. The combination of the three numbers in their relative positions represents 124 (decimal).

Ralph would go through the same thought process if asked to represent the 124 (decimal) marbles using the binary numbering system (see Figure B–3). To make the binary conversion process easier to follow, the computations in Figure B–3 are done in the more familiar decimal numbering system. See if you can trace Ralph's steps as you work through Figure B–3.

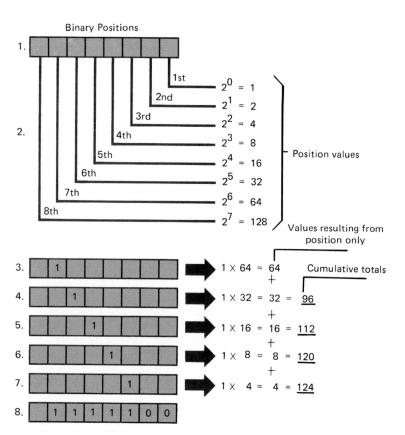

FIGURE B–3   Representing a Binary Number

To represent 124 marbles in binary, we would follow the same thought process as we would in decimal (see Figure B–2), but this time we have only two digits (0 and 1). For ease of understanding, the arithmetic is done in decimal.

Input/output (alphanumeric)	S	y	s	t	e	m

Internal representation (binary)	1110	0010	1010	1000	1010	0010	1010	0011	1000	0101	1001	0100

Hexadecimal equivalent	E	2	A	8	A	2	A	3	8	5	9	4

FIGURE B–4   *System* Expressed in Different Ways
The word System *is shown as it would appear in input/output, internal binary
notation, and hexadecimal notation.*

Hexadecimal

Perhaps the biggest drawback to using the binary numbering system for computer operations is that programmers may have to deal with long and confusing
strings of 1s and 0s. To reduce the confusion, the hexadecimal, or base-16,
numbering system is used as shorthand to display the binary contents of
primary and secondary storage.

Notice that the bases of the binary and hexadecimal numbering systems
are multiples of 2: 2 and 2^4, respectively. Because of this, there is a convenient
relationship between these numbering systems. The numbering-system equivalence table shown in Figure B–1 illustrates that a single hexadecimal digit
represents four binary digits ($0111_2 = 7_{16}$, $1101_2 = D_{16}$, $1010_2 = A_{16}$, where
subscripts are used to indicate the base of the numbering system). Notice
that in hexadecimal, or "hex," *letters* are used to represent the six higher
order digits.

Two hexadecimal digits can be used to represent the eight-bit byte of an
EBCDIC equals sign (=) (01111110_2 is the same as $7E_{16}$). Figure B–4 illustrates
how a string of EBCDIC bits can be reduced to a more recognizable form
using hexadecimal.

We will now examine how to convert one number in a numbering system
to an equivalent number in another numbering system. For example, there
are occasions when we might wish to convert a hexadecimal number into its
binary equivalent. We shall also learn the fundamentals of numbering-system
arithmetic.

CONVERTING NUMBERS FROM ONE BASE INTO ANOTHER

Decimal to Binary or Hexadecimal

A decimal number can be converted easily into an equivalent number of any
base by the use of the *division/remainder* technique. This two-step technique
is illustrated in Figure B–5. Follow these steps to convert *decimal to binary*.

Step 1. Divide the number (19, in this example) repeatedly by 2, and
record the remainder of each division. In the first division, 2 goes into
19 nine times with a remainder of 1. The remainder is always one of the
binary digits—0 or 1. In the last division you divide 1 by the base (2)
and the remainder is 1.

The problem: $19_{10} = ?_2$

The procedure:

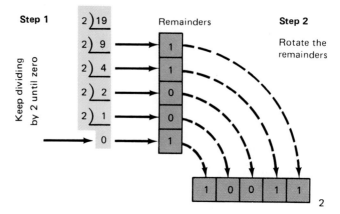

FIGURE B–5   Converting a Decimal Number into Its Binary Equivalent
Use the two-step division/remainder technique to convert a decimal number into an equivalent number of any base.

Step 2. Rotate the remainders as shown in Figure B–5; the result (10011) is the binary equivalent of a decimal 19.

Figure B–6 illustrates how the same division/remainder technique is used to convert a decimal 453 into its hexadecimal equivalent (1C5). In a *decimal-to-hex* conversion, the remainder is always one of the 16 hex digits.

FIGURE B–6   Converting a Decimal Number into Its Hexadecimal Equivalent
The two-step division/remainder technique is used to convert a decimal number into its hex equivalent.

The problem: $453_{10} = ?_{16}$

The procedure:

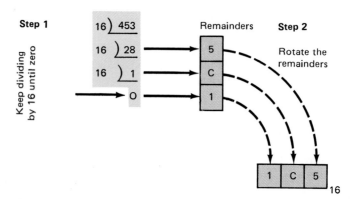

The problem: $11010_2 = ?_{10}$

The procedure:

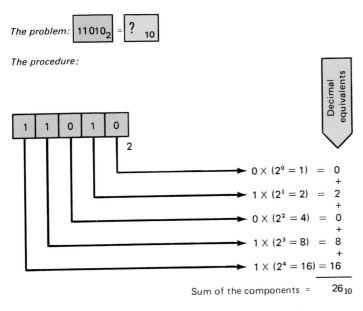

Decimal equivalents

$0 \times (2^0 = 1) = 0$
$+$
$1 \times (2^1 = 2) = 2$
$+$
$0 \times (2^2 = 4) = 0$
$+$
$1 \times (2^3 = 8) = 8$
$+$
$1 \times (2^4 = 16) = 16$

Sum of the components $= 26_{10}$

FIGURE B–7   Converting a Binary Number into Its Decimal Equivalent
Multiply the 1s in a binary number by their position values.

Binary to Decimal and Hexadecimal

To convert from *binary to decimal*, multiply the 1s in a binary number by their position values, then sum the products (see Figure B–7). In Figure B–7, for example, binary 11010 is converted into its decimal equivalent (26).

The easiest conversion is *binary to hex*. To convert binary to hex, simply begin with the 1s position on the right and segment the binary number into groups of four digits each (see Figure B–8). Refer to the equivalence table in Figure B–2, and assign each group of four binary digits a hex equivalent. Combine your result, and the conversion is complete.

Hexadecimal to Binary

To convert hex numbers into binary, perform the grouping procedure for converting binary into hex in reverse (see Figure B–8).

Hexadecimal to Decimal

Use the same procedure as that used for binary-to-decimal conversions (see Figure B–7) to convert *hex to decimal*. Figure B–9 demonstrates the conversion of a hex 3E7 into its decimal equivalent of 999.

FIGURE B–8   Converting a Binary Number into Its Hexadecimal Equivalent
Place the binary digits in groups of four, then convert the binary number directly into hexadecimal.

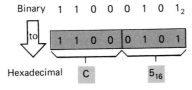

Binary   1 1 0 0 0 1 0 1_2

to

1 1 0 0   0 1 0 1

Hexadecimal   C 5_{16}

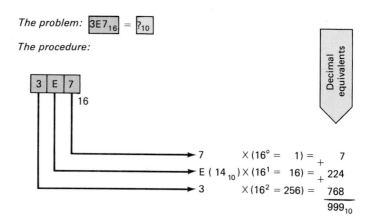

The problem: $3E7_{16}$ = $?_{10}$

The procedure:

FIGURE B–9   Converting a Hexadecimal Number into Its Decimal Equivalent
Multiply the digits in a hexadecimal number by their position values.

ARITHMETIC IN BINARY AND HEXADECIMAL

The essentials of decimal arithmetic operations have been drilled into us so that we do addition and subtraction almost by instinct. We do binary arithmetic, as well as that of other numbering systems, in the same way that we do decimal arithmetic. The only difference is that we have fewer (binary) or more (hexadecimal) digits to use. Figure B–10 illustrates and compares addition and subtraction in decimal with that in binary and hex. Notice in Figure B–10 that you carry to and borrow from adjacent positions, just as you do in decimal arithmetic.

SELF-TEST (by section)

1. The hex numbering system has a base of _____, and the binary numbering system has a base of _____.

2. The value of a particular digit in a number is determined by its relative position in a sequence of digits. (T/F)

FIGURE B–10   Binary, Decimal, and Hexadecimal Arithmetic Comparison
As you can see, the only difference in doing arithmetic in the various numbering systems is the number of digits used.

	Binary	Decimal	Hexadecimal
Addition	1111100 + 10010 ——— 10001110	124 + 18 ——— 142	7C + 12 ——— 8E
Subtraction	1111100 − 10010 ——— 1101010	124 − 18 ——— 106	7C − 12 ——— 6A

3. A single hexadecimal digit can represent how many binary digits: (a) two, (b) three, or (c) four?

4. The bases of the binary and decimal numbering systems are multiples of 2. (T/F)

5. The binary equivalent of a decimal 255 is _____.

6. The binary equivalent of a hexadecimal 1C is _____.

7. The decimal equivalent of a hexadecimal 1B6 is _____.

8. The hexadecimal equivalent of a decimal 129 is _____.

9. The decimal equivalent of a binary 110101 is _____.

10. The hexadecimal equivalent of a binary 1001 is _____.

11. The binary equivalent of a decimal 28 is _____.

12. The binary equivalent of a hexadecimal 35 is _____.

13. The decimal equivalent of a hexadecimal 7 is _____.

14. The hexadecimal equivalent of a decimal 49 is _____.

15. The decimal equivalent of a binary 110110110 is _____.

16. The hexadecimal equivalent of a binary 1110 is _____.

17. The result of $101_2 + 11_2$ is _____ (in binary).

18. The result of $A1_{16} + BC_{16} + 10_{16}$ is _____ (in hexadecimal).

19. The result of $60_{10} + F1_{16}$ 1001001_2 is _____ (in decimal).

20. The result of $11_2 + 27_8 + 93_{10} - B_{16}$ is _____ (in decimal).

Self-test answers   **1.** 16, 2. **2.** T. **3.** 4. **4.** F. **5.** 11111111. **6.** 11100. **7.** 438. **8.** 81. **9.** 53. **10.** 9. **11.** 11100. **12.** 110101. **13.** 7. **14.** 31. **15.** 438. **16.** E. **17.** 1000_2. **18.** $16D_{16}$. **19.** 228_{10}. **20.** 108_{10}.

C

Using
a Microcomputer

- ▶ Interacting with a Personal Computer
- ▶ User-Friendly Software
- ▶ Care and Maintenance of a Micro

This appendix prepares you for using microcomputers and microcomputer software. It does so by presenting those concepts and procedures universally applicable to most microcomputers and virtually all micro software. In the sections that follow you will learn about the keyboard, menus, macros, and much more.

INTERACTING WITH A PERSONAL COMPUTER

To interact effectively with a personal computer, you need to be knowledgeable in four areas:

1. The operation of microcomputer hardware (such as the keyboard)
2. General microcomputer software concepts (for example, windows and scrolling)
3. The operating system (the program that resides in RAM and controls the execution of all other software, the most popular being MS-DOS, Macintosh DOS, OS/2, and UNIX)
4. The specific applications programs you are using (for example, the electronic spreadsheet program Lotus 1-2-3)

The first three areas of understanding are prerequisites to the fourth; that is, you will need a working knowledge of micro hardware, software concepts, and the operating system before you can make effective use of applications programs like dBASE IV (a data management program), WordPerfect (a word processing program), or any of the thousands of micro software packages. The first two areas of knowledge are discussed in this appendix. The third area, operating systems (MS-DOS), is discussed in Appendix D, "MS-DOS Tutorial and Exercises." Popular applications software for micros, the fourth area of knowledge, is discussed in Appendix E, "WordPerfect Tutorial and Exercises"; Appendix F, "Lotus 1-2-3 Tutorial and Exercises"; and Appendix G, "dBASE III Plus Tutorial and Exercises."

Micros throughout this engineering company provide engineers with design and computational capabilities. However, before they can use their systems, they must load DOS to RAM.

Getting Started

Once all the micro components have been connected to the processor unit, the operating system has been installed, and the various components are connected to an electrical power source, you are ready to begin processing. Micros are similar to copy machines, toasters, and other electrical devices: You must activate them with electrical power. If you have a micro with a permanently installed hard disk, all you have to do is turn on the computer and, perhaps, the monitor and printer. After a short period, a beep signals the end of the *system check*, and the operating system is loaded automatically from disk to RAM. If your micro does not have a hard disk and is configured with one or two diskette drives, you must insert the diskette containing the operating system software before turning on the system.

Entering Commands and Data

Micros can be very picky. A personal computer is responsive to your commands, but it does *exactly* what you tell it to do—no more, no less. If you do something wrong, it tells you and then gives you another chance.

Whether entering an operating system command or an applications program command, you must be explicit. For example, if you wish to copy a word processing document file from one disk to another, you cannot just enter

"copy", or even "copy MYFILE". You must enter the command that tells the micro to copy MYFILE from Disk A to Disk B (for example in MS-DOS, "copy a:myfile b:"). If you omit necessary information in a command or the format of the command is incorrect, an error message will be displayed and/or an on-screen prompt will request that you reenter the command correctly.

Micros are not always so picky. You can enter DOS commands and filenames as either uppercase or lowercase characters. For example, the system interprets the command "copy a:myfile b:" and "COPY A:MYFILE B:" to be the same command. Some software packages do not distinguish between uppercase and lowercase *commands*; however, all software packages do make the distinction between uppercase and lowercase entries for *keyed-in data* (for example, an employee's last name).

The Keyboard

A microcomputer's *keyboard* is normally its primary input and control device. You enter data and issue commands via the keyboard. Besides the standard typewriter keyboard, most micro keyboards have **function keys**, also called **soft keys** (see Figure C–1). When pressed, these function keys trigger the execution of software, thus the name "soft key." For example, pressing one function key might call up a *menu* of possible activities that can be performed. Another function key might cause a word processing document to be printed. Some keyboards have permanently labeled function keys: COPY, FIND, SAVE, and so on. Others are numbered and assigned different functions for different software packages. The software packages usually are distributed with **keyboard templates** that designate which commands are assigned to which function keys. For example, HELP is often assigned to F1, or Function Key 1. The templates usually are designed to fit over the keyboard or be attached with an adhesive.

FIGURE C–1   A Microcomputer Keyboard
This is a representative microcomputer keyboard being configured with the latest IBM-compatible micros. In the figure, the alphanumeric characters follow the commonly used QWERTY layout. The positioning of the function keys, cursor-control keys, and the 10-key pad may vary substantially from keyboard to keyboard. On earlier versions of IBM-PC–compatible keyboards, the 10 function keys were aligned in two columns on the left end.

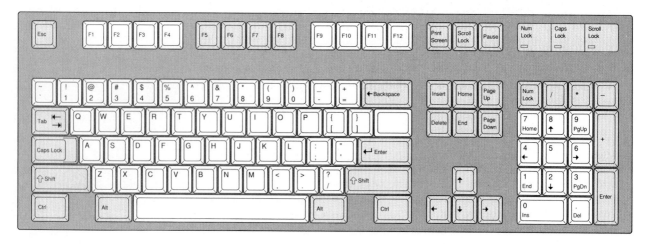

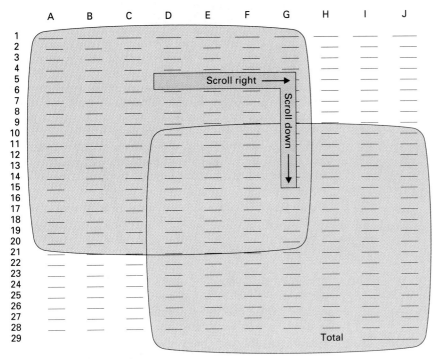

FIGURE C–2   Scrolling

When an electronic spreadsheet does not fit on a single screen, you can scroll horizontally (to the right as shown in the figure) and vertically (down in the figure) to view other portions of the electronic spreadsheet.

Most keyboards are equipped with a *10-key pad* and **cursor-control keys** (see Figure C–1). The 10-key pad permits rapid numeric data entry. It is normally positioned to the right of the standard alphanumeric keyboard. The cursor-control keys, or "arrow" keys, allow you to move the text cursor up and down (usually a line at a time) and left and right (usually a character at a time). The text cursor always indicates the location of the next keyed-in character on the screen. To move the cursor rapidly about the screen, simply hold down the desired cursor-control key.

For many software packages, you can use the cursor-control keys to view parts of a document or worksheet that extend past the bottom, top, or sides of the screen. This is known as **scrolling**. Use the up and down cursor-control keys to *scroll vertically* and the left and right keys to *scroll horizontally*. For example, if you wish to scroll vertically through a word processing document, move the up or down cursor-control key to the edge of the current screen and continue to press the key to view more of the document, one line at a time. Figure C–2 illustrates vertical and horizontal scrolling.

In summary, there are three basic ways to enter a command on the keyboard:

- *Key in* the command using the alphanumeric portion of the keyboard.
- Press a *function key*.
- Use the *cursor-control keys* to select a *menu option* from the display of a menu. (Menus are discussed in detail in the next section.)

Other important keys common to most keyboards are the *Enter* or *Carriage return* (ENTER or RETURN), HOME, END, *Page up* and *Page down* (PGUP and PGDN), *Delete* (DEL), *Insert-overstrike toggle* (INS), *Backspace* (BKSP), *Escape* (ESC), SPACE, *Control* (CTRL), and *Alternate* (ALT) keys (see Figure C–1).

ENTER Normally the ENTER key is used to send keyed-in data or a selected command to RAM for processing. For example, when you want to enter data into an electronic spreadsheet, the characters you enter are displayed in an edit area until you press ENTER, also called the *carriage return*, or RETURN. When you press ENTER, the data are displayed in the appropriate area in the spreadsheet. When you highlight a menu option in a software package with a cursor-control key, press ENTER to select that option. Like most of the special keys, ENTER has other meanings, depending on the type of software package you are using. In word processing, for example, you would designate the end of a paragraph by pressing the ENTER key.

HOME Pressing the HOME key results in different actions for different packages, but often the cursor is moved to the beginning of a work area (the beginning of the screen or document in word processing, the upper lefthand corner of the spreadsheet, or the first record in a data base).

END With most software packages, press END to move the cursor to the end of the work area (the end of the screen or document in word processing, the lower right corner of the spreadsheet, or the last record in a data base).

PGUP, PGDN Press PGUP (*page up*, or previous) and PGDN (*page down*, or next) to vertically scroll *a page (screen) at a time* to see parts of the document or spreadsheet that extend past the top or bottom of the screen, respectively. PGUP and PGDN are also used to position the cursor at the previous and next record when using database software.

DEL Press DEL to *delete* the character at the cursor position.

INS Press INS to **toggle** (switch) between the two modes of entering data and text—*insert* and *replace*. Both modes are discussed and illustrated in the word processing discussion in Chapter 7, "Productivity Software: Word Processing and Desktop Publishing." The term *toggle* is used to describe the action of pressing a single key to alternate between two or more modes of operation (insert and replace), functions (underline on or underline off), or operational specifications (for type of database field: character, numeric, date, memo).

BKSP Press the BKSP, or *backspace*, key to move the cursor one position to the left and delete the character in that position.

ESC The ESC, or *escape*, key may have many functions, depending on the software package, but in most situations you can press the ESC key to negate the current command.

SPACE Press the SPACE bar at the bottom of the keyboard to key in a space at the cursor position.

CTRL, ALT The CTRL, or *control*, and ALT, or *alternate*, keys are used in conjunction with another key to expand the functionality of the keyboard. You hold down a CTRL or ALT key to give another key new meaning. For example, on some word processing systems you press HOME to move the cursor to the top left corner of the screen. When you press CTRL and HOME together, the cursor is positioned at the beginning of the document.

Each keystroke you enter is sent first to an intermediate *keystroke buffer* that can save from 15 to hundreds of keystrokes. Under normal processing conditions, the keystroke is sent immediately from the buffer to the processor; however, in many instances you may have to wait for processing to finish (such as during a disk read operation). When this happens, you can key ahead. For example, if you know that the next prompt to be displayed is "Enter filename:" you can enter the desired filename in anticipation of the prompt. When the prompt appears, the filename you entered is loaded from the keystroke buffer and displayed after the prompt. Judicious use of the keystroke buffer can make your interaction with micro software packages much more efficient.

The Mouse

Another device used for input and control is the *mouse* (introduced in Chapter 4, "Input/Output Devices). The hand-held mouse is connected to the computer by an electrical cable (the mouse's "tail") and the mouse is rolled over a desktop to move the graphics cursor, often an arrow or crosshair. The mouse is used for quick positioning of the graphics cursor over the desired menu item or a graphic image, called an **icon** (for example, a graphic rendering of a file cabinet or a diskette). Buttons on the mouse are activated to select a menu item or icon, or to perform certain tasks such as moving blocks of data from one part of the screen to another. The mouse also permits the random cursor movements needed for the user to "draw" lines and create images on the screen. When using a paint software program, you press and hold a mouse button to *drag* the graphics cursor across the screen and create the image.

The keyboard is our primary means of entering data into a computer system. Another input device, called the mouse (under the user's right hand), is rolled across the desktop to move the graphics cursor quickly about the screen.

Issuing Commands to Micro Software Packages

You can interact with software packages, such as electronic spreadsheet and database, at several different levels of sophistication: the *menu level*, the *macro level*, and the *programming level*. These three levels of command interaction are discussed in the following sections.

Menus

The hierarchy of menus   When using micro applications software, you issue commands and initiate operations by selecting activities to be performed from a hierarchy of **menus**. These hierarchies are sometimes called *menu trees* (see Figure C–3). When you select an item from the **main menu**, you are often presented with another menu of activities, and so on. Depending on the items you select, you may progress through as few as one and as many as eight levels of menus before processing is initiated for the desired activity.

Let's use presentation graphics software to illustrate how you might use a hierarchy of menus. One of the options on the main menu of a graphics software package might be "Type of graph." If you select this option, you are presented with another menu and an opportunity to choose one of three types of graphs.

Bar   Pie   Line

If you select *Bar* graph, another menu lets you choose whether you wish to create a new one, revise an existing one, or view an existing one.

Create   Revise   View

FIGURE C–3   A Hierarchy of Menus

This figure illustrates how a user of Lotus 1-2-3, a popular electronic spreadsheet program, progresses through a hierarchy of menus to format all numeric entries to a currency format with two decimal places (for example, the entry 1234.56 would be displayed as $1,234.56). Selecting the "Worksheet" option causes a display of the second-level menu. The "Global" option indicates that further menu options apply to all applicable spreadsheet entries. At the third and fourth levels, the user selects the "Format" and "Currency" options. Upon selecting the "Currency" option, the user is prompted to enter the desired number of decimal places.

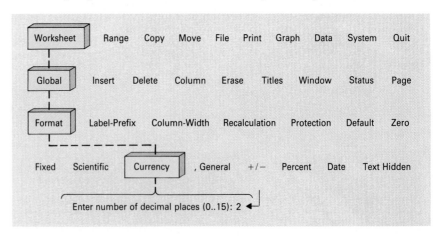

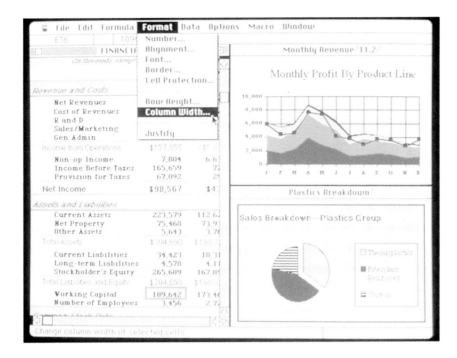

The main menu for this spreadsheet program is a bar menu at the top of the screen. The options are file, edit, formula, format, data, options, macro, and window. The pull-down menu in the display results from the user selecting the format option. The balance sheet and the two graphs are displayed in windows.

If you select *Create*, more menus are presented that permit you to describe the graph (using labels) and to identify what data are to be graphed.

Types of menus   A menu can appear as a **bar menu** in the *user interface* portion of the display, a **pull-down menu**, or a **pop-up menu**. The user interface is from one to six lines at the bottom and/or top of the screen. The menu options in a bar menu are displayed across the screen. To select an item in a bar menu, use the left and right cursor-control keys to highlight the desired menu option, and press ENTER.

The result of a menu selection from a bar menu at the top of the screen is often a pull-down menu. The subordinate menu is "pulled-down" from the selected menu option and displayed as a vertical list of menu options. The entire menu is shown in a **window** directly under the selected menu option and over whatever is currently on the screen. A window is a rectangular display temporarily superimposed over whatever is currently on the screen. Use the up and down cursor-control keys to highlight the desired menu option, and press ENTER to select it.

Like the pull-down menu, the pop-up menu is superimposed on the current screen in a window. A pop-up menu can be called up in a variety of ways, including by using function keys or as the result of a selection from a higher level pop-up menu.

Defaults   As you progress through a series of menus, you are eventually asked to enter the specifications for data to be graphed (graphics software), the size of the output paper (word processing software), and so on. As a convenience to the user, many of the specification options are already filled in for common situations. For example, word processing packages set output document size at $8\frac{1}{2}$ by 11 inches. If the user is satisfied with these **default options**, no further specifications are required. The user can easily revise the default options to accommodate less common situations. So, to print a document on legal-sized paper, the default paper length of 11 inches would have to be revised to 14 inches.

Menu summary   During any given point in a work session, the options available to the user of a micro software tool are displayed somewhere on the screen. For example, in word processing, the instructions for calling up the main menu or a help screen are prominently displayed above or below the document work area. If you are ever confused about what to do next, the options are usually displayed on the current screen.

Macros and Programming.   At the menu level of command interaction, you are initiating individual commands. At the macro and programming levels of interaction, you can string together commands and even introduce logic operations.

A handy feature available with most micro software packages is the **macro**. A macro is a sequence of frequently used operations or keystrokes that can be recalled as you need them. You create a macro by entering the sequence of operations or keystrokes and storing them on disk for later recall. To *invoke*, or execute, the macro, you either refer to it by name (perhaps in the text of a word processing file) or enter the series of keystrokes that identify it (for example, ALT-D, CTRL-F4). Three common user-supplied macros in word processing could be the commands necessary to format the first-, second-, and third-level headings in a report. For example, the user might want the first-level heading to be centered, boldface, and followed by two spaces; the second level to be flush left, boldface, and followed by an indented paragraph; and the third level to be flush left, underlined, and followed on the same line by the beginning of the first paragraph. In electronic spreadsheets, macros are commonly used to produce graphs automatically from spreadsheet data.

Some software packages allow users the flexibility to do their own *programming*—that is, create logical sequences of instructions. For example, a database software program can be written that will retrieve records from a particular data base depending on preset criteria, process the data according to programmed instructions, and print out a report. The programming capability enables users to create microcomputer-based information systems for an endless number of applications, from payroll processing to inventory control. Programming concepts are discussed in Chapter 9.

USER-FRIENDLY SOFTWARE

Virtually all vendors of micro software tout their product as being **user-friendly**. Software is said to be user-friendly when someone with limited computer experience has little difficulty using the system. User-friendly software communicates easily understood words, phrases, and icons to the end user, thus simplifying his or her interaction with the computer system. A central focus of the design of any micro software package is user-friendliness.

Help Commands

A handy feature available on most software packages is the **help command**. When you find yourself in a corner, so to speak, you can press the HELP key, often assigned to a numbered function key, to get a more detailed explanation or instructions on how to proceed. In most micro software packages, the help commands are *context sensitive*—the explanation provided relates to what you were doing when you issued the help command. For example, if you were entering data into a data base, the explanation would address how to enter data. When you are finished reading the help information, the system returns you to your work at the same point you left it.

Windows

Windows allow users to "look through" several windows on a single display screen; however, you can manipulate text or data in only one window at a time. This is called the *current window*. Windows can overlap one another on the display screen. For example, some integrated software packages allow users to view a spreadsheet in one window, a bar graph in another window, and a word processing document in a third window. With windows, you can work the way you think and think the way you work. Several projects are at the tips of your fingers, and you can switch between them with relative ease.

You can perform work in one of several windows on a display screen, or you can **zoom** in on a particular window—that is, the window you select expands to fill the entire screen. Press a key and you can return to the multiwindow display. A multiwindow display permits you to see how a change in one window affects another window. For example, as you change the data in a spreadsheet, you can see how an accompanying pie graph is revised to reflect the new data.

You can even create **window panes**! As you might expect, a window is divided into panes so you can view several parts of the same window subarea

At many colleges, microcomputers are strategically located throughout campus so that students and professors can have ready access both to a wide variety of information and to the processing capability of a micro. These Apple Macintosh micros in the library are available on a first-come, first-serve basis. Micros are extremely durable. When users use common sense in their care and maintenance, micros can go for years without being repaired, even those in libraries and student laboratories.

at a time. For example, if you are writing a long report in a word processing window, you might wish to write the conclusions to the report in one window pane while viewing other portions of the report in another window pane.

CARE AND MAINTENANCE OF A MICRO

Micros, peripheral devices, and storage media are very reliable. Apply the dictates of common sense to their care and maintenance, and they will give you months, even years, of maintenance-free operation. A few helpful hints are listed below.

- Avoid excessive dust and extremes in temperature and humidity.
- Avoid frequent movement of desktop micros.
- Install a *surge protector* between the power source and the micro. Micros as well as other electronic devices can be seriously damaged by a sudden surge of power caused by such things as a bolt of lightning striking a power line.

A blank diskette, costing only a dollar or so, has a very modest value. But once you begin to use the diskette, its value, at least to you, increases greatly. Its value includes the many hours of work you have spent entering data, preparing spreadsheets, or writing programs. Such a valuable piece of property should be handled with care. The following are a few guidelines for handling $5\frac{1}{4}$-inch diskettes and $3\frac{1}{2}$-inch microdisks.

Do

- *Do* label each diskette, and use a soft-tipped pen on the label.
- *Do* cover the *write-protect notch* on all important diskettes intended for read-only use, such as the program diskettes for micro software packages. On microdisks, slide the *write-protect tab* to its open position.
- *Do* store diskettes in their envelopes so that the exposed surface is covered.
- *Do* store diskettes vertically or, if stored flat, place no more than 10 in a stack.
- *Do* store diskettes and microdisks at temperatures ranging from 50 to 125 degrees Fahrenheit.
- *Do* keep a backup of diskettes and microdisks containing important data and programs.
- *Do* remove diskettes and microdisks from disk drives before you turn off the computer.

Don't

- *Don't* fold, spindle, or mutilate diskettes.
- *Don't* force a diskette or microdisk into the disk drive. It should slip in with little or no resistance.
- *Don't* touch the diskette or microdisk surface.
- *Don't* place diskettes or microdisks near a magnetic field, such as magnetic paper-clip holders, tape demagnetizers, or electric motors.
- *Don't* expose diskettes or microdisks to direct sunlight for a prolonged period.
- *Don't* insert or remove a diskette or microdisk from a disk drive if the red "drive active" light is on.

SELF-TEST (by section)

1. Use the _____ for rapid numeric data entry.

2. When interacting with microcomputers, you must wait until one command is executed before keying in another. (T/F)

3. A sequence of frequently used operations or keystrokes that can be activated by the user is called a: (a) menu, (b) macro, or (c) program.

4. Use the _____ and _____ cursor-control keys to scroll vertically.

5. Pictographs, called _____, are often associated with user-friendly software.

6. Window panes enable users to view several parts of the same window subarea at a time. (T/F)

7. What do you do to expand a window to fill the entire screen: (a) zip, (b) zot, or (c) zoom?

8. You should cover the write-protect notch on a diskette on those disks that are intended for read-only use. (T/F)

9. A _____ is installed between the power source and the microcomputer to protect the micro from being damaged by a sudden surge of power.

Self-test answers   **1.** 10-key pad. **2.** F. **3.** b. **4.** up/down. **5.** icons. **6.** T. **7.** c. **8.** T. **9.** surge protector.

D

MS-DOS Tutorial and Exercises

- Variations in PC Configurations
- Files, Directories, and Paths
- Booting the System
- DOS Commands
- Backup: Better Safe Than Sorry

KEYSTROKE CONVENTIONS USED IN THE STEP-BY-STEP TUTORIALS

Boxed keystroke tutorials are interspersed throughout this MS-DOS appendix, Appendix E (WordPerfect), Appendix F (Lotus 1-2-3), and Appendix G (dBASE III Plus). These keystroke tutorials are designed to give you hands-on experience with DOS, WordPerfect, Lotus 1-2-3, and dBASE III Plus. The keystroke conventions are consistent with what you might find in the vendor-supplied documentation for a particular software package.

Standard Type, Boldface, Outlined Keys, and Italic

Portions of the keystroke tutorial displayed by the program are shown in standard type. User-entered data and text commands are shown in **boldface** type.

Enter new date (mm-dd-yy): **12-14-91** ↵

For the above, you would enter "12-14-91" in response to the prompt and press the ↵ or ENTER key.

Keystroke or keystroke combination commands are boxed. In-line instructions or clarifications that are not displayed on the screen in response to an input are shown in italics (such as *Yes*). Italicized instructions or clarifications that are not extensions of commands are in italics and enclosed in parentheses, for example (*15 times*).

[HOME]**/ W**orksheet **C**olumn **S**et-Width

Enter column width (1..240): → (*15 times*) ↵

For the above, you would press the HOME key, "/", "W", "C", "S", the right cursor-control key 15 times, and ↵.

Summary of Keystroke Conventions

KEYSTROKE(S)	ACTION
↵	Press ENTER, RETURN, CR (carriage return).
← → ↑ ↓	Press the left, right, up, or down cursor-control (arrow) key indicated.
[F1]	Press Function Key 1 (or the number indicated). Boxed keys refer to specific keys (F5, HOME, ESC).
/File **S**ave	Press "/", then "F", then "S". Clarifications and instructions displayed by the program are in standard print.
[ESC]**E**nd **Q**uit	Press escape (ESC), then "E", then "Q". Clarifications and instructions not displayed by the program are in italics.
[CTRL]-[PRTSC]	Press hyphenated keys simultaneously (press and hold CTRL, then press PRTSC).

Simply stated, you press only those characters that are in boldface type, the cursor-control keys, the ENTER key, and the boxed keys. All other characters are provided for clarification or explanation.

This tutorial focuses on the features of the MS-DOS operating system fundamental to the use and application of microcomputer productivity software. MS-DOS, often referred to as DOS (rhymes with *boss*) is the primary operating system for IBM-compatible PCs. General operating system concepts are discussed in Chapter 10, "Software Concepts and Data Management."

Interspersed throughout the discussion of MS-DOS are *step-by-step* tutorial boxes that lead you, *keystroke-by-keystroke*, through the execution of the most commonly used DOS commands. These tutorial boxes enable you to interact with the computer and actually do what is being discussed.

If you have not already done so, you should read and familiarize yourself with the material in Appendix C, "Using a Microcomputer."

VARIATIONS IN PC CONFIGURATIONS

Microcomputers can be configured with or without a hard disk. Virtually all micros will have at least one diskette or microdisk drive. Some have one of each. Except for a few laptop PCs, virtually all micros manufactured in recent years are configured with a hard disk. Therefore, *this tutorial and the productivity software tutorials in Appendices D, E, and F assume that you are using a hard-disk–based PC*. The DOS prompt (for you to enter a command) when you are logged into the hard disk is either "C>" or "C:\>". Typically, MS-DOS and the productivity software (for example, WordPerfect) are stored on the hard disk. In learning situations, students usually keep their personal data files on the interchangeable diskettes.

If you are using a diskette-based PC with only one diskette, MS-DOS, productivity software, and your data diskette must share Disk Drive A. Therefore, all DOS prompts will be A>. To use the tutorials in this book, simply read the C:\> prompts as an A> and insert the appropriate diskette (MS-DOS, productivity software, or data), as needed.

If you are using a diskette-based PC with two diskettes, let MS-DOS and your applications software share Disk Drive A. Use Disk Drive B for your data disk. To use the tutorials in this book, simply read the C:\> and the A:\> prompts as A> and B>, respectively. Insert the appropriate diskette (MS-DOS, productivity software, or data) in the appropriate disk drive (A or B), as needed.

FILES, DIRECTORIES, AND PATHS

One of the prerequisites to understanding DOS commands is an understanding of how DOS deals with files.

Naming Files

On a microcomputer, a **file** is related information that is stored on disk (from memory) or retrieved from a disk (to memory) as a unit. A file can be a program, data for an electronic spreadsheet, a database of names and addresses, the text of a report, or even a game. Each file is given a name, either by a user or someone else (for example, a software vendor). The name of a file includes:

- A *filename* of up to eight characters
- An optional *extension* of up to three characters.

The filename and extension are separated by a period (.). The extension identifies files with a certain application. For example, word processing packages often append the extension DOC (for document) to a user-supplied filename (such as LETTER.DOC). The extension appended to BASIC program filenames is BAS (PAYROLL.BAS). The following are legal filenames:

NAMEADDR.DB   SALES.WK1   A

These are not legal:

N+A.DB (+ . = / \ [ ] : | < > = ; , are not allowed)
FIRSTQUARTERSALES (more than eight characters)
.out (no filename)

Referencing Files

The *file specification* includes disk drive, the filename, and the extension. A file (e.g., SALES.WK1) is associated with a particular disk drive. Diskette drives are labeled A and B. The hard-disk drive is labeled C. One of the disk drives is designated to be the *active drive* (or default drive); that is, DOS commands you issue apply to the active drive unless you state otherwise in the command. The DOS prompt indicates which drive is the active drive (for example, for a DOS prompt of A:\>, the active drive is A). If the desired file (SALES.WK1) is on Drive A and the active drive is A, the drive specifier can be omitted. If the active drive is C (i.e., the DOS prompt is C:\>), and the desired file (SALES.WK1) is on Drive A, the entire file specification is needed to reference the file (for example, A:SALES.WK1).

Active Drive	File Reference
A:\>	SALES.WK1
C:\>	A:SALES.WK1

Directories and Subdirectories

A **directory** is simply a list of the names of the files that are stored in a named area on a hard disk or diskette. A disk can have any number of directories and subdirectories. The directory feature of DOS enables us to group related files in a directory. For example, we can create a directory into which we would store only word processing document files and another directory into which we would store only spreadsheet files.

It is not uncommon for a hard disk to contain hundreds of files in 20 or more directories. To make file management and inquiries easier, users organize their files into a hierarchy, or *tree*, of directories and **subdirectories**. At the highest level of the "upside-down tree" is the **root directory** (C:\ on a hard-drive–based system). All other directories are subordinate to the root directory. When you load DOS, the root directory is the *active directory*.

Consider the directory tree illustrated in Figure D–1. Two marketing managers, Ted and Amy, and their assistant, Dennis, share the same personal computer. To keep their programs and files separate, they established directories as shown in Figure D–1. They created the subdirectories \LOTUS and \WP to which they could assign subordinate subdirectories for their personal files. The subdirectory \LOTUS contains the software for LOTUS 1-2-3 and two subordinate directories for Ted's (\LOTUS\TED) and Amy's (\LOTUS\AMY) Lotus 1-2-3 data files (SALES.WK1, BOOKFILE.WK1, and so on). The subdirectory \WP contains the software for WordPerfect and three subordinate directories for Ted's (\WP\TED), Amy's (\WP\AMY), and Dennis's (\WP\Dennis) WordPerfect document and graphics files (MEMO.DOC, REPORT.TXT, FIGURE1.WPG, and so on).

The relationship between a directory at a higher level to one at a lower level is that of a *parent* to *child* or *children*. In Figure D–1, the root (C:\) is

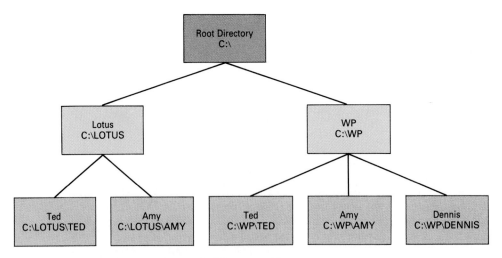

FIGURE D–1   Example Directory Tree
The first-level subdirectories \LOTUS and \WP have two and three second-level subdirectories, respectively.

the parent of the \LOTUS and \WP. The subdirectory \LOTUS is the parent of both \LOTUS\TED and \LOTUS\AMY. In the hierarchy, no directory has more than one parent. The root does not have a parent.

Files of any kind can be stored in the root directory or in any subdirectory. When working with files that are stored on a disk with a hierarchy of directories, you need to specify the **path**. The path is the logical route that DOS must follow in order to locate the specified file. For example, the path to Ted's SALES.WK1 file would be *from* the root directory (C:\) *to*

- The Lotus 1-2-3 subdirectory (C:\LOTUS) *to*
- Ted's subdirectory (C:\LOTUS\TED) *to*
- the specific file (C:\LOTUS\TED\SALES.WK1).

The filename is always the last entry in the path.

Wildcards

There are many times when you might wish to issue a DOS command that applies to several files. For such operations we use a **wildcard** character, the asterisk (*). When used in a filename.extension combination, the * is a generic reference to any combination of legal characters. A wildcard reference is applicable only to those files in the current or named directory. The following files are on the root directory (A:\>) on the diskette in the active drive (A).

SALES1Q.WK1	LETTER.WP	SALES3Q.WK1	MEMO2.WP
IDEA.OUT	SALES2Q.WK1	SALES4Q.WK1	THOUGHTS.OUT
NET.WK1	REPORT.WP	MEMO1.WP	NAMES.DB

Wildcard File Reference	Files Referenced			
*.WP	LETTER.WP	REPORT.WP	MEMO1.WP	MEMO2.WP
SALES*.WK1	SALES1Q.WK1	SALES2Q.WK1	SALES3Q.WK1	SALES4Q.WK1
.	all files in directory			

BOOTING THE SYSTEM

Before you can use a microcomputer, you must load DOS, or "boot the system." The procedure for booting the system on most micros is simply to load the operating system from disk storage into main memory.

- Turn on the monitor and the printer (if needed).
- Turn on the computer. (On a diskette-based system, insert the DOS disk in Disk Drive A [top or left drive], close the door, and turn on the computer).
- After a short period, a beep signals the end of the system check, and DOS is loaded from disk to RAM.
- At the "date" prompt, enter the date in the month (mm), day (dd), year (yy) format. At the "time" prompt, enter the time in the HOURS: MINUTES format.

  Note: Use the backspace key, as needed, to make corrections while entering data or commands.

Step 1   *DATE and TIME*

Enter new date (mm-dd-yy): **12-14-91** ↵
Enter new time: **13:35** ↵
C:\>

The entries are for December 14, 1991, and 1:35 p.m. To omit these entries tap ↵ after the prompts. Change or request the date and time at any time during a session by issuing the DATE and TIME commands (for example, C:\>DATE).

DOS Command Summary

Active drive	Change the active drive.	Step 2	DIR/W	Abbreviated directory listing.	Step 4
CD	Change current directory.	Step 6			
CLS	Clear the screen.	Step 8	DISKCOPY	Copy disk.	Step 15
CHKDSK	Check disk.	Step 16	ERASE	Delete file(s) (also DEL).	Step 11
COPY	Copy file(s).	Step 10	F3	Repeat previous DOS command.	Step 13
COPY CON	Copy from keyboard to disk.	Step 8	FORMAT	Format a disk.	Step 3
DATE	View or change date.	Step 1	MD	Make a directory.	Step 5
DEL	Delete file(s) (also ERASE).	Step 11	RD	Remove a directory.	Step 7
DIR	List contents of directory.	Step 4	REN	Rename file.	Step 12
DIR/P	Pause during directory listing.	Step 4	SHIFT-PRTSC	Print screen.	Step 14
			TIME	View or change time.	Step 1
			TYPE	Display file content.	Step 9
				Wildcard characters.	Step 10

DOS Keyboard Functions

DOS provides you with internal functions that can be invoked with a single keystroke or a keystroke combination.

■ SHIFT-PRTSC (*print screen*). Press SHIFT-PRTSC to print what is currently being displayed on the screen.

■ CTRL-PRTSC (*printer echo*). Press CTRL-PRTSC to begin echoing, or repeating, on the printer what is displayed on the screen. Press CTRL-PRTSC to discontinue printer-echo mode.

■ F1 and F3 (*repeat DOS command*). Press the F3 function key to invoke a command that causes the most recently entered DOS command to be repeated after the DOS prompt. Press F1 to repeat the most recently entered DOS command one character at a time.

■ F6 (*insert end-of-file marker*). Press the F6 func-

tion key to insert an end-of-file marker (^Z) at the end of a DOS-generated text file.

■ CTRL-S (*pause screen*). Press CTRL-S to stop the scrolling of the text, and press any key to continue. This pause-screen function is often used with the TYPE and DIR commands.

■ CTRL-BREAK (*break*). Press CTRL-BREAK to terminate a program prematurely, that is, prior to a normal and orderly finish.

■ CTRL-ALT-DEL (*restart DOS*). Press and hold down CTRL-ALT, then press DEL to reload DOS to memory. Use this keystroke combination when the computer is already on or when you are running an applications program that has no orderly *exit* (leaving the program) to DOS. If you are using a diskette-based system, make sure that the DOS disk is in Drive A.

Note: If your system is configured with a battery-powered clock, the date and time prompts may not appear after booting the system.

The C:\> prompt indicates that the system is ready to receive user commands.

*Note: These tutorials assume that your micro is configured to display the DOS prompt with a colon and a backslash. If your prompt is C>, enter "prompt pg" at the DOS prompt (that is, C> **prompt pg**).*

DOS COMMANDS

We use DOS *commands* to run our application programs, make systems inquiries, and manage files. This section contains a summary of some of the more frequently used commands.

DOS commands are of two types, *internal* and *external*. The internal commands are memory-resident (that is, they are stored in memory when you load DOS) and are therefore available to the user at any time. The external commands must be loaded to memory from the directory containing the DOS files.

Changing the Active Disk Drive

If you wish to change the active, or logged, drive, simply type the desired drive letter followed by a colon (:) at the DOS prompt. For example, if C is the active drive and you wish to make A the active drive, then do the following (make sure you have a diskette in Drive A):

Step 2   *Change the Active Drive*

   C:\> **a:** ↵
   A:\>

Now make Drive C the active drive again.

Step 2   *Change the Active Drive*   (continued)

   A:\> **c:** ↵
   C:\>

FORMAT: Preparing a Disk for Use

The *external* FORMAT command prepares a new disk for use. Before a disk can be used, it must be "formatted"; that is, the disk is initialized with the DOS recording format. If the computer you are using has a hard disk, it probably has been configured to accept external DOS commands from any directory, including the root directory (C:\). If this is not the case, your instructor will provide you with specific instructions.

   Note: Formatting an already used disk erases everything that was previously stored on it.

   Insert and FORMAT a blank disk in Drive A.

Step 3   *FORMAT a Disk*

   C:\> **format a:** ↵
   Insert new diskette for drive A:
   and press ENTER when ready . . . ↵

DOS should reply with a message that the disk is being formatted. Press ↵ if your version of DOS prompts you for a volume label. Answer "N" or no to the following prompt when it appears.

Step 3   *FORMAT a Disk*   (continued)

   Format another (Y/N)?**n** ↵
   C:\>

From now on, we'll refer to this diskette as the *data disk*. Use it for all keystroke tutorials in this appendix and in Appendices E, F, and G.

Creating, Changing, and Removing a Directory

DIR: Directory Command.   The *internal* DIR, or directory command, causes a list of all entries on the current directory to be displayed on the monitor, including the names of all files and subdirectories (indicated by a <DIR>).

The listing also includes such useful information as the size of each file (in bytes) and the number of bytes on the disk still available to the user.

Use the /p, or "pause," option (e.g., C:\> **dir/p**) if you wish to scroll through the long directory one screen at a time. Use the /w, or "wide," option (e.g., C:\> **dir/w**) if you want a list that includes only the names of the files and subdirectories on the current directory.

Note: Two types of slashes are used, one a backslash (\) and the other a forward slash (/).

Step 4   *DIRectory List*

C:\> **dir** ↵
C:\> **dir/p** ↵ (*Tap any key to advance to the next screen.*)
C:\> **dir/w** ↵

The actual list of files and subdirectories will vary markedly from computer to computer.

MD: Make Directory Command.   Create four subdirectories on your newly formatted data disk named WP (for WordPerfect files), LOTUS (for Lotus 1-2-3 files), DB (for dBASE III Plus files), and EXTRA. Use the DIR command to confirm that these subdirectories to the root directory A:\ have been created.

Step 5   *MD (Make Directory)*

C:\> **a:** ↵
A:\> **md\wp** ↵
A:\> **md\lotus** ↵
A:\> **md\db** ↵
A:\> **md\extra** ↵
A:\> **dir** ↵

CD: Change Directory Command.   Make EXTRA the current directory.

Step 6   *CD (Change Directory)*

A:\> **cd\extra** ↵
A:\EXTRA> ↵

Notice that the new prompt shows the entire path: root directory (A:\) and subdirectory (EXTRA).

RD: Remove Directory Command.   To remove a directory, it must be empty (that is, contain no files or subdirectories). Also, the directory to be removed cannot be the current directory. Use "cd\" to change to the root directory, then remove the directory named EXTRA. The backslash (\) is the symbol for the root directory.

Step 7   RD *(Remove Directory)*

A:\EXTRA> **cd** ↵

A:\> **rd\extra** ↵

A:\> **dir** ↵

Only three subdirectories are listed by the DIR command. Keep and use this data disk in the remaining DOS keystroke tutorials.

Working with DOS Files and Directories

COPY CON: Copy Input from Keyboard to Disk.   To complete the DOS tutorial, we'll need a file to manipulate. A "quick-and-dirty" way to create a file on disk is to use the COPY command to "copy" whatever you enter via the keyboard to a disk file. Use COPY to create a file called "FILE1.TXT" in the \WP subdirectory. The system-defined name for the keyboard (the source of the file) is CON: (for "console keyboard"). We'll use this form of the COPY command only to create this file. We'll look at more conventional uses of COPY later in the DOS tutorial.

Step 8   CLS *(Clear Screen)*; COPY CON

A:\> **cls** *(Clear the screen.)* ↵

A:\> **cd\wp** ↵

A:\WP> **copy con file1.txt** ↵

Key in the following sentence. Press ↵ after the word "created", the period, and the ^Z.

Step 8   CLS *(Clear Screen)*; COPY CON   *(continued)*

This one-sentence text file is created ↵

and manipulated in this DOS tutorial. ↵

[F6] *(F6 inserts an end-of-file marker)* ^Z ↵

A:\WP> **dir**

Whenever you create, copy, or delete files, confirm that you did what you wanted to do by issuing the DIR command. FILE1.TXT should be the only named file on the newly formatted disk. Figure D–2 shows the display of the DOS sequence in Step 8.

The dot (. <DIR>) and the double dot (.. <DIR>) entries at the first of the DIR listing are references to the root directory and the parent directory for A:\WP.

Use TYPE to display and examine the contents of FILE1.TXT. The TYPE command is handy when you want a quick preview of the contents of a particular text file.

FIGURE D–2   Display of the DOS Sequence in Step 8

The COPY CON: command enables text to be entered on the keyboard and stored on disk in a named file.

```
A:\> cd\wp

A:\WP> copy con: file1.txt
This one-sentence text file is created
and manipulated in this DOS tutorial.
^Z
        1 File(s) copied

A:\WP> dir

 Volume in drive A has no label
 Directory of  A:\WP

.            <DIR>      02-22-90   6:26a
..           <DIR>      02-22-90   6:26a
FILE1    TXT       79   03-01-90  11:00a
        3 File(s)     358400 bytes free

A:\WP>
```

> **Step 9**   *TYPE*
>
> A:\WP> **type file1.txt** ↵
> This one-sentence text file is created
> and manipulated in this DOS tutorial.

COPY: Copying Files.   The *internal* COPY-files command copies one or more files to the directory specified in the command. In the COPY command, the *source* file(s) specification is listed first and the *target* file(s) specification is listed second. If not specified, the current directory is assumed. If you omit the filename(s) in the target specification, the duplicate file(s) is given the same name as the source file(s).

Use COPY to create a duplicate copy of FILE1.TXT, called FILE2.TXT, on the same \WP subdirectory. Invoke the "wide" option on the directory command.

> **Step 10**   *COPY and Wildcard Characters*
>
> A:\WP> **copy file1.txt file2.txt** ↵
> A:\WP> **dir/w** ↵

Now use the * (asterisk) wildcard character to copy all files on the subdirectory \WP to the subdirectory \LOTUS and give these files the same name.

> **Step 10**   *COPY and Wildcard Characters*   *(continued)*
>
> A:\WP> **copy *.* \lotus** ↵

Now request a DIR listing for A:\LOTUS. Because you are logged into A:\WP, you must qualify your DIR request by specifying \LOTUS. Also, use the asterisk (*) wildcard character to request a listing of only those files in \LOTUS that begin with "file".

> **Step 10**   *COPY and Wildcard Characters*   *(continued)*
>
> A:\WP> **dir \lotus** ↵
> A:\WP> **cd\lotus** ↵
> A:\LOTUS> **dir file*.*** ↵

DEL or ERASE: Deleting Files.   You now have two directories with exactly the same content—two files named FILE1.TXT and FILE2.TXT. Use DEL or ERASE, which are identical commands, to delete FILE1.TXT from subdirectory A:\LOTUS. The *internal* DEL or ERASE command deletes the specified file(s) from disk storage.

Step 11   *DELete*

A:\LOTUS> **del file1.txt** ↵

A:\LOTUS> **dir** ↵

REN: Rename a File.   The *internal* REN command renames an existing file. Use REN to change the name of the remaining file on \LOTUS from FILE2.TXT to FILE3.TXT.

Step 12   *REName*

A:\LOTUS> **ren file2.txt file3.txt** ↵

Confirm that \LOTUS contains FILE3.TXT and \WP contains FILE1.TXT and FILE2.TXT. For the second DIR, tap F3 to repeat the last DOS command.

Step 13   *F3 (Repeat Previous DOS Command)*

A:\LOTUS> **cls** (*Clear the screen.*) ↵

A:\LOTUS> **dir** ↵

A:\LOTUS>   [F3]dir**/wp** ↵

Figure D–3 shows the display of the DOS sequence in Step 13. If your system includes a printer, print the display of the current screen.

Step 14   *SHIFT-PRTSC (Print Screen)*

[SHIFT]-[PRTSC]

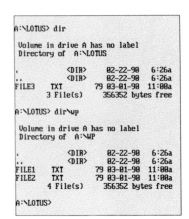

```
A:\LOTUS> dir

Volume in drive A has no label
Directory of  A:\LOTUS

.           <DIR>     02-22-90   6:26a
..          <DIR>     02-22-90   6:26a
FILE3   TXT        79 03-01-90  11:00a
        3 File(s)      356352 bytes free

A:\LOTUS> dir\wp

Volume in drive A has no label
Directory of  A:\WP

.           <DIR>     02-22-90   6:26a
..          <DIR>     02-22-90   6:26a
FILE1   TXT        79 03-01-90  11:00a
FILE2   TXT        79 03-01-90  11:00a
        4 File(s)      356352 bytes free

A:\LOTUS>
```

FIGURE D–3   Display of the DOS Sequence in Step 13
The DIR command lists the contents of the current DIR (\LOTUS) or the contents of a designated directory (\WP).

BACKUP: BETTER SAFE THAN SORRY

DISKCOPY: Copy a Diskette

The *external* DISKCOPY command makes a duplicate copy of a diskette. In the DISKCOPY command the source diskette is listed first and the target diskette is second. If the target diskette is a new disk, it is automatically formatted prior to the copy operation.

Use DISKCOPY to make a backup copy of your data disk. But first change to the DOS directory on the hard disk.

Step 15   *DISKCOPY*

A:\LOTUS> **cd** ↵

A:\> **c:** ↵

Issue the DISKCOPY command to copy the data disk (source diskette) in Drive A to a blank disk (target diskette), which will share Drive A with the source diskette.

Note: If your PC is configured with two diskette drives of the same type (both 5¼-inch or both 3½-inch), use "diskcopy a: b:" and place the source diskette in Drive A.

Step 15   DISKCOPY   (continued)

C:\> **diskcopy a: a:** ↵

Insert SOURCE diskette in drive A:

Press any key to continue . . . ↵

Insert TARGET diskette in drive A:

Press any key to continue . . . ↵

Copy another diskette (Y/N)?**n**

C:\>

CHKDSK: Check the Disk

The *external* CHKDSK command displays a status report of disk contents and storage space and of memory.

Step 16   CHKDSK *(Check Disk)*

C:\> **chkdsk a:** ↵

C:\>

Figure D–4 shows the display of the DOS sequence in Step 16.

Once you have completed the session, remove all diskettes and turn off the monitor, the printer (if needed), then the computer. Store your data disk and its backup in a safe place. You will be using them again if you plan to do the WordPerfect, Lotus 1-2-3, and/or dBASE III Plus tutorials in Appendices E, F, and G.

FIGURE D–4   Display of the DOS Sequence in Step 16
The CHKDSK command displays a status report of disk and memory. The three middle lines are not included on MS-DOS Version 3, X CHKDSK displays.

```
C:\> chkdsk a:

  362496 bytes total disk space
    3072 bytes in 3 directories
    3072 bytes in 3 user files
  356352 bytes available on disk

    1024 bytes in each allocation unit
     354 total allocation units on disk
     348 available allocation units on disk

  655360 total bytes memory
  439488 bytes free

C:\>
```

HANDS-ON EXERCISES

1. Complete Steps 1 through 7 of the keystroke tutorials in this appendix to format a floppy disk and create three subdirectories on the data disk.

2. Complete Steps 8 through 14 of the keystroke tutorials in this appendix to practice creating and manipulating files. Use the data disk from Exercise 1.

3. Complete Steps 15 and 16 of the keystroke tutorials in this appendix to copy the contents of the data disk from Exercise 2 to another disk.

4a. Format a new or blank disk. After formatting is complete, examine the directory on your work disk to confirm that no files exist on the disk. Print the screen image.

b. Clear the screen, then use the COPY CON command (Step 8) to create the following text file on your work disk.

This is a "hands-on exercise" text file.

Name the file THREE.TXT, and store it on your newly formatted work disk. Confirm that THREE.TXT is stored on your disk by displaying the contents of the file. Print the screen image and clear the screen.

c. Create a duplicate copy of THREE.TXT and call it TWO.TXT. Confirm that the copy was successful by examining the directory of your work disk.

d. Rename THREE.TXT as ONE.TXT. Confirm that only two files, TWO.TXT and THREE.TXT, are stored on the disk. Print the screen image.

5a. On the work disk from Exercise 2, create two subdirectories. Name them \ALPHA and \BETA.

b. Use the wildcard character, the asterisk (*), to copy ONE.TXT and TWO.TXT to both of the newly created directories.
(Hint: Use the F1 key to facilitate the keying of the second COPY command.)

c. Rename the ONE.TXT and TWO.TXT on \ALPHA to be THREE.TXT and FOUR.TXT. Rename the ONE.TXT and TWO.TXT on \BETA to be FIVE.TXT and SIX.TXT. Clear the screen and confirm that the copy operations were successful by examining the appropriate directories. Print the screen image.

d. Consolidate all six TXT files on the root directory (A:\>). Use a wildcard file reference to copy the four TXT files to the root directory.

e. Now delete the TXT files from the subdirectories \ALPHA and \BETA.

f. Remove the \BETA directory. Clear the screen and confirm that the root directory contains six TXT files and an empty \ALPHA directory. Print the screen image.

6a. On the work disk from Exercise 3, create two subdirectories for \ALPHA. Name them \GAMMA and \DELTA.

b. Identify all parent/child relationships among the directories on the work disk.

c. Copy ONE.TXT to \ALPHA\GAMMA as SEVEN.TXT, and copy TWO.TXT to \ALPHA\DELTA as EIGHT.TXT.

d. Clear the screen and confirm that \ALPHA and \GAMMA contain the TXT files. Print the screen image.

7a. You will need a blank disk for this exercise. Use the DISKCOPY command to make a backup of the work disk from Exercise 3.

b. With the printer on, activate the printer echo and display the directory for the backup diskette. Deactivate the printer echo.

c. What is the total capacity (in bytes) of the diskette in Drive A? How many bytes of disk storage are taken up by the six user files? What is the total capacity (in bytes) of your microcomputer's memory (RAM)?

d. What is the total capacity (in bytes) of the hard disk?

E

WordPerfect Tutorial and Exercises

WordPerfect Command Summary

Block indent	Step 24	Page break (hard)	Step 22
Boldfacing text	Step 14	Page up/down	Step 29
Cancel	Step 21	Previewing a document	Step 16
Centering text	Step 13	Printing a document	Step 17
Cursor movement	Step 5	Retrieving a document	Step 9
Deleting text	Step 11	Reveal codes	Step 25
Directory (default)	Step 8	Revising page margins	Step 3
Double-spacing	Step 26	Saving a document	Step 8
Enter	Step 4	Saving a revised document	Step 18
Entering text	Step 6	Search and replace	Step 12
Function key assignments	Step 2	Speller	Step 19
Help	Steps 2, 21	Switching documents	Step 28
Insert and typeover modes	Step 7	Tab	Step 4
Justification off	Step 27	Terminating a session	Step 18
Loading WordPerfect	Step 1	Thesaurus	Step 20
Marking text	Steps 10, 11	Typeover and insert modes	Step 7
Merging documents	Step 23	Underlining text	Step 15
Moving text	Step 10		

This appendix demonstrates commonly used features and functions of WordPerfect 5.1 by using interactive tutorials. WordPerfect, a product of WordPerfect Corporation, is the most widely used word processing software package. Once you have completed the step-by-step keystroke tutorials and exercises in this appendix, you will have acquired the WordPerfect skills needed to address most word processing tasks.

This WordPerfect tutorial assumes that you have read and understood the material in Appendix C, "Using the Microcomputer," and have a working knowledge of DOS (Appendix D, "MS-DOS Tutorial and Exercises"). Because these step-by-step tutorials parallel the conceptual coverage of word processing in Chapter 7, "Productivity Software: Word Processing and Desktop Publishing," it is recommended that you read the word processing portion (Section 7–2) of Chapter 7.

The keystroke conventions for the WordPerfect tutorial are consistent with those of the DOS tutorial in Appendix D. You might wish to review the box in Appendix D, "Keystroke Conventions Used in the Step-by-Step Tutorials."

BEGINNING A WORDPERFECT SESSION

Boot the system (see Appendix D, "Booting the System") and load WordPerfect to memory.

> ***Step 1***   *Loading WordPerfect*
>
> C:\> **wp** ↵

When the WordPerfect work screen appears, you will see a blank screen with the cursor in the upper lefthand corner. The cursor-position indicators are in the lower right-hand corner: Document 1 (Doc 1), Page 1 (Pg 1), Line 1 inch (Ln 1"), and Position 1 inch (Pos 1"). WordPerfect permits you to work with two documents (Doc 1 and Doc 2). The top margin and the page offset (left margin), are set automatically at one inch (Ln 1" and Pos 1", respectively).

Insert the data disk you created in Appendix D, "MS-DOS Tutorial and Exercises" in Drive A. (This disk should contain three subdirectories: \WP, \LOTUS, and \DB. If your data disk does not contain a \WP subdirectory, follow the procedures outlined in Step 5 of Appendix D to create the subdirectory.) You are now ready to begin your WordPerfect session.

CREATING AND FORMATTING A DOCUMENT _____

In this WordPerfect tutorial you will create and print the memo in Figure E–1. However, to do so, you will need to make a series of revisions of the draft memo in Figure E–2 to improve readability and appearance. By entering the draft memo and making the revisions, you will become familiar with WordPerfect's most commonly used features.

Before entering text, familiarize yourself with WordPerfect's function-key–based command structure. Most of the commands in WordPerfect are entered using the function keys alone or in combination with the CTRL, SHIFT, or ALT keys. Thus, each function key has four function assignments. WordPerfect supplies a handy template, for quick reference, that fits over the function keys. Tap F3 (for "help") or tap F3 twice to get an on-screen display of the function key assignments (see Figure E–3).

Step 2   *Help and Function Key Assignments*

[F3] [F3]

[SPACE]

FIGURE E–1   The Final Printed Memorandum
This memorandum is the end result of the tutorial in this appendix.

```
                        July 8, 1992

To:       Field Sales Staff
From:     Pat Kline, National Sales Manager
Subject:  June Sales Summary

     Good job! Sales for June are up 21% over the same month last
year. Our top performer for June, Phyllis Hill, set a new one-month
record--$78,167! Congratulations Phyllis.
     I've included a bar graph and a "Statistical Sales Summary."
The bar graph shows sales activity by region by product for June.
The summary should help you place your performance into
perspective.
     Our annual sales meeting is set at the Bayside Hotel and
Marina in San Diego during the first week in January. Plan your
schedule accordingly.

cc: P. Powell, President; V. Grant, VP Marketing
```

```
To:       Field Sales Staff
From:     Pat Kline, National Sales Manager
Subject:  June Sales Summary

     Good job! Sales for the month are up 21% over the same month
last year. Our top performer for the month, Phyllis Hill, set a new
one-month record--$78,167! Congratulations Phyllis.
     I've included a bar graph and a "Statistical Sales Summary."
The bar graph shows sales activity by region by product for the
month. The summary should help you place your performance into
perspective.
     Plan your schedule accordingly. The annual sales meeting is
tentatively scheduled at the Bayside Hotel in San Diego during the
first week in January.

cc: P. Powell, President; V. Grant, VP Marketing
```

FIGURE E–2   First-Draft Memorandum
This first-draft memo is used in this word processing tutorial to produce the printed memo of Figure E–1.

Change the top margin to 1.5 inches and accept the default settings for the line (justification, single spacing, tab settings, and so on); for the page (for example, bottom margin at one inch, no page numbering, and so on); and for the document.

FIGURE E–3   WordPerfect's Function Key Assignments
(a) This is WordPerfect's command template for keyboards with 10 function keys.
(b) This is WordPerfect's command template for enhanced keyboards (12 function keys).

(a)

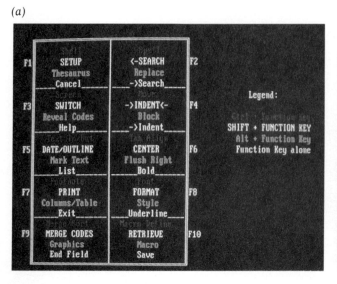

(b)

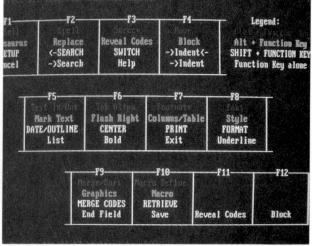

Step 3   *Revising Page Margins*

SHIFT - F8 *(format menu)*

page **m**argins

1.5 *(top margin)* ↵ *(4 times)*

Notice that WordPerfect gives you the option of selecting menu items by tapping a number (1, 2, 3, and so on) or by tapping a mnemonic, a representative letter (*L* for Line, P for Page, and so on). *Mnemonics* are used in the tutorial.

ENTERING AND ADDING TEXT

Cursor Movement

Enter the first three lines of the text of the memo (Figure E–2), and follow them with a blank line. If you wish, enter your name rather than Pat Kline's. To correct typographical errors, use the cursor-control keys along with the DEL and BKSP keys.

Step 4   *Tab and Enter*

To: TAB TAB **Field Sales Staff** ↵

From: TAB **Pat Kline, National Sales Manager** ↵

Subject: TAB **June Sales Summary** ↵ ↵

The second ENTER adds a blank line. The status line should indicate Ln 2.17", Pos 1".

Use the cursor-movement keys in combination with the HOME and CTRL keys to move about the screen. Familiarize yourself with these options.

Step 5   *Cursor Movement*

HOME HOME ↑. *(Move to beginning of document.)*

→ ↓. ← ↑.

HOME → *(Move to end of line.)*

HOME ← *(Move to beginning of line.)*

CTRL -→ CTRL -→ CTRL -→ CTRL -→ *(Move cursor to next word.)*

CTRL -← CTRL -← CTRL -← CTRL -← *(Move cursor to previous word.)*

HOME ↓. *(Move to bottom of screen.)*

HOME ↑. *(Move to top of screen.)*

HOME HOME ↓. *(Move to end of document.)*

Word Wrap

Key in the remainder of the memo in Figure E–2. Because the lines wrap automatically, *tap ENTER only at the end of the paragraph!* Use the TAB to indent the first line of each paragraph.

Step 6   *Entering Text*

   TAB **Good job! Sales for the month** . . . (*See text in Figure E–2.*) . . . **week in January.** ↵ ↵ (*Insert blank line.*)
cc: P. Powell, President; V. Grant, VP Marketing ↵

Insert and Typeover Modes

When WordPerfect is in insert mode, there is no indication on the work-screen status line, but in overstrike mode the word "Typeover" appears in the lower left corner of the screen. Toggle (switch) between insert mode and typeover mode with the INS (insert) key, and observe the indicator. Finish in typeover mode.

Step 7   *Insert and Typeover Modes*

   INS   INS   INS

Position the cursor at the "T" in the word "The" at the beginning of the last sentence of the last paragraph. In typeover mode, replace "The" with "Our". Toggle back to insert mode.

Step 7   *Insert and Typeover Modes*   (*continued*)

(*Position cursor in Ln 3.33" at the "T" in "The".*)
Our INS

In that same sentence, insert "and Marina" after "Hotel". If the text extends beyond the right margin, as in this instance, move the cursor (any direction) and the document will be reformatted to fit the defined margins.

Step 7   *Insert and Typeover Modes*   (*continued*)

(*Position cursor in Ln 3.5" at the "i" in "in".*)
and Marina / SPACE ↑

SAVING AND RETRIEVING A DOCUMENT

Change the default directory from C:\ to A:\WP on your data disk. Name and save "memo" to the WP\ directory on your data disk, then clear the screen before retrieving "memo".

Step 8   *Saving a Document*

[F5] (*List files.*)
Dir C:*.* = (*Type = to change default Dir.*)
New directory = C:\ **a:\wp** ↵
Dir A:\WP*.* ↵ (*Display all files in default directory.*)
[SPACE] (*Return to work screen.*)
[F10] (*Save.*)
Document to be saved: **memo** ↵
[F7] (*Exit.*)
Save Document? Yes (No) **n** (*Text was not modified.*)
Exit WP? No (Yes) **y**

Use one of the following keystroke sequences to retrieve "memo" from disk storage:

Step 9   *Retrieving a Document*

[F5] (*List files.*)
Dir A:\WP*.* ↵ (*Display all files in default directory.*)
(*Use arrow keys to highlight "memo" file.*)
retrieve

The following step illustrates an alternative procedure for retrieving a document. Skip it if you have already retrieved "memo" from disk storage.

Step 9 (alternative procedure)   *Retrieving a Document*

[SHIFT]-[F10] (*Retrieve a document from disk storage.*)
Document to be retrieved: **memo** ↵

The "memo" document now should be on the screen with its name listed in the lower left corner.

BLOCK OPERATIONS _____

WordPerfect permits you to move, copy, or delete a block of text. A block can be a word, a sentence, a paragraph, or any amount of contiguous text.

Marking, Moving, and Copying a Block of Text

Begin any block operation by *marking* the beginning and end of the desired text. Mark the first sentence of the last paragraph in the example, and move it to the end of the paragraph.

Step 10   *Marking and Moving Text*

(Position cursor in Ln 3.33" at the "P" in "Plan".)

`ALT`-`F4` *(Block on; notice the blinking "Block on" indicator.)*

(Position cursor in Ln 3.33" at the "O" in "Our".)

`CTRL`-`F4` *(Move.)*

Move: **b**lock *(Operation is applicable to marked block.)*

move *(The block is "cut" from the screen and placed in memory.)*

(Position cursor at the end of the paragraph after the "." in Ln 3.67".)

Move cursor: press Enter to retrieve ↵

`SPACE` *(Separate the sentences with a space.)*

Should you need to cancel the "Block on" indicator, tap ALT-F4 a second time or F1 (cancel).

If the block you wish to mark is a sentence, paragraph, or page, you can mark it quickly by placing the cursor anywhere in the text to be marked and choosing the appropriate option in the Move menu (CTRL-F4). Skip this alternative procedure if you have already moved the sentence.

Step 10 (alternative procedure)   *Marking and Moving Text*

(Position cursor anywhere in the first sentence of the last paragraph.)

`CTRL`-`F4` *(Move.)*

sentence **m**ove *(The block is "cut" and placed in memory.)*

(Position cursor at the end of the paragraph after the "." in Ln 3.67".)

↵   `SPACE`

To copy text, select the Copy option rather than the Move option. Text is copied in a manner similar to the Move operation except that the text block you select is copied to the location you designate. At the completion of a copy operation, two exact copies of the text block are present in the document.

Marking and Deleting a Block of Text

In the example, mark, then delete, the phrase "tentatively scheduled" in the last paragraph. We will eventually replace it with the word "set".

Step 11   *Marking and Deleting Text*

(Position cursor in Ln 3.33" at the first "t" in "tentatively".)

`ALT`-`F4` *(Block on; or, F12, if available.)*

(Position cursor in Ln 3.33" at the "a" in "at".)

`CTRL`-`F4` *(Move.)*

Move: **b**lock

delete

Use the DEL key to expedite a delete-block operation. Skip this alternative procedure if you have already deleted the phrase "tentatively scheduled".

Step 11 (alternative procedure)   *Marking and Deleting Text*

(Position cursor in Ln 3.33" at the first "t" in "tentatively".)

`ALT`-`F4` *(Block on.)*

(Position cursor in Ln 3.33" at the "a" in "at".)

`DEL`

Delete Block? No (Yes) **y**

When you have only a few words to delete, you might prefer the delete-word command.

Step 11 (alternative procedure)   *Deleting Text*

(Position cursor in Ln 3.33" on "tentatively".)

`CTRL`-`BKSP` *(Delete word at cursor position.)*   `CTRL`-`BKSP`

Now insert the word "set" after "is".

Step 11   *Marking and Deleting Text*   *(continued)*

(Position cursor in Ln 3.33" at the space before "at".)

set`SPACE` →

At this point your display should look like Figure E–4.

> Good job! Sales for the month are up 21% over the same month last year. Our top performer for the month, Phyllis Hill, set a new one-month record—$78,167! Congratulations Phyllis.
>   I've included a bar graph and a "Statistical Sales Summary." The bar graph shows sales activity by region by product for the month. The summary should help you place your performance into perspective.
>   Our annual sales meeting is set at the Bayside Hotel and Marina in San Diego during the first week in January. Plan your schedule accordingly.

FIGURE E–4   Display of Memo Through Step 11

SEARCH AND REPLACE

WordPerfect lets you search the text forward (F2) and backward (SHIFT-F2) for occurrences of a user-defined character string or pattern (for example, "the month"). You can also search for and replace (ALT-F2) a user-defined pattern (for example, "the month") with another user-defined pattern (such as "June"). The search-and-replace can be accomplished selectively (the user is given the option to replace at each occurrence) or globally (all occurrences are replaced).

Replace all occurrences of the phrase "the month" in the memo with the word "June". Use a global search-and-replace.

Step 12   *Search and Replace*

[HOME] [HOME] ↑ *(Position cursor at beginning of document.)*

[ALT]-[F2] *(Search-and-replace key.)*

w/Confirm? No (Yes) **n** *(Replace without confirmation.)*

-> Srch: **the month** [F2] *(Search forward.)*

Replace with: **June** [F2]

WordPerfect uses the F2 key, not the ENTER key, to signify the end of the pattern. This allows the user to include a hard carriage return in the search string, if needed.

CENTERING, BOLDFACING, AND UNDERLINING

Center a Line of Text

Add and center the date at the top of the memo. Separate the date and the memo with a blank line. Enter today's date if you wish.

> **Step 13**   *Centering Text*
>
> HOME HOME ↑ *(Position cursor at beginning of document.)*
> ↵ *(Insert a blank line at the top of the memo.)*
> ↑
> SHIFT - F6 *(Center.)*
> **July 8, 1992** ↵

To center an existing line, position the cursor at the beginning of the line and tap SHIFT-F6. The line should be terminated with a hard carriage return (ENTER).

Marking Text to Be Printed in Boldface Type

Mark "21%" in the first line of the body of the memo to be printed in boldface type.

> **Step 14**   *Boldfacing Text*
>
> *(Position cursor in Ln 2.5" at the "2" in "21%".)*
> ALT - F4 *(Block on.)*
> → *(3 times)*
> F6 *(bold)*

The "21%" is in some way highlighted to indicate bold (different color or intensity, reverse video).
  To mark text as boldface during entry, simply tap F6, enter the text to be boldfaced, then tap F6 again to signal the end of the boldface text.

Marking Text to Be Underlined When Printed

Underline the last sentence in the memo. ("Plan your schedule accordingly.").

> **Step 15**   *Underlining Text*
>
> *(Position cursor in Ln 3.83" at the "P" in "Plan".)*
> ALT - F4 *(Block on.)*
> ↓ *(Move cursor to end of next line.)*
> F8 *(underline)*

The sentence is in some way highlighted to indicate underline (different color or intensity, reverse video). On some high-resolution monitors, the text is actually underlined on the display.

To mark text to be underlined during entry, simply tap F8, enter the text to be underlined, then tap F8 again to signal the end of the underlined text.

PREVIEWING AND PRINTING A DOCUMENT

Previewing a Document

WordPerfect lets you see what a document will look like when it is printed. Let's look at the memo.

> ### Step 16   Previewing a Document
>
> `SHIFT`-`F7` (print menu)
>
> **view** document (Not available on all systems.)
> **1** (100% or actual size)
> **2** (200% or enlarged 2 times)
> **3** (full page)
> `SPACE` (Return to print menu.)
> `SPACE` (Return to work screen.)

Printing the Full Document

Turn on the printer and produce a hard copy of the memo.

> ### Step 17   Printing a Document
>
> `SHIFT`-`F7` (print menu)
>
> **full** document

Notice in the print menu you are given the option of printing the "Full Document" or a single "Page." To print a particular page of a multipage document, position the cursor in the desired page, then select the "Page" option in the print menu.

SAVING A REVISED DOCUMENT AND TERMINATING A SESSION

Save the memo to disk, end your WordPerfect session, and return to DOS. When exiting WordPerfect, you are prompted to save the document on which you are working. If any revisions have been made since the document was last saved, answer "Y" to the prompt; otherwise, the revisions will be lost.

Step 18   *Saving a Revised Document and Terminating a Session*

[F10] (*save*)

Document to be saved: A:\WP\MEMO ↵

Replace A:\WP\MEMO? No (Yes) **y** (*Text was modified.*)

[F7] (*exit*)

Save Document? Yes (No) **n** (*Text was not modified.*)

Exit WP? No (Yes) **y**

C:\>

USING THE SPELLING CHECKER

Run the WordPerfect Speller to ensure that all words in "memo" are spelled correctly. Begin a WordPerfect session (see Step 1), change the default directory (see Step 8), retrieve "memo" from your data disk (see Step 9), and run the Speller. In all likelihood there will be at least one spelling error, but in case there is not, change the spelling of "Sales" in the "To:" line (ln 1.83") to "Sals".

Step 19   *Speller*

[CTRL]-[F2] (*spell*)

document (*Check spelling in entire document.*)

WordPerfect highlights the first unrecognized word (probably "Sals"), suggests optional spellings, and displays a menu. Press the letter next to the correct spelling to replace "Sals" with "Sales".

Step 19   *Speller*   (*continued*)

e (*E. sales*)

At this point your display should look like Figure E–5.

As you spell-check the remainder of the document, you may need to select options from the Spell menu. The most commonly used options are:

1. **Skip Once**   Spell-checking continues; the Speller stops at the next occurrence of the word.
2. **Skip**   Spell-checking continues; the word is ignored for the rest of the document. Choose this option when "Bayside" and "Powell" are highlighted.
3. **Add (Word)**   The word is saved in the supplementary dictionary and spell-checking continues. (*Do not use this option at this time.*)
4. **Edit**   You can correct the spelling and then tap F7 (exit) to continue spell-checking.

Continue the procedure for each misspelled word until you reach the end of the document.

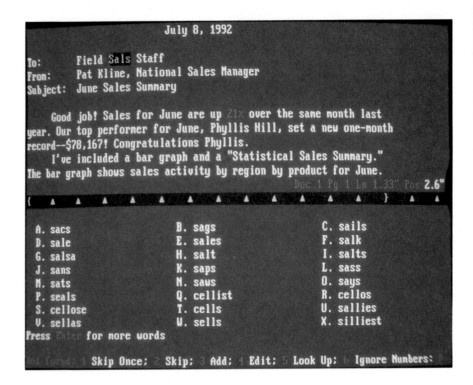

FIGURE E–5   The Spelling Checker
The WordPerfect Speller highlights "Sals", suggests optional spellings, and displays a menu.

USING THE THESAURUS

Let's assume that you are not satisfied with the word "top" in the first paragraph and want to examine some other possibilities. Use the WordPerfect Thesaurus feature to find another word for "top." The cursor must be on the desired word before you invoke the thesaurus feature.

> **Step 20**   *Thesaurus*
>
> *(Position cursor in Ln 2.67" on the word "top".)*
> `ALT`-`F1` *(thesaurus)*

The program reads the word at the cursor ("top") and suggests alternatives (synonyms). Choose any synonym from the adjectives list ("top (a)"). The "n," "a," "v," and "ant," indicators after "top" stand for noun, adjective, verb, and antonym, respectively. The following keystrokes replace "top" with "lead". Use the cursor-control keys to switch between columns and to scroll vertically.

Step 20 *Thesaurus*   (continued)

→ (*Move letters to column 2.*)
1 (*Replace word.*)
Press letter for word **g** (*Select the synonym "lead".*)
(*Save [see Step 8] and print [see Step 17] the revised memo.*)

OTHER HELPFUL WORDPERFECT FEATURES ————————

Several other frequently used features will prove helpful during WordPerfect sessions. If you are not already engaged in a WordPerfect session, load WordPerfect and retrieve the memo you created in Steps 1 through 18.

Help is just a keystroke away. Tap F3 (the help command) to get a brief explanation of any WordPerfect feature. After tapping F3, tap any letter to get an alphabetical list of features that begin with that letter. Or, after tapping F3, tap any function key (F1, Cancel) or key combination (CTRL-ENTER, page break) to get information about the use of the function key or key combination. Use the "help" facility and the following keystroke tutorials to introduce yourself to the following capabilities: Help, Cancel, Hard (user defined) page break, Merging documents, Block indent, Reveal codes, Double spacing, Justification off, Switching documents, and Page up/down. Read each screen before progressing to the next step.

Step 21 *Help and Cancel*

[F3] (*initial help screen*)

[F3] (*Display function key assignments.*)

[SPACE] (*Return to work screen.*)

[F3] (*initial help screen*)

[F1] (*Display information about the Cancel function.*)

[SPACE] (*Return to work screen.*)

Step 22 *Hard Page Break*

[F3] (*initial help screen*)

p (*Display features that begin with "p".*)

(*Locate the Page-break feature and observe Key Name: CTRL-ENTER.*)

[CTRL]-↵ (*Display information about the the Page-break feature.*)

[SPACE] (*Return to work screen.*)

[HOME] [HOME] ↓ (*Move to end of document.*)

[CTRL]-↵ (*Insert a hard page break.*)

Step 23   *Merging Documents*

[SHIFT]-[F10] (*Retrieve a document from disk storage.*)

Document to be Retrieved: **a:\wp\memo** ↵

(*"Memo" is merged with the document on the screen at the cursor position.*)

[HOME] [HOME]↓

Step 24   *Block Indent*

[F3] (*initial help screen*)

[SHIFT]-[F4] (*block indent help screen*)

[SPACE] (*Return to work screen.*)

(*Position cursor on Pg 2 Ln 2.5" Pos 1", or start of first paragraph.*)

[SHIFT]-[F4] (*Indent the first paragraph on both margins.*)

↓

Step 25   *Reveal Codes*

[F3] (*initial help screen*)

[ALT]-[F3] (*Reveal codes help screen; or, F11, if available.*)

[SPACE] (*Return to work screen.*)

[ALT]-[F3] (*Reveal codes.*)

(*Position cursor in Ln 2.5" of Pg 2 at the "G" in "Good".*)

← (*Highlight the "Tab" code to the left of "Good".*)

[DEL] (*Delete the "Tab" code.*)

[ALT]-[F3] (*Exit reveal codes.*)

(*Position cursor on Pg 2 Ln 3.17" Pos 1", or start of second paragraph.*)

↵ (*Separate the first and second paragraph with a blank line.*)

Step 26   *Double Spacing*

[F3] (*initial help screen*)

[SHIFT]-[F8] (*format help screen*)

line (*line format help screen*)

Line spacing (*line spacing help screen*)

[SPACE] (*Return to work screen.*)

(*Position cursor at start of page 2, Pg 2 Ln 1.5" Pos 1".*)

[SHIFT]-[F8] (*format*)

line

Line spacing

2 ↵ (*Double-space text from current cursor position.*)

[SPACE] [SPACE] (*Return to work screen.*)

Step 27   *Justification Off*

F3 (*initial help screen*)

SHIFT - F8 (*format help screen*)

line (*line format help screen*)

justification (*justification help screen*)

SPACE (*Return to work screen.*)

(*Position cursor at start of page 2, Pg 2 Ln 1.5" Pos 1".*)

SHIFT - F8 (*format*)

line

justification

Left (*Left justification only from current cursor position.*)

SPACE   SPACE (*Return to work screen.*)

(*The change in justification will be evident in Step 29.*)

Step 28   *Switching Documents*

F3 (*initial help screen*)

SHIFT - F3 (*switch help screen*)

SPACE (*Return to work screen.*)

SHIFT - F3 (*Switch to Document 2 screen; note cursor position
indicators.*)

SHIFT - F3 (*Switch to Document 1 screen; note cursor position
indicators.*)

Step 29   *Page Up/Down*

PGUP (*page up*)

SHIFT - F7 (*print menu*)

view document (*Not available on all systems.*)

1 (*100% or actual size*)

SPACE   SPACE (*Return to work screen.*)

PGDN (*page down*)

SHIFT - F7 (*print menu*)

view document

1 (*100% or actual size*)

3 (*full page*)

SPACE (*Return to print menu.*)

full document

F10 (*Save.*)

Document to be saved: **a:\wp\practice** ↵

> F7 (*Exit.*)
>
> Save Document? Yes (No) **n** (*Text was not modified.*)
> Exit WP? No (Yes) **y**

As you do the exercises and class assignments, refer to the step-by-step tutorials and use the Help facility liberally. Don't be afraid to experiment with the various features. With a little practice you will become a WordPerfect whiz and a lifelong advocate of word processing.

HANDS-ON EXERCISES

1. Complete Steps 1 through 18 of the keystroke tutorials in this appendix to create and print the memo of Figure E–1.

2. Complete Steps 19 and 20 of the keystroke tutorials in this appendix to run the Speller and Thesaurus on the memo created in Exercise 1.

3. Use the memo created in Exercise 2, and complete Steps 21 through 29 of the keystroke tutorials in this appendix to practice using a variety of helpful WordPerfect features, including merging documents, reveal codes, and switching documents.

4a. Enter the following text into a WordPerfect document:

    Too Much Paper!
    Last year, the Public Relations Department's paper budget was overrun by $350. Therefore, Public Relations personnel are requested to learn word processing. It is apparent that Public Relations has not taken full advantage of the word processing capabilities of its microcomputers.

   Turn justification off and accept the other default format options. Print the document.

   In the remaining portion of Exercise 4, make the changes cumulative; that is, revise whatever text is left after the previous revision. Each part of the exercise builds on the results of the previous part.

b. In insert mode, insert the word "all" before "Public" in the second sentence. In typeover mode, replace the lowercase letters in the title with capital letters. Print the document.

c. Center the title. Print the document.

d. At the end of the second sentence, add "by the end of the month". Observe how words at the end of the line wrap around to the next line. Print the document.

e. Use the Move command to move the second sentence to the end of the document. Print the document.

f. Designate the word "all" to be underlined and the title to be in boldface when printed. Print the document.

g. Place a hard page break at the end of the document and use the Copy command to produce another copy of the entire document just below the original. Print the document.

h. Use the search-and-replace command to replace all occurrences of "Public Relations" in the second document with "Research and Development". Revise $350 in the second document to be $525. Print the document.

i. Run the spell checker. Print the document. If you performed all the exercises, a–h, your printed output should be similar to the examples that follow.

TOO MUCH PAPER!

Last year, the Public Relations Department's paper budget was overrun by $350. It is apparent that Public Relations has not taken full advantage of the word processing capabilities of its microcomputers. Therefore, <u>all</u> Public Relations personnel are requested to learn word processing by the end of the month.

TOO MUCH PAPER!

Last year, the Research and Development Department's paper budget was overrun by $525. It is apparent that Research and Development has not taken full advantage of the word processing capabilities of its microcomputers. Therefore, <u>all</u> Research and Development personnel are requested to learn word processing by the end of the month.

j. Save the file in the \wp directory on your data disk.

5a. Design and compile a personal résumé using word processing software. Use appropriate word processing features to enhance the presentation of the résumé. At a minimum, include these elements: your name; address; telephone number; education (dates, school, degree); work history (dates, position title and brief description of work, employer, employer address); and a personal section (interests, special achievements, and so on).

b. Use the spell checker to check your résumé for misspelled words and typographical errors.

c. Print the résumé and save it as "resume" on your data disk.

6a. Write a cover letter to accompany the résumé you created in Exercise 5. Address the letter to Mrs. Peggy Peoples, Vice President of Personnel, Zimco Enterprises, P.O. Box 923481, Dallas, TX, 75208. In the letter, inform Mrs. Peoples of your availability, describe the type of work you are seeking, mention that your résumé is enclosed, and state that references will be supplied upon request.

b. Use a spell checker to check your cover letter for misspelled words and typographical errors.

c. Print the cover letter and save it as "letter" on your data disk.

F

Lotus 1-2-3 Tutorial and Exercises

This appendix demonstrates commonly used features and functions of Lotus 1-2-3, Version 2.2, by using interactive tutorials. Lotus 1-2-3, a product of Lotus Development Corporation, is the most widely used electronic spreadsheet software package. It is a high-performance integrated software package with electronic spreadsheet, presentation graphics, and data management capabilities. This Lotus 1-2-3 tutorial focuses on its spreadsheet and presentation graphics capabilities. Once you have completed the step-by-step keystroke tutorials and exercises in this appendix, you will have acquired the Lotus 1-2-3 skills needed to address common electronic spreadsheet tasks.

This Lotus 1-2-3 tutorial assumes you have read and understood the material in Appendix C, "Using the Microcomputer" and have a working knowledge of DOS (Appendix D, "MS-DOS Tutorial and Exercises"). Because these step-by-step tutorials parallel the conceptual coverage of electronic spreadsheet software in Chapter 8, "Productivity Software: Electronic Spreadsheet and Database," it is recommended that you read the electronic spreadsheet portion (Sections 8-1 and 8-2) of Chapter 8.

The keystroke conventions for the Lotus 1-2-3 tutorial are consistent with those of the DOS tutorial in Appendix D. You might wish to review the box opposite Appendix D, "Keystroke Conventions Used in the Step-by-Step Tutorials."

BEGINNING A LOTUS 1-2-3 SESSION

Boot the system (see Appendix D, "Booting the System"), and load Lotus 1-2-3 to memory. (You may need to change from the root directory [C:\] to the directory containing the Lotus 1-2-3 programs before loading Lotus 1-2-3. Ask your instructor.)

Step 1   *Loading Lotus 1-2-3*

C:\> **123** ↵

The Spreadsheet Display

The display includes a spreadsheet work area with numbered rows, lettered columns, and a user interface. A cell designates the intersection of a particular row and column (for example, A2 or G12). The user interface (control panel) consists of the three lines at the top of the screen.

- The first line contains status information for the current (highlighted) cell cursor (location, format, column width, location and contents) and the mode indicator (ready, point, menu, edit, wait, and so on).
- In the second line, commands are selected from a bar menu and data are edited. This line is blank until the user requests a display of the main menu.
- The third line displays a submenu or a brief description of a highlighted command in the second line.

Use your cursor-control keys to move the cell pointer around the screen and return it to A1, the home position.

Lotus 1-2-3 Command Summary

Bar graph	Step 19	Lotus Access system	Step 18
Clearing work area	Step 7	Naming a graph within a spreadsheet	Step 21
Clustered-bar graph	Step 23	Pie graph	Step 24
Copy operation	Steps 11, 17	Printing a spreadsheet	Step 14
Directory (set default)	Step 6	Printing/plotting a graph	Step 22
Displaying main menu	Step 2	Retrieving a spreadsheet file	Step 8
Editing (range and data)	Step 17	Saving a graph	Step 22
Entering numeric data	Step 9	Saving a spreadsheet file	Step 6
Entering repeating text	Step 16	Setting column widths	Step 3
Entering text/labels	Steps 4, 5	Stacked-bar graph	Step 23
Formatting spreadsheet	Step 13	Terminating a Lotus 1-2-3 session	Step 15
Formulas	Step 10	Using a graph within a spreadsheet	Step 24
Functions	Step 12	Viewing a graph	Step 20
Loading Lotus 1-2-3	Step 1		

Use the PGUP and PGDN keys to scroll horizontally and the cursor-movement keys to scroll vertically and horizontally.

The Lotus 1-2-3 Hierarchy of Menus

Display the main menu in the the user interface by pressing "/". To select a menu item, press the first letter of the desired menu item, or use the left or right cursor-control keys to highlight the desired menu item, then press ENTER. ESC erases the current menu.

> ### Step 2   *Displaying Main Menu*
>
> **/**
>
> [ESC]

Three function-key commands may prove helpful as you work through the following tutorials:

F1 is the context-sensitive Help key.
F2 permits editing the contents of the current cell.
F5 moves pointer to ("GoTo") a user-specified cell.

Insert your data disk in Drive A (the one prepared in the DOS tutorial in Appendix D). Your data disk should contain a \LOTUS subdirectory. You are now ready to begin your Lotus 1-2-3 session.

	A	B	C	D	E	F	G
1			MONTHLY SALES SUMMARY--JUNE				
2							
3			***** SALES SUMMARY BY REPRESENTATIVE *****				
4	NAME	REGION	XL-1	XL-2	MPX	TOTAL	COMMISSION
5	Rosco, R.	West	$18,750	$30,400	$12,000	$61,150	$3,639.25
6	Mann, G.	West	18,558	58,388	0	76,946	5,107.85
7	Cox, B.	Middle	25,900	38,903	280	65,083	4,158.91
8	Taylor, A.	Middle	15,570	32,005	730	48,305	3,125.90
9	Allen, H.	East	22,460	32,055	5,050	59,565	3,681.15
10	Hill, P.	East	28,067	24,660	25,440	78,167	4,287.49
11							
12	TOTALS		$129,305	$216,411	$43,500	$389,216	$24,000.55
13							
14	COMMISSION RATE		5.5%	7.0%	4.0%		

FIGURE F–1   Spreadsheet for a Monthly Sales Summary

FORMATTING THE COLUMN WIDTH

In the first portion of this Lotus 1-2-3 tutorial you will create and print the spreadsheet in Figure F–1. The planned spreadsheet template has seven columns. To make the most effective use of the display screen, revise the column widths from the default of 9 positions to 11, 6, and 11 positions for columns A, B, and G. First, change Column A to Width 11. HOME positions the pointer at A1. The command applies to the column containing the cell cursor.

Step 3   *Setting Column Widths*

HOME

*/*worksheet **c**olumn **s**et-*Width*
Enter column width (1..240): **11** ⏎

Change Column B to width 6. Use the cursor-control keys to move the pointer to B1, or use the F5 function key to go to (move pointer to) B1. (The latter is illustrated in the tutorial.)

Step 3   *Setting Column Widths*   *(continued)*

F5

Enter address to go to: **b1** ⏎
*/*worksheet **c**olumn **s**et-*Width*
Enter column width (1..240): **6** ⏎

Use the same procedure to set the column width of Column G to 11.

ENTERING TEXT DATA

An entry to a cell is classified as either *text*, *numeric*, or *formula*. In this tutorial we'll make all the text entries needed for the spreadsheet of Figure F–1. Backspace to correct entry errors. Press ENTER or a cursor-control key to enter the text to the work area. If you wish to correct an error or revise an entry in the work area, move the pointer to the desired cell and press F2 to change to edit mode. Edit the text in the edit portion of the user interface as you would edit text in a word processing document; that is, use the left and right cursor-control keys, the backspace key, and the delete key.

Enter the titles in C1 and B3.

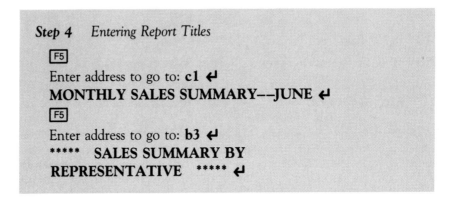

Step 4   *Entering Report Titles*

[F5]

Enter address to go to: **c1** ↵
MONTHLY SALES SUMMARY--JUNE ↵

[F5]

Enter address to go to: **b3** ↵
***** **SALES SUMMARY BY**
REPRESENTATIVE ***** ↵

Notice how the long entries in C1 and B3 spill over into empty cells.

A particular range is indicated by the addresses of the endpoint cells and separated by two periods. A range can be adjacent cells in a row (for example, A5..G5) or column (for example, A5..A10), a rectangular block of cells (for example, A5..B10), or a single cell (A5). Many electronic spreadsheet operations ask you to designate a range of cells.

In Lotus 1-2-3, text entries are normally left-justified within their respective columns. Prefacing a text entry with a double quote (") causes it to be right-justified, and prefacing it with a caret (^) causes it to be centered. Enter the column headings in Row 4. Center the entries in the range C4..G4. Enter the text data in Columns A and B.

Step 5   *Entering Remaining Text*

[F5]

Enter address to go to: **a4** ↵
NAME → **REGION** → **^XL-1** → **^XL-2** →
^MPX → **^TOTAL** → **^COMMISSION** ↵

[F5]

Enter address to go to: **a5** ↵
Rosco, R. ↓ **Mann, G.** ↓ **Cox, B.** ↓
Taylor, A. ↓ **Allen, H.** ↓ **Hill, P.** ↓ ↓
TOTALS ↓ ↓ **COMMISSION RATE** ↵

[F5]

Enter address to go to: **b5** ↵
West ↓ **West** ↓ **Middle** ↓
Middle ↓ **East** ↓ **East** ↵

At this point your spreadsheet should look like Figure F–1, but without the numeric data.

SAVING AND RETRIEVING A SPREADSHEET_____

Use the data disk you created in Appendix D, "MS-DOS Tutorial and Exercises." (This disk should contain three subdirectories: A:\WP, A:\LOTUS, and A:\DB. If your data disk does not contain an A:\LOTUS subdirectory, follow the procedures outlined in Step 5 of Appendix D to create the subdirectory.) Change the current directory to the \LOTUS subdirectory on your data disk, then save the current spreadsheet as "summary" to your data disk.

> **Step 6**   *Setting Default Directory and Save*
> **/file directory**
> Enter current directory: **a:\lotus** ↵
> **/file save**
> Enter name of file to save: A:\LOTUS**summary** ↵

A file extension *WK1* is added automatically by Lotus 1-2-3, making the filename SUMMARY.WK1.

If you had already saved "summary" to disk storage, you would have been presented with another menu warning that you will destroy the previous version of the file and replace it with the current version. In Lotus 1-2-3, the menu options are "Cancel" (cancel the Save operation), "Replace" (replace the existing file with a file containing the current spreadsheet), and "Backup" (save the current spreadsheet with a BAK extension). If you have saved "summary" previously, follow this procedure to save the updated version of the spreadsheet.

> **Step 6**   *Setting Default Directory and Save*   (continued)
> **/file save**
> Enter name of file to save: A:\LOTUS\SUMMARY.WK1 ↵
> **replace**

Now clear the work area before retrieving it.

> **Step 7**   *Clearing Work Area*
> **/worksheet erase**
> **yes**

Issue the following commands to retrieve your "summary" file and continue the tutorial.

Step 8   *Retrieving a Spreadsheet File*

/file retrieve

Name of file to retrieve: A:\LOTUS**summary** ↵

Lotus 1-2-3 assumes the WK1 extension. If you wish, you can use the left/right cursor-control keys to highlight the desired file, then tap ENTER to load the file.

ENTERING NUMERIC DATA

Continue the development of the spreadsheet template of Figure F–1 by entering the numeric data. Enter the numeric values in Columns C, D, and E for Rows 5 through 10 and Row 14. In Rows 5 through 10, enter only the number, not the comma or dollar sign. These will be formatted later. In Row 14, enter the values as .055, .07, and .04. These will be formatted to a percent format later. Formulas are entered in the next step.

Step 9   *Entering Numeric Data*

[F5]

Enter address to go to: **c5** ↵

18750 → **30400** → **12000** ↓ ← ←

18558 → **58388** → **0** ↓ ← ←

(*Use this procedure to complete the data entry for the range C7..E10.*)

[F5]

Enter address to go to: **c14** ↵

.055 → **.07** → **.04** ↵

Once you have entered the numeric data, your spreadsheet should appear as shown in Figure F–2.

ENTERING FORMULAS

Spreadsheet formulas are created by combining cell addresses with arithmetic operators: + (add), − (subtract), * (multiply), / (divide), ^ (raising to a power, or exponentiation). The formulas in the range F5..F10 (see Figure F–3) add sales for the three products for each salesperson. The formulas in the range G5..G10 (see Figure F–3) compute the commission for the salespeople, based on the commission rates listed in Row 14. In the commission formulas, sales-amount variables are represented by relative cell addresses (C5, D5, E5) and the commission rate variables are represented in absolute cell addresses ($C$14, $D$14, $E$14). The dollar signs ($), which preface both the column and row in an absolute cell address ($C$14), distinguish it from a relative cell address (C5). The relative cell address is based on its position relative to the cell containing the formula. If the content of a cell containing a formula is

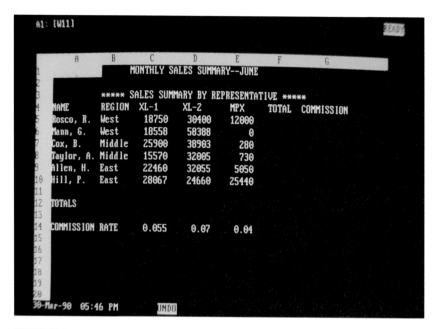

FIGURE F–2   Unformatted Spreadsheet of Figure F–1 without Formulas

copied to another cell, the relative cell addresses in the copied formula are revised to reflect their new position, but the absolute cell addresses are unchanged.

Add the calculation capability to the spreadsheet of Figure F–2. First, enter the formulas in F5 and G5.

Step 10   *Formulas*

[F5]

Enter address to go to: **f5** ↵

+c5+d5+e5 → **+c14*c5+d14*d5+e14*e5** ↵

Notice that the results, and not the formulas, are displayed in Cells F5 and G5. However, the formula is displayed on the status line. Verify that the formulas were entered correctly by comparing the results to the values displayed in Figure F–1.

FIGURE F–3   Actual Content of Formula Cells: Rows 1 through 14
This figure illustrates the actual content of the cells in Figure F–1 that contain formulas.

	A	B	C	D	E	F	G	H	I
1			MONTHLY SALES SUMMARY--JUNE						
2									
3			***** SALES SUMMARY BY REPRESENTATIVE *****						
4	NAME	REGION	XL-1	XL-2	MPX	TOTAL		COMMISSION	
5	Rosco, R.	West	$18,750	$30,400	$12,000	+C5+D5+E5	+$C$14*C5+$D$14*D5+$E$14*E5		
6	Mann, G.	West	18,558	58,388	0	+C6+D6+E6	+$C$14*C6+$D$14*D6+$E$14*E6		
7	Cox, B.	Middle	25,900	38,903	280	+C7+D7+E7	+$C$14*C7+$D$14*D7+$E$14*E7		
8	Taylor, A.	Middle	15,570	32,005	730	+C8+D8+E8	+$C$14*C8+$D$14*D8+$E$14*E8		
9	Allen, H.	East	22,460	32,055	5,050	+C9+D9+E9	+$C$14*C9+$D$14*D9+$E$14*E9		
10	Hill, P.	East	28,067	24,660	25,440	+C10+D10+E10	+$C$14*C10+$D$14*D10+$E$14*E10		
11									
12	TOTALS		@SUM(C5..C10)	@SUM(D5..D10)	@SUM(E5..E10)	@SUM(F5..F10)	@SUM(G5..G10)		
13									
14	COMMISSION RATE		5.5%	7.0%	4.0%				

Instead of entering the formulas for the range F6..G10, we can copy the formulas from F5 and G5 to other positions in their respective columns.

Step 11   *Copy Operation*

[F5]

Enter address to go to: **f5** ↵

/copy

Enter range to copy FROM: F5..F5 ↵

Enter range to copy TO: **f6..f10** ↵

[F5]

Enter address to go to: **g5** ↵

/copy

Enter range to copy FROM: G5..G5 ↵

Enter range to copy TO: **g6..g10** ↵

Separate the endpoints of the range with one period (C10.D10) or two (C10..D10). Move the pointer to F6 and G6; notice that the copied formulas apply to Row 6 and G. Mann.

USING PREDEFINED FUNCTIONS

Electronic spreadsheets offer users a wide variety of predefined operations called *functions*. These functions can be used to create formulas that perform mathematical, logical, statistical, financial, and character-string operations on spreadsheet data. To use a function, simply enter the desired function name (for example, SUM for "Compute the sum") and enter the *argument*. The argument, which is placed in parentheses, identifies the data to be operated on.

Use the predefined function SUM to calculate the totals in Row 12. Enter the formula in C12 as shown in Figure F–3. Preface functions with an @ symbol.

Step 12   *Functions*

[F5]

Enter address to go to: **c12** ↵

@sum(c5..c10) ↵

Copy C12 to the range D12..G12. Enter the "copy TO" range directly as illustrated above, or use the cursor-control keys in combination with the anchor (period). To do this, position the cell pointer at one of the endpoints of the range (for example, D12) and press the anchor. Move the pointer to the other endpoint (G12) and press ENTER.

Step 12   *Functions*   (*continued*)

/*copy*
Enter range to copy FROM: C12..C12 ↵
Enter range to copy TO: → D12. → → → ↵

FORMATTING THE CELL ENTRIES _____

Complete the spreadsheet template by formatting the cell entries to improve appearance and readability. Format the entries in C5..F12 as currency with commas and no decimal places. Format the entries in G5..G12 as currency with commas and two decimal places.

Step 13   *Formatting a Spreadsheet*

/*range* **format** **c**urrency
Enter number of decimal places (0..15): **0** ↵
Enter range to format: **c5..f12** ↵
/*range* **format** **c**urrency
Enter number of decimal places (0..15): **2** ↵
Enter range to format: **g5..g12** ↵

Reformat Rows 6 through 10 to remove the dollar sign.

Step 13   *Formatting a Spreadsheet*   (*continued*)

/*range* **format** **,**
Enter number of decimal places (0..15): **0** ↵
Enter range to format: **c6..f10** ↵
/*range* **format** **,**
Enter number of decimal places (0..15): **2** ↵
Enter range to format: **g6..g10** ↵

Format the amounts in Row 14 as a percentage with one decimal place.

Step 13   *Formatting a Spreadsheet*   (*continued*)

/*range* **format** **p**ercent
Enter number of decimal places (0..15): **1** ↵
Enter range to format: **c14..e14** ↵

The spreadsheet should look like that of Figure F–1.

PRINTING A SPREADSHEET AND
TERMINATING A SESSION

Define the range to be printed and print the current spreadsheet. Turn on the printer, adjust the paper, and reset the printer to the top of the page (*Align* in menu). *Go* prints the spreadsheet. *Page* advances the paper to the top of the next page.

> **Step 14**   *Printing a Spreadsheet*
>
> **/**print **p**rinter **r**ange **a1..g14** ↵
> **a**lign **g**o (*print spreadsheet.*)
> **p**age
> **q**uit (*to return to the spreadsheet*)

Do not exit Lotus 1-2-3 at this time if you intend to continue with the tutorial. If you wish to terminate your Lotus 1-2-3 session, save your spreadsheet to your data disk, then exit Lotus 1-2-3.

> **Step 15**   *Terminating a Lotus 1-2-3 Session*
>
> **/f**ile **s**ave
> Enter name of file to save: A:\LOTUS\SUMMARY.WK1 ↵
> **r**eplace
> **/q**uit **y**es (*Omit this line if you wish to continue.*)

EXTRACTING INFORMATION
FROM EXISTING SPREADSHEET DATA

The spreadsheet of Figure F–1 is typical in that its data provide the foundation for further analysis and more information. In Steps 16 and 17 we will use the sales data in Rows 5 through 10 to create a "Sales Summary by Region"

FIGURE F–4   Spreadsheet for a Monthly Sales Summary
A "Sales Summary by Region" is appended to the spreadsheet in Figure F–1.

	A	B	C	D	E	F	G
1			MONTHLY SALES SUMMARY--JUNE				
2							
3			***** SALES SUMMARY BY REPRESENTATIVE *****				
4	NAME	REGION	XL-1	XL-2	MPX	TOTAL	COMMISSION
5	Rosco, R.	West	$18,750	$30,400	$12,000	$61,150	$3,639.25
6	Mann, G.	West	18,558	58,388	0	76,946	5,107.85
7	Cox, B.	Middle	25,900	38,903	280	65,083	4,158.91
8	Taylor, A.	Middle	15,570	32,005	730	48,305	3,125.90
9	Allen, H.	East	22,460	32,055	5,050	59,565	3,681.15
10	Hill, P.	East	28,067	24,660	25,440	78,167	4,287.49
11							
12	TOTALS		$129,305	$216,411	$43,500	$389,216	$24,000.55
13							
14	COMMISSION RATE		5.5%	7.0%	4.0%		
15			==				
16			***** SALES SUMMARY BY REGION *****				
17		REGION	XL-1	XL-2	MPX	TOTAL	
18		West	$37,308	$88,788	$12,000	$138,096	
19		Middle	$41,470	$70,908	$1,010	$113,388	
20		East	$50,527	$56,715	$30,490	$137,732	

in Rows 15 through 20 (see Figure F–4). First, enter the repeating text (the row of =, or equal signs) to distinguish between the two summaries. Use a single backslash (\) before the text string that is repeated text (equals [=] in this example).

Step 16   *Entering Repeating Text*

F5

Enter address to go to: **a15** ↵

\= ↵

/copy

Enter range to copy FROM: A15..A15 ↵

Enter range to copy TO: → B15. → (5 *times*) ↵

Enter the text and formulas into the appropriate cells as shown in Figure F–5. Save keystrokes and time by copying the range B3..F9 to B16. Delete cells that are not applicable and edit the others as needed.

Step 17   *Copying and Editing a Range*

/copy

Enter range to copy FROM: **b3..f9** ↵

Enter range to copy TO: **b16** ↵

Because we need only one label for each region, delete Rows 19 and 20 (one "West" and one "Middle" row).

Step 17   *Copying and Editing a Range*   (continued)

F5

Enter address to go to: **b19** ↵

/worksheet **delete row** ↓ ↵

Edit the title to read "REGION".

FIGURE F–5   Actual Content of Formula Cells: Rows 15 through 20

This figure illustrates the actual content of the cells in Figure F–4 that contain formulas.

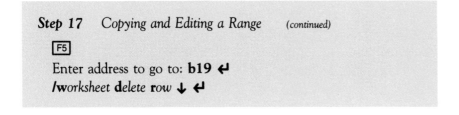

	A	B	C	D	E	F
15	===
16		***** SALES SUMMARY BY REGION *****
17		REGION	XL-1	XL-2	MPX	TOTAL
18		West	+C5+C6	+D5+D6	+E5+E6	+C18+D18+E18
19		Middle	+C7+C8	+D7+D8	+E7+E8	+C19+D19+E19
20		East	+C9+C10	+D9+D10	+E9+E10	+C20+D20+E20

> **Step 17**   *Copying and Editing a Range*   *(continued)*
>
> [F5]
>
> Enter address to go to: **b16** ↵
>
> [F2] *(Edit current cell.)*
>
> ← *(6 times)*   [BKSP] *(12 times to delete "PRESENTATIVE")*
>
> **GION** ↵

Erase the erroneous data in the range C18..E20.

> **Step 17**   *Copying and Editing a Range*   *(continued)*
>
> [F5]
>
> Enter address to go to: **c18** ↵
>
> */range erase*
>
> Enter range to erase: **c18..e20**

Enter the formulas as shown in Figure F–5 by entering those in Column C, then copying them to Columns D and E. Note that the relative formulas copied to the TOTAL column (F) were revised to reflect their new cell locations.

> **Step 17**   *Copying and Editing a Range*   *(continued)*
>
> [F5]
>
> Enter address to go to: **c18** ↵
>
> **+c5+c6** ↓ **+c7+c8** ↓ **+c9+c10** ↵
>
> */copy*
>
> Enter range to copy FROM: **c18..c20** ↵
>
> Enter range to copy TO: **d18..e20** ↵

The spreadsheet should look like that of Figure F–4. Save the spreadsheet and exit Lotus to DOS.

> **Step 17**   *Copying and Editing a Range*   *(continued)*
>
> */file save*
>
> Enter name of file to save: A:\LOTUS\SUMMARY.WK1 ↵
>
> *replace*
>
> */quit yes*

USING THE LOTUS 1-2-3 GRAPHICS CAPABILITY _____

The remainder of this Lotus 1-2-3 tutorial emphasizes the graphics capability. We will use the data in the "Sales Summary by Region" portion of the example spreadsheet (Figure F–4) to illustrate regional sales information in the form of bar, pie, and line graphs.

    Load Lotus 1-2-3; however, this time load it by using the Lotus Access system. The Access is a shell that permits access to other Lotus 1-2-3 programs, such as the PrintGraph program. (You may need to change from the root directory (C:\) to the directory containing the Lotus 1-2-3 programs before loading Lotus 1-2-3. Ask your instructor.)

> ### Step 18   Using the Lotus Access System
>
> C:\> **lotus** ↵
> *1-2-3 (load Lotus 1-2-3)*

Set the default directory to A:\LOTUS (see Step 6), and retrieve the "summary" spreadsheet (see Step 8).

PRODUCING A BAR GRAPH _____

Produce the bar graph illustrated in Figure F–6. Identify the data to be graphed and select type of graph to be "Bar".

> ### Step 19   Bar Graph
>
> */graph* **a**
> Enter first data range: **f18..f20** ↵
> *(in Graph menu)* **t**ype **b**ar

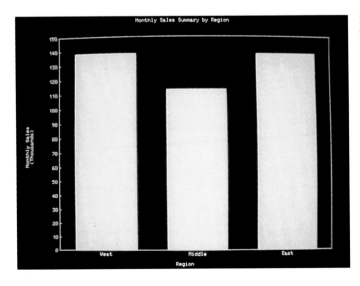

**FIGURE F–6
Bar Graph**

Add the main heading, labels for the x-axis (horizontal) and y-axis (vertical), and label the bars for each region.

Step 19   *Bar Graph*   *(continued)*

(in Graph menu) **o**ptions **t**itles **f**irst
Enter first line of graph title: **Monthly Sales Summary by Region** ↵
(in Graph/Options menu) **t**itles **x**-Axis
Enter x-axis title: **Region** ↵
(in Graph/Options menu) **t**itles **y**-Axis
Enter y-axis title: **Monthly Sales** ↵
quit *(to return to Graph menu)*
(in Graph menu) **x**
Enter x-axis range: **b18..b20** ↵

Display the bar graph.

Step 20   *Viewing a Graph*

(in Graph menu) **v**iew
[SPACE] *(Press any key to return to the graph menu.)*

A graph displayed on a monitor may or may not appear as it would when printed or plotted. On occasion, the program must make certain compromises to fit as much of the graph as possible onto the display (such as writing labels vertically rather than horizontally).

NAMING AND PRINTING A GRAPH

Lotus 1-2-3 saves the settings for the current graph when the spreadsheet is saved. However, if you wish to create and then recall more than one graph from the spreadsheet data, you will need to name each graph. Name the bar graph "bar".

Step 21   *Naming a Graph within a Spreadsheet*

(in Graph menu) **n**ame **c**reate
Enter graph name: **bar** ↵
quit

To recall the settings for a particular graph, make it the current graph. Do this by selecting "Graph" (from the main menu), "Name", "Use", then highlight and select the name of the desired graph. This is illustrated later in Step 24.

In Lotus 1-2-3, the current graph settings are saved when the spreadsheet is saved. However, if you plan to print or plot a particular graph, you will need to create a separate "PrintGraph" file. The bar graph is the current graph.

Step 22   *Saving and Printing/Plotting a Graph*

/graph **save**
Enter graph file name: A:\LOTUS**bar** ↵
quit

The foregoing commands create a file, called BAR.PIC (Lotus 1-2-3 adds the PIC extension), from which the bar graph can be printed.

Save the spreadsheet, and exit Lotus 1-2-3 to the Access system menu. Select the PrintGraph program to print the bar graph.

Step 22   *Saving and Printing/Plotting a Graph*   *(continued)*

/file **save**
Enter name of file to save: A:\LOTUS\SUMMARY.WK1 ↵
replace
/quit yes
printGraph *(Load PrintGraph program.)*

Change the default PrintGraph settings so that the program searches the \LOTUS subdirectory on Disk A for BAR.PIC, and identify the device on which the graph will be printed or plotted. Print the graph. Printing or plotting a graph may take a few minutes. After printing is complete, exit PrintGraph and return to Lotus 1-2-3.

Step 22   *Saving and Printing/Plotting a Graph*   *(continued)*

settings hardware graphs-Directory
Enter directory containing picture files
a:\lotus ↵
printer *(If needed, mark the output device.)*   `SPACE` ↵
quit quit
image-Select *(Mark BAR.)*   `SPACE` ↵
align go
page
exit
yes *(End PrintGraph session.)*
1-2-3 (Load Lotus 1-2-3.)

After returning to Lotus 1-2-3, reset the default directory and retrieve the "summary" spreadsheet (see Steps 1, 6, and 8).

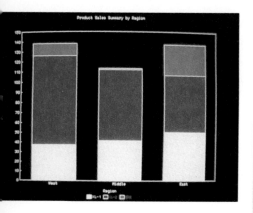

FIGURE F–7   Stacked-Bar Graph

PRODUCING STACKED-BAR AND CLUSTERED-BAR GRAPHS

Produce the stacked-bar graph illustrated in Figure F–7. Identify the range of the data to be graphed and select type of graph to be "Stack-Bar".

Step 23   *Stacked- and Clustered-Bar Graphs*
/graph **a**
Enter first data range: **c18..c20** ↵
(*in Graph menu*) **b**
Enter second data range: **d18..d20** ↵
(*in Graph menu*) **c**
Enter third data range: **e18..e20** ↵
(*in Graph menu*) **type** stack-Bar

Add the main heading and labels for the x-axis and y-axis. The heading and labels for the "bar" graph are still current in Lotus 1-2-3, so the labels for the x-axis and y-axis are unchanged. Enter a new title, and label the variables (that is, the three products).

Step 23   *Stacked- and Clustered-Bar Graphs*   (*continued*)
(*in Graph menu*) **options titles first**
Enter first line of graph title: ESC **Product Sales Summary by Region** ↵
quit (*to return to Graph menu*)
(*in Graph menu*) **options legend a**
Enter legend for first data range: **XL-1** ↵
(*in Graph/Options menu*) **legend b**
Enter legend for second data range: **XL-2** ↵
(*in Graph/Options menu*) **legend c**
Enter legend for third data range: **MPX** ↵
quit (*to return to Graph menu*)

Display the stacked-bar graph on the screen.

Step 23   *Stacked- and Clustered-Bar Graphs.*   (*continued*)
(*in Graph menu*) **view**
SPACE (*to return to the spreadsheet*)

Produce and display the clustered-bar graph illustrated in Figure F–8. All the specifications are the same for the stacked-bar and for the clustered-bar graphs except the selection of type of graph. Because the data range (C18..E20) has both rows and columns, the request for a "bar" graph is interpreted as a request for a clustered-bar graph.

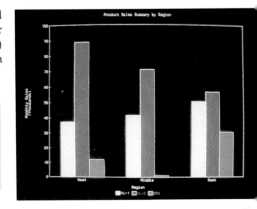

FIGURE F–8   Clustered-Bar Graph

Step 23   *Stacked- and Clustered-Bar Graphs*   *(continued)*

(in Graph menu) **type b**ar **view**

[SPACE] *(to return to the Graph menu)*

Save the graph settings in "multibar".

Step 23   *Stacked- and Clustered-Bar Graphs*   *(continued)*

(in Graph menu) **n**ame **c**reate

Enter graph name: **multibar** ↵

quit

PRODUCING A PIE GRAPH

Produce a "Monthly Sales Summary by Region" pie graph as an alternative to the bar graph in Figure F–6. All the specifications are the same for the bar graph (created in Step 19) and the pie graph except the selection of type of graph. Make the bar graph the current graph, and change the type to "Pie." Save the graph settings in "pie".

Step 24   *Pie Graph*

/graph **n**ame **u**se

(highlight "BAR") ↵

[SPACE] *(to return to the Graph menu)*

(in Graph menu) **type p**ie

(in Graph menu) **view**

[SPACE] *(to return to the Graph menu)*

(in Graph menu) **n**ame **c**reate

Enter graph name: **pie** ↵

quit

Save the spreadsheet, and exit Lotus 1-2-3 and the Access system to DOS.

Step 24   *Pie Graph*   (*continued*)

/file save
Enter name of file to save: A:\LOTUS\SUMMARY.WK1 ↵
replace
/quit yes
exit

As you do the exercises and class assignments, refer to the step-by-step tutorials and use the Help facility liberally. Don't be afraid to experiment with the various features. With a little practice you will become comfortable with Lotus 1-2-3 and make it a part of your weekly routine at home and work.

HANDS-ON EXERCISES

1. Complete Steps 1 through 15 of the keystroke tutorials in this appendix to create and print the spreadsheet of Figure F–1.

2. Complete Steps 16 and 17 of the keystroke tutorials in this appendix to expand on the spreadsheet created in Exercise 1 above.

3. Use the spreadsheet data created in Exercise 2, and complete Steps 18 through 24 of the keystroke tutorials in this appendix to create bar and pie graphs.

4. Use the specifications for the clustered-bar graph created in Exercise 3 to create a line graph.

5a. Expand on the spreadsheet created in Exercises 1, 2, and 3. In Rows 21 through 27 include a "Statistical Sales Summary" as shown below. Use the spreadsheet functions MIN (minimum, or low), AVG (average), and MAX (maximum, or high) to compute the low, average, and high for each product. Compute the range by finding the difference between the low and the high sales for each product. Format your spreadsheet like the following:

	A	B	C	D	E	F
21	= =					
22		•••••STATISTICAL SALES SUMMARY•••••				
23	SALES BY REP		XL-1	XL-2	MPX	TOTAL
24		LOW	$15,570	$24,660	$0	$48,305
25		AVG.	$21,551	$36,069	$7,250	$64,869
26		HIGH	$28,067	$58,388	$25,440	$78,167
27		RANGE	$12,497	$33,728	$25,440	$29,862

b. Print the spreadsheet.

c. Enter new amounts for R. Rosco. Print the spreadsheet and save the file as "stats".

d. Use the data in the range C24..E26 to create a clustered-bar graph. Cluster the statistical amounts for each product. Label the x-axis "Products" and the y-axis "Monthly Sales". Label each cluster of bars with the appropriate product name. Include a legend as a cross-reference to the statistical values (low, average, high).

6a. The following represent the unit sales data for the past year for Diolab, Inc., a manufacturer of a diagnostic laboratory instrument that is sold primarily to hospitals and clinics.

DIOLAB INC. SALES (UNITS)

REGION	QTR1	QTR2	QTR3	QTR4
NE REGION	214	300	320	170
SE REGION	120	150	165	201
SW REGION	64	80	60	52
NW REGION	116	141	147	180

Enter the title, headings, and data in an electronic spreadsheet. Place the title in the range B1, the column headings in the range A2..E2, the row headings in the range A3..A6, and the sales data in the range B3..E6.

In the remaining portion of this exercise, each part builds on the results of the previous one. If the exercise is to be handed in, print out the initial spreadsheets, then print them out again for each revision.

b. Add another column heading called SALES/YR in F2 of the Diolab spreadsheet. Enter a formula in F3 that adds the sales for each quarter for the NE Region. Copy the formula to the range F4..F6. SALES/YR should be 1004 for the NE Region, and 636 for the SE Region.

c. Add average sales per quarter, AVG/QTR, in Column G. AVG/QTR should be 251 for the NE Region and 159 for the SE Region.

d. Add two more columns that reflect sales per salesperson. In Column H, add number of salespeople per region: PERSONS: 5, 3, 2, and 4, respectively. In column I, add formulas that compute sales per person: SALES/PER (from the data in SALES/YR and PERSONS columns). SALES/PER should be 200.8 for the NE Region and 212 for the SE Region.

e. In the range B8..F8, use functions to total sales for each quarter and for the year. The total sales for all regions should be 2480.

f. Print the spreadsheet and save the file as "diolab".

7a. Create a spreadsheet that summarizes an individual's monthly budget in two general categories: expenditures and income. Use formulas to compute the totals for the two categories, the percent of the total, and the ratio of total expenditures to total income. Format your spreadsheet like the following:

	A	B	C
	A	B	C
1	EXPENDITURES		
2	Category	Amount	Percent of Total
3	Housing	495.00	33.01%
4	Utilities	125.45	8.37%
5	Food	369.29	24.63%
6	Clothing	85.00	5.67%
7	Transportation	265.17	17.68%
8	Entertainment	100.00	6.67%
9	Other	59.50	3.97%
10		- - - - - - -	
11	TOTAL	$1,499.41	
12	= =		
13	INCOME		
14	Category	Amount	Percent of Total
13	Wages	2,400.00	96.00%
14	Tips	0.00	0.00%
15	Gifts	100.00	4.00%
16	Other	0.00	0.00%
17		- - - - - - -	
18	TOTAL	$2,500.00	
19	= =		
20	Ratio of expenditures to income:		.60

b. Print the spreadsheet and save the file as "budget".

c. Enter new amounts for various categories of expenditures and income. Print the spreadsheet.

8a. Create a spreadsheet that will allow you to compare this year's monthly electric bills with last year's. Use the data shown here or use your own. Format your spreadsheet like the following:

	A	B	C	D
	A	B	C	D
1	Month	This Year	Last Year	Difference
2				
3	January	140.23	154.24	−14.01
4	February	160.54	168.30	−7.76
5	March	90.77	87.22	3.55
6	April	65.12	56.61	8.51
7	May	30.98	50.15	−19.17
8	June	50.00	48.08	1.92
9	July	69.33	74.04	−4.71
10	August	45.20	48.59	−3.39
11	September	35.61	22.62	12.99
12	October	70.02	69.11	0.91
13	November	98.87	106.04	−7.17
14	December	128.09	140.01	−11.92
15		- - - - - - - - - - - - - - - -		
16	TOTAL	$984.76	$1025.01	

b. Print the spreadsheet and save the file as "bills".

9a. Use the Diolab, Inc., sales data in Exercise 6. Produce a bar graph showing the total unit sales by region for Diolab, Inc. Entitle the graph "Total Sales by Region" with the subtitle "Diolab, Inc."; label the y-axis "Unit Sales", and label the bars "NE Region", "SE Region", "SW Region", and "NW Region".

   Each of the remaining parts of this exercise deal with the Diolab, Inc., data or graphs produced from these data.

b. Produce a pie graph showing the total unit sales by region for Diolab, Inc. Entitle the graph "Total Sales by Region" with the subtitle "Diolab, Inc." Label the pieces "NE Region", "SE Region", "SW Region", and "NW Region".

c. Compare the information illustrated in the bar and pie graphs above.

d. Produce a clustered-bar graph showing quarterly unit sales by region for Diolab, Inc. Entitle the graph "Quarterly Sales by Region" with the subtitle "Diolab, Inc." Label the y-axis "Unit Sales", label the clusters of bars "Qtr1", "Qtr2", "Qtr3," "Qtr4", and include a legend as a cross-reference to the four regions (NE, SE, SW, NW).

e. Produce a line graph showing quarterly unit sales by region for Diolab, Inc. Enitle the graph "Quarterly Sales by Region" with the subtitle "Diolab, Inc." Label the y-axis "Unit Sales", points on the lines "Qtr1", "Qtr2", "Qtr3", "Qtr4", and include a legend as a cross-reference to the regional lines (NE, SE, SW, NW).

f. Compare the information shown in the clustered-bar and line graphs.

G

dBASE III Plus Tutorial and Exercises

This appendix demonstrates commonly used features and functions of dBASE III Plus by using interactive tutorials. Although dBASE III Plus, a product of Ashton-Tate, was introduced in the mid-1980s, it remains the most widely used database software package. Once you have completed the step-by-step keystroke tutorials and exercises in this appendix, you will have acquired the dBASE III Plus skills needed to address common database tasks.

This dBASE III Plus tutorial assumes you have read and understood the material in Appendix C, "Using the Microcomputer," and have a working knowledge of DOS (Appendix D, "MS-DOS Tutorial and Exercises"). Because these step-by-step tutorials parallel the conceptual coverage of database software in Chapter 8, "Productivity Software: Electronic Spreadsheet and Database," it is recommended that you read the database portion (Section 8–3) of Chapter 8.

The keystroke conventions for the dBASE III Plus tutorial are consistent with those of the DOS tutorial in Appendix D. You might wish to review the box opposite Appendix D, "Keystroke Conventions Used in the Step-by-Step Tutorials."

BEGINNING A dBASE III PLUS SESSION

The relational database management system dBASE III Plus enables users to create, maintain, and manipulate a data base and allows flexibility in making inquiries and in generating reports. The organization of the data in a data base is similar to the traditional hierarchy of data organization. Related fields, such as company name, region, representative name, and so on are grouped to form records (for example, the customer records in the KEY_ACCT data base in Figure G–1). A collection of related records make up a file or a data base. (In microcomputer database software terminology, *file* and *data base* are often used interchangeably.)

In this tutorial we will create the KEY_ACCT data base in Figure G–1 and manipulate its data to generate information. The KEY_ACCT data base contains a record for each of a company's nine major accounts. Each record contains the following fields:

- COMPANY (the name of a key-account company)
- REGION (sales region: West, Middle, or East)
- REP_NAME (name of field representative who services the account)
- XL1_NO (the number of XL1s installed at the account)

FIGURE G–1   The KEY_ACCT Data Base
The KEY_ACCT data base contains a record for each of a company's nine key accounts.

COMPANY	REGION	REP. NAME	PRODUCTS			
			XL1 NO.	XL2 NO.	MPX NO.	LAST ORDER
Hi-Tech	West	Rosco	22	35	5	01/11/91
Electronic	East	Allen	48	21	15	02/06/91
Compufast	Middle	Taylor	103	67	42	02/07/92
Zapp. Inc.	West	Rosco	71	85	40	01/16/92
Whizzard	East	Hill	35	45	20	10/12/91
SuperGood	Middle	Cox	24	55	4	12/24/91
Bigco	East	Hill	38	50	21	09/09/91
Actionpak	Middle	Cox	24	37	14	11/01/91
Zimco	West	Mann	77	113	40	01/13/91

- XL2_NO (the number of XL2s installed at the account)
- MPX_NO (the number of MPXs installed at the account)
- LAST_ORDER (the date of the last order for one or more XL1s, XL2s, or MPXs)

Boot the system (see Appendix D, "Booting the System"), and load dBASE III Plus to memory. (You may need to change from the root directory, C:\, to the directory containing the dBASE III Plus programs before loading dBASE III Plus. Ask your instructor.)

Step 1   *Loading dBASE III Plus*

C:\> **dbase** ↵

---

dBASE III Plus provides two methods for interacting with the system, Assist mode and Command mode. The default user interface is the Assist mode, its menu-driven interface with the system. The initial screen displays the main menu as a bar menu at the top of the screen with a pull-down menu for the "Set Up" option of the main menu. The Command mode provides a command-driven user interface. This tutorial will expose you to both methods of entering dBASE III Plus commands.

Set the default disk to be Drive A in Assist mode, then tap ESC to switch from Assist mode to Command mode. The dBASE III Plus dot prompt (a period, ".") at the bottom of the screen indicates that you are in Command mode.

Step 2   *Setting Default Drive*

Tools

Set drive (*Highlight this option with up/down cursor keys.*) ↵

A: (*Highlight this option.*) ↵

[ESC] (*Change to Command mode.*)

Several function-key commands will prove helpful as you work through the following dBASE III Plus tutorial:

F1 dBASE III Plus's context-sensitive Help key.

F2 Changes from Command to Assist mode.

F3 Displays contents of active database file.

F4 Displays the database files on a specified directory.

F5 Displays the structure (fields) of current database file.

F9 Permits the addition of records to the current database file.

F10 Permits editing of records in the current database file.

dBASE III Plus uses the terminology "database file" to refer to the actual data base and uses "database structure" to refer to the definition of the structure of the data base (fields and their characteristics).

Insert your data disk in Drive A (the one prepared in the DOS tutorial in Appendix D). Your data disk should contain a \DB subdirectory. You are now ready to begin your dBASE III Plus session.

dBASE III Plus Command Summary

Activating a data base	Step 9	Fields and field types	Step 3
Adding records to a data base	Step 6	Inquiries—one condition	Step 10
Assist mode	Step 2	Inquiries—two conditions	Step 12
Browsing through a data base	Step 7	Inquiries—statistical	Step 13
Character field	Step 3	Inquiries—summary	Step 13
Command mode	Step 2	Listing a file	Step 5
Creating a data base	Step 3	Loading dBASE III Plus	Step 1
Date field	Step 3	Numeric field	Step 3
Defining the database structure	Step 3	Printing results	Step 11
Deleting a record	Step 7	Saving a data base	Steps 8, 9
Directory (default)	Step 2	Setting default drive	Step 2
Editing a data base	Step 7	Sorting a data base	Step 14
Entering data	Step 4	Terminating a session	Step 8
Exiting the data entry screen	Step 5		

CREATING A DATA BASE

To create the KEY_ACCT data base of Figure G–1, it is necessary to define its structure.

Step 3   *Defining the Database Structure*

. **create \db\key_acct** ↵

Study the input and editing keystroke options at the top of the screen, the record-definition work area, and the status/user-instruction interface at the bottom of the screen. In the keystroke options box, the ˆ (carat) means to press and hold the CTRL key, then tap the adjacent key.

In the field-definition work area for Field Number 1, define the COMPANY field. (Use the backspace or delete keys to correct errors in data entry.) The five types of fields are *character* (the default), *numeric*, *date*, *logical*, and *memo*. To select a field type, press the first character of the desired field type or press the space bar to toggle through the options. Define the width of the field, sometimes called field length, to be 10 character positions.

Step 3   *Defining the Database Structure*   *(continued)*

COMPANY ↵

Character

10 ↵

The cursor is automatically positioned for the next field definition because fields of type "Character" do not require a "Dec", or definition of decimal positions.

Define the other two character fields in the KEY_ACCT data base.

Step 3 *Defining the Database Structure* (continued)

REGION ↵ **C 6** ↵
REP_NAME ↵ **C 8** ↵

The fourth, fifth, and sixth fields are of type "Numeric." Set the "Width", which includes the decimal point, to four. Set "Dec", or the number of spaces to the right of the decimal, to zero.

Step 3 *Defining the Database Structure* (continued)

XL1_NO ↵ Numeric **4** ↵ **0** ↵
XL2_NO ↵ Numeric **4** ↵ **0** ↵
MPX_NO ↵ Numeric **4** ↵ **0** ↵

The last field is of type "Date." The width of the date type is set automatically at eight.

Step 3 *Defining the Database Structure* (continued)

LAST_ORDER D*ate*

Tap ENTER with the cursor at the "Field Name" prompt to signify the end of the record definition for the KEY_ACCT database file. Tap ENTER again to confirm that the definition is correct. Return to the dot prompt with a "No" response to the question.

Step 3 *Defining the Database Structure* (continued)

↵ ↵
Input data records now? (Y/N) **n**

A "Yes" response would display the data entry screen for the KEY_ACCT data base.

ADDING DATA BASE RECORDS

At this point the KEY_ACCT data base has no records. Use the system-generated data entry screen (Figure G–2) to enter the first record to the KEY_ACCT data base.

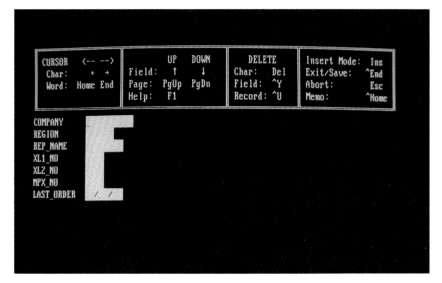

```
┌──────────────────┬────────────┬─────────────┬──────────────────────┐
│ CURSOR  <-- -->  │      UP DOWN│   DELETE    │ Insert Mode:  Ins    │
│   Char:    ←  →  │ Field:  ↑  ↓│ Char:   Del │ Exit/Save:   ^End    │
│   Word: Home End │ Page: PgUp PgDn│ Field:  ^Y │ Abort:        Esc   │
│                  │ Help:   F1  │ Record: ^U  │ Memo:       ^Home    │
└──────────────────┴────────────┴─────────────┴──────────────────────┘

COMPANY
REGION
REP_NAME
XL1_NO
XL2_NO
MPX_NO
LAST_ORDER   /  /
```

FIGURE G–2   Data Entry Screen for the KEY_ACCT Data Base

Step 4   Entering Data to a Data Base

. F9 *(Display data entry screen.)*

Hi-Tech ↵

West ↵

Rosco ↵

22 ↵

35 ↵

5 ↵

011191

Because "01/11/91" is exactly as long as the field-width definition, the cursor is automatically positioned at the next field or record. There may be a warning beep.

Before proceeding to Step 5, follow the procedure in Step 4 and enter Records 2 and 3 of the KEY_ACCT data base (Figure G–1). After entering the third record, the record counter in the status line should read "Rec: EOF/3", indicating that the current data entry screen represents the EOF (end-of-file) record in a data base that contains three records (numbered 1, 2, and 3).

In Step 5, page up (PGUP) to view Records 1, 2, and 3, then return to the dot prompt and list the data base.

Step 5   Exiting the Data Entry Screen

PGUP *(3 times)*

CTRL – END *(Exit to the command interface.)*

. F3 *(List the current file.)*

Enter the next record (Record 4) of the KEY_ACCT data base (Figure G–1).

Step 6   Adding Records to an Existing Data Base

. F9 (*Display data entry screen.*)

Zapp, Inc.
West ↵
Rosco ↵
71 ↵
85 ↵
40 ↵
011692

Before continuing with Step 6, enter the remaining records (Records 5 through 9) of the KEY_ACCT data base (Figure G–1). After entering the last record, you should be at the end of file (EOF) and at Record Number 9.

In the continuation of Step 6, enter the last record (Zimco) again. (This is to create an unwanted record that will be deleted in the next step.)

Step 6   Adding Records to an Existing Data Base   (*continued*)

Zimco ↵
West ↵
Mann ↵
77 ↵
113 ↵
40 ↵
011391

Page up (PGUP) to view Records 1 through 10, then return to the dot prompt and list the data base.

Step 6   Adding Records to an Existing Data Base   (*continued*)

PGUP (*10 times*)

CTRL — END

. F3 (*List the current file.*)

Always exit the data entry screen (CTRL-END) with a completed record and its data being displayed. If you exit on a blank record, the blank record will be added to the file. To avoid this, use the PGUP key to display a completed record, then exit the data entry screen.

MODIFYING AND DELETING RECORDS IN A DATA BASE

At this point the active data base is KEY_ACCT. Any commands you issue are applied to the active data base. Enter the "BROWSE" command and position the cursor at the first record in the data base.

Step 7   *Browse and Edit a Data Base; Delete a Record*

. **browse** ↵

⎡CTRL⎤ = ⎡HOME⎤ (*Display the Set Options menu.*)

Top (*Highlight first record in data base.*)

Use the left/right cursor-control keys (to move one character at a time), the up/down cursor-control keys (to move one record at a time), and the home/end keys (to move one field at a time), and browse through the records of the data base. Make any needed corrections by positioning the cursor at the proper location and keying-in the correct data. Use the INS key to toggle between the Insert and Replace data entry modes.

In the continuation of Step 7, delete the extra Zimco record and return to the dot prompt. In dBASE III Plus, deleting a record is a two-step process. First, mark the record to be deleted. Do this by highlighting the desired record and tapping CTRL-U (CTRL-U also undeletes a record marked for deletion.) When you do this, a "Del" appears in the right side of the status/user-instruction interface at the bottom of the screen. The "Del" indicates that this record is marked for deletion. The second step is to "pack" the file to eliminate all records marked for deletion.

Step 7   *Browse and Edit a Data Base; Delete a Record*   (continued)

(*Highlight record 10 with up/down cursor keys.*)

⎡CTRL⎤ – ⎡U⎤

⎡CTRL⎤ – ⎡END⎤

. ⎡F3⎤ (*List the current file and note the "*" by Record 10.*)

. **pack** ↵ (*Permanently remove records marked for deletion.*)

. ⎡F3⎤ (*List the current file.*)

An alternative to viewing or modifying records of the active data base is to tap F10 (edit) or issue the "EDIT" command at the dot prompt (or Update/Edit in Assist mode), and then to PGUP or PGDN to select the appropriate record. Another alternative, if you know the record number, is to go directly to the desired record with the "EDIT" command (to edit Record Number 4: . EDIT 4). Call up the edit screen and page through the records. Check them again for errors and, if needed, make corrections.

> **Step 7**   *Browse and Edit a Data Base; Delete a Record*   *(continued)*
>
> [F10] *(Edit the data base.)*
>
> *(PGUP/PGDN as needed to examine the data base records.)*
>
> [CTRL] − [END]

SAVING A DATA BASE AND
TERMINATING A SESSION _____

The active, or "open," database file is not saved to disk storage until it is closed (deactivated). Typically, you would close an active file by exiting dBASE to DOS or loading another database file to RAM. Another way to save the active database file is to reactivate the current file. (This is demonstrated later.) Exit dBASE III Plus to DOS.

> **Step 8**   *Terminating a dBASE III Plus Session*
>
> **. quit** ↵

If the active database file has been modified, QUIT saves it to disk storage.

　　　If at any time you cannot continue with the tutorials, use the above procedure to terminate your dBASE III Plus session and save your work for your next session.

MAKING A DATA BASE THE ACTIVE DATA BASE _____

Begin another dBASE III Plus session. Set the default drive to A, and enter Command mode (see Steps 1 and 2). If needed, insert your data disk in Drive A.

　　　Make the KEY_ACCT data base in the \DB subdirectory on your data disk the active directory. Display the active data base to confirm that it is KEY_ACCT.

> **Step 9**   *Activating a Data Base for Processing*
>
> **. use \db\key_acct** ↵ *(to activate KEY_ACCT)*
>
> . [F3] *(List the current file.)*

You are now ready to manipulate the data in KEY_ACCT to produce information.

MAKING DATA BASE INQUIRIES

Inquiries That Involve Conditions

With dBASE III Plus, it is easy to make inquiries of the data base. To do this, you set conditions for the selection of records by compiling a *conditional expression*. A conditional expression normally compares one or more field names to numbers or character strings using the *relational operators* (= [equal to], > [greater than], < [less than], and combinations of these operators). Several conditions can be combined with *logical operators* (AND, OR, and NOT).

Display records based on the condition that REGION is equal to "East". It is good practice to clear the display screen.

> ***Step 10***   *Making a Simple Inquiry*
>
> . **clear** ↵
> . **list for region='East'** ↵

Notice that the character string "East" is in upper- and lowercase type, just as it is in the database file, and it is enclosed in single quotes.

Display and print only the COMPANY and REGION for the records that meet the above condition. Append the qualifier, TO PRINT, to the end of the LIST command to route LIST selections from the active database file to the printer. If needed, turn on the printer.

> ***Step 11***   *Printing the Results of an Inquiry*
>
> . **clear** ↵
> . **list company, rep_name for region='East' to print** ↵

As an alternative to keying in the LIST command above, you may edit the first LIST command. Use the ↑ and ↓ cursor-control keys to scroll through previous commands. In this instance, you can simply press ↑ until the desired command is displayed at the dot prompt and edit it as needed. Press ENTER to effect the command. You may need to toggle between Replace and Insert modes with the INS key. (Use the Insert mode to insert "COMPANY, REGION" in the first LIST command to create the second.)

In the next example, we will display those companies from the Eastern region that have not submitted an order since July 1, 1991. This criterion requires a compound condition—that is, one that involves a logical operator. dBASE III Plus requires that the data types on either side of the relational operator be the same. If you were to include the condition "LAST_ORDER < 7/1/91" in a command, you would get an error message. In this situation, the LAST_ORDER field is defined as type "date" in the data base structure and 7/1/91 is interpreted as type "character"—a data type mismatch. To overcome this inconsistency, apply the CTOD (character-to-date) conversion function to the date character string.

> *Step 12*   *Making an Inquiry with a Compound Condition*
>
> . **clear** ↵
> . **list for region='East' .and. last_order<=ctod('7/1/91')** ↵

Electronic is the only company that satisfies this compound conditional expression.

Inquiries That Involve Calculations

dBASE III Plus has many helpful functions, several of which assist in generating summary and statistical information.

Display the total number of XL1s, XL2s, and MPXs installed in the "Middle" region. The results should be 121, 116, and 56, respectively.

> *Step 13*   *Making Summary and Statistical Inquiries*
>
> . **clear** ↵
> . **sum xl1_no, xl2_no, mpx_no for region='East'** ↵

Display the average number of XL1s, XL2s, and MPXs installed in all key accounts. The result should be 49, 56, and 22, respectively.

> *Step 13*   *Making Summary and Statistical Inquiries*   *(continued)*
>
> . **clear** ↵
> . **average xl1_no, xl2_no, mpx_no** ↵

Display the total number of key accounts in the "Middle" or "West" regions. The result should be 6.

> *Step 13*   *Making Summary and Statistical Inquiries*   *(continued)*
>
> . **clear** ↵
> . **count for region='West' .or. region='Middle'** ↵

SORTING A DATA BASE

Sort the KEY_ACCT data base by REP_NAME field (secondary key) within the REGION field (primary key). Create a temporary database file called KEY_SRT1 on the \DB subdirectory on your data disk. Make it the active file and display it.

Step 14   *Sorting a Data Base*

. **clear** ↵
. **sort to \db\key_srt1 on region, rep_name** ↵
. **use \db\key_srt1** ↵
. [F3] (*List the current file.*)

The USE command makes KEY_SRT1 the active database file. Your display should be similar to that in Figure G–3.

Appending the /D qualifier to a field in the Sort command causes the records to be sorted in descending order for that field. Sort KEY_ACCT on the XL1_NO in descending order. Create a temporary database file called KEY_SRT2 on the \DB subdirectory on your data disk. Make it the active file and display it. Exit dBASE III Plus.

Step 14   *Sorting a Data Base*   (continued)

. **clear** ↵
. **use \db\key_acct** ↵
. **sort to \db\key_srt2 on xl1_no/d** ↵
. **use \db\key_srt2** ↵
. [F3] (*List the current file.*)
. **quit** ↵

As you explore the capabilities of dBASE III Plus, you will soon realize why it is the software foundation for millions of operational information systems.

FIGURE G–3   Display of the dBASE III Plus Sequence in Step 13.
The sort command creates the file KEY_SRT1.

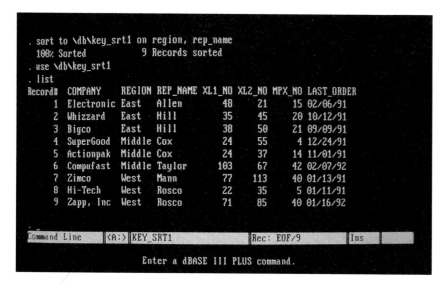

HANDS-ON EXERCISES

1a. Create a data entry screen to accept the following sales data for Diolab, Inc., a manufacturer of a diagnostic laboratory instrument sold primarily to hospitals and clinics. Name the data base DIOLAB.

DIOLAB INC. SALES (UNITS)				
REGION	QTR1	QTR2	QTR3	QTR4
NE REGION	241	300	320	170
SE REGION	120	150	165	201
SW REGION	64	80	60	52

Each of the remaining parts of this exercise builds upon the previous part.

b. Enter the Diolab data into a data base.

c. Revise the NE Region first-quarter sales to be 214.

d. Add the following NW Region record to the data base.

REGION	QTR1	QTR2	QTR3	QTR4
NW REGION	116	141	147	180

e. Obtain a printout of the data base.

f. Select and list all Diolab regions (records) that sold more than 150 units in the fourth quarter (all but the SW Region).

g. Select and list all Diolab regions (records) that sold more than 150 units in the fourth quarter *and* for which fourth-quarter sales are greater than third-quarter sales (SE and NW regions).

h. Select and list only the REGION and QTR4 fields of those Diolab regions for which the average sales for the first three quarters is less than the sales for the fourth quarter (SE and NW regions). *Hint: Use the arithmetic expression (QTR1+QTR2+QTR3)/3 in a conditional expression.*

i. Make an inquiry to the Diolab data base that results in a display of the average unit sales for each quarter (QTR1=128).

j. Make an inquiry to the Diolab data base that results in a display of the total unit sales for each quarter (QTR1=514).

k. Sort the Diolab data base in ascending order by QTR1 sales. Print out the sorted data base.

l. Sort the Diolab data base in descending order by QTR4 sales. Print out the sorted data base.

2a. Create a name-and-address data base. Sort and list the data base in various ways.

Create a data base called NAMES that includes the following fields: FIRSTNAME, LASTNAME, ADDRESS, CITY, ST, ZIP. Use the following field information.

FIELD NAME	TYPE	WIDTH
FIRSTNAME	Character	12
LASTNAME	Character	15
ADDRESS	Character	15
CITY	Character	15
ST	Character	2
ZIP	Numeric	5

b. Enter the following data into the data base.

FIRSTNAME	LASTNAME	ADDRESS	CITY	ST	ZIP
Phil	Cline	1915 N.W. 25th	Oklahoma City	OK	73107
Sherry	Howard	3587 Lee Dr.	Jackson	MS	39208
Bill	Allred	630 W. Call	Tallahassee	FL	32308
Warren	Sherman	3745 Rogers	Fort Worth	TX	76109
Malcolm	Haney	642 Tulane Av	Little Rock	AR	72204
Sharon	Bias	125 Lake View	Gainesville	GA	30501
Janet	Roche	432 Oak St.	Nashville	TN	37203
Joyce	Phinney	345 Pratt Dr.	New Orleans	LA	70122
Michael	Howard	3587 Lee Dr.	Jackson	MS	39208
Alison	Haney	933 Hilltop	Little Rock	AR	72204
Kristine	Haney	3216 West End	Nashville	TN	37203

c. List and print the data base.

d. List the records of those people who live in Arkansas (AR).

f. List and print the records of those people who live in Arkansas or Mississippi.

g. Sort the data base alphabetically in ascending sequence by last name. List only the LASTNAME field.

h. Sort the data base alphabetically in ascending sequence by STATE. List only the LASTNAME and STATE fields.

i. Sort the data base alphabetically in ascending sequence using LAST-NAME as the primary field and FIRSTNAME as the secondary field. List and print only the LASTNAME and FIRSTNAME fields.

3a. Create a data base named AUDIO to keep track of an individual's library of recordings: compact discs (CDs), long-playing (LP) records, and audio tapes. The data base should have the following fields defined:

(1) FORMAT (CD, LP record, or tape)

(2) ARTIST

(3) TITLE

(4) [Playing] TIME

(5) [Number of] SONGS

b. Enter the following data into the AUDIO data base.

FORMAT	ARTIST	TITLE	TIME	SONGS
CD	Depeche Mode	Some Great Reward	38.59	13
CD	The Cure	The Cure?	32.32	10
RECORD	London Symphony	Mozart: Requiem	61.25	1
TAPE	Pet Shop Boys	Please	32.15	10
CD	Depeche Mode	Black Celebration	41.19	12
RECORD	Depeche Mode	People Are People	32.37	11
TAPE	O.M.D.	The Pacific Age	43.00	12
CD	The Cure	Standing on the Beach	52.18	15
RECORD	The Ramones	End of the Century	36.28	16

c. Use the original and sorted versions of the AUDIO data base and appropriate criteria to generate and print reports that contain

(1) The entire data base sorted alphabetically by title.

(2) All LP records and tapes sorted by playing time.

(3) All CDs recorded by Depeche Mode.

(4) All LP records and tapes with playing times in excess of 40 minutes.

d. Make the following inquiries to the AUDIO data base.

(1) The total number of songs on all CDs.

(2) The average playing time for all recordings.

Glossary

Abacus Probably the original mechanical counting device, which can be traced back at least 5000 years. Beads are moved along parallel wires to count and perform arithmetic computations.

Absolute cell address A cell address in an electronic spreadsheet that always refers to the same cell.

Access arm The disk-drive mechanism used to position the read/write heads over the appropriate track.

Access time The time interval between the instant a computer makes a request for a transfer of data from a secondary storage device and the instant this operation is completed.

Accumulator The computer register in which the result of an arithmetic or logic operation is formed (related to *arithmetic and logic unit*).

Acoustical coupler A device on which a telephone handset is mounted for the purpose of transmitting data over telephone lines. Used with a modem.

Ada A multipurpose, procedure-oriented language.

Add-on boards Circuit boards that contain the electronic circuitry for a wide variety of computer-related functions (also called *add-on cards*).

Add-on cards See *add-on boards*.

Address (1) A name, numeral, or label that designates a particular location in primary or secondary storage. (2) A location identifier for terminals in a computer network.

ALGOL [ALGOrithmic Language] A high-level programming language designed primarily for scientific applications.

Algorithm A procedure that can be used to solve a particular problem.

Alpha A reference to the letters of the alphabet.

Alpha test The in-house testing of a software product by the vendor prior to its release for beta testing. (Contrast with *beta test*.)

Alphanumeric Pertaining to a character set that contains letters, digits, punctuation, and special symbols (related to *alpha* and *numeric*).

Analog computer A computer that operates on data expressed as a continuously changing representation of a physical variable, such as voltage. (Contrast with *digital computer*.)

Analog-to-digital (A–D) converter A device that translates an analog signal into a digital signal. (Contrast with *digital-to-analog converter*.)

ANSI [American National Standards Institute] An organization that coordinates the setting of standards in the United States, including certain software standards.

APL [A Programming Language] An interactive symbolic programming language used primarily for mathematical applications.

Application A problem or task to which the computer can be applied.

Application generator A very high-level programming language in which programmers specify, through an interactive dialog with the system, which processing tasks are to be performed (also called *code generator*).

Applications portfolio The current mix of existing and proposed information systems in an organization.

Applications software Software designed and written to address a specific personal, business, or processing task.

APT [Automatically Programmed Tools] A special-purpose programming language used to program machine tools.

Architecture The design of a computer system.

Arithmetic and logic unit That portion of the computer that performs arithmetic and logic operations (related to *accumulator*).

Arithmetic operators Mathematical operators (add [+], subtract [−], multiply [*], divide [/], and exponentiation [^]) used in electronic spreadsheet and database software for computations.

Array A programming concept that permits access to a list or table of values by the use of a single variable name.

Array processor A processor composed of several processors, all under the control of a single control unit.

Artificial intelligence (AI) The ability of a computer to reason, to learn, to strive for self-improvement, and to simulate human sensory capabilities.

ASCII [American Standard Code for Information Interchange] An encoding system.

ASCII file A generic text file that is stripped of program-specific control characters.

Assembler language A low-level symbolic language with an instruction set that is essentially one-to-one with machine language.

Assistant system A type of knowledge-based system that helps users make relatively straightforward decisions. (Contrast with *expert system*.)

Asynchronous transmission Data transmission at irregular intervals that is synchronized with start/stop bits. (Contrast with *synchronous transmission*.)

Attribute A data element in a relational data base.

Auto-answer A modem function that permits the automatic answering of a call from a remote computer.

Auto-dial A modem function that permits the automatic dialing of the number of a remote computer.

Automatic teller machine (ATM) An automated deposit/withdrawal device used in banking.

Automation The automatic control and operation of machines, processes, and procedures.

Auxiliary storage See *secondary storage*.

Back-end processor A host-subordinate processor that handles administrative tasks associated with retrieval and manipulation of data (same as *data base machine*).

Backup Pertaining to equipment, procedures, or data bases that can be used to restart the system in the event of system failure.

Backup file Duplicate of an existing production file.

Badge reader An input device that reads data on badges and cards (related to *magnetic stripe*).

Bar code A graphic encoding technique in which vertical bars of varying widths are used to represent data.

Bar graph A graph that contains vertical bars that represent specified numeric values.

Bar menu A menu in which the options are displayed across the screen.

BASIC A popular multipurpose programming language.

Batch file A disk file that contains a list of commands and/ or programs that are to be executed immediately following the loading of the operating system to main memory.

Batch processing A technique in which transactions and/ or jobs are collected into groups (batched) and processed together.

Baud (1) A measure of the maximum number of electronic signals that can be transmitted via a communications channel. (2) Bits per second (common-use definition).

Benchmark test A test for comparing the performance of several computer systems while running the same software, or comparing the performance of several programs that are run on the same computer.

Beta test Testing a software product in a live environment prior to its release to the public. (Contrast with *alpha test*.)

Binary notation Using the binary (base-2) numbering system (0, 1) for internal representation of alphanumeric data.

Bit A *binary digit* (0 or 1).

Bits per second (bps) The number of bits that can be transmitted per second over a communications channel.

Block A group of data that is either read from or written to an I/O device in one operation.

Blocking Combining two or more records into one block.

Boilerplate Existing text in a word processing file that can in some way be customized so that it can be used in a variety of word processing applications.

Boot The procedure for loading the operating system to primary storage and readying a computer system for use.

BPI [Bytes Per Inch] A measure of data-recording density on secondary storage.

Bridge A protocol-independent hardware device that permits communication between devices on separate local area networks.

Bubble memory Nonvolatile solid-state memory.

Buffer Intermediate memory that temporarily holds data that are en route from main memory to another computer or an input/output device.

Bug A logic or syntax error in a program, a logic error in the design of a computer system, or a hardware fault. (See *debug*.)

Bulletin-board system (BBS) The electronic counterpart of a wall-mounted bulletin board that enables end users in a computer network to exchange ideas and information via a centralized data base.

Bus An electrical pathway through which the processor sends data and commands to RAM and all peripheral devices.

Bus architecture See *open architecture*.

Bus topology A computer network that permits the connection of terminals, peripheral devices, and microcomputers along an open-ended central cable.

Business Systems Planning (BSP) A structured process for MIS planning based on the premise that data are a corporate resource that must be evaluated carefully with respect to organizational needs.

Byte A group of adjacent bits configured to represent a character.

C A transportable programming language that can be used to develop both systems and applications software.

Cache memory High-speed solid-state memory for program instructions and data.

CAD See *computer-aided design*.

CAI See *computer-assisted instruction*.

Callback procedure A security procedure that results in a remote user being called back by the host computer system after the user password and authorization code have been verified.

CAM See *computer-aided manufacturing*.

Capacity planning The process by which MIS planners determine how much hardware resources are needed to meet anticipated demands.

Carrier Standard-sized pin connectors that permit chips to be attached to a circuit board.

Carrier, common [in data communications] A company that furnishes data communications services to the general public.

CASE [Computer-Aided Software Engineering] A collective reference to a family of software development productivity tools (also called *workbench technologies*).

Cathode ray tube See *CRT*.

CBT See *computer-based training*.

CD-ROM disk [Compact Disk Read-Only Memory disk] A type of optical laser storage media.

Cell The intersection of a particular row and column in an electronic spreadsheet.

Cell address The location—column and row—of a cell in an electronic spreadsheet.

Central processing unit See *CPU*.

Certificate in Computer Programming (CCP) A certification for programmers.

Certificate in Data Processing (CDP) A general certification in the area of computers and information systems.

Certified Data Educator (CDE) A certification for educators in the general area of computers and information systems.

Certified Information Systems Auditor (CISA) A certification for information systems auditors.

Certified System Professional (CSP) A general certification in the area of computers and information systems.

Channel The facility by which data are transmitted between locations in a computer network (e.g., workstation to host, host to printer).

Channel capacity The number of bits that can be transmitted over a communications channel per second.

Character A unit of alphanumeric datum.

Chargeback system A system designed to allocate the cost of computer and information services to the end users.

Checkpoint/restart When a system fails, backup files/data bases and/or backup transaction logs are used to re-create processing from the last "checkpoint." The system is "restarted" at the last checkpoint, and normal operation is resumed.

Chief information officer (CIO) The individual responsible for all information services in a company.

CIM [Computer-Integrated Manufacturing] Using the computer at every stage of the manufacturing process, from the time a part is conceived until it is shipped.

Clip art Prepackaged electronic images that are stored on disk to be used as needed in word processing or desktop publishing documents.

Clone A hardware device or a software package that emulates a product with an established reputation and market acceptance.

Closed architecture Refers to micros with a fixed, unalterable configuration. (Contrast with *open architecture*.)

Cluster controller See *down-line processor*.

Clustered-bar graph A modified bar graph that can be used to represent a two-dimensional set of numeric data (for example, multiple product sales by region).

Coaxial cable A shielded wire used as a medium to transmit data between computers and between computers and peripheral devices.

COBOL [COmmon Business Oriented Language] A programming language used primarily for administrative information systems.

CODASYL [COnference on DAta SYstems Languages] An organization chartered to oversee and approve software tools and procedures, such as programming languages and database management systems.

Code (1) The rules used to translate a bit configuration into alphanumeric characters. (2) The process of compiling computer instructions in the form of a computer program. (3) The actual computer program.

Code generator See *application generator*.

Cold site A backup site equipped for housing a computer system. (Contrast with *hot site*.)

Collate To combine two or more files for processing.

Column A vertical block of cells that runs the length of a spreadsheet and is labeled by a letter.

COM [Computer Output Microfilm/Microfiche] A device that produces a microform image of a computer output on microfilm or microfiche.

Command An instruction to a computer that invokes the execution of a preprogrammed sequence of instructions.

Command-driven Pertaining to software packages that respond to user directives entered as commands.

Common carrier [in data communications] See *carrier, common*.

Communications See *data communications*.

Communications channel The facility by which data are transmitted between locations in a computer network (same as *line* and *data link*).

Communications protocols Rules established to govern the way data are transmitted in a computer network.

Communications software Software that enables a microcomputer to emulate a terminal and to transfer files between a micro and another computer.

Compatibility (1) Pertaining to the ability of one computer to execute programs of, access the data base of, and communicate with, another computer. (2) Pertaining to the ability of a particular hardware device to interface with a particular computer.

Competitive advantage A term used to describe a company's leveraging of computer and information technologies to realize an advantage over its competitors.

Compile To translate a high-level programming language, such as COBOL, into machine language in preparation for execution.

Compiler Systems software that performs the compilation process. (Compare with *interpreter*.)

Computer See *processor*.

Computer console The unit of a computer system that allows operator and computer to communicate.

Computer network An integration of computer systems, workstations, and communications links.

Computer system A collective reference to all interconnected computing hardware, including processors, storage devices, input/output devices, and communications equipment.

Computer-aided design (CAD) Use of computer graphics in design, drafting, and documentation in product and manufacturing engineering.

Computer-aided manufacturing (CAM) A term coined to highlight the use of computers in the manufacturing process.

Computer-assisted instruction (CAI) Use of the computer in the educational process. (Contrast with *computer-based training*.)

Computer-based training (CBT) Using computer technologies for training and education. (Contrast with *computer-assisted instruction*.)

Computerese A slang term that refers to the jargon associated with computers and information processing.

Concatenation The joining together of labels or fields and other character strings into a single character string in electronic spreadsheet or database software.

Concentrator See *down-line processor*.

Configuration The computer and its peripheral devices.

Connectivity Pertains to the degree to which hardware devices, software, and data bases can be functionally linked to one another.

Contention A line-control procedure in which each workstation "contends" with other workstations for service by sending requests for service to the host processor.

Contingency plan A plan that details what to do in case an event drastically disrupts the operation of a computer center (same as *disaster plan*).

Control clerk A person who accounts for all input to and output from a computer center.

Control field See *key data element*.

Control total An accumulated number that is checked against a known value for the purpose of output control.

Control unit The portion of the processor that interprets program instructions, directs internal operations, and directs the flow of input/output to or from main memory.

Conversion The transition process from one system (manual or computer-based) to a computer-based information system.

Cooperative computing An environment in which businesses cooperate internally and externally to take full advantage of available information and to obtain meaningful, accurate, and timely information (see also *intracompany networking*).

Coprocessor An extra processor under the control of the main processor that helps relieve it of certain tasks.

Core memory A main memory technology that was popular in the 1950s and 1960s.

Cottage industry People who do work-for-profit from their homes.

Counter One or several programming instructions used to tally processing events.

CPU The main processor in a computer system (see also *host processor*).

Critical Path Method (CPM) A network modeling technique that enables managers to show the relationships between the various activities involved in a project and to select the approach that optimizes the use of resources while meeting project deadlines (similar to *Project Evaluation and Review Technique*, or *PERT*).

Critical success factors (CSF) A procedure by which a manager identifies areas of business activity that are critical to the successful operation of the functions within his or her scope of responsibility.

CRT [Cathode Ray Tube] The video monitor component of a workstation.

Cryptography A communications crime-prevention technology that uses methods of data encryption and decryption to scramble codes sent over communications channels.

Cursor, graphics Typically an arrow or crosshair which can be moved about a monitor's screen by an input device to create a graphic image or select an item from a menu. (See also *cursor, text*.)

Cursor, text A blinking character that indicates the location of the next keyed-in character on the display screen. (See also *cursor, graphics*.)

Cyberphobia The irrational fear of, and aversion to, computers.

Cylinder A disk storage concept. A cylinder is that portion of the disk that can be read in any given position of the access arm. (Contrast with *sector*.)

Daisy-wheel printer A letter-quality serial printer. Its interchangeable character set is located on a spoked print wheel.

DASD [Direct-Access Storage Device] A random-access secondary storage device.

Data Representations of facts. Raw material for information. (Plural of *datum*.)

Data base (1) An organization's data resource for all computer-based information processing in which the data are integrated and related to minimize data redundancy. (2) Same as a file in the context of microcomputer usage. (Contrast with *database*.)

Data base administrator (DBA) The individual responsible for the physical and logical maintenance of the data base.

Data base machine See *back-end processor*.

Data base management system (DBMS) A systems software package for the creation, manipulation, and maintenance of the data base.

Data base record Related data that are read from, or written to, the data base as a unit.

Data bits A data communications parameter that refers to the number of bits in a message.

Data cartridge Magnetic tape storage in cassette format.

Data communications The collection and distribution of the electronic representation of information from and to remote facilities.

Data communications specialist A person who designs and implements computer networks.

Data dictionary A listing and description of all data elements in the data base.

Data diddling The unauthorized revision of data upon being entered into a system or placed in storage.

Data element The smallest logical unit of data. Examples are employee number, first name, and price; same as *field*. (Compare with *data item*.)

Data entry The transcription of source data into machine-readable format.

Data entry operator A person who uses key entry devices to transcribe data into a machine-readable format.

Data flow diagram (DFD) A design technique that permits documentation of a system or a program at several levels of generality.

Data item The value of a data element. (Compare with *data element*.)

Data link See *communications channel*.

Data management software See *database software*.

Data processing (DP) Using the computer to perform operations on data.

Database An alternative term for microcomputer-based data management software. (Contrast with *data base*.)

Database software Software that permits users to create and maintain a data base and to extract information from the data base (also called *data management software*).

DB2 IBM's mainframe-based relational DBMS.

Debug To eliminate bugs in a program or system. (See *bug*.)

Decimal The base-10 numbering system.

Decision support system (DSS) An interactive information system that relies on an integrated set of user-friendly hardware and software tools to produce and present information targeted to support management decision making involving semistructured and unstructured problems. (Contrast with *executive support system* and *management information system*.)

Decision table A graphic technique used to illustrate possible occurrences and appropriate actions within a system.

Decode To reverse the encoding process. (Contrast with *encode*.)

Default options Preset software options that are assumed valid unless specified otherwise by the user.

Density The number of bytes per linear length of track of a recording medium. Usually measured in bytes per inch (bpi) and applied to magnetic tapes and disks.

Departmental computing Any type of computing done at the departmental level.

Departmental computing system Computer systems used both as stand-alone systems in support of a particular department and as part of a network of departmental mini-computers, all linked to a large centralized computer.

Desktop computer Any computer that can be placed conveniently on the top of a desk (same as *microcomputer*, *personal computer*, *PC*).

Desktop film recorders An output device that permits the reproduction of high-resolution computer-generated graphic images on 35-mm film.

Desktop page printer A small printer that uses laser technology to print near-typeset-quality text and graphics one page at a time.

Desktop publishing Refers to the hardware and software capability of producing near-typeset-quality copy from the confines of a desktop.

Diagnostic The isolation and/or explanation of a program error.

Dial-up line See *switched line*.

Dictionary See *information repository*.

Digital computer A computer that operates on data that are expressed in a discrete format (such as an on-bit or off-bit). (Contrast with *analog computer*.)

Digital-to-analog (D–A) converter A device that translates a digital signal into an analog signal. (Contrast with *analog-to-digital converter*.)

Digitize To translate data or an image into a discrete format that can be interpreted by computers.

Digitizing tablet A pressure-sensitive tablet with the same x-y coordinates as a computer-generated screen. The outline of an image drawn on a tablet with a stylus or puck is reproduced on the display.

DIP [Dual Inline Package] A toggle switch that is typically used to designate certain computer-system configuration specifications (such as the amount of RAM).

Direct access See *random access*.

Direct conversion An approach to system conversion whereby operational support by the new system is begun when the existing system is terminated.

Direct-access file See *random file*.

Direct-access processing See *random processing*.

Direct-access storage device See *DASD*.

Director of information services The person who has responsibility for computer and information systems in an organization.

Directory A list of the names of the files stored on a particular diskette or in a named area on a hard disk.

Disaster plan See *contingency plan*.

Disk, magnetic A secondary storage medium for random-access data storage. Available as microdisk, diskette, disk cartridge, or disk pack.

Disk drive, magnetic A magnetic storage device that records data on flat rotating disks. (Compare with *tape drive, magnetic*.)

Diskette A thin, flexible disk for secondary random-access data storage (same as *floppy disk* and *flexible disk*).

Distributed data processing Both a technological and an organizational concept based on the premise that information systems can be made more responsive to users by moving computer hardware and personnel physically closer to the people who use them.

Distributed DBMS Software that permits the interfacing of data bases located in various places throughout a computer network.

Distributed processor The nucleus of a small computer system linked to the host computer and physically located in the functional area departments.

Documentation Permanent and continuously updated written and graphic descriptions of information systems and programs.

Domain expert An expert in a particular field who provides the factual knowledge and the heuristic rules for input to a knowledge base.

DOS [Disk Operating System] A generic reference to a disk-based operating system.

Down-line processor A computer that collects data from a number of low-speed devices, then transmits "concentrated" data over a single communications channel (also called a *concentrator* and *cluster controller*).

Download The transmission of data from a mainframe computer to a workstation.

Downtime The time during which a computer system is not operational.

DP Abbreviation for *data processing*.

Driver module The program module that calls other subordinate program modules to be executed as they are needed.

Dump The duplication of the contents of a storage device to another storage device or to a printer.

E-mail See *electronic mail*.

E-time See *execution time*.

Earth station An earth-based communications station that can transmit and receive data from communications satellites.

EBCDIC [Extended Binary Coded Decimal Interchange Code] An encoding system.

EDP Abbreviation for *electronic data processing*.

Education coordinator The person who coordinates all computer-related educational activities within an organization.

EFT [Electronic Funds Transfer] A computer-based system allowing electronic transfer of money from one account to another.

EGA [Enhanced Graphics Adapter] A circuit board that enables the interfacing of high-resolution monitors to microcomputers.

EISA [Extended Industry Standard Architecture] An architecture for microcomputers that use the Intel 80386 or 80486 microprocessors.

Electronic bulletin board A computer-based "bulletin board" that permits external users access to the system via data communications for the purpose of reading and sending messages.

Electronic data interchange (EDI) The use of computers and data communications to transmit data electronically between companies.

Electronic data processing Same as *data processing*.

Electronic dictionary A disk-based dictionary used in conjunction with a spelling-checker program to verify the spelling of words in a word processing document.

Electronic funds transfer See *EFT*.

Electronic mail A computer application whereby messages

are transmitted via data communications to "electronic mailboxes." Also called E-mail. (Contrast with *voice message switching*.)

Electronic spreadsheet   See *spreadsheet, electronic*.

Encode   To apply the rules of a code. (Contrast with *decode*.)

Encoding system   A system that permits alphanumeric characters to be coded in terms of bits.

Encyclopedia   See *information repository*.

End user   The individual providing input to the computer or using computer output (same as *user*).

End user computing   A computing environment in which the end users handle both the technical and functional tasks of the information systems projects.

End-of-file (EOF) marker   A marker placed at the end of a sequential file.

EPROM   Erasable PROM [Programmable Read-Only Memory]. See *PROM*.

Exception report   A report that has been filtered to highlight critical information.

Execution time   The elapsed time it takes to execute a computer instruction and store the results. Also called E-time.

Executive support system (ESS)   A system designed specifically to support decision making at the strategic level. (Contrast with *decision support system* and *management information system*.)

Expansion slots   Slots within the processing component of a microcomputer into which optional add-on circuit boards can be inserted.

Expert system   An interactive knowledge-based system that responds to questions, asks for clarification, makes recommendations, and generally helps users make complex decisions. (Contrast with *assistant system*.)

Expert system shell   The software that enables the development of expert systems.

Facilities management company   For a fee, employees of facilities management companies physically move into a client company's computer center and take over all facets of the center's operation.

Facsimile   Equipment that transfers images of hard-copy documents via telephone lines to another office.

Fault-tolerant system   A computer system that can operate under adverse environmental conditions.

Feasibility study   A study performed to determine the economic and procedural feasibility of a proposed information system.

Feedback loop   In a process control environment, the output of the process being controlled is input to the system.

Fetch instruction   That part of the instruction cycle in which the control unit retrieves a program instruction from main memory and loads it to the processor.

Field   See *data element*.

File   (1) A collection of related records. (2) A named area on a secondary storage device that contains a program, data, or textual material.

Filtering   The process of selecting and presenting only that information that is appropriate to support a particular decision.

Firmware   Logic for performing certain computer functions that is built into a particular computer by the manufacturer, often in the form of ROM or PROM.

Fixed disk   See *hard disk*.

Flat files   A traditional file structure in which records are related to no other files.

Flat-panel monitor   A monitor, thin from front to back, that uses liquid crystal and gas plasma technology.

Flexible disk   See *diskette*.

Floppy disk   See *diskette*.

Flops   Floating point operations per second.

Flowchart   A diagram that illustrates data, information, and work flow via specialized symbols which, when connected by flow lines, portray the logic of a system or program.

Font   A typeface that is described by its letter style, its height in points, and its presentation attribute.

Footprint   The evidence of unlawful entry or use of a computer system.

FORTH   A programming language particularly suited for microcomputers that enables users to tailor the language's set of commands to any application.

FORTRAN   [FORmula TRANslator]   A high-level programming language designed primarily for scientific applications.

Fourth-generation language (4GL)   A programming language that uses high-level English-like instructions to retrieve and format data for inquiries and reporting.

Frame   A rectangular area in a desktop publishing-produced document that holds the text or an image of a particular file.

Frequency division multiplexing   A method of simultaneously transmitting several communications signals over a transmission medium by dividing its band width into narrower bands, each carrying a communications signal.

Front-end processor   A processor used to offload certain data communications tasks from the host processor.

Frozen specifications   System specifications that have been approved and are not to be changed during the system development process.

Full-duplex line   A communications channel that transmits data in both directions at the same time.

Full-screen editing   This word processing feature permits the user to move the cursor to any position in the document to insert or replace text.

Function   A predefined operation that performs mathematical, logical, statistical, financial, and character-string operations on data in an electronic spreadsheet or a data base.

Function key   A special-function key on the keyboard that can be used to instruct the computer to perform a specific operation (also called *soft key*).

Function-based information system   An information system designed for the exclusive support of a specific application area, such as inventory management or accounting.

Functional specifications   Specifications that describe the logic of an information system from the perspective of the user.

Functionally adjacent systems   Information systems that feed each other, have functional overlap, and/or share all or part of a data base.

Gateway   Software that permits computers of different architectures to communicate with one another.

Gateway computer A subordinate computer that translates communications protocols of remote computers to a protocol that is compatible with the host computer, thereby enabling the transmission of data from external sources.

General-purpose computer Computer systems that are designed with the flexibility to do a variety of tasks, such as CAI, payroll processing, climate control, and so on. (Contrast with *special-purpose computer*.)

Geostationary orbit See *geosynchronous orbit*.

Geosynchronous orbit An orbit that permits a communications satellite to maintain a fixed position relative to the surface of the earth (also known as *geostationary orbit*).

Gigabyte (G) Referring to one billion bytes of storage.

GIGO [Garbage In, Garbage Out] A euphemism implying that information is only as good as the data from which it is derived.

Global memory Pertaining to random-access memory that is shared by several processors.

Grammar checker An add-on program to word processing software that highlights grammatical concerns and deviations from conventions in a word processing document.

Grandfather–father–son method A secondary storage backup procedure that results in the master file having two generations of backup.

Graphics cursor A symbol on a display screen which can be positioned anywhere on a display screen by a light pen, joystick, track ball, digitizing tablet and pen, or mouse to initiate action or to draw.

Graphics workstation A terminal with a high-resolution graphics monitor for the sophisticated user that is endowed with its own processing capability as well as the ability to interface with a mainframe.

Gray scales The number of shades of a color that can be presented on a monochrome monitor's screen or on a monochrome printer's output.

Hacker A computer enthusiast who uses the computer as a source of recreation.

Half-duplex line A communications channel that transmits data in both directions, but not at the same time.

Handshaking The process by which both sending and receiving devices in a computer network maintain and coordinate data communications.

Hard carriage return In word processing, a special character that is inserted in the document when the carriage return is pressed. Typically, the character denotes the end of a paragraph or of a string of contiguous text.

Hard copy A readable printed copy of computer output. (Contrast with *soft copy*.)

Hard disk A permanently installed, continuously spinning magnetic storage medium made up of one or more rigid disk platters. (Same as *fixed disk*; contrast with *interchangeable magnetic disk*.) See also *Winchester disk*.

Hard-wired Logic that is designed into chips.

Hardware The physical devices that comprise a computer system. (Contrast with *software*.)

Hashing A method of random access in which the address is arithmetically calculated from the key data element.

Head crash A disk drive malfunction that causes the read/write head to touch the surface of the disk, thereby resulting in the loss of the disk head, the disk, and the data stored on the disk.

Help command A software feature that provides an online explanation of or instruction on how to proceed.

Help screen The display that results from initiating the help command.

Hertz One cycle per second.

Heuristic knowledge Rules of thumb that evolve from experience.

Hexadecimal A base-16 numbering system used as a programmer convenience in information processing to condense binary output and make it more easily readable.

Hierarchical data base A data base whose organization employs the tree data structure. (Contrast with *relational data base* and *network data base*.)

High-level programming language A language with instructions that combine several machine-level instructions into one instruction. (Compare with *machine language* or *low-level programming language*.)

HIPO [Hierarchical Plus Input-Processing-Output] A design technique that encourages the top-down approach, dividing the system into easily manageable modules.

Historical reports Reports generated from data that were gathered in the past, and do not reflect the current status. Reports based solely on historical data are rare in practice. (Contrast with *status reports*.)

Host computer See *host processor*.

Host processor The processor responsible for the overall control of a computer system. The host processor is the focal point of a communications-based system (also called *host computer*).

Hot site A backup site equipped with a functioning computer system. (Contrast with *cold site*.)

I/O [Input/Output] Input or output, or both.

I-time See *instruction time*.

Icons Pictographs used in place of words or phrases on screen displays.

Idea processor A software productivity tool that allows the user to organize and document thoughts and ideas (also called an *outliner*).

Identifier A name used in computer programs to recall a value, an array, a program, or a function from storage.

Image processor A device that uses a camera to scan and digitize an image that can be stored on a disk and manipulated by a computer.

Index file Within the context of database software, a file that contains logical pointers to records in a data base.

Index sequential-access method (ISAM) A direct-access data storage scheme that uses an index to locate and access data stored on magnetic disk.

Inference engine The logic embodied in the software of an expert system.

Information Data that have been collected and processed into a meaningful form.

Information center A facility in which computing resources are made available to various user groups.

Information center specialist Someone who works with users in an information center.

Information engineering A term coined to emphasize using the rigors of engineering discipline in the handling of the information resource.

Information management systems (IMS) IBM's mainframe-based hierarchical DBMS.

Information network Same as *information service*.

Information overload The circumstance that occurs when the volume of available information is so great that the decision maker cannot distinguish relevant from irrelevant information.

Information repository A central computer-based storage facility for all system design information (also called *dictionary* and *encyclopedia*).

Information resource management (IRM) A concept advocating that information be treated as a corporate resource.

Information service An on-line commercial network that provides remote users with access to a variety of information services (same as *information network*).

Information services auditor Someone who is responsible for ensuring the integrity of operational information systems.

Information services department The organizational entity that develops and maintains computer-based information systems.

Information society A society in which the generation and dissemination of information becomes the central focus of commerce.

Information system A computer-based system that provides both data processing capability and information for managerial decision making.

Information technology A collective reference to the combined fields of computers and information systems.

Information-based decision See *nonprogrammed decision*.

Input Data to be processed by a computer system.

Input/output-bound operation The amount of work that can be performed by the computer system is limited primarily by the speeds of the I/O devices.

Inquiry An on-line request for information.

Insert mode A data entry mode in which the character entered is inserted at the cursor position.

Instruction A programming language statement that specifies a particular computer operation to be performed.

Instruction register The register that contains the instruction being executed.

Instruction time The elapsed time it takes to fetch and decode a computer instruction. Also called I-time.

Integer Any positive or negative whole number and zero.

Integrated circuit (IC) Thousands of electronic components that are etched into a tiny silicon chip in the form of a special-function electronic circuit.

Integrated information system An information system that services two or more functional areas, all of which share a common data base.

Integrated software Two or more of the major microcomputer productivity tools integrated into a single commercial software package.

Intelligent Pertaining to computer aided.

Intelligent terminal A terminal with a built-in microprocessor.

Intelligent workstation A workstation endowed with its own sophisticated processing capability as well as the ability to interface with a mainframe.

Interactive Pertaining to on-line and immediate communication between the end user and computer.

Interactive computer system A computer system that permits users to communicate directly with the system.

Interblock gap (IBG) A physical space between record blocks on magnetic tapes.

Interchangeable magnetic disk A magnetic disk that can be stored off-line and loaded to the magnetic disk drive as it is needed. (Contrast with *hard disk*, or *fixed disk*.)

Intercompany networking See *electronic data interchange*.

Interpreter Systems software that translates and executes each program instruction before translating and executing the next. (Compare with *compiler*.)

Interrupt A signal that causes a program or a device to stop or pause temporarily.

Intracompany networking The use of computers and data communications to transmit data electronically within a company (see also *cooperative computing*).

ISAM See *index sequential-access method*.

ISO [International Standards Organization] An organization that coordinates the setting of international standards.

Job A unit of work for the computer system.

Job control language (JCL) A language used to tell the computer the order in which programs are to be executed.

Job stream The sequence in which programs are to be executed.

Joystick A single vertical stick that moves the cursor on a screen in the direction in which the stick is pushed.

Kb See *kilobyte*.

Kernel An independent software module that is part of a larger program.

Key data element The data element in a record that is used as an identifier for accessing, sorting, and collating records. (Same as *control field*.)

Keyboard A device used for key data entry.

Keyboard templates Typically, a plastic keyboard overlay that indicates which commands are assigned to particular function keys.

Keyword See *reserved word*.

Kilobyte (Kb) A computerese abbreviation for 2 to the 10th power, or 1024.

Knowledge acquisition facility That component of the expert system shell that permits the construction of the knowledge base.

Knowledge base The foundation of a knowledge-based system that contains facts, rules, inferences, and procedures.

Knowledge engineer Someone trained in the use of expert system shells and in the interview techniques needed to extract information from a domain expert.

Knowledge worker Someone whose job function revolves around the use, manipulation, and dissemination of information.

Knowledge-based system A computer-based system that helps users make decisions by enabling them to interact with a knowledge base.

Large-scale integration (LSI) An integrated circuit with a densely packed concentration of electronic components. (Contrast with *very large-scale integration*, or *VLSI*.)

Layout A detailed output and/or input specification that graphically illustrates exactly where information should be placed/entered on a VDT display screen or placed on a printed output.

Layout line A line on a word processing screen that graphically illustrates appropriate user settings (margins, tabs). Also called a format line.

Leased line A permanent or semipermanent communications channel leased through a common carrier.

Lexicon The dictionary of words that can be interpreted by a particular natural language.

Librarian A person who functions to catalog, monitor, and control the distribution of disks, tapes, system documentation, and computer-related literature.

Light-emitting diode (LED) A device that responds to electrical current by emitting light.

Limits check A system check that assesses whether the value of an entry is out of line with that expected.

Line See *communications channel.*

Line graph A graph in which conceptually similar points are plotted and connected so they are represented by one or several lines.

Linkage editor An operating system program that assigns a primary storage address to each byte of an object program.

Liquid crystal display (LCD) An output device that displays characters and other images as composites of actuated liquid crystal.

LISP [LISt Processing] A programming language particularly suited for the manipulation of words and phrases that is often used in applications of artificial intelligence.

Live data Test data that have already been processed through an existing system.

Load To transfer programs or data from secondary to primary storage.

Local area network (LAN or local net) A system of hardware, software, and communications channels that connects devices on the local premises.

Local memory Pertaining to the random access memory associated with a particular processor or peripheral device.

Log on procedure The procedure by which a user establishes a communications link with a remote computer.

Logic bomb A Trojan horse that is executed when a certain set of conditions are met.

Logic operations Computer operations that make comparisons between numbers and between words, then perform appropriate functions, based on the result of the comparison.

Logical operators Used to combine relational expressions logically in electronic spreadsheet and database software (such as AND, OR). See also *relational operators.*

Logical record See *record.*

LOGO A programming language often used to teach children concepts in mathematics, geometry, and computer programming.

Loop A sequence of program instructions that are executed repeatedly until a particular condition is met.

Low-level programming language A language comprising the fundamental instruction set of a particular computer. (Compare with *high-level programming language.*)

Machine cycle The cycle of operations performed by the processor to process a single program instruction: fetch, decode, execute, and place result in memory.

Machine independent Pertaining to programs that can be executed on computers of different designs.

Machine language The programming language that is interpreted and executed directly by the computer.

Macro A sequence of frequently used operations or keystrokes that can be recalled and invoked to help speed user interaction with microcomputer productivity software.

Magnetic disk See *disk, magnetic.*

Magnetic disk drive See *disk drive, magnetic.*

Magnetic ink character recognition (MICR) A data entry technique used primarily in banking. Magnetic characters are imprinted on checks and deposits, then scanned to retrieve the data.

Magnetic stripe A magnetic storage medium for low-volume storage of data on badges and cards (related to *badge reader*).

Magnetic tape See *tape, magnetic.*

Magnetic tape drive See *tape drive, magnetic.*

Magneto-optical disk An optical laser disk with read and write capabilities.

Mail merge A computer application in which text generated by word processing is merged with data from a data base (e.g., a form letter with an address).

Main memory See *primary storage.*

Main menu The highest level menu in a menu tree.

Mainframe computer A large computer that can service many users simultaneously.

Maintenance The ongoing process by which information systems (and software) are updated and enhanced to keep up with changing requirements.

Management information system (MIS) An integrated structure of data bases and information flow throughout all levels and components of an organization, whereby the collection, transfer, and presentation of information is optimized to meet the needs of the organization. (Contrast with *decision support system* and *executive support system.*)

Manipulator arm The movable part of an industrial robot to which special-function tools are attached.

MAP [Manufacturing Automation Protocol] A communications protocol, developed by General Motors, that enables the linking of robots, machine tools, automated carts, and other automated elements of manufacturing into an integrated network.

Master file The permanent source of data for a particular computer application area.

Maxicomputers That category of computers that falls between minicomputers and supercomputers.

Mb See *megabyte.*

MCA [Micro Channel Architecture] The architecture of the high-end IBM PS/2 line of microcomputers.

Megabyte (Mb) Referring to one million bytes of primary or secondary storage capacity.

Memory See *primary storage.*

Memory-resident program A program, other than the

operating system, that remains operational while another applications program is running.

Menu   A workstation display with a list of processing choices from which an end user may select.

Menu driven   Pertaining to software packages that respond to user directives that are entered via a hierarchy of menus.

Message   A series of bits sent from a workstation to a computer, or vice versa.

Metal-oxide semiconductor (MOS)   A technology for creating tiny integrated circuits in layers of conducting metal that are separated by silicon dioxide insulators.

Methodology   A set of standardized procedures, including technical methods, management techniques, and documentation, that provides the framework for accomplishing a particular task (e.g., system development methodology).

MHz [megahertz]   One million hertz.

MICR inscriber   An output device that enables the printing of characters for magnetic ink character recognition on bank checks and deposit slips.

MICR reader-sorter   An input device that reads the magnetic ink character recognition data on bank documents and sorts them.

Micro/mainframe link   Linking microcomputers and mainframes for the purpose of data communication.

Microchip   An integrated circuit on a chip.

Microcomputer (or **micro**)   A small computer (same as *desktop computer, personal computer, PC*).

Microcomputer specialist   A specialist in the use and application of microcomputer hardware and software.

Microdisk   A $3\frac{1}{2}$-inch flexible disk used for data storage.

Microframe   A high-end microcomputer.

Microprocessor   A computer on a single chip. The processing component of a microcomputer.

Microsecond   One millionth of a second.

Milestone   A significant point in the development of a system or program.

Millisecond   One thousandth of a second.

Minicomputer (or **mini**)   A midsized computer.

MIPS   Millions of instructions per second.

MIS   See *management information system*.

MIS planner   The person in a company who has the responsibility for coordinating and preparing the MIS plans.

MIS steering committee   A committee of top executives who are charged with providing long-range guidance and direction for computer and MIS activities.

Mnemonics   Symbols that represent instructions in assembler languages.

Modem [MOdulator-DEModulator]   A device used to convert computer-compatible signals to signals suitable for data transmission facilities, and vice versa.

Modula-2   A general-purpose language that enables self-contained modules to be combined in a program.

Monitor   A televisionlike display for soft-copy output in a computer system.

Motherboard   A microcomputer circuit board that contains the microprocessor, electronic circuitry for handling such tasks as input/output signals from peripheral devices, and memory chips.

Mouse   A small device that, when moved across a desktop

a particular distance and direction, causes the same movement of the cursor on a screen.

MS-DOS [MicroSoft Disk Operating System]   A microcomputer operating system.

Multicomputer   A complex of interconnected computers that share memory while operating in concert or independently.

Multidrop   The connection of more than one terminal to a single communications channel.

Multifunction add-on board   An add-on circuit board that performs more than one function.

Multiplexing   The simultaneous transmission of multiple transmissions of data over a single communications channel.

Multiprocessing   Using two or more processors in the same computer system in the simultaneous execution of two or more programs.

Multiprogramming   Pertaining to the concurrent execution of two or more programs by a single computer.

Multiuser microcomputer   A microcomputer that can serve more than one user at any given time.

Nanosecond   One billionth of a second.

Natural language   A programming language in which the programmer writes specifications without regard to the computer's instruction format or syntax—essentially, using everyday, human language to program.

Nested loop   A programming situation where at least one loop is entirely within another loop.

Network, computer   See *computer network*.

Network data base   A data base organization that permits children in a tree data structure to have more than one parent. (Contrast with *relational data base* and *hierarchical data base*.)

Node   An endpoint in a computer network.

Nonprocedural language   A programming language that can automatically generate the instructions needed to create a programmer-described end result.

Nonprogrammed decision   A decision that involves an ill-defined and unstructured problem (also called *information-based decision*).

Nubus   The architecture of high-end Apple Macintosh computers.

Numeric   A reference to any of the digits 0–9. (Compare with *alpha* and *alphanumeric*.)

Object program   A machine-level program that results from the compilation of a source program. (Compare with *source program*.)

Object-oriented language   A programming language structured to enable the interaction between user-defined concepts (such as a computer screen, a list of items) that contain data and operations to be performed on the data.

OCR scanner   A light-sensitive input device that bounces a beam of light off an image to determine the value of the image.

Octal   A base-8 numbering system used as a programmer convenience in information processing to condense binary output and make it easier to read.

Off-line   Pertaining to data that are not accessible by, or hardware devices that are not connected to, a computer system. (Contrast with *on-line*.)

Office automation (OA) Pertaining collectively to those computer-based applications associated with general office work.

Office automation specialist A person who specializes in the use and application of office automation hardware and software (see *office automation*).

On-line Pertaining to data and/or hardware devices accessible to and under the control of a computer system. (Contrast with *off-line*.)

On-line thesaurus Software that enables a user to request synonyms interactively during a word processing session.

Opcode Pertaining to that portion of a computer machine–language instruction that designates the operation to be performed. Short for operation code. (Related to *operand*.)

Open architecture Refers to micros that give users the flexibility to configure the system with a variety of peripheral devices. (Contrast with *closed architecture*; also called *bus architecture*.)

Open systems interconnect (OSI) A standard for data communications within a computer network established by the International Standards Organization (ISO).

Operand Pertaining to that portion of a computer machine–language instruction that designates the address of the data to be operated on. (Related to *opcode*.)

Operating environment (1) A user-friendly DOS interface. (2) The conditions under which a computer system functions.

Operating system The software that controls the execution of all applications and systems software programs.

Operation code See *opcode*.

Operator The person who performs those hardware-based activities necessary to keep information systems operational.

Operator console The machine–room operator's workstation.

Optical character recognition (OCR) A data entry technique that permits original-source data entry. Coded symbols or characters are scanned to retrieve the data.

Optical fiber A data transmission medium that carries data in the form of light in very thin transparent fibers.

Optical laser disk A read-only secondary storage medium that uses laser technology.

Optical scanners Devices that provide input to computer systems by using a beam of light to interpret printed characters and various types of codes.

Orphan The first line of a paragraph that is printed as the last line on a page in a word processing document.

Outliner See *idea processor*.

Output Data transferred from primary storage to an output device.

Packaged software Software that is generalized and "packaged" to be used with little or no modification in a variety of environments. (Compare with *proprietary software*.)

Packet switching A data communications process in which communications messages are divided into packets (subsets of the whole message), transmitted independent of one another in a communications network, then reassembled at the source.

Page A program segment that is loaded to primary storage only if it is needed for execution (related to *virtual memory*).

Page break In word processing, an in-line command or special character that causes the text that follows to be printed on a new page.

Page offset The distance between the left edge of the paper and the left margin in a word processing document.

Page-composition software The software component of desktop publishing software that enables users to design and make up pages.

Pagination The word processing feature that provides automatic numbering of the pages of a document.

Parallel Pertaining to processing data in groups of bits versus one bit at a time. (Contrast with *serial*.)

Parallel conversion An approach to system conversion whereby the existing system and the new system operate simultaneously until the project team is confident that the new system is working properly.

Parallel host processor A redundant host processor used for backup and supplemental processing.

Parallel port A direct link with the microcomputer's bus that facilitates the parallel transmission of data, usually one byte at a time.

Parallel processing A processing procedure in which one main processor examines the programming problem and determines what portions, if any, of the problem can be solved in pieces by other subordinate processors.

Parallel processor A processor in which many, even millions, of processing elements simultaneously address parts of a processing problem.

Parity bit A bit appended to a bit configuration (byte) that is used to check the accuracy of data transmission from one hardware device to another (related to *parity checking* and *parity error*).

Parity checking A built-in checking procedure in a computer system to help ensure that the transmission of data is complete and accurate (related to *parity bit* and *parity error*).

Parity error Occurs when a bit is dropped in the transmission of data from one hardware device to another (related to *parity bit* and *parity checking*).

Parsing A process whereby user-written natural language commands are analyzed and translated to commands that can be interpreted by the computer.

Pascal A multipurpose, procedure-oriented programming language.

Password A word or phrase known only to the end user. When entered, it permits the end user to gain access to the system.

Patch A modification of a program or an information system.

Path The logical route that an operating system would follow when searching through a series of directories and subdirectories to locate a specific file on disk storage.

PBX A computer that electronically connects computers and workstations for the purpose of data communication.

PC [Personal Computer] See *desktop computer* and *microcomputer*.

PC-DOS [PC Disk Operating System] A microcomputer operating system.

Performance monitoring software Systems software used

to monitor, analyze, and report on the performance of the overall computer system and the computer system components.

Peripheral equipment   Any hardware device other than the processor.

Personal computer (PC)   See *desktop computer* and *microcomputer*.

Personal computing   A computing environment in which individuals use microcomputers for both domestic and business applications.

Personal identification number (PIN)   A unique number that is assigned to and identifies a user of a computer network.

Phased conversion   An approach to system conversion whereby an information system is implemented one module at a time by either parallel or direct conversion.

Pick-and-place robot   An industrial robot that physically transfers material from one place to another.

Picosecond   One trillionth of a second.

Pie graph   A circular graph that illustrates each "piece" of data in its proper relationship to the whole "pie."

Pilferage   A special case of software piracy where a company purchases a software product without a site-usage license agreement, then copies and distributes it throughout the company.

Pilot conversion   An approach to system conversion whereby the new system is implemented by parallel, direct, or phased conversion as a pilot system in only one of the several areas for which it is targeted.

Pipe   Under the Unix operating system, the "connection" of two programs so that the output of one becomes the input of the other.

Pitch   Horizontal spacing (characters per inch) in printed output.

Pixel   An addressable point on a display screen to which light can be directed under program control.

PL/I   A multipurpose, procedure-oriented programming language.

Plotter   A device that produces hard copy graphic output.

Plug-Compatible Manufacturer (PCM)   A company that makes peripheral devices that can be attached directly to another manufacturer's computer.

Point-of-sale (POS) terminal   A cash-register-like terminal designed for key and/or scanner data entry.

Point-to-point connection   A single communications channel linking a workstation or a microcomputer to a computer.

Pointer   The highlighted area in an electronic spreadsheet display that indicates the current cell.

Polling   A line-control procedure in which each workstation is "polled" in rotation to determine whether a message is ready to be sent.

Pop-up menu   A menu that is superimposed in a window over whatever is currently being displayed on the monitor.

Port   An access point in a computer system that permits communication between the computer and a peripheral device.

Post-implementation evaluation   A critical examination of a computer-based system after it has been put into production.

Prespecification   An approach to information systems de-

velopment where users determine their information processing needs during the early stages of the project, then commit to these specifications through system implementation.

Primary storage   The memory area in which all programs and data must reside before programs can be executed or data manipulated. (Same as *main memory*, *memory*, and *RAM*; compare with *secondary storage*.)

Printer   A device used to prepare hard copy output.

Printer spooler   A circuit board that enables data to be printed while a microcomputer user continues with other processing activities.

Private line   A dedicated communications channel between any two points in a computer network.

Problem-oriented language   A high-level language whose instruction set is designed to address a specific problem (such as process control of machine tools, simulation).

Procedure-oriented language   A high-level language whose general-purpose instruction set can be used to produce a sequence of instructions to model scientific and business procedures.

Process control   Using the computer to control an ongoing process in a continuous feedback loop.

Processor   The logical component of a computer system that interprets and executes program instructions (same as *computer*).

Processor-bound operation   The amount of work that can be performed by the computer system is limited primarily by the speed of the computer.

Program   (1) Computer instructions structured and ordered in a manner that, when executed, cause a computer to perform a particular function. (2) The act of producing computer software (related to *software*).

Program register   The register that contains the address of the next instruction to be executed.

Programmed decisions   Decisions that address well-defined problems with easily identifiable solutions.

Programmer   One who writes computer programs.

Programmer/analyst   The title of one who performs both the programming and systems analysis function.

Programming   The act of writing a computer program.

Programming language   A language programmers use to communicate instructions to a computer.

Project Evaluation and Review Technique (PERT)   A network modeling technique that enables managers to show the relationships between the various activities involved in the project and to select the approach that optimizes the use of resources while meeting project deadlines (similar to *Critical Path Method*, or *CPM*).

Project leader   The person in charge of organizing the efforts of a project team.

Prolog   A descriptive programming language often used in applications of artificial intelligence.

PROM   [Programmable Read-Only Memory]   ROM in which the user can load read-only programs and data. (See *EPROM*.)

Prompt   A program-generated message describing what should be entered by the end user operator at a workstation.

Proportional spacing   A spacing option for word processing documents in which the spacing between characters remains relatively constant for any given line of output.

Proprietary software Vendor-developed software that is marketed to the public. (Related to *packaged software*.)

Protocols Rules established to govern the way data are transmitted in a computer network.

Prototype system A model of a full-scale system.

Pseudocode Nonexecutable program code used as an aid to develop and document structured programs.

Puck A flat hand-held device with cross hairs used in conjunction with a digitizing tablet to translate an image into machine-readable format.

Pull-down menu A menu that is "pulled down" and superimposed in a window over whatever is currently being displayed on a monitor.

Purging The act of erasing unwanted data, files, or programs from RAM or magnetic memory.

Quality assurance An area of specialty concerned with monitoring the quality of every aspect of the design and operation of information systems, including system efficiency and documentation.

RAM [Random Access Memory] See *primary storage.*

Random access Direct access to records, regardless of their physical location on the storage medium. (Contrast with *sequential access.*)

Random file A collection of records that can be processed randomly. (Same as *direct-access file.*)

Random processing Processing data and records randomly. (Same as *direct-access processing*; contrast with *sequential processing.*)

Range A cell or a rectangular group of adjacent cells in an electronic spreadsheet.

Raster scan monitor An electron beam forms the image by scanning the screen from left to right and from top to bottom. (Contrast with *vector scan monitor.*)

Read The process by which a record or a portion of a record is accessed from the magnetic storage medium (tape or disk) of a secondary storage device and transferred to primary storage for processing. (Contrast with *write.*)

Read/write head That component of a disk drive or tape drive that reads from and writes to its respective magnetic storage medium.

Real-time computing The processing of events as they occur, usually in a continuous feedback loop.

Reasonableness check A system checking procedure that determines whether entered or generated data is reasonable when compared to historical data.

Record A collection of related data elements (such as an employee record) describing an event or an item. Also called *logical record.*

Recursion Pertaining to the capability of a program to reference itself as a subroutine.

Register A small high-speed storage area in which data pertaining to the execution of a particular instruction are stored. Data stored in a specific register have a special meaning to the logic of the computer.

Relational data base A data base in which data are accessed by content rather than by address. (Contrast with *hierarchical data base* and *network data base.*)

Relational operators Used in electronic spreadsheet and database formulas to show the equality relationship between two expressions ($=$ [equal to], $<$ [less than], $>$ [greater than], $\leq$ [less than or equal to], $\geq$ [greater than or equal to], $\neq$ [not equal to]). See also *logical operators.*

Relative cell address Refers to a cell's position in an electronic spreadsheet in relation to the cell containing the formula in which the address is used.

Replace mode A data entry mode in which the character entered overstrikes the character at the cursor position.

Report generator Software that produces reports automatically based on user specifications.

Request for information (RFI) See *RFI.*

Request for proposal (RFP) See *RFP.*

Reserved word A word that has a special meaning to a software package. (Also called *keyword.*)

Resolution Referring to the number of addressable points on a monitor's screen. The greater the number of points, the higher the resolution.

Response time The elapsed time between when a data communications message is sent and when a response is received. (Compare with *turnaround time.*)

Responsibility matrix A matrix that graphically illustrates when and to what extent individuals and groups are involved in each activity of a systems development process.

Reusable code Modules of programming code that can be called and used as needed.

Reverse video Characters on a video display terminal presented as black on a light background; used for highlighting.

RFI [Request For Information] A request to a prospective vendor for information about a particular type of product.

RFP [Request For Proposal] A formal request to a vendor for a proposal.

Ring topology A computer network that involves computer systems connected in a closed loop, with no one computer system the focal point of the network.

Robot A computer-controlled manipulator capable of locomotion and/or moving items through a variety of spatial motions.

Robotics The integration of computers and industrial robots.

ROM [Read-Only Memory] RAM that can only be read, not written to.

Root directory The directory at the highest level of a hierarchy of directories.

Row A horizontal block of cells that runs the width of a spreadsheet and is labeled by a number.

RPG A programming language in which the programmer communicates instructions interactively by entering appropriate specifications in prompting formats.

RS-232-C A "recommended standard" 25-pin plug that is used for the electronic interconnection of computers, modems, and other peripheral devices.

Run The continuous execution of one or more logically related programs (such as printing payroll checks).

Scheduler Someone who schedules the use of hardware resources to optimize system efficiency.

Schema   A graphical representation of the logical structure of a CODASYL data base.

Screen formatter   Same as *screen generator.*

Screen generator   A system design tool that enables a systems analyst to produce a mockup of a display while in direct consultation with the user. (Also called a *screen formatter.*)

Screen-image projector   An output device that can project a computer-generated image onto a large screen.

Scrolling   Using the cursor keys to view parts of a word processing document or an electronic spreadsheet that extends past the bottom or top or sides of the screen.

Secondary storage   Permanent data storage on magnetic disk and/or tape. (Same as *auxiliary storage;* compare with *primary storage.*)

Sector   A disk storage concept: a pie-shaped portion of a disk or diskette in which records are stored and subsequently retrieved. (Contrast with *cylinder.*)

Self-booting diskette   A diskette that contains both the operating system and an applications software package.

Semiconductor   A crystalline substance whose properties of electrical conductivity permit the manufacture of integrated circuits.

Sequential access   Accessing records in the order in which they are stored. (Contrast with *random access.*)

Sequential files   Files containing records that are ordered according to a key data element.

Sequential processing   Processing of files that are ordered numerically or alphabetically by a key data element. (Contrast with *direct-access processing* or *random processing.*)

Serial   Pertaining to processing data one bit at a time. (Contrast with *parallel.*)

Serial port   A direct link with the microcomputer's bus that facilitates the serial transmission of data, one bit at a time.

Serial printer   Printers that print one character at a time.

Serpentine   A magnetic tape storage scheme in which data are recorded serially in tracks.

Service bureau   A company that provides almost any kind of information processing service for a fee.

Service request   A formal request from a user for some kind of computer- or MIS-related service.

Set   A CODASYL data base concept that serves to define the relationship between two records.

Shelfware   Software that was purchased but never used or implemented.

Simplex line   A communications channel that transmits data in only one direction.

Situation assessment   An MIS planning activity that results in a definition of where the information services division and the functional areas stand with respect to their use of computer and information technologies.

Skeletal code   A partially complete program produced by a code generator.

Smalltalk   An object-oriented language.

Smart card   A card or badge with an embedded microprocessor.

Smart modems   Modems that have embedded microprocessors.

SNA [Systems Network Architecture]   IBM's scheme for networking its computers.

Soft carriage return   In word processing, an invisible special character that is automatically inserted after the last full word within the right margin of entered text.

Soft copy   Temporary output that can be interpreted visually, as on a workstation monitor. (Contrast with *hard copy.*)

Soft key   See *function key.*

Software   The programs used to direct the functions of a computer system. (Contrast with *hardware;* related to *program.*)

Software engineering   A term coined to emphasize an approach to software development that embodies the rigors of the engineering discipline. (Also called *systems engineering.*)

Software package   One or more programs designed to perform a particular processing task.

Software piracy   The unlawful duplication of proprietary software (related to *pilferage*).

Sort   The rearrangement of data elements or records in an ordered sequence by a key data element.

Source code   See *source program.*

Source data   Original data that usually involves the recording of a transaction or the documenting of an event or item.

Source data automation   Entering data directly to a computer system at the source without the need for key entry transcription.

Source document   The original hard copy from which data are entered.

Source program   The code of the original program. (Compare with *object program.*) Also called *source code.*

Special-purpose computer   Computers designed for a specific application, such as CAD, video games, robots. (Contrast with *general-purpose computer.*)

Speech synthesizers   Devices that convert raw data into electronically produced speech.

Spelling checker   An add-on program to word processing software that checks the spelling of every word in a word processing document against an electronic dictionary.

Spooling   The process by which output (or input) is loaded temporarily to secondary storage. It is then output (or input) as appropriate devices become available.

Spreadsheet, electronic   Refers to software that permits users to work with rows and columns of data.

Stacked-bar graph   A modified bar graph in which the bars are divided to highlight visually the relative contribution of the components that make up the bar.

Star topology   A computer network that involves a centralized host computer connected to a number of smaller computer systems.

Statement   See *instruction* (for a computer program).

Status reports   Reports that reflect current status. (Contrast with *historical reports.*)

Streamer tape drive   Tape drive for 1/4-inch tape cartridges that stores data in a serpentine manner.

Structured Analysis and Design Technique (SADT)   A top-down design technique in which a system is conceptualized as being composed of things and activities and the relationships between them.

Structured programming   A design technique by which the logic of a program is addressed hierarchically in logical modules.

Structured Query Language (SQL)   The ANSI and ISO standard data access query language for relational data bases.

Structured walkthrough   A peer evaluation procedure for programs and systems under development. It is used to minimize the possibility of something being overlooked or done incorrectly.

Style checker   An add-on program to word processing software that identifies deviations from effective writing style in a word processing document (for example, long, complex sentences).

Stylus   A penlike device used in conjunction with a digitizing tablet to translate an image into computer format.

Subdirectory   A directory that is subordinate to a higher-level directory.

Subroutine   A sequence of program instructions that are called and executed as needed.

Subscripts   Characters that are positioned slightly below the line of type.

Summary report   A report that presents a summary of information about a particular subject.

Supercomputer   The category that includes the largest and most powerful computers.

Superscripts   Characters that are positioned slightly above the line of type.

Supervisor   The operating system program that loads programs to primary storage as they are needed.

Switched line   A telephone line used as a regular data communications channel. Also called *dial-up line.*

Synchronous transmission   Transmission of data at timed intervals between terminals and/or computers. (Contrast with *asynchronous transmission.*)

Syntax   The rules that govern the formulation of the instructions in a computer program.

Syntax error   An invalid format for a program instruction.

Sysop [*system operator*]   The sponsor who provides the hardware and software support for an electronic bulletin board system.

System   Any group of components (functions, people, activities, events, and so on) that interface with and complement one another to achieve one or more predefined goals.

System development methodology   Written standardized procedures that depict the activities in the systems development process and define individual and group responsibilities.

System integrators   See *turnkey company.*

System life cycle   A reference to the four stages of a computer-based information system—birth, development, production, and death.

System maintenance   The process of modifying an information system to meet changing needs.

Systems analysis   The analysis, design, development, and implementation of computer-based information systems.

Systems analyst   A person who does systems analysis.

Systems engineering   See *software engineering.*

Systems software   Software that is independent of any specific applications area.

Systems testing   A phase of testing where all programs in a system are tested together.

Tape, magnetic   A secondary storage medium for sequential data storage. Available as a reel or as a cartridge.

Tape drive, magnetic   The hardware device that contains the read/write mechanism for the magnetic tape storage medium. (Compare with *disk drive, magnetic.*)

Tape reel   Magnetic tape storage in reel format.

Task   The basic unit of work for a processor.

Technology transfer   The application of existing technology to a current problem or situation.

Telecommunications   Communication between remote devices.

Telecommuting   "Commuting" via a communications link between home and office.

Teleconferencing   A meeting in which people in different locations use electronic means to see and talk to each other and to share charts and other meeting materials.

Teleprocessing   A term coined to represent the merging of telecommunications and data processing.

Template   A model for a particular microcomputer software application.

Terminal   Any device capable of sending and receiving data over a communications channel.

Terminal emulation mode   The software transformation of a microcomputer so that its keyboard, monitor, and data interface emulate that of a terminal.

Test data   Data that are created to test all facets of an information system's operational capabilities.

Test data base   A data base made up of test data.

Text cursor   A blinking character on a display screen that indicates the location of the next keyed-in character on the screen.

Thesaurus, on-line   See *on-line thesaurus.*

Third-party provider   An intermediary who facilitates electronic data interchange between trading partners with incompatible hardware and software.

Three-tier network   A computer network with three layers—a host mainframe at the top, which is linked to multiple minicomputers, which are linked to multiple microcomputers.

Throughput   A measure of computer system efficiency; the rate at which work can be performed by a computer system.

Throwaway system   An information system developed to support information for a one-time decision, then discarded.

Time-division multiplexing   A method of concurrently transmitting several communications signals over a transmission media.

Timesharing   Multiple end users sharing time on a single computer system in an on-line environment.

Toggle   The action of pressing a single key on a keyboard to switch between two or more modes of operation such as insert and replace.

Top-down design   An approach to system and program design that begins at the highest level of generalization; design strategies are then developed at successive levels of decreasing generalization, until the detailed specifications are achieved.

Trace A procedure used to debug programs whereby all processing events are recorded and related to the steps in the program. The objective of a trace is to isolate program logic errors.

Track, disk That portion of a magnetic disk face surface that can be accessed in any given setting of a single read/write head. Tracks are configured in concentric circles.

Track, tape That portion of a magnetic tape that can be accessed by any one of the nine read/write heads. A track runs the length of the tape.

Trackball A ball mounted in a box that, when moved, results in a similar movement of the cursor on a display screen.

Transaction A procedural event in a system that prompts manual or computer-based activity.

Transaction file A file containing records of data activity (transactions); used to update the master file.

Transaction-oriented processing Transactions are recorded and entered as they occur.

Transcribe To convert source data into machine-readable format.

Transfer rate The number of characters per second that can be transmitted between primary storage and a peripheral device.

Transistor An electronic switching device that can be used to vary voltage or alter the flow of current.

Transparent A reference to a procedure or activity that occurs automatically. It does not have to be considered in the use or design of a program or an information system.

Trap door A Trojan horse that permits unauthorized and undetected access to a computer system.

Trojan horse A set of unauthorized instructions hidden in a legitimate program, such as an operating system.

Tuple A group of related fields (a row) in a relational data base.

Turbo Pascal A microcomputer version of the Pascal programming language.

Turnaround document A computer-produced output that is ultimately returned to a computer system as machine-readable input.

Turnaround time Elapsed time between the submission of a job and the distribution of the results. (Compare with *response time*.)

Turnkey company A company that contracts with a client to install a complete system, both hardware and software (also called *system integrators*).

Twisted-pair wire Two twisted copper wires. The foundation of telephone services through the 1970s.

Two-tier network A computer network with two layers—a host mainframe at the top that is linked directly to multiple minicomputers and/or microcomputers.

Uninterruptible power source (UPS) A buffer between an external power source and a computer system that supplies clean and continuous power.

Unit testing That phase of testing in which the programs that make up an information system are tested individually.

Universal product code (UPC) A 10-digit machine-readable bar code placed on consumer products.

Upload The transmission of data from a workstation to the mainframe computer.

Uptime That time when the computer system is in operation.

Upward compatibility A computing environment that can be upgraded without the need for redesign and reprogramming.

User See *end user*.

User acceptance testing That stage of testing where the system is presented to the scrutiny of the user managers whose departments will ultimately use the system.

User interface A reference to the software, method, or displays that enable interaction between the user and the applications or system software being used.

User liaison A person who serves as the technical interface between the information services department and the user group.

User sign-off A procedure whereby the user manager is asked to "sign off," or commit, to the specifications defined by the systems development project team.

User-friendly Pertaining to an on-line system that permits a person with relatively little experience to interact successfully with the system.

Utility program An often-used service routine, such as a program to sort records.

Vaccine An antiviral program.

Value added network (VAN) A specialized common carrier that "adds value" over and above the standard services of common carriers.

Value-added reseller (VAR) A company that integrates the hardware and software of several vendors with its own software, then sells the entire package.

Variable A primary storage location that can assume different numeric or alphanumeric values.

Variable name An identifier in a program that represents the actual value of a storage location.

VDT [Video Display Terminal] A terminal on which printed and graphic information are displayed on a televisionlike monitor and into which data are entered on a typewriterlike keyboard.

Vector scan monitor An electron beam forms the image by scanning the screen from point to point. (Contrast with *raster scan monitor*.)

Version number A number that identifies the release version of a software package.

Very large-scale integration (VLSI) An integrated circuit with a very densely packed concentration of electronic components. (Contrast with *large-scale integration*, or *LSI*.)

VGA [Video Graphics Array] A circuit board that enables the interfacing of very high-resolution monitors to microcomputers.

Video display terminal See *VDT*.

Videodisk A secondary storage medium that permits storage and random access to video or pictorial information.

Videotext The merging of text and graphics in an interactive communications-based information network.

Virtual machine (VM) The processing capabilities of one computer system created through software (and sometimes hardware) in a different computer system.

Virtual memory The use of secondary storage devices and primary storage to expand effectively a computer system's primary storage.

Virus A program written with malicious intent and loaded to the computer system of an unsuspecting victim. Ultimately, the program destroys or introduces errors in programs and data bases.

Vision input systems A device that enables limited visual input to a computer system.

Voice data entry device A device that permits voice input to a computer system (also called a *voice recognition device*).

Voice message switching Using computers, the telephone system, and other electronic means to store and forward voice messages. (Contrast with *electronic mail*.)

Voice recognition device See *voice data entry device*.

Voice response unit A device that enables output from a computer system in the form of user-recorded words, phrases, music, alarms, or anything that might be recorded on tape.

Walkthrough, structured See *structured walkthrough*.

Widow The last line of a paragraph that is printed as the first line on a page in a word processing document.

Wildcard (character) Usually a ? or an * that is used in microcomputer software commands as a generic reference to any character or any combination of characters, respectively.

Winchester disk Permanently installed, continuously spinning magnetic storage medium that is made up of one or more rigid disk platters. (See also *hard disk*.)

Window (1) A rectangular section of a display screen that is dedicated to a specific activity or application. (2) In integrated software, a "view" of a designated area of a worksheet, such as a spreadsheet or word processing text.

Window panes Simultaneous display of subareas of a particular window.

Word For a given computer, an established number of bits that are handled as a unit.

Word processing Using the computer to enter, store, manipulate, and print text.

Word wrap A word processing feature that automatically moves, or "wraps," text to the next line when that text would otherwise exceed the right margin limit.

Workbench technologies See *CASE*.

Workstation The hardware that permits interaction with a computer system, be it a mainframe or a multiuser micro. A VDT and a microcomputer can be workstations.

Worm A program that erases data and/or programs from a computer system's memory, usually with malicious intent.

WORM [Write-Once, Read-Many disk] An optical laser disk that can be read many times after the data are written to it, but the data cannot be changed or erased.

Write To record data on the output medium of a particular I/O device (tape, hard copy, workstation display). (Contrast with *read*.)

WYSIWYG [What You See Is What You Get] A word processing package in which what is displayed on the screen is very similar in appearance to what you get when the document is printed.

XMODEM A standard data communications protocol for file transfers.

XON/XOFF A standard data communications protocol.

X.12 An ANSI communications protocol that has been adopted for electronic data interchange transactions.

X.25 A standard communications protocol for networks that involves packet switching.

X.75 A standard communications protocol for networks that involves international interconnections.

Zoom An integrated software command that expands a window to fill the entire screen.

Index

Note: When several page references are noted for a single entry, boldface denotes the page(s) on which the term is defined or discussed in some depth. Page references refer the text, photo, and figure-caption material.

Photo Acknowledgments

COVER Photo by Roberto Brosan.

CHAPTER 1 **2:** AT&T Technologies; **4:** EDS photo by Steve McAlister; **5:** courtesy of International Business Machines Corporation; **6:** Chrysler Motors Corporation; **7:** courtesy of International Business Machines Corporation; **8:** used by permission, Gannet Co., Inc.; **9:** Digital Equipment Corporation; **10:** Microsoft Corporation; **11:** courtesy of International Business Machines Corporation; **14:** courtesy of Apple Computer, Inc.; **16:** Sun Microsystems, Inc.; **17:** reproduced with permission of AT&T; **18, 20:** courtesy of International Business Machines Corporation; **21:** Mead Data Central, Dynatech Corporation; **22:** photo courtesy of Hewlett-Packard Company; **23:** Texaco, Inc., Control Color Corporation; **24:** courtesy of International Business Machines Corporation; **25:** Santa Fe Industries.

CHAPTER 2 **30:** AT&T Technologies; **33:** courtesy of International Business Machines Corporation; **34:** Eaton Corporation; **35:** Grid Systems Corporation, courtesy of International Business Machines Corporation; **36, 38:** courtesy of International Business Machines Corporation; **39:** Harcom Security Systems Corporation; **43:** courtesy of International Business Machines Corporation; **47:** photo courtesy of Hewlett-Packard Company; **48:** courtesy of International Business Machines Corporation; **49:** Cray Research, Inc.; **50:** Genigraphics Corporation.

CHAPTER 3 **54:** AT&T Technologies; **56, 57:** courtesy of International Business Machines Corporation; **62:** Andor Systems, Inc.; **63:** Amdahl Corporation, AT&T Technologies; **66–67:** 1, 7, 8, 12—courtesy of International Business Machines Corporation, 2—Micron Technology, 3, 4—© M/A-COM, Inc., 5, 10—courtesy of Unisys Corporation, 6—AT&T Technologies, 9—National Semiconductor Corporation, 10—courtesy Intel Corporation; **71:** Cray Research, Inc.; **72:** courtesy of International Business Machines Corporation.

CHAPTER 4 **76:** photo courtesy of Hewlett-Packard Company; **78:** courtesy of International Business Machines Corporation; **79:** Dynatech Corporation; **80:** courtesy of International Business Machines, Inter-ad, Inc.; **81:** GE Research and Development Center; **82:** courtesy of Apple Computer, Inc., courtesy of International Business Machines Corporation; **84:** GRiD Systems Corporation; **85:** photo courtesy of Motorola, Inc.; **86:** courtesy of International Business Machines Corporation; **88:** Xerox Imaging Systems/Kurzweil, a Xerox Company; **90:** courtesy of International Business Machines Corporation, NCR Corporation; **92:** courtesy of Unisys Corporation; **93:** photo courtesy of Hewlett-Packard Company; **94:** courtesy of International Business Machines Corporation; **96:** NCR Corporation; **97:** Storage Technology Corporation, Dataproducts Corporation; **98:** Dataproducts Corporation; **99:** AST Research Inc.; **100:** photo courtesy of Hewlett-Packard Company, Houston Instrument; **101:** photo courtesy of Hewlett-Packard Company; **102:** Franklin Electronic Publishers, Inc.

CHAPTER 5 **106:** Micron Technology; **108:** courtesy of International Business Machines Corporation; **110:** Seagate Technology; **111:** Nashua Corporation; **112:** courtesy of International Business Machines Corporation; **113:** copyright © Wang Laboratories, Inc. 1989; **115:** courtesy of International Business Machines Corporation; **116:** Cray Research, Inc.; **118:** Nashua Corporation; **121:** courtesy of International Business Machines Corporation, Storage Technology Corporation; **122:** courtesy of International Business Machines Corporation; **126:** Philips and DuPont Optical Company; **127:** Storage Technology Corporation.

CHAPTER 6 **132:** Seagate Technology; **134:** courtesy of International Business Machines Corporation; **137:** Phillips Petroleum Company; **138:** used with permission of Borland International, Inc.; **140:** photo courtesy of Hewlett-Packard Company; **143:** AT&T Technologies; **145:** photo courtesy of Motorola, Inc., Electronic Data Systems Corporation; **146:** Dynatech Corporation; **147:** Western Union Corporation; **148:** NASA; **149:** used by permission, Gannet Co., Inc.; **151:** courtesy of International Business Machines Corporation; **153:** Compaq Computer Corporation; **154:** Compuserve; **155:** Copyright Viewdata Corporation of America 1984.

CHAPTER 7 **162:** courtesy of International Business Machines Corporation; **164:** NASA; **166:** courtesy of International Business Machines Corporation; **169:** photo courtesy of Hewlett-Packard Company; **177:** photo courtesy of NeXT, Inc.; **178:** Reference Software; **180:** Zenith Data Systems; **183, 184:** photo courtesy of Hewlett-Packard Company.

CHAPTER 8 **190:** courtesy of International Business Machines Corporation; **192:** courtesy of Compaq Computer Corporation; **194:** Funk Software; **198:** courtesy of On Technology; **202:** Long and Associates; **205, 209:** courtesy of International Business Machines Corporation; **211:** Computerland; **215:** photo courtesy of Hewlett-Packard Company.

CHAPTER 9 **222, 224:** courtesy of International Business Machines Corporation; **230:** USAA; **235:** NCR Corporation; **238:** courtesy of International Business Machines Corporation; **240:** official U.S. Navy photo; **241:** courtesy of International Business Machines Corporation; **243:** NASA; **244:** courtesy of International Business Machines Corporation; **245:** photo courtesy of Hewlett-Packard Company; **248:** GE Research and Development Center.

CHAPTER 10 **252:** courtesy of International Business Machines Corporation; **254:** GE Research and Development Center; **257, 258:** courtesy of International Business Machines Corporation; **260:** Cray Research, Inc.; **264:** AT&T Technologies, photo courtesy of Hewlett-Packard Company; **269:** TRW Inc.; **270:** courtesy of International Business Machines Corporation; **272:** The Cullinane Group, Inc.; **276:** USAA.